THE OXFORD HISTORY
OF THE PRISON

THE OXFORD HISTORY OF THE PRISON

The Practice of Punishment in Western Society

Edited by
Norval Morris and David J. Rothman

New York · Oxford
Oxford University Press · 1998

Oxford University Press

Oxford   New York

Athens Auckland Bangkok Bogotá Bombay Buenos Aires
Calcutta Cape Town Dar es Salaam Delhi
Florence Hong Kong Istanbul Karachi
Kuala Lumpur Madras Madrid Melbourne
Mexico City Nairobi Paris Singapore
Taipei Tokyo Toronto Warsaw

and associated companies in
Berlin Ibadan

Issued as an Oxford University Press paperback in 1998

Published by Oxford University Press, Inc.
198 Madison Avenue, New York, New York 10016

Oxford is a registered trademark of Oxford University Press

Library of Congress Cataloging-in-Publication Data
The Oxford history of the prison / edited by Norval Morris, David J. Rothman.
p. cm.
Includes bibliographical references and index.
ISBN 0-19-506153-5 (cl.)
ISBN 0-19-511814-6 (pbk.)
1. Prisons—History. I. Morris, Norval. II. Rothman, David J.
HV8501.O94 1995
365'.9—dc20   95-6280
                                                     CIP

Frontispiece: The interior of an imaginary prison from *Carceri d'Invenzione* (circa 1745), a series of etchings
by Italian artist Giambattista Piranesi.

The editors would like to extend their thanks to the following scholars for their review of the manuscript for
this volume at various stages: Paul S. Boyer, Michael D. Coogan, Anthony N. Doob, Eric Gruen, Roger G.
Hood, James R. Hugunin, Seán McConville, Michael H. Tonry, Nigel Walker, and Franklin Zimring.

The following publishers have granted permission to reprint previously published material:

Greenwood Publishing Group, Inc.: From "Western European Perspectives on the Treatment of Young
Offenders" by Gordon Hawkins and Franklin E. Zimring from *Intervention Strategies for Chronic Juvenile
Offenders*, edited by Peter Greenwood. Copyright 1986. Reprinted with permission of Greenwood Publishing
Group, Inc., Westport, CT.

University of Michigan Press: From *The Works and Days, Theogony, The Shield of Herakles* by Hesiod, translated by Richmond Lattimore. Copyright © 1959, 1986 by the University of Michigan. Reprinted by permission of the publisher.

1 3 5 7 9 8 6 4 2

Contents

Part II: Themes and Variations

INTRODUCTION

For many readers, the most novel contribution of *The Oxford History of the Prison* may well be its demonstration that prisons do have a history. In the popular imagination, institutions of incarceration appear so monumental in design and so intrinsic to the criminal justice system that it is tempting to think of them as permanent and fixed features of Western societies. The massive quality of the buildings, with their walls and turrets jutting out of the landscape and visible over great distances, conveys immutability. Meting out punishment by a calculus of time to be served seems so commonsensical today, that it becomes difficult to conceive of a moment when prisons were not at the core of criminal justice.

In fact, the history of incarceration is marked by extraordinary changes. As the table of contents to this book indicates, before the eighteenth century the prison was only one part, and by no means the most essential part, of the system of punishment. Moreover, once invented and implemented, the prison underwent fundamental alterations in appearance and organization. In the 1830s prisons were organized around the principles of order and regularity and hence isolated each prisoner in a cell and enforced rules of total silence. By the early 1900s the institutions modeled themselves on the outside community, affording inmates the opportunity to mix in the yard and work in groups; the prison thus became a testing ground for judging readiness for release. All the while, over the course of the nineteenth century prisons began to specialize, so that juveniles entered one type of institution, women another, the mentally ill still another. The process continued into the twentieth century, with inmates eventually confined to minimum-, medium-, maximum-, or lately, maximum-maximum-security prisons according to the severity of their offense and the extent of their criminal record. Thus, the English prison of 1790 or the American prison of 1830 had little in common with the prisons of 1900 or 1990, regardless of whether the yardstick is the daily routine, the amount of time served, the methods of release, or as we shall see, the public's understanding of the purposes of confinement. In brief, prisons not only have a history, but a rich history.

Uncovering the History of the Prison

It is a tribute to recent scholarship that the contours of these developments are so well mapped. To create this book as recently as twenty-five years ago would have been impossible. Practically all of the contributors to this volume are pioneers in the field, and the results of their research began to appear only in the 1970s. Indeed, the historians' attention to the prison is so new that one has to ask why they were inspired to take up this subject in the first place.

Part of the answer rests in the emergence of a keen interest in social history and a determination to understand the organization of a society in terms not only of the activities of the elite (the leaders of government, diplomacy, and business) but also of the role of ordinary people, including workers, women, minorities, and even those who ended up in jails, prisons, and reformatories. Some of the inspiration for this analysis came from one of the founders of modern sociology, Emile Durkheim. Durkheim first demonstrated that to expose the fundamental norms of a society, often so fundamental as to remain hidden and unarticulated, it was useful to investigate the fate of those who openly violated the norms. The history of the deviant became a way to understand the history of the normal, or in our terms, the history of the prison serves to illuminate the history of all social institutions.

Theory aside, it was almost inevitable that once historians began to follow people to work and church, they would also follow them to public festivals and outings—which, as contributor Pieter Spierenburg discovered, in the seventeenth century included the public execution. At first, the execution spectacle was scary and intimidating, and the monarch and his subordinates zealously used the occasion to bolster the authority of royal government. But in time, executions became the occasion for rowdiness and disgust—both because the crowd had begun to identify with the victim, not the executioner, and because the spectacle had become revolting, offending a new sensibility about pain and bodily integrity. Thus, it became desirable to mete out punishment away from the public gaze and to find alternatives to the gallows. So the historian who opened an inquiry into public gatherings ended up writing a critical chapter in the history of the prison.

The historians' engagement with the prison also builds on the fact that social history has joined with political history to explore how societies and governments maintain social order. To this end, punishment becomes not a detour on the historical landscape but a critical element in evaluating the exercise of authority. Thus in the American case, it is no accident that in the 1820s and 1830s, when democratic principles were receiving their most positive support and ordinary citizens were participating in politics to an unprecedented degree, incarceration became the core feature of criminal justice. In effect, those who want to understand the special features of Jacksonian America must grapple with the origins and development of the prison.

Perhaps no one better demonstrated the value of this approach than the French moral philosopher Michel Foucault. Not by training or temperament a historian, Foucault used history as a text on which to ground a discussion of power and authority in Western civilization. As exemplified by his book *Discipline and Punish,* he eschewed archival research and had little appreciation for the nuances of time and place. He wrote as though phenomena separated by decades were one and as though all the universe were France. Most important, he frequently conflated official rhetoric and daily realities; let public officials announce a program for the surveillance or the reform of criminals, and he presumed its realization. But however serious these flaws, Foucault endowed the history of incarceration with a special meaning. The prison became the representative institution of industrial society, the perfect realization of the modern state. Study the prison and understand bourgeois society: this enticing formulation inspired a number of historians.

That prisons captured the attention of historians is the result, too, of the declining legitimacy of the institutions both in Europe and in the United States throughout the 1960s and 1970s. Once established organizations become suspect, the curiosity of historians is immediately stimulated. In the United States, for example, prison riots, particularly the one at Attica State Prison in New York, highlighted the wretchedness of institutional conditions. At the same time, the prisoners' rights movement equated confinement with cruel and unusual punishment, and litigation on behalf of prisoners successfully persuaded federal judges to intervene directly in the administration of the institutions and to abandon a hands-off policy that had given deference to wardens' expertise. These developments prompted historians to question the heretofore accepted explanation of the rise of the prison, an explanation stating that the prison, in comparison with the gallows and the whipping post, represented a burgeoning spirit of benevolence and humanitarianism. If the prison had turned into so grim a place, historians asked, why was it invented in the first place? As Randall McGowen and Seán McConville explain in chapters three and five, reformers such as John Howard in England did play an important role in provoking changes in the system of punishment. Nevertheless, the history of the prison must be framed in the context of developments in the larger society, which made social, administrative, and political concerns even more determinative than benign philanthropy.

Why the Prison?

Even while studying the prison in a variety of places and periods, historians of the institution have asked many of the same questions. What are prisons for? What purposes do they serve? What purposes should they serve? In what conditions should the prisoners be held? What are prisoners obliged to do, and to forfeit? These themes resonate throughout the history of the prison and, thus, throughout this volume.

To read this book is to discover that whatever the current realities of the prison and however the prison has been used, each of these questions generated a full and elaborate debate. Over the years these topics attracted the leading philosophers and political scientists of their generations—Kant, Bentham, Mill, Hart, and many others. The serious search for a justification of the prison and for the definition of its purposes has continued through the centuries.

Applying the American distinction between *prison* and *jail* helps to launch the inquiry into the purposes of the prison. Oversimplifying, jails hold mainly those awaiting trial and awaiting punishment; prisons hold convicted offenders as a punishment. Of course, some alleged criminals have to be held secure until brought to trial and, if convicted, until punishment. In this sense the system of trials presupposes the existence of the jail. If the cage exists, and if we do not know what else to do with a convicted offender who does not need to be killed or whipped or exiled yet who cannot be allowed to escape adverse consequences for his crime, why not continue the caging? So, we are suggesting, the original justification for the prison may well have been incapacitation. Whatever else, incarceration serves to remove a potential offender from the community.

The conventional contemporary answer to "Why the prison?" includes the desire to deter crime, to express society's urge for retribution, and to reform the deviant, but adds as well the desire to incapacitate dangerous criminals. We will not canvass the libraries of studies on the extent to which the prison manages to fulfill these four purposes, but some comment on the broad state of current knowledge about the efficacy of each of them is useful.

Incapacitation: At least for the period during which a prisoner is in prison, he is unlikely to inflict criminal harm on those outside the walls. To this extent, the prison clearly helps to reduce crime. But this effect may not be very great; it all depends on the natural history of criminal careers. Most serious crime fluctuates with the life cycle: a tendency toward violence flourishes in males aged fifteen or sixteen, stays high in their twenties, wanes in their thirties, and virtually disappears at about thirty-five. The question, then, is whether the prison sentence simply occupies some of this time or whether it merely defers the experiential processes of maturating away from criminal behavior.

Deterrence: The criminal justice system as a whole appears to have a deterrent and reductive effect on criminal behavior, but it is not at all clear whether marginal changes in any one element of that system has any effect at all. So far, at least, it has proved impossible causally to relate changes in the quality of conditions of imprisonment or in the length of imprisonment to changes in its crime rates—and, similarly, impossible causally to relate changes over time between the two. Likely, the prison deters some citizens and some prisoners from crime, but equally likely, it confirms other prisoners in their criminality.

Retribution or Expiation: The talionic law originated as a restraint on punishment. It is best understood not as an eye for an eye, a life for a life, but as *only* an eye for an eye, *only* a life (not torture and then death) for a life. But the quantum of punishment deserved is not easy to assess. Much depends on whose measure of appropriate vengeance governs the equation. Indeed, the victim's sense of what constitutes appropriate suffering for the criminal may change between the time of the loss and a few months later. And, is it the victim's sentiment of vengeance that should control the assessment? The social justification for retribution as an appropriate purpose of imprisonment states that otherwise, individuals who had been wronged would take the law into their own hands and exact retribution. Historically, punishment under the aegis of the law, and not that of the victim, prevents lasting and socially debilitating blood feuds. But in modern society this understanding does not help very much in deciding who should go to prison and for how long and under what conditions of incarceration. All one can say about public sentiment on these issues is that whatever practices are followed in a society at any time, the majority of citizens perceive these practices as too lenient toward the criminal.

Reformation: It is entirely sensible that, so far as is practicable, the prisoner's time in prison should be devoted to fitting him to live a law-abiding life on release. To this extent, reformation is an unexceptionable purpose of incarceration. But it does not justify the prison. Indeed, the prison turns out to be an ineffective and undesirable venue for reformative efforts—be they educative, psychological, social adaptive, or whatever. It is hard to train for freedom in a cage.

These four conventional justifications of the prison are so routinely put forward to justify punishment under the aegis of the criminal law—any punishment, all punishments—that they provide little insight at all into the "why" of the particular punishment of the prison. If one feels that suffering should be imposed on whoever has inflicted suffering on another (he made another suffer, let him suffer too) then the prison is only one possible means among many. If one's guiding belief is that an offender must be banished, either permanently or temporarily (because of what he has done he is no longer allowed to be a member of our group) such a banishment may be achieved by capital punishment, by exile or transportation, or by imprisonment for life or for a period of time. So why opt for the prison? Why invest in cells and walls?

Without simplifying or condensing the answers, it is apparent that Western societies typically carry expectations of the prison that are unreal and contradictory. It is rare for prison administrators to seek to define their purposes, but sometimes they try. Consider one recent effort. Her Majesty's Prison Service is responsible for providing prison services in England and Wales. It is a substantial organization, consisting on March 1, 1993, of 38,233 staff, 128 prisons, and 42,870 prisoners. Its "Statement of Purpose" declares that it "serves the public by keeping in custody those committed by the courts." Its duty is to "look after them with humanity and help them lead law-abiding and useful lives in custody and after release." These purposes are then broken down into a series of principal goals, namely, to:

- keep prisoners in custody
- maintain order, control, discipline and a safe environment
- provide decent conditions for prisoners and meet their needs, including health care
- provide positive regimes which help prisoners address their offending behavior and allow them as full and responsible a life as possible
- help prisoners prepare for their return to the community.

These are clear and modest goals, but it is not surprising that such expectations are not often met. The rhetoric of imprisonment and the reality of the cage are often in stark contrast. Nowhere is this more obvious than in the issue of prison labor, an issue that also resonates throughout this book. The expectation is that prisoners will do hard and punitive labor, be productive, and help to meet the costs of their incarceration but, at the same time, will not compete unfairly with free labor or with entrepreneurship. The tensions here are obvious and troublesome, and they have generated sometimes brutal and generally uneven results. There is a grim history of prisoners being intentionally worked to death—in the salt mines and quarries of the ancient world, in the galleys of the Mediterranean, and in the Soviet Gulag. But nowhere was this brutal purpose more clearly realized than in the Nazi concentration camps, with their cruelly cynical and mendacious motto *Arbeit Macht Frei* (Work Makes You Free).

But one must confront the contrast. If temporary banishment from the community were the leading purpose of the prison, there would seem to be no reason that the community, the prisoner, and those who are dependent on him should be denied the product of the prisoner's labor. Hence one model of imprisonment, developed most adequately in the Scandinavian countries, is a full-wage prison—a "factory with a fence," as described with approval by a chief justice of the U.S. Supreme Court. The prisoner earns roughly as much as he would were he free and from his earnings meets the cost of his board and keep in prison, compensates the victims of his crime, supports his dependents, and saves for his release. However, these sensible purposes are rarely realized, and there is frequently abuse in the exploitation of prison labor—far less than in the brutal lethality of the Gulag and the concentration camp, but abuse enough. There is a history of the exploitation of prison labor in the fields and chain gangs of the pre–Civil War South and in the labor camps and factories of contemporary China.

Today, in more advanced countries, there is little productive work for prisoners to do, so that deadening idleness deepens the pangs and inefficiencies of prison life. This lack springs, of course, from the opposition of organized labor and of organized business to having to compete with prison labor. The most common resolution, or amelioration, of this problem has been to confine prison production to "state use," thereby at least concealing if not eliminating the continuing and obvious conflict with free labor and enterprise. But the paradox remains: the prisoner should work and yet he is denied work. The essays in this volume describe the many different arrangements that have been made for prison labor; not one seems to have reached a satisfactory compromise to make the prison a place of useful and profitable production.

The Expectations of the Prison, Past and Present

This brief survey of the difficulty of defining the proper role of labor in the prison provides a clue to the basic dysfunction of the prison itself. Most students of the prison have increasingly come to the conclusion that imprisonment should be used as the sanction of last resort, to be imposed only when other measures of controlling the criminal have been tried and have failed or in situations in which those other measures are clearly inadequate. The usual public response to such a proposition is that it could be made only by someone who cared not at all, or certainly too little, for citizens' safety. This reaction is not surprising: as this book shows, the public has always overwhelmingly supported whatever punishments were inflicted as a means of either reducing or preventing an increase in crime. However, research into the use of imprisonment over time and in different countries has failed to demonstrate any positive correlation between increasing the rate of imprisonment and reducing the rate of crime.

It is also true that countries with very similar crime rates have startlingly different rates of imprisonment. How can this be? Certainly, while prisoners are in prison they cannot (with very few exceptions) commit crimes in the community; there must be some incapacitative effect of their caging. So why *don't* crime rates decline as imprisonment rates increase? This question is made more pointed by the observable fact that some prisoners do indeed use their time in prison (or that time uses them) so that they do not offend again. The answer may be found in the criminogenic force of imprisonment itself, or the idea that prison serves as, in nineteenth-century language, "a school for criminals." Possibly the self-image that the prison generates for its inhabitants outweighs the crime-reducing influence of deterrence, efforts at rehabilitation, and biological influences of the passage of time on human behavior. Admittedly, this idea is speculative, but so is the opposing view that incapacitation and deterrence truly do lower the crime rate.

Another line of argument insists that the duty of the prison is to reform the criminal, to change him from a social danger and an economic liability into a peaceful and useful citizen. The small group of prisoners who, by their past behavior and recent crimes, have demonstrated their dangerousness should receive all the forces of reform, coercively if necessary, and not be released until they have demonstrated their fitness to live in society without committing criminal acts. For them, at least, prison should be an indeterminate sentence to be served until their fitness for complete release is confirmed. To this end, release itself should be a gradual and closely controlled process, with expanding degrees of freedom in which the fitness of the inmate for complete freedom can be tested. If the prisoners fail the tests, they should remain confined.

These are the seductive ideas that underlay the movement toward the indeterminate sentence, parole release decision, conditional release and supervision, and habitual criminal laws. In their literary incarnation, the ideas are excellently presented as the "Ludovici Technique" in Anthony Burgess's *A Clockwork Orange* and in other less-compelling science fiction. Their defect is that they grossly exaggerate the present capacity of the social sciences both to predict and to change human behavior. But, as we shall see time and again in the chapters that follow, modesty in rhetoric is not a standard feature in the prison literature.

What of the Prisoners?

So much, then, for what the community and the prison staff can properly expect of the prison. What of the prisoners? Who are they, and what can they reasonably expect of the institution?

The inmates are the best and the worst among us. They include Mahatma Gandhi, Martin Luther King, Nelson Mandela, Thomas More, Oscar Wilde, Bertrand Russell—a very mixed group but not lacking in virtue—and a long list of highly principled dissenters. There is no point in cataloguing the worst. Prisoners are ourselves writ large or small. And, as such, they should not be subjected to suffering exceeding fair expiation for the crimes for which they have been convicted. Below that admittedly vague ceiling of suffering, they are entitled to a reasonably safe, clean environment. They must be spared cruelty, *cruelty* being defined as violations of their bodily and psychological integrities beyond the legitimate necessities of their punishment. There is one theme, however, that has complicated this whole analysis of appropriate prison conditions—the alleged principle of "less eligibility." It is the idea, which dates back at least to the nineteenth century, that the prisoner's conditions must not in any particular be preferable, more comfortable, or more adequate than those of the worst-off members of the community who have *not* been convicted of a crime. Otherwise, it is suggested, a positive incentive is created for those worst-off citizens to commit crime so as to improve their conditions. This is a daft idea, but it captures men's minds. Happily, it is not taken seriously by prison administrators who know that if they are not to operate death camps, their prisons must be run by consent. The administrators hold the ultimate power at the periphery, but within the walls power lies with the prisoners. In the end, the prison embodies the largest power the state exercises over its citizens in time of peace. If the balance between authority and autonomy is struck fairly here, it is not likely to go far wrong elsewhere.

One last word on the scope and limits of this book: the history of the prison is so extensive and diverse that inevitably, as editors, we have had to make hard choices. Thus, for example, we did not include a chapter on the concentration camps because in their design and horror they are outside the history of the prison. The genocidal practices that went on within the camps did not take their inspiration from the conduct of criminal punishment; however gross the violations to dignity and decency within the prison, they do not match up to the Nazi experience.

Moreover, to keep the book to manageable proportions, we limited ourselves to Western countries, and even there we focused our attention on the Anglo-American story. Had we dared to venture more fully outside it, excepting the chapters on the European continent and Australia, we would have had to create a second volume. Our hope is that what we have sacrificed in coverage we have compensated for in depth. And we do anticipate that others will explore the history of the prison in still other places, and, in so doing, take the story in new directions.

—Norval Morris and David J. Rothman

PART I

PRISONS IN HISTORY

CHAPTER ONE

PRISON BEFORE THE PRISON

The Ancient and Medieval Worlds

Edward M. Peters

The prisons of the ancient world have disappeared. Those of late antiquity and medieval Europe have fallen into ruin, have been recycled into other uses, or have been preserved as museums, their varied history usually explained only in terms of modern concepts of penology. Like the buildings that once housed them, the sources for the early history of prisons are also lost, diverse, fragmentary, or otherwise difficult to interpret. The collaborative work of archaeologists, philologists, and historians has been required to illuminate the character of the Babylonian bit asiri and the "Great Prison" of the Egyptian Middle Kingdom. For the prisons of ancient Athens, we must turn to the Greek oratorical literature and the writings of Plato. For the prisons of the ancient Hebrews, we must consult the central Jewish religious text, the Bible. And if we want properly to understand these and other ancient and medieval prisons, we must approach them from a broad cultural perspective.

Imprisonment of any sort and for whatever purpose is in essence the public imposition of involuntary physical confinement. In the Western tradition the practice occurs as early as the Greek myths and the Book of Genesis, and it is usually classified as part of the wider category of physical punishments that restrict an individual's freedom of movement. In the broadest sense, this category includes practices foreign to modern ideas of imprisonment, such as public sale into slavery or publicly imposed forced labor, the exhibition of offenders to public shame—like the stocks that are often seen in reconstructed American colonial villages—and exile and deportation (banishment to a remote place). Imprisonment included temporary custodial detention pending trial or the infliction of some other punishment. The abandonment of an offender, confined and left to starve to death, shaded into another category of physical punishment: the punishment of the body by death, mutilation, or beating. An examination of these ancient practices will assist our understanding of the past functions of imprisonment.

This chapter will describe the role of prisons and related ideas of crime and punishment in early Greece, ancient Egypt, Persia and Israel, Rome, and medieval Europe (the latter including both the law and practices of the Latin Christian Church and the learned law and practices of England and the Continent). Each of these cultures is introduced by a brief overview of its social and legal history, a description and analysis of its ideas and practices of crime and punishment, its specific use of prisons, and a discussion of its single important—or most striking—source of information about prisons. Each section concludes with a discussion of the uses of prison imagery in religious, philosophical, and literary works produced by each of the cultures; that is, prisons and imprisonment are considered as part of the imagination as well as the penal practices of past cultures.

The chapter as a whole deals with prisons as part of a broader spectrum of modes of physical punishment, including confinement, well before the large-scale period of prison building and imprisonment that began in seventeenth-century Europe. Our subject is prisons in the ages before the prison.

CRIMINAL LAW IN ANCIENT ATHENS

Writing around 700 B.C., the Greek poet Hesiod made an eloquent claim that the capacity for living according to law and justice was what made humans uniquely human:

> Here is the law, as Zeus established it
>   for human beings;
> as for fish, and wild animals, and the flying birds,
>   they feed on each other, since there is no idea
>   of justice among them;
> but to men he gave justice, and she in the end
>   is proved the best thing
> they have.

For Hesiod, justice meant a set of dispute-settling procedures that reduced the inequalities of wealth, power, or status between contestants and allowed for a decision based solely on the issue in dispute between them.

In the century after Hesiod, the *polis*, the autonomous Greek city-state, created a collective, public authority that controlled the settlement of private disputes, issued written laws, and created the category of crime. From the law on homicide attributed to Drakon around 620 B.C. through the more extensive laws of Solon around 594 B.C. and additions and revisions in the later sixth and fifth centuries, the *polis* claimed a monopoly over written laws, the regulation of dispute settlement, and the punishment of criminals. At the end of the great age of independent city-states, in the middle of the fourth century B.C., the philosopher Aristotle offered yet another definition of human nature: man is an animal differentiated from all other animals by living in the society of the *polis*—the original meaning of the often misunderstood phrase, "man is a political animal." Greek city-states provide the earliest evidence for public punishment in the Western tradition—and for its roots in ideas of law and justice.

Of all the Greek city-states, Athens is the best documented. Athenian documentation ranges from the writings of orators and philosophers to the tragedies of the Greek dramatists. The identification, first, of law with justice and, second, of law and justice with the city-state is expressed dramatically in the plays of Aeschylus (525–456 B.C.). In one of these, the issue of involuntary confinement is central. Hesiod had told the story of the anger of Zeus at the titan Prometheus because Prometheus had stolen fire from heaven and given it as a gift to humans. Zeus had Prometheus chained to a great mountain and subjected to insufferable torments. Aeschylus took up the theme of Zeus's anger and power—and the epic confinement of Prometheus—in the drama *Prometheus Bound*. There, as in his other dramas, Aeschylus explored the relationship between power and justice, ostensibly at the mythical level of gods and titans but to his audience in the language of their own understanding and experience. Even the Greek title of the play, *Prometheus desmotes*, reflects a term and a practice contemporary with Aeschylus and his audiences: *desmotes* meant, literally, "chained," and one of the names of the prison in Athens was the *desmoterion*—"the place of chains."

The most concise statement concerning a rationale for the punishment of criminals in Greece is found not in the legal literature but in a remark of the philosopher Plato. In the dialogue *Gorgias* (525A-B), Plato has Socrates observe:

> Now the proper office of all punishment is twofold: he who is rightly punished ought either to become better and profit by it, or he ought to be made an example to his fellows, that they may see what he suffers, and fear to suffer the like, and become better. Those who are improved when they are punished by gods and men, are those whose sins are curable; and they are improved, as in this world so also in another, by pain and suffering; for there is no other way in which they can be delivered from their evil. But they who have been guilty of the worst crimes, and are incurable by reason of their crimes, are made examples; as they are incurable, they get no good themselves, but others get good when they behold them enduring forever the most terrible and painful and fearful sufferings as the penalty of their sins—there they are, hanging up in the prison-house of the world below just as examples, a spectacle and warning to all unrighteous men who come thither.

Socrates' sharp analogy between punishments inflicted by civil authorities in this life and those administered by the gods after death is echoed elsewhere in Plato's writings, notably in *Laws* (881B): "Hence we must make the punishments for such [terrible] crimes here in this present life, if we can, no less stern than those of the life to come."

Plato's argument on behalf of exemplary deterrence became a commonplace in ancient and medieval thought. But his argument for correction, based on his ideas that evil acts are the result of ignorance and that punishment should consist of instruction and correction of those offenders who are capable of being reformed (*Protagoras* 324B-D, and below), remained largely unheeded until the European Middle Ages—and then was viewed in a very different cultural context. Although Plato rejected the idea of retribution, or vengeance, his own Greek language in dealing with terrible crimes and uncurable criminals is extremely violent, and there is evidence that a considerable aspect of Athenian criminal justice did focus on retribution as well as deterrence.

Athenian legal procedure also determined the forms of punishment that could be inflicted: stoning to death (lapidation); throwing the offender from a cliff (precipitation); binding him to a stake so that he suffered a slow death and public abuse while dying (*apotympanismos*, an early form of crucifixion); or the formal dedication of the offender to the gods, by a ritual cursing him or forbidding all from any social communication with him. Dedication to the gods reflects the religious sanction that homicide and other crimes were thought to invoke. In other instances, the dishonored dead might be forbidden burial, and their houses might be destroyed.

Besides these physical punishments, Athens and a number of other ancient societies recognized and used "patrimonial" punishments—confiscation of property, fines, and the destruction of the condemned offenders' houses. The free citizen, Demosthenes the orator once observed, was usually punished in his property, the slave in his body. But the distinction was not categorical; the range of punishments described here could be applied to slaves, foreigners, and citizens alike. Athens and other ancient societies also used "moral" punishments: the public exposition of the offender, the infliction of posthumous punishments, the publicly imposed status of shamefulness (*atimia*, "with severe civil disabilities"), and public denunciation.

The well-known case of Socrates illustrates a number of aspects of the Athenian system of punishment. Charged in 399 B.C. with the offense of impiety—in Socrates' case, of corrupting youthful minds and of believing in "new" gods instead of the gods recognized by the city—Socrates was tried before a jury of five hundred members in a trial that, by Athenian law, lasted only a single day. Socrates' defense was the long speech attributed to him in Plato's dialogue *Apology*. Found guilty of impiety by a slim majority of thirty jurors, Socrates had the right to propose his penalty—as did the prosecution. Socrates' prosecutors proposed the death penalty, and Socrates himself considered, but rejected, imprisonment (*Apology* 37C):

> Shall I [propose] imprisonment? And why should I spend my days in prison, and be the slave of the magistrates [elected for just one] year—a slave of the Eleven? Or shall the penalty be a fine, and imprisonment until the fine is paid? There is the same objection. I should have to lie in prison, for money I have none, and cannot pay. And if I say exile (and this may possibly be the penalty which you will affix), I must indeed be blinded by the love of life, if I am so irrational as to expect that when you, who are my own [fellow] citizens, cannot endure my discourses and arguments, and have found them so grievous and odious that you will have no more of them, [that] others are likely to endure them.

Probably because Socrates himself rejected the alternatives, the jury condemned him to death. Because of a delay imposed by the Athenian religious calendar (Plato, *Phaedo* 58B), Socrates was confined in prison—from which his friends urged him to escape—until he drank poison in a form of execution that was also an Athenian penalty: compulsory suicide. The case of Socrates offers a spectrum of early fourth-century Athenian criminal law and modes of punishment—not only the death penalty but also the possibility of a fine with prison until it was paid and of exile.

Sixth-century Athens instituted a number of different bodies to enforce its criminal law. Among these was The Eleven, a board of public officials charged with dealing with those described as *kakourgoi* (literally, "evildoers"). These were the annually elected magistrates whom Socrates brusquely dismissed as tyrants ruling over slaves. The Eleven assumed custody of all arrested people, maintained several prisons, and supervised the application and removal of chains to some classes of prisoners (Plato, *Phaedo* 59E). Among the magistrates' duties were opening and closing the prison for visiting hours (Plato, *Phaedo* 59D, *Crito* 43A) and announcing to the condemned the day of their execution (Plato, *Phaedo* 59E). Prisons were also, as in the case of Socrates, often the scenes of executions, as well as the torture of slaves and of citizens accused of certain serious crimes. The general term for prison was *phylake*, although the word for the place of chaining, *desmoterion*, was sometimes generically used for the prison itself in Athens and elsewhere in Greece.

Socrates' speech in his own defense also suggests some of the range of functions that Athenian prisons served. Plato's *Apology* implies that punitive imprisonment was at least a legitimate possibility in 399, as was imprisonment in cases of debt to the state (in Socrates' case, an unpaid and perhaps unpayable fine) and in the case of the detention of those condemned to death until the sentence was carried out. Other sources indicate that The Eleven were responsible for receiving and securing all those accused of certain kinds of flagrant crime, especially those who initially denied guilt and always in the cases of foreigners and slaves, whose legal status in Athens, as in much of the rest of the ancient world, was considerably inferior to that of free citizens.

Besides these uses of imprisonment illustrated in the case of Socrates, other offenses also entailed short or long terms in prison. All foreigners accused of a public or private offense were jailed if they could provide no sureties, in order to prevent their flight. Imprisonment was also used to coerce a debtor to meet his obligations, especially obligations to the state. Some evidence indicates that prisoners were temporarily paroled during certain civic festivals, although they remained under the supervision of The Eleven. Within the prison-*desmoterion* itself, prisoners might have freedom of movement, or again as in the case of Socrates, they might be chained, fettered, or put into the stocks, head or neck braces, or wooden beams or blocks restricting leg or arm movement. For example, a passage in a speech by Lysias in the late fourth century B.C. refers back to one of Solon's laws: "He shall have his foot confined in the stocks for five days, if the court shall make such addition to the sentence." Lysias says that in his own day, this was called "confinement in the wood."

Plato devoted considerable thought to the reform of such punishment, particularly in *Laws*, in which he describes the utopian commonwealth of Magnesia. *Laws* considers various offenses against piety and morals and proposes three distinct kinds of prison depending on the reformability or incorrigibility of the offender. The first, a public building near the marketplace, was for general offenders and was expected to hold a large number of these, although none for longer than two years. The second class of prison, called a reform center, was for those who had committed more serious offenses but had done so because they were foolish, rather than intrinsically bad. They were to be confined for no less than five years, with no contact with other citizens except for visits from the Nocturnal Council, a kind of moral and civil police, near whose meeting place the prison was located. These visits were intended to improve their moral character. The third kind of prison was for incorrigibles and was to be located far from the city in the wildest part of the commonwealth. No visitors were allowed, and the inmates, who were to be imprisoned for life, were guarded and fed by slaves. When a prisoner died, his body was to be cast out beyond the frontiers of the state and left unburied.

These notions of prisons reflect much of Plato's distinctive view of crime as error and of punishment as instruction, but they also tell us about some of the functions of actual Athenian (and perhaps other Greek) prisons. Prisons as places of temporary custody for those about to be tried or those sentenced to punishment, as structures for coercive detention for certain kinds of debtors, as sites of torture and execution, and as institutions for long-term, perhaps even lifelong, punishment all find echoes in *Laws*. Prisons did not play the largest punitive role in Athenian penology, since capital punishment, fines, and exile were more frequently used. But they were regularly used in a variety of instances, and their existence and conditions were well-known.

Prisons and images of confinement exercised the Athenian imagination, not only in Aeschylus's depiction of the torment of Prometheus but also in Plato's account of Socrates and of his own idealized Magnesia. They also supplied metaphors for philosophical discussions of significant aspects of the human condition. In Plato's *Cratylus* (400C), Socrates observed that some philosophers regard the body as a prison in which the spirit is incarcerated. Other thinkers argued that the *kosmos* (the orderly universe) itself is a kind of prison (*desmoterion*) for human beings. As institution and as familiar metaphor, the prison occupied a significant place in Athenian civilization. The later influence of Athenian prisons lay less in their continuous history than in their use in literary imagery and philosophical literature, as in the case of Socrates. As such, they created images and scenes that have influenced the Western imagination ever since.

Ancient Egypt, Mesopotamia, and Assyria

The earliest records of prisons in Egypt date from the period of the Middle Kingdom (2050–1786 B.C.). The pharaohs of the Middle Kingdom acknowledged a sacred duty to preserve public order. Every injury inflicted on (or by) an Egyptian troubled the sacred order, which the pharaohs were bound to reestablish through their judiciary, legal procedures, and punishments. On these principles, expressed in the concept of *maat* ("justice" or "order"), depended the equilibrium of the universe. Pharaohs and their servants could be neither arbitrary nor cruel, and Middle Kingdom pharaohs appear to have preferred public beatings and imprisonment to the death penalty.

One of the most useful accounts of prisons in ancient Egypt is the passage in the Book of Genesis (39:20–40:5) describing the confinement of the Hebrew slave Joseph by the Egyptian royal official Potiphar. Pharaoh's prison in Genesis appears to have been a granary that housed foreign offenders, who performed forced labor while in confinement. Imprisonment of this kind could be lengthy. One rabbinic tradition says that Joseph remained in prison for as long as twelve years. Genesis states that he rose to the position of supervisor of other prisoners and was finally freed only because Pharaoh heard that he had a knack for interpreting dreams.

Joseph's fellow inmates included royal servants temporarily confined for dereliction of duty and frequently foreigners captured in war or thought to be spies. Joseph's own brothers were arrested and confined in prison for three days because they were suspected of being spies. All of these instances appear to be consistent with what else is known of the practice of imprisonment in the Egypt of the Middle Kingdom.

Joseph's prison was the "Great Prison," the *hnrt wr* at Thebes, present-day Luxor, whose existence is unrecorded before the period of the Middle Kingdom. The Egyptian word *hnrt* derives from the verb *hnr*, "to restrain," hence *hnri*, "prisoner" or "one who is restrained." The prisons of Egypt (the prisons of places other than Thebes were generally designated *ith*, a generic term for any place of confinement) might have resembled fortresses with cells and dungeons or institutions like a workhouse or labor camp, since Egyptian prisoners appear to have been expected to work during their time of confinement. This practice was not unique to Egypt. When Samson was captured by the Philistines (Judges 16:22) he too was put to prison work grinding corn.

There seems to have been no classification of prisoners according to their offenses. Prisoners who were awaiting the disposition of their cases, those who were being held for execution after conviction, and those who—like Joseph—had been confined indefinitely at the order of a royal official were all confined together with deserters from state labor forces, suspected spies like Joseph's brothers, and disgraced officials of the state. Escape from prison was an additional—and very serious—crime. The prisons were directed by an overseer with a staff of scribes and guards. Prison records were meticulously kept, and prisons themselves seem to have housed the criminal courts. Such institutions appear to have survived in Egypt long after the age of the pharaohs and were still in existence, together with forced labor by prisoners, at the beginning of the Common Era.

In another area, the series of civilizations that arose between 3000 and 400 B.C. between the Tigris and Euphrates rivers produced codes of law very early, the best known being that of Hammurabi (1792–1750). Hammurabi stated that his law was intended to maintain justice and destroy evil so that the strong did not oppress the weak. These early Babylonian codes provided for several kinds of punishment, including various forms of capital punishment and such lesser punishments as mutilation. The early laws speak little of prisons, but sources in other literature indicate their use in cases of debt, theft, and bribery, as well as for rebellious slaves and, as in Middle Kingdom Egypt, for foreign captives.

The Assyrian empire (746–539 B.C.) imprisoned smugglers, thieves, deserters from royal service, tax evaders, and like its predecessors in the ancient Near East, foreign captives, often on a very large scale and often involving forced labor. The Old Babylonian term *bit asiri* seems to refer specifically to the forced labor of foreign captives. Like Samson among the Philistines (and Hebrews and others among the Egyptians), foreign prisoners among the Assyrians largely labored at grinding flour, and their prisons were close to or inside granaries. Some prisoners were confined in dry cisterns that were otherwise used for the storage of grain. *Bit kili*, another Babylonian term for prison, appears to have had a somewhat broader meaning, indicating any location used to confine criminals, hostages, rebels, or those detained for any other reason.

These practices extended from Hammurabi through the period of Assyrian domination down to the Persian empire that succeeded Assyria in 539 B.C. We know of them both from internal Mesopotamian sources and from the observations and narratives of those people who experienced firsthand the penal practices of Middle Kingdom Egypt, Assyria, and Persia: the Hebrews.

Ancient Israel

Between the floodplain civilizations of Egypt and Mesopotamia, small, largely nomadic, clan-based societies of shepherds and traders, led by patriarchal chieftains, arose. These Semitic-speaking peoples drew on the cultures of neighboring civilizations, but they rejected both the great cities and the gods of the Egyptians and Babylonians. One of these groups, identifying itself as the descendants of Abraham, fled Egypt around the thirteenth century B.C. under the leadership of Moses and moved east into Palestine and Syria.

The memory of the exodus from Egypt and the experience of establishing themselves in Palestine shaped the refugees into a new people possessed of a powerful new religion. That religion was based on a covenant between God and the Hebrew people and was spelled out in the law attributed to Moses.

The chief source of ancient Hebrew history is the Bible, but the Bible is also far more than a lawbook. It consists of literary works belonging to different literary genres, written at different times and for different purposes. Its components are not always accurately datable, and for purposes of historical description they are not always clear. The core of ancient Hebrew law (as well as modern Jewish law) is Torah (in Hebrew, meaning "law," "wisdom," "teaching"; in Greek, *Pentateuch,* the "five books" of Genesis, Exodus, Leviticus, Numbers, and Deuteronomy). At the heart of Torah is the covenant between God and Moses on behalf of the entire Hebrew people (Exodus 19–34, Deuteronomy 4–10), expressed in the Ten Commandments (Exodus 20:1–17, Deuteronomy 5:6–21) and subsequent legal commands. The rest of the Bible originally consisted of two other kinds of text, "the prophets" and "the writings," both of which are also of considerable historical and legal importance.

The Bible describes the law and civilization of the Hebrew people and many aspects of other civilizations in the ancient Near East, including criminal law and penology. It is worth noting, for example, that of the seventeen instances of imprisonment in the narrative parts of the Bible, twelve are described as taking place outside Hebrew society proper, and they show various types and functions of imprisonment in societies as different as Egypt and Assyria.

The first recorded offense in Jewish history, Adam and Eve's disobedience to God, was punished by exile. So was the second, Cain's killing of Abel. Both offenses were punished by God himself, in Cain's case with the addition of a protective or shaming "mark" placed on Cain. Jewish law itself can be traced only from the thirteenth century B.C.

During the period of the judges (thirteenth to eleventh centuries), local councils of elders appear to have administered the law of each village (Ruth 4:2), law that was customary and unwritten. The inhabitants witnessed the deliberations and participated in the execution of sentences. Besides the elders, exceptional individuals might also give judgment (1 Samuel 2:18–21). In the period of the early monarchy (David [1000–961] and Solomon [961–922]), kings began to assert authority throughout the kingdom, accepting appeals from village courts. During the period of divided kingship (Judah in the south, Israel in the north, 871–609; the term "Jew" derives from the descendants of the kingdom of Judah), royal rule in Judah grew more assertive: royal judges were appointed for each village; and a high court at Jerusalem heard appeals and formulated jurisprudence. In addition, during the reign of Josiah (640–609) a lawbook was discovered during the restoration of the Temple (2 Chronicles 34:14–33), a book now recognized as the original form of the Book of Deuteronomy. Josiah's acceptance of the book and his declaration of a new covenant provided the kingdom of Judah with a written law for the first time.

The last years of the Judean monarchy were marked by the growing threat from Assyria in the east, the destruction of the kingdom of Israel in 722, and the conquest of Judah in 586. The conquest led to the period of Jewish exile in Babylon and the slow restoration of a Jewish protectorate kingdom under later Persian, Egyptian, and Syrian domination during the post-Exilic period (537–142), until the resurgence of the monarchy under the Maccabees and the later dependence on the Roman Empire. In the post-Exilic period, judicial authority among the Jews was held by the priestly class and was centered at the seventy-one-member court of the Sanhedrin, presided over by the high priest in Jerusalem.

The history of criminal law in the Bible is colored by the precepts of Deuteronomy. Crime was regarded as a violation of the covenant with God, as deliberate disobedience to categorical commandments. Because the covenant created the Hebrews as a people, the principal early punishments were death and exile, both forms of removal from the community. The earliest references to confinement (Leviticus 24:10–23, Numbers 15:32–36) indicate simply that offenders were placed in temporary custody until capital sentences could be carried out.

Like exile, the death penalty was used to remove those whose offenses disrupted public order and purity and threatened to bring down the wrath of God on the whole community (Deuteronomy 17:12, which also suggests a theory of deterrence, and Joshua 7). The argument in favor of using punishment as a deterrent is made in Deuteronomy 19:16–21, which also states that exact reprisal, "life for life, eye for eye, tooth for tooth, hand for hand, foot for foot," should be taken on a false witness precisely as the witness had intended his opponent to suffer.

The principal forms of the death penalty were lapidation (dramatic instances are Numbers 15:32–36 and Joshua 7:25–26, which echo the earlier form of community participation in village trials), burning (which consisted of forcing the mouth open and pouring molten lead into the stomach), decapitation (Deuteronomy 13:13–17), and strangulation. Corporal punishments included beating and mutilation. Compensation, fines, and compulsory sacrifices could also be ordered. There is an interesting tendency in post-Exilic Judaism to mitigate the harsher punishments, including the death penalty, in favor of other forms of punishment, several of which appear to have originated outside Israel.

The Deuteronomic laws say nothing of prisons, and the few early instances of confinement mentioned above are obviously custodial, although Hebrew writers certainly noted the practice among other peoples, as in the story of Joseph in Egypt. Prisons first appeared among the Hebrews during the monarchy, when King Ahab ordered the imprisonment of the prophet Michiah on a diet of bread and water until the king returned from battle (1 Kings 22:26–28, 2 Chronicles 18:25–27). In another incident, King Asa put the "seer" Hanani in stocks (2 Chronicles 16:10). Neither king had any religious warrant for such an action, but imprisonment, like other forms of bodily punishment, appears to have been introduced by the early kings, perhaps in imitation of the practices of neighboring states, Egypt to the west or the great empires of the east.

In terms of legal and religious history, one of the most influential books of the Bible has been the Book of Ezra. The work was composed around 400 and recorded the reestablishment of the Jewish community in Palestine after the Babylonian captivity. The Persian king Artaxerxes II retained political control of the territory, and it was Artaxerxes' permission, which Ezra recorded, that laid down the enforceability of religious regulations and procedures of criminal law: "Whoever will not obey the law of your God and the law of the king, let judgment be rigorously executed upon him, be it death, banishment, confiscation of property, or imprisonment" (Ezra 7:26). These forms, two of which—imprisonment and the confiscation of property—had not before existed in Jewish law, were adopted by later Jewish law enforcement officials and were retained until well into the Common Era. The power of Assyria was long remembered in post-Exilic Jewish society—for both ordinary Jews and Jewish kings had endured the hardships of Assyrian imprisonment, including five kings of Judah (2 Chronicles 35:11, 2 Chronicles 36:6, 2 Kings 17:4, 2 Kings 25:7, 2 Kings 25:27).

The most informative instance of imprisonment in Jewish society is the case of the prophet Jeremiah. The prophets, claiming divine inspiration and command, proved particularly irritating to both kings and priests, and Jeremiah was one of the greatest irritants. His prophecy of divine vengeance on Judah so irritated Pashur, son of Immer the priest, that Pashur had Jeremiah flogged and then confined overnight in stocks, "in the prison in the Upper Gate of Benjamin" (Jeremiah 20:1–2). Shemaiah the Nehelamite complained that all prophets should be jailed (Jeremiah 29:24–29) and that this was the duty of the priests. King Zedekiah (himself later imprisoned in Assyria: 2 Kings 25:27) also imprisoned Jeremiah "in the court of the guardhouse attached to the royal palace" (Jeremiah 32:2–5). Later, Jeremiah was arrested by a royal officer who had him flogged "and imprisoned him in the house of Jonathan the Scribe, which they had converted into a prison; for Jeremiah had been put into a vaulted pit beneath the house, and here he remained for a long time" (Jeremiah 37:13–16). Interrogated by Zedekiah, Jeremiah was transferred to the court of the guardhouse, where he again remained for some time (Jeremiah 37:21). But the soldiers, infuriated by his prophecies, received the king's permission, took Jeremiah, and let him down with ropes into a water cistern that still had mud and slime at its bottom (Jeremiah 37:6–13). Rescued by a friend's petition, Jeremiah returned to the court of the guardhouse until the fall of Jerusalem.

The conventions of biblical translation require that the text of the Bible be rendered in such a way that it is understandable to contemporary readers. But in the case of imprisonment, such translation rules prove to be misleading. The description of the places and uses of imprisonment in the case of Jeremiah alone suggests a far greater variety of types of confinement than what the simple modern terms "prison" and "stocks" can adequately convey. In fact, the trials of Jeremiah illustrate a collection of practices that are consistent with—and probably derivative from—others in non-Jewish societies in the ancient world.

The functions of imprisonment that had been adopted by Jewish society by the time of the writing of the Book of Jeremiah survived through the Maccabean monarchy and the juridical importance of the Sanhedrin down to the Roman world. Some echoes of them can be found in the Christian Bible. The overnight detention of Peter and John by the Sanhedrin (Acts of the Apostles 4:3) and of the apostles by the high priest, from which they were freed by an angel (Acts 5:18–19), Saul's imprisonment of Christians (Acts 8:3, 9:2), and the now-converted Paul's reminder to fellow Christians that some of them had been imprisoned and had had their possessions confiscated (Hebrews 10:34) are all early Christian testimonies to the continuing practice of imprisonment in Jewish penology.

Like the case of Socrates and the Greek uses of images of imprisonment as literary metaphors, the Jewish legacy was also one of images. The Jewish philosopher Philo, around the turn of the Common Era, interpreted the imprisonment of Joseph in Egypt in terms of the Platonist image of the soul's imprisonment in the body. But the greatest influence of Jewish images of imprisonment was religious rather than philosophical. The influence of the Jewish Bible reached a far wider audience than Plato or the Greek orators, and that audience paid particular attention to its vivid expressions of human helplessness and terror, particularly in its language of confinement and release, of captives ransomed by God, of refuge and sanctuary, and of exile and return.

Psalms 40, 69, and 107 use the imagery of God's drawing a prisoner "up out of the muddy pit, out of the mire and clay," echoing the next-to-last imprisonment of Jeremiah. Psalm 102 states that the Lord will hear the groaning of prisoners; Psalm 105 retells the story of Joseph as prisoner; Psalm 142 requests, "Set me free from prison that I may praise thy name." Psalm 146 says that the Lord will set the prisoner free, and the Book of Isaiah (61:1) states that the Lord has commanded the prophet "to proclaim liberty to the captives and release those in prison." The Books of Job, Psalms, Isaiah, Lamentations, and Zechariah also abound in prison images. The eloquence of the religious imagery of the Jewish Bible joined the philosophical imagery of the Athenians as part of the historical and intellectual legacy of Mediterranean antiquity. But neither of these traditions focused on scientific jurisprudence or law. The third legacy, that of Rome, addressed both.

THE LAW OF ROME

The city-state of Rome was built in the farmsteaded countryside of central Italy on a series of hills close to convenient crossing-points of the Tiber River. The legendary date of its founding was 753 B.C., and from that date until 509 B.C. it was ruled by kings. In 509 a republic was established, at whose head were two magistrates, called consuls, as well as various subordinate magistrates, some of whom, the praetors, performed the chief legal functions of the magistracy. The Republic directed the expansion of Roman military power, and eventually Roman government, throughout Italy and the Mediterranean and Near Eastern worlds and into Southern and Central Europe. The expansion of Roman authority created social and economic strains, flooded Rome with enormous wealth, and made political power the object of a number of civil wars. By the last quarter of the first century B.C., the Republic was replaced by the rule of a single man, the emperor, and by a large imperial bureaucracy and army. From the reign of Constantine on (A.D. 312–37), the emperors, with one exception, were all Christians. The Roman Empire is conventionally said to have lasted in the West until A.D. 476 and in the East until A.D. 1453. Its influence, particularly its legal influence, lasted much longer.

In 451 B.C. the Twelve Tables, the first written laws of Rome, were issued. These dealt chiefly with private disputes between individuals, and even the few instances of offenses against the Roman state—receiving bribes and aiding an enemy of Rome—had to be prosecuted privately before the assembly of the people. Such offenses as physical assault, theft, insult, the theft or destruction of crops, and perjury were all considered offenses against private persons (delict) to be prosecuted by the offended individual in the presence of the appropriate magistrates and before the assembly of citizens.

Conviction for some offenses required the payment of compensation, but the most frequent penalty was death. Among the forms of capital punishment in effect were burning (for conviction of arson), precipitation from the Tarpeian Cliff (for perjury), clubbing to death (for composers of scurrilous songs about a citizen), hanging (for theft of the crops of others, apparently a form of punitive human sacrifice to the goddess Cebes), and decapitation. Although not mentioned in the Twelve Tables, several other forms of capital punishment were also used in early Rome. The *culleus*, the practice of confining the offender in a sack with an ape, a dog, and a serpent and throwing the sack into the sea, was used for those who had killed close relatives. Vestal virgins who violated their oaths of chastity were buried alive. The powerful features of the laws of delict suggest that these punishments emerged originally as a substitute for private revenge. In addition, although it was not a formal punishment, exile might be chosen by a convicted offender as an alternative to execution. Those who chose to go into exile in these circumstances lost their citizenship, freedom, and immovable property and could be killed by any citizen if they returned to Rome.

The only instance of imprisonment in the Twelve Tables occurs in the laws concerning debt. Debtors who could not or would not pay were to be held in private confinement by their creditors for sixty days and were to have their debts publicly announced on three successive market days, on the last of which they might be executed or sold into slavery outside the city. Narrative sources add one further category of imprisonment. The limitless powers of the male heads of Roman households included the right to maintain a domestic prison cell to discipline members of the household. This cell, the *ergastulum,* could be a work cell for recalcitrant or rebellious slaves or a place of confinement at the pleasure of the father for any family member for any infraction of household discipline.

The Twelve Tables were never officially abolished as Roman law, but changes in the administration and application of law from the fifth to the second century B.C. greatly widened the range and expanded the procedures used. To give legal advice was both an obligation and one of the few acceptable public roles for members of the ruling class (the others were military command, holding public office—including judicial office—and managing one's own estates). Although technically amateurs, legal experts achieved considerable fame, and their advice was offered and accepted at all stages of a litigation procedure. Cicero (106–43 B.C.), who made his own reputation as an orator in the law courts, noted the intense interest in discussing even minor points of law on the part of those who held the highest offices in the Roman state. When legal experts held the office of praetor they were able to influence the law by their right to control its application. By the end of the second century B.C. some jurists had begun to write specialized treatises on particular questions of law. Other amateurs, Cicero among them, specialized in speaking against or on behalf of defendants in court—further developing the Greek genre of forensic oratory.

From the mid-second century B.C. the Roman state began to establish specific courts, the *quaestiones perpetuae*, to try particular offenses. These courts were presided over by a praetor, although accusation and prosecution were still conducted by private individuals. The penalties inflicted by these courts were statutory—there was no discretion on the part of the court—and there was no appeal from their verdicts. The *quaestiones perpetuae* represented the next stage in the formation of Roman criminal law.

Several other aspects of Roman culture also contributed to this process. For the bottom strata of Roman society there appears to have been a summary police procedure exercised by the lower magistrates, notably by the *tresviri capitales*. Only the highest Roman magistrates—the consuls, the assembly of citizens, occasional dictators, and the highest military command ranks—held what the Romans called *imperium*, the power of life and death over Roman citizens. But even magistrates like the *tresviri capitales* possessed the right of *coercitio*, the authority to punish violations of their commands and instances of public disorder by a number of means short of capital punishment. References in Roman literature, including the comic drama, indicate that the *tresviri capitales* could imprison offenders temporarily, although of these prisons little is known. In the provinces of the empire local governors and their staffs had great latitude in the administration of the law, including criminal law. Military courts too had considerable power over those who came before them. It is possible that the summary police procedure used by lesser magistrates in the city of Rome, by governors in the provinces, and by military courts constituted something closer to a true criminal legal system than the *quaestiones perpetuae*.

At the end of the first century B.C. a series of revolutions placed Augustus at the head of the Roman state. The period between Augustus and the death of the jurist Ulpian (A.D. 222/224) is termed the classical period of Roman law. Although the emperor himself became the chief source of law, Augustus and most of his successors relied on the advice of legal specialists, not only in their legal administration but in the composition of the very laws they issued. Besides the increasingly prominent role of jurists and imperial officials in the administration of the law, particularly the criminal law, the other distinguishing feature of the classical period is the flowering of a technical literature of jurisprudence produced by the imperial jurists, a body of legal literature that has no counterpart in the ancient world. During the last century of the Republic, the social upheavals and internal violence that characterized the period had led to the expansion of the sphere of public law (including constitutional and criminal law), law that dealt with the endangering of the order or authority of the state itself. The emperors, with the advice of the jurists, greatly expanded the sphere of criminal law.

Emperors and their legal advisers added new offenses to the competence of the *quaestiones perpetuae*, and they created still other new offenses by imperial edict. In some instances imperially delegated officials assumed the functions of the older *quaestiones perpetuae*, trying cases on the basis either of charges brought by private citizens or of charges generated by their own investigation—*inquisitio*. In both instances the central role of the state indicates that the older conception of many offenses as private injuries—delicts—was giving way to a conception of some of these, at least, as crimes, to be treated under public law by public authorities.

Under the new imperial system, a number of hitherto infrequent practices became more common, notably the use of torture. Torture had always been required in the testimony of slaves, since they were assumed to have no honor and no reason to tell the truth except when compelled. The application of torture to others gradually expanded to defendants of low social status and even to witnesses in some cases, particularly treason, a category that itself greatly expanded under the emperors.

The increasingly public character of offenses that had once been prosecuted privately made social status more important, especially while it still served to determine the way an offense might be tried and punished. Older Roman social distinctions had by the early Empire given way to the social distinction between strata called *honestiores* and *humiliores*. One sign of the difference between these two levels was the nature of punishments that were normally inflicted on members of each. This difference became more important during the imperial period, when punishments themselves became more and more severe.

Under the emperors, exile—formerly a choice enabling one to avoid capital punishment—became an inflicted punishment, either as *relegatio* (exile from Rome) or as *deportatio* (banishment to a particular place, often remote and harsh). Emperors also condemned some offenders to forced labor at public works for a specific period of time, to the mines, or to gladiatorial combat. The last two of these, usually inflicted on *humiliores*, were really death sentences, as was, of course, the other new punishment of being thrown to the beasts in public games, another punishment chiefly inflicted on *humiliores* but under some emperors used on anyone who displeased or offended them.

Being thrown to the beasts, being publicly burned to death, or suffering the Roman form of *apotympanismos* (crucifixion) belonged to a class of spectacular punishments known as the *summa supplicia*, "the highest punishments." These were reserved for horrendous offenses (or offenses that were thought to be horrendous), and they were aspects of the increasing pursuit of exemplary deterrence through spectacular and aggravated executions, which demonstrated the limitless power of the emperors. These punishments began under the early emperors and reached a peak during the third and early fourth centuries, when they reached a level of ferocity that had rarely, if ever, been equaled in the ancient world. During this period the literature describing Christian martyrs (see below) offers graphic depictions of large numbers of examples of such forms of execution.

The later fourth- and fifth-century emperors, however, began to reduce both the variety and the severity of capital punishment. This process occurred in the context of the last major stage in Roman legal history, the compilation of extensive collections of legal literature under imperial patronage. In 438 the emperor Theodosius II issued the *Theodosian Code,* containing imperial edicts from the fourth and early fifth centuries. A century later, Justinian issued the *Institutes* (533), the first introductory book for beginning law students, the *Code* (534), a new compilation of imperial legislation from the second century through the early sixth, and the *Digest* (533), a rich collection of legal science written by the great jurists of the imperial period. These texts, known since the thirteenth century as *Corpus Iuris Civilis* ("Body of Civil Law"), influenced the law of

Europe and the Americas until the end of the eighteenth century and are still the basis for learned law in countries with civil law systems. The treatment of Roman criminals in Book 9 of Justinian's *Code* and in Books 47 and 48 of the *Digest*, even though Justinian himself termed them "the terrifying books," was considerably closer to the forms of execution in the late Republic and early Empire than to those of more recent Roman history.

Aside from the references in the Twelve Tables to imprisonment for debt and for the practice of the domestic *ergastulum*, sources for the history of the early use of prisons in Rome are largely the narratives of historians. The first-century historian Livy described an episode that had taken place in 385 B.C., suggesting an early use of prison other than for debt or the domestic *ergastulum*. After an attempt to free a number of imprisoned debtors, the military hero Marcus Manlius was hauled before the dictator of Rome (dictators were occasionally appointed during political crises in the Roman Republic) and put into prison in chains, "to draw his breath in darkness, at the mercy of the executioner."

Livy's Latin uses two terms for the action against Manlius: *vinculum* (chaining) and *carcer* (prison). These correspond exactly to the Greek terms *desmoterion* and *phylake*, and when Latin writers translated the Greek terms they used the Latin *vinculum* and *carcer*. The cases of Manlius and several others from the fourth to the second centuries B.C. suggest something of the instances of imprisonment but little of the character of prisons in the early Republic. The Roman writer Aulus Gellius mentions Naevius the satirist: "He wrote two plays in prison, *The Soothsayer* and *The Lion,* when by reason of his constant abuse and insults aimed at the leading men of the city, after the manner of the Greek poets, he had been imprisoned at Rome by the triumvirs." The triumvirs in Gellius's story of Naevius are the *tresviri capitales,* the lower-ranking magistrates possessing the power of *coercitio.* Naevius's imprisonment was coercive: he was released when he promised to stop insulting important people. The otherwise unknown C. Cornelius was convicted of sexually corrupting a young boy. One of the *tresviri capitales* placed him in prison, where he either remained until he died or was executed.

One of the earliest references to the prison at Rome occurs in another passage by Livy. After the successful suppression of a revolt by Carthaginian prisoners of war in 198 B.C., the consuls ordered the lower magistrates to double their prison precautions. "So at Rome watchmen patroled the streets, the minor magistrates were ordered to make inspections, and the three officials in charge of the quarry-prisons to increase their vigilance, and the praetors sent letters around to the Latin confederacy, that the hostages kept should be placed in close custody, with no opportunity to come out into public places, the prisoners loaded with chains of not less than ten pounds' weight, and guarded only in a public prison."

The quarry-prisons and their three officials were the *tresviri capitales* and the prisons known as *latumiae.* The *latumiae* were part of a prison complex located on the southern slope of the Capitoline Hill, where rock had once been quarried. They were adjacent to the underground chamber called the *Tullianum,* later called the *carcer Mamertinus,* the Mamertine prison. This stood at the northwest corner of the Roman forum, in an area known as the *Comitium,* the seat of the magistrates and the site of much of their judicial business. The prison that survives today is below the present-day church of San Giuseppe dei Falegnami. The *Tullianum* was built in the third century B.C., probably as a convenient place of confinement close to the courts. In the late second century B.C. a room was added above the *Tullianum* proper, and the *latumiae* stood close by. The lower chamber appears to have been used indifferently as both a place of confinement and an execution chamber. The second-century A.D. historian Sallust described the chamber: "In the prison . . . there is a place called the *Tullianum*, about twelve feet below the surface of the ground. It is enclosed on all sides by walls, and above it is a chamber with a vaulted roof of stone. Neglect, darkness, and stench make it hideous and fearsome to behold. Into this place Lentulus was let down, and the executioners then carried out their orders and strangled him."

Sallust wrote around the middle of the first century B.C., when the *tresviri capitales,* with a relatively small number of subordinates, still seem to have constituted the effective police force in Rome. The rapid growth of the city, however, and the needs of the emperors at the end of that century began the development of other forms of policing and probably the building of other prisons. Juvenal, the second-century A.D. Roman satirist, complained that he longed for the days when only a single prison had met the needs of the city of Rome. Under the Empire too, provincial governors certainly built prisons, so that by the end of the second century, if not considerably earlier, the number of prisons within the city and the Empire had increased considerably.

Even under the Republic there were prisons outside Rome. In the early second century B.C., Perseus, king of Macedonia, was captured by a Roman army and placed by the praetor of Rome with his family in a prison at Alba Fucens in central Italy. The first-century B.C. historian Diodorus Siculus described the prison:

> The prison is a deep underground dungeon, no larger than [a dining-room that could hold nine people], dark and noisome from the large numbers [of people] committed to the place, who were men under condemnation on capital charges, for most in this category were incarcerated there at this period. With so many shut up in such close quarters, the poor wretches were reduced to the appearance of brutes, and since their food and everything pertaining to their other needs was all so foully commingled, a stench so terrible assailed anyone who drew near it that it could scarcely be endured.

Many of Perseus's fellow inmates were awaiting execution, but it is not clear that Perseus was. Nevertheless, his jailers threw down a sword and a noose to him, urging him to commit suicide, which he refused to do. He had nearly died from mistreatment when he was removed to a more comfortable place of confinement. Perseus lasted there for two years, until his guards undertook to kill him by depriving him of sleep.

As a prisoner of war, Perseus was in a special category. Elsewhere Livy wrote of the confinement and chaining of prisoners of war (some of them in the *latumiae* in Rome) and of hostages, a custom seen elsewhere in the ancient world. The details the account of Perseus preserves about the prison at Alba Fucens are important. The cell below ground level—with its stench and filth, the invitation to suicide, and the possibility of the chamber as a place of execution—indicates a variety of functions. Perseus's prison at Alba Fucens too was below ground, and it echoes the water cistern into which Jeremiah was thrown, as well as the *Tullianum* in Rome.

It is difficult to see the *Tullianum*, at least, as a prison intended for long-term punitive imprisonment, since its physical conditions were so terrible and dangerous. But it is possible to see the chamber above it and the *latumiae* as places of more than temporary custodial confinement, not only in the indefinite detention of prisoners of war but also in the detention of others who might have been imprisoned for long terms or for life. Such cases, however, were rare, and although we know considerably more about the prison at Rome than, for example, that at Athens, punitive imprisonment for any length of time seems to have been infrequent.

By the early fourth century, imperial edicts indicated a general concern for at least the minimal physical well-being of inmates. An edict of Constantine in the *Theodosian Code* dated 320 referred to anyone held in custody awaiting the appearance of his accuser: "[He] shall not be put in manacles of iron that cleave to the bones, but in looser chains, so that there may be no torture and yet the custody may remain secure. When incarcerated he must not suffer the darkness of an inner prison, but he must be kept in good health by the enjoyment of light, and when night doubles the necessity for his guard, he shall be taken back to the vestibules of the prison and into healthful places. When day returns, at early sunrise, he shall be forthwith let out into the common light of day so that he may not perish from the torments of prison."

Constantine's edict and other sources, notably those concerning the imprisonment of Christians, reveal other important features of Roman prisons. They appear to have had different sections, for example. One was an inner (or deeper), more obscure chamber in which the accused might be shut up in darkness, locked into stocks or tightly chained, unattended to, unfed, suffering from heat or cold and filth, abused by jailers, or otherwise tortured while in prison. Such sections are referred to in another passage of the *Theodosian Code* in reference to crimes "that deserve prison barriers and squalid custody." A century after Constantine's edict, St. Augustine, in a passage in one of his *Tractates on the Gospel of John*, also mentioned the different parts of a Roman prison: "And it makes a difference for each one who is later to be brought before the judge with what kind of guard he is taken. For, in fact, detentions under guard are exercised in accordance with the merits of the cases. Lictors are ordered to guard some, a humane and mild duty and appropriate to a citizen; others are handed over to jail-ers. Others are sent into prison; and in the prison itself not all, but in accordance with the merits of more serious cases, [some] are thrust into the lowest parts of the prison." The *Theodosian Code* also directed judges to inspect prisons every Sunday to see that the guards had not accepted bribes from prisoners, that the prisoners were provided with a ration of food at public expense, and that the prisoners were conducted to the baths under guard. The prison registrar was responsible for any escapes and for any excessive brutality toward the prisoners.

Emperors sometimes performed gratuitous acts of mercy. In one such case we can see the distinction between two different kinds of crime and the treatment of criminals. An edict of 367 announced the emptying of the prisons in honor of Easter, except for those prisoners guilty of treason, crimes against the dead, sorcery, adultery, rape, and homicide. These crimes, which merited the *summa supplicia* as punishment, were generally termed *crimina excepta*—crimes so awful that ordinary criminal procedures were suspended in their prosecution.

The category of *crimen exceptum* also explains some of the erosion of the status distinctions that had earlier marked Roman forms of punishment. In the Republic and during the first century of the Empire, those who came to be termed *honestiores* either were quickly executed—usually by decapitation—or were allowed to flee into exile. But from the third century on, if not earlier, *honestiores* and *humiliores* alike underwent torture and suffered the *summa supplicia* in the case of the excepted crimes.

The actual policing practices of the Empire and the increase in the size of the imperial administration, including the administration of justice, appear to have outrun the doctrines of the jurists. The jurists of the classical period preserved the older categories of offenses tried by the Republican *quaestiones perpetuae*, even though these had long since fallen into disuse with the rise of the imperial civil service and criminal legal procedures. During the third and early fourth centuries, the combination of the limitless power of the emperors and their servants and their arbitrary use of it made the formulation of a doctrine of criminal justice very difficult, if not irrelevant.

Justinian's *Code* and *Digest* nonetheless offer a number of ideas concerning imprisonment, all from the classical period and one of which became extremely influential. The *Code*, for example, contained an edict from the second-century emperor Antoninus, who stated his position on life imprisonment: "Your statement that a free man has been condemned to imprisonment in chains for life is incredible, for this penalty can scarcely be imposed [even] upon a person of servile condition." The later jurist Callistratus indicated that an even earlier second-century emperor, Hadrian, had issued an edict specifically forbidding life imprisonment by provincial governors.

Among the jurists whose work on criminal law does survive, the most influential of all was Ulpian, whose death in 222/224 conventionally marks the end of the classical period of Roman law. In the matter of prison, Ulpian left one phrase that resonated through many centuries and came to be understood (erroneously) as the sole doctrine of imprisonment in Roman law: "Governors are in the habit of condemning men to be kept in prison or in chains, but they ought not to do this, for punishments of this type are forbidden. *Prison indeed ought to be employed for confining men, not for punishing them.*"

In matters of criminal law, the *Code* and the *Digest* of Justinian represent an attempt by the later Roman emperors to mitigate the arbitrary harshness of the third-century Empire by recovering the laws of such moderate second-century emperors as Hadrian and Antoninus and the opinions of the classical jurists. The laws of the Christian emperors after Constantine also reflected a mitigating of the most ferocious aspects of Roman criminal procedure.

The largest single group of Roman prisoners whose sources provide extensive detail for life in Roman prisons are the Christians, not only from accounts in the gospels, the epistles, and the Acts of the Apostles, all parts of the Christian New Testament, but also from a group of texts known generally as the "Acts of the Christian Martyrs." Although the exact legal basis for the Roman prosecution of Christians is still a matter of scholarly debate, accounts from different parts of the Empire are in considerable agreement concerning the prisons in which the Christians were held.

Like other accused criminals, Christians were remanded to prison for custodial purposes, to await the arrival of a competent judicial official or the attention of the local magistrate or to await the execution of a capital sentence (Acts of the Apostles 22–26), sometimes for years. In at least one case, that of Ptolemaeus, the account states that when Ptolemaeus admitted to being a Christian, an officer "put him in chains and punished him for a long time in prison (*desmoterion*)." The text is not clear whether the imprisonment was for the purposes of aggravated physical punishment such as torture or for punitive confinement, since Ptolemaeus was later executed. In general, however, Christians do not seem to have been imprisoned as a punishment. In spite of formidable gates, walls, security measures, overcrowding, and filth, prisons were certainly not the harshest punishments known to imperial whim, as the *summa supplicia* testify.

The "Acts of the Christian Martyrs" corroborate the point that prisons had several sections. One was the inner chamber, cited above by both Constantine and Augustine. Other parts of the prison were less terrible. Some had windows. There were policies, at least, concerning minimal food rations, although one martyr preferred to fast and share his small ration among the other prisoners. The more desirable parts of the prison could sometimes be obtained by purchasing them from the jailers, as did the friends of St. Perpetua in Carthage in 202. Christians may have been routinely placed at first in the inner part of the prison because of their jailers' fear that they might escape by means of magic.

From the third-century account of the martyrdom of Pionius, it is clear that many jailers could expect to extort a percentage of the gifts given to prisoners in their charge, since the jailers became angry at Pionius for refusing to accept gifts from friends outside the prison. Visitors were sometimes permitted, but they could also be arbitrarily refused access to the prisoners. Among Christians, the duty of visiting prisoners was recognized as soon as the persecutions began in earnest in the second century. It was inspired by Jesus' prediction that at the Last Judgment, those who had visited prisons would be counted among the righteous (Matthew 25:36), and by other scriptural texts (Hebrews 13:3), as would those who suffered imprisonment during the persecutions (Hebrews 10:34). For a brief time, St. Perpetua was permitted to have her newborn baby with her in prison. She noted, "And my prison suddenly became a palace to me, and I would rather have been there than anywhere else."

The contribution of Rome to the history of criminal law and prisons was the jurisprudence of the *Code* and the *Digest* and the moving narratives of the Christian martyrs. The acts of the martyrs were read by later Christians, along with the books of Job, Psalms, Lamentations, Isaiah, and Zechariah, and these shaped later Christian attitudes toward both the use of prisons and the needs of prisoners. The earliest Christian literature urged charity and forbearance toward offending fellow Christians (Romans 2:1), or fraternal admonishment (Matthew 18:15), but the expansion of Christianity and the Christianization of the entire Roman Empire by the end of the fourth century made such attitudes ethically compelling but very difficult to adopt as criminal policy. Although Christianity did mitigate some of the savage *summa supplicia* and although churchmen such as St. Augustine did urge mercy for the condemned whenever possible, the texts of the *Code* and the *Digest* remained the measure of Roman—and later learned—criminal law. Those texts of scripture and the "Acts of the Christian Martyrs" offered a religious and moral framework for understanding prisons and criminal justice in general.

Early Medieval Europe

Justinian's *Code* and *Digest* did not find a ready home in Western Europe until the twelfth century. From the late fifth century on, imperial rule in Italy and in the Western European provinces of the Roman Empire was largely swept away by the migrations of Germanic and other peoples and the internal collapse of the administrative, political, and financial apparatus that had long provided for the governance of the state and the administration of the laws. In 554, Justinian successfully reconquered Italy from one such people, the Ostrogoths, who had occupied it since 491, and sent to Italy the newly codified Roman law. But Italy was invaded—and much of it was conquered—by the Lombards three years after Justinian's death in 565, and there was no immediate need for the learned law of a lost empire.

The Germanic kingdoms that were carved out of the old imperial provinces and Italy itself—the kingdoms of the Visigoths in the Iberian peninsula, the Franks in Gaul, the Lombards in Italy, and the Angles, Saxons, and others in Britain—all produced written bodies of law, usually with the help of their Roman subjects. But these laws were personal; that is, each free man or woman had to be judged by the law of the people of which he or she was a member. This practice is known as that of the personality of law. Even "Roman" law, including the surviving *Theodosian Code,* was applicable only to those subjects of Germanic kings who were Romans and, to a large extent, to church personnel and property. The Germanic laws were far less complex than Roman learned law had been, and they contained only rudimentary ideas of public law. The laws were chiefly devoted to establishing the rights of the king and his household and regulating the settlement of private disputes.

Between the fifth and the twelfth centuries yet another legal system grew up in Western Europe, that of the Latin Christian Church. In theory, the common doctrines of belief and religious practice of the church were applicable to all Christians, but until the twelfth century they remained extremely localized. Only from the ninth century on, chiefly under the influence of Charlemagne (747–814) and his successors, was there an effective movement to shift from the personality to the territoriality of law, that is, to make a single legal system applicable to all inhabitants of a territory regardless of their political origin and to make ecclesiastical law effectively binding on all Christians everywhere.

Prisons are occasionally mentioned among the few punishments indicated in the Germanic laws, but very rarely. In Lombard Italy the early eighth-century king Liutprand issued a law stating that an apprehended thief had to compound for his theft (pay some multiple of its value) and then spend two or three years in an underground prison, which each Lombard judge was ordered to have constructed in his district. In Paul the deacon's narrative *History of the Lombards,* written in the late eighth century, some Lombards invading Gaul in 570 discovered a man in chains in a tower whose entrances were sealed. Although the "prisoner" turned out to be St. Hospitius, who chose to live in this fashion as an act of penance, the Lombards' assumption that chained confinement was a punishment for murder suggests that prisons served other purposes among the Lombards besides punishing theft.

The use of prisons for private purposes is also reflected in the narrative sources for Frankish Gaul. Of these, Gregory of Tours's *History of the Franks* and the narratives of a large number of saints' lives are the most important. Gregory also tells the story of how the invading Lombards mistook St. Hospitius for a condemned murderer (VI.6), but for the most part narrative sources suggest that imprisonment for ransom was far more prevalent among the Franks than was any form of judicial imprisonment. Kings sometimes used monasteries as prisons for captured rebels, as Chilperic used St. Calais in the diocese of le Mans in 576 for the imprisonment of his rebellious son Merovech. The monasteries of St. Denis and Fulda were used as prisons by later kings of the Franks. But for the most part, prisons were used infrequently. Like the Lombards, the Franks used fines, enslavement, mutilation, and capital punishment far more often than they used prisons.

There are two exceptions to this general statement. The laws of Visigothic Spain distinguished sharply between private injury and crime, although royal judges supervised the adjudication of both. Visigothic judges used a number of legal practices, including torture and other procedural rules, in such a way as to indicate a strong influence from Roman criminal law. Visigothic laws indicate certainly the use of custodial confinement, including private custodial confinement and imprisonment pending the execution of a capital sentence, since these laws discuss the crimes of escaping from prison and aiding in the escape of prisoners. There is also mention of the amount of money that jailers could accept from prisoners. But there is little more in either the laws or the narrative sources indicating the extent or character of imprisonment.

A second exception is the case of Ostrogothic Italy before it fell to Justinian's armies in 554. The Ostrogothic king Theoderic (491–526) attempted to rule his Ostrogothic and Roman subjects separately, as king of the Ostrogoths and as military leader of Italy. But Theoderic's rule was never secure, and in 524 Theoderic imprisoned his Roman servant, the scholar, diplomat, and theologian Boethius, on a charge of treason. While in prison in Pavia, Boethius wrote his moving work in prose and verse, *The Consolation of Philosophy*, a dialogue between the imprisoned author and Lady Philosophy on the nature of human fortune and misfortune. The work, smuggled out of prison by members of Boethius's family, became one of the most widely read works of Latin Christian literature, and it has remained immensely popular down to the present. Among its translators into English have been King Alfred the Great, Geoffrey Chaucer, and Queen Elizabeth I. Boethius's imprisonment, torture, and execution became for later readers the last Christian martyrdom of the ancient world.

The strong Roman tinge to Ostrogothic and Visigothic legal practice did not characterize the rest of European society until the ninth century. For many prisoners, the only hope was not in human justice but in divine. Boethius was tortured and executed in prison, but others were freed by saintly intervention.

An important role of churchmen in early medieval Europe, regardless of the folk to which they belonged, was that of peacemaker between enemies, both private and public. Churchmen often had few resources or material powers in these affairs, but they had one advantage that violent layfolk did not: they could invoke supernatural powers. Among those to whom both churchmen and laypeople turned were those saints known for their miraculous ability to liberate prisoners.

Few early Christian martyrs were released from prison by divine or saintly intervention, although the apocryphal literature did depict a few miraculous escapes. But in Gaul the liberator-saint had appeared by the sixth century and remained popular for centuries afterward. In his *History of the Franks* (V.8), Gregory of Tours recounts the story of how the body of the recently deceased St. Germanus (the St. Germanus of Saint-Germain-des-Prés, now part of Paris) became heavier to its pallbearers as his funeral procession passed a prison and then became miraculously lighter to carry after the prisoners were freed. We know little else about the people liberated from prison by Frankish saints, but it seems that many were the powerless, those who had run afoul not of public law and public authority but of private holders of public authority who used imprisonment as a means of coercing the weak, of obtaining ransoms, and of punishing personal enemies. Besides the relics of St. Germanus, Gregory also notes the liberating function of St. Eparchius (VI.8) and states that direct divine intervention freed Bishop Aetherius of Lisieux (VI.36). The narrative life of St. Eligius notes that when the saint approached the prison in Bourges, the gates opened miraculously and the prisoners' chains fell off. All the miracles attributed to St. Gaugericus of Cambrai concern the freeing of prisoners, often against the will of officials. Of all the liberating saints, the most popular was probably St. Leonard, whose cult began among the weak but appealed more to the knightly and aristocratic social strata in the later Middle Ages, indicating that the weak and powerless were not the only people who had reason to fear imprisonment and who had the need to seek saintly assistance.

Other kinds of liberators were less saintly. Medieval kings often performed gratuitous acts of mercy in pardoning prisoners, often at the urging of churchmen, but royal mercy was not to be routinely expected. Other moral obligations, however, were more regularly practiced. The early Christian conviction that aiding prisoners with alms and other services, as well as praying for them, was a proper work of Christian charity led pious individuals and groups to contribute to the aid and occasionally the ransom of prisoners throughout the Middle Ages.

From the eleventh century on, significant numbers of hospitals, religious orders, and religious associations called confraternities began to devote themselves to aiding the poor, the sick, the lepers, the pilgrims, and the abandoned children and the old people of medieval Europe. By the twelfth century, prisoners came to be included in this category—generally termed "the poor of Christ"—and donations in private wills in the form of bequests and endowments to aid the poor became a standard part of the general obligation of charity. Occasionally entire religious orders devoted themselves to the ransom of prisoners—including prisoners captured in wars or in conflicts across the religious divide between Christendom and the Islamic world. One of the most active of these was the Order of St. Mary of Merced in Barcelona.

If churchmen and acts of charity on the part of ordinary Christians could only slightly ease the lot of prisoners, the charitable component of behavior toward prisoners on the part of clergy and laity should not be neglected. It inspired not only individuals and groups but also the legal system that grew up alongside the secular laws of the Germanic and later kingdoms: the canon law of the Latin Christian Church.

The Discipline and Law of the Latin Church, 550–1550

Ecclesiastical Discipline and Canon Law

Scriptural references to relations among Christians in the earliest communities were shaped by the charismatic and fraternal character of those communities. Christians were admonished not to pass judgment on fellow Christians (Luke 6:37), to act with forbearance (Romans 2:1), and to exercise fraternal admonition (Matthew 18:15) and forgiveness of personal offenses (Matthew 18:21–35). In some cases, however, scriptural texts allow for a more severe response to sinful conduct: 1 Corinthians 5:1–13 permits exclusion from the community in a case of incest. Authority had been given by God to the Christian community to "bind and loose" (Matthew 18:18) in matters among themselves. That authority was assumed particularly by the community's leaders, the bishops.

The legalization of Christianity in the Roman Empire and the legal privileges given to Christian communities and their leaders beginning in the fourth century helped to create a hierarchy of authority among Christians. Emperors recognized the spiritual authority of bishops in matters of maintaining discipline and establishing dogma in the communities ruled by the bishops, and in many instances they also recognized the bishops' authority in civil affairs.

Bishops assumed judicial responsibility for all matters concerning Christian clergy and church property and for immoral behavior within their communities. Assemblies of bishops—the church councils—increasingly legislated for all of Christianity. The writings of individual churchmen and respected individual bishops, particularly those of the city of Rome, also contained advisory and legislative acts that were accepted throughout most of the Christian world. From the sixth century on, local ecclesiastical assemblies, the rulings of Germanic kings, private handbooks of penance, liturgical books, and other texts produced still more legal materials. Many scholars attempted to collect and rationalize this vast body of material between the eighth and the twelfth centuries, but not until the collection of Gratian of Bologna around 1140—*The Concordance of Discordant Canons,* or *Decretum*—did a single collection come to be widely accepted as the starting point for all study of ecclesiastical, or canon, law. Gratian's collection was the basis for later laws and legal collections issued by popes and councils and for the *Liber Extra* of Pope Gregory IX in 1234, the *Liber Sextus* of Pope Boniface VIII in 1298, and the *Extravagantes* of Pope John XXII in 1317. Canon law was also recognized in all of the territorial monarchies, principalities, and independent city-republics of medieval Europe at least until the Reformations of the sixteenth century.

The disciplinary aspects of canon law were based on the bishop's responsibility for the salvation of those he ruled by the proper application of "discipline" and "correction." In the name of God, bishops were expected to determine the nature of spiritual offenses and to apply the appropriate penances so that a sinner might be corrected and led to salvation by a combination of discipline, correction, and mercy.

Early Christian writers had used some of the terminology of Roman criminal law to describe spiritual offenses. These offenses were considered sins—acts against God and duly constituted spiritual superiors who acted in God's name. Church courts rejected any penitential punishment that resulted in death, mutilation, or the shedding of blood or any form of discipline that might lead the offender to despair, thus preventing the penance that would lead to salvation and restoration to the Christian community. Here, in a very different form, was an echo of one of Plato's justifications for punishment in the *Gorgias*—the correction and improvement of wrongdoers.

The development of canon law in the cases of monks, secular clergy, and laypeople was the earliest articulation of an institutionalized disciplinary system, one that based itself on the idea of sin and its correction, penitential expiation. In this process the prison emerged with an entirely new function.

Monastic Prisons

Of all Christian clergy, only members of monastic orders lived lives of continual prayer and penitence. Monks were considered to have withdrawn from this world to a life of penitence in preparation for the next. Those who entered monastic orders took special vows that included the vow of obedience to the ruler of the monastery, the abbot. Different monastic orders were governed not only by canon law but also by constitutions designed specifically for each order. By the twelfth century the most influential monastic rule was that of St. Benedict of Nursia (d.547), a rule supplemented by later constitutions issued by church councils, popes, and the orders themselves.

In matters of discipline, the Rule of Benedict spoke only of the isolation of serious offenders, banning them from the common table and the collective liturgical services that constituted the center of monastic life and forbidding them both the company and the speech of other monks. The isolated monk was made to labor, "persisting in the struggle of penitence; knowing that terrible sentence of the Apostle [Paul, 1 Corinthians 5:5] who said that such a man was given over to the destruction of the flesh in order that his soul might be saved at the day of the Lord" (c.25). The Rule of Benedict continued: "The refection of food, moreover, shall he take alone, in the measure and at the time the abbot shall appoint as suitable for him. Nor shall he be blessed by anyone who passes by, nor shall any food be given to him."

The Benedictine Rule does not mention a term for prison, but an earlier canon law source, a letter of Pope Siricius (384–98) to Himerius, bishop of Tarragona, stated that delinquent monks and nuns should be separated from their fellows and confined in an *ergastulum,* a disciplinary cell within the monastery in which forced labor took place, thus moving the old Roman punitive domestic work cell for slaves and household dependents into the institutional setting of the monastery. The letter of Siricius was reissued in 895 at the Synod of Tribur, and it made its way into Gratian's *Decretum* in 1140. Not all monastic constitutions became part of canon law, but from the sixth century on, a number of them used the Latin term *carcer* as a designation of penitential confinement, and most of them agreed that such confinement might continue solely at the discretion of the abbot, in the most severe cases entailing confinement for life.

The systematization of canon law tended to homogenize Latin monasteries, and by the late twelfth century each monastery was expected to contain a prison of one sort or another. By the thirteenth century some instances of monastic penitential imprisonment were designated by the formal term "punishment," and later legal writers pointed out that imprisonment for life for a monastic offender was comparable to the death penalty in secular justice.

In monastic usage the term *murus* ("a wall") came to be used as a designation for the room "appropriate for imprisonment" that the Benedictine Rule called for. Some historians have suggested that the term indicates that monastic offenders were "walled up," but *murus* simply seems to have been a common term for monastic imprisonment of any kind. The related terms (used in other clerical and in lay instances) *murus strictus* and *murus largus* ("close confinement" and "more liberal confinement") suggest two distinct aspects of confinement depending on the nature of the offense.

Monastic imprisonment was used in conjunction with other disciplinary measures, including restricted diet and beating with rods. In general, no form of monastic discipline differed qualitatively from individual penances that monks might voluntarily undertake for spiritual benefit. But excessive punishment was occasionally inflicted in cases of monastic imprisonment, although most of the sources that record it usually criticized excessiveness. Peter the Venerable of Cluny, one of the most influential abbots of the twelfth century, told disapprovingly of a prior who confined an offending monk in a subterranean chamber for life. Other abbots imposed chains and fetters on imprisoned monks. In fourteenth-century Toulouse, monks lodged a protest against a monastic prison called *Vade in pace* ("Go in peace"), which seems to have been far more severe than the usual place of monastic confinement. Monastic prisons and their severities survived into early modern times, and the great Benedictine monk and scholar Jean Mabillon criticized them in a short tract written around 1690, "Reflections on the Prisons of the Monastic Orders."

The most severe examples of monastic imprisonment, however, cannot be taken for the norm. The horror stories of monastic prisons that circulated during the eighteenth and nineteenth centuries must not be read back and assumed to be an accurate generalized portrait of monastic confinement everywhere.

Nor were monks the only religious subject to confinement. The twelfth-century Cistercian writer Ailred of Rievaulx told the story of the nun of Watton, who, around 1160, became pregnant by another religious, was discovered, and was chained by fetters on each leg and placed in a cell with only bread and water to live on. After her lover had been castrated, the nun remained in prison, but through divine intervention all traces of pregnancy miraculously disappeared and her chains and fetters fell off. The stories of Peter the Venerable, the prison called *Vade in pace,* and the nun of Watton seem to be memorable precisely because they were considered unusual, not because they illustrated a common practice. They do represent, however, a distinctive monastic contribution to the history of prisons: the first instan-ces of confinement for specific periods and occasionally for life for the purpose of moral correction.

Monastic prisons also served for the confinement of secular clergy under discipline by their bishops. The process was known as *detrusio in monasterium* ("confinement in a monastery"), and it might entail either living as a monk under normal monastic discipline or being held in a monastic prison. During the twelfth century, bishops were expected to have their own diocesan prisons for the punishment of criminal clergy. The episcopal use of imprisonment as punishment was regularized in an executive order entitled "Quamvis" and issued by Pope Boniface VIII in his lawbook, the *Liber Sextus,* in 1298. Addressing the Roman law doctrine that prisons should serve as places of confinement, not punishment, Boniface nevertheless permitted abbots and bishops to punish offenders by the *poena carceris* ("punishment of prison") either for periods of time or for life. Boniface VIII is the first sovereign authority in the Western tradition to determine that imprisonment as punishment was a legitimate instrument of a universal legal system.

Clerical Discipline of the Laity

The disciplinary obligations of bishops, councils, and popes were not restricted to clerical personnel. Laypeople too sinned and required penance to expiate sin. The key to clerical jurisdiction over laypeople—including, in theory and often in practice, nobles and kings—was the necessity of penance on the part of all sinners. In all cases, the clergy's duty was to impose penance. Lesser and secret sins might be privately confessed, and in most cases private penance was imposed, since, as canon lawyers said, "The Church does not judge hidden things."

But in the case of sins that were publicly known or of such enormity that they required public penance, the "internal forum" of conscience and private confession and penance gave way to the "external forum" of ecclesiastical judgment. Such sins might be intrinsically serious, or they might be serious offenses that were notorious and caused *scandalum,* public knowledge that injured the Christian community and therefore had to be dealt with publicly. "Criminal sins," as the most severe sins were called, required public exclusion from the church and the sacraments, and they required public penance of various kinds, including penitential confinement, the same *detrusio in monasterium* that applied to secular clergy. For some particularly offensive criminal sins—incest, magic, divination—several eighth- and ninth-century councils insisted on actual punitive incarceration, and the Latin sources specifically use the term *carcer.*

The extensive development of canon law after the work of Gratian in the mid-twelfth century tended to regularize ecclesiastical criminal procedure and formally extended the competence of ecclesiastical courts, especially after the decretal *Novit* of Pope Innocent III (1198–1216) in 1204, which asserted ecclesiastical jurisdiction in any case involving sin. At the same time, Innocent III established a new legal procedure for ecclesiastical courts. The traditional procedure had been accusatorial: a case required a private accuser in order to begin a legal process. This procedure also operated in secular courts. Innocent revived an older method of procedure, the inquisitorial procedure, which had been developed in Roman imperial courts, had occasionally been used in the early Christian communities, but since then had only rarely been used, chiefly by bishops who were required to visit the religious institutions in their dioceses and inquire into the moral conduct of those in the institutions. The new inquisitorial procedure introduced by Innocent III applied to both clerics and laypeople, particularly in serious and publicly known matters.

The Prisons of the Inquisitors

Perhaps the best-known instances of the clerical discipline of the laity are found in the work of a number of inquisitorial tribunals established in the early thirteenth century chiefly to deal with cases of heterodoxy, that is, active dissent from ecclesiastical doctrine. The revival of inquisitorial trial procedure by Innocent III appears to have been used initially in the cases of criminal clergy. But with the perception by churchmen and lay rulers of widespread dissent in religious matters in the twelfth and thirteenth centuries, the older doctrines of forbearance, pastoral admonition, and the accusatorial procedure appeared insufficient to protect Christian society against a new and formidable enemy. From the late twelfth century, both churchmen and lay rulers issued stiffer laws regarding the discovery and punishment of people who were considered enemies of both God and Christian society. These laws also contributed to the simultaneous development of secular criminal law, considered in the next section of this chapter. In the early thirteenth century the popes created the special office of "inquisitor of heretical depravity," an instance of papally delegated jurisdiction to a specific individual to investigate the presence of heterodoxy in a particular place for a specified period of time.

Inquisitorial investigations required time—to notify people of the inquisitors' arrival and the purpose of their visit, to establish contact with local ecclesiastical and secular authorities, and to investigate matters that were generally concealed and difficult to establish with clarity. Because the investigations often took a long time, inquisitors used prisons to hold those accused until the investigation was complete. Although inquisitors could not inflict the death penalty, they were permitted to establish the orthodoxy or lack of it on the part of the accused and then "relax" the heretic to "the secular arm," the secular court that could execute a convicted heretic once heterodoxy had been established by the appropriate theological jurisdiction, in this case, that of the inquisitor.

Only in extreme cases, however, were convicted heretics executed. If there was hope of changing the views of heretics or of inducing heretics to repent, they were often imprisoned, some for life. The new work of the inquisitors at first greatly overloaded the capacity of existing prisons, and from the mid-thirteenth century on, both the confiscated property of convicted heretics and grants from the royal treasury, especially in France and Sicily, led to the construction of special inquisitorial prisons. These were expensive to maintain, however, and thus proved to be a continuous source of dispute among the different authorities responsible for them. The inquisitors and their secular counterparts were the first to discover the financial impact that even a modest system of prisons could have. The inquisitors' frequent use of imprisonment also increased officials' awareness of prison conditions. Early in the fourteenth century, Pope Clement V sent a commission of inspectors into the inquisitorial prisons of southern France; finding these prisons to be in great disrepair, the inspectors issued strict and apparently successful orders for improvement. From the fourteenth century on, inquisitorial prisons were probably the best-maintained prisons in Europe.

The authority of ecclesiastical courts, including inquisitorial courts, over monks, secular clergy, and laypeople was not substantially challenged in most of Europe until the various Reformations of the sixteenth century and the movements for the secularization of ecclesiastical property and the elimination of clerical privilege in the eighteenth and nineteenth centuries. As part of the associated polemic, a largely mythical image of the ominous and terrible "Inquisition" was used effectively against any manifestation of clerical authority over lay-people. One of the most popular images was the case of Joan of Arc. Fighting on behalf of the king of France against the English and their Burgundian allies in 1430, Joan was captured by the Burgundians, sold by them to the English, and tried as a heretic in 1431 by an inquisitorial court that the English established with French clerical collaboration. Promised leniency by the court, Joan pleaded guilty to a reduced charge. But when she was sentenced to life imprisonment because her judges believed that she had recanted only out of fear of death (a common reason for sentences of life imprisonment in inquisitorial courts), Joan revoked her confession and was burned at the stake. Another inquisitorial tribunal posthumously rehabilitated her in 1456.

For the most part, the inquisitorial tribunals were far more regularized than the ad hoc tribunal that tried Joan. In their extension of clerical authority to discipline the laity, inquisitorial tribunals brought a new kind of imprisonment, hitherto restricted to the world of monks and secular clergy, into the world of lay criminal justice. They also brought Boniface VIII's rule that prisons could indeed be used for temporary or perpetual punishment, regardless of what Roman law said about the matter. The influence of ecclesiastical courts in general from the twelfth century on coincided with the revived study of Roman law and the reform of criminal law in virtually all the states of Europe.

LEARNED LAW AND PUNISHMENT IN EUROPE, 1150–1550

The Revival of Roman Law and Local Law

The *Institutes* and *Code* of Justinian were known in Europe from 554 on. But the *Digest*, the key to late Roman jurisprudence, was not. Late in the eleventh century a single manuscript of the *Digest* surfaced in northern Italy, and from then on, Roman law was taught at a number of schools, especially at the great law university of Bologna. From the twelfth century on, learned law became the most popular subject of study in Europe, partly because it also served the needs of rulers.

The formal study of learned law gave considerable impetus to efforts by secular rulers to expand and legitimize their authority, especially their authority over wrongdoing. On a number of fronts—academic study, the design of lawmaking bodies, and the practical activity of lay courts throughout Europe—learned law became a prominent part of a general transformation of European society and culture in the twelfth century and after. Although Roman law was the formal subject of most study, it was the learned and scientific character of that law that most strongly influenced contemporary societies. Learned law did not necessarily become identical with Roman law in France, Italy, the Iberian peninsula, and England, but these places too increasingly invoked the principles of learned law. A mixture of Roman law and local learned law shaped what legal historians call the *ius commune*, the "common learned law," of early modern Europe, with the term used in Latin only so as not to confuse it with the English common law, the other major legal system of medieval and early modern Europe. A number of elements in the learned law influenced public law, particularly its criminal law component. Prominent among these was the general shift from the accusatorial to the inquisitorial legal procedure, the institution of written evidence, and the use of specialized professional personnel, including judges with wide discretion in admitting evidence and sentencing. The social, political, economic, and intellectual changes of the twelfth century have long been regarded by historians as a turning point in European history. The growth and development of cities, many of them asserting virtual independence of any superior authority, especially in northern Italy, the increasingly public character of kingship, and the familiarity and attractiveness of canon law transformed early medieval Europe into the civilization of proto-modern Europe. Legal study occupied a prominent place in the dynamics of the twelfth-century renaissance.

But European societies did not change everywhere at once, nor did they all change at the same pace or in the same ways. A survey of the doctrines that governed crime and punishment in the two systems of the English common law and the continental *ius commune* reflects the variances among different regions and the survival of older ideas and methods alongside the new. The universal claims of learned Roman law and canon law often made little impression on areas not prepared to receive or use them.

Prisons and the Common Law of England

The Germanic law codes of Anglo-Saxon England record the use of imprisonment for theft and witchcraft, but the most common forms of punishment were those used in the rest of Europe—mutilation, death, exile, or compensation. In the violent century following the Norman conquest of England in 1066, William I (1066–87) and his successors attempted to impose their authority throughout the kingdom, but a strong public law and administration did not emerge until the second half of the twelfth century under Henry II (1154–89). Among the steps toward a strengthened public law was the construction of the Tower of London by William I as the first royal prison in England, built to hold the king's enemies. Other early royal prisons were the Fleet in London, used chiefly for the custody of those confined by London justices as well as for occasional prisoners of war and hostages, and the "baulk house" at Winchester, whose functions were similar. Instances of using prisons to hold private enemies, particularly in the civil wars of 1135–54, abound in narrative histories. When Henry II issued the Assizes of Clarendon in 1166, he ordered that sheriffs should build jails in each county to hold those accused of felonies until they could be tried by itinerant royal justices.

During the later twelfth and thirteenth centuries, coercive imprisonment in the Fleet or the Tower for debtors of the crown became more common, as did the imprisonment of contumacious excommunicates, those who interfered with the working of the law, failed appellants, attainted jurors, perjurers, frauds, and those who misinformed the courts. These reasons for confinement fall generally within the conventional categories of custodial and coercive imprisonment. In the early thirteenth century the great English jurist Ralegh-Bratton could comfortably quote the Roman jurist Ulpian to the effect that prisons were for custody only, not for punishment. Ulpian's Roman rule certainly seemed to apply in Ralegh-Bratton's England.

But from the 1270s on, the number of prisons in England and of imprisonable offenses increased rapidly. By 1520 there were 180 imprisonable offenses in the common law. A significant number of these new offenses dealt with vagrancy, breaking the peace, infamy, illegal bearing of arms, morals offenses, and other similar acts. Besides the proliferation of imprisonable offenses, there also occurred in the thirteenth century a restriction of those devices that permitted an offender to stay out of prison—bail, frankpledge, and property attachment. There was a corresponding increase in offenses for which no bail could be obtained—treason, arson, jailbreaking, and arrest by the direct order of the king or the king's chief justice.

The prison-building program begun by Henry II placed royal prisons throughout the kingdom. Nobles who had more limited rights of justice also kept prisons, ranging from suites of rooms in the gatehouses of monasteries to castles, mills, and parts of houses, the "makeshift prisons" that are evident in German lands as well as parts of England. Some English prisons were franchisal—that is, the right to arrest and hold a free man was given (or sold) by the king to a person who derived an income from the difference between money spent maintaining the prison and the prisoners and money received for their upkeep.

Towns too were compelled by the king to build and maintain jails as part of their corporate responsibility for keeping the peace. London, for example, held not only the Tower and the Fleet but also the following, from the late twelfth century: Newgate, largely for debtors and state prisoners; Ludgate, for freemen of the city confined for debt, trespass, contempt, and other lesser offenses; the Marshalseas (prisons of the royal Marshall); the Counters (prisons for the sheriffs of London and Middlesex County), and the Tun, chiefly for moral delinquents. Other towns also had prisons, and the Bristol Tun is depicted in one of the earliest English drawings of a prison.

Punishment in English criminal law was intended to be quick and public to serve as a deterrent to other crime. Thus, forms of punishment ranged from shaming display—the pillory, mutilation, branding, public stocks, and ducking stools—to severe and aggravated capital punishments—hanging, drowning, burning, burial alive, or decapitation—and any of these could be preceded by the infliction of torments before the execution itself. Besides the prisons of London, there was also the official place of execution, Tyburn Hill, which was used for several centuries.

The increase in criminal legal business strained the capacity of the jails, and during the thirteenth century, the crown appointed special commissions to clear, or "deliver," the jails. These commissions of "gaol delivery" greatly speeded up the process of criminal justice and emptied the prisons—by convictions as well as releases—so that the next group of prisoners could be assembled. When the system worked efficiently, gaol delivery could clear jails two or three times a year.

In royal prisons the types of accommodations varied from foul to comfortable, the latter usually reserved for high-ranking prisoners. Jailers charged fees for what they termed *suavitas* ("gentle keeping"), and these fees were regulated by a London ordinance of 1346. Food, fuel, bedding, and other items of comfort were sold to prisoners, and debts to jailers had to be cleared before a prisoner could be freed. Irons were used inside prisons to confine dangerous prisoners, although a number of laws stated that these were not to be used for aggravating confinement but rather for security. "Iron fees" might be paid to alleviate the prisoner's condition. The prisoners thus bore much of the cost of their own confinement because of the low fees allowed by the crown and because of the expenses and narrow profit margins of the franchisal prisons. The practice of private charity greatly aided prisoners, especially the poorest, some of whom depended on it for their very survival.

At their worst, English prisons resembled those on the Continent and earlier Roman prisons as well. Below the comfortable rooms were common chambers for groups of prisoners, and below these were the cells of harshest confinement: "Juliansbourne" in Newgate, "Bolton's Ward" in the Fleet, and other notoriously named cells in other prisons.

Jailers were subject to severe penalties for escapes. In the later Middle Ages, convicted felons who had escaped and been recaptured were treated as traitors. Boredom and despair still drove many prisoners to escape. In 1244 the prisoner Gryffud ap Llewellyn fell to his death while attempting to escape from the Tower of London, an attempt commemorated in contemporary chronicle accounts and in a striking manuscript illustration.

England was a compact kingdom, efficiently ruled by a series of kings who based many of their claims to legitimacy on the strength of the common law. England also had courts of canon law, and the two laws in England produced a remarkable homogeneity throughout the kingdom in law and punishment, as well as in the use of prisons. The English legal system and its doctrines of criminal law spread throughout the later English colonies and the British Empire, constituting one of the major legal systems of the modern world.

Prisons on the Continent and the Ius Commune

One of the chief differences between the common law of England and the evolving *ius commune* of the Continent was the degree to which the latter was strongly influenced by Roman law. The greatest centers of this influence were the kingdom of Sicily and the city-republics of northern Italy, much of southern France, and the kingdoms of France and Castile in general, especially from the thirteenth century. But not all of continental Europe was equally influenced by Roman and other learned law, and it is advisable to begin with those areas influenced least and latest.

Germany was the most regionalized and fragmented of European kingdoms. Princes, ecclesiastical rulers, and cities wielded virtually unchecked local power, and the scope of royal authority—including royal justice—was limited. The older personal law codes of earlier Germanic peoples and the laws of later kings and emperors developed after the tenth century into diffuse local usages. Regional accounts of legal custom appeared in the thirteenth century in Saxony and Swabia, although these accounts were privately made and not legally binding. Canon law too operated in the German lands, but it remained strictly in the ecclesiastical courts and had little impact on legal change outside these courts. Learned Roman law did not enter German courts until the end of the fifteenth century. And not until 1532 did there emerge a full-fledged criminal code, the *Carolina* of Emperor Charles V.

Crime and punishment in the German lands rested on local custom, often followed archaic legal procedures, and operated largely at the discretion of the local ruler. Much of what became criminal law elsewhere in Europe remained in the realm of private injury; cases were tried by tribunals of lay jurors who were merely the prominent men in the local community and were directed by a judge appointed by the lord who controlled the court. Procedure was oral, and law lay in the conscience and local knowledge of jurors. Public law was limited, and its resources were few.

Custom dictated both procedure and punishment. Nobles were beheaded, and serious offenders of lower social status were broken on the wheel, burned, or hanged. These forms of shameful execution, often accompanied by mutilation, were inflicted by the executioner in the service of the local holder of the rights of "high justice." The division of judicial competence into the spheres of "high," "middle," and "low" justice occurred throughout Europe from the eleventh century on, originally by delegation from the king but later appropriated by any lord strong enough to do so. These rights were as much financial as judicial—the higher the justice one's court wielded, the greater the ruler's income in fines and confiscations.

On the rare occasions when prisons are mentioned, they serve either as a mitigation of capital punishment or as an alternative to a fine if the offender was insolvent. Except for mitigated death sentences, prison terms were usually short, although by the fifteenth century, particularly in the courts of cities, terms of imprisonment varied more widely. In some territories a visit by the king customarily entailed the freeing of prisoners. The German king-emperors themselves often used the castle at Trifels to hold enemies and those charged with crimes against them.

For the most part, prisons in German lands consisted of rooms and holes in the foundations of local fortifications, in the cellars of town halls, and in subterranean chambers known as Löcher: the Bornheimer Loch was a prison in Frankfurt under the Bornheim gate, and the Brückenloch was located under the bridge tower in Mainz. Such ad hoc prisons were regulated only by the local authorities who administered them. Imprisonment in the German lands remained local and unreformed until well into the early modern period.

The Scandinavian countries, like Germany, favored punishments that entailed property loss, death, or mutilation and, occasionally in Iceland, penal servitude. Although imprisonment was used in canon law courts in Northern Europe, and in Iceland and probably elsewhere as temporary confinement in the sheriff's house pending trial and execution, there appears to have been no wider use of imprisonment in any Scandinavian law until the sixteenth century, when confinement at forced labor was gradually introduced. In the Low Countries too, canon law courts used prisons, but secular courts generally did not, except for preventive detention—as in Iceland and elsewhere—until the growth of a widespread use of prisons throughout Europe in the late sixteenth and seventeenth centuries.

Like Germany, tenth-, eleventh-, and twelfth-century France consisted of territorial principalities created by warlords in the wake of the fall of the Carolingian monarchy and the invasions of the later ninth and tenth centuries. The kings of "France" made extensive claims to superiority over the territorial princes, but for much of the period between 987 and 1180 they effectively ruled only in the middle Seine Valley in the territory known as the Ile-de-France. The emergence of strong kings in the late twelfth century, particularly Philip II (Philip Augustus, 1180–1223), and the extension of royal authority over many of the territorial principalities through inheritance, marriage, and conquest led to the creation of a strong and centralized monarchy that ruled a country of distinctive regions in the thirteenth century, a monarchy best exemplified by the kings Louis IX (1226–70) and Philip IV (Philip the Fair, 1285–1314). The French monarchy survived the disasters of the long war with England during the fourteenth and early fifteenth centuries and emerged at the end of the fifteenth century with its authority restored and its powers and governing institutions increased.

The royal centralization of law and justice that characterized England by the second half of the twelfth century did not occur in France until the mid-thirteenth century. In fact, until Napoleon, civil and criminal law in France remained largely regionally based, although royally supervised. During the twelfth and thirteenth centuries royal, lordly, municipal, and ecclesiastical courts and courtholders with differing levels of judicial competence and very different levels of legal science existed side by side. By the thirteenth century the right to administer justice itself had become categorized—as it was in German lands and England—as "high," "middle," and "low" depending on the sphere of competence of the courtholder. Part of the centralizing of royal power in the thirteenth century was the monopolizing of high justice by royal officials and courts directly responsible to the kings of France.

By the thirteenth century the local customs and practices in the different regions of France were written down in volumes called *coutumières*, or customaries. In these, offenses and punishments were generally fixed, the accusatory process operated in both private and public matters, and the rules of evidence were vague. In royal courts, however, judges adopted the inquisitorial procedure, generally termed Romano-canonical, as well as written evidence and stricter rules of evidence generally, enjoyed broad judicial discretion, and became legal specialists in the new learned law.

In Old French the Latin term *prisio*, derived from a Latin term meaning "to arrest" or "to take custody of," acquired a variety of distinct meanings. It might mean the act of arrest, the right to try someone arrested, the right to arrest a free person, the state of privation of liberty, or the actual place of detention itself. In French, Italian, and English it displaced the older and more formal Latin term *carcer* and the medieval Latin term *geola*, which became, in English, "jail."

Custodial imprisonment existed in France, as it did elsewhere, for those accused of certain kinds of crimes, for those whose flight was considered likely, for those who were considered infamous, and for those without status or privilege. Imprisonment as a punishment also developed in thirteenth-century France, not only in royal justice but in collections of regional customary law as well. The customary law written in thirteenth-century Normandy (1248–70) allowed for punitive imprisonment, and the fourteenth-century *Ancient Customary of Brittany* included punitive imprisonment for offenders of low estate when their offenses insulted those of higher estate. The greatest of the customaries, that written by Philippe de Beaumanoir (1247–96) for the county of Clermont and the region around Beauvais, was a private collection but was extremely wide-ranging and virtually encyclopedic. Beaumanoir routinely stated that punishment should consist of death, punitive imprisonment, or loss of property. Beaumanoir echoed the Brittany customs regarding the insulting of a superior by an inferior—and he added an argument for deterrence. He allowed imprisonment for debt, as well as for perjury and conspiracy.

Throughout thirteenth-century France, blasphemy was punishable by imprisonment, in close confinement at the judge's discretion; imprisonment was also used for the misuse of the right to imprison, in some instances of theft, and occasionally as an alternative to the execution of capital punishment. In 1312 Perceval d'Aunay, convicted of breaking into a house at night for the purpose of robbery and kidnapping, was sentenced to two years of close confinement on bread and water, to be followed by exile from the kingdom of France. In 1317 Simon Braielez, implicated in the assassination of an advocate of the Parlement of Paris, was sentenced to imprisonment for life in the Châtelet in Paris.

The Châtelet is the best known of the early French prisons. A fortress on the right bank of the Seine, it came around 1200 to house the court and prison of the provost (royal governor) of the city. The prison itself was a tower in the northeast corner of the fortress. The comfortable highest rooms were maintained for nobles who paid their own expenses of fourpence a night for a bed and twopence a night for a room. On a lower level was a single room shared by prisoners of lower social status, and below this, as in English prisons, was the *fosse* or *oubliette*, into which prisoners were lowered from the floor above, although even there prisoners had to pay one penny per night for their room.

The jurisdiction of the provost of Paris extended widely beyond the city proper and eventually came to include most of northern France. The procedures of the provost's court were compiled into the *Custom of Paris,* ultimately the most influential of French regional collections of customary law. The records of the Châtelet are far from complete, but a number of scholars have successfully used them in studies of criminality and punishment. Although the Châtelet served most frequently as a custodial prison, the sentences of Perceval d'Aunay and Simon Braielez indicate that punitive imprisonment was not unknown, although it was infrequent.

In principle, royal prisons were to be regularly inspected—for physical conditions as well as for the supervision of jailers—and they were to be reasonable and airy, as royal instructions stated, so that the punishment of prison did not cause death or injury. The sexes were routinely separated, and if possible, female prisoners were to have female jailers. One of Joan of Arc's complaints was that she had not been given female guards while in prison. Hardened criminals were to be separated from offenders who were not thought to be dangerous. Jailers were also responsible for preventing escapes and for providing their charges with food, at least bread and water, although in some cases prisoners were permitted to pay for better food or to have relatives and friends bring food. On occasion some fraternal, professional, or charitable associations donated food and wine to prisoners at the Châtelet, as did the goldsmiths' guild, which gave an Easter dinner to all the prisoners in the city of Paris. In royal prisons, prisoners were deprived of their own clothing and forced to wear a simple garment that was easily identifiable and helped to mark escapees and to identify prisoners mingling with visitors either in the prisons or on those occasions when prisoners were permitted briefly to be outside prisons.

Outside Paris, there was little systematization of prisons, except in the royal castles, where provosts kept prisoners until they were transferred to the Châtelet. Royal prisons began to increase in number during the reign of Louis XI (1461–83), who expanded the fortress at Loches, near Tours, with towers and dungeons and transformed the chateau at Vincennes into an elaborately secure fortress and prison. The most famous royal prison, the Bastille, was originally a gate in the fortifications constructed for the military defense of Paris. From 1370 until the early fifteenth century the Bastille was enlarged; it had dungeons, eight towers with places of confinement inside thick stone walls, and physically debilitating living conditions.

The system of prisons that emerged from French customary regional and royal law lasted until the French Revolution in 1789. In the late seventeenth and eighteenth centuries, penal reformers, under the influence of Ulpian's old maxim that prisons should be used only for confinement and not for punishment, insisted that prison conditions be improved and prison practices reformed. By the eighteenth century, however, new forms of punishment had been introduced—including the galleys and the workhouses. All of Europe stood on the eve of a vast program of political and legal reform, one of the most symbolic acts of which was the storming of the Bastille—by then an insignificant prison that held few prisoners. But as a symbol of the power of the Old Regime, the Bastille illuminates the position that prisons had come to occupy in French society and in the revolutionary imagination.

In the Christian kingdoms of the Iberian peninsula in the tenth and eleventh centuries, most law was local and customary. Its legitimacy usually depended on the existence of a local charter of settlement issued, by a ruler, to Christian settlers of reconquered Muslim lands *(cartas de población)* or on more detailed *fueros*, charters given by a ruler to the inhabitants of a district and used by them to administer their own affairs. Some *fueros* were so detailed that they circulated widely within large regions, thus making legal practice uniform, at least within areas influenced by a single *fuero*. Legal procedures were similar to those of other European societies: privately initiated, supervised by royally appointed judges, largely oral, and unlearned. In criminal cases the kings and royal officials could impose fines, confiscation, exile, mutilation, and hanging. The only traces of imprisonment in the eleventh and early twelfth centuries were its infliction for failure to appear in court and the practice of imprisoning those defendants who could not post bonds to the plaintiff.

As rulers began to legislate more actively in the eleventh century, a number of larger and more inclusive legal works appeared. Particularly important were the *Usatges* of Barcelona and the legislation of Alfonso IX of Léon-Castila at the end of the twelfth century. Royal legislation and royally appointed, specialized judges considerably expanded criminal law, affirming the king's right to inflict capital punishment (hanging, drowning, boiling alive) as well as mutilation (punitive amputation of hands and feet, and noses, lips, ears, and breasts in the case of women), blinding, and fines and imprisonment. Iberian scholars and rulers also drew on the renewed study of Roman law after the mid-twelfth century and attempted to create uniform legal systems within the kingdoms of Aragon, Castile, and Portugal. Although their attempts often encountered stiff local resistance, much of their work was successful.

The most impressive and wide-ranging legislative work in medieval Iberia was the collection called *Las Siete Partidas* ("The Collection in Seven Parts"), issued by King Alfonso X shortly after 1265. Although the applicability of the *Siete Partidas* varied within Castile, the work contains the most extensive discussion of the uses of prison of any royal legislation in medieval Europe.

Title XXIX of the seventh part of the *Siete Partidas* contains fifteen laws pertaining to prisons and prisoners, ranging from the process of prison commitment to penalties for escape and for erecting new prisons without royal permission. Prison security is emphasized, as is the insistence that female prisoners be segregated from males for fear of scandal, either by placing them in a convent or putting them in the custody of good women. The regulations for guarding prisoners are detailed: the chief jailer must report regularly to the judges about the condition of the prisons and prisoners, and undue severity—branding and mutilation of prisoners—was forbidden. The penalty for permitting or aiding prison breaks was severe.

We do not know the extent to which the laws of the *Siete Partidas* applied to actual prisons in Castile—or elsewhere in the peninsula—nor do we know about the prison buildings themselves. But the breadth of Alfonso X's concerns with prisons suggests more than a mere imitation of Roman and French royal law.

France and Castile illustrate the difficulties faced by royal authorities in the thirteenth and fourteenth centuries when they tried to impose systematic criminal law on large territorial monarchies. The numerous societies in Italy, however, display a very different pattern. Nowhere else in Western Europe is the broad spectrum of legal innovations in the twelfth and thirteenth centuries as evident as in Italy. The Kingdom of Sicily, the papal states, and the powerful city-republics of the north—Venice, Florence, Milan, and Genoa—offer an astonishingly ambitious address to the problems of crime and criminal law. This approach, at its most developed, comes closest to later developments in criminal law and modes of punishment.

Italy was the home not only of the first major center of learned legal study—Bologna—but also of the first university created to serve the interests of a single state, that of Naples. From the universities, legal specialists, rapidly creating a new profession, moved on to careers in the church, royal and princely chanceries and courts, and the legal judgeships and advocacies of the cities. They effected the reform of the older Lombard law into a general territorial law for much of Italy. They contributed to the making and administration of canon law, not only in the papal states (which had a separate system of secular law as well) but also in the cities. They also shaped and administered the new urban legal codes. Results of their work included the first learned written law code of the kingdom of Sicily, the *Constitutions of Melfi* of 1231, the written versions of regional and urban customs (at Milan in 1216, followed quickly by Brescia, Como, and Piacenza), and the formal promulgation of urban statutes. In criminal law the legal specialists produced the first handbooks of criminal procedure, notably Albertus Gandinus's *Treatise on Crimes* of 1270 and, in the fourteenth century, the first treatise specifically devoted to penal law, the *Treatise on Prisons*, attributed to the great jurist Bartolus of Sassoferrato.

In spite of the diversity of jurisdictions across the Italian peninsula, a common result of the influence of learned law on local custom and practice here, as in the royal courts of France, was its impact on the area of legal procedure and the rules of evidence. Most jurisdictions adopted the inquisitorial procedure of Roman law and canon law, the rules of evidence in learned law, the specialization of a legal profession, and the institutions of punishment for criminal offenses. One feature of the new learned law that did not derive from Roman precedents or doctrine, however, was the use of punitive imprisonment.

Among the variety of state-inflicted punishments, prison was not originally conspicuous. Fines, capital punishments by various means, exile, and public shaming were far more frequent. In the *Constitutions of Melfi*, for example, a period of imprisonment, usually for one year, was prescribed only for those who falsely claimed to be physicians. In this instance imprisonment was a supplementary punishment to the confiscation of the offender's property. Like other tribunals that received convicted heretics from church courts, the Sicilian kingdom also prescribed life imprisonment for heretics who had recanted out of fear of death.

In Sicily, as elsewhere in Italy, public authorities used as prisons whatever suitable space was available for the purpose. One of the best-known instances of imprisonment in the kingdom of Sicily was that of Pietro della Vigna, chancellor of the king-emperor Frederick II and author of the *Constitutions of Melfi*. In 1249 the chancellor fell into the king's disfavor and was blinded and put into prison, where, in despair, he committed suicide. He makes an eloquent and moving appearance in Dante's *Inferno* (Canto XIII), composed around 1310 and itself a rich source of imagery touching on criminal justice, tortures, and imprisonment.

In Rome the famous Castel San Angelo, originally the tomb of the second-century Roman emperor Hadrian, seems to have been referred to as early as the seventh century as "The Prison of Theoderic," although there is no evidence that the early-sixth-century Ostrogothic king ever used it as such. The Castel was used frequently as a fortified residence for Roman aristocrats and popes, however, and as a place of confinement for local criminals. The *prigione storiche* ("historical prisons") within it are still shown to visitors. In Florence, before the construction of the official city prison, Le Stinche (1297–1304), the city government leased private buildings, although these were used only to hold those awaiting trial for certain offenses and those awaiting the execution of capital sentences.

In the Roman law that guided much of the law learning and lawmaking in thirteenth-century Italy, Ulpian's statement that prisons should be used for confinement, not for punishment, was generally understood to be the formal doctrine on the subject. In other learned law, however, notably canon law, prisons were certainly used for both punishment and correction. This conflict was more apparent than real. Roman law by itself did not hold in very many places in Italy or the rest of Europe. Moreover, Roman law gave considerable discretion to the presiding judge in criminal cases, and the statutory authority of many city-republics not only permitted them to establish their own statutory punishments but also allowed judges to create new punishments when the occasion seemed to call for them and to punish by analogy—that is, to apply known punishments to offenses not specifically defined by statute. Especially in cases in which the harshest of punishments seemed inappropriate, for one reason or another, imprisonment offered an appealing alternative. Judges also knew that a prison sentence was reversible if new evidence was forthcoming and that a capital sentence was not.

In preambles to collections of statute law, treatises on crime and punishment, lectures of the legal scholars, oaths of public office, instructions to magistrates, and opinions of practicing jurists, criminal law was regarded as both a punishment for wickedness and a means of reforming the offender—in modern terms, both retribution and reform. The growth of the northern Italian cities was accompanied by increased crime and increased official attention paid to crime and criminals. During the fourteenth and fifteenth centuries the lawmakers of the cities became willing and able to fit punishments to crimes with considerable rational precision, including, in Italy and elsewhere, a reduction in the physical severity of many punishments.

Some historians have identified a sequence in styles of public punishment from the twelfth to the sixteenth centuries, according to which initially harsh physical punishments were succeeded by fines, and fines often were combined with imprisonment during the fourteenth and fifteenth centuries. In both Venice and Florence the increased use of punitive imprisonment suggests that imprisonment represented a major aspect of the legal revolution that had begun in the twelfth and thirteenth centuries.

In 1297 the city of Florence began the construction of its public prison, Le Stinche. The construction of the prison shortly followed the publication of the *Ordinances of Justice* in 1293. Florence revised its criminal statutes twice more in the fourteenth century, in 1322–23 and in 1355, and again in the fifteenth century, in 1415. The statutes of criminal justice and the prison both represented a considerable investment of communal energy and resources, and both reflected a new interest in making imprisonment a regular part of criminal punishment.

Le Stinche was sometimes used to incarcerate children for their correction and improvement. It segregated its inmates according to age, gender, degree of sanity, and the seriousness of the offense. So well-known did it become that the prisons that later appeared in other cities—Siena and Pistoia among them—although formally known as *carceri di Comune* ("prisons of the Comune"), were also informally called Le Stinche. In 1559 the architect Antonio da Ponte was commissioned to construct a large public prison in Venice, containing four hundred individual cells in which would be incarcerated prisoners whose capital sentences had been commuted to life in prison, suggesting that the increasing visibility and the novelty of the use of prisons did not constitute an isolated Florentine and Venetian phenomenon.

The legal learning and innovative character of the northern Italian city-republics in the thirteenth and fourteenth centuries overcame the objections of Roman law to the use of punitive imprisonment, possibly on the model of contemporary canon law and certainly out of the experience of lawmaking and law administering in the new societies the cities created. The lessons about punitive imprisonment learned in these cities and in canon law courts were not lost on the royal courts of France and Castile or, eventually, on most other Western European societies.

In the age of the "birth of the prison" in the eighteenth and early nineteenth centuries, criminal law reformers, artists, novelists, and polemicists looked back on what they thought they knew of medieval European prisons with a mixed attitude of fascination, horror, and contempt. In terms of the new purposes of punishment and the immense scale of prisons, nothing in the ancient or medieval worlds seemed to resemble the institutions that followed from Pentonville, Eastern State, or Auburn. Compared with the new, large-scale, scientifically managed and organized prisons of the modern world, those of the ancient and medieval worlds looked like ghastly dungeons of the sort that eighteenth- and nineteenth-century Romantic artists like Giambattista Piranesi and the illustrators of fantastic novels about the Spanish Inquisition loved to draw. But long before the new penal institutions and the modern age of penology heralded by these institutions, the small-scale societies of medieval Europe, working with what they could of Roman law and driven by the conviction that in some cases, however few, punitive confinement was preferable to capital punishment, exile, or the confiscation of property, created punitive imprisonment in both ecclesiastical and secular courts.

Thirteenth-century Europeans knew little about the prisons of Mediterranean antiquity except for their treatment in Roman law and their echoes in scripture. But just as these Europeans carved out a new legal science and a new legal system for themselves, so they created a new system of punishment. At worst, the new criminal punishments indeed appeared to be what Richard van Dülmen has called "a theater of horror." Especially in the frequency of and the mechanical use of torture and in aggravated executions, these punishments came close to the *summa supplicia* of third-century Rome. The body of the condemned became the map of the offense and the sole subject of legal vengeance.

But there is another side to the penal practices of the thirteenth century and later, one that is especially evident in the history of prisons. In some instances, at least, those who held the power of life and death chose the confined life of prison. Some, like Boniface VIII, instituted punitive imprisonment statutorily, sweeping aside the conventional Roman objections. Others—the independent city-republics of northern Italy and the kings of Sicily, England, France, and Castile—introduced imprisonment into traditional systems of criminal punishment. After 1200, the criminal law practices of Europe resembled less and less those of Mediterranean antiquity and the earlier Middle Ages and more and more those of later centuries.

Acknowledgments

I am grateful to my colleagues Ruth Mazo Karras, Jeffrey Tigay, Marvin Wolfgang, and Robert L. Rowen for their suggestions and advice.

Bibliographic Note

A much fuller bibliography is available from the author. The references here follow the sequence of topics treated in the chapter.

The best and most recent general surveys of punishment in the ancient and medieval worlds are the volumes entitled *La Peine* (Punishment), Recueils de la Société Jean Bodin pour l'histoire comparative des institutions, vols. 55–56 (Brussels: De Boeck Université, 1988, 1991). The best introduction to law and justice in early Greece, as well as a remarkably successful placing of this development within the framework of recent general scholarship on criminal legal theory and practice in the twentieth century, is Mary Margaret Mackenzie, *Plato on Punishment* (Berkeley: University of California Press, 1981). A recent survey of the entire ancient world is Israel Drapkin, *Crime and Punishment in the Ancient World* (Lexington, Mass: Lexington Books, 1989). Trevor J. Saunders, *Plato's Penal Code: Tradition, Controversy, and Reforms in Greek Penology* (Oxford: Clarendon Press, 1991), focuses on Plato's thought in great detail.

The best study of prisons in ancient Hebrew culture is the wide-ranging and indispensable work of David Louis Blumenfeld, "The Terminology of Detention and Forced Imprisonment in the Bible" (Ph.D. diss., New York University, 1977), which ranges across the ancient Near East and offers a rich collection of comparative material. See also the articles by M. Greenberg in *The Interpreter's Dictionary of the Bible* (New York: Abingdon Press, 1962), vol. 1, "Crimes and Punishments," pp. 733–44, and vol. 3, "Prisons," pp. 891–92. There is a brief and stimulating treatment of Jewish criminal law in Drapkin, *Crime and Punishment in the Ancient World*, pp. 54–83, and an outline of Talmudic teaching in Hermann L. Strack, *Introduction to the Talmud and Midrash* (reprint, New York: Atheneum, 1969), pp. 48–54, 183–87.

On ancient Egypt, see William C. Hayes, *A Papyrus of the Late Middle Kingdom in the Brooklyn Museum [Papyrus Brooklyn 35.1446]* (Brooklyn, N.Y., 1955; reprint, Brooklyn, N.Y.: Brooklyn Museum, 1972), pp. 34–43, 137–43, as well as Blumenfeld, "The Terminology of Detention." On Mesopotamia and Assyria, see Blumenfeld.

The history of Roman law is efficiently laid out in Alan Watson, *The Law of the Ancient Romans* (Dallas: Southern Methodist University Press, 1970), and is vividly described in its social context in J. A. Crook, *Law and Life of Rome, 90 B.C.–A.D. 212* (Ithaca: Cornell University Press, 1967). The fundamental work on Roman criminal law is still that of Theodor Mommsen, *Römisches Strafrecht* (Leipzig: Duncker and Humblot, 1899). There is a summary in Drapkin, *Crime and Punishment in the Ancient World*, pp. 213–43.

On torture specifically, see Edward Peters, *Torture* (New York: B. Blackwell, 1985), and Page DuBois, *Torture and Truth* (New York: Routledge, 1991).

On the *Tullianum*, see Tenney Frank, "The *Tullianum* and Sallust's Catiline," *Classical Philology*

19 (1923–24): 495–98, and Tenney Frank, *Roman Buildings of the Republic*, Papers and Monographs of the American Academy in Rome, vol. 3 (Rome: American Academy, 1924), pp. 39–47, and for the *Comitium*, pp. 61–66. There is an important discussion of prisons in O. F. Robinson, *Ancient Rome: City Planning and Administration* (London: Routledge, 1992), especially pp. 175–79, 193–94. On the relation between social status and punishments, see Peter Garnsey, *Social Status and Legal Privilege in the Roman Empire* (Oxford: Clarendon, 1970), especially pp. 103–52.

A recent and reliable review of forced labor and penal slavery in the ancient and modern worlds is J. Thorsten Sellin, *Slavery and the Penal System* (New York: Elsevier, 1976).

On the Christian martyrs, see W.H.C. Frend, *Martyrdom and Persecution in the Early Church* (Oxford: Basil Blackwell, 1965). The relevant texts are in Eusebius, *The History of the Church from Christ to Constantine*, trans. G. A. Williamson (Baltimore: Penguin, 1965), and Herbert J. Musurillo, *The Acts of the Christian Martyrs* (Oxford: Clarendon, 1972).

For the case of Boethius, see Margaret Gibson, ed., *Boethius* (Oxford: Basil Blackwell, 1991). The best general description of the transformations of European legal history from Rome to the present is O. F. Robinson, T. D. Fergus, and W. M. Gordon, *An Introduction to European Legal History* (Abingdon, England: Professional Books, 1985); for private law, see R. C. Van Caenegem, *An Historical Introduction to Private Law* (Cambridge: Cambridge University Press, 1992), and Manlio Bellomo, *The Common Legal Past of Europe, 1000–1800*, trans. Lydia G. Cochrane (Washington, D.C.: Catholic University of America Press, 1995).

On Merovingian saints as liberators of prisoners, see Steven D. Sargent, "Religious Responses to Social Violence in Eleventh-Century Aquitaine," *Historical Reflections/Réflexions Historiques* 12 (1985): 219–40. The best study of a ransoming religious order is that of James William Brodman, *Ransoming Captives in Crusader Spain: The Order of Merced on the Christian-Islamic Frontier* (Philadelphia: University of Pennsylvania Press, 1986). On fraternal pious orders that served the spiritual needs of prisoners, see Samuel Y. Edgerton, Jr., *Pictures and Punishment: Art and Criminal Prosecution during the Florentine Renaissance* (Ithaca: Cornell University Press, 1985).

Monastic prisons are discussed extensively in Ralph B. Pugh, *Imprisonment in Medieval England* (London: Cambridge University Press, 1968), ch. 18, "Monastic Prisons," and in Thorsten Sellin, "Dom Jean Mabillon: A Prison Reformer of the Seventeenth Century," *Journal of the American Institute of Criminal Law and Criminology* 17 (1927): 581–602.

On the case of the nun of Watton, see Giles Constable, "Ailred of Rievaulx and the Nun of Watton: An Episode in the Early History of the Gilbertine Order," in *Medieval Women*, ed. Derek Baker (Oxford: B. Blackwell, 1978), 205–26, and Sharon K. Elkins, *Holy Women of Twelfth-Century England* (Chapel Hill: University of North Carolina Press, 1988), 106–11. On the nature of inquisitorial ecclesiastical tribunals, see Edward Peters, *Inquisition* (New York: Free Press, 1988), and Walter L. Wakefield, "Inquisition," *Dictionary of the Middle Ages* (New York: Charles Scribner's Sons, 1982), 6:483–89.

The legal revolutions of the twelfth century have generated a very large literature, much of it conveniently summarized and noted in the essays by Stephan Kuttner, "The Revival of Jurisprudence," and Knut Wolfgang Nörr, "Institutional Foundations of the New Jurisprudence," both in *Renaissance and Renewal in the Twelfth Century*, ed. Robert L. Benson and Giles Constable, with Carol D. Lanham (Cambridge, Mass., 1982; reprint, Toronto: University of Toronto Press, 1991), 299–323, 324–38; and the essays by R. C. Van Caenegem, Kenneth Pennington, and J. P. Canning in *The Cambridge History of Medieval Political Thought, c.350–c.1450*, ed. J. H. Burns (Cambridge: Cambridge University Press, 1988). On the emergence of a criminal law literature, see Richard Fraher, "Conviction According to Conscience: The Medieval Jurists Debate Concerning Judicial Discretion and the Law of Proof," *Law and History Review* 7 (1989): 23–88. All of these works offer substantial bibliographies.

For a discussion of the consequences of some of these changes from the perspective of early modern Europe, see Pieter Spierenburg, *The Spectacle of Suffering* (Cambridge: Cambridge University Press, 1984), and Richard van Dülmen, *Theatre of Horror: Crime and Punishment in Early Modern Germany*, trans. Elisabeth Neu (Cambridge, England: Polity Press, 1990).

On English prisons, see the following: Pugh, *Imprisonment in Medieval England*; John Bellamy, *Crime and Public Order in England in the Later Middle Ages* (London: Routledge and Kegan Paul, 1973), ch. 6; Christopher Harding, Bill Hines, Richard Ireland, and Philip Rawlings, *Imprisonment in England and Wales: A Concise History* (London: Croom Helm, 1985), chs. 1–2; Richard W. Kaeuper, "Jail Delivery," *Dictionary of the Middle Ages* 7:44–45; Edward Powell, *Kingship, Law, and Society: Criminal Justice in the Reign of Henry V* (Oxford: Clarendon, 1989).

For Germany, see *Criminal Justice through the Ages from Divine Judgement to Modern German Legislation*, trans. John Fosberry, Publications of the Medieval Crime Museum, Rothenburg ob der Tauber, vol. 4 (Rothenburg: Medieval Crime Museum of Rothenburg ob der Tauber, 1981).

For France, see Annik Porteau-Bitker, "L'Emprisonment dans le droit laique du moyen age," *Revue historique du droit francais et étranger*, ser. 4, 46 (1968): 211–45, 389–428, and Fredric L. Cheyette, "Châtelet," *Dictionary of the Middle Ages* 3:278–79. The work of Beaumanoir is available in *The "Coutumes de Beauvaisis" of Philippe de Beaumanoir*, trans. F.R.P. Akehurst (Philadelphia: University of Pennsylvania Press, 1992). The records of the Châtelet have been studied in the work of Bronislaw Geremek, *The Margins of Society in Late Medieval Paris*, trans. Jean Birrell (Cambridge: Cambridge University Press, 1987).

For Spain, see E. N. van Kleffens, *Hispanic Law until the End of the Middle Ages* (Edinburgh: Edinburgh University Press, 1968), and Joseph F. O'Callaghan, *A History of Medieval Spain* (Ithaca: Cornell University Press, 1975), both with extensive further references.

There are many good studies of the place of northern Italy in twelfth- and thirteenth-century European history, for example, J. K. Hyde, *Society and Politics in Medieval Italy* (New York: St. Martin's Press, 1973). On the laws of Sicily, see James M. Powell, ed. and trans., *The Liber Augustalis; or, Constitutions of Melfi, Promulgated by the Emperor Frederick II for the Kingdom of Sicily in 1231* (Syracuse: Syracuse University Press, 1971). For general legal history, the older work of Carlo Calisse, *A History of Italian Law* (Boston: Little, Brown, 1928), must be read in the light of considerable revision indicated in the work of a number of more recent scholars, notably Laura Ikins Stern, *The Criminal Law System of Medieval and Renaissance Florence* (Baltimore: Johns Hopkins University Press, 1994), and John K. Brackett, *Criminal Justice and Crime in Late Renaissance Florence, 1537–1609* (Cambridge: Cambridge University Press, 1992).

On Bartolus, see Anna T. Sheedy, *Bartolus on Social Conditions in the Fourteenth Century* (reprint, New York: AMS Press, 1967). On the Florentine *Le Stinche*, see Marvin E. Wolfgang, "A Florentine Prison: *Le Carceri delle Stinche*," *Studies in the Renaissance* 7 (1960): 148–66, and Marvin E. Wolfgang, "Crime and Punishment in Renaissance Florence," *Journal of Criminal Law and Criminology* 81 (1990): 567–84. On the legal system that created and operated Le Stinche, see Stern, *The Criminal Law System of Medieval and Renaissance Florence*.

On the fabric of medieval prisons, see Norman Bruce Johnston, "The Development of the Radial Prison: A Case Study of Cultural Diffusion," 3 vols. (Ph.D. diss., University of Pennsylvania, 1958), especially 1:7–29.

CHAPTER TWO

THE BODY AND THE STATE

Early Modern Europe

Pieter Spierenburg

In 1757 Robert-François Damiens was sentenced to be publicly quartered in Paris for attempting to take the life of King Louis XV. Because the unusual strength of his muscles and joints prevented the horses from tearing his arms and legs apart, the executioner had to make incisions to carry out the punishment. But the affecting drama of Damiens's suffering, detailed by Michel Foucault at the opening of his *Discipline and Punish*, should not mislead us into thinking many offenders were treated as harshly. On the contrary, Damiens's execution was altogether exceptional. The judges, uncertain what punishment to inflict for so heinous a crime, decided to impose the same sentence that the previous regicide, François Ravaillac, had received in 1610. French authorities had not quartered anyone in the intervening years, and they would never do so again.

Courts in early modern Europe already made frequent use of less severe corporal punishments as well as a variety of other sanctions. Between the early seventeenth and the mid-eighteenth centuries, the penal system changed greatly. At the center of this transformation was the emergence of the prison as the chief institution for combating crime. To understand the rise of the prison, one must examine changing social attitudes toward offenders, the family, and the human body itself. A general pattern of development in Western Europe does emerge, but it is also important to consider national and regional distinctions.

The executioner's scaffold is one vivid example of the wider cultural context on which punishment occurs. For most contemporary legal theorists, the staging of executions, the ceremonial behavior of magistrates, and the adornment of scaffolds represent mere inherited social conventions rather than significant aspects of the punishment. In fact, spectators (and probably the authorities as well) most likely saw a whole constellation of meanings in the ritual of the scaffold. The manner in which sentences were executed was at least as important as the content of the sentences.

Court activities provide another example of how broad cultural perspectives affected the evolution of penal systems. Torture, for example, was a tool for questioning prisoners and so qualified as part of the fact-finding process. As an officially accepted form of physical injury, however, it is akin to corporal punishment. Both torture and corporal punishment reflected a particular attitude toward the body, an attitude that was long widespread in Europe and that gave little thought to pain or bodily integrity. Various semijudicial measures also reflected wider cultural significance. Relatives or guardians, for instance, could imprison unruly family members who, strictly speaking, had committed no crime. This type of imprisonment, recorded in the Netherlands, France, and Germany, went beyond private discipline, for relatives wanting to apply it had to obtain magistrates' permission.

THE VARIETY OF AGENCIES DISPENSING JUSTICE

In early modern Europe, a variety of agencies had the right to exercise justice. Besides the "regular" courts, special ecclesiastical tribunals and law enforcement officials had jurisdiction in certain areas. Sometimes these rights dated from the feudal period, as in the case of the seigneurial courts in France, which, alongside the royal courts, continued to deal with common criminals until the eighteenth century. In England, beyond the proceedings at assizes and quarter sessions, many judicial affairs of lesser magnitude were handled summarily, usually by justices of the peace. Germany, with its many principalities and free towns, had a more complicated system. In independent cities such as Hamburg, the senate, the supreme political body, also acted as a high court. Several European countries had special law enforcement agencies charged with detecting and trying particular types of offenders; for example, forestry courts passed judgment on poachers, and farm-tax officials punished smugglers. In all nations, military courts-martial constituted another special law enforcement agency.

Perhaps most prominent of all the branches of separate jurisdiction was the church. It meted out justice through two types of institutions: courts that were dependent on the ecclesiastical hierarchy, and the Inquisition. The courts' concerns transcended religion, encompassing a number of offenses that the regular courts handled in countries where such forms of ecclesiastical jurisdiction were absent. The English church courts handled all kinds of matters in the realm of marriage and sexuality and also prosecuted such offenses as usury and defamation. Bishops' courts in Sweden played a similar role. So too, in Portugal, Spain, and several Italian states in the early modern period, the Inquisition prosecuted offenses such as bigamy, prostitution, astrology, and magic healing. Officially, the inquisitors' authority was restricted to heresy, but that broadly defined concept included many deviant activities. Both prostitutes and their clients, for example, could be tried for clinging to the erroneous belief that paid love was not sinful.

The prevalence of ecclesiastical justice meant that the state gave over part of its judicial authority to the church. To be sure, church officials normally acted in league with the secular rulers. In a similar manner, the family also acted in league with the state. The custom of private confinement typifies this alliance. When families had their sons, wives, or other relatives imprisoned for misconduct, they acted together with the state to maintain order in private homes and local communities. The state, for its part, also relied on the family. The authorities viewed the hierarchically governed nuclear family as a model of the benevolent rule they supposedly exercised over their subjects.

The Variety of Punishments

Although different legal bodies sometimes resorted to different types of penalties, they relied more often on common forms of punishment. Special state tribunals and law enforcement agencies usually drew on the same set of punishments that the regular state courts used. Like the French royal judges, French farm-tax officials often sent offenders to the galleys. Unlike the higher courts, though, most special courts could not pronounce the severest sentences, which were reserved for the most serious offenders. For example, Dutch village courts, which exercised "low jurisdiction," could not try cases that might carry the death penalty.

Military courts-martial frequently employed sanctions all their own. "Running the gauntlet" represented one such exclusively military punishment. This technique required the offender to run between two rows of men who struck at him with clubs. The execution of military punishments often fell to the offender's peers, which meant that he retained his "honor." But even courts-martial relied on the standard fare of punishment. Military judges in seventeenth-century France regularly pronounced galley sentences, and their Dutch counterparts in the eighteenth century often imposed terms in a prison workhouse.

Church justice stood further apart regarding its types of punishments. Ecclesiastical judges were often content with relatively mild sanctions. Although the Inquisition in Mediterranean countries had the authority to pronounce death sentences (carried out by the agents of secular justice), it did so only in a minority of cases. Very often church judges condemned the offender to wear a penitential garment for a certain time. English church courts, which in the Middle Ages regularly sentenced offenders to be flogged, stopped doing so after the Reformation. In the early modern period they often imposed a public penance, obliging the offender to go barefoot while dressed in a sheet. They also suspended punishment or used excommunication or fines. In fact, the types of punishment invoked by religious courts eventually spread to the secular realm. Public penance, for example, gained a role in secular justice in seventeenth-century Germany.

The regular state courts also had a wide range of sentences at their disposal, depending on the nature of the case. Throughout preindustrial Europe, sentencing always involved a choice; judges had more varied alternatives than they do today or, for that matter, than they did in the late nineteenth century. Penal options during this period ranged from aggravated forms of the death penalty (such as breaking on the wheel) to minor sanctions (such as a warning not to repeat the offense). In between lay more and less serious forms of corporal punishment (such as mutilation), exposure on the scaffold or the pillory, forms of bondage (such as galley servitude or confinement in a prison workhouse), banishment, fines, and a host of minor obligations or prohibitions.

Among these many punishments, two types held the greatest interest for the people of early modern Europe. One—execution on the scaffold or at a similar public spot—most clearly embodied contemporary attitudes. The other—punishment involving bondage and labor—suggested the direction criminal justice would take in the future. The scaffold served as a stage on which the drama of justice was enacted in its most visible and conspicuous form before the people of the day. For authorities, it was the most forceful means of exerting social control. Although the scaffold retained its importance well into the nineteenth century, already by the late sixteenth century its use had changed. As conspicuous forms of mutilation disappeared, execution on the scaffold became more (so to speak) routine and less dramatic. The scaffold eventually yielded its primacy to imprisonment and to transportation, which first appeared around 1600. These gradually evolved to the point where confinement to a prison workhouse became a major penal sanction. The prison, of course, remains the primary means of punishment today. To trace its development is the principal task of this chapter.

Historians today no longer describe the evolution of criminal justice in simple terms, such as a gradual progress away from cruelty. Several major social and cultural processes come into play, including privatization, the development of new attitudes toward the body, and the changing character of the family. Privatization involves the gradual withdrawal of various features of life from the public arena to private space. By the middle of the eighteenth century, for example, death no longer took place in the presence of servants or even of casual passersby. It became an intimate family affair. At the same time, cemeteries lost the character of public meeting places and were often relocated outside the boundaries of towns. As death shed its public nature, the open infliction of capital punishment was bound to be affected.

Penal changes also reflected new attitudes toward the body. Growing sensitivity to violence and an aversion to physical suffering had an impact on ideas about appropriate forms of punishment. Finally, developments in the family were crucial to the evolution of imprisonment in the early modern period. Offenders who served a term in prison were viewed as having escaped the disciplining bonds of the family. As inmates, therefore, they received a quasi-patriarchal form of discipline. Thus the history of punishment and prisons entails not only political and institutional processes, such as the formation of national states and the refinement of systems of justice, but also changes that belong to the realm of social history.

Corporal Punishment

Theatrical punishment and the scaffold were closely linked in early modern Europe. Noncapital physical punishments, though not everywhere carried out on a scaffold-like structure, were usually dispensed in public, giving them a theatrical character. The legal infliction of pain and death was a show before an audience. In most countries the penal system included a clearly circumscribed class of punishments defined as public and an equally clearly circumscribed class of punishments affecting the offender's life or bodily integrity. For example some offenders, especially juvenile delinquents, received floggings in the courtroom. But this practice, familiar in France and the Netherlands, was exceptional. The distinction between public and physical punishments is deceiving, since as a rule, the two classes largely overlapped.

A range of nonphysical, public sanctions usually had a shaming function. Thus women accused of immoral conduct had to wear an outfit or carry a symbol that marked their degradation. Offenders appeared before the public wearing a rope around their neck, as in the case of the perpetrators of carnival excesses in Rome. In the Netherlands a mock beheading often took place when the judges could not unequivocally establish the guilt of someone suspected of stabbing a victim to death. Exposure could of course turn into physical punishment when the audience harassed the offender or when he or she had to stand in some uncomfortable posture. In eighteenth-century Bremen, for example, some thieves had to stand in the market square wearing a neck-iron for half an hour before leaving for prison. Well into the eighteenth century, standing in the pillory in England entailed the risk of harassment by the audience.

Punishments that were both physical and public can be divided into five degrees of severity. Whipping, the least severe, was the most common form of corporal punishment in all countries. In the Netherlands as well as Germany, the executioner generally administered public floggings with whips of various materials, such as rope or birch branches.

The next degree of severity involved burning the convict's skin. Authorities most often branded with red-hot irons, but in Amsterdam they sometimes used a heated sword. Branding usually left a permanent scar, the mark by which the judges literally made their imprint on the convict. In France, where all justice derived ultimately from the king, the mark functioned symbolically as the king's imprint. The practice of branding was equally prevalent in republics and relatively autonomous cities, such as those of the northern and southern Netherlands. There, the mark showed the city coat of arms or a part of it. The court of Brussels, for example, adorned the backs of branded criminals with an angel, which also figured in the city coat of arms.

To a degree, branding was a preindustrial method for identifying recidivists. Judges, who took marks as sure signs of a previous conviction, often ordered the executioner to inspect the suspect's body. Of course, this method worked only if the suspect had committed a crime serious enough to warrant branding. In fact, among those who submitted to corporal punishment, only a minority received this penalty, but those who did sometimes bore specific evidence of their prior criminal record. In France during the 1810s and 1820s, the skin of criminals condemned to forced labor showed the letter T (for *travaux forcés*) or V (for *voleur*) instead of a mark.

Relatively rare, the third degree of corporal punishment, mutilation, involved more serious encroachments on bodily integrity. In Amsterdam, some violent offenders received a cut in the cheek. Other punishments amounted to outright mutilation. The amputation of hands, an always infrequent practice, continued in some countries for a longer period than in others. In Europe no judicial sentence ever ordered a person's feet to be cut off. Blinding, however, did occur occasionally until about 1600. No doubt the most common form of mutilation was cutting off an ear. In several countries this practice continued well into the seventeenth century. In the eighteenth century, offenders lost their thumbs, usually when they perpetrated large-scale fraud.

Capital punishment involved either a "merciful" instant death, the fourth degree of corporal punishment, or a prolonged death, the fifth and severest form. Never imposed lightly, the death penalty required recidivism or other aggravating circumstances, except in cases of murder and homicide. Tradition held beheading, hanging, garroting, and burying alive among the "merciful" forms of capital punishment. Throughout Europe, decapitation was considered the most honorable method, particularly when performed with a sword, the noble weapon. The few aristocrats who ended their life on the scaffold were all beheaded. Malefactors of more humble origins had the privilege of decapitation only if the court did not consider them hardened criminals. First offenders who had killed their opponent in a tavern brawl fell into this category. Hanging was the standard nonhonorable form of the death penalty, imposed on robbers and burglars, recidivists (usually), and everyone else who the judges thought deserved it. In theory women could not be hanged for reasons of decency, but in Amsterdam a few women did meet their end in a noose. Still, most women there received the death penalty by garroting. Supposedly a more acceptable alternative to hanging, garroting meant a slower death. Even slower was burying alive, which represented the decent alternative to hanging in France until the sixteenth century.

The severest category of capital punishment comprised prolonged forms of execution. In France, burning alive was occasionally practiced until the eighteenth century, particularly in serious cases of arson. French convicts could spare themselves a prolonged death by naming accomplices after hearing their sentence. In that case they earned the *retentum*: an instruction to the executioner to strangle the convict before lighting the pyre. The executioner had to do this secretly so that the audience would not notice that the show was a fake; authorities did not want the mercy shown to an individual offender to cause the public to doubt the severity of justice. In the northern and southern Netherlands and most parts of Germany, breaking on the wheel represented the most common form of prolonged death penalty. The convict's bones were broken with an iron bar before he received the coup de grace to his heart. In early modern England, by contrast, prolonged death was practically unknown. Capital punishment there did not go beyond hanging, although a famous pamphlet of 1701 argued that hanging did not effectively deter potential lawbreakers.

Forms of the Death Penalty: The Theater of the Scaffold

As the secrecy surrounding the custom of the *retentum* indicates, staging played a leading role in the theater of physical punishment. A custom of the Amsterdam prosecutor further reveals the importance of staging: the prosecutor determined the number of lashes given at a public whipping not in the courtroom but on the spot, gesturing with his hand to tell the executioner when to stop. But most theatrical of all public punishments was the execution of death sentences. In the early modern period, execution rituals developed throughout Europe, with many similarities from nation to nation. One key element was the ceremonial presence of the magistrates. In Amsterdam the judges and the prosecutor, dressed in special ceremonial robes, took their seats in the windows of a gallery overlooking the scaffold and the audience. Burgomasters attended too, and the town secretary recited the sentences of the condemned.

Religious officials appeared as well, whatever the dominant religion. In a strict sense, their task was to prepare the condemned for eternity, but the plainly visible and public way in which they fulfilled their duties also served to legitimate the punishment. The Amsterdam magistrates knelt down to pray together with the preacher and the condemned criminals before the hangman took charge. In other cities the priest or minister invited the audience to join in the prayer.

Another theatrical element, the execution procession, sometimes figured into the drama. Smaller Dutch towns as well as large cities like London, Paris, and Seville marched prisoners through the streets. In London, for example, the person about to be hanged was led from his cell at Newgate jail through several of the most densely populated districts of the town to the gallows at Tyburn. All the town churches rang their bells to announce the event. Some of the more adventurous spectators climbed the wall enclosing Hyde Park, which was also en route to Tyburn, for a better view. The raucous custom persisted until the late eighteenth century.

The execution ritual incorporated yet another characteristic feature in the early modern period: the ceremony of the execution itself. In Dutch towns during the sixteenth century, executions underwent a metamorphosis—from brief, sober events held at varying locations to ornate, ceremonious occasions conducted at a central place. The English instituted elaborate rituals to accompany public hangings in Tudor times. Wherever it occurred, this shift accompanied the growth of the state and changing attitudes toward violence and suffering. In medieval times, because state authority was fragmented and no superior source of justice could assert itself, justice could take rather casual forms. From the sixteenth century onward, however, large areas of Europe came under direct political control, and public authority was established more firmly. As a result, governments paid more attention to the symbolic force of the law. Public executions bolstered the power of monarchs and magistrates and made it concretely visible. Authorities did not want to display naked oppression but rather a theater of righteousness and repentance.

Accordingly, magistrates took great pains to organize a "beautiful execution." Ideally, the convict behaved humbly on the scaffold, showing repentance. In the Netherlands, offenders who had just been whipped or branded were obliged to kneel down in front of the judges and express their gratitude for the mercy shown them. So too, audiences at executions expected that those about to die would heed the minister's admonitions and approach eternity with a clean conscience. Reports of the period indicate that both magistrates and audiences appreciated such "beautiful" executions. When, in 1767, an Amsterdamer who had killed his wife showed a repentant attitude on the scaffold, reciting a line from a religious hymn, the judges, the minister, and thousands of spectators apparently rejoiced.

Just as people attached importance to the convict's contrition, so they expressed disgust at the sight of convicts who refused to repent or who even displayed their impertinence on the scaffold. A recidivist whipped and branded in Amsterdam in 1653 exclaimed, at the very moment when he should have thanked the judges for their mildness, that he intended to commit a hundred more crimes. The magistrates ordered him flogged anew immediately. Two other impertinent Amsterdam offenders in the early eighteenth century showed their contempt for the watching crowd, one by putting out his tongue to the spectators and the other by screaming abuse at them. In England, audiences also disliked being deprived of a beautiful execution. When a Yorkshire murderer obstinately refused to acknowledge his guilt on the scaffold in 1682, an observer noted that the majority of onlookers went away disappointed.

Another element in the theater of punishment was the use of dead bodies as warnings to the living. Most European towns and villages kept a gallows field or gallows mountain on which they displayed the corpses of selected capital offenders. The bodies hung in public until they decomposed; those who had died on the wheel were propped up on the device, supported by a harness. Towns always located their gallows field at a conspicuous spot. Amsterdam, for instance, placed it on the main water route for all incoming ships to see. For this defamation the courts selected criminals who had committed particularly heinous offenses or who had refused to name accomplices.

Although the theater of punishment shared many similarities regardless of region, practices differed somewhat from place to place. In England, exposure of the body, called hanging in chains, was uncommon. When the executioner did carry it out, he left the corpse to rot at the scene of the crime rather than on a gallows mountain. English criminals feared another fate—the anatomy room—even more. During the second half of the eighteenth century, authorities permitted London surgeons to claim the bodies of criminals hanged at Tyburn, but they had to compete for the bodies with other interested parties. Relatives, friends, and workmates of the executed often fought over the bodies with the journeymen surgeons.

England differed from other countries, such as the Dutch Republic, on another point as well. In the Netherlands the courts made no distinction between the execution of corporal and of death penalties. On "justice days" in Amsterdam a number of criminals were flogged, some were branded, and one or two were put to death, all in a single ceremony. The executioner dealt with all of them together on the scaffold, beginning with the capital convicts. Offenders sentenced to mere exposure sometimes stood there during the ceremony, tied to the scaffold railing. (Only minor offenders were exposed on the *kaak*, a kind of mini-scaffold. This took place on separate days and constituted the only occasion of public punishment besides the justice days.) In England, by contrast, the authorities drew a sharp line between the execution of death penalties on the scaffold and other occasions for public and physical punishment. Hangings did not accompany floggings. Put into effect at a whipping post, the whippings seem to have drawn less public interest and were often imposed summarily by a justice of the peace.

Another area of national and regional variation entailed the amount of self-expression allowed convicts on the scaffold. In some places they delivered a speech from the scaffold; in others they remained silent. Dutch executions were comparatively sober events in this regard. Convicts could pray or sing psalms, but otherwise they remained passive. No one objected when the notorious murderess Hendrina Wouters kept on praying while the executioner broke her bones in Amsterdam in 1746. But in 1800, when a robber condemned in The Hague declared he wanted to make a speech, the magistrates silenced him. Convicts occasionally addressed the public in southern France and parts of Germany; in England they did so often. In fact, clergymen wrote most of their speeches, which all adhered to a stereotypical pattern. Each speech outlined a familiar pattern of vices in the condemned's earliest youth, vices that inevitably led to a grave misdeed or a criminal existence. For the public the lesson was plain: every child who disobeyed his or her parents, every adolescent who refused to go to church, and every husband who spent his time in an alehouse stood the chance of ending up at the gallows.

The precise location of the scaffold also varied from town to town, determined partly by the geographic particularities of a jurisdiction. In the larger towns on the continent, the scaffold stood somewhere near the center, and the corpses destined for public display were taken to the gallows field afterward. In smaller towns or villages, notably towns in Germany, both activities often took place at the same spot. Because the scaffold and the gallows mountain had to be accessible to the entire population, capital convicts were hanged on the gallows mountain itself, where they subsequently remained if they had been denied a burial. In some German towns the form of capital punishment determined the location. Beheading took place at the market square, and hanging, burning, or breaking on the wheel was conducted on the gallows mountain. In sixteenth-century Cologne, the market square was reserved for the execution of political offenders. These local idiosyncrasies of setting, however, serve only to highlight the theatrical character of public punishment.

Finally, regional differences affected the religious content of the execution. In general, executions had a slightly more prominent religious component in Catholic countries. To be sure, in German Protestant regions, schoolchildren sang songs of death, and people referred to the convict as *Armesünder* (poor sinner). But executions in France and the Mediterranean countries seem to have featured more baroque religious staging. In the execution procession at Seville, for example, the convict usually rode a donkey, reminding the public of Jesus' entry into Jerusalem a few days before his crucifixion. France, meanwhile, followed the custom of the *amende honorable*. On their way to the place where they would be put to death, convicts stopped for a while at a church or a chapel to perform a public act of penitence, asking forgiveness from God. All the while they had a rope around their neck and carried a burning candle.

Despite these variations, public executions encompassed a familiar theatricality. The courts designed executions as public rituals, staged so as to make the deepest impression on the spectators. Along with the theme of deserved punishment, these events prominently featured motifs of repentance and righteousness. The formal participation of the magistrates marked the execution as an official expression of the force of law.

The Audience for Execution

The theater of the scaffold changed over time. To understand the mechanisms of the change, one must examine both the reactions of the audience and the attitudes of the elite. The crowd consisted for the most part, but not exclusively, of lower-class people; for example, the seventeenth-century Lille artisan Chavatte reported in his chronicle that he regularly went to see capital executions as well as whippings and exposure at the pillory. Although the audience often appreciated the spectacle exactly in the manner the authorities hoped, not everyone was moved by the show of repentance and justice. Many spectators no doubt paid as little attention to the moral lesson as they did to the suffering and pain of the condemned. They simply attended to witness the spectacle. And in certain cases the crowd felt favorably toward the offenders: lower- and lower-middle-class people looked sympathetically on smugglers, for instance, because they did not consider smuggling a genuine crime.

Executions that followed riots presented special problems for the magistrates. When the rebels were condemned for participation in tax revolts or disturbances over food prices, the majority of spectators strongly sympathized with them. In Amsterdam during the seventeenth and eighteenth centuries, such post-riot executions always took place in an atmosphere of extreme tension, and soldiers stood ready to restrain the crowd. Because they attached such great value to the theater of justice, the authorities proceeded with unpopular executions nevertheless. Not until their confidence in public punishment declined for other reasons did they come to fear the possibly rebellious crowd of spectators.

During the eighteenth century the reactions of crowds at ordinary executions changed. Most of the evidence comes from London, but the transformation may have occurred in other European cities as well. According to contemporary reports, the crowds assembling at Tyburn did not play the part of passive and receptive spectators. Instead of taking a moral lesson to heart, they approached the spectacle of execution with irreverence and sometimes even showed admiration for bold men who were about to die fearlessly. This defiant attitude, which in earlier centuries showed up only in picaresque novels, apparently infected the majority of London's population. As onlookers cheered on the convicts or offered them drinks, the procession from Newgate to Tyburn became a special occasion of merriment. The condemned responded to this new attitude by putting on their finest costumes and adopting the posture of heroes. As a consequence, the authorities increasingly viewed executions as problems of public order. The spectacle of the scaffold had turned into a kind of popular festival. In 1783 the London magistrates abolished the procession to Tyburn, but the actual hangings continued to draw large, vulgar crowds.

Modern historians once assumed, incorrectly, that executions had always been popular festivals. But when the perceptions of a large part of the audience changed, the execution ritual could no longer convey a moral lesson or buttress the power of the authorities. Instead, the ceremony became the occasion for merriment or even for mockery of the law. As a result, nineteenth-century officials lost confidence in public punishment.

The changing attitudes of the elite also reduced the appeal of the execution ceremony. Judges and legislators, of course, belonged to the elite and had the power to alter penal law or at least to discontinue certain penal practices. Indeed, the disappearance of some punishments constituted the earliest sign of a change of attitude among the elite. Penalties involving the mutilation of a person's body, notably the cutting off of ears, were discontinued around the middle or end of the seventeenth century. A related development that occurred even earlier concerned branding. In the sixteenth century the executioner often imprinted the mark on the convict's hand or forehead; later he branded only the offender's back, where clothing would hide the mark. Admittedly, the court continued to sentence some serious offenders to mutilation, but only as a prelude to the death penalty. In other words, mutilation was acceptable only if the convict died subsequently and was thus removed from the community. Convicts who did not receive the death penalty escaped maiming as well.

The elite of the Dutch Republic showed the first signs of mild distaste at the sight of executions toward the end of the seventeenth century. Upper-class people usually expressed this distaste by disparaging the curiosity and behavior of the lower-class spectators. Constantijn Huygens, the seventeenth-century poet and diplomat, wrote as much. He also raised his voice against the maintenance of a stone scaffold at The Hague, calling it the most villainous of all constructions. Indeed, most Dutch towns replaced their permanent stone scaffolds with removable wooden ones during the seventeenth century so that the sight of gallows and wheels was no longer a daily experience. Greater sensitivity to public punishment, however, did not appear until a century later. From the 1770s onward, literary expressions of opposition to the spectacle became increasingly frequent in several European countries. In 1773 an anonymous citizen of Amsterdam wrote that he trembled and grew ice cold at every step the convicts took up the ladder on their way to be hanged; to his relief he noticed a similar horror in the eyes of many other spectators. During this period, revulsion against the display of dead bodies also increased. In the Netherlands, exposure was abolished in 1795 as a relic of older, barbarous days.

Quantitative data substantiate the gradual decline in public punishment, particularly capital punishment. During the Middle Ages, the lack of a strong central system of justice resulted in rather infrequent use of the death penalty. In the county of Warwickshire, England, during the late fourteenth century, and in the Dutch city of Utrecht during the fourteenth and fifteenth centuries, courts sentenced fewer than one-tenth of convicted felons to capital punishment. The early modern period witnessed first a rise in capital punishment, as monarchs and other rulers displayed their newly acquired power, and then a gradual decline. In England the proportion of convicts who were hanged rose sharply during the Tudor period, reaching its height in the middle of the sixteenth century. Then a marked decline set in. In Cheshire, for instance, the average number of death sentences dropped from about ten per year around 1600 to under two per year in the second half of the century.

At the same time, courts redefined the types of crimes that required the death sentence: Cheshire authorities demanded execution for seven-eighths of all crimes against property in 1600, a figure that dropped to one-half by the middle of the century, whereas for homicide that figure rose from one-tenth to one-third during the same period. Thus, the death penalty was aimed more and more at serious crimes against the person. Everywhere throughout England, except in London, capital convictions for property offenses dropped considerably between the end of the sixteenth and the middle of the eighteenth centuries.

The Netherlands experienced a similar trend during the early modern period. In Amsterdam the peak employment of capital punishment came relatively late, with about five per year in the first half of the eighteenth century; the comparable figures are three per year for the preceding half-century and only one per year for the following fifty years. Between the first and second halves of the eighteenth century, six small towns and rural districts in the Netherlands saw the number of executions drop by half. Evidently, the decline of capital punishment in the Netherlands was especially marked in the second half of the eighteenth century. Dutch courts simultaneously started to reserve this penalty for homicide, just as in England. Germany and Switzerland also showed a trend similar to that in England, with a peak of death sentences in the sixteenth century and a decline afterward. Historians have observed this pattern in the cities of Frankfurt, Augsburg, Nuremberg, and Zurich.

In addition, judicial torture came under sustained attack during the eighteenth century. Long a customary aid to questioning in all European jurisdictions, torture methods varied widely. Certainly the torture was not always as gruesome as the modern reader might imagine. The Parlement of Paris, for example, used a form of forced drinking that must have been mild, since almost no one confessed under it. Some French convicts, however, had to undergo two phases of torture: one to make them confess and another, after they had been sentenced, to make them name their accomplices. But though we know something about methods of torture, we know much less about its incidence. Some data from Amsterdam give us a rough picture. From the bills submitted by the "indoor executioner," it appears that the court used the severest forms of torture with declining frequency during the eighteenth century. Shin- or thumb-screws or hanging with weights tied to the toes was used on two persons per year in the twenty-year period ending in 1741, but on only one person per year in the following twenty-year period. The Netherlands legally abolished judicial torture in the late 1790s, as did most other European countries at around the same time.

Although imprisonment began its triumphant rise in the late eighteenth century, public punishment continued for some time. In England, for example, scholars mark the beginning of the "modern" penal regime around 1870, when transportation ended and executions took place in private. Certainly, among the elites, sensitivity toward the proceedings on the scaffold intensified after 1800, but well into the nineteenth century their feelings of revulsion could not overcome the idea that public physical punishments were necessary. Advocates of imprisonment, notably those favoring solitary confinement, spoke most strongly against the scaffold. By the middle of the nineteenth century the authorities abolished most corporal penalties or, as with flogging in England, removed them from the public realm.

Then, between 1850 and 1870, capital punishment moved from the scaffold to within prison walls. France was the exception, continuing to execute the death penalty in public until 1939. A few countries, such as the Netherlands, abolished capital punishment altogether. The last execution in the Netherlands—except for the episode of extraordinary justice after World War II—took place in 1860. Elsewhere, indoor executions retained some public elements. When convicts were put to death in German prisons, for example, officials handed out some fifty to one hundred entrance tickets to interested persons from the civil service. This custom came to an end in 1908. Other public elements also disappeared by the early twentieth century, completing the movement toward private, or "concealed," punishment.

LESSER PUNISHMENTS

The movement toward private punishment and the eventual triumph of imprisonment stand as the most conspicuous changes in the long-term evolution of the penal system. Nevertheless, throughout the centuries, courts routinely applied a host of minor sanctions below this layer of conspicuous evolution. Historians have not systematically studied these punishments in their own right, probably because they have little spectacular appeal. Still, these penalties often constituted the larger part of the sentences imposed by early modern courts. Especially when confronted with large numbers of lawbreakers, judges usually dealt with the bulk of petty offenders in the cheapest way. Even today we often forget this simple fact; we think of the prison as the primary penal institution, but the most common judicial sanction is a fine (usually for violating traffic rules). Likewise, in the early modern period, the public thought of justice primarily in terms of the scaffold, but the courts imposed banishment much more frequently.

Moreover, authorities often condemned offenders to suffer two or more different punishments as the result of one conviction. English offenders, for example, might be whipped and then imprisoned in a house of correction. Combined sentences were extremely common in the Netherlands. A court condemned a burglar to a flogging on the scaffold and to confinement in a prison workhouse afterward. Banishment could be imposed as the only punishment in a trial or could be combined with a corporal penalty, a prison sentence, or both.

Whether or not they combined lesser sentences with heavier sanctions, courts resorted to banishment and other minor punishments with varying frequency. The approach depended partly on the type of judicial agency. A court concentrating on the prosecution of serious criminals was likely to pronounce few sentences that included only petty sanctions. Farther down the judicial hierarchy, the number of such sentences increased. At the bottom of the ladder, special colleges of judges tried to keep the peace between parties rather than enforce the criminal law. These courts imposed the lightest punishments. In England, for instance, two villagers with a long-standing quarrel might be "bound over" to keep the peace; often this measure proved sufficient to effect a reconciliation.

Banishment

At first glance, banishment might not seem a minor punishment. When a condemned man had roots in his community, owned a house, and had employment and friends too, he must have found banishment an ordeal. If he wanted to remain united with his wife and children, they had to follow him. But if the convict was a vagabond, without family or work in the first place, banishment merely continued a marginal existence. In short, banishment represented a severe punishment for the settled but a relatively light one for outsiders. Who, then, received this punishment?

In the Roman Empire exile served as a penalty for political dissidents, most of them from the upper classes. This tradition continued when urban courts in the Middle Ages also banished citizens in political cases. Medieval courts introduced the practice of banishing nonresident troublemakers, which seemed a convenient and inexpensive way to be rid of them; the problems they might cause in another town or in the countryside were of little concern. In the early modern period, banishment of the settled as well as of outsiders continued. Possibly, it befell established citizens only in special cases, but the available literature does not allow a firm conclusion.

In Holland, adultery or concubinage could warrant a fifty-year banishment from the province, a penalty the local courts imposed occasionally. In these cases, the condemned usually belonged to the settled population and had done something particularly obnoxious to the community. But wealthy people accused of adultery—married men caught with prostitutes, for example—commonly bought off the prosecution. Adulterous members of the Reformed Church, as a rule, were censured only by the consistory. Concubinage and adultery among the nonsettled did not attract the special attention of Dutch courts except as an additional charge when such people were sentenced for property offenses.

Most trials conducted by the Amsterdam court in the early modern period involved people from a floating population of professional criminals, those without a fixed residence. A number of petty thieves and first offenders were banished. Recidivists and professional criminals often suffered other penalties in addition to banishment. No less than 97 percent of the Amsterdam court's public noncapital sentences between 1650 and 1750 included banishment. Banishment imposed on thieves from the floating population functioned essentially as a local police measure. Many of the convicts were caught again in Amsterdam under suspicion of new thefts, but these crimes were often hard to prove. Hence, when a recognized recidivist persisted in denying his subsequent crime, he might be charged with infraction of banishment and punished for this instead. From about 1715, the use of both whipping and imprisonment as a penalty for infraction of banishment increased. Most of the offenders involved had denied initial charges of property crime.

Banishment also served to keep offenders away from a town or a rural jurisdiction. Although courts in Holland had the authority to banish offenders from the whole province, this seldom yielded a real advantage. Only for the crime of vagrancy in the seventeenth century did the Estates (parliament) of Holland insist that local courts pronounce banishments from the province. Because the prison workhouses could not accommodate the large numbers of vagrants, the Estates offered a bonus to every court that banished one.

Banishments from an entire country were probably rare throughout Europe, for a court would have difficulty putting such a sentence into effect. This sort of banishment resembled transportation to some extent, with the difference that the banished person was free to go where he or she pleased outside the country. Still, authorities had trouble forcing the banished person beyond the border. As a result, only a few persons were sentenced to remain away from the Dutch Republic.

Just as banishment had no great effect on vagrants, so fines could not be collected from the poor. Amsterdam courts nonetheless levied nominal fines on the poor in trials for smuggling. The parties involved in this crime often recruited middlemen from among the poor, who could never pay the fine required by law. In effect, the flogging that they received in addition to the fine turned out to be their one punishment. Throughout Europe, a fine was normally a penalty reserved for the rich. The criminal justice system generally favored the upper and middle classes; a monetary sanction often took the place of a more shameful or painful type of punishment. Members of the lower-middle class also paid fines on occasion. The Amsterdam court tried misdemeanors according to a separate procedure, registering the proceedings on the so-called *schoutsrol*. Almost always the penalty was a small fine, often imposed for a transgression of one of the city by-laws but also, in a considerable number of cases, for petty violence. Those who were fined instead of being tried by the regular criminal procedure belonged to the settled population of guild members, shopkeepers, and "respectable" workers.

Amsterdam also provides an illustration of the final class of minor punishments, the petty sanctions. Its court dealt with a number of arrested people whom it did not really want to punish but whom it refused to release without a sanction. Almost half of this group suffered some kind of restriction on its freedom of movement within the city. Pickpockets, for example, were denied access to Dam Square or the Stock Exchange. People who had caused disturbances in one neighborhood had to move to another. Prostitutes were often denied access to inns and brothels and sometimes to coffeehouses as well. Like banishment, all these restrictions made it possible to arrest someone and treat him or her as a recidivist simply on the grounds that the person showed up at a certain location. The Amsterdam authorities used this tool until recent times. Petty drug dealers and troublesome addicts were forbidden for fourteen days to frequent the street where most of the trade went on. In 1990, however, a court deemed such prohibitions illegal.

Penal Bondage

A new type of judicial sanction, midway in severity between the scaffold and the minor punishments, grew popular during the early modern period. Courts came to use it almost as frequently as physical sanctions. Instead of being flogged or hanged, some offenders were incarcerated in workhouses or forced to perform labor in some other setting. We may use the term "bondage" to denote any punishment that puts severe restrictions on the condemned person's freedom of action and movement, including but not limited to imprisonment. Indeed, the term embraces both punitive and penal institutions, a distinction worth making because several forms of punitive bondage become penal, in the sense of fully belonging to the criminal justice system, only later in their history.

Bondage always carried the loss of liberty and usually involved forced labor as well. Especially in early modern prisons, the work program supposedly disciplined and punished the inmates. The obligation to work distinguished prisons from almshouses, asylums, and hospitals, as well as from workhouses, whose inmates worked voluntarily and not as punishment.

Imprisonment and other forms of bondage grew increasingly popular in several European countries as early as the sixteenth century. Thus, far from representing a radical change in the penal system, the proliferation of penitentiaries in Europe after 1800 was the product of gradual developments during the preceding centuries. One such development, the emergence of bondage, reflected changing ideas about idleness and labor on the one hand and renewed interest in enforcing morality on the other. Ideas about idleness and labor had already started to change before the Reformation, and an interest in vigorous moral enforcement emerged from both the Reformation and the Counter Reformation.

More often than other forms of bondage, imprisonment was designed to enforce morality. Confinement as a punitive sanction had several unique features. Because its execution spanned more than a single moment in time, confinement implied a longer-term effort to change the behavior of people. Indeed, many of those sent to prisons during this period were confined because of their way of life. Within the prison, the agents of discipline tried to correct bad habits rather than to punish actual crimes. Phrases like "evil conduct," "laziness," and "disreputable behavior" occurred frequently in documents describing the conduct that workhouses strove to eliminate. Relatively unspecific, these terms simply referred to behavior that, according to the agents of discipline, ought to be improved.

Sometimes termed "civilization offensives," these efforts to reform immoral people were recurrent in the early modern period. Churchmen as well as laymen organized these moral campaigns. Protestant and Catholic clergy directed their efforts at concubinage, premarital intercourse, and a number of "superstitious" popular practices. Laypeople, meanwhile, tended to favor "societies for the reformation of manners," founded in England from the 1690s onward. These societies promoted the imprisonment of drunkards, gamblers, and similar offenders. In general, the early modern period was one of increasing moral entrepreneurship aimed at "civilizing" the behavior of the whole populace. Since anyone might lead a life that his or her peers judged immoral, upper-class people were also imprisoned for this reason.

Idleness, the other target of reformers, was considered the habit of a specific sort of people. This well-defined social group, the stratum of vagrants and beggars, figured very prominently in the founding documents of prison workhouses. The idle not only were imprisoned but also, in certain countries, were sent to row the galleys of the fleet. They were among the first to experience the full weight of bondage as a punitive sanction. This policy reflected a change of attitudes toward poverty, marginality, and idleness, a change that in turn led to more repressive sanctions.

The earlier, medieval attitudes toward the poor had been more tolerant. Clerical people and laypeople, speaking of "the poor of Jesus," saw poverty almost as a sacred state. Men and women without possessions followed in the footsteps of Christ, and as long as their numbers remained within reasonable limits, they were not a source of anxiety. The poor provided the rich with an opportunity to give alms and thereby to earn entrance to heaven. Whether they appeared as beggars, vagrants, or needy people in one's parish or as poor laity or members of the mendicant orders, they all deserved charity. The populace and the learned elite shared this attitude. Ordinary laypeople probably did not think that everyone, without exception, was worthy of alms, but in individual cases they most likely did not inquire whether a beggar who held out his hand did so with good reason. Learned scholastics, meanwhile, were reluctant to inquire into the causes of a beggar's misery, which finally provided an occasion for charity and a God-pleasing act. Thomas Aquinas found it self-evident that everyone should beg if poor or unable to earn a living by labor, although this begging should not bring luxuries.

After 1500 a new attitude emerged, one that was far more suspicious. Increasingly, people thought it necessary to inquire whether the beggar bore the blame for his misery; potential almsgivers distinguished the deserving poor from the undeserving. Even the clergy no longer automatically found the image of Christ in the poor. And the secular authorities now considered the poor a threat to the stability of society and sought to supervise them strictly. With a few exceptions, the public tolerated idleness only from the sick, the disabled, or the aged. All others should be compelled to work.

It may appear odd that social attitudes toward poverty, rather than attitudes toward crime, provided the ideological basis for the emergence of bondage. But bondage—at least its two most prominent forms—originated as a noncriminal category of sanctions. Imprisonment and galley servitude did not start out as criminal punishments but as disciplinary institutions meant to deal with problems of poverty and marginality. At first, when the itinerant poor became unwanted strangers, the reaction was to chase them away from one's town or rural district. In a world of localism, this seemed the most logical solution. But during the sixteenth century, local authorities had no choice but to start cooperating with each other, recognizing that banishing marginals from one town meant foisting them on another. At the same time, the public's intensifying disapproval of idleness gave rise to the idea that people who refused to work should be forced to do so. At this point, the positive sanction of bondage appeared alongside the negative sanction of banishment.

Sixteenth-century Europeans did not invent punitive bondage. As we have seen, the ancient Romans, among others, practiced it, and the Renaissance interest in classical antiquity may very well have contributed to its reintroduction. Early modern Europe recognized four basic forms of bondage: the galleys, public works, imprisonment at forced labor, and transportation. France pioneered the first form. Already in the fifteenth century, French vagabonds manned the country's galleys, either because they were being punished or because they had been impressed, that is, seized and forcibly made to serve. At that time, however, vagrants and delinquents represented only a small minority among the oarsmen. Almost every Mediterranean state kept a galley fleet and manned it with volunteers who could find no other employment, as well as with non-Christian slaves captured at sea or bought in Asian markets.

In France, Spain, and most Italian states, galley sentences became more common from about 1500 onward. On Italian galleys, for example, offenders outnumbered volunteers by the middle of the sixteenth century. Only in Venice did a reasonable supply of lower-class locals (along with oarsmen from the Dalmatian and Greek coasts) delay this process; but toward the end of the century, forced laborers were the largest group in the Doge's fleet also. Many of the offenders who received galley sentences were vagrants; France, Spain, and some Italian states occasionally rounded them up for this very purpose. When Venice's poorhouse hospitals became overcrowded in the 1540s, for instance, a number of unlicensed beggars housed in those institutions were condemned to serve in the fleet. Thus, galley servitude came to represent a mostly but not entirely noncriminal punishment. It befell beggars and vagrants in particular but also extended to convicts. This combination turned out to be crucial to future developments.

Public works as a form of punishment appeared in Europe only slightly earlier than imprisonment. Spanish records contain examples of penal servitude by the middle of the sixteenth century. Unlike imprisonment and galley servitude, public work was a criminal sanction from the outset. Those subjected to it were always people who had been condemned for some crime by a court. Although in the broadest sense the term "public works" referred to every form of compulsory labor, it most commonly referred to labor that took place in the street or underground. Convicts dug ore in mines, repaired ramparts, built roads or houses, or went from door to door collecting human waste.

Following on the Spanish experience, the public works penalty grew especially popular in Germany and Switzerland in the seventeenth and eighteenth centuries. In those countries, it was often associated with imprisonment. Some male inmates of prison workhouses actually stayed within the walls only at night, working in chain gangs during the daytime. In Celle at the beginning of the eighteenth century, for example, male convicts were sentenced to build the *zuchthaus* (prison) in which they or their successors would later be confined.

Imprisonment constituted the third form of bondage. Although the courts had incarcerated people throughout the Middle Ages, convicts did not at first inhabit separate, punitive institutions. The prison workhouses established in Europe from the second half of the sixteenth century onward differed from their predecessors in that they were single-purpose institutions where inmates performed forced labor. To highlight the novelty of this approach, we must distinguish between jails and prisons. The population of jails largely consisted of debtors and people under provisional detention (for example, awaiting trial), together with an occasional sentenced offender; they did not have to work. By contrast, prisons primarily housed offenders sentenced by a court or committed there by another authority for purposes of chastisement or correction. The inmates had obligations to fulfill, largely through forced labor. Early modern Europeans made a linguistic distinction between jails and prisons, referring to prisons as "bridewells" or "houses of correction" (in England), *tuchthuizen* (in the Netherlands), and *zuchthäuser* (in Germany), the latter two terms literally meaning "houses of discipline." Although the British led the way, the Dutch and the Germans most fully developed the model of the prison workhouse.

This form of bondage originated in northern Europe. Records show that the first towns to establish prisons included London (1555) and other English towns (from 1562), Amsterdam (1596) and other Dutch towns (from 1598), Copenhagen (1605), Bremen (1608) and other North German towns (from 1613), Antwerp (1613) and other towns in the southern Netherlands (from 1625), Lyon (1622), Madrid (1622), and Stockholm (1624). This geographic concentration of early prisons in the north obviously reflected the rarity there of galley servitude, which provided an alternative sanction in the Mediterranean areas.

Transportation, the fourth form of bondage, was used most frequently in England, where King James I introduced it as a penalty in a royal decree of 1615. In the preamble to the decree, the king announced his desire to take care that "justice be tempered with mercie" in view of "the severity of our laws." The notion that a combination of severity and mercy should define any approach to crime remained a key idea in the English criminal justice system well into the eighteenth century. In 1615, economic motives may also have played a part in the introduction of the new punishment, which required offenders to perform a "profitable service to the Commonwealth." This service, of course, consisted of indentured servitude in Britain's American colonies. Hence, transportation belongs in the category of bondage, for offenders were not simply shipped overseas and then set free.

Transportation was imposed only infrequently in Britain until 1718; we have little information about its practice before that date. Toward the end of the seventeenth century a few other European countries experimented with this penalty. The court of Amsterdam sentenced a number of criminals to work for the governor of Surinam but soon dropped the practice. Swedish courts sent convicts to the country's Baltic dominions and a few to New Sweden (the present state of Delaware).

The Early Modern Workhouse

We are relatively well informed about the daily experiences of convicts confined to early modern workhouses. Records illuminate two significant aspects of workhouse life: the concept of the prison workhouse as a household and the role of its managers in this household; and the nature of the institutional regime and the inmates' reactions to it.

The management of prison workhouses did not change very much between the introduction of the first such institutions around 1600 and the first half of the nineteenth century, when solitary confinement and the panoptic principle took center stage. Most workhouses were managed by a complex hierarchy of supervisors consisting of four levels of officers, the third of which bears particular relevance to our discussion. The first level included the magistrates who founded and ultimately directed the prison. The second, consisting of the administrators, was responsible for the institution's finances and for passing disciplinary sentences on inmates who seriously misbehaved. Both the magistrates and the administrators spent little actual time at the prison. The third level, the resident staff, reported to the administrators and oversaw the internal affairs of the prison. Subordinate to them was the fourth level in the managerial hierarchy, the assistants.

The role of the resident staff, the group with the most direct responsibility for running the workhouse, most clearly reveals the nature of the prison program. The staff had three main tasks: to keep the inmates busy with work, to provide them with food, and to ensure internal order. In the Hanseatic towns, these tasks often fell to three separate officials. Both the *zuchthaus* and the spinhouse at Hamburg had a *werkmeister* (work master), an *oeconomus* (household manager), and a *zuchtmeister* (discipline master), although one person sometimes served as both *werkmeister* and *zuchtmeister*. In the Amsterdam rasphouse, the head of the staff, known as the "indoor father," took care of meals and the work program; a "master of discipline" assisted him. Likewise, the Haarlem prison had an indoor father, but in his relations with other staff members he was merely the first among peers. In Delft, however, the *concherge* was the central figure, who controlled all the institution's internal affairs.

Whenever they spoke of the officials who dealt with prisoners, contemporaries preferred paternalistic terminology, using the word "father" intentionally. This usage shows up only faintly in the examples just given, but in unofficial speech the term "father" crops up repeatedly. Prisoners usually conferred the term on the Delft *concherge*; Amsterdam inmates used it for several members of the staff. The title also appeared in Germany. In Bremen, prisoners referred to the *speisemeister* (food master) and his wife as the *speisevater* (food father) and *speisemutter* (food mother); the Hamburg *oeconomus* was admonished to act as a good *hausvater* (house father). Paternalistic titles for prison personnel were recorded throughout Germany, from Danzig to München, and in the Habsburg Empire. The fact that Austria and Bavaria also used such terms proves that the father imagery extended beyond Protestant areas. A paternalistic spirit also pervaded the administration of the Austrian *zuchthäuser*.

The word "mother" was just as important, for fathers were only fathers if assisted by mothers. As a result, married couples almost always managed prison affairs. In the Hanseatic towns, when new personnel were sworn in, husband and wife took the oath together. When one of the partners died, the other could not easily continue in the job, especially if it was the husband who had died. For example, in the Hamburg Zuchthaus, on December 16, 1643, authorities assigned the task of feeding the prisoners to an *oeconome* named Gesche Heimb. We do not know whether she was the widow of the previous *oeconomus*, but whatever exceptional situation put a woman in charge, it lasted for only nine months. On September 9, 1644, Gesche Heimb married Jacob Schumacher, who took the oath as *oeconomus* on October 17. When he died in February of the next year, Gesche Heimb exercised her function alone again until December 1646. The administrators finally bought her off, appointing a new couple in her place. They explicitly noted that they did not think her incompetent, for she had always performed her duties well. The problem was simply that she had no desire to marry again.

Records from Delft offer similar evidence that the authorities preferred to appoint couples to direct prison affairs. The administrators in 1736 advertised a job opening in the Delft, Leiden, and The Hague newspapers: "The regents of St. George's Hospital, also prison workhouse, in the town of Delft notify everyone that the post of concherge in the said house is due to be vacated at the last day of September of this year 1736. Everyone interested, who is married, has a knowledge of the fabrication of cloth, worsted, and baize, and possesses the required capabilities, is invited to report to the regents of the said house before 1 February 1736." Six candidates replied, but only two merited serious attention. The administrators met and, having considered "the personalities, wives, and other circumstances" of the two applicants, voted unanimously for Leendert van den Heuvel. Thus, not only did candidates have to be married but their wives' character formed an essential part of their qualifications. Delft followed similar procedures later in the eighteenth century; the word *concherge* was then defined as "indoor father."

Staff members usually lived in prison, in part to shore up the household structure. Unlike modern penitentiaries, which maintain a clear separation between confined inmates and an outside staff, early modern workhouses provided staff living quarters that were part of the building as a whole. In Amsterdam, for example, both the indoor father and the master of discipline lived in the rasphouse. When Jan de Lange resigned as master of discipline because of old age, his successor moved into his living quarters. De Lange moved into one of the rooms of the indoor father, who happened to be his son-in-law.

De Lange was eighty-four years old when he resigned, which was probably exceptional. The ages of staff members in Dutch prisons were very seldom recorded, but most of the fathers and mothers in Hanseatic towns were in their forties or fifties. The mother of the Bremen Zuchthaus, for example, was fifty-five in 1726, when officials questioned her because of an escape. Her daughter, who also worked in the house, was twenty-six (it was very common for sons and daughters of staff members to assist them). The age as well as the marital status of personnel helped qualify them to play the role of fathers and mothers over the inmates.

Of course, the staff served merely as surrogate fathers and mothers. Contemporaries never referred to inmates as pseudo-children. Interestingly, records from the early years frequently called male inmates "journeymen." The common use of the term "master" for staff members makes sense in light of this. At the time, the terminology of employment and that of paternalism were quite compatible. In free society, master craftsmen and shopkeepers acted as surrogate fathers over their apprentices and journeymen. Shop and household were not yet distinct. In prison the situation was no different. The indoor father and mother had a shop to run, which happened to be a prison workhouse.

To help manage the journeymen-inmates, the staff relied on journeymen-assistants. The assistants, never very numerous, reported directly to individual members of the resident staff. Records show the presence of assistants to the indoor father and of maids who helped the indoor mother. Although they obviously ranked above the inmates, assistants performed tasks similar to those performed by prisoners. Indeed, prisoners themselves often earned the privilege of performing such assistance tasks if they behaved well. The prison, in effect, was a complex household.

The workhouse notions of "family" and "household," however, may tell us more about the ideas of staff and magistrates than about the reality of inmates' experience. For prisoners, the punitive character of the environment may have remained central. They did not always spend their time in the manner the authorities wanted them to. We know of three main inmate activities, two that complied with official prison order and one that hoped to subvert it: labor, religious exercises, and preparations for escape.

The prison regime revolved around forced labor. Prison trades varied widely, but rasping and cloth work were most important. Cloth work, the prison trade practiced most frequently, included spinning, weaving, and fabricating such cloths as bombazine, canvas, or linen. Rasping involved the pulverization of logs of dyewood to produce powder for coloring material. This very strenuous job fell only to males convicted of the most serious crimes. Women did most of the spinning, whereas both men and women with light sentences did weaving. Whatever the task, the prison normally required a minimum output from each inmate. In the case of rasping, staff measured output as the weight of the powder produced. In Amsterdam and Bremen a pair of strong inmates, who worked together handling a rasping-saw, had to produce fifty pounds a day. According to various prison ordinances, workdays lasted about ten to twelve hours, comparable to the working hours of free laborers. Some inmates managed to exceed their minimum output during these hours and, as a rule, received a small sum of money, with which they could buy extras from the indoor father.

On weekdays, the religious routine consisted of an obligation to say a morning and an evening prayer, probably a universal requirement easily enforced by the staff. Inmates performed no labor on Sundays, and the Lord's day served as the main occasion for religious exercises. The prisoners usually assembled in a special room for a service and sometimes received religious instruction as well. In the Netherlands, authorities in the early years harbored great hope that such instruction could hasten reformation. But by the middle of the seventeenth century they acknowledged that certain people could not be saved at all. In addition, the staff found it too dangerous to gather particular inmates for services. The hardest convicts in the Amsterdam rasphouse, for example, were simply given a pocket Bible in hopes that at least one inmate could read and would recite from it to his fellows. In Haarlem, where comparable conditions prevailed, the managers found a different solution: the Sunday sermon was delivered in one of the raspers' rooms so that the inmates of the adjacent rasping rooms could hear it too. The male weavers and the female inmates assembled separately in the courtyard of the institution.

The religious character of imprisonment was more pronounced in North German towns. Regular ministers from parish churches preached in prisons on most Sundays. The records of the Hamburg Zuchthaus around 1630 show that "students and instrumentalists" provided "a nice music" during these services. Together with the inmates, the general public attended services at the prison in a room normally called the church. This practice was recorded at the Hamburg spinhouse and in the *zuchthaus* at Celle, where the "free community" sat between the groups of male and female prisoners, separated from them by bars. Hamburg citizens could pay for a reserved seat, if they so desired.

The third major inmate activity, preparing for escape, was not the only one that subver-ted official order. There were also conflicts and violence among inmates, sexual contacts be-tween inmates or between staff and prisoners, refusals to work or other forms of disobedience to the superiors, and insubordinations and revolts. Preparations for escape, however, represented by far the most common subversive activity and lay at the heart of a developing inmate subculture. Still, actual escapes happened infrequently. Between the mid-seventeenth and the mid-eighteenth centuries, the percentage of inmates who escaped was very small, usually well under 10 percent. In Brussels, over twenty years during the eighteenth century, seventy-five men and six women broke out from the *tuchthuis*. Later in the eighteenth century, the number seems to have declined even further. But unsuccessful attempts must have outnumbered successful escapes at all times. Probably no day passed in early modern prisons without one or more inmates at least contemplating a breakout.

The escape methods inmates used fall into three categories. The most "archaic" manner, arson, appeared mainly in the seventeenth century. Prisoners who set their room on fire hoped to create a situation of total chaos in which they could run away. The physical circumstances in early modern prisons favored this method. Buildings were made with a good deal of wood, and much of the equipment for work was combustible as well. But arson seemed a notorious act of desperation, and officials recorded it less frequently in the eighteenth century. The second method, getting keys by force or trickery or using violence to coerce the staff into complicity, occurred with no particular pattern over time. The third method, breaking out, increased in frequency as arson declined. Even though these methods too yielded success in only a minority of cases, breaking and digging out were more clever approaches.

Attempts at these forms of escape constituted the inmates' major nocturnal activity, just as labor was their daytime business. Eighteenth-century male convicts made themselves especially busy digging tunnels and trying to break walls or bars almost every night. By keeping up their hopes and maintaining the myth that one day they would all be free as a result of their own efforts, these prisoners made their situation tolerable. Preparations for escape boosted morale, and that principle shaped the prison subculture that emerged in the eighteenth century.

THE DEVELOPMENT OF THE PRISON AS A PLACE OF PUNISHMENT

There was one major exception to the regime of forced labor in prison. Some inmates were in prison because their relatives could not cope with them, or because the family feared that the unruly member might damage the family reputation, or both. In such cases, imprisonment served as a tool of private discipline. The family drew up a petition explaining why the individual should be imprisoned, and the authorities decided whether or not to consent. Usually, private offenders were confined because of conduct considered immoral. Most of them had to work too. But a minority from wealthy and distinguished families avoided the labor program. Their relatives, who could well afford to pay for their upkeep, wanted merely to separate the black sheep from the outside world. Inmates from such wealthy backgrounds belonged to the prison population from the start. Both in the Amsterdam rasphouse and the Hamburg Zuchthaus, for example, the authorities established separate wards for these privileged few at the beginning of the seventeenth century.

These wards signaled the creation of a new type of confinement, one that differed from that of the prison workhouse. Separation from the outside world, rather than forced labor, defined this regime. Although the prisoners did not suffer complete solitude, their treatment foreshadowed the nineteenth-century system of solitary confinement. In the Dutch Republic, the new system eventually gave rise to a different sort of prison, in which the inmates performed no work at all. Enterprising individuals were the first to establish such institutions, in the mid-seventeenth century. We read of them in Delft, where they began with private people who lodged a small number of the insane in their own homes. An ordinance of December 1662 opens with the statement that ever more citizens were making a business of this; further on, it mentions "the insane and other confined persons." Everyone who housed these prisoners was henceforth obliged to request the magistrates' permission and to submit to official visitations.

During the decades that followed, private institutions, for the insane as well as for misbehaving people, emerged in other places. In Amsterdam in 1694 two men hired on as "landlord" and *betermeester* of the *beterhuis* that was about to open. The ordinance establishing the institution spoke of "malicious and obstinate persons" rather than the insane. It also included the phrase "to the exclusion of all other betermeesters in town," which gave the managers a monopoly and suggests that private entrepreneurs had previously accommodated prisoners in Amsterdam.

From the end of the seventeenth century, such institutions, referred to as *(ver)beterhuis*, became common in the Netherlands. Quite a number opened in small villages or rural areas, instituting a form of confinement distinct from that of the older prison workhouses. All *beterhuizen* adhered to a regime of separation from the outside world without forced labor. The proprietors sought profit, and the relatives of the inmates paid for their stay. Institutions for the confinement of family embarrassments proliferated in eighteenth-century France, where they were often managed by monastic orders. England had its private prisons too, but admission seems to have been restricted to the insane.

The emergence and the spread of such institutions in the Netherlands were spurred in part by the simultaneous evolution of prison workhouses. Because the latter increasingly admitted common criminals, upper- and middle-class families no longer found these places desirable for the detention of their own. Their distaste for workhouses created a demand for private prisons. As a result, in the period before 1800, public imprisonment was more firmly established as a criminal sanction, replacing other forms of bondage. A brief review of the penal history of four European countries—the Dutch Republic, Germany, France, and England—illustrates this shift.

The Dutch experience was the simplest. Because the Dutch had always preferred imprisonment to other forms of bondage, the transformation of their prison workhouses into penal institutions went smoothly. From the beginning, the town courts of Amsterdam and Haarlem had sentenced thieves and comparable offenders to the *tuchthuizen*. After 1654, when the Amsterdam workhouse opened as a prison for vagrants and minor delinquents, the rasphouse housed convicts only. It thus represented the first criminal prison in Europe. The Amsterdam spinhouse, too, soon filled mostly with criminal women. Other towns in the Dutch Republic maintained just one prison, with a ward for each sex. These facilities did not evolve into exclusively criminal prisons, but convicts made up most of their population in the eighteenth century. By then, courts frequently imposed sentences of imprisonment. During the third quarter of the seventeenth century, the Amsterdam court did so in one-fifth of its criminal cases; a century later, it did so in three-fifths. By the 1670s the court of Groningen-City imposed imprisonment in two-fifths of criminal cases.

By contrast, Germany was slow to replace public works with imprisonment as a criminal sanction. For many years in the Holy Roman Empire, the courts faced strong opposition to using prison workhouses for the confinement of criminals. This opposition came from prison administrators, who profited from board money paid by the families of nonconvict inmates, and from citizens reluctant to spend public money to support inmates. Both feared a loss of revenue if workhouses were too closely associated with the criminal element of society. The German notion of honor, which the populace cherished with particular tenacity, viewed everything connected with crime and criminal justice as tainted. In this view, any prison workhouse used to confine criminals would become an infamous or dishonorable place, even if the authorities proclaimed it decent. Since the presence of common criminals would deter families from committing undisciplined members to prison, the prison masters would lose income and the public would have to spend more on the punishment of criminals.

The Hamburg magistrates found a solution first by establishing a new prison, the spin-house, to which only infamous convicts were committed. Opened in 1669, it was the second criminal prison in Europe. Without paying inmates, of course, the institution required another source of financing, which it found in the public treasury. Other German towns either had fewer financial options or were more reluctant to spend their money on separate prisons for convicts. In the second half of the eighteenth century, however, authorities overcame the popular hostility to infamous institutions. By that time, imprisonment was a common penal sanction throughout the Empire.

In France, the change in approach to penal bondage started with galley servitude, which was first instituted in the sixteenth century as a form of punishment primarily for vagrants. During the seventeenth century, criminals sentenced by courts, especially deserters condemned by courts-martial, came to predominate in the galley fleet. After 1715, however, galleys lost their importance as naval tools, which doomed them as a military institution. As a result, the composition of the oarsmen population changed. Whereas during the thirty years before 1715 almost half the oarsmen had been condemned by a court-martial, usually for desertion, during the following third of a century nine-tenths of the oarsmen had been sentenced for smuggling and common-law crimes. At the same time, those condemned to galley servitude increasingly served their sentences as workers rather than oarsmen. After 1715, more and more convicts remained in the harbor of Marseilles during the winter season, laboring in the arsenals or for private merchants on a for-hire basis.

In 1748 the galleys were abolished, and the complex at Marseilles was dismantled. French law, however, did not change. Courts continued to impose galley servitude; to execute these sentences, the condemned were put to work in the naval arsenals at Toulon, Brest, and Rochefort. They had to carry heavy loads, turn wheels, drive pumps, or pull cables; others labored in joinery, drilling, or caulking, and a few assisted in building ships. At night they slept in barracks, chained to their beds. This kind of punishment survived the Revolution and endured until 1854. The arsenals were in fact labor camps where convicts had to remain within an enclosed space, so the penalty was more akin to imprisonment than to public works. In one respect, however, these labor camps had fewer penal possibilities than the prison workhouses of other countries: only men worked in the arsenals, for only men had rowed the galleys.

For the confinement of both women and men in France we must turn to another institution, the *hôpitaux généraux*. In most places these were asylums rather than prisons, with limited facilities for locking up criminals. In Paris, though, the situation was different, for many convicts were imprisoned in its hospital general. The institution actually consisted of several physically distinct establishments joined administratively. Two of these had a separate ward, *la force*, which was in fact a prison within the institution: the Salpêtrière for women; and Bicêtre, which originally housed only men but from the early eighteenth century on also housed syphilitic women. The prisoners in *la force* had been committed at the request of their families, by a court, or by the lieutenant of police. In the last case, they were either prostitutes or suspect people arrested at night and charged with vagabondage or petty theft. On the eve of the Revolution, *la force* at Bicêtre and at the Salpêtrière accounted for about one-seventh of the total hospital general population of Paris, about 650 and 1,000 inmates, respectively. Even though a minority of the inmates of both institutions were incarcerated in *la force*, the two wards ranked among the largest prisons in Europe at the time.

The regular courts sentenced convicts to imprisonment in a hospital less often than they did to galley servitude. This preference for the galleys shows up in the penalties imposed on food thieves by the Parlement of Paris during the eighteenth century. At no time in this period were more than one-twentieth of all food thieves imprisoned in a hospital general. In the first half of the century about one-sixth were sent to the galleys, but before the end of the century about one-third received a galley sentence, which now meant confinement in one of the arsenals. Indeed, by the 1780s, galley punishment constituted half of all sentences handed down by the Parlement of Paris.

England too had its own peculiar developments, but eventually imprisonment grew. Although the English had pioneered imprisonment, courts and legislators remained reluctant to use the bridewell system for the detention of felons. Vagrants and servants who cheated their employers made up the bulk of those confined to bridewells. For a long time, transportation was the preferred form of penal bondage. The Transportation Act of 1718 made it a primary penalty rather than a means to avoid capital punishment; the act also decreed that henceforth the government would pay for the shipment of convicts. In all, some fifty thousand British convicts were transported to America between 1718 and 1776, condemned not only by English courts but also by Irish and, to a lesser extent, Scottish courts. Among the Irish convicts, vagrants were relatively numerous, but most of the English and Scottish convicts were thieves indicted for grand larceny.

More than half the persons transported were in their twenties and four-fifths were male. Maryland and Virginia were the most frequent destinations, although some convicts landed in the Caribbean. In America, the shipping contractors sold the convicts to private employers, mostly middle-sized planters who owned a small number of black slaves. Because the price of a convict averaged about a third of that of an African, the larger slaveholders protested the system. They suggested, in vain, that England adopt galley servitude or public works as punishments.

Evidence from eighteenth-century Surrey, England, illustrates the fate of men and women condemned to noncapital punishments for property offenses. As the century progressed, more and more received sentences of transportation, so that by 1772 three-fifths of male convicts were transported (women were transported less often during every period). Imprisonment, meanwhile, was statistically insignificant during the first half of the century; even in the third quarter of the century, no more than one-tenth of convicts received prison sentences. But from that point onward, despite a revival of transportation in the 1790s, imprisonment gained steadily, accounting for at least two-thirds of criminal sentences by the end of the century. The decline of transatlantic transportation before the American Revolution shows that imprisonment gained for reasons other than the troubles in the colonies. Hence, in England as well as in the Dutch Republic, Germany, and France, imprisonment was well established toward the end of the early modern period.

Acknowledgments

I wish to thank Sjoerd Faber and Jim Sharpe for their comments. Their works, too, were important for composing this chapter.

Bibliographic Note

This essay draws on my own work in the history of punishment and discipline in preindustrial Europe: *The Spectacle of Suffering: Executions and the Evolution of Repression, from a Preindustrial Metropolis to the European Experience* (Cambridge: Cambridge University Press, 1984); *The Prison Experience: Disciplinary Institutions and Their Inmates in Early Modern Europe* (New Brunswick, N.J.: Rutgers University Press, 1991). For a theoretical comparison of European and American developments in punishment, see my article "From Amsterdam to Auburn: An Explanation for the Rise of the Prison in Seventeenth-Century Holland and Nineteenth-Century America," *Journal of Social History* (Spring 1987), 439–61.

The major competing theory on executions and the rise of imprisonment is to be found in Michel Foucault, *Surveiller et Punir: Naissance de la Prison* (Paris: Gallimard, 1975) (translated in English as "Discipline and Punish"). See also his *Folie et Deraison: Histoire de la Folie a l'Age Classique* (Paris: Gallimard, 1961) (translated in English as "Madness and Civilization"). An older but still valuable overview is Georg Rusche and Otto Kirchheimer, *Punishment and Social Structure* (New York: Russell and Russell, 1939).

Important works dealing with specific types of judicial sanctions are the following: A. Roger Ekirch, *Bound for America: The Transportation of British Convicts to the Colonies, 1718–1775* (Oxford: Clarendon Press, 1987), on deportation overseas; Andre Zysberg, *Les Galeriens: Vies et Destins de*

60,000 Forcats sur les Galeres de France, 1680–1748 (Paris: Editions du Seuil, 1987), on galley servitude; Bronislaw Geremek, *La Potence ou la Pitie: L'Europe et les Pauvres du Moyen Age a Nos Jours* (Paris: Gallimard, 1987), and Robert M. Schwartz, *Policing the Poor in Eighteenth-Century France* (Chapel Hill: University of North Carolina Press, 1988), on disciplining the poor; John H. Langbein, *Torture and the Law of Proof: Europe and England in the Ancien Regime* (Chicago: University of Chicago Press, 1977), and Edward Peters, *Torture* (New York: B. Blackwell, 1985), on judicial torture.

The major works dealing with separate countries are, for England: J. M. Beattie, *Crime and the Courts in England, 1660–1800* (Princeton: Princeton University Press, 1986), and J. A. Sharpe, *Judicial Punishment in England* (London: Faber and Faber, 1990); for France: Nicole Castan, *Justice et Repression en Languedoc a L'Epoque des Lumieres* (Paris: Flammarion, 1980); for the Netherlands: Sjoerd Faber, *Strafrechtspleging en Criminaliteit te Amsterdam, 1680–1811: De Nieuwe Menslievendheid* (Arnhem: Gouda Quint, 1983); for Sweden: Eva Österberg and Dag Lindström, *Crime and Social Control in Medieval and Early Modern Swedish Towns* (Uppsala: Academia Upsaliensis, 1988); for Germany: Richard van Dülmen, *Theater des Schreckens: Gerichtspraxis und Strafrituale in der Frühen Neuzeit* (München: Beck, 1985) (also available in English); for Italy: Gaetano Cozzi, ed., *Stato, Societa e Giustizia nella Repubblica Veneta, Sec. 15-18* (Roma: Jouvence, 1980); and for Spain: Ruth Pike, *Penal Servitude in Early Modern Spain* (Madison: University of Wisconsin Press, 1983).

CHAPTER THREE

THE WELL-ORDERED PRISON

England, 1780–1865

Randall McGowen

The contrast between a prison in 1780 and one in 1865 could scarcely have been greater. Disorder and neglect were the dominant features of the eighteenth-century prison. On entering the jail, one was confronted with the noise and smell of the place. It was seldom easy to distinguish those who belonged in the prison from those who did not. Only the presence of irons differentiated the felons from the visitors or from the debtors and their families. The jail appeared to be a peculiar kind of lodging house with a mixed clientele. Some of its inhabitants lived in ease while others suffered in squalor. There was little evidence of authority. Some prisoners gambled while others stood drinking at the prison tap. On the other hand, the prison in the mid-nineteenth century was quiet and orderly, if also drab and functional. The eeriness of the building was exaggerated by the ghostly forms of convicts in uniforms and masks. Only prisoners and jailers were present, and the difference between the two groups was apparent at a glance. Conversation and pleasure had been outlawed, but the prison was clean and healthy. Prisoners were confined to identical cells and subjected to a similar diet. Their lives were carefully regulated. A prison had assumed an unmistakable appearance.

Although the difference between the two points seems clear, the history of the transformation is difficult and complex. For one thing, the story begins long before 1780. England had experienced significant changes in penal policy on several earlier occasions. And although the late eighteenth century witnessed a particularly intense and innovative discussion of imprisonment, the actual transformation of imprisonment was slow and halting. The only constant in the period from 1780 to 1850 was a nearly uninterrupted increase in crime and the number of prisoners. This increase lent a sense of urgency to the debate over punishment, but it scarcely explains why particular solutions were proposed. Although these decades saw momentous change in the character of English society, especially in the rise of urban and industrial civilization, focusing too insistently on this vast transformation will only produce reductionist explanations of penal reform.

Penal change was a complicated affair, full of contradictory impulses and policies. With so many causes operating, it is probably futile to search for one decisive cause or one particular moment when the modern prison was "born." Reform came in waves. It was often the product of compromises among competing ideas and between abstract schemes and practical limitations. Despite the sensation created by John Howard's investigations, prison reform between 1780 and 1820 tended to be carried out at the local level. It was only after 1810 that a national campaign, conducted in part by Quakers, shifted attention to parliamentary investigation and legislation. Even in the early nineteenth century, Parliament was reluctant to impose central direction on local authorities. By the 1820s, critics of reform argued that confinement had become too lenient and needed to be more deterrent. By the 1830s prison chaplains pushed what came to be called the separate system at both the local and the national levels. The proponents of this system triumphed in the construction of the national prison at Pentonville in 1842. Yet debate over penal policy continued into the 1850s, with many people echoing criticisms that had first been uttered in 1780. The average prisoner's life in 1865 was profoundly different from his life in 1780, but despite the large new prisons and the greater numbers incarcerated, the prison remained an institution strangely resistant to the intentions of its designers.

THE EIGHTEENTH-CENTURY PRISON EXPERIENCE

Eighteenth-century English justice employed a wide variety of measures to punish crime. For misdemeanors, English courts typically imposed fines or resorted to public and symbolic inflictions such as the pillory or whipping. Offenders were sometimes encouraged to join the military. Many of those condemned to death were pardoned on the condition that they be transported to the American colonies. The hierarchy of punishments climaxed in the drama of the gallows, where secular authority invoked the image of divine sanction to perfect human justice. Punishment spoke of the majesty of God and the king. It was inflicted to avenge their honor. The condemned were invited to earn forgiveness by confessing to the correctness of the sentence and the goodness of human justice. But punishment, although it expected the participation of the convicted, existed for the public. It was offered as an example and a lesson. The spectacle of human suffering was intended to put the crowd in mind of the vastly greater terrors of hell, the only fear that most magistrates believed could over awe a fallen humanity. Such occasions ran the risk of participation by an unpredictable crowd, which might sympathize with the condemned or become enraged at a bungled execution. But since the fundamental goal of punishment was publicity, this risk had to be taken.

Although whipping, the pillory, and the gallows more fully expressed the aim of early modern justice, confinement had a familiar place in the judicial process. People were confined while awaiting trial or the execution of a sentence. Only a small minority were actually imprisoned as punishment, usually for such minor offenses as vagrancy. In theory two types of institutions existed, the jail and the house of correction. The former contained felons and debtors, as well as those held for trial, whereas the latter received petty offenders sentenced for short terms. But the distinction between the establishments was not always observed, and even within a particular institution, different categories of prisoners often mingled together. Indeed, the terms *jail* and *prison* were often used interchangeably, and they will be so used in this chapter.

There were an extraordinary number of places of confinement, probably more than three hundred. The possession of such an establishment was a jealously guarded privilege for a borough, manorial, or ecclesiastical franchise holder. Yet many of these local jails consisted of no more than a gatehouse, room, or cellar. They seldom contained inhabitants for any length of time. Only a few establishments held a significant number of prisoners. The prison population of the county jail at Warwick, for instance, fluctuated considerably depending on whether it was near time for the assizes, the twice-yearly trials of serious crimes before the judges on their tour of the country. John Howard, the prison reformer, found 33 felons in the jail in January 1776, along with 24 debtors, whereas in October he discovered only 7 felons and 22 debtors. London contained the largest prisons and a disproportionate share of the prison population. The most important London prison, Newgate, often held as many as 300 felons in the late eighteenth century. The city also possessed large separate establishments for debtors such as the Fleet and the Marshalsea. Responsibility for these various prisons lay with different local authorities who exercised widely varying degrees of oversight.

If confinement was not strictly associated with punishment in the eighteenth century, part of the explanation was the presence of large numbers of debtors. Debtors constituted a larger portion of the long-term inhabitants of a jail than felons. In Newgate, Howard found between 30 and 50 debtors in the 1770s, and in county jails there were often as many debtors as felons even at assize time. Of the 4,084 prisoners Howard counted on his tours, 2,437 were debtors. It is hard to overstate the importance of imprisonment from debt in shaping the popular image of confinement as well as the jail itself. The incarceration of debtors resulted from a civil process, a contest between two private citizens. Imprisonment was not meant to punish a debtor but rather to secure the debtor until the debt was paid. Government fulfilled its responsibility to uphold credit relations by providing a place of confinement for those who had betrayed a trust. Although debtors and felons were confined together, debtors were not felons, and the authorities were limited in their responsibility for and control over debtors. The jailer had little power over them. They proved an unruly element within the jail, resisting efforts to police their conduct. They were ever ready to complain of infringement of their rights as Englishmen. They often brought their wives and children into the prison, further contributing to the problem of regulating the institution. In 1776 Howard found 242 debtors in the Fleet, along with 475 wives and children. In theory the creditor was supposed to provide subsistence to the debtor, but this did not always occur. In some counties debtors were offered food, but in many instances debtors had to provide for themselves and their families. They depended on the wider community, family, friends, or charity. The situation of debtors formed the basis for a money economy in the prisons. Debtors not only rented space from the jailer and bought his food or beer but also sold goods and services to others confined. As a result the prison experience depended more on what one could afford than on the particular reason for confinement.

The presence of so many debtors in prison had long been a source of complaint. The power of the creditor over the debtor seemed at times an unconstitutional assumption of influence in private hands, and the plight of so many innocent families confined in hunger and sickness aroused widespread concern. Jailers in particular, accused of the greedy exploitation of those trapped by circumstances, became targets of outraged popular opinion. The exposure of abuses occasionally prodded the authorities to investigate prison conditions. At various times Parliament passed insolvency acts to secure the release of debtors. Wills sometimes included bequests to provide food or clothing for poor prisoners. But legal authorities regarded imprisonment for debt as a valuable sanction that secured responsible conduct in business. It seemed, at the very least, a necessary evil. In part because of this practice, confinement consisted of a series of private arrangements in which there was a wide degree of latitude for all the parties involved.

The fluid character of prison life was reinforced by the peculiar position of the jailer. Prisons were largely self-financing operations, and the jailer was supposed to derive his income from the fees owed by prisoners for various legal services. In addition the jailers enjoyed the profits from whatever commercial opportunities they could organize. They might collect fees from visitors, charge for bedding, or benefit from the sale of beer in the prison. In the larger prisons the office was so lucrative that it was widely sought after. One family jealously guarded the possession of the Bedford jail through several generations. The sources of profit came to be considered a form of property legitimately belonging to the jailer. Many of the judicial decisions on confinement concerned the rights of the parties involved rather than the rules regulating discipline. In an important case in 1669 the judge supported the claims of a jailer who continued to confine a man found innocent at his trial because he had not paid his fee. The man claimed that he was too poor to pay. The judge, Matthew Hale, held, "[I cannot] help that, nor can I give away other men's rights; if they will not remit their fees, you must pay them." Such a decision accorded with the general attitude toward office-holding. Although it might seem that such a judgment exposed the prisoners to unlimited extortion, this was seldom the case. More typically the jailer treated prisoners as customers. He cultivated the trade of those who could pay while simply neglecting those who were without resources. Jailers had little interest in securing a more rigorous regime; a generous tolerance increased their profits while keeping down their costs. Their rapacity was also kept in check by the freedom of prisoners to petition magistrates or assize judges. Jailers did not want trouble. A riot would attract the attention of authorities and result in an unwanted inspection of the establishment. The relative infrequency of petitions and riots suggests that the occupants of jails were in some measure reconciled to their conditions.

Even if jailers had possessed the ambition to impose tighter control, they usually lacked the means to do so. They had almost no staff, and those few assistants they employed came from their own families or were often recruited from among the prisoners. Instead they tolerated a wide measure of self-government on the part of those confined. Prisoners often developed elaborate rules and procedures for keeping order among themselves. In the larger jails they had courts that heard complaints, assigned fines, and settled disputes that arose in their community. The order of the prison mirrored that of society to a surprising degree. Prisoners entering the prison paid garnish as a form of initiation just as if they were entering a trade. In most prisons no effort was made to regulate the prisoner's day. Some worked at an occupation, but at their own initiative and for their own profit. Others were permitted to beg. The usual complaint about prisons was that occupants passed their time in games, gambling, and drunkenness. Jailers tolerated the almost unrestricted admission of friends and the curious, who mingled with the prisoners. They profited from selling this privilege. The prison wall scarcely separated the community created among the prisoners from the wider world. The internal organization of the prison was dominated by custom and the rough compromises that governed relations between prisoners and jailers. Life in an eighteenth-century prison could be tumultuous, but it would be a mistake to confuse disorder with anarchy.

THE BRIDEWELL, TRANSPORTATION, AND THE HULKS

The preceding paragraphs should not be taken to suggest the existence of an unchanging regime. The early modern period saw many attempts to remedy immediate problems or develop new solutions to deal with crime. Time and again an outbreak of jail fever or a surge in crime attracted the attention of local justices or Parliament. Local records often record expenses for repairing prisons. Parliamentary legislation in 1670 sought to ensure that debtors and felons were kept separate. An act of 1699 vested new powers in the county justices to build and repair jails. The Society for the Promotion of Christian Knowledge conducted an investigation of Newgate and the Marshalsea in 1702. In addition to listing abuses, it praised the idea of keeping prisoners in separate cells. James Oglethorpe secured a parliamentary committee to examine the Fleet and the Marshalsea in the 1720s. In 1728 a statute required jailers to post a schedule of fees, and in 1751 the sale of liquor in prisons was forbidden. Although some of this legislation was mandatory, local authorities were required to enforce these statutes. These measures do not indicate a consistent record of intervention; bequests were forgotten and rules went unobserved. But they remind us that there were important periods of innovation in punishment well before the last decades of the eighteenth century.

The most dramatic evidence of an earlier effort to transform confinement in the centuries before 1780 lay in the existence of the house of correction, or bridewell. This institution emerged in late-sixteenth-century London in response to the growing problem of vagrancy. By the early seventeenth century perhaps 170 such houses had been opened across the country. The distinctive purpose of these institutions was to reform as well as to punish. They were intended to employ their inhabitants so that the prisoners would learn industrious habits. Many of the proposals offered by penal reformers in the 1780s were foreshadowed here, even in smaller details. For example, the keeper of a bridewell was to be paid a salary, and magistrates were responsible for the oversight of the institution. In one gloomier sense the history of the house of correction offered an ominous lesson as well. Even after these institutions failed to produce the intended reform they were nonetheless adopted by justices who appreciated the advantages of short periods of confinement. Magistrates became convinced that these sentences were an effective way to deter vagrants and to discipline disobedient servants. The bridewell became the focus of several later efforts to reform punishment. For instance, between 1690 and 1720 a number of new houses were created. A measure of Parliament's continuing interest in the institution was legislation passed in 1706 permitting judges to sentence felons to the house of correction for up to two years. Significantly, the act further specified that the sentence could include hard labor.

If the house of correction was a significant area of experimentation with secondary punishments, transportation to the American colonies was just as important. Both initiatives were part of the same search for an alternative intermediate punishment at a time when there was little choice between the gallows and branding. Indeed the early-eighteenth-century legislation on bridewells and transportation suggests that this period marks a decisive break in penal thought and practice. Both forms of punishment signaled a shift away from penalties that employed the body in a public spectacle to sentences defined in terms of labor and time. A sentence of hard labor already had a double meaning, promising both suffering and reform. Proponents of transportation believed that a term spent facing the severe conditions of the colonies would transform the idle as well as provide them with a new opportunity. Although the transportation of felons had been experimented with in the seventeenth century, the legislation that restored the penalty in 1718 arose at central government initiative and with state funding. Faced with a rising tide of crime in the aftermath of a war, the authorities acted decisively to transform the character of punishment. The sentence was an immediate success, at least as measured by its acceptance and use. Some thirty thousand people were transported to the American colonies between 1718 and 1775. Yet its widespread employment did not indicate uniform enthusiasm for the penalty. By the 1750s critics argued against a punishment that seemed insufficiently deterrent. Opponents pointed out that the reputation of the sentence could not be controlled. The rumor that those who were sent out prospered rather than suffered undercut the effectiveness of the penalty. Sentencing patterns suggest that even before the disruption produced by the American Revolution, judges were returning with renewed interest to confinement as a better way to punish offenders.

By the 1770s English justice was buffeted from several different directions. Most immediately, the number of those convicted of crimes was on the rise, and the resulting overcrowding in prisons was compounded by the presence of more debtors. The abrupt interruption of the transportation penalty in 1775 produced a crisis. The government, in scrambling to find a solution, settled in 1776 on the use of old vessels, which came to be called hulks, as places of temporary confinement. Although an emergency measure, this expedient revealed the shifting currents in penal thought. The plan adopted for the management of the hulks was more rigorous than anything found in most of the jails of England. A restrictive diet was imposed on the prisoners, and they were set to hard labor clearing the Thames and other seaports. Well into the nineteenth century the hulks continued to be a major repository for convicts retained in England, but they never lost the taint of being a half measure. They earned popular disapproval by being expensive and at least initially unhealthy. Critics repeated tales of the immorality and violence that prevailed when the hatches were closed.

Penal expedients during these years were adopted, in large part, out of a sense of desperation. Especially in the aftermath of the American Revolution, England seemed deluged by crime. For a brief period the authorities turned to the gallows. By 1783 the clamor was growing for a return to transportation. In 1787 the first fleet sailed for Australia. Yet this revival of transportation did not diminish the discussion of confinement, as it had seventy years earlier. The arguments in favor of the hulks and transportation tended to be pragmatic rather than principled and merely sharpened the urgent sense that a more adequate form of punishment was required.

THE RISE OF REFORM

In addition to these practical pressures, the whole question of punishment was again being discussed, in a changed political and intellectual environment. The imperial crisis associated with the American Revolution produced a far-ranging questioning of English institutions and morality. The political radical Josiah Dornford expressed this feeling in 1785 when he wrote, "Nothing but a *real reform* can save us from ruin as a nation." He argued, "Were our prisons new modelled, it would be one considerable step toward reform of the lower orders of the people." Dornford was one of a number of authors who published works on prisons and punishment in this period. London was a center for such agitation, and radical doctors and lawyers took a lead in the movement. Reformers focused on two aspects of prison administration, health and religion. "With grief I speak it," Dornford complained, "we take little care of the bodies, and less of the souls of our prisoners." The plight of prisoners was described in the most heartrending terms. They were trapped in prisons, victims of disease, hunger, and jailers' greed. Parliamentary legislation displayed a sensitivity to such concerns when, in 1773, magistrates were permitted to appoint chaplains to jails and to provide them with a salary and when, in 1774, magistrates were empowered to select surgeons to attend to the prisoners.

In concentrating so insistently on the bodies and souls of individual prisoners, the reformers indicated an intensification of concern that had found expression for over a century. They rejected the idea of punishment as spectacle, suggesting that such displays produced callousness. Society should show a tender regard for the individual, thus fostering gentler manners. These goals demanded more attention to punishment, not to its relaxation. Nearly every author during these years had favorable words for some kind of solitary confinement. Even a defender of the gallows such as William Paley praised the ability of solitude to frustrate vice and promote virtue among prisoners.

Among the foremost advocates of solitude was the philanthropic entrepreneur Jonas Hanway. In 1776 he published *Solitude in Imprisonment*. The interruption of transportation, he argued, offered an opportunity to reexamine the arrangements for dealing with prisoners. He complained that earlier discussions had failed to consider the importance of reforming the offender. Hanway was part of a rising evangelical tide that inspired many advocates of reform in the late eighteenth century. By "reformation" he meant religious conversion. "This confinement," he wrote, took place between this world and the next and was "calculated to qualify" prisoners for either. "However nauseous it may be, for a time, it will cooperate with necessity, like medicine for the body, and those wretched beings may be induced to submit to that which is so apparently intended to preserve both body and soul." Suffering was no longer physical pain exploited in a drama intended for an audience but was a spiritual ordeal provoked for the prisoner's own good. The prison was simply the passive setting for such a struggle; the prisoner's own conscience inflicted the suffering. Hanway saw the prison as a more suitable emblem of divine justice, displacing the gallows, which had for centuries been considered an appropriate representation of the human predicament before an omnipotent judge. "The walls of his prison will preach peace to his soul," Hanway proclaimed, "and he will confess the goodness of his Maker, and the wisdom of the laws of his country."

The insistent demand for solitude marked a new development in the conception of the form and purpose of punishment. The house of correction had long targeted idleness, using labor to produce reform. But Hanway went beyond such an analysis in attacking a particular form of sociability. Whatever the source of crime, the remedy lay in the isolation of the individual soul. Only by becoming an individual could the convict discover the right principles to guide his life. True religion needed the assistance of institutions in a corrupt world. Solitude cut the offender off from his false community. A proper confinement taught a lesson of heightened responsibility for one's life. It promoted the internalization of more exacting rules for regulating private conduct.

These proposals for reform soon influenced a few leading individuals to experiment with local prisons. The most significant effort was undertaken by the Duke of Richmond in rebuilding the Sussex county jail at Horsham in 1775. The prison brought together a wide number of the measures proposed by the reformers. The jail was well situated, and the building was strong and well suited to its purpose. Each prisoner had a separate cell. The prison was built on arches to aid in the circulation of air. Each room was equipped with bed and blankets. The jail made a break with the past in striving to achieve an equalization of treatment. The felons were washed on entrance and clothed in a uniform. Debtors were permitted a quart of strong beer or a pint of wine a day, but felons had only water to drink. The county had abolished all fees as well as the tap, and it provided the jailer with a salary. A chaplain had been appointed, with a regular salary, to give a sermon once a week and prayers every day. Horsham revealed a frustration with waste, disorder, and sickness; it displayed a confidence in what could be achieved through the rationalization of institutional life.

John Howard

Although authors like Hanway and Dornford discussed the various elements that composed a proper penal regime—religion, work, severity—the book that had the widest impact on penal arrangements was published by John Howard in 1777, *The State of the Prisons in England and Wales* captured public attention. Although this work popularized prison reform, it did so less by the force of its originality than by its synthesis of existing thought. It was a peculiar book to attract such acclaim. Howard recorded in several paragraphs a few simple facts regarding the condition of each English prison he visited. Yet contemporaries read through the tedious details to the passion that fired his investigations. Howard was a middle-aged country gentleman when he was appointed sheriff of Bedfordshire. This official's responsibility included the jail, but Howard was unusual in going so far as to visit it. He shared with other religiously inclined reformers a sense that his beliefs required an energetic commitment to transform the world. What he found in the jail shocked him: prisoners were ill, and rules went unobserved. The prison symbolized the antithesis of Christian charity. Magistrates abdicated responsibility. In particular he was appalled to discover that prisoners who had been acquitted were still confined because they could not pay the jailer's fees. He protested to the magistrates, who asked him for evidence that other counties acted differently. In seeking to provide an answer, Howard began an investigation that took him to all the prisons in England. Soon he roamed the continent examining the forms of confinement in other countries. Finally in 1791 these exhausting and dangerous investigations led to his death in Russia while he was visiting prisons there.

Although Howard was drawn to his mission by his particular religious disposition, and although the appointment to a peculiarly English office provided the occasion for his effort, once Howard visited the continent he discovered a Europe-wide interest in confinement. One consequence of his book was to expose the English to these other practices and to suggest that England lagged behind other countries. Howard never claimed originality when it came to prisons. He simply sought to bring the English up-to-date and to adopt the best practices he could discover. Everywhere he went he found people concerned with similar questions and conducting parallel experiments. The Dutch in particular won his admiration. They had already achieved the perfection he hoped to introduce in England: prisons were "so quiet, and most of them so clean," that a visitor could "hardly believe" he was in a jail. Howard did not know "which to admire most, the neatness and cleanliness appearing in the prisons, the industry and regular conduct of the prisoners, or the humanity and attention of the magistrates and regents." At a moment of crisis in English penal practice Howard introduced the idea that a proper prison regime already existed, only somewhere else.

Howard's advocacy of prison reform, however conventional in some respects, was in more subtle ways a powerful intervention. If justices and the public in England were beginning to reconsider confinement, Howard's contribution was to make the prison the center of focus, shifting all other forms of punishment to the margins. He fostered a vital change of perspective at the very time that judges were sentencing greater numbers of felons to confinement. Howard's book created the impression that the prison was the natural and inevitable shape of punishment. Yet he also sought to show that imprisonment in England was deeply flawed, that it was riddled with abuses. It required immediate reformation. Still, the prison was its own cure. Howard had an ideal of what the prison should be, not so much as a particular architecture or regime, although he had thoughts on both issues, but as an institution, as a way of handling people. The difference between Hanway and Howard was that the former concentrated on the offender and on constructing a regime appropriate to his moral condition, whereas Howard focused on what made for a healthy and efficient institution. In his travels Howard visited schools, hospitals, and poorhouses as well as prisons. His emphasis was less on the character of the people confined and the mission of the institution than on the common features of all such places. If he found an institution well managed and clean, he was full of praise for it. He had nothing more to inquire of its inhabitants. He had an almost sublime faith in the ability of institutions with a common shape and regime to solve social problems.

When Howard visited a prison, what offended him was the evidence of disorder and inattention, the failure to post rules, the indiscriminate mixing of inhabitants, and the unregulated boundary between the prison and the community. Although he characterized such disorder as oppressive for the prisoners, what he meant was that it pained him. His concern was to establish a new organization of the prison, one grounded on principles of rationality, health, and a warm sense of religious purpose. He often described as an abuse what was in part simply variety in penal practice and saw as anarchy what was a different form of order. He took the independence of the prison culture as one more symptom of general maladministration. He focused on simple points, the fees taken by jailers, the absence of magisterial oversight, and the level of illness. Yet these so-called abuses were not incidental but went to the heart of existing arrangements. In proposing to remedy them, Howard was in fact trying to create a new institution. He wanted a prison that was less like the actual world. The life of the jail should stand as a counterpoint to the disorder from which crime sprang. Howard believed that jailers should be paid a salary so that they would have no interest in collaborating in the circumvention of established laws. Local officials should take a far more active role in inspecting prisons to ensure that these regulations were observed. He wanted to extinguish the petty pleasure indulged in by the prisoners. They should not be able to gamble, drink, or pass their time in idleness. Those confined should be submissive; swearing should not be tolerated. Howard's target was not simply filth and physical afflictions but also the noise and disorder, the "audacious spirit of profaneness and wickedness." He made no distinction among the various ills he discovered. He attacked with equal fervor the presence of disease and the autonomy of prisoner culture, seeing them as part of a common failure.

The Years of Local Prison Reform

The agitation that coincided with the publication of Howard's book in one sense climaxed in the passage of the Penitentiary Act of 1779. This statute was drawn up by William Blackstone and William Eden with Howard's influential support. The proposal combined many of the features Howard had admired in continental institutions—solitary confinement, religious instruction, a labor regime. Prisoners were to wear uniforms and be subjected to a coarse diet. The work was to be arduous and servile. The act proposed to pay officials a salary, but its authors expected the costs to be recovered from the profits of prison labor. The prisoners would also enjoy a share of the earnings. The act called for a kind of progressive class system in which prisoners could earn a remission of part of their sentence by good conduct and effort. The legislation summarized the most advanced thinking of the day on the prison question. Two penitentiaries were to be built, one for men and the other for women. The program was invested with impeccable philanthropic credentials when Howard, the Quaker physician John Fothergill, and George Whately, treasurer of the Foundling Hospital, were appointed to oversee the construction. Yet the committee soon fell into disagreement about the location of the buildings, and support for the project waned. The act exceeded the national government's enthusiasm for reform. The constraints imposed by the war against France and practical doubts about the wisdom of building so centralized a facility combined to undermine the program. Far from inaugurating a new era, the Penitentiary Act revealed the limits of what could be expected of reform at the national level in the eighteenth century.

The surprising dimension of the agitation of the 1770s lay less in the failure of the national legislation than in the burst of activity that followed at the county level. Perhaps forty-five prisons were rebuilt in the years before 1790 in a largely uncoordinated effort. A second wave of prison construction occurred in the 1820s. What made this success so unexpected was the role of the traditional landed classes and their representatives at the quarter sessions in carrying out the reform. From 1780 to 1865 most English prisons remained under local control. The decision to rebuild a prison or change its administration rested with the royally appointed justices of the peace who gathered at the county quarter sessions. They voted the sums needed to carry out reform, and the new prisons were not cheap. Prisons could account for anywhere between one-quarter and one-half of the county budget, contributing to the sharply rising burden of county rates. Intellectuals and political radicals may have made the penitentiary idea a cherished project, but it was the support of more conservative and cautious local politicians that provided the approval and funding for the new constructions.

Prison reform was not one of the partisan political issues of the period. Of the two major political parties, the Whigs contained the more advanced and systematic reformers. The Tories, fearful of reforms justified by abstract principles, supported more modest and pragmatic alterations. Typically a Whig interested in reform initiated a discussion on local penal arrangements, although there were even exceptions to this generalization. In Bedfordshire the Whig Samuel Whitbread pushed penal change, while in Lancashire T. B. Bayley and in Sussex the Duke of Richmond played the central roles. Such men were familiar with the most advanced thinking on the prison question and shared a confidence in the potential of the reformed establishment. They took a leading part in collecting information and studying architectural designs. But they had to carry more conservative magistrates with them in order to advance reform. The acquiescence of the bench in these bold initiatives can be explained in part by a crime threat at a time when traditional punishments seemed unsatisfactory. Provincial authorities faced a rising tide of crime in the 1780s and with it the threat of jail fever. Local facilities were simply not up to the challenge. The attack on the disorder of the prison also coincided with other efforts to "civilize" popular culture, such as the attempts to control alehouses and to abolish cockfighting and bullbaiting. Rural justices faced an increasing population and a dramatic rise in poverty. Enclosures and conflicts over such customary practices as gleaning produced greater judicial activity. The struggle over poaching intensified. Employers turned to the courts to punish the indiscipline of servants. The reformed prison came to be accepted as a convenient remedy to petty criminality.

But the justices were responding to more than these circumstances when they initiated the rebuilding of prisons. For they not only expanded the size of county prisons but also rebuilt them with new architectural proposals in mind. They enforced measures that imposed a stricter regime on the jail and secured tighter control over the activities of the jailer. Both through their own activity and in their actions to foster a new ethic of administration on the prison, these magistrates displayed their own altered notions of the responsibilities that went with office-holding. These principles required a more energetic involvement in administration as well as a more professional and impersonal style of government. A public office involved a trust that raised service above self-interest and party consideration. Justices who possessed this ethic looked with suspicion on those who derived profit from an office, especially when the officer exercised an unrestricted power over those paying the fees. Such a description fit all too well the situation of the jailer.

This heightened sense of administrative responsibility made the magistrates sensitive to the abuses catalogued in Howard's work. His book publicized lapses that reflected on their administration of the county. Disease in the jail not only indicated a faulty regime in the prison but also implied a judgment on the moral integrity of those responsible for the oversight of the institution. Although Howard was cautious in his attribution of blame to jailers or magistrates, his proposals involved a higher level of oversight and accountability. Howard urged justices to take a more aggressive role in the supervision of prisons. Parliamentary measures sanctioned such increased activity. The legislation that influenced the justices was less the Penitentiary Act than the measures passed in 1782, 1784, and 1791 that provided magistrates with the power to repair prisons, separate classes, and pay a salary to the jailer. By the 1780s justices were less inclined to treat the prison as a franchise and were beginning instead to view the office of jailer as involving a trust. This philosophy triumphed in the passage in 1815 of a statute that abolished jail fees and required that magistrates come up with some other arrangement for paying jailers.

In some English counties the task was taken up with enthusiasm, but others lagged behind. Not every locality responded readily or sympathetically to Howard's revelations. The initial effort to rebuild the prison in Howard's own Bedfordshire failed. Only in 1797 did the grand jury present the jail as "insufficient." A committee of justices formed to investigate the matter proposed the construction of a new prison, which opened in 1801. The pattern varied from county to county. In 1783 Dorset rebuilt its jail at a cost of four thousand pounds, a considerable sum for county government. Yet when Howard visited the site, he found it still inadequate. Led by William Morton Pitt, the justices resolved to build a new jail at a cost of sixteen thousand pounds. Much depended on the presence of an influential individual who would adopt the prison as a personal cause. The Duke of Richmond's efforts in Sussex did not stop with the Horsham jail. In 1789 he was responsible for the construction of a new house of correction at Petworth. This bridewell not only included separate cells but also introduced stalls to keep prisoners apart in chapel.

If Howard played a crucial role in accelerating prison change, as important an influence was exercised by the architect William Blackburn. Before he died in 1790 he had designed some nineteen prisons and influenced the shape of many more. He was Howard's favorite architect. Blackburn expressed the ambition to use space and stone to shape human nature. His designs revealed the implicit belief that architecture could promote the goals of confinement. Geometry and symmetry triumphed in these designs, which pursued health, order, and more equal conditions. A rationally organized space, he believed, would foster the development of reason and self-regulation in its inmates. His plans also sought to strengthen the position of the jailer within the prison by promoting inspection. Above all Blackburn sought to secure classification and separation; he set the main task of prison architecture as the regulation of human sociability. The disease analogy produced a search for the sources of contagion and ways to disrupt its spread. Prison reformers feared the contamination that resulted when the untried mingled with the convicted, debtors shared the same wards as felons, or those convicted of misdemeanors intermixed with those guilty of more serious offenses. Reformers were especially anxious about the effects of men and women intermingling and the danger of allowing young offenders to communicate with mature criminals. The categories were mundane and predictable, but the reformers invested immense energy in the discovery of these distinctions. It was the belief in the contagious nature of crime that spawned the investment of time and money in prison construction. Blackburn's designs promised to separate these classes and so prevent contamination. Prison walls were the cure. The challenge presented to prison reformers was to identify the dangerous and endangered groups and to properly allocate offenders among these various categories.

For the two decades after the death of Howard, the leading advocate of prison reform was George Onesiphorus Paul. In the aftermath of Howard's visit to Gloucester, local officials stirred themselves to reform the city jail, but the effort became mired in acrimony over the cost and scope of reform. Paul's intervention in 1783 dramatically transformed the situation. Paul was the son of a successful clothier, and after the death of his father he settled down to enjoy the status of a landed gentleman. Frustrated in his efforts to gain election to Parliament, he turned to prison reform. In a speech delivered to a county meeting he pointed to the deaths from jail fever of five prisoners recently released from confinement. He listed the abuses that existed in the local prisons and proposed an ambitious program of reform. The meeting approved his proposal and sanctioned the effort to secure parliamentary legislation to authorize the building of a new county jail and five bridewells.

By 1785 Parliament approved the plan and Paul secured designs from Blackburn. The new facilities were opened by 1792, with room for some four hundred prisoners and at a cost of forty-six thousand pounds. The regime established at Gloucester included a stage imprisonment system, with the first third of a sentence passed in solitude. In 1792 Paul summarized the main ambition of his program: "Their clothing is comfortable, yet humiliating; secluded from the society of their friends, they are daily visited by gentlemen attentive to their spiritual and bodily welfare; food is prepared for them sufficient for all the purposes of life and health, whilst the use of money is denied and, by this denial, every means of luxury, or partial indulgence, and of corruption, is prevented." Paul's proposals for the management of the prison were just as important. A governor held central power in the prison, and Paul desired that this official be drawn from a higher class than were the jailers of the past. He lent his support to the search for ex-military men to fill the post. It was not enough that the officers of the prison would have no interest in fees or profits; the governor had new responsibilities for record-keeping, inspecting prisoners, and disciplining subordinates. The chaplain was given independent authority to report on the governor's conduct, and a committee of justices was made responsible for visiting the prison three times a quarter. Paul's efforts remind us not only of the importance of the local level as the scene for most penal innovation between 1770 and 1820 but also of how many of the basic elements of reform were widely accepted by this time.

THE NATIONAL DEBATE OVER PUNISHMENT

Significantly, penal reform did not become a partisan issue during the years of the wars with revolutionary France. At a time when many other humanitarian causes were viewed with suspicion because they were tainted with revolutionary associations, prison reform advanced. The explanation lies in the fact that the prison remained an institution firmly under the control of traditional local authorities. They initiated changes. Parliamentary legislation enhanced their power and their prestige, as well as their responsibility. The improved jail also aided justices concerned about the challenges of vagrancy and rural crime; it provided a more effective short-term punishment for petty offenses. It promised to produce moral reform without upsetting the old social order.

The lack of sharp debate over the prison is all the more striking because this situation contrasts with what would seem a closely related issue, capital punishment. The increasing use of confinement was also accompanied by a growing disinclination to impose any public punishment, such as whipping and the gallows, that relied on the spectacle of human suffering. Many penal reformers were critical of a criminal code that imposed death for a wide range of offenses, but there was no consistent effort to alter that code in the eighteenth century. Justices by 1800 were less likely to impose such penalties, but few spoke out against them in principle. It was only in 1808 that Samuel Romilly inaugurated a campaign to ameliorate the criminal law by radically circumscribing the use of the death penalty. Despite the steady advance of prison reform, Romilly's proposals met with heated opposition and made headway only slowly over the next two decades. Although the two causes were intimately related, the difference in the reaction to them reveals the fissures in the seemingly monolithic movement. But the contest over the gallows took place on another plane. Even though fewer individuals were being executed, the symbolic significance of the execution remained as important as ever to conservative politicians. The execution offered a public display of the power of the state. Political authority sought to find legitimacy in a ritual form that enlisted religious meanings and symbolism. It was because this form of punishment was so closely identified with a particular conception and practice of social relations that Tory politicians sought to defend it with such tenacity.

Reformers like Romilly condemned the gallows precisely for the reasons the conservatives defended it: it was public and emphasized the discretionary element of justice. They demanded a justice that was neutral and predictable, that celebrated its procedural fairness rather than its ultimate moment. They wanted to circumscribe the authority of the judge to exercise discretion. Such acts drew too much attention to the personal element in judicial practice. Punishment should not depend on a personal decision but should be so mechanical that it could be calculated. The reformers also condemned the public nature of punishment. The execution excited the wrong kind of emotions; it hardened those who watched rather than softening them and making them gentler. The reformers invariably turned to the prison as embodying the proper form of punishment. The image of the gallows repeated the worst aspects of the unreformed prison, its turbulence and unpredictability. The reformers wanted to achieve a greater control over punishment, to regulate its operation and effect. In the prison, punishment was carried out in private. The reformed prison sought to reduce the autonomy of the convict at the same time that it left no place for the observer. In the reform arguments the rituals of public displays of power gave way to the technologies of institutions for managing people and shaping minds. Prisons did not inflict needless and excessive pain; they merely employed a minimal level of severity in order to secure the proclaimed goal of reforming the individual.

In 1810 Romilly rose in Parliament to propose resurrecting the Penitentiary Act of 1779. The government responded by appointing the Holford Committee to examine the whole question of penal reform. This committee canvassed many who had been active in prison reform in the preceding decades. Paul testified on the reform principles he had tried to realize in Gloucestershire. Jeremy Bentham was questioned about his twenty-year struggle, beginning in 1792, to design and construct his model prison, the panopticon. Bentham's scheme for the prison emphasized inspection and labor. Although both themes had been discussed in the eighteenth century, Bentham produced an idiosyncratic vision that carried each to a pitch that had not been achieved before. Yet the real significance of his appearance was that it afforded the committee the occasion to reject decisively the idea that prisons could be privately managed for profit. Bentham had offered to run the penitentiary under contract. Such an idea was intolerable to other reformers. Their revulsion revealed how deeply the new principles of administrative responsibility had penetrated. Prison reform had been carried forward by those who condemned the old system of a jailer relying on fees. Reformers of all stripes feared the danger of abuse in a prison not subject to oversight. They also mistrusted the operation of the profit motive both on prison managers and as an inducement for prisoners. They wanted to see the prison operated along humanitarian lines and with the goal of producing a religious conversion in the convict.

The Holford Committee itself testified to the growing strength of a prison reform movement that once again came to occupy a national stage. Parliamentary investigation of prison conditions became a setting within which reformers could advance their more radical measures. One product of this attention was the decision to undertake the construction of a national penitentiary at Millbank. Although it cost a half million pounds to construct and was immediately subject to much criticism, the prison represented an important step in the nationalization of the question of imprisonment. Millbank, opened in 1816, was a huge prison, designed to hold one thousand inmates. Its prominent location in London, as well as its complicated arrangement of pentagons surrounding a hexagon, precipitated unprecedented public discussion.

By the 1820s reformers were less likely to look to the local bench and more likely to turn to national agitation to secure their schemes. Although not always openly expressed, reformers' positions became more hostile to the traditional power exercised by the magistracy. The success of measures taken to improve health and impose a degree of order left idealists discontented. They thought the prison should do more, that it had not yet realized its purpose. H. G. Bennet, a prominent Whig politician who had played a role in prison reform in Bedfordshire, was one such critic. "The occasional humanity of a sheriff," he argued, "remedies one abuse, relieves one misery, redresses one wrong, cleanses a sewer, whitewashes a wall; but the main evils of want of food, air, clothing, bedding, classification, moral discipline, and consequently moral amendment, remains as before." In part the problem arose from the increase in the numbers confined, which overwhelmed existing arrangements. At both Gloucester and Petworth, overcrowding undermined earlier reforms. But such criticism implied a heightened demand for uniformity and an increased expectation for thoroughness. Ironically many of the prisons that were criticized in the second decade of the nineteenth century had been "reformed" in the wake of Howard's visits. The appearance of such articles in journals with a national readership marked one other aspect of this nationalization of the prison question. In this milieu the tendency was to define local arrangements not as occasions for experimentation but as excuses for the continuation of abuses. If the aims of penal reformers and magistrates had harmonized in the late eighteenth century, they had begun to diverge by the early nineteenth century.

The Influence of the Quakers

A leading role in the revival of penal activism through national organization and with a national audience was occupied by a small group of evangelically minded Quakers. Prison reform, however, was only one of a wide number of issues that claimed the attention of the Quakers during these years. William Allen, a proprietor of a London pharmaceutical concern, illustrates the character of Quaker involvement. Allen was active in the antislavery cause, in Lancastrian school reform, and in the operation of a Spitalfields soup kitchen. He was one of the founders of the Society for Diffusing Information on the Death Penalty in 1808, and he also pressed the cause of criminal law reform in a journal, *The Philanthropist*, which he launched in 1811. In 1813 he began visiting prisoners in Newgate on a regular basis. In the same year his coreligionist Elizabeth Fry entered the female side of Newgate to bring clothes to the prisoners there. Appalled by the disorder and riot she encountered, she soon began to preach to the prisoners. After a four-year hiatus she returned to Newgate at the head of a female committee, while her brother-in-law, Samuel Hoare, began to visit another London prison, Cold Bath Fields. Fry became a celebrity, aided by the series of articles describing her activities and published by her brother, the Quaker theologian J. J. Gurney. Prominent Londoners flocked to the prison to hear her sermons and to marvel at her effect on the prisoners. Here seemed proof not only that religion could reform but that it produced the only true alteration in character. This activity lent luster to a campaign that demanded a wider role for religion in defining the purpose of the prison.

This activism sprang in part from a deep sense of personal unworthiness, which shared much with the evangelical spirituality of the day. Nonetheless the Quakers displayed a confidence in a divine providence that exerted itself to improve humanity. They believed in the availability of an "inner light" to all people. Their worldly success in banking and industry created in them an internal agony that not only led them to identify with the outcasts of the world but also produced in them a desire to witness to their faith by their philanthropic activity. The awareness of suffering testified to one's own spiritual condition. While they constantly struggled against their own fallen natures, these Quakers were so confident of the power of faith to reform the convicts that they hurried to the prisons. The seeming incorrigibility of the criminal was the result not of human nature but of a mistaken punishment.

The Quakers opposed punishments that afflicted the body. Such penalties produced a hardness and insensitivity that found its fullest expression in the disorder of the prison. The "idleness, clamor, and dissipation . . . the mixed din of fiddling, laughing," and profanity appalled them. They demanded order and quiet in the prison. Quaker penal thought was distinguished by a belief in reformation as the only real task of punishment and the conviction that this goal could be achieved by the exercise of personal influence. In a well-run prison, Gurney advised, "the prisoners are ruled by kindness; chains are therefore unnecessary." He noted, "They appeared to us to be subdued and softened by the gentleness with which they were treated." Fry and Gurney did not advocate any particular regime of work and religious influence. Rather they relied on personal contact to produce a consciousness of true religious principles. The social relationship established between the humanitarian and the prisoner produced reform. The prisoner's proof of reform came not only in the avowal of belief but also in the openness to this relationship. The Quakers put great faith in the value of voluntary efforts carried out by groups of laypeople within the jails. Displaying considerable organizational ability, they set up committees and produced regular schedules for visiting the prisons. "If throughout the country," wrote one proponent of these arrangements, "committees to visit and reform the prisoners were to become general, the evils of captivity would be lightened, numbers would be softened into virtue, and kindness would become the means of producing reform, instead of misery operating to deepen crime."

The Quakers galvanized the public by their activity in the immediate aftermath of the Napoleonic Wars, renewing the prison question by exposing abuses. In particular they created a heightened anxiety around the figure of the individual prisoner, creating both a sympathy for his plight and a demand for a regime appropriate to his condition. In doing so, they established religion as a more central medium for articulating the failure of existing arrangements and proposing a new vision for the goal of reformation. In their own visiting and in their publication of proposals to the public they circumvented the magistracy. Their call for voluntary action as the basis for a permanent penal policy proved utopian, but their organizational flair and zeal for publicity had a considerable impact on political discussions.

One of their most successful efforts was the creation of the Society for the Improvement of Prison Discipline (SIPD), founded in 1816. This group enlisted the support not only of prominent philanthropists but of powerful politicians as well. It applied pressure at both the national and the local levels. Its reports were frequently reprinted in the press, and its members appeared before parliamentary committees, providing a new kind of expert testimony. The SIPD sought to influence architectural plans for constructing prisons, offering detailed comments on every aspect of design. The society brought a new level of precision and expertise to penal questions, ironically displacing and discrediting the voluntary efforts lauded by a Quaker like Fry. The SIPD focused more attention on the practical arrangements of institutions than on a concern for the prisoner. The discussion of proposals for new prisons was increasingly conducted in a more technical language that limited the influence of the amateur philanthropist.

The SIPD became an advocate for greater centralization of English prisons and helped to advance this cause through its activities. Committee members visited prisons and collected information for its reports. They lobbied for the adoption of a radial design for the prison, a design that promised not only the rational organization of space but also the fullest measure of inspection within the prison. Although the SIPD announced that its object was reform of the offender, it pursued its policy through an ever more total system of policing the prison. Design would frustrate all attempts at communication and any efforts on the part of the convicts to see the world inside or beyond the prison wall. Perhaps more revealing of the society's conception of the prison was its advocacy of the treadwheel. This device, introduced in the second decade of the century, was composed of a series of steps on a giant wheel and was propelled by the prisoners' climbing motion. By 1824 some fifty-four prisons had adopted the mechanism. The treadwheel had many virtues in the eyes of the SIPD. It could be operated by the uneducated and provided the prisoners with exercise. It deprived the convicts of all independence in regulating their own labor while supposedly exposing each individual to the same burden. It gave the authorities the fullest measure of control because they set the pace and the resistance of the wheel. The regime was also one that could be imposed in every prison. Above all it promised to reconcile the competing aims whose conflict overshadowed every discussion of punishment: the struggle between reform and severity. The SIPD turned to the technologies of construction and machinery to support its claim to have perfectly satisfied each ambition. In each case the SIPD proposed to realize its goal by replacing human discretion with mechanical force, the properly constructed cell and the treadwheel.

The Critics of Reform

Although the idea that a prison should deter potential offenders was always a part of the penal philosophy of those who sought the reform of the prison, critics from the beginning maintained that too much deterrence was sacrificed to the elusive goal of reform. But the activities of the Quakers and the rising influence of the prison chaplain produced a more strident and self-conscious reaction. The public debate over the prison increasingly centered on the following dilemma: was too much being done to the convict, or was too much being done for the convict? So long as the gallows remained the symbolic center of punishment, the prison advanced under the banner of reform. But once the prison emerged as the dominant form of punishment, some critics contended that it was flawed. The earliest complaints suggested that prisoners were coddled, that they were fed too well, that county funds were wasted to provide indulgences that the average working family was denied. "Those salutary ideas of loathsomeness and misery," wrote one author in 1823, "which men associate with a jail, and which naturally tend to the prevention of crimes, cannot fail to be much weakened by a sight of the cleanliness and order, the decent apparel and seeming comfort, which are found within the walls." He concluded, "A prison ought to be a place of terror to those without, of punishment to those within." Despite their discontent with the direction of reform, these critics did not have an alternative to the prison.

What they did have was a different story about the prisoner. If the reformers appealed to sentiment in their highly charged portrayals of suffering humanity abandoned in dungeons, the critics used a scathing humor to mock what they saw as the misguided and naive efforts of humanitarians. They provided a sketch of the convict as clever, immoral, and hypocritical. The Whig essayist Sydney Smith was an early master of such attacks on the "softness" shown to criminals. The successful prison, he feared, might well do a disservice to society. "Hence it is," he complained, "we object to that spectacle of order and decorum—carpenters in one shop, taylors in another, weavers in a third, sitting down to a meal by ring of bell, and receiving a regular portion of their earnings. We are afraid it is better than real life on the other side of the wall, or so very little worse, that nobody will have any fear to encounter it." In expressing this thought, Smith shared with most authors an undervaluing of what might have seemed the main cost of punishment—the loss of freedom. He was able to do so because he portrayed criminals as caring more for luxury than freedom. Felons also lived lives devoted to the pursuit of an illicit freedom, one of indulgence and debauch. He wanted a prison that was an antidote to such freedom, a place of "sorrow and wailing." "A return to prison," he advised, "should be contemplated with horror—horror, not excited by the ancient filth, disease, and extortion of jails; but by calm, well-regulated, well-watched austerity—by the gloom and sadness wisely and intentionally thrown over such an abode." The striking feature of Smith's recommendations was that they employed the same language and ideas as the reform schemes: the regulation of space, time, and diet. He feared that the SIPD erred on the side of "a system of indulgence and education in jails." He wrote, "A prison may lose its terror and discredit, though the prisoner may return from it a better scholar, a better artificer, and a better man." Whereas the reformers appealed to the good of the prisoner as the justification for their regime, Smith appealed to the well-being of society to justify what were essentially the same measures but directed now toward the goals of severity and deterrence.

Punishment in the 1820s offered a confused picture. Many prisons had been rebuilt and so were more healthful as well as more rigorous for those confined. The Gaol Act of 1823, passed through the initiative of Robert Peel at the Home Office, marked a dramatically intensified effort to impose uniformity throughout the country. It forbade the use of alcohol in prisons and called for the appointment of a surgeon and a chaplain. Facilities for instruction were to be provided. A committee of justices was required to visit jails on a regular basis. The act also proposed a system of classification for the prisons. But in most respects the act was a compromise. It left a wide measure of latitude in the hands of local authorities, and no effort was made to close small jails. The legislation also failed to empower the government to enforce these measures. Prisons had become more forbidding places after forty years of intermittent reform, but they lacked the staff to enforce the most severe regulations. More than one hundred prisons had fewer than ten officers, whereas only fifteen had more than fifteen officers as late as 1835. There was still an intimacy and informality in the operation of most prisons. Debtors continued to be a special case, preserving their rights and customs and remaining difficult to control. But they were more isolated and a much smaller proportion of the prison population. Both reform groups such as the SIPD and critics of reform such as Smith continued to be discontented with this situation. Punishment still seemed too haphazard and uncertain.

It is tempting to portray each stage in the transformation of the prison as culminating in a self-confident victory for some scheme or design. But more often those involved with making policy expressed frustration or a sense of impotence. Peel said as much in a letter he sent to Smith in 1826. He wrote at a time when several thousand offenders were being transported to Australia every year and when the hulks confined many of the serious offenders who remained in England. "I admit," he conceded, "the inefficiency of transportation to Botany Bay, but the whole question of what is called secondary punishment is full of difficulty." He did not think that the hulks represented a desirable solution, but he feared that solitary punishment required "too delicate a hand in the enforcement of it to be generally available." He concluded by returning to the theme that there were simply too many convicts to handle in any other way: "The real truth is the number of convicts is too overwhelming for the means of proper and effectual punishment." Peel acknowledged the importance of every idea advanced by the reformers even as he justified his failure to institute any of them.

The Controversy over Systems of Discipline

By the 1830s a sense of crisis over the direction of penal policy prevailed. In 1820 some 13,700 people had been committed for trial for serious offenses; by 1840 the number had increased to 27,200. The number of prisoners nearly doubled between 1820 and 1840. The range of punishments, especially transportation and the hulks, seemed to have no effect on this inexorable rise. The growth in crime was as great in rural as in urban areas. The criminal statistics assumed an even darker form when considered in the context of the general state of society. The disorders that accompanied the Reform Bill agitation were quickly followed by a deeply disturbing outbreak of incendiarism as rural laborers across southern England protested against new machinery. There were riots connected with the interdiction of the "new" Poor Law, particularly in northern areas of the country. These movements were overshadowed in turn by the rise of Chartism and the disturbing image of an organized working class. Police and penal reform were offered as possible remedies to the ills that afflicted the nation.

In seeking to explain the failure of traditional arrangements, prison reformers turned to a familiar argument, that the inadequately reformed prison was itself the source of the trouble. The feeling was that prisoners were still too free to communicate among themselves. In doing so, prisoners gave each other support and passed along information. The hardened offenders contaminated the younger or less-experienced prisoners. Critics complained that classification had failed to stem this contagion because an offender was assigned to a class on the basis of the offense committed rather than the degree of his guilt. What had begun in the 1780s as an attempt to defeat prisoner culture now climaxed in the effort to gain the total elimination of that culture by imposing a regime of silence. If prisoners could be prevented from communicating, they would be less resistant to the regime intended to reform them and less able to seduce others to a life of sin and idleness.

By this date the English had become fascinated with penal experiments being conducted in America. William Crawford, of the SIPD, published a report in 1834 that offered a survey of two systems of prison discipline, the silent and the separate systems. Each promised to disrupt prison communication but in different ways and with different costs. The silent system was employed at Auburn in New York State. Under it, prisoners worked together but in a silence reinforced by punishments for those who violated the rule. Guards were instructed to detect even the smallest gesture. This system placed its emphasis on the development of work habits and took a somewhat more pessimistic view of the chances of converting the offender. It also vested in the governor a considerable discretion to decide which offenses needed punishment and what penalty to impose. Despite the necessity of employing more staff to achieve such control, the system could claim to be less expensive than its alternative. To an ex-military man like G. L. Chesterton, governor of Cold Bath Fields, the system imposed a necessary severity upon a class that was incapable of reform. He defended the system as a practical compromise between the extreme goals of the separatists and the too lenient measures that still prevailed in most prisons. Chesterton was a reformer; he ended illegal trading at the prison and imposed tighter control on the turnkeys. Despite its many classes of prisoners, Cold Bath Fields was a large prison, difficult to manage. The average sentence was only six weeks, scarcely long enough to permit the kind of reform idealized by others. Chesterton believed that the silent system acknowledged the danger of contamination while offering the kind of harsh sentence that represented the most that could be expected of normal punishment.

But it was the separate system that attracted the more enthusiastic supporters in the 1830s. Although similar ideas had been offered by Hanway in the 1780s, and occasional efforts had been made to realize them, the years between 1835 and 1850 saw the most sustained effort to reconstruct the prison along separatist lines. As practiced in Philadelphia, the system isolated the convict for long hours in his own cell to commune with his conscience. The skill of architects and builders was devoted to preventing communication between prisoners in their cells and to depriving them of any glimpse of the outside world. The sight of a hillside or distant buildings beyond the wall was believed to frustrate reform. The separation prepared the mind to receive better impressions and the soul to hear the message offered by the chaplain. English advocates of this system, such as Crawford, believed prisoners should be set to work in their cells, but they did not think that labor alone would produce the necessary changes. The separate system promised a true conversion, not the temporary obedience produced under the silent system. Proponents of separation complained that the other system was a mere compromise defended by half-measure men. The silent system was condemned because it vested too much discretion in the governor and relied too heavily on physical inflictions such as whipping.

The separate system employed the passive weight of architecture to secure its ends. Solitude was broken only by the soothing influence of a Christian message offered by the chaplain. Not surprisingly, a talented group of chaplains became the foremost defenders of the system. John Clay at Preston, John Field at Reading, and Joseph Kingsmill and John Burt at Pentonville became celebrities in their day. They challenged magistrates and prison governors over who should control the prison. Clay attacked both the system of classification established by the Gaol Act of 1823 and the activities of Fry and the Quaker visitors. He held that only the chaplain had the necessary insight into the true character of the offender. The advocates of separation could call for support upon the idea, pervasive in this period, that the revitalization of religion was the solution to a host of social problems afflicting English society. The prison achieved prominence as a central battleground in this struggle. Crime was sustained in society by the spread of irreligion and immorality among the lower orders, but it could be isolated and counteracted by the application of religion to the souls of the worst offenders.

The separate system was significantly promoted by the 1835 report of a committee of the House of Lords. The committee concluded that more uniformity in prison practice was desirable and proposed two measures to secure it. On the one hand prison rules and diets were to be reported to the secretary of state. On the other the government was to appoint inspectors to visit all English prisons. The legislation that followed gave these inspectors only limited powers. In particular they could not order the adoption of reform or even demand the resignation of an incompetent jailer. But of the five inspectors chosen, two—Crawford and the Reverend Whitworth Russell—proved unstinting advocates of separation. They used their reports to coerce local authorities to make changes favorable to their system. They displayed little tact in pursuit of this goal and were unwilling to compromise on any point to their regime. Since Russell was the cousin of the Whig politician Lord John Russell, he was particularly well placed to influence government policy. Even after their deaths in 1847, Russell and Crawford continued to exercise an influence over English prison policy.

Their greatest triumph came with the opening of Pentonville prison in 1842. The prison was a monument to faith in an ideal. It became the model for the construction of many local prisons in the decades that followed and attracted worldwide attention. The prison held 520 prisoners in separate cells. Four wings radiated out from a central point, from which one could observe each cell door. The construction of the walls hindered communication between prisoners, and even the guards wore padded shoes so that they would not disturb the silence. The guards were as strictly controlled as the prisoners, forbidden to talk to the convicts and kept to a steady patrol by a system of time clocks. The prison was also a monument to English engineering; every detail was ingenious, from the plumbing to the lighting. Each cell was exactly the same—thirteen feet deep, seven wide, and nine high. For a regime that was intended to individualize punishment, it did its best to erase any trace of individuality. Prisoners wore hoods when they emerged from their cells. Their names were replaced by numbers. They had separate stalls in chapel as well as separate exercise yards. Pentonville represented the apotheosis of the idea that a totally controlled environment could produce a reformed and autonomous individual.

The Rise of the Prison Administrators

Whereas the 1840s seemed to mark the triumph of a particular and rigorous conception of the prison, the 1850s revealed a retreat from this ideal. Even as the prison emerged as the central institution in the struggle against crime, the fundamental assumptions that had supported its rise were being questioned. The separate system was not repudiated, but it was modified to accommodate pragmatic considerations and was reinterpreted by proponents of greater severity. The man who oversaw these adjustments, succeeding Russell and Crawford, was Major Joshua Jebb. Jebb first served as surveyor-general of prisons, responsible for approving plans for the construction of new jails, and then as chairman of the Directors of Convict Prisons until his death in 1863. Although Jebb began his career under Russell and Crawford, and contributed to the spread of the separate system, he was never a fanatical supporter of that system. He was more pragmatic in his attitude toward various regimes. His rise to power symbolized the resurgence of the ex-military men who dominated the post of prison governor. Even as a number of chaplains published memoirs that defended their system, their influence was in decline. Yet this decline in no way hindered the spread of the Pentonville model. Separation found ready support among those who criticized a regime of chaplains and the extravagant hopes of reform. What recommended it to such figures was the hatred the regime produced in convicts. Although the separate system had been advanced as a method for securing the reformation of offenders, it imposed a scheme of such rigorous severity that it was easily embraced by those whose main interest was in punishing criminals and producing deterrence.

The central challenge Jebb faced was the task of fashioning a prison regime that would replace the hulks and transportation. Rather than adopt any particular scheme, he oversaw the rise of what came to be called the progressive stage system. Each segment of the regime seemed to satisfy some constituency, whereas its overall shape reflected the orderly mind of a military man faced with the task of organizing a large prison establishment. The first stage consisted of a term of separate confinement, although there was little agreement about its purpose or length. Complaints about the effects of separation on the prisoner's sanity led to a reduction of the term from eighteen to twelve and eventually to nine months. During the second stage the prisoners were sent to public works prisons, where they worked together at arduous tasks that would benefit the public. Major facilities were opened at Portland, Dartmoor, Portsmouth, and Chatham between 1847 and 1856. Prisoners were set to work building breakwaters and fortifications or working in gangs to reclaim moorland. Although it was argued that such associated labor would produce contamination, popular opinion was now on the side of hard work that would produce some useful result.

The third stage involved the most controversial element. It offered conditional release to convicts based on their good conduct while in prison. This step represented an acknowledgment of what proponents of the separate system had ignored: that prison administrators had management concerns that conflicted with ideological purity and that no system could render prisoners simply passive targets of a penal regime. A remission of sentence was a standard device for securing the cooperation of prisoners during confinement by holding out a promise of early release. Those who administered prisons knew how important such a policy was. But to both penal reformers and advocates of deterrence, this policy looked like a dangerous relaxation of penal discipline. The contest arose from a dispute over how remission was earned, by minimal observance of the rules or by some extraordinary proof of reform. Penal servitude acts of 1853 and 1857 wrestled with these complicated questions, whereas a series of riots reminded the authorities that prisoners were not passive observers of these decisions. In the end, administrative considerations triumphed over ideological purity; prisoners earned remission by not giving their jailers problems.

Public opinion in the 1850s, alarmed in part by the impending end of the system of transportation, was turning away from sympathy with convicts. Panics associated with several violent robberies committed by convicts released on ticket-of-leave served to focus the issue. The influence of the prison in shaping the experience of crime for the wider public can be seen here. Writers complained of the "criminal classes," a group most easily identified as those who returned time and again to jail. Newspapers and politicians both demanded longer sentences under a more severe regime. The popular cry was for "hard labor, hard fare, and a hard bed." The prison had become the inescapable center for the debate about crime. The fact that this reaction against the language of reform did not result in any significant alteration of the regime created by reform casts a revealing light on the earlier efforts. The reformers had created the belief that the prison was the right way to deal with criminals, and they had produced a regime for gaining control over the individual, a regime that lent itself to both reformist and retributivist interpretations.

The Carnarvon Committee and the Ideal of Deterrence

Surprisingly, the bitterest complaints against the compromises involved in the mid-century prison regime came not from reformers but from advocates of greater severity. Such sentiments dominated the proceedings of a committee of the House of Lords, the Carnarvon Committee, appointed in 1863 to reexamine the question of discipline in local prisons. The committee was composed of politicians aroused by what they saw as an indulgence of convicts. Although they targeted reform as the problem, they shared more with the earlier campaigns than they perhaps realized. Above all they continued to believe that if the prison was shaped in an appropriate fashion, it would significantly reduce crime. They favored a policy of deterrence, but the specific measures they advocated were consistent with a half century of penal effort. These retributivists were as willing as earlier reformers to override the autonomy of local authorities in an effort to secure greater uniformity of penal practice. As a result of their investigations, the number of prisons declined from 187 in 1850 to 126 in 1867. They sought to have their proposed rules embodied in parliamentary legislation and enforced by the threat of withdrawal of a treasury grant. The members bemoaned the "many and wide differences, as regards construction, labor, diet, and general discipline," existing in "the various Gaols and Houses of Correction in England and Wales, leading to an inequality, uncertainty, and inefficiency of punishment, productive of the most prejudicial results." No one called for a return to the relaxed standards of an earlier day. On the contrary, they demanded more rigid observance of procedures and more centralization. The prison failed not because it did not reform prisoners but because it tried to reform people who could not be changed.

Consistent with their skepticism about the reformability of criminals, the Lords were critical of those who assigned a major role to industrial labor or education in the penal regime. They insisted that only the "more strictly penal" portion of the sentence could achieve the central goal of all punishment, deterrence. They applauded the separate system because it disrupted communication and was feared by convicts. What particularly appalled them was the lack of any settled definition of the phrase "hard labor." In some prisons mat-making was considered light labor, but in others it was defined as hard labor. The treadwheel and the crank were, the committee members insisted, the only punishments worthy of the name "hard labor." The Lords argued that the sentence should not be undercut in any fashion that would console the prisoner with the thought that he was doing something useful. No relaxation of diet, labor, or separation should be permitted except in the most extreme cases. And they wanted to put obstacles in the way of surgeons, chaplains, or governors exercising such an option. The details of punishment attracted their attention. They proposed to reduce prison diets and to make each prisoner sleep on planks during part of his term. They saw health less as something to be preserved than as a minimal standard that the prison regime should approach as closely as possible in order to punish thoroughly.

The Lords soon discovered that their real opponents were the pragmatic and stubborn prison officials, not the sentimental reformers. Those most intimately involved in prison administration revealed how often practical considerations rather than consistent policy goals governed the actual operation of the prison. Governors and surgeons provided anecdotal information rather than clear solutions to penal problems. Each official seemed to possess his own interpretation of existing practice and of what needed to be done. The members of the Carnarvon Committee frequently expressed frustration when dealing with their witnesses. Ironically the politicians had a more consistent position than the penal "professionals" they examined. The Lords held stubbornly to the idea that the purpose of the prison was deterrence. They did not flinch in the face of contrary evidence. Yet even witnesses friendly to their position seldom gave answers as clear-cut and decisive as they wanted.

After fifty years of attempts to turn the prison into a machine, imprisonment still remained subject to personal discretion. Governors in particular had a strong sense of their independence. One prison surgeon reported that he had written to sixty governors to inquire into their practices. Based on their responses, he noted, "It is not merely in different gaols that there are different instruments of punishment, but in the same gaol the kind of punishment is varied from day to day, and at different parts of the day." Whipping and irons were used only rarely, but solitary confinement and the withholding of food were often employed to punish difficult prisoners. Prisons still lacked an adequate staff. In 1865 there were only about one thousand wardens to cope with an average prison population of eighteen thousand. Despite the Lords' aggressive insistence that punishment should be hard and unpleasant, some of their witnesses stubbornly dissented. One of the prison inspectors, John Perry, particularly annoyed them by his challenge to their contention that deterrence was the one certain effect that could be produced by the prison. Perry replied that he had "not so much confidence" as many other people did in the "deterring power of prison punishments."

By the 1850s many had come to doubt the ability of the prison to reform. Some then turned to the hope that it could deter. A few, like Perry, confessed that they were not sure what imprisonment could do but acknowledged that society could not do without it.

THE MID-VICTORIAN PRISON EXPERIENCE

While reformers and retributivists tried to shape the prison regime to suit their purposes, both the reality of the prison and the use made of imprisonment by the judicial system displayed the substantial limits of their achievement. Judges and magistrates used the prison, but not in a way that cooperated with the ambitions of the designers of penal regimes. Both reformers and retributivists believed that long sentences were needed to reform or deter offenders. But sentencing policy moved in the opposite direction. Of some 74,000 sentenced by magistrates to imprisonment by the early 1860s, 52,000 were for terms of one month or less. Of the 12,000 sentenced to jails by higher courts, nearly 7,000 were for a period of six months or less. Only 2,100 were subjected to the harshest penalty, penal servitude. By contrast some 9,000 debtors were sent to prison, where they remained, as debtors had a century earlier, a separate group subject to special rules. The Carnarvon Committee acknowledged that little could be done for the typical prisoner beyond a short, sharp sentence. The average occupant of the prison—

the drunkard or the individual who could not pay a fine—was seldom the professional criminal who was so graphically described in popular debate.

If the central features of the eighteenth-century prison had been abolished by 1865, the various penal ideals of the reformers had been only imperfectly realized. This failure made imprisonment a different kind of experience from what had been imagined. For instance, the reformers believed in the power of a rationally planned and minutely articulated architecture to transform human character. Far from being neutral and anonymous, however, the actual mid-Victorian prison building possessed a distinctive personality. The smell of the prison was offensive. The cold produced a level of suffering that approached cruelty. The silence was incomplete, broken by the sobs and cries of prisoners at night or the movements of guards and the constant opening and closing of doors. Although the goal of separation led to refinements in the prison, these changes often only complicated the task of moving large numbers of prisoners about the building. Convicts were given only a few minutes in the bathroom in the morning, and it could take up to an hour to get prisoners in and out of the stalls at chapel.

Similarly the rituals of prison life often worked differently than had been desired. Reformers introduced a regime whose ambition was to erase the old identity of the offender and to destroy the immoral sociability that was thought to sustain bad habits. Imprisonment was supposed to create this change by the combined action of stone, routine, labor, and religion. No aspect of life was thought too insignificant to contribute to this result. The initiation into prison life symbolized this quest. New prisoners were given a bath and a haircut. They were clothed in uniforms and assigned a number in place of their names. These measures were intended to facilitate the creation of a new identity, but numerous prisoners testified to a different outcome. They felt demeaned and humiliated. The bathwater was foul. The uniforms were coarse and ill-fitting. The shoes were cheap and uncomfortable. The physical inspection of the prisoner's body established from the outset that he had no right of privacy, a lesson reinforced every day by the spy hole in the cell door.

Whatever high-minded goals inspired the regime, these aims tended to be lost in the multiplication of rules and rituals that governed prison life. Both reformers and their opponents agreed that comfort and pleasure had no place in the prison, that privation was a necessary element of any penal scheme. In practice this agreement led to a relentless hunt to check communication or deny any petty pleasure. The threat of punishment hung over every proceeding. The ex-military men who staffed prisons were far better at detecting infractions than at contributing to moral reform. The morning inspection of the cell became a contest during which the discovery of poorly folded blankets or a stained cup resulted in a mark against one's name. During the early part of their terms, prisoners slept on a plank bed. Their food was monotonous, unpleasant, and barely adequate. Short-term prisoners received bread and an oatmeal gruel. Those confined for more than three weeks were given in addition potatoes and soup. Prisoners sentenced to hard labor and long sentences were provided with a few scraps of meat. The food was often of dubious quality and ill-prepared. Hungry prisoners were ready to eat anything they came across, whether weeds, candles, or paper. The deprivation of food was the mainstay of punishment within the prison. Convicts who failed to fulfill their work quota, were caught talking, or proved sulky might find themselves on a diet of bread and water. The pettiness and spitefulness of these measures did far more to set the tone for imprisonment than any of the lofty words of spiritual consolation.

One of the main aims of the reformed penal regime was to render prisoners passive so that their characters could be reshaped. But the evidence offered by prison memoirs told a different story. Prisoners were inventive in discovering ways to subvert penal discipline. Only the new convicts challenged the regime head-on, and a beating or a week of reduced diet demonstrated the folly of such attempts. The old hands avoided direct confrontations; they were the model prisoners whom many commentators suspected of hypocrisy but against whom nothing could be proved. They taught new prisoners methods for communicating with each other, shortcuts in finishing work, and the names of guards who could be played upon. Convicts shared food and warned of the approach of guards. They developed a form of ventriloquism, the art of talking without moving one's lips. The prison at night was filled with the sound of tapping as pipes became the medium for telegraphic communication. Some prisoners created chat holes through which they could speak to each other. They relayed information on where to find nails that would make oakum picking, the separation of strands of old rope, easier. They told how to step on the treadwheel so as to make that ordeal less exhausting. Some engaged in an illegal trade with guards and among themselves for tobacco and other small luxuries. Witnesses before parliamentary committees testified to the intransigence of prison culture and the solidarities formed among prisoners.

No other area of prison life exposed the contradictions and tensions of imprisonment so much as health. The reform of incarceration had arisen out of a concern with the sickness and suffering that existed in the old jails. The claim that modern prisons protected health served to justify their existence. But critics worried that too much relaxation of a necessary severity had crept into the regime under this banner. Prison officials were often skeptical of reports of sickness, yet they were afraid of the scandal that arose from illness and death. Since the prison surgeon had considerable authority to grant a prisoner release from labor or a better diet, convicts had a powerful incentive to take advantage of this chink in the penal order. Some were so desperate that they deliberately injured themselves to avoid dangerous or unpleasant work. Others became masters of feigning illness to gain access to the relaxed discipline of the hospital. The reformers and retributivists who debated possible forms of imprisonment always imagined reducing the autonomy of the prisoners and the guards to a minimum. Prison memoirs revealed how elusive this goal could be.

CONCLUSION

In the period between 1780 and 1865, confinement was given a more uniform and exacting shape. The ideals of reformers often played a decisive role in defining this shape, even though the penal practices fostered by reformers long survived the decay of their ideals. For instance, the classification of prisoners was born from a desire to limit the spread of moral contagion. It came to constitute a way of organizing the prisoner's progression through his sentence and enlisting his cooperation. All too often strategies that were intended to reform prisoners found acceptance because they increased the severity of confinement or aided in the management of convicts. The most enduring accomplishment of these years was the creation of the prison as a place apart from the world. It was a realm defined by an ever more thorough loss of freedom. Prisoners suffered few physical punishments, but they were denied any control over their days. They were permitted almost no visitors. Even their letters were censored. Communication was conducted under a constant threat of punishment. Any contact that might resemble normal sociability among prisoners or with the outside world became a target for controls and prohibitions.

Even as the prisoners were more closely controlled and observed, punishment disappeared from the experience of most people. The general public became less familiar with the inside of the prison. Society came to rely on the wide dissemination of literary and journalistic reports about the prisons. Here was the other enduring consequence of this period. The prison loomed even larger in the public's imagination as the prisoner disappeared from view. The prisoner out of sight produced more, rather than less, anxiety. The public was alarmed at the occupant of the "other" world and the possibility of his return to their world. This separate time and space had been created for the benefit of the offender, as a way of reforming him. The order and morality of the prison world was supposed to mirror that of respectable society. But the prison regime remained an order of unfreedom and severity. And as such, it branded those who had passed through it. The witnesses before the Carnarvon Committee returned time and again to the power of the stigma that attached to those who came out of prison. The prison was supposed to individualize treatment, to produce a "new man." But the public never came to accept this claim. On the contrary, they regarded the prison as discovering the true identity of those who passed through its gate. Thus the prison, far from curing crime, created a uniform criminality whose taint clung to anyone who had been confined. Prisons were supposed to civilize their occupants, but it was difficult for most in society to admit that the institution or its residents belonged to the civilized world. Yet this was an effect that no one who contributed to the penal debates had intended. The prison regime of 1865 not only was the product of the ideals of reformers and the practices of prison administrators, of local initiatives and government intervention, but also was the outcome of an institution that had created its own logic and powerful necessity.

Acknowledgments

Randall McGowen would like to acknowledge John Beattie and Joanna Innes for their many helpful comments.

Bibliographic Note

Anyone interested in the subject of penal change in the period between 1750 and 1850 should consult Michel Foucault's *Discipline and Punish: The Birth of the Prison,* trans. Alan Sheridan (New York: Vintage Books, 1979). This book is a brilliant, if difficult and controversial, interpretation of the prison and its relationship to modern society. For my own comments on Foucault, see "Power and Humanity, or Foucault among the Historians," in *Reassessing Foucault: Power, Medicine, and the Body,* ed. Colin Jones and Roy Porter (London: Routledge, 1994). David Garland's *Punishment and Modern Society: A Study in Social Theory* (Chicago: University of Chicago Press, 1990) offers an intelligent discussion of both historical and theoretical treatments of the transformation of punishment.

J. M. Beattie's *Crime and the Courts in England, 1660–1800* (Princeton: Princeton University Press, 1986) provides an essential introduction to the operation of justice in early modern England. This work is particularly significant for its discussion of the rise of transportation. Two essays by Joanna Innes have forced us to rethink our understanding of early modern confinement. In the first, "The King's Bench Prison in the Later Eighteenth Century," in *An Ungovernable People: The English and Their Law in the Seventeenth and Eighteenth Centuries,* ed. John Brewer and John Styles (New Brunswick, N.J.: Rutgers University Press, 1980), she offers a careful examination of imprisonment for debt, illuminating both the law on debt and the internal organization of the debtors' prison. In the second essay, "Prisons for the Poor: English Bridewells, 1555–1800," in *Labour, Law, and Crime: A Historical Perspective,* ed. Francis Snyder and Douglas Hay (London: Tavistock Publications, 1987), she provides a revisionist account of the bridewell, whose history tells us so much about the rhythms of reform in early modern England.

Christopher Harding et al., *Imprisonment in England and Wales: A Concise History* (London: Croom Helm, 1985), is a good introduction to the general history of confinement in England from medieval times to the present. Michael Ignatieff, *A Just Measure of Pain: The Penitentiary in the Industrial Revolution, 1750–1850* (New York: Pantheon, 1978), emphasizes the ideological sources of the prison and the role of class conflict in its development. Robin Evans, *The Fabrication of Virtue: English Prison Architecture, 1750–1840* (Cambridge: Cambridge University Press, 1982), is an architectural history of the prison but one that uses design along with other sources to cast new light on prison reform. For a different treatment of the role of ideas in producing change, see my articles "The Body and Punishment in Eighteenth-Century England," *Journal of Modern History* 59 (1987), and "A Powerful Sympathy: Terror, the Prison, and Humanitarian Reform in Early Nineteenth-Century Britain," *Journal of British Studies* 25 (1986). Margaret DeLacy's *Prison Reform in Lancashire, 1700–1850: A Study in Local Administration* (Stanford: Stanford University Press, 1986) provides us with the best study of local prison reform, based on careful analysis of archival sources. Eric Stockdale's *A Study of Bedford Prison, 1660–1877* (London: Phillimore, 1977) is another useful local study of an important prison and includes short biographical sketches of some of the central prison reformers. Philip Priestley, *Victorian Prison Lives: English Prison Biography, 1830–1914* (London: Methuen, 1985), offers an account of prison life in Victorian England based on two hundred autobiographies written by prisoners. For a detailed history of administrative change, consult Seán McConville, *A History of English Prison Administration, 1750–1877* (London: Routledge and Kegan Paul, 1981). Martin J. Wiener, *Reconstructing the Criminal: Culture, Law, and Policy in England, 1830–1914* (Cambridge: Cambridge University Press, 1990), charts changes in penal thought in Victorian England and links them to wider cultural currents.

CHAPTER FOUR

PERFECTING THE PRISON

United States, 1789–1865

David J. Rothman

The history of the origins and development of the prison system in the United States confronts what appears to be an extraordinary paradox. In the 1820s and 1830s, when democratic principles were receiving their most enthusiastic endorsement, when the "common people"were participating fully in politics and electing Andrew Jackson their president, incarceration became the central feature of criminal justice. At the very moment that Americans began to pride themselves on the openness of their society, when the boundless frontier became the symbol of opportunity and equality, an idea developed: those convicted of crimes would be confined behind walls, in single cells, and would follow rigid and unyielding routines. As principles of freedom became more celebrated in the outside society, notions of total isolation, unquestioned obedience, and severe discipline became the hallmarks of the captive society. Indeed, to make the puzzle more intriguing, Jacksonian Americans took enormous pride in their prisons, were eager to show them off to European visitors, and boasted that the United States had ushered in a new era in the history of crime and punishment.

The European visitors, on the whole, tended to agree with this assessment. They came in numbers to tour the prisons—the typical itinerary of a visit to America included New England (with a stop at a textile factory), a western settlement (Cincinnati was a favorite), a plantation (to see slavery at work), and one of the new penitentiaries. And the visitors were distinguished, including such notables as Alexis de Tocqueville and Gustave de Beaumont from France. The purported purpose of Tocqueville's tour of the United States in 1831 was to advise the French government on the American prison system. The unexpected spin-off from this mission was his classic analysis *Democracy in America.*

Why did Jacksonian Americans adopt a prison system? How did they organize it, and what routines did they impose? Why were they so delighted with it, and why did others flock to inspect their solutions? Answering these questions requires moving between the prison and the society, reckoning not only with crime and punishment but with ideas about social order, social disorder, and the destiny of a new republic.

The Colonial Legacy

In the seventeenth and eighteenth centuries, the American colonists, like the British themselves, shared a keen apprehension about criminal behavior. They included within the category an exceptionally wide range of conduct, incorporating what we would think of as sinful actions (idolatry, blasphemy, and witchcraft) along with social transgressions (theft, arson, and murder). But however much they worried about the extent of crime, they saw no prospect of eliminating it from their midst. From their perspective, crime reflected on the human condition and failings—men were born in sin—and not on any basic flaws in social order. As one clergyman informed his audience immediately before the public execution of a criminal, "The natural man defiles every step he takes, and the filth thereof redounds to himself." Such sentiments confirmed that the criminal, like the poor, would always be with us, endemic to the society, and that citizens and magistrates were to cope with it as best they could.

What little effort colonial Americans spent in trying to analyze the sources of crime beyond the sinfulness of human nature went to a careful distinction between insiders and outsiders, town residents and nonresidents. Although anyone might commit a crime, the major source of the threat seemed to emanate from those who wandered from town to town, rogues and vagabonds as they were then called. Because the towns lacked formal mechanisms of law enforcement—police forces were an invention of nineteenth-century cities, and the militia was called on only to respond to major riots—the basic means for controlling crime was to regard with deep suspicion anyone who entered the town and to "warn out," or banish, those who came without introductions (for example, a letter from the minister in the home community) or without artisanal skills and sufficient property to demonstrate respectability.

When crimes did occur, colonial towns, like their counterparts in England, meted out a wide range of punishments. The most popular sanctions included fines, whippings, mechanisms of shame (the stock and public cage), banishment, and of course, the gallows. What was not on the list was imprisonment. The local jails held men (and it was almost always men) going through the process of judgment, that is, those awaiting trial or convicted but not yet punished, or men who were in debt without having satisfied their obligations. Which one of the existing sanctions would be applied to a given offender depended almost as much on who he was as on the act that he had committed.

If the offender was a resident of the town, a person of means, and the crime was not a very serious one, the magistrates would levy a fine. If the townsman had no property, he might well end up on display in the stocks or public cage, to be sneered at or spit upon by his neighbors. In Massachusetts, for example, anyone guilty of drunkenness was fined five shillings; offenders unable to pay spent three hours in the stocks. If on the other hand the criminal was an outsider to the town, he would most often be whipped and then banished. In New York City, for example, the Mayor's Court between 1733 and 1743 whipped and banished practically every nonresident guilty of theft.

The primary goal in dispensing one or another of these penalties was deterrence, in the hope that the punishment would serve to keep the offender from repeating the crime in this particular community. For a town resident to be displayed as an object of derision before one's neighbors would be so embarrassing that the offender would mend his ways; to be whipped would be so painful that he would not repeat the offense. By the same token, banishment represented the town's effort to avoid the repetition of a crime by getting rid of the offender, even if it put an adjoining town at risk.

Magistrates in colonial America never considered the possibility of rehabilitation through punishment. Their aim was not to reform the offender but to frighten him into lawful behavior. Only when the crime was very grievous, as in the case of murder, did the idea of just deserts—the offender who deserves to be executed—enter into the calculus.

In all, criminal justice in the colonial period had a tenuous and haphazard character. To an exceptional degree, the efficacy of the punishment depended on the active compliance of the offender; the agencies of law enforcement were so weak and underdeveloped that the punitive and coercive aspects of the law bore an unusually heavy burden. What if the whipping did not discourage the culprit, or if he repeatedly ignored an order of expulsion? What if the offender considered the risk of a fine worth taking in his search for illegal returns, or if he lost all shame and embarrassment before his neighbors? Were these contingencies to occur, the only recourse for the colonists was to execute the offender. In effect, capital punishment had to compensate for all the weaknesses in the criminal justice system, which is why capital crimes were defined so very broadly. The Massachusetts assembly, for example, in 1736 ordered that a thief, on first conviction, be fined or whipped. The second time he was to pay treble damages, sit for an hour upon the gallows platform with a noose around his neck, and then be carted to the whipping post for thirty stripes. For the third offense, he was to be hung. The colonial system, then, vacillated between comparatively lenient and harsh punishments. Townspeople were let off with fines or some lashes—but the recidivist, whether a pickpocket, horse thief, or counterfeiter, might well find himself mounting the gallows.

Reforming the Law

In the immediate aftermath of independence and nationhood, Americans repudiated their British legacy and, along with it, the British methods for dispensing criminal justice. Attracting the most republican scrutiny and disapproval were the numerous statutes that punished criminal behavior with execution. As Benjamin Rush, the Pennsylvania physician and signer of the Declaration of Independence, argued: "Capital punishments are the natural offspring of monarchical governments. . . . Kings consider their subjects as their property; no wonder, therefore, they shed their blood with as little emotion as men shed the blood of their sheep or cattle. But the principles of republican governments speak a very different language. . . . An execution in a republic is like a human sacrifice in religion." In fact, in a curious twist, the new Americans, embracing the ideas of such Enlightenment thinkers as Cesare Beccaria, blamed the codes themselves for the persistence of crime. "The severity of punishment itself emboldens men to commit the very wrongs it is supposed to prevent," Beccaria had insisted. "The countries and times most notorious for severity of penalties have always been those in which the bloodiest and most inhumane deeds were committed." The logic of the argument was particularly powerful to Americans. They looked back on the colonial period as a case in point: since British laws were so severe, juries had been loathe to convict anyone except the most terrible of criminals. And once punishment lost its certainty, criminals were encouraged to pursue their misdeeds.

This analysis of past failure carried with it an answer through which the new nation would be able to reduce, perhaps even eliminate, crime. At the same time, adopting this solution would bring glory to a republican government and demonstrate its inherent moral superiority to other forms. Confident that his proposals would fulfill both these ends, Thomas Eddy, one of the leaders in this movement, insisted that New York had to revise its criminal codes. The state should no longer tolerate laws of "barbarous usages, corrupt society, and monarchical principles . . . [that were so] imperfectly adopted to a new country, simple manners, and a popular form of government." As soon as it did so, punishment would become a certainty, and crime would disappear. In accordance with these views, most of the states amended their criminal punishment statutes. Pennsylvania in 1786 eliminated the death penalty for robbery and burglary and in 1794 restricted it to first-degree murder; in 1796 New York, New Jersey, and Virginia reduced their roster of capital crimes. Other states followed their example so that by 1820, practically all had abolished the death sentence except for the crime of first-degree murder or had strictly limited it to a handful of the most serious crimes.

As they enacted these reforms, the states immediately confronted the question of what punishment should substitute for execution. If they were not to hang the convicted criminal, what penalty should they impose? The answer was incarceration, to have the offender serve a term, a very long term, in prison. Pennsylvania led the way in turning the old Philadelphia jail at Walnut Street into a state prison. In 1796, New York appropriated funds to build the Newgate state prison in Greenwich Village. New Jersey completed its state penitentiary in 1797 and Virginia and Kentucky theirs in 1800. That same year, Massachusetts made an appropriation for the prison at Charlestown, and in short order Vermont, New Hampshire, and Maryland followed suit.

In this first burst of enthusiasm, Americans expected that a rational system of punishment that was at once certain and humane would dissuade all but a handful of offenders from a life in crime. Unlike their colonial predecessors, they did not locate the roots of deviancy in the corrupt nature of humankind or, in more practical terms, worry most about the dangerous outsider. They blamed British law and were confident that distinctively American statutes would inaugurate a new era. Although these ideas led immediately to the construction of the first prisons, the facilities themselves were not endowed with any special attributes. Incarceration was not the critical feature of the reformed system, and rehabilitation was not its expected goal. A repulsion from the gallows, rather than any faith in the powers of the penitentiary itself, spurred the construction. Americans were still thinking in terms of deterrence. What mattered most was the certainty of the punishment, not the internal routine or management of the prison.

By the beginnings of the 1820s, the faith in the efficacy of legal reform had declined. For one, statutory changes had no discernible impact on the level of crime. For another, the prisons had become the scene of rampant disorder, with escapes and riots commonplace. Prisoners lived together in large rooms and took their meals in one common dining area. They mingled freely, shared booty (which included alcohol), and had ample time to plot their escapes or to share the secrets of their trade. Institution life was casual, undisciplined, and irregular. "Our favorite scheme of substituting a state prison for the gallows," concluded one New York lawyer, "is a prolific mother of crime. . . . Our state prisons as presently constituted, are grand demoralizers of our people." A few conservatives aside, no one wanted to go back to the gallows. But it was clear that the elimination of capital punishment would not eliminate crime and just as clear that something had to be done about organization of the prisons. The way Americans resolved this predicament brings us to the second and most critical stage in the history of American prisons.

REPUBLICAN THINKING

Over the period 1820–50, Jacksonian Americans, in marked contrast to their colonial predecessors, believed that crime was posing a fundamental threat to the stability and order of republican society. The idea of the prison was rooted in this perception, reflecting the fear that once stable social relationships were now in the process of unraveling, that social order and cohesion were in danger of collapsing. It became the task of the prison to do nothing less than ensure the future safety of the republic.

To judge by the numerous articles, pamphlets, and legislative reports that discussed the issues, Americans in the antebellum era were frankly puzzled by the persistence of crime. They were not surprised that it continued to plague Old World countries; where great disparities of wealth existed between classes, where the common people had no voice in government, and where laws were harsh, crime was the inevitable result. But the new republic had eliminated these evils—not only had the states reformed their criminal codes, but economic opportunity was widespread and a marked equality existed between the social classes. Why, then, should crime disturb this country? Why was it maintaining a place in the new society?

The answer that Jacksonian Americans arrived at suggests that their great pride in the openness of their society was qualified by a nagging fear that this very openness was producing disorder and disarray. As they viewed it, all of the institutions that had once stabilized the social order were declining in influence. The outstanding case in point was the family. Fathers were losing their authority to discipline children, either because they were devoting too much time to securing their own economic advancement or because the children quickly left home to try to make their own marks. As one group of concerned reformers concluded, "It is the confession of many convicts . . . that the course of vice which brought them to the prison commenced in disobedience to their parents, or in their parents' neglect."

What was true for the family was even more apparent in the church. Once the mainstay of the community, the church was now losing its authority. Worse yet, the schools were not able to fill the gap, for undisciplined youths ignored their lessons just as they did those of the family and church. All the while, of course, the community itself was losing its leverage. Americans were too much on the move—to the frontier, to the cities—to believe that neighbor could any longer influence neighbor.

From one angle of vision, all these developments were exciting. Here was a new society in which every man was free to follow his own inclinations, where inherited traditions counted for very little. But from another angle, all these changes were scary.

Could a society characterized by so much mobility, both social and geographic, cohere? Could it maintain stability amid all this motion? To judge by the incidence of crime, the answer might well be "no." Dorothea Dix, the most energetic and celebrated of all Jacksonian reformers, declared, "It is to the defects of our social organization, to the multiplied and multiplying temptations to crime that we chiefly owe the increase of evils doers."

Were these fears justified? Was the social crisis real or imagined? It may be that European countries were experiencing a degree of social disturbance more severe than anything found in the United States. But it is nearly impossible to calculate the actual rates of crime in antebellum America—the recording of crime statistics was as primitive as the policing mechanisms themselves. Nevertheless, the likelihood is that the preoccupation with crime had less to do with the real incidence of crime and more to do with general social attitudes about a society in change. Whatever the reality, there was a subjective vision of disorder. Indeed, it is this perspective that is most helpful in enabling us to understand the resulting form of the public response to crime. It is in the realm of perceptions that we will find the answers to why the country adopted the idea of the prison and devised so novel a routine for it.

The Rehabilitative Ideal

Americans in the pre–Civil War period moved on a variety of fronts to combat the disorder that they perceived around them. Over these years dozens of advice books, with titles like *The Father's Book* and *The Rollo Code of Morals*, instructed the family on how to raise an obedient child. At the same time, a generation of educators sought to make the school a more powerful force in students' lives, and clergymen organized Sunday school classes to reach out to the younger generation. In this same spirit, and with even greater intensity, Jacksonian reformers discovered the prison and attempted to make it an institution that would teach inmates the lessons of order and discipline. The prison would transform the deviant into a law-abiding citizen, that is, rehabilitate the offender.

It was a heady assignment requiring imagination and innovation, and American prison reformers were equal to the task. In the 1820s New York and Pennsylvania set out the models that soon spread throughout the country. New York devised the Auburn, or what became known as the congregate, system of penitentiary organization, implementing it first at Auburn State Prison and then at Ossining, better known as Sing Sing. Pennsylvania set out a rival plan, the separate system, at the Pittsburgh penitentiary and the Philadelphia prison.

In retrospect, the differences between the two plans do not seem very notable. Both, as we shall see, emphasized isolation, obedience, and a steady routine of labor. Nevertheless, their respective merits were the subject of a fierce debate. Every report from New York and from Pennsylvania penitentiaries constituted an explicit defense of its own organization and an attack on its opponent. The rival systems had their own fervent supporters drawn from the ranks of American reformers—Samuel Gridley Howe and Dorothea Dix, for example, preferred the Pennsylvania system, Mathew Carey and Louis Dwight the New York system—many of whom produced pamphlets leveling charges and rebutting countercharges about their arrangements. If the literature on

Auburn versus Pennsylvania never quite matched the outpouring of material on the pros and cons of slavery, it came remarkably close.

Under the Auburn plan, prisoners slept alone, one to a cell. They came together to eat and to work in the prison shops, but the rules prohibited all talking and even the exchanges of glances. The Pennsylvania system, on the other hand, confined prisoners to individual cells for the entire period of their confinement. They worked, ate, and slept in solitary confinement and were allowed to see only selected visitors.

For all their enmity, the advocates of Pennsylvania and Auburn were both committed to the rehabilitative potential of the prison and were both convinced that the routines imposed on the inmate would transform him into a law-abiding citizen. Reform, not deterrence, was now the aim of incarceration. The shared assumption was that since the convict was not innately depraved but had failed to be trained to obedience by family, church, school, or community, he could be redeemed by the well-ordered routine of the prison. The penitentiary would succeed precisely where other community institutions had failed. Just as the defects in the social environment had led the inmate into crime, the disciplined and disciplining environment of the institution would lead him out of it.

To fulfill this mandate, prison reformers focused their attention on the divisions of time and space within the facilities. One of the most influential of the reform associations, the Boston Prison Discipline Society, deemed architecture one of the most important of the moral sciences. "There are," the society observed, "principles in architecture, by the observance of which great moral changes can be more easily produced among the most abandoned of our race. . . . Other things being equal, the prospect of improvement in morals, depends, in some degree, upon the construction of buildings."

In fact, the reformers hoped that the solutions that they devised to prison design problems would be relevant to the wider society. With no ironies intended, they talked about the penitentiary as serving as a model for the family and the school. The prison was nothing less than "a grand theatre for the trial of all new plans in hygiene and education." Or as one prison chaplain insisted: "Could we all be put on prison fare, for the space of two or three generations, the world would ultimately be the better for it. . . . As it is, taking this world and the next together . . . the prison has the advantage." It was no wonder, then, that Tocqueville and Beaumont came away convinced that reformers had been caught up in "the monomania of the penitentiary system," which to the reformers seemed to be "a remedy for all the evils of society."

And it was no wonder, then, that Auburn and Pennsylvania supporters defended their positions so staunchly. With the stakes so high and with results almost entirely dependent on the internal design of the prison, every element in prison organization assumed overwhelming importance. Intense partisanship was inevitable when the right program would reform the criminal and reorder the society and the wrong one would encourage vice and crime.

The Pennsylvania camp saw itself as purist, taking the idea of reform through isolation to its logical conclusion. It separated inmates from each other—to the point of placing hoods over the heads of newcomers so that as they walked to their cells they would not see or be seen by anyone. Over the course of their sentence, they were given nothing to read except the Bible and were prevented from corresponding with friends and family; they were given work to do in their cells (spinning wool was one common activity), in the expectation that they would learn steady habits and discipline. In this way, they would be released to the community cured of vice and idleness, ready to take their places as law-abiding citizens.

From the perspective of Pennsylvania supporters, the Auburn plan was an incomplete and inconsistent version of their own superior plan. Auburn tempted the prisoners—forbidding conversation but placing them next to each other at meals and at work. Inevitably, guards would be forced to punish those prisoners who broke the silence, giving the congregate institutions an atmosphere of cruelty and corruption. Pennsylvania, by contrast, would be humane, secure, ordered, and ultimately, successful.

For its part, the Auburn school responded not by defending its own compromises (which was not easy to do) but by finding flaws in the Pennsylvania arrangements. Supporters argued that Pennsylvania was impractical, citing the difficulty of feeding and employing hundreds of inmates in the individual cells. They contended that the walls at the Pennsylvania prisons were not thick enough to prevent conversation, a claim that prompted a rebuttal from Pennsylvania, which stated that the walls were indeed thick enough; in short order, pamphlets were pouring out that analyzed the measurements of prison walls and the layout of pipes. Auburn proponents also insisted that total isolation was so unnatural that it literally drove prisoners mad. Perhaps most important, they maintained, altogether accurately, that Auburn was considerably less expensive to build and maintain and that prison labor in congregate workshops would bring greater returns to the state. Why bother to incur the greater costs when Auburn could do the job of reform as well as Pennsylvania?

The Prison System

The very intensity of the debate, as well as the shared premise that criminals could be rehabilitated, made prison reform a central concern for state legislatures in the antebellum period. One after the other they appropriated the considerable funds necessary to construct or renovate penitentiaries. In the late 1820s, Connecticut built a state prison at Wethersfield, Massachusetts reorganized its prison at Charlestown, and Maryland erected a new facility at Baltimore. In the 1830s, New Jersey, Ohio, and Michigan constructed their state prisons, and in the 1840s, so did Indiana, Wisconsin, and Minnesota.

Almost all the states adopted the Auburn plan, eager to realize the rehabilitative influence of the prison without incurring the greater costs required by the Pennsylvania system. But the fact that they were prudent in terms of their expenditures should not suggest that the ideology of rehabilitation was any the less important. An amazingly diverse group of constituents lined up in support of such an expensive and complex undertaking. Without appreciating the larger goals of the project, one cannot understand the extent of the investment in the prison and the degree of enthusiasm for it. If the incapacitation of the inmate had been the exclusive concern, it would have been unnecessary to invest so extravagantly in prisons or to organize such elaborate and disciplined routines. To punish the criminal through service on some form of a chain gang would have been considerably cheaper and more efficient.

To be sure, there were naysayers to the idea of the prison. Some critics did not want to see the burden of taxation increased, and others were convinced that the only punishment that criminals respected was capital punishment. But a shared sense of crisis and emergency overrode these objections. Too much was at stake to postpone action; something had to be done lest republican order be subverted. In other words, the prison captured support, and dollars, because of its very grandeur, its promise to reform the deviant.

The decision to build prisons was reserved to the separate states, but nowhere does it appear to have sparked political confrontations between supporters and opponents. The consensus was broad, undoubtedly because the idea of the asylum had something for everyone. There were those who supported it because they thought that juries would not hesitate to convict the guilty if jury members knew that a prison sentence, not the gallows, awaited the convicted; others, probably the majority, advocated confinement because of its rehabilitative potential. The appeal of the prison was so diffused through the society that to identify proponents with a party or regional label belies the nature of the coalition as well as its motives. Nor will it do to identify them, as some historians have done, with an emerging commercial or manufacturing class. Clearly, those who invented the prison and were its most avid enthusiasts were people of property, those with social standing in the society. But their leadership—and their ideas on punishment—reflected their general education and their concern for the future of the republic as much as their economic interests. Moreover, their fear of disorder was far more a fear of moral dissoluteness than of class warfare; it was the weakened authority of the family and the community, not the aggressive demands of a submerged laboring class, that frightened them. Accordingly, their solutions, as exemplified in the prison routine, looked more to individual reformation (in a secular sense) than to the needs for a compliant and disciplined labor force in the new factories.

As Americans began to build and administer the prisons, they learned that although the idea of isolation and the general orientation maxims produced by advocates for the Auburn and Pennsylvania systems did provide a general scheme to follow, running a prison on a daily basis also required solving a large number of specific, and important, details. For example, what should prisoners be forced to wear? How should they be moved from place to place? How should the prison maintain internal security, and how should it discipline the refractory prisoner?

These questions were particularly difficult to answer because Americans were embarking on a new venture. "Reform in prison discipline was an experiment," one participant in the process noted. Americans "had no model prison to visit; no pioneers in the march of reform, to warn them of errors or guide them to truth." The English experience could have provided guidance in resolving these issues, but both because of their own insularity and because of their dislike of things foreign, officials were not well informed about developments there. For example, Jeremy Bentham's 1791 design for the panopticon was almost unknown in the United States, although his emphasis on the need for the segregation, employment, and surveillance of the criminal offender was consistent with the aims of American prisons. In the end, the Americans' intellectual debt to England was not great. Few Americans read Bentham, and even fewer took him seriously. (One should also remember that Bentham had a genius for spinning off ideas and trying, almost desperately, to give them a practical bent, but there was always something fantastic about his schemes, and the English prison that might be thought to represent his ideas, Pentonville, did not open until 1842.) In effect, Americans contrived their own homegrown solutions.

Perhaps the most distinctive feature of American prisons in the pre–Civil War decades, and certainly the element that European visitors most frequently commented on, was the silence that pervaded the institutions. The injunction to isolate the inmate, an idea that ran through both the Auburn and the Pennsylvania plans, was rigidly and effectively translated into practice. As Tocqueville and Beaumont noted after their visit to Auburn in 1831, "Everything passes in the most profound silence, and nothing is heard in the whole prison but the steps of those who march, or sounds proceeding from the workshops." After the inmates returned to their cells, "the silence within these vast walls" was "that of death." The two wrote, "We felt as if we had traversed catacombs; there were a thousand living beings, and yet it was a desert solitude." As would be expected, they found that the same conditions held at Pennsylvania: "It is uncontestable that this perfect isolation secures the prison from all fatal contamination."

Officials were able to maintain the rule of silence in part because in the period 1820–50, overcrowding was not a problem. Given the promise of reform, legislatures readily appropriated the funds for construction, and when more cells were needed, they made the funds available. Perhaps even more important, prison wardens and guards were fully prepared to punish, and harshly punish, any inmate who broke the rules. Sing Sing was particularly well-known for the severity of its discipline, for which it made no apologies. A prison, as one of the assistant wardens told the New York legislature in 1834, "should not be governed in a manner as to induce rogues to consider it as a comfortable home. They must be *made to submit* to its rules, and this by the most energetic means; corporeal punishments for transgression, which to be effectual must be certain, and inflicted with as little delay as possible."

Other institutions were also more intent on securing obedience than on inflicting cruel and unusual punishments. The whip was commonplace in the prisons of New York, Massachusetts, and Ohio; Pennsylvania tied an iron gag on disobedient inmates, and Maine had recourse to the ball and chain. The rehabilitative ideal certainly helped to legitimate the severity of the correctional schemes. A state investigation in Pennsylvania unhesitatingly justified the iron gag because convicts were "men of idle habits, vicious propensities, and depraved passions," and because obedience was the necessary first step to reformation. "Only relax the reins of discipline," commented one prison chaplain, "and a chaplain's labors would be of no more use here than in a drunken mob." Since the end of rehabilitation was so significant, any and all means of securing it were justified.

The prisons enforced not only rules of silence but also regular labor, and the inmate who shirked his tasks would quickly find himself the object of harsh discipline. Most facilities compelled the men to work eight to ten hours a day, a routine that was to serve to inculcate habits of diligence even as it brought the state a financial return on its prison investment. In New York, for example, convicts were up at five o'clock to work two hours before breakfast; they then went back to work for three hours and forty-five minutes, had a lunch break, and returned to work for another four hours and forty-five minutes. The only limitations on the length of the work week were a respect for a Christian Sunday and the absence of artificial lighting.

Translating the ideas of silence, labor, and discipline into the prison routine inspired prison officials to adopt quasi-military models. At almost every possible point, they imposed regimentation. Thus, convicts did not saunter from place to place but went in close order and single file, each looking over the shoulder of the man in front, faces inclined to the right, feet moving in unison, in lockstep. In fact, the lockstep became the trademark of American prisons in these years (and thereafter as well, as attested to by 1930s prison movies). It was a curious combination of march and shuffle, the march aiming to impose discipline, the shuffle trying to make certain that the men did not become too prideful. With the prisoners' heads pointed to the right, guards could make certain that no one carried on a conversation.

The daily routine also followed a military model. At the sound of a horn or bell, the guards opened the cells, and the prisoners stepped onto the deck and then in lockstep went into the yard. In formation they emptied their night pails, which they then washed; they took a few more steps and placed the pails on a rack to dry. They then moved in lockstep to the shops and worked at their tasks while sitting in rows on long benches. When the bell rang for mealtime, they grouped again in single file, passed into the kitchen, picked up their rations (the rules ordered them not to break step), and continued either to their cells (in some institutions) or to a common mess hall (in others), where they ate their meals while, by regulation, sitting erect with their backs straight. At the bell they stood, reentered formation, and in lockstep returned to their shops or cells.

The same commitment to regimentation dictated that inmates wear uniforms, not elegant ones of course but ones made of crude and simple design, with stripes (to keep the men humble and to increase the likelihood of recapture in case of escape). In keeping with a commitment to military regimentation, the convicts' hair was cut short, and the cells were sparsely furnished with a cot, a pail, and tin utensils. Indeed, the military model extended to the prison guards, who wore uniforms, were mustered at specific hours, and kept watch like sentries. The wardens, who often came to their positions after military service, issued regulations commanding the guards to act in a "gentlemanly manner," as though they were officers, and to avoid laughter, ribaldry, or unnecessary conversation while on duty. Guards, as Sing Sing's rules announced, "were to require from the convicts the greatest deference, and never suffer them to approach but in respectful manner; they [were] not to allow them the least degree of familiarity, nor exercise any towards them; they should be extremely careful to *command* as well as to compel their respect."

These characteristics were apparent in the architectural design of the prison. Most of the facilities looked like medieval fortresses, monumental, as befit so noble an experiment. The thick walls and turrets were assurances that the prison was secure, even as it promised to promote isolation and separation. The buildings themselves were long and low slung, symmetrically arranged with evenly spaced windows, all very regular and methodical. Thus in appearance and in routine, these were institutions that would inculcate fixity and order.

The internal and external design of the prison suggests some affinity between these institutions and the new factories that were simultaneously transforming the manufacturing sectors of the American economy. In appearance and routine, the prison and the factory did bear a resemblance. Both emphasized regularity and punctuality. Indeed, starting from this observation, a number of historians have located the origins of the prison in the new economic order. They acknowledge the depth of anxiety and insecurity in Jacksonian America about social order and the fate of the new republic, but the source of these fears they locate not in the imbalance between inherited ideas on social order and new realities but in the emergence of separate and hostile social classes, the factory owners and their associates on the one hand and the workers on the other. In this interpretation, the purpose of the prison was to segregate the working class from the criminal element so as to make certain that lawlessness did not pervade the lower ranks. Thus, by instilling order in its inmates, the prison was, in effect, helping to guarantee discipline and regularity in those who arrived each morning at the factory gate. They would understand that there was no alternative to wage-earning, that an effort to ignore or violate the precepts of the new industrial order was futile. They would line up at the sound of the bell in the factory yard or line up at the bell in the prison yard.

Although this vision may have persuaded some citizens to favor the prison solution, it would be erroneous to maintain that the inspiration for the prison is to be found in the organization and needs of the factory. More was at stake than owners bringing discipline to their workers. Surely the manufacturing enterprises had sources of recruitment broad enough to ignore the determined felon, and the prison was hardly in a position to be a purveyor of values to the laboring classes. In fact, in the United States, the prison spread not only through the Northeast—where factories were springing up—but also through the Midwest and the West—where industrial development was still decades away. It seems far more likely, as the historian Michael Ignatieff has concluded, that to the degree that prisons and factories resembled each other, it was "because both public order authorities and employers shared the same universe of assumptions about the regulation of the body and the ordering of time."

REFORM GONE AWRY

From its moment of origin, the American prison never lacked for critics, for the system had a harshness to it that was unmistakable and dismaying. Charles Dickens, on his 1842 tour of the United States, went to Philadelphia expressly to see the prison and found it "cruel and wrong." Its intentions, he conceded, were humane and reformatory. But its designers, he was convinced, did not know what it was that they were doing. He noted: "I believe that very few men are capable of estimating the immense amount of torture and agony that this dreadful punishment, prolonged for years, inflicts upon the sufferers. . . . I hold this slow and daily tampering with the mysteries of the brain, to be immeasurably worse than any torture of the body." Concluded Dickens, "Those who have undergone this punishment MUST pass into society again morally unhealthy and diseased."

Tocqueville and Beaumont were more measured in their summary judgments. "We have no doubt," they wrote, "but that the habits of order to which the prisoner is subjected for several years, influence very considerably his moral conduct after his return to society. . . . Perhaps, leaving prison he is not an honest man, but he has contracted honest habits." Between Auburn and Pennsylvania, they preferred Pennsylvania. "The Philadelphia system produces more honest men, and that of New York more obedient citizens." But these points notwithstanding, the prisons that they visited did not fit with the America that they saw. "While society in the United States gives the example of the most extended liberty, the prisons of the same country offer the spectacle of the most complete despotism. The citizens subject to the law are protected by it; they cease to be free when they become wicked."

With the passage of time, whatever saving graces these visitors could find in the prison system weakened. At least for the period 1820–50, the founders could justifiably claim that the institutions were faithful to reform principles in enforcing the congregate and separate systems. Whatever reservations one might have had about the validity, or even the humanity, of either of the plans, there was a genuine correspondence between the ideal and the real, between blueprint and actuality. However, by the 1860s, and even more obviously by the 1870s and 1880s, the unique arrangements of the Auburn and Pennsylvania plans had disappeared.

Prisons in the post–Civil War era became modern, that is, characterized by overcrowding, brutality, and disorder. Nevertheless, they continued to occupy the central place in criminal punishment. Massive walls enclosed prison space, and heavy gates swung open to admit a steady stream of convicts.

There can be no question of the dimension of the decline. The most thorough account of the nation's prisons in the post–Civil War era was the 1867 report of E. C. Wines and Theodore Dwight to the New York legislature, and their findings were unambiguous: "There is no longer a state prison in America in which the reformation of the convicts is the one supreme object of the discipline." By this standard they noted, "There is not a prison system in the United States which . . . would not be found wanting."

As legislative reports in New York itself made unmistakably clear, the state's own prisons were no exception to this rule. Already in 1852 an investigation had found that the prisons did serve to incapacitate the offender, preventing him from committing crimes during his stay. "But if the object is to make him a better member of society so that he may safely again mingle with it . . . that purpose cannot be answered by matters as they now stand." Twenty years later, another commission found conditions still worse. Not only were cruel punishments pervasive throughout the state prisons (it was not uncommon to hang convicts by their thumbs), but so also was corruption (inmates regularly bribed guards to get a more favorable work assignment).

Overcrowding was everywhere the rule of the day. By 1866 even the institution most famed for keeping only one prisoner to a cell, the Pennsylvania penitentiary at Philadelphia, had so many inmates to hold that separation was no longer possible. Wines and Dwight estimated that nationwide roughly one-third of all prisoners were double celled. And as isolation broke down, the opportunities for prisoner unrest increased, which prompted wardens and guards to become all the more harsh in their discipline of inmates. But why did the system at once fail to live up to its original ideals, and why did this failure not have any impact on its longevity? Why did the reform impulse fade without uprooting the prison from the criminal justice system?

Part of the answer rests in the original reform design for the prison. The doctrine of rehabilitation through obedience and discipline was particularly susceptible to abuse. In the name of reform, wardens had the excuse to mete out the most severe punishment while still believing that they were doing more than satisfying their own convenience. By the same token, it was too easy to succumb to the belief that incarceration in and of itself would accomplish reform, that all wardens had to do was to confine the inmate and the result would be beneficial. In other words, the rhetoric of the reform program continued to cloak the prison with the mantle of legitimacy long after the reality of reform had disappeared.

Part of the answer too rests in the nature of the prison population. The Jacksonian reformers had presumed that inmates would not be hardened criminals but "good boys gone bad," who after a period of corrective training would go on their way, not to return again. In fact, the prisons came to hold a very diverse group of inmates, not so much the petty embezzler as the recidivist and the murderer—and indeed, since the latter had longer sentences, inevitably the prison became the holding ground for the toughest of criminals. For example, of the 839 convicts who served time in the Connecticut state prison between 1828 and 1840, 60 percent were guilty of crimes of violence: they were burglars and robbers (343), murderers and attempted murderers (78), rapists (42), and arsonists and escaped inmates (45). And by all accounts, the Connecticut experience was typical of other state prisons before the Civil War. Inmates in the 1860s and 1870s were an even more hardened group—manslaughter, murder, robbery, and rape were what brought men to prison.

This development reflected not only the (understandable) decision of judges to send the toughest cases to prison—they used jails or suspended sentences for the more minor offenders—but also the structure of the sentencing process itself, more specifically, the very long sentences meted out in the United States to offenders. (To this day, American sentences and actual time served are two to three times longer than European ones.) As formulated in the 1790s, the prison sentence was to substitute confinement for execution, and although no records survive that tell us how legislators initially equated crime with time, it seems likely that their reckonings went from the top down. If murder once brought death, it now brought thirty years. And if murder was worth life, then robbery should bring ten or fifteen years; rape, twelve or fourteen; assault, seven or nine; and burglary six or seven. The very long sentences carried over into the Jacksonian period on the grounds that rehabilitation took time; a felon might well require a decade of confinement in order to acquire the habits of discipline.

Such sentencing practices filled the prisons with the most serious offenders and set off a mutually reinforcing series of considerations, all of which made rehabilitation less relevant to the actual administration of the prison. For one, guards and wardens inevitably became cynical about the idea of reform, trotting it out only at convenient times and places. For another, when serious offenders were crowded together within a prison, wardens and guards had the incentive, and in their eyes the justification, to increase again and again the severity of prison discipline. For still another, as legislators and citizens came to understand the nature of the prison population, they became more satisfied to let the operation be essentially custodial. Why spend money to ensure single cells for this kind of criminal?

All of these changes were reinforced by one more critical development in the 1850s and 1860s: an increasing number of prison inmates were drawn from new immigrant groups, specifically from the Irish. Between 1830 and 1835, 20 percent of the inmates at Auburn had been born outside the United States; the comparable figure from Pennsylvania was 18 percent. In the 1850s, the percentage of foreign-born in New York prisons rose to 32 percent, by 1860 to 44 percent. In 1860, in Massachusetts immigrants were 40 percent of the prison population, in Illinois 46 percent. And all of these percentages swelled in the 1870s and again thereafter. State legislators, with little sympathy for the immigrant, saw even less reason to invest in making the prisons anything but custodial. As bad as conditions were, they seemed good enough for the Irish.

Thinking about Prisons: Social Control versus Reform

An interpretation that locates the origins of the prison in a profound uneasiness about the fragility of the social order is often characterized as part of a school of "social control." But the label is ill-suited, obfuscating more than it clarifies. The term itself comes from sociological studies in the 1920s and 1930s. Theorists like George Herbert Mead and E. A. Ross used it to promote a sharper appreciation of the role of subjective and qualitative values in binding social groups together. Rather than assuming that the good order of the society rested on the regulatory authority of the prison or the police, they sought to link social stability to shared values and principles. Social order became the product not of fiat and force but of ideas and sympathy. Accordingly, they were concerned with other institutions of social control: the family, the church, and the school. In fact, they searched so broadly for the elements instilling social harmony that they conceived of social control in a manner that made it indistinguishable from socialization. They found social control everywhere and applauded its presence.

In the 1950s, the meaning of the term changed, actually reversing itself. Social control became synonymous not with persuasion but with the imposition of state or class authority over the lower classes. Social control was equated with repression and coercion, with the formal and informal mechanisms that were intended to compel order and obedience. It was with this negative connotation that social control first came to the attention of historians.

When historians first used social control to think about the prison, the concept served a highly useful function. It helped to stimulate a series of novel questions and served as a necessary corrective to the prevailing idea that the prison was best understood as a "reform." Until then, the origins of incarceration had been interpreted as the triumph of humane impulses. Good-hearted citizens and generous philanthropists had been appalled at the condition of jails, at the use of corporeal and capital punishment, and had invented the prison to introduce a less cruel and more benevolent mode of punishment. But the difficulty was that, by simply describing the innovation as a reform, historians assumed that the prison was a logical step in the progress of humanity; they failed to ask why the prison was invented in the 1820s and 1830s and why it adopted its special attributes. Indeed, the subsequent history of the prison becomes much more difficult to explain if one thinks only in terms of progressive sentiments. By the 1950s, the prisons were anything but humanitarian, so an interpretative framework that focuses narrowly on the spirit of benevolence does not help us to understand changes in the prison and its continuing centrality to the system of punishment. To view the degeneration of the prison as a series of incremental changes that unexpectedly and unpredictably produced a horror show is to avoid the challenge of historical analysis. To insist on the moral purity of state intervention and paternalism, to absolve the prison administrators of all responsibility for the decline (on the grounds that human institutions are inevitably fallible), is to sidestep the important historical questions. Why did the state and would-be reformers fail to recognize the fallibility of their creations? Why, even decades later, did proponents of the prison maintain their positions and continue to legitimate the practice of confinement even in the face of declension? In this sense, the idea of social control was liberating, encouraging a group of historians to start investigating the purposes, benign or not so benign, that a purported reform might fulfill.

But now that these questions have been asked, and answered, using the term "social control" has little value. It is not always evident whether the term is being invoked as a statement of fact (this organization or institution is charged to maintain social order), or whether it is being invoked as a proposition (this is an organization that attempted to buttress the social order by coercing or deceiving the lower classes). "Social control" may be used as the equivalent of the formal exercise of state power—meaning that the police are agents of social control and are duty-bound to maintain public order—or it may be used in a more sweeping, if ill-defined manner, to make it a weapon (secret?) in the arsenal of the ruling class. In all events, the term in present usage neither advances knowledge nor clarifies subtle differences.

As one looks back on the origins of the prison, there should be no doubt that humanitarian impulses had an important place in its history. However irresistible the urge to make rigid dichotomies in historical interpretations, no one would want to dismiss considerations of humanity or denigrate the benevolent impulses of reformers. The pre-prison modes of punishment (as chapters one, two, and three make eminently clear) were brutal, whether the practice was torture and executions or sentences of transportation. The accounts of the convict origins of Australia are replete with heartbreaking stories of what it meant to men and women, often guilty of no more than petty thievery, to be separated forever from spouses, children, and relatives.

Nevertheless, benevolent motives take us only part of the way to understanding the origins of prisons. No matter how empathetic one may be to the reformers' impulse to find a substitute for garroting the condemned, the fundamental question still remains: why invent a system of incarceration, why substitute confinement in segregated spaces and design a routine of bell-ringing punctuality and steady labor? Why channel the impulse to do good into creating something as strange as the prison, a system that, over 150 years later, can still prompt an inmate to want to meet the man who dreamed it all up, convinced that he must have been born on Mars?

Should the prison be judged an advance when compared with the practices it replaced? Was it not an improvement over the gallows and the whip? Even this seemingly self-evident judgment, however, must be qualified, for the prison extended its reach and brought into its orbit many who would have been spared punishment in an earlier era. It is likely that some among the deviant suffered less because of the prison, but some may have suffered more; a number of prisoners who previously would have been shamed before their neighbors and then left to resume their lives instead spent years in a cell. The calculus of benefits and losses is too exquisite to render an unambiguous verdict.

Finally, is the history of the prison relevant to our understanding of the present and our imagination of the future? Are there lessons that we should draw from the record? Clearly, the past is no predictor of the future, and the fact that prisons failed to deliver on their promise is no warrant to find that they have outlived their usefulness and should now be abandoned. At the same time, we would be foolhardy not to raise our level of skepticism. We cannot afford to forget that designs that promise the most grandiose results often legitimate the most unsatisfactory methods. In light of this history, the burden of proof falls on those who would claim that confinement can serve all ends, benefiting both the inmate and the society.

Bibliographic Note

This chapter draws on my own work in the history of the prison: *The Discovery of the Asylum: Social Order and Disorder in the New Republic*, rev. ed. (Boston: Little, Brown, 1990), and *Conscience and Convenience: The Asylum and Its Alternatives in Progressive America* (Boston: Little, Brown, 1980). For a fuller discussion of my ideas and those of others on the issue of social control, see Stanley Cohen and Andrew Scull, eds., *Social Control and the State* (New York: St. Martin's Press, 1983).

The two rightfully famous reports by European visitors are Gustave de Beaumont and Alexis de Tocqueville, *On the Penitentiary System in the United States and Its Application in France* (reprint, Carbondale: Southern Illinois Press, 1964), quotations in the text from pp. 79, 90, and Charles Dickens, *American Notes* (London: MacDonald and Sons, 1850), quotations from pp. 129, 142.

On public executions, see Louis P. Masur, *Rites of Execution: Capital Punishment and the Transformation of American Culture, 1776–1865* (New York: Oxford University Press, 1989).

Other accounts of the pre–Civil War penitentiary include the following: W. David Lewis, *From Newgate to Dannemora: The Rise of the Penitentiary in New York* (Ithaca: Cornell University Press, 1965); Negley K. Teeters, *The Cradle of the Penitentiary: The Walnut Street Jail at Philadelphia, 1773–1835* (Philadelphia, 1955); Negley K. Teeters and John D. Shearer, *The Prison at Cherry Hill: The Separate System of Penal Discipline, 1829–1913* (New York, 1957); and Blake McKelvey, *American Prisons: A History of Good Intentions* (Montclair, N.J.: Patterson Smith, 1977).

For other antebellum efforts to control the deviant, see Paul S. Boyer, *Urban Masses and Moral Order in America, 1820–1920* (Cambridge: Harvard University Press, 1978), and John R. Sutton, *Stubborn Children: Controlling Delinquency in the United States, 1640–1981* (Berkeley: University of California Press, 1988).

CHAPTER FIVE

THE VICTORIAN PRISON

England, 1865–1965

Seán McConville

If I had the means of giving every man who is sentenced to hard labour in Stafford prison the full amount of discipline I am empowered to do by Act of Parliament, for two years, no man alive could bear it: it would kill the strongest man in England.

—Major William Fulford, governor of Stafford jail, 1863

Victorian imprisonment embodied several curious contradictions. Arrive in prison as the result of a minor offense, and you would be treated more severely than had you committed one of the great crimes. Commit a grave offense (short of murder), and you would be punished ostensibly more with an eye to reformation than had you been modest in your crime. Commit no offense at all, other than destitution, and as pauper, you would have workhouse food markedly less generous than that which Her Majesty granted to convicted felons. How the Victorians got themselves into this tangle is only one part of the fascinating history of ideas, policy, administration, and personages of this hundred years of punishment.

TERMINOLOGY

Penal history is littered with unfulfilled promises, abandoned hopes, and discarded institutions, and punishment is a process that most people find unpleasant to contemplate. The subject is therefore crowded with euphemisms and forsaken designations. The word *prison* is apt to prove confusing because of different American and British usage and because the uninstructed may apply it anachronistically. *Prison* is the generic term for all institutions and many devices that hold captives. A house of correction is a type of prison, as is a jail—but neither term can be used generically. Had legislators and administrators been consistent in appellations, all would be clear and simple, but government has obvious needs to choose and use terms suggestive of progress and change, especially when little or nothing has been or will be altered.

Today in the United States, *prison* is reserved for state and federal institutions that receive offenders sentenced to imprisonment for more than one year. One might, all the same, look in vain for state use of the term: *correctional facility* or *correctional institution* have replaced *penitentiary* in most jurisdictions, just as *penitentiary* replaced *prison*. States no longer have prison departments, preferring departments of correction, though the federal government has stuck to its Bureau of Prisons. But name changing means little, especially in the tables of the Bureau of Justice Statistics. These make no concession to penal cosmetics and refer only to *prisons* and *prisoners*.

Whether or not the Americans and the British are two great peoples divided by a common language, as Oscar Wilde suggested, it is the apparently familiar that confuses and embarrasses transatlantic communications rather than the unusual and arcane. The British still use the word *jail* (often spelled "gaol") to mean imprisonment. But imprisonment in Britain is not what it seems. There are, officially, no jails, but some prisons function as jails, holding remanded (pretrial) prisoners and short-sentence convicted offenders. These institutions are called local prisons or, when they hold only pretrial detainees, remand prisons or centers. Prisons for long-term prisoners are known as training prisons or long-term prisons, which in the United States would be called simply prisons.

Finally, there are a few terminological niceties about the inhabitants of these places. Historically, the only distinction of note was between the felon and the misdemeanant. In modern usage *felon* became *convict*, very likely as a contraction of *convicted felon*. In this, as in a number of other English usages, the United States is truer to eighteenth-century tradition than is Britain. The terms *felon* and *misdemeanant*, which appear in everyday speech in the United States and are certainly legal currency, are almost archaic in Britain. A felon in the United States is liable to imprisonment in a state or federal prison for more than a year, a misdemeanant to imprisonment in a local (county or municipal) jail for up to a year. There is a connection here with past practice in England, where a felon who was not to be executed was the responsibility of central government, but a misdemeanant went to a local jail. *Convict*, when the term is used today, has lost its precise meaning and is usually an emphatic form of *prisoner*, which is the term most used in Britain. The squeamish, on both sides of the Atlantic, prefer *inmate* to *prisoner* and may even urge the use of the thoroughly evasive *resident*.

The Victorian English Prison System

By the early 1860s there were two distinct types of prison in England. The older, stretching back to Saxon times and probably beyond, was the local prison. This was made up of two historically distinct components, the jail and the house of correction. Both of these are discussed elsewhere in this book but may conveniently be described here. In medieval and early modern times, the jail was primarily used for detention and much less often for punishment. It held people awaiting trial and those found guilty and awaiting the execution of sentence. These sentences were likely to be corporal or capital, and the period of posttrial detention was therefore brief. It was common, for example, for a person to be sentenced and hanged or flogged on the same day. From the early seventeenth century onward, transportation overseas became a more common fate for felons, who would wait in jail until they were delivered to the central government collection depot. Later still, penal servitude at home was substituted for transportation, and convicted felons would wait in jail until they were sent to a government convict prison.

Jails were also used to detain witnesses whose appearance at trial was in doubt or, occasionally, to protect them or prevent their subornation. From the fourteenth century onward, jails were also used to enforce the payment of private debts, by means of holding the debtor until he paid or otherwise satisfied his creditor. There had probably always been a small amount of punitive jailing, but corporal and capital punishment and fining were preferred. It is impossible to be precise about how often jail was used as a punishment, but the practice did gradually become more common over the centuries, though even by the early eighteenth century those given jail sentences were apparently the minority of those held.

The history of the house of correction is shorter. The first was located in the former palace at Bridewell, in the City of London, and opened (or shut) its doors for business in December 1556. Bridewell became the model for similar institutions in other English towns, which were concerned with the apparent inefficacy of traditional remedies for beggary, moral offenses, and other petty criminality. Elizabethan legislation allowed and encouraged the magistrates to provide a bridewell (now known by its general and functional name as a house of correction) in every county. At this point the house of correction was used more to underpin social than criminal policy and was intended especially to suppress idleness and vagrancy. A law of James I in 1609 made a house of correction obligatory for all English counties.

The Prison Act of 1865, which was the major consolidator of nineteenth-century prison law, formally amalgamated the jail and the house of correction. It abolished a distinction that by this time had ceased to denote a difference. The resulting institution was known as a prison. Because there were other prisons in existence—those run by central government for the confinement of convicts—it became customary to speak of the new hybrid as local prisons and to refer to the government prisons as convict prisons. The local prisons did not cease to perform the functions of jails: the detention of those awaiting trial, debtors, and capitally condemned prisoners. But they also now served as places of punishment for those sentenced for terms of up to two years.

Local prisons were owned and administered by county and borough magistrates. Besides their judicial role, the county magistrates had constituted the rural local government of England and Wales for several centuries (and continued to do so until the advent of elected county councils in 1888); the borough magistrates were usually also members of their municipal corporation or council. Local prisons were largely financed from the rates (local taxes) with, from the mid-1840s onward, a significant and increasing subvention from central government. Some local prisons also contracted with the army and navy, which paid them to hold soldiers and sailors sentenced by courts-martial. In 1867 there were 145,184 committals to 126 local prisons in England and Wales.

The convict system in 1867 comprised nine convict prisons, an asylum for criminal lunatics, and a refuge (a prerelease prison) for female convicts. These central government prisons had a much shorter history than either the jail or the house of correction. They dated back no further than 1776, when the loss of the American convict depositories obliged central government to take a reluctant hand in prison administration. Believing that providence would provide a penal alternative to America, the government simply extended its holdings of hulks—disused and decommissioned warships—which had previously been used to marshal the convicts before their transportation to the American colonies. Put to dockyard, arsenal, and similar work during the day, convicts returned to the hulks for sleeping and feeding. These prisons provided their own kind of security but were also prone to corruption and abuse of all kinds. They were managed by a private contractor, to whom the government paid a fee.

The apparently irremediable condition of the hulks (though they could, in fact, be run fairly decently, as later civil-service administrations showed), and the enthusiasm for "penitentiaries" in the last decades of the eighteenth century, eventually persuaded central government to set up its own land-based prisons. The first of these was the General Penitentiary, a massive, costly, impractical, and mock-medieval pile erected on the Thames, at Millbank. This received its first prisoners in 1816 and was a constant source of administrative, financial, and health problems until it was pulled down in 1893. Two good things came out of Millbank: after demolition, its sixteen-acre site was used for housing the poor, and its leveling provided work for some of London's unemployed.

Until the end of the nineteenth century, the two prison systems—convict and local—continued as largely separate administrations. There were fewer of both types of prison than in earlier decades. This was the result of falling committals and shorter sentences and of increased central government pressure on the localities to improve their prisons or to amalgamate the smaller ones. So distinct were local from convict prisons, and so separate their administrations, that there was great ignorance, even by the staff, of how the other's system was run. A white-collar offender who in the late 1870s received five years of penal servitude (as convict imprisonment was then called) noted this mutual ignorance in his memoirs. As the law required, he was held locally during his trial, and after sentencing he was removed to a convict prison. At Newgate (the City of London local prison) he found that "everyone, warders and officials, were perfectly ignorant of the system and discipline pursued at the convict establishments. Not one knew anything of convict life."

In the late nineteenth century there was heated controversy about the decline in the prison committals. Administrators claimed that falling numbers were evidence that, among other things, convict and local prisons were doing their job, deterring or reforming criminals. Skeptics, on the other hand, saw the falling numbers as the result of shorter sentences. The whole picture was complicated by a rising general population, the creation of new offenses such as failing to send one's child to school or for vaccination, and at the same time, the introduction of several means of curtailing the use of imprisonment (probation, time to pay fines). A careful sifting of the statistics by an 1894 Home Office committee concluded that although sentencing changes had undoubtedly played a major part in the reduction of prison numbers, crime had also diminished.

In retrospect, this fall is hardly surprising, since in those years all the institutions and instruments of order and socialization were being refined and extended in England. The effects of the crude mobilization and exploitation of labor, and the consequent civic upheaval and social disorganization, which marked the first phase of the industrial revolution, began to fade. Working people began to enjoy a higher standard of living, together with a predictability and security in their circumstances that wedded them more firmly to the status quo (to the increasing despair and disgust of revolutionaries, such as Marx and Engels). And indeed the status quo was itself changing, with ever greater political participation and representation being extended to working people. Add to the picture vast sanitary, transportation, educational, financial, municipal, and social security changes and a proliferation of civil organizations—political, labor, religious, cultural, recreational, and self-help—and one has elements for stabilization, incorporation, and empowerment, elements that today's politicians, on both sides of the Atlantic, might envy. It is salutary and humbling to reflect that in late Victorian England, prison closures, with their attendant loss of local employment and trade, constituted a recurring criminal justice problem and a source of quarrels, long and bitterly fought.

Penal Servitude and Progressive Stages

The convict prisons, which had grown out of problems with the transportation of convicts overseas, eventually replaced transportation altogether. Expense, a growing belief that transportation had little deterrent value, and an antipathy to the practice in some of the Australian colonies were the principal reasons for its demise. The last batch of convicts arrived in Western Australia in January 1869, but by then the flow had dwindled to an annual selection of some 600 suitable long-sentence prisoners. (The last consignment numbered 279 and included 63 Fenians from the abortive 1867 uprising in Ireland.)

From first to last, it is estimated that about 162,000 men and women were transported to Australia. Between 1719 and 1772 some 30,000 had been transported to the American colonies from England alone. Although the flow of convicts overseas was gradually reduced over a period of years by weeding out those who had shorter sentences or were unfit, there was understandable public alarm at the prospect of the retention and eventual release at home of all convicts. Political and judicial opinion, transmitted to the public through inflammatory journalism and the Victorian equivalent of "true crime" pulp publications, portrayed transported convicts as the most dangerous and wicked of offenders. These convicts were seen as a national threat, people whose implacable criminal natures were compounded by an animalistic sexuality and profound immorality and who were therefore likely to expand a dangerous subversive class. Any alternative to transportation had to be cast in a form that would quiet public fears.

For several decades prison administrators had experimented in managing penal discipline by means of "progressive stages." Breaking the prisoner's sentence into successively less restrictive and punitive parts was a feature of the regime at the pioneering (and prototypical) penitentiary established at Gloucester in 1791, and this approach was adopted when central government set up its own penitentiary at Millbank. The penal discipline at Pentonville penitentiary, established in 1842 to embody and exemplify the latest elements in penal thought and prison design, also included progressively easing stages. The notion was simple. Good behavior assured the authorities that the prisoner could be trusted in easier conditions of confinement and earned him advancement. The system was supposed to test, encourage, and deter—the last because a lapse in behavior could result in degradation to a lower stage.

Pentonville convicts were supposed to be the pick of the criminal crop—young, in good health, relatively inexperienced in crime, and carefully chosen for reformation. All who entered Pentonville at this time (the early 1840s) were doomed to be transported after the exceptionally severe test of eighteen months of separate confinement (eventually reduced to nine months because of the toll it took on physical health and sanity). The prisoner was to be softened up: the chaplain spoke of softening hard hearts; critics referred to a softening in the head. Once the prisoner was in a compliant and cooperative state, he would be taught the basics of a handicraft trade, would be terrorized by preaching, and would in other ways be prepared for life overseas. The best behaved were not spared transportation but were granted a certificate that allowed conditional release almost immediately on their arrival in Australia. The obdurate and ill-conducted were delivered in chains to a penal colony—the nearest the British came to Devil's Island—for several years of debilitating toil, harsh living, and crushing discipline.

The philosophy of progressive stages and penal servitude was set out in November 1842 in a declaration by Lord Stanley, secretary for war and the colonies. His statement so succinctly embodied the thinking of this and several successive generations that it is worth quoting in full.

> We do not . . . contemplate a state of things in which the convict, suffering under the sentence of the law, should ever be excluded from the hope of amending his condition by blameless or meritorious behaviour, or from the fear of enhancing the hardships of it by misconduct. On the contrary, to keep alive an invigorating hope and a salutary dread at every stage of the progress of the prisoner . . . appears to us to be an indispensable part of the discipline to which he should be subjected. Further, we contemplate the necessity of subjecting every convict to successive stages of punishment, decreasing in rigour at each successive step, until he reaches that ultimate stage . . . of a pardon, either absolute or conditional, though not ever entitled to demand the indulgence of right. (*Correspondence on Convict Discipline*, 1843)

Twentieth-century tyrants have made full use of the terrible properties of separate confinement. Nineteenth-century penologists were every bit as aware of its capacity to break the spirit, even though they were ignorant of the psychological mechanisms involved. The Reverend John Burt, sometime assistant chaplain at Pentonville, in 1852 proclaimed separation to the world (or at least to the how-to-do-it group of magistrates who constituted his readership): "The passions of the criminal by which he is chiefly actuated, are usually excessive and malignant. Penal discipline finds the will vigorous, but vicious, propelled powerfully, but lawlessly. It is this vicious activity that is subjugated by protracted seclusion and wholesome discipline. . . . The will is . . . subdued . . . bent or broken, and the moral character is . . . made plastic by the discipline. . . . The will is bent in its direction; it is broken in its resistance to virtue, its vicious activity is suppressed only to leave it open to the control of better motives." The nine-month duration of this first stage in penal discipline suggested what was being sought—a rebirth, a new being, a person purged of criminal instincts and malign attitudes and ready for the carefully graduated series of rewards and threats that constituted the later stages of the system.

This system of inducements and threats, and a period of initial purging and breaking, became the basis of the home-based convict system. The numbers of convicts retained in Britain were gradually increased by transporting only fit males with the longest sentences. In 1853 this informal practice, which had been based on the use of the Royal Prerogative and executive discretion, was put on a proper legal footing and called penal servitude.

Prisoners are most animated by the prospect of freedom, and giving them a way to affect the duration of their confinement is a powerful form of behavioral control. Accelerated release for good behavior was the basis of the convict system proposed as a substitute for transportation by Sir Joshua Jebb, chairman of the Directors of Convict Prisons. It was agreed in 1853 that a convict who would have served fifteen years if transported would be imprisoned at home for eight to ten years; a ten-year man might be released in six; and a seven-year sentence could be served in Britain in four. The proportion of time that could be remitted was changed again in 1857, on a sliding scale of from one-sixth for the shortest sentence of penal servitude to one-third remission for those serving fifteen years and more.

There was some ingenuity in Jebb's system. Nine months of separate confinement would be followed by time at a public works prison, where the prisoner would be allowed the (supposedly) carefully controlled company of his fellows. These prisons got their names from the work the convicts performed—building fortifications, laboring at naval dockyards, or (eventually) reclaiming marginal farmland. A three-stage promotion was necessary for a prisoner to obtain early release. A book, rather like that of the recording angel, noted every convict's progress. Sentences were converted into marks, and prisoners were informed of the total number standing between them and liberty. Jebb insisted that "at every opportunity" prisoners should be reminded of the book and of the conduct it ineluctably charted. Each of the three stages was denoted by conduct badges. Every prisoner had his own status, as well as that of his fellows, constantly thrust before him. In addition, bad behavior forfeited marks already earned; very bad behavior incurred flogging and the appalling discomfort and aggravation of living in chains. Even indifferent behavior could cause one to wait out the whole of a sentence. Energy, commitment, and complete submission were the supposed prerequisites of early release.

Nor, when he left the prison, was the prisoner finished with the calculus of invigorating hopes and salutary dreads. Except for the recalcitrants who sat out their sentences, release was conditional, on a "ticket of leave" (the forerunner of parole). Those who won early re-lease knew that they were being watched and could be recalled even if their misbehavior was not criminal. A recalled convict served out the unexpired portion of his sentence, often under even more punitive conditions.

The Local Prisons

While penal servitude was being established, consolidated, and refined as a substitute for transportation, local prisons (as we may conveniently call the combined jails and houses of correction) were also undergoing great change. The administrative source of that change was the strengthening of central government, which as a consequence of the 1832 Reform Act took the first steps toward representative democracy. Hard on the heels of national political reform came an overhaul of local government, then immensely

more important to the life of the nation than now. Among numerous changes, the reform-minded Whig government established a national inspectorate for local prisons.
Simultaneous legislation obliged local authorities to improve prison management and
to tighten discipline, and grants-in-aid from the Treasury coated the pill. These subsidies were wheedled out of Parliament with the argument that since central government
was mandating expensive changes, it ought to help meet some of the costs. But like all
such bounties, grants transformed the donor-recipient relationship. Theoretically, the
local authorities could refuse the grants and maintain their autonomy. In practice, they
incorporated the grants into their financial expectations and then generally lived up to
their income. The new standards of management imposed by legislation, combined
with regular and effective inspection and growing financial dependency, brought extensive changes in the local prisons.

The first and most obvious of these was a wave of closures. So little reliable
information was available that it was only after central government inspectors had
been working for a few years that the number of local prisons could confidently be
stated. In 1812, James Neild, the prison investigator and reformer, reported that
there were 317 prisons in England and Wales. Seven years later a parliamentary
return gave the number as 335. This probably did not indicate an increase but was
rather the result of an undercounting by Neild. Central government's inspection
and regulation exerted such pressure on localities, however, that by 1862 the judicial statistics reliably reported only 193 local prisons in England and Wales. By
1877 this number had dropped to 112.

The right of a county, municipality, or liberty to operate a jail or house of correction was valued for several reasons. It confirmed civic identity and importance and
usually provided an amount of patronage; and through legal business, the provisioning
of the prison, and the spending of salaries, a jail was a stimulus to local trade. But for
some of the very small authorities, benefits were outbalanced by the legal and financial
obligations. In 1862, for example, one-third of local prisons in England and Wales
admitted fewer than twenty-five prisoners in the whole year, and one-seventh received
fewer than six prisoners. Some local prisons were completely unoccupied. But, empty
or not, the prisons cost money. The fabric of the building had to be maintained and
improvements made to allow for classification and separation and to meet the requirements of the inspectorate and legislation. Somehow or other (usually by combining
several municipal offices) staff had to be retained. The honor and benefits of being a
prison holder in these small jurisdictions simply did not justify the cost to the local
taxpayer.

But one could not simply close up shop and let the courts send the prisoners elsewhere. The right to own and operate a jail, a right often secured by strenuous effort and
maintained with extraordinary tenacity, required an act of Parliament to be extinguished.
A local authority that grew dissatisfied with its bargain had to pay to get out. The least
complicated arrangements were either to amalgamate with another local prison or to
contract.

Whether amalgamation or contracting was chosen, the principle was the same:
local taxpayers who wished to discontinue a prison had to pay for the accommodation
of their prisoners elsewhere. Amalgamation was a more drastic step, since it terminated

the right to have a local prison. Contracting held out at least the possibility of the resumption of in-dependent authority. The usual type of arrangement was for a small municipality to contract with the county authority—a county town such as Worcester, for example, would contract with the county of Worcestershire. National improvements in transportation (particularly railways) and a desire to cut costs also led some counties, which had operated more than one jail or house of correction (such as Berkshire, which had jails at both Abingdon and Reading), to close the smaller of their two establishments.

Closures, contracting, and amalgamations adjusted prison populations to changes in the distribution of the general population, changes that grew ever more marked as industrialization and urbanization took hold. But for a time the flow of prisoners was not all one way. As counties and small towns lost their populations, the occupancy rate of their prisons declined. In the 1860s, therefore, a few of the overcrowded industrial towns and cities contracted with counties to receive some of their overflow. To make this cost-effective, only longer-term prisoners (those serving several months rather than a few days or weeks) were dispatched to the country. In time, contracting, closures, and amalgamations might have led to a fairly efficient, flexible, and rational distribution of accommodation, especially since there was a significant overall decline in the number of prisoners. But difficulties remained, of course. Even with populations and levels of crime increasing rapidly, some industrial towns, such as Newcastle and Liverpool, were unwilling or unable to build or to contract for their swollen prison numbers. There was also some irrationality in the existing system of county and municipal administrations, which clung to age-old prerogatives, boundaries, and privileges. Decisions were sometimes made on the basis of sentiment, custom, or inertia rather than efficiency.

Nationalization of the Local Prisons

The phrase "improvements in transportation" vastly understates the changes wrought in England by the railways between the 1840s and the 1870s. Journeys that had taken days, and were apt to be hampered by weather, could by mid-century be made in comfort, with a very high degree of reliability, in a matter of hours. This assisted prison authorities in the rationalization of their accommodation and was incorporated into the argument that crime, and therefore its punishment, had become a national rather than a local responsibility. Indeed, greater mobility and better communications were causes of the breakdown of localism in England, from which emerged a profound change in how people viewed the world, including crime and its punishment.

From the origins of Anglo-Saxon policing (in its original broad sense) the precept that communities should themselves be responsible for the maintenance of law and order was fundamental. Over the centuries this notion was buttressed by numerous experiences confirming fears that central government would abuse power and could not be trusted with peacekeeping, which for safety's sake had to remain a function of the localities. Broadly speaking, this is why continental countries had state-controlled police services many centuries before the English, who were, against their very strong instincts, cajoled by Sir Robert Peel to consent to their first professional city police force in 1829. Even when that first hesitant step had been taken, police forces were locally managed and financed (the London Metropolitan Police being the exception). The very notion of a national penal system was therefore a radical departure from what many politicians—Tory and Whig alike—considered to be the ancient constitution of England.

But a change in opinions about the balance of local and national responsibilities began in 1842 when Peel repealed the protectionist Corn Laws, in the interests of cheap food and free trade. Bowing to the argument that the abolition of agricultural tariffs would have adverse consequences for the landed interest, Peel and his supporters agreed to relieve some of the burden of property taxation by paying a proportion of law and order expenses out of central government revenues (which were not property-based). Not all local prison costs were taken over, but central government thenceforward paid maintenance costs for both felons and misdemeanants. Localities still had to find the bulk of prison funding—for unsentenced and civil prisoners, for staffing, and for capital costs: the ratio of local to central funding was about 85 percent to 15 percent.

An important constitutional line had already been redrawn, and the country had become comfortable with the new arrangements, when in 1872 it was proposed that there should be a further redistribution in prison costs. The economy as a whole had entered a period of unparalleled prosperity, yet agriculture was beginning to experience clear intimations of what was to become its prolonged decline. The vast extension of the electoral franchise in 1867 through the Second Reform Act, and the undoubted wealth of industry, were put forward as reasons for the removal of prison costs from local taxation. The franchise reform had granted the vote to virtually all adult males, and the reasoning was that they should assume a greater burden as taxpayers. This meant another shift from property to personal taxation: the former was locally raised, the latter nationally. The proliferation of central government regulations, it was further argued, had reduced the magistrates who administered the local prisons to the status of agents of the central authority.

There was also a criminological argument in favor of the cost redistribution. The increased mobility of criminals, thanks to the railways, supposedly made them a national problem, and their punishment became a central rather than a local responsibility. These arguments drifted around for a while. They had an abstract plausibility but little urgency. Various schemes were considered to enable central government to take over a greater proportion of prison costs, but no decisions were made. These proposals all stopped well short of an actual appropriation by central government, although both politicians and senior civil servants agreed that increased central funding should be matched by greater government control.

To this stew, various penologists—by then a marginal and uninfluential group—added their own herbs and condiments. There had long been abroad the notion that crimes were planned according to the comparative severity of local punishments. Criminals, with an eye to their fate if caught, supposedly planned their depredations for a jurisdiction with a "soft" prison. Evidence for this theory—which became received wisdom—was purely anecdotal and was based on a gross overestimation of most criminals' capacity to plan and decide. But since it sounded plausible and gave an indication of how crime might be suppressed, localities vied with each other to be feared by criminals and vagrants. The argument for uniformity in prison discipline was strengthened by these preoccupations and by the contention that lax localities attracted criminals and also failed in their broader duty, which was to contribute to the national repression of crime. And since uniformity could best be ensured by a greater amount of central direction, this argument dovetailed with those urging a national redistribution of penal costs and power.

Another version of the argument had been current for much longer than the notion of uniformity as deterrence: that it was inequitable that similar crimes should be punished in a dissimilar way. Why should mere geography determine the amount and type of punishment? The inspectorate of the prisons and the proliferation of laws and national regulations on imprisonment had largely been born out of this concern. Parity in sentencing and punishment had wide political appeal and no theoretical opposition.

All of these interests and concerns came together in 1874 and were given urgency when Benjamin Disraeli formed his second (and last) government. His election platform had been cautious and vague but had included unambiguous promises to reduce local rates and central government taxation. We now know that he had little idea how he would honor his pledges and that he asked the various members of his cabinet to make suggestions. There were increasingly urgent political pressures from the agricultural interest, which was suffering from market stagnation and falling prices. The removal of prisons completely from local government became attractive as a means of bringing swift relief. Accordingly, in 1876, Home Secretary Richard Assheton Cross (a politician who had never previously held ministerial rank) was given cabinet permission to bring in the necessary legislation.

The case looked attractive. There were apparently sound criminological and penological reasons to enforce greater uniformity in prison discipline. The exclusive links between localities and law enforcement had already been weakened by fiscal changes and by the transportation revolution. To these was added a clinching argument: if local prisons were nationalized, there would be a net saving of expenditure, thus reducing the total tax burden, local and national.

This last argument, which time and experience would show to be fallacious, was put forward by the person who had become the government's chief penal adviser— Colonel Edmund Du Cane. Du Cane's experience of local prisons was minimal. He was chairman of the Directors of Convict Prisons, and the two systems, as we have seen, were not in the least inclined to acquaint themselves with each other. They received very different types of prisoners, and the management problems and priorities of convict and local prisons were very different. Having spent virtually the whole of his career as a soldier in civil administration, Du Cane had an overly high regard for the personnel and machinery of central government and a contempt for local government, which he saw as amateur and inefficient.

But it was Du Cane's nationalization calculations that proved to be amateur. His figures were flawed and misleading, yet the cabinet accepted them uncritically. Home Secretary Cross had no experience of central government administration and finance, and members of Parliament, much more taken with the penal and constitutional issues involved, proved incapable of dealing with the financial side of the decision. Leaving aside the largely theoretical arguments about local and national responsibilities, equity in punishment, and the supposed rationality of criminals, we find that Disraeli's government embarked on the nationalization of prisons on the basis of a misleading prospectus drawn up by one of its most senior and most trusted advisers, a prospectus accepted uncritically by the home secretary and his senior officials and passed unchecked by Parliament. At every stage the checks and balances failed to work.

When viewed in retrospect, the financial projections verge on the absurd, but even at the time, their weakness would have been apparent to anyone who had taken the trouble to probe. By closing down half the local prisons in the country—thus carrying to a logical conclusion the process of contracting and amalgamations already under way—Du Cane hoped to save a sum of money almost equal to the extra expense of taking over the running of the remaining prisons. Something, in other words, could be had for nothing. With the speculator's self-deceiving ingenuity, Du Cane also calculated that confining unproductive penal labor, such as the crank and treadwheel, to the first month of a sentence, instead of the three months required by existing legislation, would cause a substantial increase in revenue from prisoners' enhanced industrial productivity. This increased revenue would further offset the costs of nationalization.

These computations and projections were riddled with fallacies, errors, and omissions. In the first place, there was no uniform system of accounts in the local prisons: every locality had its own bookkeeping system. Balance sheets were no more than estimates, each one of which had been arrived at according to local custom and practice. The claims that were made for the profitability of the prison industries were unreliable, often reflecting nothing more than wishful thinking. To extrapolate from this mishmash simply added whimsy to fantasy. Having dealt previously only with convicts, Du Cane did not understand the minimal productive capacities of short-term prisoners. Ill health, lack of work experience, poor skills, low motivation and rapid turnover, and the psychologically depressing effects of the harsh prison environment were all fierce brakes on productivity. More generally, this was a period in British economic history when handicrafts, and even small-scale workshop labor, were in an increasing and irreversible decline in competition with capital-intensive production.

There was another inexcusable error in the reckonings. Any commercial enterprise thinking of an acquisition consisting so substantially of buildings would have insisted on a thorough inspection by an independent surveyor. By omitting this elementary precaution, Du Cane lumbered central government with a penal estate in need of substantial and urgent investment. Since the prisons had been built at different times to meet diverse prison legislation and according to the crotchets and nostrums of various groups of magistrates, nationalization entrusted the government with a wonderful architectural cross-section of English history, in the form of hopelessly costly encumbrances.

Newgate dated back to the eighteenth century; other prisons, such as Oxford, dated to early medieval times. Newcastle was modern but was jerry-built and inadequate even before it opened. Among those in apparently good condition, some had inadequate health and dangerous sanitary facilities. Nationalization in one form or another had been sufficiently discussed for most of the 1870s to console some local authorities in their assumption that there was little point in improving, or even maintaining, buildings that could soon pass to central government. Certified as adequate by the surveyor-general and inspectors of prisons, the prisons had not been inspected to see if they should be purchased but only to judge if they met the limited requirements of the various prison acts. And even the inspectorate had lost its energy in the 1870s, with nationalization in the offing. Central government, for political and legal reasons, could not afford to be as lackadaisical as the local authorities. Takeover meant major improvements in those buildings that were to be kept in operation as prisons.

Unrelated fiscal and political pressures, and the policy vacuum of Disraeli's second administration, thus created the pressure to go forward with this half-baked scheme. The government's chief adviser, who should at the very least have acted as an impartial broker, was apparently motivated by that pervasive passion, bureaucratic empire building. If this were not enough, he was given a further push toward unbalanced judgment by the promise of a very large cash bonus to carry the thing through—and Du Cane was particularly responsive to the stimulation of money. It was from a plethora of such bonus-based judgments that the banking crisis of the sophisticated 1980s emerged, after all; so what chance was there for a headstrong civil servant serving ill-equipped ministers and bemused parliamentarians in the 1870s?

Despite his flawed calculations and ill-considered judgments in this matter, Du Cane was intelligent, hard working, and resourceful. He spent much of the first decade of nationalization covering his financial tracks. Although his tactics now look obvious, they were effective at the time, and he had the great good fortune to serve a succession of home secretaries who were inept, inexperienced, or indifferent to prison administration. The higher civil servants, who should have alerted ministers, were ferociously kept at bay by Du Cane, who headed the commission that had been set up to run the local prisons. By the time the Home Office mandarins had acquired sufficient prison expertise and confidence to begin seriously to encroach on Du Cane's territory, he escaped through retirement.

Management and finance issues can be boring; in addition Du Cane had possessed, for a time, a conjurer's flair—seemingly essential in higher civil servants—for distracting his masters' attention. There was the useful old routine of revelation, shock, and hand-wringing over the previous regime. Has there ever been a takeover, political or organizational, that has not afforded the new boss a honeymoon of immunity from criticism? This dispensation was long and fully exploited in annual reports and official correspondence. The fetish of uniformity, which had been employed to support nationalization, also served to divert. Even the least sympathetic observers of Du Cane's persona and performance (including some senior civil servants in the Home Office and prison reform leaders) were impressed by his Procrustean ability to force more than sixty prisons into a new administrative framework. That and numerous improvements in management procedures, health, sanitation, and buildings provided abundant grist for lengthy, detailed, and self-congratulatory annual reports. All this work and every innovation were implicit condemnations of the old order.

The misleading basis on which nationalization was represented to the home secretary, the cabinet, the Parliament, and the country has been overlooked by prison historians. This is a curious oversight and needs some explanation, since the government's takeover of the local prisons was the major penal event of the late nineteenth century, with consequences that are still being felt today. The inaccurate and tendentious accounts of English prisons under local government, accounts written by Du Cane and by two important committees of inquiry (the Carnarvon Committee of 1863 and the absurdly overvenerated Gladstone Committee of 1894–95), have become the conventional view instead of being seen for what they were—respectively, the misrepresentations of a zealot and the dabblings of dilettantes.

This strange reading of penal history is readily explained. Scholars (and it is a small troupe that has taken on this topic in history and public administration) have almost invariably espoused the doctrine of centralization and state supremacy. First in this succession were Sidney and Beatrice Webb, with their impressively researched *English Prisons under Local Government* in 1922, which remained the substantially unchallenged text for some fifty years. The Webbs were wholehearted and unabashed statists. They were distinguished social reformers, but they were also naive elitists and, like so many of their generation, were besotted with the benign possibilities of social engineering through the centralization of authority. This worship of power led them in 1935 to publish the most voluminous of the many whitewashing accounts of Joseph Stalin's empire, under the title *Soviet Communism: A New Civilization?*, and to remove the question mark for successive editions. Of course the Webbs welcomed the centralization of the English prisons. And since it was part of an inevitable progression, centralization was in their view morally and organizationally superior to what it replaced.

Others concurred. Evelyn Ruggles-Brise, who followed Du Cane as the head of the English prisons, performed the obligatory ritual of castigating his predecessor in his version of prison history. Prison Commissioner Lionel Fox did the same thing to Ruggles-Brise when he wrote for his generation. But both took care to uphold the shibboleth of prison nationalization and to disparage local government. By the 1930s the ascendancy of central over local government was so complete in England, and the state was so imbued with benign properties, that a defense of the achievements of nineteenth-century local government would have appeared quixotic. Both "progressive" and official opinion accepted the superior virtues of prison nationalization as dogma, and to this day not a single voice of dissent has been raised. The passage of time confers its own legitimacy. Chronology, even in this bloodiest of all centuries, is only too easily seen as progress.

Hard Labor, Hard Board, and Hard Fare

It is impossible fully to understand imprisonment in England in the last two centuries without a knowledge of its administration. Uniformity was an argument for nationalization, a defining characteristic of the punishment, and a statement of beliefs about human nature. The punishment had to be of such a character that it could be made uniform, and uniformity made sense only if one adopted a general view of prisoners' capacities for choice and actions. The life of the prisoner was directly shaped by the notion of uniformity and the possibilities that nationalization offered for achieving it.

In any institutional action, the quest for uniformity necessitates a curbing of officials' discretion. It also means that activities must have a high degree of quantifiability, since "how much?" commands a much more precise answer than qualitative questions such as "how painful?," "how degrading?," and "how encouraging?" To attain a uniform end in punishment is much more difficult than to pursue uniformity in administering punishment. The latter, as shall be seen, can be reduced to quantities, to be directed and monitored with comparative ease.

And there are other ways in which administration affected a prisoner's life. Given the lingering localism of English life, even after the railway revolution, there were apt to be ties of familiarity and sentiment between local officials and their prisoners. Family names, backgrounds, and places allowed officials and offenders to meet on a human plane. This did not vanish entirely, of course, when the local prisons came under national administration, but the requirement that senior prison officials should be rotated through several prisons in the course of their careers inevitably meant that prisoners and subordinate staff would be treated more by the book and less in terms of their individual characteristics or the customs of the locality. The rationale, after all, for moving officials and managers through different institutions and departments on promotion was the same then as now—to teach, test, bind to the organization, and above all, homogenize the administrators.

Uniformity was also more likely to increase severity than to promote lenity. Apart from the equity argument (similar crimes deserve similar punishment), uniformity was based on crude behaviorist assumptions. Criminals, it was theorized, acted to minimize pain and the risk of pain and to maximize pleasure or the prospect of gain. Uniformity in punishment throughout the country would remove the possibility of matching risk to locale. But it was inconceivable that in striving for a uniform level, administrators would reduce punishment to the level of the least severe locality or even to the average level. To a behaviorist, good punishment was that which was most deterrent, and the most deterrent was likely to be as severe as public sentiment and political opinion would tolerate. The move from locally administered local prisons to nationally administered local prisons was therefore bound to mean an overall increase in severity.

Since there was no national lobby for the mollycoddling of criminals, Du Cane earned only praise when he described in his annual reports and numerous articles how he was making punishment ineluctable and more severe. He was no penal innovator, nor did he need to be. He developed and refined an approach that had been advocated in 1863 by a Lords' Select Committee led by Lord Carnarvon. Under hysterical political pressure, the proposals of this committee had been largely acceded to by a reluctant home secretary and were embodied in the Prison Act of 1865. This set out in great detail, by means of codified rules and regulations, a severely deterrent regime based on hard labor, hard board, and hard fare. With the invulnerable certainty of one who had experienced a religious revelation, Carnarvon (who, incidentally, was a leading campaigner against cruelty to animals) had come to believe that crime could be repressed and the growth of a swelling criminal class reversed by making imprisonment truly deterrent. Because of the "low, brutish nature" of offenders this could be accomplished only by working on the senses to produce a state of constant misery, discomfort, and even some pain. Taking this basic assumption and formula, Du Cane fashioned it into a national penology for the last quarter of the nineteenth century and set about applying it in all the local prisons that had come under his control.

By the last decades of Victoria's reign, and with the science-versus-belief controversies of the 1850s and 1860s left largely behind or at least put to one side, science had begun to claim primacy in public debate because of its purported intellectual and moral superiority. Its ascendancy incorporated a misunderstanding of the ethical content of scientific judgment, leading to evil and disastrous consequences in the twentieth century. Using committees of puppet scientists and medical men, Du Cane refined and legitimized dietary, labor, and living arrangements to fashion the penal discipline to which Carnarvon had aspired as a national goal but had only glimpsed in practice.

Imprisonment with hard labor had become a near universal substitute for flogging and other corporal punishments by the middle of the nineteenth century. "Hard labor" meant more than working hard; it denoted an intensification of the pains of imprisonment. The magistrates who ran the local prisons before nationalization were equivocal about too doctrinaire an implementation of the punishment, since if the rules were conscientiously followed, they were bound to interfere with prisoners' industrial labor. This, in turn, would prevent the profits of prisoners' productivity from being applied to the local tax burden. The phrase "hard labor" was, however, helpfully vague, and in many localities industrial labor was deemed to be hard labor. To close this loophole, and to compel uniform penal labor, Carnarvon had demanded labor that quickened the breath and opened the pores. This was embodied in the 1865 statute by listing examples of approved hard labor, including the treadwheel, the crank, and the capstan. The obligation to enforce this type of labor was a major feature of the 1865 Prison Act.

Noting this requirement, Du Cane appointed a medical and scientific committee to advise on the quantity of daily hard labor that could safely be extracted. With fitting gravity and authority, the committee concluded that prisoners sentenced to hard labor should daily ascend 8,640 feet on the treadwheel (equivalent to six ascents of the Sears Tower). Because this was an objective scientific judgment, touching on quantity and physical capacity, the basic notion of hard labor was taken for granted by the committee. Yet what this amounted to was the coerced application of a vast quantity of labor to completely nonproductive purposes. (The coercion was the threat of the whip and starvation.) And as a bonus, providing a mental dimension to the torment, the prisoners had the galling and demoralizing knowledge that their toil was completely wasted. This was scarcely veiled torture and yet was accepted with hardly a murmur of dissent from penal reformers and journalists. When one contemplates the 150,000 or so people then annually committed to the English local prisons, with perhaps 100,000 sentenced to hard labor, 75,000 being declared fit for the treadwheel, and all treading and grinding uselessly for six hours a day, one realizes that at times even the most cruel and absurd of practices will be countenanced if presented with appropriate authority.

The prints and photographs that remain of prisoners on the treadwheel fail to capture its full penal properties. They do not convey the motion, the noise, the palpable strain and smell of intense physical effort. To go on the wheel was to be cast into a machine. A slip could bring injury or even death to the novice, and at the very least the experience was grueling. Yet despite the claims of enthusiasts that the wheel inexorably extracted labor from all, experienced prisoners apparently learned to coast on the labor of others. According to the surgeon of Glasgow prison, beginners or men incapacitated through drink found the wheel "very trying, if not dangerous." A prisoner who served a sentence in the late 1870s, but who did not himself go to the wheel, "pitied the treadwheel men as they went out to their labour" and noted how they sweated when they came back in. Sometimes, big strong prisoners would be led away crying. It is ironic that today gymnasiums can command large fees from devotees of physical fitness for allowing them to use modern versions of the wheel, and thus some readers may imagine that the prisoner's life was not as hard as I have suggested. But it should be remembered that in the local prisons of 1870s England, the customers were more likely to be emaciated than overweight, and they performed their wheel labor for six hours a day on a diet of oatmeal, bread, and water, after nights and days of extreme discomfort.

Other bodily vulnerabilities were diligently exploited. A "progressive" dietary was established. This provided for an allowance of food so meager in the early stages as to constitute scientific starvation. And since local prison sentences were so short, few prisoners stayed long enough to get beyond the first or second stage to a marginally improved allowance. "It appears to us," pronounced Du Cane's scientists, "to be a self-evident proposition that imprisonment should be rendered as deterrent as is consistent with the maintenance of health and strength." The penal dietary might, they reflected, be seen as a benign infliction: "It is a matter of universal experience that partial abstinence from food for a limited period is not only safe under ordinary circumstances, but frequently beneficial, and we think that a spare diet is all that is necessary for a prisoner undergoing a sentence of a few days or weeks." To give more than a minimum diet, the committee cautioned, would be "to forego an opportunity for the infliction of salutary punishment; it would constitute an encouragement to the commission of petty crimes." Laxness, indeed, "would assist in the manufacture of the habitual criminal."

But since these experts were to science and medicine what Du Cane had been to accountancy when he foisted nationalization on the government, their conclusions and recommendations inevitably and conveniently overlooked some important facts. Prisoners were generally drawn from the lowest sections of society. Many came off the streets—starving, drunken, demented, filthy, lousy, and tubercular, suffering from mental and physical illnesses and weaknesses associated with long-term malnutrition and dissipation. These facts were so obvious that they were perhaps not so much overlooked as selectively interpreted. Near-starvation was justified as unavoidable when punishing those already hungry, to deter them from committing crime and from using the prison as a boardinghouse. Yet the *effects* of dietary were considered in relation to a well-fed person, to whom, indeed, "partial abstinence . . . is not only safe . . . but frequently beneficial." And that was not the only sleight of hand. Many of the drunks, beggars, tramps, prostitutes, nuisances, and petty thieves who populated the local prisons were habitual offenders. They would go to prison for a week or two on minimum diet, debilitating labor, and depressing conditions, would come out for a day or two of free-range starvation and sleeping rough on the streets, and would go back inside for another dose of the same, scientifically administered. The cumulative effects of the prison dietary on such people, "serving life by installments," as it is sometimes described, were devastating and destructive.

There is insufficient space here fully to discuss Du Cane's recommended dietary, which is indicative of the temper and penal methods of those years. Consistent with their crude utilitarianism, the scientists and officials were not satisfied with meals that provided minimum nutriment. They issued detailed instructions on how to cook it in such a way and from such ingredients that it had a smell, taste, and consistency so repulsive that it made some prisoners nauseous and even diarrheic. These experiences run through prisoners' memoirs, from the persistent driving hunger of imprisoned labor leader John Burns in the 1880s to Oscar Wilde's gastrointestinal troubles at Reading Gaol in the 1890s (and neither was on the lowest diet).

Burns never forgot the hardships of his six weeks of imprisonment. (Du Cane might have argued that this lasting remembrance of punishment proved that his formula worked.) Burns eventually moved his politics from the streets to the House of Commons. There, ten years after his incarceration, he told MPs of his experience with Du Cane's dietary: "I am not ashamed to say that at one or two o'clock in the morning I have wetted my hands with my spittle, and gone down on my hands and knees on the asphalted floor in the hope of picking up a stray crumb from the meal I had ten hours before."

In what, for all its sentimentality, is one of the great prison poems, Wilde, who served a two-year sentence in local prisons for sexual offenses, wrote in *The Ballad of Reading Gaol* of "Lean Hunger and Green Thirst." He reported to friends, and in articles published after his release, that the food was revolting and insufficient, that diarrhea was so common that astringent medicines were issued as a matter of routine, and that on three occasions he had seen prison staff vomit when they unlocked cells in the morning. (There was no integral sanitation in the cells, and the prisoners were issued chamber pots.)

Michael Davitt was one of several Irish revolutionists turned constitutional politicians who sat in the House of Commons in the last decades of the nineteenth century and whose interest in prison matters arose from their own experiences with the system (Davitt had served eight years of a fifteen-year sentence of penal servitude). He described the dietary as a "scale of scientific starvation." Hunger turned life into misery: "There is no bodily punishment more cruel than hunger—that remorseless, gnawing, human feeling which tortures the mind in thinking of the sufferings of the body, and tending to make life an unbearable infliction under a denial of the elementary cravings of nature." The Commons and the nation were shocked as Davitt recalled how he had seen men devour candle ends, the grease provided for their boots, the marrow of the putrid bones they had been set to break and grind, and even a used poultice retrieved from the prison garbage heap by the cesspool. Thus the measure of Du Cane's extremism and the indolence or irresponsibility of his political masters were eventually broadcast, for a time at least, to the country.

Without the aid of either a scientific committee or Shakespeare, Du Cane grasped the penal possibilities of denying sleep. He endorsed Carnarvon's decree that, as far as possible, the prisoner's "ravell'd sleave of care" was to be left undone. Low brute natures would surely not—particularly not—be permitted the indulgence of "sore labor's bath, Balm of hurt minds." Punishment could be pushed past the boundaries of consciousness by obliging emaciated prisoners to chase sleep on a hard board. The hours of repose were curtailed, and any attempt to doze, relax, or fall into a reverie after six hours of laboring on the treadwheel or grinding the crank was foiled by requiring the prisoner, under threat of even more drastic punishment, to sit on a backless stool or his upturned slop pail and by setting as a cell task a stiff quota of oakum picking. Wilde told a friend that the plank bed caused him to shiver all night long and that, as a consequence of its rigors, he had become an insomniac; Davitt made the same complaint.

Low brutes were, of course, gregarious. Misery might be diminished by company, which was also corrupting. The crushing oppressiveness of the discipline was intensified by keeping the prisoner alone to the greatest extent possible. This sequestration extended outside the prison; only the small minority of long-term prisoners could earn the boon and encouragement of a letter or a short visit from family and friends. On the same basis, the solace of reading was restricted to the Bible or to books of religious exhortation whose turgidity complemented the contrived nauseousness of the maize stirabout.

From the convict service, Du Cane introduced progressive stages and marks into the local prisons. Progress was by means of merit and the passage of time combined. Twenty-eight days had to be spent in a stage in order for a prisoner to be eligible to be promoted; actual promotion was obtained only by earning the required number of marks. The stage system was supposed to provide inducements and to enable the prisoner to take some charge of his punishment by good behavior. In fact, it was irrelevant to the vast majority of those who passed through the local prisons, since their sentences were so short that no matter how well behaved they were, they could win no improvement in their circumstances. In 1877, for example, three-quarters of the prison sentences in English magistrates courts (which handled the vast bulk of criminal work) were for one month or less. Even in the higher courts, which handled the most serious criminal cases, over one-quarter of all sentences of imprisonment were for three months or less.

For the tiny minority of prisoners whose sentences were long enough to allow them to win promotion to the highest (fourth) class, the inducements were paltry. At this disciplinary summit, they were allowed to work together and received some improvement in dietary and in reading material. They had also earned, by this time, mattresses instead of boards. Each month they could have a half-hour visit and a letter, and on their release they were given a slightly larger discharge gratuity.

Most important, people sentenced to imprisonment in the local prisons (that is, all sentences up to two years) did not have the inducement and advantage of a remission in sentence. A man or a woman sentenced to two years of imprisonment served the entire sentence, no matter how good his or her conduct. Progressive stage easements were not so much positive inducements as the removal or easing of conditions that, in the earlier stages, took the prisoner to the extreme limits of physical and psychological endurance. This still left a lengthy sentence of local imprisonment as an extraordinarily severe punishment. Very rarely (in 1877 there were only two such cases) a man might be sentenced to four years of imprisonment—the maximum penalty on two counts. A prisoner who served time in the 1870s described such a sentence as "the severest punishment, with the exception of death, known in the English law." According to his account, a judge who passed such a sentence remarked that he had given the sentence only twice before. "In the one case the man died, in the other he went raving mad; and I believe it a sentence that no man can survive and retain his senses."

Inverting Deserts

Although the local prisons had a harsher regime than the convict establishments, it must not be imagined that conditions in the latter were easy. The reform-minded Prison Commissioner Alexander Paterson in the 1930s made much of his aphorism—"Men are sent to prison as a punishment, not for punishment." Victorian administrators believed the opposite: that imprisonment and penal servitude were intended to be active punishment, not simply the absence of freedom. The convict prisons, therefore, although in some respects less harsh than the local prisons, were still places of onerous and grinding punishment.

With the passage of time and with constant obedience and good behavior, a convict might obtain for himself employment that was not too arduous, but if he was physically fit, he would almost certainly spend some time at manual labor on the public works. This work was conducted in large, closely guarded gangs. Labor might involve sea or riverbed excavation for a dockyard, the building of fortifications, or heavy "spade labor" on marginal farmland. Where work quotas were set, as in the excavation of Chatham dockyard, the prisoners were frantically driven on by their guards, who themselves would be in trouble if the day's allotted tasks were not completed.

Convicts endured a dietary that Du Cane and his meanspirited advisers considered appropriate for men engaged in prolonged and heavy manual labor. This did not prevent repeated criticism from members of the public, certain politicians, and even prison reformers who complained about excessive generosity. William Tallack, of the prison-reforming Howard Association, was an artless believer in harsh punishment as a means of deterring prisoners from crime. In one of his many letters to *The Times*, in the cause of what he saw as penal reform, Tallack argued that there was overfeeding of convicts: "Humane prison officers state that certain classes of prisoners are so well fed and well-treated that the necessary conditions of due deterrence for the protection of society from crime and violence are thereby weakened." He went on to quote a prison chaplain who had compared convict dietary with that of able-bodied paupers in the workhouse. The convict was given 280 ounces of solids a week, the pauper 166.

This was the obvious and widely accepted inversion of punishments in late Victorian England. Sentences of penal servitude were a minimum of three years, as compared with the maximum of two years in the local prisons. But after nine months of separate confinement (during which convicts were in some ways treated as though they had reached the final and easiest stage of local imprisonment), the pains of the sinister-sounding penal servitude were lighter than those of local imprisonment. Even the duration of confinement scarcely differentiated the punishments. A well-behaved convict sentenced to three years' penal servitude would serve only two years and six months because he could earn up to one-sixth remission of sentence; the two-year prisoner in the local system, by contrast, served every day of his allotted punishment. And many of those who went to the local prisons were caught in the revolving door of repeat offending, serving years in installments of days or weeks.

How was such an apparently absurd system justified? The notion of proportionality was deeply embedded in English sentencing policy, whatever obeisance deterrence or reform might extract. But there was also a widely accepted line of reasoning that justified the harsher treatment of the minor offender. Sir Joshua Jebb, who dominated central government's penal policy from the late 1840s until his death in 1863, raised this notion to the level of national policy. He contended that since punishment had several objectives, some evidently in conflict with others, the best way to reconcile them was to dedicate particular parts of the sentence to the different ends. The first nine months of penal servitude, for example, would be used to achieve deterrence or retribution; later imprisonment would see a diminution of retributive elements and an increased emphasis on reformation.

This reasoning was applied by Du Cane in his joint management of local and convict prisons. After he gained a few years' experience of local imprisonment, he came to argue, not implausibly, that sentences of imprisonment (as distinct from penal servitude) were so short that reformative efforts were wasted. Since it was futile to attempt reform in the local prisons, it was misguided to distract them from their principal task, which was to deter petty offenders. And because it was from the hordes of lesser criminals that the greater offenders were thought to emerge, harsh treatment at an early stage might prevent the offender from slipping deeper into crime. Should deterrence fail, or should an offender leapfrog into serious crime, prolonged detention would be appropriate, and it was during that extended confinement that efforts might be made at reformation.

Politicians, judges, magistrates, and others were sufficiently taken by this theory to overlook the contradictions and inconsistencies. There was no logical reason, for example, even if one accepted the "short and sharp" and "prolonged and reformative" bifurcation, why the two types of imprisonment should not be integrated and the resulting continuum be made available to sentencers. But custom has a powerful effect in shaping perceptions, more perhaps in the administration of law than in any other department of public life. (Until relatively recently, for example, long-term sentencing in England was inordinately affected by the seven-year, fourteen-year, and life-imprisonment matrix, which originated two hundred years ago, in the days of transportation, and was passed on to imprisonment through penal servitude.) Only after another generation would the full disparities in the punishment of minor and greater offenders be somewhat leveled out, and even then, as we shall see, the Victorian inheritance continued to exercise a powerful influence.

Closing the Prison Gates

From his surviving correspondence, official papers, publications, and the tenor of his testimony to committees of inquiry, it is clear that Du Cane always regarded the local prisons as inferior to the convict service. When, after nationalization, the staffing of the local prisons came into his hands, he fiercely guarded his prerogatives—from ministers and colleagues alike—and imported convict-service officials to fill many key posts. Convict-service methods were adapted to the local prisons, and the various prison advisory committees were well leavened with convict-service functionaries. Since at least the late eighteenth century, the English magistrates had been a continuing source of penological debate and innovation, yet overnight they were shut out of the prisons, confined to a marginal inspectorial and advisory role (which they miserably failed to develop) and discouraged at every turn. Convinced that they were meddling and uninformed amateurs—"the great unpaid"—Du Cane turned his back on them, scornfully dismissing their opinions and experience. It was an astonishing piece of administrative and personal arrogance.

The gates were slammed against the magistrates and society at large. Under local government, from 1836 until at least the late 1860s, there had been a vigorous and effective system of central government inspection. The first generation of these inspectors pursued their duties impartially and with fearless energy. They were not overawed by local bigwigs, and government made no attempt to censor their annual reports, which were published by the Stationery Office. They delivered numerous public rebukes to dilatory or noncom-pliant magistrates. These reports (which had no equivalent in the convict prisons) brought together a mass of information and opened the local prisons of the country to the educated world.

Not all interest in the prisons was commendable. There were numerous occasions when magistrates treated their prisons as freak-houses or human zoos, places of diversion for friends and entertainment for visiting notables. (Newgate in particular was a type of entertainment park available to the Lord Mayor and Corporation of London: distinguished foreigners came to expect a tour as one of the sights of London.) Turning prisons into places of amusement is indefensible, but the showmanship was generously extended to legitimate inquirers and to the press. It is doubtful if any respectable middle-class person who knew a magistrate directly or indirectly would have failed to gain entry into an English prison under local government. Henry Mayhew and John Binny's lavishly illustrated conspectus, *Criminal Prisons of London*, compiled in the 1850s, shows the freedom of access then routinely permitted. No such publication appeared during Du Cane's years or since. Traditions of prison secrecy became so firmly established, rationalizations so finely honed, and public and politicians so acquiescent that reasonable access to journalists and investigators did not again become regularly available until the 1970s and 1980s. Yet the public has many legitimate interests in this expensive and sensitive state service, and these dark places in our system of government have been notorious for their abuses through the ages. They always need the check of responsible scrutiny and publicity.

Disdaining, impeding, and dismissing the magistrates who were supposed to be keeping watch on his prisons, and with scarcely less concern for politicians, Du Cane achieved and held an unprecedented sway over English imprisonment—local and convict alike—until 1895. The inevitable occurred: unchecked authority amplified the strong domineering traits in the man's personality. He outwitted politicians, terrified his subordinates, and sowed dragon's teeth among the ranks of the increasingly formidable higher civil service. When the times changed and a radical new home secretary was convinced, by a campaigning journalist and a rebellious chaplain, that the prisons also had to change, all criticism focused on Du Cane, who had to bear the age-old consequences of gathering unto oneself all power and authority and of carelessly making enemies. After a year spent malingering to avoid appearing before a committee of inquiry (which in the end he handled masterfully), Du Cane was compelled to exit on the very day he reached retirement age.

THE TWENTIETH CENTURY AND THE VICTORIAN INHERITANCE

Twentieth-century imprisonment in England has been marked by a tenacious Victorian inheritance, both in affirmation and repudiation. A major part of this was bricks and bars. Never in English history have so many prisons been built or rebuilt as during Victoria's reign. The separate system required buildings of a special (and expensive) design. These were particularly difficult to adapt to new types of discipline that allowed the prisoners to congregate. There were long and easily supervised galleries of cells but few workshops, dining halls, or dayrooms. Chapels were the only part of local prisons where any appreciable numbers of prisoners were expected to gather. The sites added to the difficulties of adaptation. Many were originally in city centers; if prisons had been put on the outskirts, development had gone on around them. Expansions, rebuilding, and reconfigurations were in some places all but impossible.

And in these years funds were urgently required for other needs. First came the human, demographic, and political devastation of World War I, next the depression of the 1930s, and then World War II and the destructive impact on British cities. When, after 1945, prison numbers started to rise, two considerations stood in the way of increased funding. The first was the vast and pressing program of repairing war damages; the second was the social and penal reformers' assurance that successive governments could not be blamed for wanting to believe (it was indeed part of their election message)—that crime would yield to social amelioration, that it was part of the passing turmoil of wartime upheaval, and that the need for prisons would decline. The temper of those years was such that spending on prisons would have seemed like a hope betrayed. This folly of wishful thinking combined disastrously with a dramatic rise in crime and in prison numbers. In 1927 there were about 11,000 people in the English prisons. This rose to 15,000 in 1945 and to 42,000 in 1978. Caught between inadequate funding and increased demands, British prisons inevitably declined to levels of sordidness that would have appalled and shamed Victorian administrators, politicians and public alike. The low level of investment through most of the twentieth century was evident in the ages of the buildings in use at the end of the 1970s. The majority of prisoners in England and Wales were then being held in forty-two establishments built before 1900 and in another four built between 1900 and 1939. Less than one-quarter of accommodation was twentieth-century, purpose-built. Even a casual visitor who glimpses English prisons in the hearts of cities and towns immediately sees a style of architecture that bears the unmistakable stamp of the last century and cannot fail to be struck by the abiding Victorian nature of imprisonment in England. Walls and bars most certainly this prison system make.

Hegel could have been replying to an invitation to contribute to this volume when he expostulated, "What experience and history teach is this—that people and governments never have learned anything from history, or acted on principles deduced from it." If this century has seen English prison administrators grapple with their Victorian inheritance, their decisions have been erratic, uncertain, and marked by periods of administrative inertia and philosophical coma. With all the hubris and delusion that the twentieth century has invested in the word *progress,* penal history, where it has been studied at all, has been a source of self-congratulation rather than of warnings. We continue to use Victorian prisons but have rejected their objects and methods; renouncing some of their prison-keeping axioms, we have put nothing adequate in their place. Victorian administrators, for example, had good reason to abhor the congregation and free movement of prisoners. Unthinking attempts to humanize prisons led to an abandonment of this wisdom, even in some maximum-security prisons. In consequence, prison riots, all destructive and some murderous, have become a regular occurrence in England. Even when we attempt to invent and adapt, neither reformers nor administrators consider it worth while seriously to ponder the experience of earlier generations.

Selective incapacitation, a nostrum of the 1980s, was mooted throughout the 1880s and 1890s and given legislative form in England in 1908. In the practice of cumulatively sentencing repeat offenders, its origins go back to medieval times. At the other end of the criminal continuum, special treatment for the less hardened offender was one of the rationales for penitentiaries. Parole grew out of the ticket-of-leave schemes of the 1840s. Control units, which are intended to bring to heel the subversive and recalcitrant prisoner, use the time-tested methods of separation and progressive stages. History offers important lessons about virtually all reforms, but, of course, it needs to be studied carefully. A closer look at some changes that were presented as innovations is a useful way to get an overview of some of the main currents of twentieth-century imprisonment in England. In comparison with developments in the last century, many more modern penal schemes seem both pallid and meandering. Yet those are not necessarily bad qualities in themselves, since much depends on the available alternatives.

Preventive Detention

The idea of preventive detention was simple. Those who by their repeated criminality disdained or otherwise showed themselves immune to the deterrent or reformative elements in imprisonment would receive treatment different from that of "ordinary" criminals. The object was social protection rather than deterrence, reform, or retribution. A two-stage system of sentencing was established under the Prevention of Crime Act of 1908. The offender, having been found to be a habitual offender, was liable to an add-on of at least five years of preventive detention, to be served as well as whatever the court had determined was a suitable punishment for the crime. Conditions in the special preventive detention prison were supposed to be superior to those of other prisons, since neither retribution nor deterrence (nor even reformation) was being sought. Evidently the image in the minds of the politicians and administrators was of graying habituals—"old lags"—whiling away their years in a secure bucolic setting as the fires of crime dwindled into embers. Actual differences in the quality of punishment were trivial, although those in the quantity were not. Preventive detainees were still prisoners, subject to control, restriction, repression, and privation and excluded from the world of free people. The only difference was that they were being punished for what they were rather than for what they had done.

The prison commissioners were enthusiasts for the new scheme and energetically touted its virtues. But Winston Churchill's liberal and humane values—his sense of Englishness—recoiled from the concept of imprisoning someone for preventive reasons. When, in 1910, he succeeded Herbert Gladstone (son of the famous statesman) as home secretary, he immediately ordered an investigation of the brave new sentence. "I have serious misgivings," he wrote to one of his senior officials, "lest the institution of preventive detention should lead to a reversion to the ferocious sentences of the last generation. After all preventive detention is penal servitude in all essentials, but it soothes the conscience of judges and of the public and there is a very grave danger that the administration of the law should under softer names assume in fact a more severe character."

Churchill's inquiries turned up scores of cases where grotesquely heavy sentences had been imposed on petty habitual criminals, for stealing food and trivial amounts of property. He told judges that preventive detention should not be seen as a solution to the difficult issue of habitual crime but should rather be viewed as "an exceptional means of protecting society from the worst class of professional criminals." His observations were effective. In 1910, the year that he became home secretary, 177 sentences of preventive detention were imposed. The following year the number had dropped to 53; by the 1920s the annual average was 31.

There was an attempt in the 1948 Criminal Justice Act to revive preventive detention. As is frequently the case, a new generation of enthusiasts believed that if the small print was altered, all would be changed. In this case they thought that they could refine the qualifying criteria and thus equitably and accurately remove serious offenders from circulation for a long time. But the same disappointing results ensued. A few big fish were landed, in the company of shoals of pathetic repeat offenders, whose harm to society amounted only to annoyance. The sentence underwent various modifications, but the fundamental notion was so flawed that it petered out in the 1970s as an order that ensured compulsory postrelease supervision. Its revival in the United States two decades later, with a smart new set of statistical clothes and bearing the impressively scientific-sounding name of "selective incapacitation," predictably acknowledged no historical provenance.

The Rise and Fall of Borstals

The call for central government to involve itself in juvenile reformation was made during the hearings of the 1894–95 Gladstone Committee on Prisons. Judicial statistics showed that criminal propensity peaked from the mid-teens to the mid-twenties. Herbert Gladstone took the view that central government should break the cycle of offending and imprisonment, by establishing a new type of reformatory. This would differ from existing institutions in being managed by central government (as distinct from private philanthropic bodies) and also in taking young criminals up to the age of twenty-one, including repeat offenders.

Opinion was divided. Using his chairmanship of the committee, Gladstone repeatedly cajoled and led witnesses to conjure up endorsements for the idea. And when he wrote up the report, he gave the scheme a quite insupportable prominence. It is interesting to note how opinion on the matter (and it did not amount to much) divided. With his deeply held belief in the superior management powers of central government, Edmund Du Cane, commenting from the sidelines of his forced retirement, had no trouble giving approval. A colleague in retirement, former Home Office Permanent Under Secretary Sir Godfrey Lushington, took the opposite view—perhaps in part because he had seen Du Cane in action for the better part of his professional career. He was distrustful of the existing reformatories, which for their own financial reasons, he suggested, unnecessarily prolonged confinement. The whole prospect of extended incarceration for the young, whatever it was called, dismayed him. "I do not like prisons much, but in some respects I prefer them to reformatories; that is to say, I would far rather send a lad of 17 or 18 to a comparatively brief term of imprisonment than I would shut him up in a reformatory between 18 and 21." He also disputed the naive belief that a change of name would make a difference in the way the prisoners and society saw the proposed institutions; the same stigma would attach to a government-run reformatory as to a prison, he asserted. Even though the private reformatories claimed they were not penal, they could not help being so. He added, "I think they are a great deal too much so."

But the Borstal idea won out. (The name came from the village in Kent where the scheme got its first full-scale trial.) Ten years later Herbert Gladstone became home secretary and immediately ordered work to begin on the unimplemented recommendations of his committee. Among these was the government reformatory, which in the meantime had been proceeding on a limited trial basis. The results were deemed to be promising, and Gladstone's enthusiasm was undimmed. In 1908 Borstal institutions were put on a statutory footing.

The novel feature of the new measure was the indeterminant sentence (although Americans had been using it for more than thirty years, at New York's Elmira Reformatory). Criminals age sixteen to twenty-one, convicted of offenses for which they could be sent to penal servitude or to imprisonment, might instead be sent to a Borstal for between one and three years. The Prison Commission, which administered the Borstals, could release on license at any time after six months (or three months for girls) and could also recall for misbehavior.

Whatever their purposes and structure of management, the success of most organizations, and especially those that deliver services, will be determined by the spirit in which they conduct their affairs. An ability to inspire enthusiasm within and build support without is critical. Borstals, and through them the prison system, were greatly affected in these ways by Alexander Paterson, who in 1922 became a prison commissioner. Paterson was never chairman, but for the following quarter-century he was the leading light of the Prison Commission and proved to be one of that very select group who might be described as genuine innovators. Drawing on an experience of social work going back to his undergraduate days at Oxford, Paterson refashioned the Borstal system for the new generation, just then coming into power, whose social ideas had been traumatized by World War I. With a showman's flair, Paterson promoted the Borstal as a form of social service for the middle classes, and he won solid support from political leaders and also from the communities in which the Borstals were located.

For the military type of training, followed in the early Borstals, Paterson substituted delegated authority and encouragement of personal responsibility. This device had been at the heart of the ethos of the English public school (i.e., private boarding school) since the middle of the nineteenth century. One of his aphorisms showed the transformation he sought: "You cannot train lads for freedom in an atmosphere of captivity and repression." (The term "lad" was Paterson's preference; it was later revealingly replaced by the bureaucratic "trainee.") By being given more responsibility in the institution, the lads could make more decisions. It was only by making their own decisions, Paterson believed, that people could change: this could not be imposed, only offered and encouraged.

The methods and style that Paterson introduced now seem jejune. On the public school model, cellblocks were designated as "houses" by giving names to the various cellblocks. Institutional loyalty was cultivated through interhouse sports, house-based recreational and social activities, and distinctive colors. In keeping with the formula, each house had a housemaster, who was told that he was expected to work long hours for little pay and to take a close interest in the lads. All staff wore civilian clothes, and subordinates were also encouraged to get to know the lads individually. This now seems unexceptional, but it was thought revolutionary in the 1920s, when prison officers, under pain of disciplinary proceedings, were forbidden to speak to prisoners except to issue orders. The introduction of the post of matron, to oversee housekeeping and to provide a softening, feminine influence, was another indication of how closely Paterson stuck to the public school design.

As the Borstals gained experience and public esteem, Paterson's colleagues on the Prison Commission agreed to allow experiments. Cross-country walks and camping were started in 1924 and were immediately successful. No one ran away, and there were visits of endorsement and support from senior officials, including the home secretary. These experiments culminated in a long march in 1930, which became one of the high points of Borstal history. Led by the charismatic Borstal governor Bill Llewellin, a group of staff and boys marched 150 miles across the country, from Feltham to Lowdham Grange, where they took over a country estate as a new Borstal and constructed further accommodation.

Success and public esteem peaked between the wars. The Borstal formula seemed to work, and innovation and success were self-propelling. Because the Borstals were part of the Prison Commission, it was easy to move staff from a Borstal into an adult prison and vice versa. In the mid-1920s, for example, the newly recruited deputy-governor of Rochester Borstal (i.e., the original Borstal), Major Benjamin Grew, was moved after his first three years of service to Dartmoor prison, a convict establishment with a fearsome reputation for toughness and brutality. By such transfers, the prison commissioners sought to change the spirit of their service. Borstals were training grounds for staff, as much as for inmates.

The Borstal notion—training prisoners through personal relations, trust, and responsibility—gradually had an impact on the prison system as a whole. The extent and the depth of that influence are hard to gauge. An impressive amount of commitment and esprit de corps was achieved, and housemasters rose to senior positions in the adult system. But there was another side. A prison, to paraphrase Lushington, is a prison. Subordinate staff could be hard to win for a reformatory approach to imprisonment, especially one based on the subtleties of personal relations, and the keenest of expectations and highest of hopes faltered when faced by institutional inertia and the repressive miasma of the Victorian prisons. And although the movement of housemasters into the prison system was supposed to lead to a permeation of Borstal values and methods, the converse could happen, and idealistic young men could become cynics and timeservers.

Two Borstal elements were, however, transplanted into the adult system, with long-lasting effects. In 1936 the first minimum-security (open) prison was established at New Hall, near Wakefield. This initiated other open prisons and also marked the realization that the prison populations could (and should) be accommodated in a variety of security settings. In turn, this meant acceptance of the likelihood that some prisoners would abscond. Commissioners, politicians, and the public proved willing to take the risk, and it was rare that anything very serious occurred during one of these escapades.

The other successful transplant was the housemaster. Renamed assistant governors, these officials were treated as governors in training and were given responsibility for a section of an adult prison. As in the Borstal, they were expected to know and assist their prisoners. Casework—helping with a prisoner's work, family, social, and personal problems—thus came to be undertaken during a sentence, instead of being left to the discharged prisoners' aid societies, as before. The whole period in prison could be seen as a preparation for release and resettlement. And dealing with a prisoner "in the round" inevitably had some humanizing effects on policy and administration.

The spirit of Borstal faltered after 1945. Success rates (as measured by reconvictions) declined. Paterson died in 1947, and although many ardent believers in the system remained—in prisons, politics, and the community—there were among them no innovators capable of adapting the basic doctrine and Edwardian techniques to meet the needs and opportunities of the times. A whole generation of senior prison officials was Borstal trained. This preserved Borstal language and methods but could not regenerate confidence and vigor. Within a few years of the end of the war, moreover, penal priorities began to be driven by steep increases in crime and prison numbers. The administration of Margaret Thatcher acted unimaginatively, perhaps, but not particularly ideologically when, in 1982, it formally abolished the Borstal system: this was simply a long-delayed interment. The Borstal was replaced by a determinate sentence of imprisonment for young people. Euphemisms are ubiquitous—de rigueur—in this field, and the new-old prison hid shyly under the appellation "Youth Custody."

Postwar Developments

The Borstal restatement of reformatory imprisonment, and attempts to restrict the use of imprisonment, had an unintended consequence. Since the mid-Victorian years, various steps had been taken toward a lesser use of imprisonment—easier bail, probation, time to pay fines, a reduction in time to be served for a partial payment of fines, reformatories for juveniles, curtailment of imprisonment for debt, and more facilities for the insane and for habitual drunkards. These diversionary measures made it easier to treat the imprisoned residue as a hard core, unequivocally deserving of punishment. In 1928, for example, Home Secretary Sir William Joynson-Hicks described Dartmoor convict prison as "the cesspool of English humanity." He went on, "I suppose there must be some residuum which no training or help will ever improve." In itself, and in its influence on the adult prisons, the Borstal represented the opposite view and resurrected the possibility (buried in the collapse of the penitentiaries in the late 1840s) of reformatory imprisonment. The combination of the two apparently contradictory tendencies—one promoting incapacitation, the other reform—contributed to a lengthening of sentences. Neither for deterrence nor for reform was the short sentence acceptable. This convergence constituted one of the elements in the English prison crowding crisis, which became acute in the 1970s and 1980s and with which the country is still wrestling.

Alexander Paterson was influential across the whole range of penal measures. He and his colleagues drew on their ideas, experience, and discussions to frame comprehensive legislation on punishment in 1938. The measure was deferred by war but reappeared as the Criminal Justice Act of 1948. This removed some of the last vestiges of the old dual system of imprisonment, by formally abolishing penal servitude. The division of imprisonment into hard labor, without hard labor, and various classes of misdemeanants was also discontinued. Flogging, as a prison punishment, had been on the verge of abolition fifty years before, when the 1898 Prisons Bill was before Parliament, but it survived even in the 1948 act and was not discontinued until 1967.

Other types of sentences and new institutions were established. Some were half-baked, conceived out of a theory or even a desire for symmetry and launched without a jot of evidence to support their underlying assumptions. Crude deterrence made a comeback, in a form that may have coaxed a smile from Du Cane's ghost. Highly regimented, overtly and actively punitive youth prisons were established and misleadingly called detention centers. These were intended to subject boys (and, halfheartedly, some girls) who were thought to be on the verge of a custodial career to a last-chance "short sharp shock"—another idea recently and ahistorically introduced into the United States, under the wholesome and nostalgic name of "boot camp."

An idea that had great practical potential for changing the English prison system, and possibly for making it more just, appeared in the 1938 draft bill but did not find its way into the 1948 act. This was a proposal to establish completely separate institutions for pretrial prisoners. These would be custodial but nonpenal institutions. Unfortunately, in 1948 the country was still digging itself out of the debris of total war and had no funds or sympathy to spare for unconvicted detainees. Thick skins and short purses ever since have ensured that English pretrial prisoners were treated worse than they were for virtually all of Victoria's reign and much worse than their fellows who were convicted and sentenced. The spectacle of three prisoners crammed into a cell, which was built a hundred years ago to house one and from which the sanitary facilities originally provided had been removed, and of a regime that allowed them out of this disgusting confinement for only one hour a day was a disgrace to a civilized country. Several parliamentary committees and politicians affected shock at these conditions, but relief was long delayed and in places is still awaited.

In 1963 the Prison Commission was abolished, and the management of the prisons became the direct responsibility of the Prison Department of the Home Office. One part of the Prison Commission dated to 1850, when the Directors of Convict Prisons was established to give unified control over central government's several convict prisons. When local prisons were nationalized in 1877, the Prison Commission was established to manage them. The headship of both organizations was then held by Sir Edmund Du Cane, until 1895. Home Office civil servants took an increasingly active role in mediating the relationship between these two bodies and the home secretary. After Du Cane's departure, the Directors of Convict Prisons was fully assimilated into the Prison Commission, although the joint title continued to be used.

Over the years, Home Office civil servants continued to build a corporate experience in prison management. The elements of independence and the direct access to the home secretary, together with the inconvenience arising from another layer of management, became unacceptable—thus the 1963 decision to abolish the Prison Commission. Readers who have borne with the twists and turns so far will realize that penal thought and policy exemplify, par excellence, the truth that all ideas endlessly circulate. A review of prison service management, published at the end of 1991, recommended what amounts to the reestablishment of the Prison Commission—1990s style, of course.

Progress and Lessons Learned?

It is difficult to assess the progress that occurred in the hundred years between the Carnarvon Committee of 1863 and the mid-1960s, not least because this century has taught us to be extremely careful in our use of the word *progress*. Perhaps the best way to end this brief excursion is to look at the daily life of the prisoner in the 1860s and then of his counterpart in the 1960s.

In the 1860s we would occasionally have found, in many local prisons, people who were not convicted of a criminal or shameful offense but who had been given the status of first-class misdemeanant by the magistrate or judge. Life for such a prisoner usually involved no more than the loss of liberty. He wore his own clothes, could order food from an outside kitchen and a ration of beer from an inn, and had a very liberal allowance of visitors and letters. He could pay to have an ordinary prisoner clean his cell. This category of imprisonment no longer existed by the 1960s. A criminal offense was just that, irrespective of motive and context. The direct-action campaigner against nuclear weapons or animal cruelty would be treated in exactly the same way as a person who robbed a pensioner or committed some disgusting act of personal violence.

The unconvicted prisoner of the 1860s was usually allowed to provide himself with food, clothing, bedding, and any other necessities or to have the prison allowance. He had few restraints on visits or letters. By the 1960s these entitlements for the unconvicted prisoner had shrunk to the right to buy cooked food from outside the prison and to receive a liberal allowance of visits and letters. Any apparent advantages that the pretrial detainee had over the convicted prisoner would largely have been nullified because of his other conditions of confinement. Solitude would have been insisted on in 1860, but in 1960 the pretrial detainee would very likely have to share that same Victorian cell (minus its toilet) with two other prisoners. By design, or by pressure of work, his privileged free-world food would probably be cold by the time it arrived; and it could hardly be appetizing to eat the food on a bunk bed, in an atmosphere permeated with body and waste smells.

The 1860s debtor had much the same regime as the first-class misdemeanant, except that he had the additional privilege of use of a dayroom, in which he could mix with the other civil prisoners. He could also, within reason, follow his trade and retain the whole of his earnings. By the 1960s, there were very few civil prisoners left, and their regime was that of the pretrial detainee. From the time of the Gladstone Committee on, their privileges had been restricted, and in the official view they were little better than criminals.

The convicted and short-sentence petty criminal prisoner of the 1860s undoubtedly underwent hard punishment in most jurisdictions. If pronounced fit by the prison surgeon, he would perform hard labor on the treadwheel or crank for not less than six hours a day or more than ten. For the balance of the day (and gaslight was welcomed as a means of extending the hours of punishment) he toiled alone in his cell at second-class hard labor—usually picking oakum (teasing apart "junk," as the pieces of tar-encrusted rope were called). His separation would be as absolute as practicality would allow and his diet barely enough to keep him alive. He would sleep on a board, receive no visits or letters, and have only the Bible to read.

The convicted local prisoner of the 1960s would very likely share a cell and would have work of the simplest kind—boring but certainly not arduous. His diet would be considerably better than that of his predecessors and, apart from its starchy and institutional character, was not in any way penal. He had good access to books, newspapers, and magazines. Out of his earnings he could purchase indulgences such as tobacco, confectionery, and toiletries. Several forms of recreation would be available, from physical education to television. But the relatively free association of prisoners exposed the weak and unpopular to bullying and extortion (though not at this time to the appalling extent prevailing in many big American jails and prisons). A social worker would be available to deal with problems affecting his release, helping to find him employment and, if necessary, accommodation. Except for the sordid conditions of confinement, and possible fear of his companions, his lot in prison was definitely better than it would have been a hundred years previously, but he would serve several months rather than days or weeks.

The convicted felon of the 1860s had a minimum sentence of three years to serve. His day would depend on his stage and the privileges it conferred. Once past his nine months of separate confinement, he was put to heavy manual work, in a public works prison. Older or unfit convicts, or educated prisoners, might be assigned to some form of institutional maintenance, such as cleaning, working in the kitchen or library, or clerking for the chaplain. Communications with the free world would also depend on his stage, but they would be few and the visits of short duration, conducted under unpleasant, degrading, and restrictive conditions. At all times he would be under close command. Clothing had been carefully designed to be uncomfortable and to humiliate, as were the regulations concerning his appearance. Hair was cut to the "convict's crop"; faces were covered with stubble, since prisoners were not permitted a razor, and facial hair was removed with clippers. His clothing, boots, and all institutional property were marked with the government's broad arrow.

In the strict sense of penal servitude, there were no convicts by the 1960s; their equivalents were the long-term prisoners. Stages, with their associated privileges, had been abolished, and the quality of institutional life was determined by one's security classification. Those considered to be the greatest risks lived in the close confines of a very secure section of a prison and were subject to numerous restrictions and constant surveillance. Infamous prisoners, such as informers and sex offenders, lived in a prison within a prison, always kept apart and always guarded, lest they be attacked. Should offense and record place a prisoner at the opposite end of the security classification scale, his life would be almost indistinguishable from that of the free citizen in a residential institution. Twice a day he would have to answer roll call. He might sleep in a dormitory but could probably aspire to a room to which he had the key. He would have to work at his assigned task—anything from printing to pig-keeping—and would constantly be reminded of his position subordinate to the staff. He could be in part-time or even full-time education in the prison and would receive counseling and social-work support. Home leave was possible, with a good prison record and reasonable proximity to release. Letters and visits were liberally granted, and food was good enough that the staff regularly paid for and ate it as well.

What lessons have been learned from these one hundred years of imprisonment?

Some are banal, such as the periodic dangerousness, even wickedness, of those who take their own good intentions as sufficient warrant for action. Four years before he himself entered Pentonville and Reading prisons, Oscar Wilde uncannily drew this lesson, which he fashioned into one of the paradoxes that so delighted him: "As one reads history . . . one is absolutely sickened not by the crimes the wicked have committed, but by the punishments the good have inflicted." Another lesson at this grand level—and who knows whether we are not just frightening ourselves—is the seemingly inexorable gathering of all power into the center, despite the terrible lessons of the twentieth century. Other implications of prison history during this period are shocking, but perhaps less worrisome because we can hope to avoid their repetition—the occasions on which personal, trivial, and even accidental considerations moved the levers of public policy.

But surely it is to the prisoners and their keepers that we must inevitably return. *Pace* Wilde, the wickedness of both is abundantly obvious in this history, as are their occasionally displayed virtues of endurance, courage, and compassion. The exhausted vagrant who so fruitlessly worked the handle of his cell crank, or trod the wheel until his breath quickened and his pores opened, marked his own shame and degradation and, just as surely, that of the politicians, reformers, and officials whose imagination and human sympathy had so failed him. The warder who risked his tiny wage and good name to give a morsel to a child prisoner did something to redeem the just purposes of punishment. Churchill's famous 1910 admonition to the House of Commons, one of many such declarations made in that place by those who have known imprisonment, remains the best justification for the study of penal history: "The mood and temper of the public in regard to the treatment of crime and criminals is one of the most unfailing tests of the civilization of any country." Where may we rank ourselves?

Bibliographic Note

A good though "progressivist" and certainly statist overview may still be had in Sidney Webb and Beatrice Webb's *English Prisons under Local Government* (London: Longmans, Green, 1922; reprint, London: Cass, 1963). Writing in the same tradition, but with more emphasis on liberal values, Sir Leon Radzinowicz and Roger Hood take the story up to 1912, with great virtuosity, unraveling numerous strands of penal policy and skillfully placing imprisonment in its broader setting in *A History of English Criminal Law*, vol. 5 (London: Stevens, 1986). They do not, however, deal with the local prisons. The first volume of my own *History of English Prison Administration* (London: Routledge and Kegan Paul, 1981) is a study of convict and local imprisonment up to 1877, with a second volume—*English Local Prisons 1860 to 1900: "Next Only to Death"* (London: Routledge, 1994)—concentrating on the local prisons.

Readers will find Christopher Harding et al., *Imprisonment in England and Wales: A Concise History* (London: Croom Helm, 1985), exactly what it claims to be and probably the most helpful short guide and overview available. W. J. Forsythe has also produced two valuable and concise books. The first is *The Reform of Prisoners, 1830–1900* (London: Croom Helm, 1987), and the most recent is *Penal Discipline, Reformatory Projects, and the English Prison Commission, 1895–1939* (Exeter, England: University of Exeter Press, 1990). David Garland's *Punishment and Welfare: A History of Penal Strategies* (Aldershot, England: Gower, 1985) is a much acclaimed attempt to place penal history into a broader context of social policy and control.

Senior prison administrators have written various histories and biographical accounts of their systems of imprisonment. Given his many duties, it is impressive that Sir Edmund Du Cane was such a prolific contributor to contemporary journals. Most of his articles can be located through the *Wellesley Index to Victorian Periodicals*. Early in his career he wrote a booklet on penal servitude, *An Account of the Manner in Which Sentences of Penal Servitude Are Carried Out in England* (London: Convict Service, 1872). The work is timid, turgid, and clumsily put together. Better and more substantial, but still heavy-footed, is *The Punishment and Prevention of Crime* (London: Macmillan, 1885). Sir Evelyn Ruggles-Brise, the next English prison supremo, provides an attenuated view of prison history, and a flattering account of progress during his own stewardship, in *The English Prison System* (London: Macmillan, 1921). Another top administrator, Sir Lionel Fox, produced *The Modern English Prison* (London: George Routledge and Sons, 1932) and *The English Prison and Borstal Systems* (London: Routledge and Kegan Paul, 1952). Since then, the very highest Prison Department officials seem to have foresworn publication. This is regrettable, but perhaps in recent years life at the higher levels of prison management has not been the stuff of stirring reminiscences.

Sir Alexander Paterson never produced a major work on imprisonment, but the selection of his writings edited by S. K. Ruck (*Paterson on Prisons* [London: Frederick Muller, 1951]) gives a good flavor of the man. Sir Rupert Cross, a distinguished lawyer, compared Paterson and his predecessors in *Punishment, Prison, and the Public: An Assessment of Penal Reform in Twentieth Century England by an Armchair Penologist* (London: Stevens, 1971). Victor Bailey has produced a scholarly and substantial account of interwar penal policy toward juveniles in *Delinquency and Citizenship: Reclaiming the Young Offender, 1914–1948* (Oxford: Oxford University Press, 1987).

Prison governors, fortunately, have been less shy about publication than their more exalted Home Office brethren—and it is obvious that life with prisoners generally produces better anecdotes. Gerald Clayton was born in Chatham convict prison, where his father was deputy governor in the 1880s. He followed in the family trade, starting as deputy governor at Portland convict prison in January 1920 and retiring just before the 1948 Criminal Justice Act came into effect. See Gerald Clayton, *The Wall Is Strong* (London: John Long, 1958).

Benjamin Grew was recruited by Alexander Paterson two years after Clayton, and the two men leapfrogged in their postings. Grew also published his memoir, *Prison Governor*, in 1958 (London: Herbert Jenkins). This book is particularly useful for its account of the various postwar ameliorations and experiments in the regime of the prisons. One of Alexander Paterson's most effective disciples, who remained a major influence in the English prisons until the early 1960s, was John Vidler. His memoir (*If Freedom Fail* [London: Macmillan, 1964]) should be read by all who want to understand what drove that generation of reform-minded prison officials. The very different prison world of women is the subject of Joanna Kelley's *When the Gates Shut* (London: Longmans, 1967).

Prisoners have produced many instructive, moving, and entertaining memoirs. *Five Years Penal Servitude,* by "One Who Has Endured It" (London: R. Bentley, 1878), is well-written and informative, as is the 1883 *Her Majesty's Prisons: Their Effects and Defects,* by another anonymous (but presumably unrelated) author, "One Who Has Tried Them" (London: Sampson, Low, 1881). As a variation on "One Who . . . ," we have "No 7," who wrote *Twenty-five Years in Seventeen Prisons* (London: F. E. Robinson and Co., 1903). Michael Davitt was an Irish patriot who suffered a lengthy and particularly brutal imprisonment for his part in a Fenian conspiracy. His memoirs, *Leaves from a Prison Diary; or, Lectures to a "Solitary" Audience,* 2 vols. (London: Chapman and Hall, 1885), are impressive for their lack of bitterness and many astute observations on crime, punishment, and his fellow convicts.

The socialite Constance Lytton was determined to go to prison for her female suffragist activities. The authorities found her high political and social connections an embarrassment and tried to keep her out; this enraged her, and with a suitable disguise she managed to get convicted and to do her time. Her story is given in Constance Lytton and Jane Warton, *Prisons and Prisoners: Some Personal Experiences* (London: W. Heinemann, 1914). A more recent prisoner's account of female imprisonment is given by Jane Buxton and Margaret Turner in *Gate Fever* (London: Cresset, 1962).

Stephen Hobhouse and Fenner Brockway were imprisoned for their pacifist beliefs and activities during World War I, and three of their books are worth attention. *English Prisons To-day: Being the Report of the Prison System Enquiry Committee* (London: Longmans, Green, 1922) is a massive description and policy analysis by both men. Stephen Hobhouse's *Forty Years* (London: James Clarke and Co., 1951) has a chapter on his imprisonment and another on the writing of *English Prisons To-day*. Fenner Brockway's *Inside the Left: Thirty Years of Platform, Press, Prison, and Parliament* (London: George Allen and Unwin, 1942) is also valuable.

Among postwar memoirs, I most like Brendan Behan's *Borstal Boy* (London: Hutchinson, 1958), though it is probably more a work of art than a strictly factual account of the playwright's imprisonment in the 1940s. One of the best, least sentimental, and most impressive accounts of life imprisonment in the 1950s and 1960s is given by "Zeno" in his *Life* (London: Macmillan, 1968). Peter Wildeblood was imprisoned for homosexual offenses, in the days when the law thought that was sensible, and his *Against the Law* (London: Weidenfeld and Nicolson, 1955) is an eloquent account of imprisonment in postwar England.

Philip Priestley is heavily addicted to prison memoirs and shares the fruits of his enthusiasm and expertise in two very useful anthologies: *Victorian Prison Lives: English Prison Biography, 1830–1914* (London: Methuen, 1985) and, dealing with the later years, *Jail Journeys: The English Prison Experience since 1918, Modern Prison Writings* (London: Routledge, 1989). A book that started off as the first sociological account of an English prison and that provoked much controversy and interest at the time of its publication in 1963 has now, with the passage of time, itself become an important part of prison history: Terence Morris and Pauline Morris's *Pentonville* (London: Routledge and Kegan Paul).

Lastly, there are the various parliamentary and official papers. Both the Carnarvon Committee of 1863 and the Gladstone Committee of 1894–95 had axes to grind, selected their witnesses for effect, and produced tendentious reports. Their minutes of evidence nevertheless offer valuable insights into contemporary practices and attitudes. Two inquiries into penal servitude (1871 and 1878) give a similar quantity and quality of information. These and numerous other committees, and a great variety of documents touching on English prison history, such as the annual reports of the Commissioners, the Inspectors, and the Directors of Convict Prisons, may be located by consulting the index to the British Sessional Papers. Finally, because the activities of members of the House of Commons sometimes landed them in prison, their speeches and the interventions of radicals, socialists, Irish Nationalists, and political eccentrics are instructive on prison matters (as indeed on many other subjects) and are well worth reading, especially for the years 1880–1920. These are available in *Hansard,* which has excellent running indexes.

CHAPTER SIX

The Failure of Reform
United States, 1865–1965

Edgardo Rotman

In 1867, Enoch Wines and Theodore Dwight, having concluded an extensive survey of American prisons, published a monumental report describing the flaws of the existing system and proposing remedies for it. One hundred years later, the President's Commission for Law Enforcement and Administration of Justice published its own extensive survey, no less discontented with the state of affairs and no less enthusiastic about the prospect for reforms. Indeed, over the hundred years that elapsed between these two reports, other would-be reform groups proposed their own initiatives, sharing a despair about ongoing problems, a lofty idealism, and a dogged optimism that prisons could be improved. The cycle seems never ending: exposés, reports, proposals, then more exposés.

Although the fate of reform efforts is distressingly similar—each generation provides its successor with scandals to correct—the models that would-be reformers set forth over the period 1865–1965 frequently differed one from the other. The original design of the prison in pre–Civil War America, as we have seen, called for the systematic isolation of the inmate both from fellow prisoners and from the society at large. In this way, prisoners would be shielded from contaminating influences, allowing the influence of religion, steady discipline, and regular work to transform unruly criminals into law-abiding citizens. After 1865, the emphasis on seclusion and isolation was relaxed, and a gradual liberalization took hold, providing incentives as well as deterrents to shape obedient behavior. By the opening decades of the twentieth century, a frankly therapeutic model was in effect: offenders were "sick" and were to be "cured" of their criminality in a setting that approximated, as far as possible, a normal society. During the same period, a parallel social learning model of prison reform became popular. Crime was the result of learned behavior, and rehabilitation programs in a prison setting were to compensate for the inadequate socialization that followed family breakup or neglect. The prison was to become a problem-solving community.

None of these models, however attractive conceptually, altered the fundamental reali-ties of prison life. Most of the experiments that constitute the history of prison reform were isolated, pioneering undertakings at odds with a prevailing repressive system of punishment. The concrete manifestations of the rehabilitative idea thus were only a small factor in the overall field of crime control. The reform programs do testify to the benevolent impulses of a number of would-be innovators, but the very existence of the rhetoric of reform and the reality of a few limited successes in particular institutions may well have provided an excuse to avoid wider and more fundamental changes. In effect, the language of rehabilitation legitimated a prison system that was all too commonly abusive. As a result, the core theme of the one-hundred-year history of American prisons after 1865 portrays a grim reality and a persistent but ultimately unsuccessful effort to ameliorate it.

The State of the Prison, 1865–1900

By 1865, the elements of the original penitentiary design, based on regimentation, isolation, religious conversion, and steady labor, had been subverted by a pervasive overcrowding, corruption, and cruelty. Prisoners were often living three and four to a cell designed for one, and prison discipline was medieval-like in character, with bizarre and brutal punishments commonplace in state institutions. Wardens did not so much deny this awful reality as explain it away, attributing most of the blame not to those who administered the system but to those who experienced it. Because the prisons were filled with immigrants who were ostensibly hardened to a life in crime and impervious to American traditions, those in charge had no choice but to rule over inmates with an iron hand. In fact, the closing decades of the nineteenth century were the dark ages for America's prisons.

The adult incarcerative facilities of the United States in the immediate post–Civil War period consisted of state prisons, county jails, and prisons of an intermediate grade between the state prisons and the county jails. State prisons confined sentenced convicts; county jails held people arrested and awaiting trial, along with those awaiting transfer to a state prison or serving out relatively short sentences. In the intermediate prisons, called houses of correction or workhouses or bridewells, prisoners were generally guilty of lesser crimes (such as vagrancy) and were required to perform menial labor.

In organizational terms, most state prisons in the post–Civil War decades described themselves as operating according to the principles of the Auburn, not the Pennsylvania, system. Auburn, as originally designed in the 1830s, isolated prisoners at night but placed them into congregate workshops under rules of silence during the day; Pennsylvania, on the other hand, isolated the prisoners for twenty-four hours a day, providing them with tools and raw materials for labor in their cells. The Pennsylvania system did persist, albeit in attenuated fashion, in Philadelphia's Cherry Hill penitentiary. Almost everywhere else, prisons followed the Auburn plan, mostly because common workshops seemed to make prison labor more profitable. But a debate that had once divided penal experts into warring camps had now become almost irrelevant. When inmates were packed two or three into a cell designed for one, it made no sense to talk about the reformatory impact of silence or isolation.

The design of prisons in the post–Civil War period was not driven by ideas about penal theory but by budgets, by how to confine the largest number of inmates at the lowest possible cost. Small cells within multitiered blocks were the common answer, but the cells were so small as to endanger the physical health, as well as the psychological well-being, of the inmates. The cells in the Connecticut state prison at Whethersfield, for example, were seven feet long, three and a quarter feet wide, and about seven feet high. In the Michigan state prison at Jackson the cells were three and a half feet wide, six and a half feet long, and seven feet high. At Charlestown Prison near Boston, which was considered a model prison at the time, the cells were eight and a half feet long, four and three-quarters feet wide, and seven and two-thirds feet high. In addition, large windows admitted much more light than in the average Auburn system cell.

The administration of the prisons was as inadequate as the physical structures. Wardens were generally more interested in holding on to their jobs than in accomplishing anything more than keeping inmates quiet and secure. Wherever possible, wardens relied on guards and other line staff to accomplish these goals, giving them practically unlimited power over inmates' bodies and lives.

No central state authority exerted general power of control and direction over the particular prisons. Some states, like Massachusetts and New York, had boards and agencies that were empowered to visit the prisons and to issue recommendations. But even these boards were little more than advisory, and if they did offer findings on punishments or proposals for change, they had no power of enforcement. Moreover, most board staffs were part-time workers with no expertise or commitment. In effect, the administration of the prisons was left to individual superintendents.

Whereas most state prisons were grossly deficient in their operations, conditions in the county jails were even more deplorable. The overcrowding was severe, the filth awful, the ventilation primitive, and the food scanty. Not even the most rudimentary classification of inmates existed, so that the old mixed with the young, the hardened criminals with the first offenders. The jails were unable to provide opportunities for work or for education. That a majority of the inmates were presumed innocent—that is, were awaiting trial and as yet guilty of nothing—made the circumstances all the more scandalous. There were also numerous police lockups, also called station houses or guardhouses, where inmates typically remained for a few hours after their arrest until being brought before a judge. These lockups were so miserable that the jail might actually have seemed a relief.

The Wines and Dwight Report

Despite the many inadequacies of American prisons and despite the novelty of the institutions—most of the prisons were no more than thirty years old—very few observers, whether they belonged to reform societies or to state legislatures, were ready to abandon a system of incarceration. The more common aim was to improve the prisons. In part, the insistence of reform reflected a belief that specific improvements would make incarceration work better; in part too, it appeared that the most likely alternative to punishment by confinement would be a return to corporal and capital punishment, which was unacceptable to well-meaning citizens intent on doing good. But in part too,

1865 seemed an especially propitious moment to achieve far-reaching changes. With the sectional conflict resolved and a spirit of optimism about the prospects for national development widespread, a new departure for criminal justice policies seemed necessary and feasible.

With this outlook in mind, the New York Prison Association commissioned Enoch Cobb Wines and Theodore Dwight to conduct a nationwide survey and evaluation of penal methods. After visiting penitentiaries and houses of correction in eighteen states and several institutions in Canada and collecting seventy bound volumes of documents, they wrote their *Report on the Prisons and Reformatories of the United States and Canada.* Theirs was a forceful call for prison reform, comparable to the renowned report written in 1777 by John Howard for England and Wales.

Dwight was a noted lawyer and educator with a long history of concern for prisons. Wines represented a new type of professional penologist, interested in behavioral methodologies and scientific data but not without religious zeal. Wines and Dwight made a good team, and their 1867 report supported their conviction that the whole prison system needed "careful and judicious revision."

Their critical finding was that not one of the state prisons in the United States was seeking the reformation of its inmates as a primary goal or deploying efficient means to pursue reformation. More specifically, their pages were filled with a litany of shortcomings. They criticized the inadequacies of the physical plants, the lack of training of the staffs, and the absence of centralized state supervision of the systems. They strenuously objected to the regular reliance on corporal punishment for disciplinary purposes. Six of the states they investigated employed the punishment of the lash; New York used the yoke—putting inmates into a contraption that consisted of a heavy flat bar of iron five or six feet long with a center ring for the neck and wrist manacles. It also punished prisoners by "bucking": tying the wrists together, putting the arms over the bended knees, and forcing a stick under the knees and across the elbow joints. Wines and Dwight found such punishments "at once cruel and degrading, and would have them banished from all prisons."

The reform agenda that they laid out in the *Report on the Prisons* called for a variety of particular changes: enlarge the size of cells, train guards, set up state boards to inspect prisons, and so on. But they also had a larger vision for reform: prisons should prepare inmates for release by allowing them to demonstrate and earn their advance toward freedom by moving through progressively liberal stages of discipline. This reformative methodology was inspired by the bold experiment carried out in 1840 by Captain Alexander Maconochie in the Australian colony of Norfolk Island and by its development in Ireland by Sir Walter Crofton in 1854. It became the rallying cry for American reformers, endorsed not only by Wines and Dwight but also by the resolution of the National Congress of Penitentiary and Reformatory Discipline held in Cincinnati in 1870.

This congress declared, "Neither in the United States nor in Europe, as a general thing, has the problem of reforming the criminal yet been resolved." The majority of inmates still left the prison "hardened and dangerous." Therefore the congress stated, "Our aims and our methods need to be changed. [In the first instance,] the prisoner's self-respect should be cultivated to the utmost, and every effort made to give back to him his manhood." The inherited system of isolation, lockstep, and striped uniforms was now perceived as humiliating and deleterious to the reform effort, in effect robbing inmates of their manhood.

Turning this theory into practice, the congress explained, required that "the prisoner's destiny should be placed, measurably, in his own hands; he must be . . . able through his own exertions to continually better his own condition. A regulated self-interest should be brought into play." So the convention framed its Sixth Principle: "Since hope is a more potent agent than fear, it should be made an ever-present force in the mind of the prisoners, by a well devised and skilfully applied system of rewards for good conduct, industry and attention to learning. Rewards, more than punishments, are essential to every good prison system."

The rewards were to come through a revision of the existing sentencing system. Until the 1870s, sentencing in the United States fixed only a maximum penalty (European codes set a minimum and a maximum term of imprisonment) for each offense. Once a judge selected a particular sentence, it was immutable, and the convict was bound to serve it to completion. The only exception was a governor's pardon, which was sometimes used to partially reduce a prison term. What reformers like Wines and Dwight, as well as others such as Franklin Sanborn and Zebulon Brockway, wanted to substitute was an indeterminate sentencing, wherein the actual term to be served was not set down by the judge immediately after conviction but at a later date and with considerable range by another body, such as a parole board or other sentencing authority. Under this scheme, indeterminate sentences would provide inmates with incentives to participate in activities that were reformative, at least in the estimate of their organizers. Thus, the congress resolved that sentences should be limited only "by satisfactory proof of reformation."

The Elmira Reformatory

The ideas discussed at the Cincinnati congress received their most publicized translation into practice by Zebulon Brockway at the Elmira Reformatory in New York. The institution, which opened in 1876, became a model for other institutions and exerted a worldwide influence on prison reformers of the period. Brockway's system combined indeterminate sentencing and release on parole with an institutional commitment to educational programs. At Elmira, however, the indeterminacy of sentences was not absolute; inmates who did well could be released early, but no one had to serve more than the maximum sentence established in the criminal code.

At the core of the design for Elmira was an educational program that drew on the ideas and contributions of college professors, public school principals, and lawyers. The program included classroom coverage of general subjects, sports, religion, and military drill. For the less capable, Elmira offered vocational education in which tailor cutting, plumbing, telegraphy, and printing were taught. Indeed, it was the emphasis on education, either trade training or academic, that was the hallmark of Brockway's contribution to post–Civil War penology. He graded inmates according to their educational accomplishments and their work performance as well as their conduct. High marks earned eligibility for privileges and for release through parole; low marks brought penalties and longer periods of confinement.

But Elmira never did quite approximate a school. Brockway, on occasion, did allow guards to resort to physical punishment, and as a state investigation revealed in 1894, discipline at Elmira was not consistent with its proclaimed humane attitude. Indeed, there is good reason to believe that rhetoric and institutional realities diverged widely. Order was maintained at Elmira largely through the fear of severe corporal punishment, not through the promise of rewards for educational achievement or good behavior.

One reason Elmira did not live up to its promise was the grave difficulties it faced in carrying out a reformatory program under conditions of major overcrowding. By the 1890s, Elmira held two times as many inmates as it was designed for—which militated against effective rehabilitation programs as well as discipline. Moreover, the inmates were not the type that Brockway had expected. The institution had been intended for first offenders between sixteen and thirty-one years of age, but in practice recidivists always constituted one-third of the inmates. Brockway apparently could not control admissions; a program designed to keep the novice from entering a life of crime had to serve older and much more seasoned offenders.

Despite the shortfall in achieving its goals, Elmira inspired many imitators. During the 1890s, it was the model for institutions at Ionia in Michigan, Sherborn and Concord in Massachusetts, and Huntingdon in Pennsylvania, as well as at Saint Cloud in Minnesota, Pontiac in Illinois, Mansfield in Ohio, and Jeffersonville in Indiana. But most of these institutions confronted and failed to resolve the very same problems that affected Elmira. In the twenty-odd reformatories for men in the first decades of the twentieth century, the average age of inmates, their criminal records, and their length of time served were not substantially different from the age, records, and time served in regular, adult prisons. Indeed, the reformatory buildings resembled ordinary prisons both in design and in size, the labor system in both places involved less vocational training than buddy work, and disciplinary regimens were equally harsh. No wonder, then, that Sheldon Glueck and Eleanor Glueck, among the leading criminologists of the period, pronounced the reformatory experiment a failure.

Prison Conditions in the Late Nineteenth Century

The reformatory movement of the 1870s—as advanced in the 1870 congress or as administered in the state reformatories—did little to halt the deterioration of the country's prisons. Most prisons continued a dreary life of their own, unaffected by the ambitious proposals of the new reformers. Brutality and corruption were endemic; overcrowding and understaffing were also omnipresent. In such chaotic prison atmospheres, wardens often resorted to cruel and unusual forms of punishment to maintain their authority over the convicts. Despite statutory abolishment, corporal punishment to enforce institutional discipline continued to be a generalized practice for the rest of the century, mainly in the form of lashing.

Rudimentary educational programs, prison libraries, and the intercessions of official chaplains affected only an insignificant portion of the prison population. Various inmates' accounts of life in prison during the period describe the pernicious effects of enforced idleness, arbitrary punishments, and persistent overcrowding. But in 1890, even more so than in 1865, the high percentage of foreign-born and first-generation inmates, especially in industrial states, lessened the public reaction against the substandard prison conditions.

There were, it is true, some changes in prison administration after 1870. A number of states, including New York and Massachusetts, did centralize prison oversight in statewide commissions. Better methods of prisoner identification lent some weight to expanding parole on release. There was more use of grades and incentives to control behavior, with greater reliance on "good time" laws, which reduced, even if only slightly, the length of terms for obedient inmates. And there was some greater specialization among prisons. But these advances were too modest when compared with the inadequacies that remained.

The history of American prisons in the southern states is a glaring case in point. These institutions, in which blacks made up more than 75 percent of the inmates, took their inspiration from slavery. The result was a ruthless exploitation with a total disregard for prisoners' dignity and lives. The states leased prisoners to entrepreneurs who, having no ownership interest in them, exploited them even worse than slaves. During the day the prisoners, organized into chain gangs under the watch of armed (white) guards, typically built and repaired roads. In the southwestern states, prisoners were more commonly used on large farms or plantations. In Mississippi, practically all inmates were engaged in agricultural work. The farm at Parchmann, known as the Sunflower Farm, was a 16,000-acre spread, divided into twelve camps for men and one for women. All of them were surrounded by barbed-wire fences dotted with strategically placed guard posts. The buildings that housed the convicts in each camp were appropriately called cages. A peculiar feature of the Mississippi system made prison discipline even more harsh: surveillance was performed by prisoners—or trustees, as they were called—who were every bit as cruel and unyielding as the guards who were hired.

FROM THE PROGRESSIVE ERA TO WORLD WAR II

The Progressive Era was a period of extraordinary urban and industrial growth and of unprecedented social problems. The assimilation of immigrants and minorities into the industrial urban centers was particularly difficult to achieve, creating a deep anxiety about social order among many Americans. Some of them responded by advocating exclusionary policies, such as immigration restriction. But others sought answers in a paternalistic version of the state and in the articulation of a broad reform plan. These Progressive reformers shared a faith in government to carry out ambitious social undertakings and a faith in scientific achievements to resolve social and individual conflict.

Progressives' agenda for social reform included ambitious plans to transform the prison. Kate Richards O'Hare, an opponent of World War I who spent fourteen months at the Missouri penitentiary in Jefferson City in 1919 and 1920, vividly described some negative aspects of prison life. In her book *In Prison* (1923), she depicted the cell area as "very dirty and, in most essentials, shabby and unsanitary." She wrote, "Every crack and crevice of the cellhouse was full of vermin of every known sort, which no amount of scrubbing on the part of the women could permanently dislodge" (p. 63). Rats "overran the place in swarms, scampered over the dining tables, nibbled [at the food], played in [the] dishes, crept into bed, chewed up shoes and carried off everything not nailed down or hung far above their reach" (p. 65). The dining room was equally filthy; the walls were "streaked with grime," and the ceiling was covered with fifteen years' accumulation of dead flies. The inmates were segregated and seated at long wooden tables infested with cockroaches. "The dishes were of rusty battered tinware, the knives and forks of cast iron, and the spoons were non-existent. If a woman wished to use a spoon she was compelled to buy it with her own money and carry it about in the one pocket she possessed, along with her pocket handkerchief and other movable property." Health conditions were seriously neglected. No effort was made to separate inmates infected with contagious diseases, nor were disinfectants in use, with the consequence that all prisoners bathed in the same few tubs and frequently contacted highly contagious, even life-threatening diseases. O'Hare recounts a particularly gruesome incident in which she was ordered to bathe immediately after a women infected with syphilis, whom she characterized: "From her throat to her feet she was one mass of open sores dripping pus . . . with clothes so stiff from dried pus that they rattled when she walked. A women about whose neck live maggots had been seen working out of the filthy bandages" (p. 67). O'Hare was ultimately forced to feign taking a bath rather than risk becoming infected herself.

Joseph Fishman, in *Crucibles of Crime* (1923), reported another flaw of prison life: the development of drug addictions by inmates after their admission. Doctors at the parish prison in New Orleans and at the Kansas City Jail acknowledged the existence of widespread morphine addiction in the 1920s, facilitated by inventive smuggling schemes of the prisoners' friends. Drugs were often concealed in food—especially fruit—which was hollowed out and filled with illegal substances. In one famous story a jailer stuck a spoon into a large box of ice cream delivered to an inmate only to dig out a large package of morphine. Drugs were also sent in packages and were hidden in belts, in the hems of handkerchiefs, and in the heals of hollowed-out slippers. They were even placed in small amounts under the postage stamps of letters or in pockets made inside envelopes. Drug use by prisoners was not limited to morphine. According to the U.S. inspector of prisons, inmates would avail themselves of "any substance which [would] give them the desired kick or jolt, [including] cocaine, heroin, opium, yenshee (the residue of smoked opium) and in fact anything they can obtain which has any narcotic effect whatsoever." Some prisoners even went so far as to "eat the crust remaining in the bowl of a tobacco pipe after it had been used for a long time, to use bay rum from the prison barbershop, and even hashish from India" (p. 21).

In transforming criminal justice programs, Progressives relied heavily on the emerging principles of behavioral science. Confident that the key to deviant behavior lay in social and psychological causes, reformers insisted that an individualized design for the administration of criminal justice, a design responding to each offender's particular needs, would cure the offender and promote the good order of society. Under this banner, the field of penology became as much the territory for social workers, psychologists, and psychiatrists as lawyers.

The Psychotherapeutic Model of Prison Reform

At the turn of the century, psychiatric interpretations of social deviance began to assume a central role in criminology and policy making. The success of medicine in finding the causes of such diseases as tuberculosis and rabies gave a new prestige to the entire field; thus those who labored on its margins, such as criminologists and penologists, began to invoke medical language and concepts in their own areas. As a result, Progressives fully endorsed a medical or therapeutic model of rehabilitating inmates, on the assumption that criminal offenders suffered from some form of physical, mental, or social pathology.

Once crime had been diagnosed as an illness, it was logical to use the methods and language of medicine to "cure" offenders of their criminality. Indeed, the normal mechanisms of criminal law were inadequate to prevent recidivism. By 1926, sixty-seven prisons employed psychiatrists, and forty-five had psychologists. At the same time, of course, the ratio of professional to inmate (one psychiatrist or two psychologists per five hundred or one thousand cell institutions) was so small as to render the programs ineffective. No less important, therapeutic failure reflected just how little was actually known about the origins of deviant behavior or about how to respond to it in therapeutic fashion.

Nevertheless, however limited the effectiveness of the interventions, the ambitions and the language of the helping professions transformed the basic mechanisms of criminal justice. The opening of penology to psychiatrists and behavioral scientists spurred on the design and appeal of indeterminate sentencing statutes. Release from prison became the equivalent of release from a hospital. Just as no legislature would tell a doctor when to discharge a patient from a hospital as cured, so no legislature should tell a warden or any other prison official when to discharge an inmate as cured. The same discretion that the one enjoyed should belong to the other. In ideal terms, an offender found guilty of an offense—any offense, whether major or minor—should receive the same open-ended sentence: one day to life. It would be up to the prison officials, especially the warden and the parole board members, to determine where in that scheme of things the individual inmate belonged.

The limits and weaknesses of theory about criminal behavior did not hamper the application of the vocabulary of medical science to situations of purely punitive nature. The terms most frequently invoked in the context of criminal justice were "individualized treatment" and "case work." The term "clinical" was also frequently used in phrases such as "clinical method of reformation" or "clinical criminology." Despite the therapeutic pretense, prescriptions were in fact not very different from the old reformatory methods. Indeed, the therapeutic model of rehabilitation remained, during the first decades of the twentieth century, much more of a labeling than a curative instrument. So prisons in the Progressive Era picked up and extended the nineteenth-century practices of giving time off for good behavior and keeping troublemakers in for more of their sentences. The difference was that the "bad" prisoner was now the "maladjusted prisoner."

On the other hand, the new emphasis on diagnosis made classification a critical concern for the Progressive penal system. Classification according to psychological type did not lead to effective treatment. There were an insignificant number of qualified therapists on the prison staffs, a no less notable lack of well-designed programs, and at the same time, only a primitive therapeutic methodology. But although classification did not bring about effective treatment, it did revamp custodial practices. It became a practical device to segregate troublemakers and to create categories, within the prison system, that ranged from maximum to minimum security, depending on the degree of surveillance. Minimum security brought confinement in barracks or colonies in which rules rather than walls and turrets kept the inmates from escaping; honor farms might be freestanding (as at Allenwood in Pennsylvania) or attached to the main prisons (as at the Stateville and Menard Prisons in Illinois). Maximum security meant very secure cells and exercise yards and well-guarded walls. In effect, the classifications extended the range of incarcerative institutions, loosening up security at the one end and tightening it at the other. In this way, transfer to a minimum-security institution was the reward for good behavior in a maximum-security regime, which, in turn, justified harsher treatment for those classified as untreatable in the maximum-security setting. In short, classification became a powerful tool for institutional order.

Classification also fostered special consideration for mentally disabled offenders, segregating them from the rest of the prison population. A leading scholar at the time declared that what constituted a "defective delinquent" had no uniform meaning and that several more years of experimental work were needed before a clear understanding would emerge. But classification aimed at prisoners who were not considered insane but could not be classed as mentally normal. The first special institution for defective delinquents was opened at Napanoch, New York, in 1921. In 1922, a special department for the mentally defective was opened at the State Farm at Bridgewater, Massachusetts. In New York, until 1931, conviction was not a prerequisite for commitment as a defective; a charge and an arraignment for a crime were considered sufficient. In Massachusetts, a 1928 law allowed commitment as a defective delinquent for first offense if the court felt that the individual had a tendency to recidivism, even before conviction. In effect, the prevailing medical model that equated prisons and hospitals allowed commitment for an indefinite period of time, not on the basis of a criminal act but because of a state of mind.

The Social Learning Model: The Opening of the Prison to the Community

However often Progressive penologists invoked the hospital to justify broad discretion in sentencing practices, they took their design for the everyday routine of the prison not from the hospital itself but from the community. Reformers tried not only to reinforce offenders' bonds with the community but also to instill in them a sense of responsibility for their own conduct. The prison should be democratized so as to pave the way for the future reintegration of the inmate into a free society. This vision was best realized in Thomas Mott Osborne's attempt to introduce the concept of inmate self-government into the penitentiary. Osborne was inspired by the operation of the George Junior Republic, which sought to apply the idea of self-government to juvenile delinquents. The "Republic," located in Freeville, New York, held one hundred delinquent boys and half as many girls and tried, with some success, to incorporate such democratic practices as voting, officeholding, and peer participation in deciding guilt and punishment of those who broke its rules. Osborne had also participated in settlement house programs that had sought to Americanize immigrant newcomers and teach them the American way in government.

In 1913, Osborne became chairman of a commission for the reform of the New York penal system and set about applying the idea of self-government and self-support to adult inmates of the Auburn prison. His motto, borrowed from British Prime Minister W. E. Gladstone, was "It is liberty alone that fits men for liberty." The Mutual Welfare League, which Osborne established at Auburn, included a committee of forty-nine prisoners appointed by secret ballot among the prison's fourteen hundred inmates. This committee participated in the planning of disciplinary procedures, for which a special grievance court composed entirely of prisoners was created. In 1914 Osborne was appointed warden of Sing Sing Prison, where he organized another Mutual Welfare League. He was also a pioneer of the later anti-institutional approach, which replaced rigid and stultifying routines with a more varied prison day, including both a change in dress (putting away the stripes) and the introduction of recreation and movies. At least for a time, Osborne achieved a prison atmosphere in which the inmates could develop a sense of responsibility by trusting each other to exercise meaningful decision-making powers. Eventually, however, opposition from correctional officers and politicians brought about Osborne's departure and the collapse of his Mutual Welfare League in 1929.

Innovations in Prison Management: The Norfolk Prison Colony

Another outstanding example of the innovative prison based on the Progressive creed was the Norfolk Prison Colony in Massachusetts. The building of Norfolk began in 1927 as a way to alleviate overcrowding at the old Charlestown prison, which itself had been considered a model prison in the nineteenth century. Howard Gill, an economist, was in charge of overseeing the construction of the outside wall by convict laborers. The contact with these prisoner-laborers provoked in Gill an enthusiasm for rehabilitation and committed him to the idea of making Norfolk into the model reforming prison. Gill would apply the ideal Progressive medicine: individualized treatment based on psychological and sociological categories in an institution that should emulate as far as possible the atmosphere of the normal community.

Specifically, Gill's aim was to add new social, medical, psychological, and educational techniques to the traditional reformative, industrial, and religious instruction. The plan contemplated the classification of prisoners and their division into small groups of under fifty so as to manage inmates and their problems in small cohorts. Each group was to be housed and fed separately, under the supervision of its own special house-officer, and every man would have an individualized physical, mental, social, vocational, and avocational program. The groups would also be the organizing basis for the Norfolk Council, which operated on the principle of joint officer-inmate responsibility for the governance of the institution. As Gill concisely expressed it, the Norfolk system was neither an "honor system" nor "self-government" but was a system of cooperation between staff and inmates. The group system of housing and supervision promoted both individual programs for effective treatment and the development of social responsibility.

Gill, encouraged by the prominent criminologist Thorsten Sellin, kept a diary of his institution for research purposes. "The Diary of the State Colony" recorded daily activities at Norfolk over 1932 and 1933 as set down through interviews with and entries by the institutional staff. The pages offer a very special insight into the fate of a reform enterprise, clarifying the fate of a most significant penal experiment in the period.

In the first instance, the diary reveals the conflicts between the treatment staff and the custodial staff over decision-making authority. House officers supervised the inmates in their housing units—and they, not unlike other prison guards, had little respect or tolerance for the social workers, who ran the educational and training programs. The house officers considered the social workers too soft and coddling of prisoners; the social workers, in turn, found the guards ignorant and cruel. Although Gill tried to side with the social workers, the guards had an enormous day-to-day authority and were well positioned to undercut the letter and the spirit of rehabilitative programs.

Moreover, the social workers did not have a very powerful armamentarium at their disposal. They lacked the know-how and the resources to change people's lives. In the end, rehabilitative measures, applied tentatively by a staff lacking reliable methods, did not fundamentally alter the punitive structure of the prison or have any leverage on the custodial and disciplinarian tone that differentiated a prison from a hospital.

The basic flaw in Norfolk's design was the Progressive illusion that casework would ultimately reveal the cause of crime and dictate the course of treatment. This belief colored the Norfolk treatment classification, known as the SCAMP plan. Inmates were divided into five categories: situational cases, comprising occasional offenders; custodial cases, in which treatment was not possible because of age or mental insufficiency; asocial cases, composed of sociopaths; medical cases, in which crime was connected to physical illness; and personality cases, represented by the mentally ill. But the categories were ill-defined and overlapping, and the staff ended up disagreeing on where any particular inmate was supposed to fit. Gill had intended the classifications to determine the type of practitioner to which each inmate would be assigned; for example, situational cases would go to educators, asocial cases to psychiatrists. But in fact, the classifications were neither diagnostic nor predictive and had only the most minimal value. And if this was true at Norfolk, imagine how ineffective they were at more ordinary prisons.

Ultimately, the Norfolk experiment, like so many of its predecessors, fell victim to the fact that the head of the institution, in this case Gill, could not control admissions into the institution. In violation of his original agreement with the state commissioner of correction, Gill had to take in a large number of hard-core and difficult inmates. Both the numbers and the types of prisoners subverted the casework methods. The amendable type of inmates, who had originally stirred Gill's high hopes, were replaced by a core of hardened prisoners who forced Gill to shift the primary concern from rehabilitation to custody and enforced discipline. In fact, inmates became so unruly that Gill had to resort to solitary confinement with bread and water to restore control. In 1934, Gill himself was dismissed in the aftermath of several escapes and general criticism that Norfolk was too soft on criminals. But even before he left, Norfolk had revealed many of the weaknesses of the prison-reform agenda.

Alternatives to Imprisonment

Progressives also attempted to devise a new range of alternatives to incarceration. Probation—the release of a convicted offender to the community under supervision without serving prison time—was one essential component. Invented in Massachusetts half a century earlier, probation was invested with a new seriousness and energy by Progressives, making it a basic tool of the flexible individualized sentencing strategy. At the same time, parole as a mode of conditional release from prison became the indispensable complement of the rapidly expanding indeterminate sentencing.

Both procedures revealed the dangers inherent in vesting wide discretion in criminal justice officials. Judges, in practice, tended to give sentences of probation to those who in an earlier period would have been given a suspended sentence or let off with a verbal warning; in effect, probation became more of a supplement to incarceration than an alternative to it. The abuses and inadequacies of the procedure of parole are reflected in the record of parole hearings. They were arbitrary to a fault, with the board exercising its authority without review. Moreover, supervision, whether on probation or on parole, was minimal. The officers themselves rarely were professionally trained; their caseloads numbered several hundred, making assistance or surveillance practically impossible. At the same time, the officers could revoke the probation or parole status without going through a full trial or satisfying the full rigor of due process. The result was a system that usually neglected the offender, except when it disciplined in capricious fashion.

Because of the visibility of crimes committed by parolees, the institution of parole was constantly attacked by the press and became highly unpopular. Judges also opposed it because it required them to surrender sentencing prerogatives to the administrative power of the parole boards. Police chiefs, in turn, resented the boards' lack of communication regarding the location of parolees in the community. Parole boards withheld the information to protect parolees against police harassment. In the event of a crime wave, for example, the police might have been tempted to bring in all known parolees. But the police defined this cautionary behavior as hostile, and they lined up against parole. Unlike this group of detractors, prison wardens backed parole because it was used as a reward for good behavior and, as such, contributed to a smoother administration of their institutions, helping to keep peace among the inmates and to prevent riots. Legislators also favored parole, as a way to alleviate prison overcrowding and avoid appropriations for new prison construction. District attorneys were supportive of parole because of the encouragement of plea bargains that would have been hindered by the prospect of long sentences without parole and also because of the absence of impediments to a prompt return to custody in cases of parole violations. It was an evenly balanced match, but more often than not, the proponents of parole had their way.

Liabilities and Assets of Progressive Reforms

The Progressive prison-reform movement fell considerably short of its aims. The adoption of its main tenets in the areas of classification, work, discipline, education, and vocational training was partial and uneven. Rehabilitative programs were rarely executed. The Progressive ideal of treating rather than correcting criminals had only scant application. Psychological treatment hardly affected daily practices and, at best, never went beyond diagnosis. Moreover, despite reformers' efforts to model prisons on the community, the routines remained markedly different. Shabby facilities, lack of space, inadequate opportunities for work, and more profoundly still, an institutional routine lived under the eyes of guards in which security was the single most important consideration made life behind bars fundamentally different from life in the free society. In effect, custody prevailed over treatment. The Progressive prison was as maladaptive as its predecessors.

Although some historians and sociologists believe that this dismal record of reform was an inevitable by-product of incarceration, that the very idea of trying to carry out reform behind bars is flawed from the start, the causes of the Progressive failure may also be found in ongoing prison policies. For one, badly paid and incompetent personnel subverted the possibility of creating a rehabilitative prison environment. Wages for prison officers were low, and little possibility existed for advancement or higher emolument. As one Illinois report noted in 1929, the position of the guard was well-nigh intolerable; not only a meager salary but also long hours behind the walls meant that he, no less than the inmate, was imprisoned. Not surprisingly, the turnover in the ranks was high: for example, 50 percent of the staff annually in New York prisons. To make matters worse, these unskilled and uneducated officers were directed by wardens who had no serious interest in promoting rehabilitation or, for that matter, in doing much else than maintaining a secure facility and keeping the inmates in line. If the wardens had any expertise at all, it was in maintaining security, as demonstrated by their previous careers in police or military service.

Not only guards but also would-be teachers and their educational programs left much to be desired. Despite some efforts, particularly in the late 1920s, to increase the level of programs, and despite some particular advances (as in the federal prison at McNeil Island, Washington, and at San Quentin Prison in California), change was at most modest. In 1928, the great majority of prisons lacked any vocational education programs; indeed, they offered no opportunity for schooling beyond the lower grades. Austin McCormick, a highly renowned prison educator, declared in 1929 that prison education was a failure; he was unable to cite a single well-structured and effective education program in American prisons.

If prisons offered no chance for improvement, were they at least safe for inmates? Was bodily integrity protected? Progressive reformers hoped to effect the gradual extinction of corporal punishment, and most states did officially prohibit it. But not all states did; the last whipping in Delaware's prisons was in 1954, and the law sanctioning it remained on the books until 1972. In Colorado, in early 1925, the Civil Service Commission declared flogging a legal form of punishment. The Colorado officials also punished prisoners by making them wear a heavy ball and chain, riveted to the ankle, for ninety days or for even longer periods.

Even where solitary confinement had officially replaced corporal sanctions, punishments remained unfair and even brutal. Physical force, either surreptitiously or under the pretext of controlling unruly prisoners, continued to be applied, and one could still find the most primitive practices in use. The National Society for Penal Information reported that in 1929 in the state penitentiary at Frankfort, Kentucky, it found a dozen men standing with one hand cuffed at the cell door and the other cuffed to the post supporting the upper gallery; the report noted that the prisoners remained so throughout the working hours, for five to twenty days.

Solitary confinement of very long duration was also commonly used during the 1920s and 1930s. The "pit" or the "hole" was a dark and unventilated cell where prisoners were deprived of decent food, exercise, and any human contact. The Wyoming State Penitentiary at Rawlins, in the late 1920s, placed inmates in pitch-black underground cells. In 1926, in Ohio, prisoners in solitary confinement stood eight or more hours a day confined in a close-fitting semicircular steel cage. In the prison at Joliet, Illinois, men were held in solitary cells on a diet consisting of four ounces of bread and one quart of water a day, the confinement lasting from a day to a week. In addition, they were cuffed to the door of the cell for twelve hours a day. In Nevada, these cells were infested with mice and gopher snakes. Conditions were slightly better in some eastern prisons: darkness gave way to light or semilight confinement cells.

Over these decades, prisoners depended entirely on administrative goodwill to rectify situations—and that goodwill was in short supply. Inmates could not claim any rights or protections in courts of law. Invariably judges refrained from intervening in prison management, deferring to the expertise of the wardens. The only limit on wardens' discretion was the inspections of state prison boards, but membership was more honorific than meaningful, and the boards rarely held wardens to account.

Although Progressive reform fell far short of its goals, it did mitigate some of the most destructive practices of the inherited system. Prison life became less depersonalized. The vestiges from the Auburn system, such as striped uniforms, lockstep marching, and the rules of silence, were eradicated. The new "freedom of the yard" allowed intercommunication and exercise during the break period. Prison routine was also mitigated by sports, movies, and music, a beginning of what would gradually lead to the admission of radio and television. The Progressive prisons encouraged correspondence and visits, which also became part of prison life. Thus, these innovations gave initial content to the future roster of prisoners' rights.

THE BIG HOUSE

Progressive reform resulted in the "Big House," a new type of prison managed by professionals instead of short-term political appointees and designed to eliminate the abusive forms of corporal punishment and prison labor prevailing at the time. These prisons coexisted, however, with state prisons that maintained late-nineteenth-century practices. The Big Houses were large prisons that held, on average, 2,500 men, prisons such as San Quentin in California, Sing Sing in New York, Stateville in Illinois, and Jackson in Michigan. In 1929 there were two prisons with a population of more than 4,000 inmates each; there were four with more than 3,000 each; six with more than 2,000 each, and eighteen with more than 1,000 prisoners. Despite amenities such as cell furnishings and decorations, cell blocks overall were described as stenchy, noisy, and excessively cold in the winter and hot in the summer. The Big House exemplifies the superficiality of Progressive reforms in recreation, work, and assimilation with the open society. Indeed, in the world of granite, steel, and cement, the dominant features were stultifying routines, monotonous schedules, and isolation. The 1931 report to the National Commission of Law Observance and Enforcement pointed out that in most prisons, the life of the inmate was controlled for the prisoner, giving him or her no chance for initiative or judgment. Penal institutions, with their treadmill and mechanical quality of existence, did little to prepare for the resumption of a law-abiding social life.

The Big House attracted the interest of sociologists. The first study was Donald Clemmer's at Menard, a maximum-security prison in southern Illinois, in the late 1930s. Clemmer focused mainly on analyzing the internal group life. The predominant criminal type was the thief. Thieves composed a group with a special status in the prison and with a rigid code of conduct, built on the basic prohibition of snitching. Thieves and those who lived by their rules were called "yeggs," "Johnsons," "right guys," or "regulars." There was a series of other types, ranging from prison "politicians," "merchants," and "gamblers," who controlled and exchanged prison commodities, to "rapos" and "stool pigeons," who were, respectively, child sex abusers and snitches. All these categories were organized in a hierarchical order, which was associated with power and privileges. Social stratification generated various internal codes of behavior.

At the New Jersey State Prison, Gresham Sykes in 1958 saw in the prison a unique social system that accommodated the interests of the administration and those of a number of prison leaders, who obtained power and benefits in exchange for their hidden allegiance to the administration. Through a corrupt group of leaders, who falsely appeared as antagonistic, the administration was able to keep under persuasive control a larger number of potentially rebellious inmates. The pressure of prisoners' problems was controlled by a system of roles that informally legitimized and empowered prison leaders and validated their arrangements with prison authorities.

In 1963, John Irwin and Donald Cressey argued that the prison was not so overwhelming in its impact on most prisoners as to obliterate their preprison identities. The social realities of prison could be better understood through an "importation" model of corrections, which maintains that the inmate code was imported into the prison by professional thieves and organized criminals. The past "deprivation" or "adaptation" model interpreted prisons as closed organizations, with a particular code of norms to which prisoners had to adapt in order to cope with deprivations inherent in total institutions. The adoption of the "importation" model led to recognition of the need for action at the social and cultural levels, such as reorganizing the community and neutralizing the action of gangs.

The Emergence of the Federal Prison System

Until the late nineteenth century, the U.S. government housed prisoners convicted of federal crimes in state penitentiaries. In return, the state penitentiaries received boarding fees and were permitted to use the federal prisoners in their prison labor system. Two problems unsettled the arrangements. First, the number of federal prisoners began to rise, from 1,027 in 1885 to 2,516 in 1895. Second, Congress in particular became uncomfortable with the leasing system; in 1887, it outlawed the practice of contracting federal prisoners to private employers. As a result, many state penitentiaries began refusing federal prisoners.

In 1891, Congress decided to enter the prison business. The first site chosen for the construction of a federal prison was Leavenworth, Kentucky. Construction of a twelve-hundred-cell institution began in 1897 and lasted for some thirty years, with many of the prisoners sleeping in dark basements on cots or on beds arranged in double rows along the corridors. As one would expect, idleness was rampant. Thus at

Leavenworth, there was not much to distinguish the federal penitentiary from state penitentiaries.

But the federal system soon began to depart from the state mold. In 1902, Atlanta became the site of the second federal prison and broke with several traditions. Atlanta was one of the earliest prisons to feed prisoners in a dining hall at eight-person tables, instead of relying on one-way bench tables. Atlanta also ushered in the eight-hour workday for prison guards. In 1928 the first federal women's prison was built at Alderson, West Virginia, and it too had some innovative features. Alderson lacked a surrounding fence, housed the inmates in cottages, and decorated dining rooms and living rooms with curtains.

In 1910, President William Howard Taft signed the first Federal Parole Law, giving federal prisoners the opportunity for parole. To promote uniformity among the federal institutions, the superintendent of prisons was designated as the chairman for each federal prison board of parole; the remaining two positions on the board were filled by the prison's warden and chief medical officer. In addition, the superintendent of prisons traveled to state prisons to serve on the parole board for federal prisoners held in state institutions.

Federal prisons erected in the early 1900s were generally run as separate entities without any central organization. The problems caused by prison congestion, and the need for a more efficient record-keeping system to facilitate the goal of proper classification and segregation of prisoners, led to the creation of the federal Bureau of Prisons in 1929. The first director of the bureau was Sanford Bates, who was responsible for a number of important improvements. Bates altered the method of selecting wardens, substituting a merit system for political patronage. Wardens were trained at a special bureau facility and were promoted up the ranks within the bureau. In 1937, the Bureau of Prisons placed all prison employees under the Federal Civil Service, throwing off the last vestiges of political patronage. Also, the bureau began a system of staff rotation whereby any promotion was accompanied by a transfer to another facility. Prior to these changes, prison employees had moved up within the same prison and became entrenched in that prison, which had led to inflexibility and idiosyncrasies within the separate facilities.

The federal system of classification of prisoners was based on the Bureau of Prisons criminological study of prisoners. Low-risk offenders were sent to the new noncustodial camps, serious offenders to Leavenworth and Atlanta, those that would benefit from agricultural education to McNeil Island, and physically and mentally ill inmates to the hospital prison at Springfield. The bureau's conscientious efforts here made classification far more systematic in federal than in state facilities.

The increase in hard-core federal prisoners, perhaps caused by the crime waves associated with Prohibition, prompted the Bureau of Prisons to open a prison of last resort. In 1934, Alcatraz was awarded this distinction. Its purpose was to isolate the criminals of the "vicious and irredeemable type," those with no hope of rehabilitation. Prisoners for Alcatraz were selected from other federal prisons and were transferred back to other prisons before their release. Alcatraz inmates had virtually no privileges and little contact with the outside world. To prevent secret messages, officials never allowed prisoners to receive original copies of their mail, only transcribed ones. In the early years, conversation among inmates was prohibited except when indispensable. To compensate for these restrictions, Alcatraz had a fairly extensive library with many classics, and its food was above the average. Although the rest of the federal system was overcrowded, Alcatraz maintained its original purpose as a jail for the worst of the worst, a purpose that resulted in a surplus of beds. During the thirty years Alcatraz was in use, it housed a total of only 1,557 prisoners, with the highest average of daily prisoners occurring in 1937 at 302. Because of deterioration of the physical plant, Alcatraz was closed in 1963 and was replaced by the federal penitentiary at Marion, Illinois.

During World War II, the federal prison industries were greatly expanded to make goods for the war effort, including shoes, mattresses, bomb racks, and bomb fins. Also, World War II witnessed the incarceration in federal prisons of highly educated conscientious objectors; out of this came discussions on the propriety of segregating black and white inmates, but no action was taken by the bureau until after the school desegregation cases were decided by the Supreme Court.

Developments after World War II

The American prison system was shaken by a series of riots in the early 1950s. When the new concessions to inmates were thwarted by bureaucratic inefficiency, economic hardship, or unmanageable overcrowding, tensions were created that found in violence their only outlet.

Riots took place at the Trenton Prison and at the Rahway Prison Farm in New Jersey, at Jackson, Michigan, at the Ohio State Penitentiary, at the Menard State Prison in Illinois, and in various institutions in California, Oregon, New Mexico, Massachusetts, Washington, and Minnesota. The usual scenario was the destruction of costly state property, the taking of hostages, rampages, looting, and the vandalizing of prison grounds. The early 1950s also witnessed a large number of less serious rebellions in the form of sit-down strikes or isolated acts of escape or self-mutilation. Because of the particular rural structure of the penal farms of the South, self-mutilation was the main channel of revolt there.

The usual complaints that triggered the riots were the deficiency of prison facilities, lack of hygiene or medical care, poor food quality, lack of treatment, and guard brutality. All the demands of the rebels generally coincided with what in the next decade would become rights recognized by the courts. A sensitive point of contention was the formation of inmate councils as a way to channel and work out grievances. Frequently demanded by the inmates, these councils were strongly resisted by prison administrators, who considered them a threat to the hierarchical principle.

Prison riots exposed the fact that the reforms of the Progressive era had largely remained at the rhetorical level. The acute tensions created by the monotony and boredom of the Big House proved the fragility of its apparent order. The mere promise embodied in Progressive programs or even piecemeal realizations had created relentless expectations in prisoners. On the other hand, Progressive concessions, which implied the surrender of part of the autocratic power that had ruled prisons in the earlier penitentiary models, created destabilization and anarchy in the prison social system.

The study of riots brought a new understanding of the contradictions, power structures, and social arrangements that pervaded prison systems. The causes of riots were identified by the American Prison Association in 1953 as lack of financial support, official indifference, substandard personnel, enforced idleness, lack of professional leadership and professional programs, excessive size and overcrowding of institutions, political domination and motivation of management, and unwise sentencing and parole practices. But except for isolated efforts to transform prison environments, the sociological diagnosis of prison ills did not offer widespread remedies. The generalized conclusion that prison unrest was the result of insufficient rehabilitative programs led, however, to an intensification of the therapeutic thrust in prisons after the early 1950s spate of prison riots.

The New Rehabilitative Thrust

The postwar treatment era led to the creation of treatment-oriented correctional institutions and to the replacement of the Big House of the 1940s. After World War II, the penological arena was permeated by a general rehabilitative thrust caused by the international reconstructive optimism and the relative prosperity of the 1950s. The low crime rates in the 1950s, declining for some types of crime—the murder rate had a 6.9 decrease from 1946 to 1962—gave foundation to rehabilitative optimism. Enthusiasm for psychological treatment, influenced by psychoanalytically oriented professionals emigrating from Europe, increased the input of behavioral scientists in the correctional system. More psychologists and caseworkers gave a more technical orientation to the therapeutic model of rehabilitation. The assumption was that offenders were psychologically disturbed and needed individualized treatment to cope with their emotional problems, which were considered to be the cause of their criminal activities.

Further, the international rehabilitative emphasis was formalized in the 1955 United Nations Standard Minimum Rules for the Treatment of Prisoners, which provided in Article 58 that a sentence of imprisonment can be justified only when it is used "to ensure, so far as possible, that upon his return to society, the offender is not only willing but able to lead a law-abiding and self-supporting life."

The therapeutic orientation had some benefits insofar as it replaced purely discretional prison management with treatment-oriented administrative decisions. But despite the rhetoric of rehabilitation, this new wave of treatment euphoria shared with previous reform efforts the same paucity of practical realizations. Because of the limited professional possibilities offered by the penitentiary setting, the treatment staff was still generally composed of less qualified individuals. In addition, there was a permanent conflict, ideological and professional, between the custody and the treatment staffs regarding issues of discipline and security.

Closely connected to the growth of the rehabilitative ideal, inmate classification systems had developed throughout the first half of the twentieth century. When in 1929 the Federal Bureau of Prisons had turned rehabilitation into a policy, its main concern was the development of an institutional network that would allow an effective classification system and individualized decisions regarding discipline and treatment. After World War II, classification was carried out by a team of professional psychologists, caseworkers, sociologists, vocational counselors, and psychiatrists, who all worked in creating the case history of the convict. Special classification committees examined and evaluated the data to assign the prisoner to the appropriate prison, to plan the future rehabilitative action, and periodically to review the rehabilitative status of the inmate. Still, custody considerations and managerial convenience usually prevailed over treatment in the committees' decisions.

The rehabilitative optimism was shared by prison reformers, lawmakers, and prison officials. In 1954 the American Prison Association changed its name to the American Correctional Association and counseled its members to redesignate their prisons as "correctional institutions" and to label the punishment blocks in them as "adjustment centers." The Soledad Prison, also labeled a "California Treatment Facility," was the first of the men's prisons built after the war. One of its main qualities was its pleasant physical atmosphere. Fences and gun towers substituted for granite walls, and the internal structure made communal life more encouraging. Cell blocks with dayrooms and outside windows, inside walls with pastel colors, spacious and well-equipped libraries, gyms and educational facilities, acceptable food and more relaxed discipline, and a broad selection of vocational training and group counseling programs created a relatively friendly atmosphere more prone to rehabilitative treatment.

After World War II, rehabilitative strategies also shifted back to the social learning perspective, which considered criminal behavior as a learning disorder in the socialization process. Correctional innovation was guided by newly conceived, psychiatric experiments on the therapeutic community, as well as the growing awareness of the need to counteract the negative effects of institutions.

This need was made plain by the seminal work of Irving Goffman, *Asylums*, which in 1961 provided fundamental insight into the nature of "total institutions" in general and prisons in particular. Total institutions, such as prisons, army training camps, naval vessels, boarding schools, or monasteries, were characterized by their encompassing character symbolized by the barrier to social intercourse with the outside. In total institutions, human needs are handled by the bureaucratic organization, and decisions are made without the participation of inmates. Goffman pointed to the loss of the inmates' fundamental capacity to communicate and cooperate. He explained how inmates are dispossessed and degraded from the time they arrive at the institution and are stripped of the identity equipment they use for presenting their usual image of themselves to others. The social learning rehabilitative experiments attempted to transform these desocializing patterns of prison settings.

A good example of such an experiment was the therapeutic community at Chino Prison in the early 1960s, when Commissioner Richard McGee was the innovative administrator of the California Department of Correction. According to the evaluative research units set up by McGee, the Chino experiment demonstrated the effectiveness of the therapeutic community method to change the antisocial behavior of offenders. The institution was decentralized into small units, with counselors housed in each of them. Convicts were used as therapists. The prison became a community center for special training, work release, and family contacts. Therapeutic communities focused on the transformation of the institutional environment, creating a network of compensatory social interactions, a network that was intended to replace the hierarchical structure of the institution with a horizontal association of mutually responsible human beings who would resolve their common problems through a process of intensive social interaction. The vehicles of this process were the frequent meetings and group discussions in which decisions were reached through the participation of both inmates and staff. The demand for active participation was intended to counteract such notorious negative effects of institutions as depersonalization, dependency, and loss of initiative.

The emphasis on the therapeutic model of rehabilitation led to abuses that in the 1970s would generate a movement of general opposition to and discrediting of the rehabilitative idea. In practice, attempts at rehabilitation were only peripheral, but the prevailing indeterminate sentencing statutes led to disparities, arbitrariness, and disproportionately high penalties. Another negative aspect of the therapeutic model of rehabilitation was the abuse of intrusive therapies. After 1960 different forms of behavioral modification programs were used in American correctional institutions. Many of these programs, discontinued in the 1970s, were disguised versions of highly punitive practices.

The Beginnings of the Prisoners' Rights Movement

Until the beginnings of the prisoners' rights movement, inmates had practically no rights, and U.S. Supreme Court decisions precluded their access to courts. Judges reasoned that interference in prison matters would disrupt institutional discipline. Furthermore, they considered that such intervention was prevented by the doctrine of separation of powers and that judges lacked the expertise to run institutions. Courts were declared not to have jurisdiction or power over the internal management of prisons. In the 1960s this was retrospectively referred to as a "hands-off" doctrine, which virtually abandoned penal institutions to the unchecked power of their administrators, who were entitled to pursue whatever punitive or despotic methods they chose to apply.

The courts intervened in extreme cases. Violation of the cruel and unusual punishment proscription of the Eighth Amendment resulted in a few isolated, though important, decisions in the 1940s and 1950s. One particularly significant decision and notorious case, *Johnson v. Dye* (1949), involved a Georgia chain gang. The plaintiff had escaped from the gang and had been arrested in Pennsylvania. He there applied for a writ of habeas corpus, alleging brutal treatment from the Georgia prison officers and danger to his life if he returned to the chain gang. The district judge denied him habeas corpus relief, but the Court of Appeals of the Third Circuit reversed. For the first time, a federal court declared that a prison environment could entail the infliction of cruel and unusual punishment. The flexible interpretation of the Eighth Amendment of the U.S. Constitution led to the condemnation not only of physically barbarous punishments but also, as early as 1910, of punishment grossly disproportionate to the severity of the crime. In this decision the Court recognized that the concept of cruel and unusual punishment changes as "public opinion becomes enlightened human justice."

In this respect it is important to underscore that the concession of benefits and privileges during the Progressive Era had become accepted social practices that ultimately gave substance to the nascent prisoners' rights movement. Those concessions were largely the result of the policy of patterning the prison on the community. The recognition of the needs of inmates for successful reintegration into society, a view widely shared by public opinion and the press, paved the way for the recognition of their rights.

The recognition of prisoners' rights is also an aspect of the general expansion of civil rights and liberties after World War II, impelled by new expectations of prisoners together with other vulnerable social groups, such as racial minorities, women, children, and the mentally ill. This movement was given force by the appointment of Earl Warren, an advocate of social change, as the Supreme Court's chief justice in 1953. The 1954 U.S. Supreme Court landmark decision in *Brown v. Board of Education*, prohibiting racial segregation, particularly contributed to the creation of a legal atmosphere that would allow the development of rights for prisoners. The recognition of prisoners' rights was preceded and encouraged by a series of U.S. Supreme Court decisions that emphasized the rights of the individual. President John F. Kennedy, elected in 1960, initiated policies in support of minorities and the poor. These policies inspired a civil rights movement, which decidedly influenced the history of American prisons.

In the early 1960s, prisoners began to seek enforcement of their constitutional rights through two main legal devices: the writ of habeas corpus and the Civil Rights Act. The writ of habeas corpus is a means that all people have to challenge in a court of justice their illegal confinement. The prevailing liberal trend of the 1960s led the courts to interpret the habeas corpus procedure as a way to attack in federal courts state convictions flawed by constitutional violations. In 1963 three Supreme Court decisions reaffirmed the power of the federal courts to review constitutionally challenged state court decisions, triggering an unprecedented expansion of the scope of the writ. These decisions minimized the habeas corpus requirements and set liberal standards both for the granting of new evidentiary hearings in federal courts and for successive applications of the writ against the same judgment.

The second and most significant legal tool used to enforce constitutional rights of prisoners was the Civil Rights Act. This nineteenth-century law had been incorporated into the U.S. Code, which is a codification of the federal statutes, and became the basis of modern civil rights litigation. Section 1893 of Chapter 42 of the U.S. Code, originally enacted after the Civil War to protect freed slaves from civil rights abuses, began increasingly to be used by state prisoners for violations of their federal rights.

Until 1961 it was necessary for a plaintiff to sue on constitutional issues before the state courts, where allegations of state breaches of constitutional rights were often not well received. Through a 1961 police misconduct case, *Monroe v. Pape*, the U.S. Supreme Court unearthed the Civil Rights Act of 1871 and allowed plaintiffs to sue on constitutional issues directly before the federal courts, thus avoiding the sometimes prejudiced state courts.

The Black Muslim religious movement generated the first decisions that led to the abandonment of the Supreme Court's "hands-off" doctrine concerning prison management. In the mid-1950s there was a significant change in the inmate populations as a consequence of the large migrations of southern blacks into northern and western cities. Thus many northern prisons came to hold a black majority. Also, the civil rights movement on the streets gave support and inspiration to the pioneers of prisoners' rights litigation. The Black Muslims were a nationalistic and separatist group that tried to vindicate the situation of blacks through the affirmation of their sense of worth. The organization grew during the 1950s, under the teachings of Elijah Muhammad. The first victories of the prisoners' rights movement were in the early 1960s in the area of freedom of religion, a subject to which the courts were traditionally highly receptive. Black Muslim prisoners mainly demanded to obtain copies of the Koran, receive their newspaper, eat pork-free meals, and hold religious services and other meetings. After much resistance from apprehensive prison authorities, they won their right to exist in 1965, as a result of *Cooper v. Pate.* Thomas Cooper had filed a civil rights complaint alleging that he had been confined in segregation to punish his religious beliefs and demanding access to Muslim literature and clergy. The U.S. Supreme Court reversed the lower courts' dismissal and ordered the district court to hold a trial on Cooper's complaints, which led to the recognition of the Black Muslims as a religious group.

The State of Prisons in 1965

The state of corrections in 1965 was mirrored in the survey for the President's Commission on Law Enforcement and Administration of Justice, a survey carried out by the National Council on Crime and Delinquency from February to September 1966. The project was undertaken with the help of three thousand correctional administrators, wardens, probation and parole officers, sheriffs, statistical chiefs, and other professionals. The situation of American penal institutions was characterized with these words: "Life in many institutions is at best barren and futile, at worst unspeakably brutal and degrading. To be sure, the offenders in such institutions are incapacitated from committing further crimes while serving their sentences, but the conditions in which they live are the poorest possible preparation for their successful reentry into society, and often merely reinforce in them a pattern of manipulation or destructiveness."

In the foreword, Milton R. Rector pointed out, "One cannot read the report without being struck by the fact that American correctional philosophy is a philosophy of institutionalization." The figures also stress excessive reliance on institutions as the nation's principal correctional method. During 1965 more than 125,000 persons were received in adult correctional institutions in the United States. Of this number almost 80,000 were felons. The survey findings established that on any one day in the United States, about one and a quarter million persons were under the jurisdiction of state and local correctional agencies and institutions. In addition, many thousands more were serving from a few days to a few weeks in a variety of local lockups and jails not included in the survey. Of the total reported, 28 percent were juveniles, and 72 percent were adults. One-third of all offenders reported were under probation or parole supervision. Although judged insufficient, the use of probation and other community alternatives had already altered the overall trend of increasing prison populations. Between 1961 and 1965, there was an exceptional annual decline.

The survey noted, "Judges and juries evidently place a high degree of reliance on institutional commitment." As the survey pointed out, the high commitment rates were challenged in 1963 by the Saginaw Probation Demonstration Project, which offered evidence of the comparatively greater success achieved with offenders through increased use of effective probation. It also stressed the enormous savings that a lower commitment rate produces not only in manpower but also in taxes. The survey indicated that prospects for establishing a variety of alternatives to mass custody and mass caseloads could become reality through joint state and federal planning.

The survey reflected an anti-institutional movement in American society at the time, a movement that led to the development of the reintegration model of correctional change. This model tried to avoid imprisonment by keeping offenders in the community and helping them, through various programs, to reintegrate. The President's Crime Commission indicated that the task of corrections was to build or rebuild solid ties between the offender and community life, through "restoring family ties, obtaining employment and education," and "securing in the large sense a place for the offender in the routine functioning of society." The aspirations of this anti-institutional approach included changes in the community to create resources for convicts and an adequate environment for successful reintegration.

CONCLUSIONS

At the beginning of the period of our survey, in 1865, Samuel Gridley Howe, a leading American philanthropist and prison reformer, warned, "Institutions . . . so strongly built, so richly endowed . . . cannot be got rid of so easily." Institutional structures proved their tenacity during the hundred years between 1865 and 1965. The basic belief that prisons were the most effective means for reacting against crime led to excessive institutionalization and to endemic overcrowding. Indeed, overcrowding became a prevailing feature of the history of American prisons. One hundred years after Howe's warning, the Task Force Report of the President's Commission on Law Enforcement and Administration of Justice denounced the excessive reliance on imprisonment in the United States. As a result of this unchecked trend, the U.S. rate of incarceration today (519 per 100,000 population) is second in the world, after Russia, and at least five times greater than that of most other industrialized nations.

Despite the appeals of numerous prison reformers, most of these overcrowded institutions maintained their original nineteenth-century structure. In 1967 the New York state prison at Auburn, built in 1816, remained in operation, and the President's Crime Commission reported that forty-three penitentiaries, seven reformatories, and one women's institution built before 1900 were still in use in thirty-six states, "grim reminders of an age of ignorance and inhumanity."

The Progressive aspiration to individualize and democratize the prison resulted in the abolishment of practices such as the lockstep and striped uniforms. This aspiration also motivated changes such as the introduction of bands, orchestras, sports, exercise, and movies. But the overall Progressive goals of modeling the prison on the community and of transforming the prison into a treatment institution basically failed. Psychiatrists were unable to move beyond diagnosis, and the quality of prison life remained subordinated to the prevalent custodial aim. The priority given to institutional order, discipline, and security reduced true rehabilitative efforts to a few insufficient and scattered attempts.

Although the balance of change was meager, prisons could not remain impervious to momentous technological and economic progress. Despite the persistence of old external structures, there have been significant transformations in their infrastructures. Prison life was profoundly changed by technological advance in the fields of housing, sanitation, plumbing, and ventilation. An example is the introduction into prison cells at the turn of the century of the first toilets with running water, to replace the sordid and antihygienic buckets. These toilets were installed for the first time in Maryland, in 1899. However, in 1900 most prisons were still using the bucket system, which was a major cause of the rampant spread of diseases throughout the prison population. Raising prison living conditions was first a matter of prison officials' discretion and good judgment. But with time, this became an issue of general health legislation. During the 1960s, standards of housing and sanitary conditions became the subject of constitutional litigation and statutory recognition.

The methods used to maintain order and discipline in penal institutions also changed significantly. Whipping and other forms of corporal punishment, already condemned in the Wines and Dwight report of 1867, were replaced by solitary confinement as the extreme punishment. The gradual expansion of statutes abolishing corporal punishment was not always followed by penal practices. Unofficial forms of barbarous punishment continued well into the twentieth century and were eradicated later only through the scrutiny of activist courts and the imposition of due process safeguards in disciplinary proceedings. There is an endemic tendency to inflict cruel physical punishment in prison environments, a tendency that even now constitutes a major source of prisoner litigation.

Another prison practice that has acquired particular significance since the late nineteenth century in American prisons is recreation. High levels of overcrowding plus the idleness resulting from the reduction of prison industries created an acute need for recreational activities as an incentive to maintain order and discipline. The main recreational activities were first the slowly growing libraries, orchestras, organized sports, and what was called the freedom of the yard. Sunday morning services were also regarded as a relief from the boredom of incarceration. Later, movies and television became important elements in breaking the monotony of prison life.

There have also been numerous efforts to open the prison to the community, to create a series of alternatives to imprisonment, to improve medical and psychological treatment, and to rehabilitate inmates. The diversification of institutions and the new classification methods constitute another remarkable development, to the extent that the history of American prisons has been envisioned as a history of different systems for classifying prisoners.

In 1871 Woody Ruffin, convicted of murder, appealed his death sentence, which had been constitutionally flawed by procedural errors. The Virginia court rejected his appeal because it considered him "a slave of the state," suffering "civil death." If one compares Ruffin's legal status with that of prisoner litigants in the 1960s, one can appreciate a significant change. The introduction of law and the courts into prisons in the early 1960s contrasts with the lawlessness, arbitrariness, and cruelty that had been routine in penitentiary management practice. The emergence of prisoners' legal status was the cumulative result of all the changes in prison life and social practices brought about by reformers since 1865.

Acknowledgments

I am grateful to the staff of the Harvard University libraries and of the Boston Public Library, where I completed my original draft. I later found important materials at the University of Miami libraries. Nora de la Garza, Head of Retrieval Services at the University of Miami Law

Library, provided valuable interlibrary-loan assistance. Allison Berman and Keith Gaudioso were effective research assistants.

Bibliographic Note

The leading analysis of the period covered by this chapter is David J. Rothman's *Conscience and Convenience: The Asylum and Its Alternatives in Progressive America* (Boston: Little, Brown, 1980). This work is indispensable to understanding the constellation of factors that shaped American prisons during most of the twentieth century. Blake McKelvey's *American Prisons: A History of Good Intentions* (Montclair, N.J.: Patterson Smith, 1977), the standard book on the subject, is a necessary source of information. Other, less detailed accounts of the evolution of American prisons include the following: Harry Elmer Barnes, *The Story of Punishment: A Record of Man's Inhumanity to Man*, 2d ed. rev. (Montclair, N.J.: Patterson Smith, 1972), written from a Progressive's perspective; Howard Gill, "State Prisons in America: 1787–1937," in U.S. Department of Justice, *The Attorney General's Survey of Release Procedures*, 5 vols. (Washington, D.C.: Government Printing Office, 1939–40), a useful panoramic view of the history of American prisons until 1937; Larry Sullivan's well-informed *The Prison Reform Movement: Forlorn Hope* (Boston: Twayne Publishers, 1990); and Mabel A. Elliott's *Coercion in Penal Treatment: Past and Present* (Ithaca, N.Y.: Pacifist Research Bureau, 1947).

Edgardo Rotman's *Beyond Punishment: A New View on the Rehabilitation of Criminal Offenders* (Westport, Conn.: Greenwood Press, 1990) includes a detailed analysis of the successive models of rehabilitation that underlay prison reform initiatives during the period covered by this chapter. Francis A. Allen's *The Decline of the Rehabilitative Ideal: Penal Policy and Social Purpose* (New Haven, Conn.: Yale University Press, 1981) examines the social and ideological context in which the twentieth-century rehabilitative ideal flourished, whereas Francis T. Cullen and Karen E. Gilbert's *Reaffirming Rehabilitation* (Cincinnati, Ohio: Anderson, 1982) assesses twentieth-century rehabilitative and sentencing policies.

On particular periods or aspects of the time covered by this chapter, see the following: J. E. Baker, *Prisoner Participation in Prison Power* (Metuchen, N.J.: Scarecrow Press, 1985), a detailed historical account of inmates' participation in prison government; Torsten Eriksson, *The Reformers: An Historical Survey of Pioneer Experiments in the Treatment of Criminals* (New York: Elsevier, 1976), a study of major penal institutions and protagonists; Glen A. Gildemeister, *Prison Labor and Convict Competition with Free Workers in Industrializing America, 1840–1890* (New York: Garland Publishing, 1987), a view of the development of American prisons from 1840 to 1890, from the labor perspective; and Paul W. Keve, *Prisons and the American Conscience: A History of U.S. Federal Corrections* (Carbondale: Southern Illinois University Press, 1991), a history of U.S. federal corrections. James B. Jacobs's *Stateville: The Penitentiary in Mass Society* (Chicago: University of Chicago Press, 1977) is an informative view of the post-1925 period through the study of a particular institution, and John Irwin's *Prisons in Turmoil* (Boston: Little, Brown, 1980) provides insight into the evolution of American prisons in the mid-twentieth century.

In addition, this essay draws on, among others, the following publications: the chapter on correctional history in Todd R. Clear and George F. Cole, ed., *American Corrections*, 2d ed. (Pacific Grove, Calif.: Brooks/Cole, 1990); Thomas O. Murton's interpretation of the vicissitudes of prison reform in *The Dilemma of Prison Reform* (New York: Holt, Rinehart, and Winston, 1976); J. Thorsten Sellin's analysis of the exploitation of convict work in America as part of a history of penal slavery, in *Slavery and the Penal System* (New York: Elsevier, 1976), and Michael Sherman and Gordon Hawkins's historical interpretations in *Imprisonment in America: Choosing the Future* (Chicago: University of Chicago Press, 1981). The following sources should also be mentioned: Michael Stephen Hindus, *Prison and Plantation: Crime, Justice, and Authority in Massachusetts and South Carolina, 1767–1878* (Chapel Hill: University of North Carolina Press, 1980); Leonard Orland, *Prisons: Houses of Darkness* (New York: Free Press, 1975); President's Commission on Law Enforcement and Administration of Justice, *Task Force Report on Corrections* (Washington, D.C.:

Government Printing Office, 1967); David J. Rothman, "Sentencing Reform in Historical Perspective," *Crime and Delinquency* (October 1983); Sol Chaneles, ed., *Prisons and Prisoners: Historical Documents* (New York: Haworth Press, 1985); Enoch C. Wines and Theodore W. Dwight, *Report on the Prisons and Reformatories of the United States and Canada* (Albany: Van Benthuysen, 1867); Louis N. Robinson, "Institutions for Defective Delinquents," in *Journal of Criminal Law and Criminology* 24 (1933); Marjorie J. Seashore and Steven Haberfeld, *Prisoner Education: Project Newgate and Other College Programs* (New York: Praeger, 1976); Kate Richards O'Hare, *In Prison* (New York: Alfred A. Knopf, 1923); Joseph F. Fishman, *Crucibles of Crime: The Shocking Story of the American Jail* (1923; reprint, Montclair, N.J.: Patterson Smith, 1969); Erich H. Steele and James B. Jacobs, "Minimum Security," in *Correctional Institutions*, ed. Robert M. Carter, Daniel Glaser, and Leslie T. Wilkins, 3d ed. (New York: Harper and Row, 1985); Jim Thomas, *Prisoner Litigation: The Paradox of the Jailhouse Lawyer* (Totowa, N.J.: Rowman and Littlefield, 1988); James B. Jacobs, *New Perspectives on Prisons and Imprisonment* (Ithaca: Cornell University Press, 1983); Jonathan Simon, *Poor Discipline: Parole and the Social Control of the Underclass, 1890–1990* (Chicago: University of Chicago Press, 1993); and Larry W. Yackle, *Reform and Regret: The Story of Federal Judicial Involvement in the Alabama Prison System* (New York: Oxford University Press, 1989).

CHAPTER SEVEN

THE PRISON ON THE CONTINENT

Europe, 1865–1965

Patricia O'Brien

The penal institutions of a people should be, like all laws, the expression of its social state." So spoke the French reformer Léon Faucher, who at mid-nineteenth century was intent on redesigning the French prison system to reflect the progress and achievements of his own society. Prisons were expected to change and develop in accord with democratic and moral principles of equity, fairness, and improvement. As an institution, the modern prison system has always been porous, permeated by political cultural assumptions and social values. The history of prisons in Europe from 1865 to 1965 is, therefore, a story of continual change that parallels the changing cultural, economic, political, and social realities of modern states. Moreover, as earlier chapters have demonstrated, the prison was also the product of pressure to reform existing methods of punishment and to find a more enlightened, humane, and effective answer to punishing crime.

Almost as soon as the prison itself became central to criminal punishment, it became the focus of reform efforts. Many different prison reform movements appeared throughout this period, advocating a variety of methods to reach distinct goals. All these movements, however, took their inspiration from the same sources: advances in the new fields of knowledge, including criminology and sociology; changes in beliefs about the causes and proper treatment of deviance; and shifts in social attitudes toward crime and criminals.

Each European nation formed and maintained its own prison system. In spite of distinct, national institutions, however, the prison systems that developed throughout Europe in the nineteenth century were remarkably similar, reflecting a commonly held penal philosophy. Shared ideas about how to create prisons that were secure, sanitary, and rehabilitative produced similar prison populations, architecture, work systems, and inmate subcultures.

Toward the end of the nineteenth century, imprisonment became the subject of increasing criticism and gradually lost the absolute position it had gained as the dominant form of punishment. In its place, many European states invented new, noncustodial punishments, such as the suspended sentence and supervised parole. In some countries, these new nonincarcerative punishments produced only a minor change in penal practice; in others, they substantially replaced imprisonment.

Penal philosophies began to diverge significantly in the twentieth century. Development of nonincarcerative punishments continued energetically in some countries while others aggressively expanded their prison systems. The forced labor camps of the former Soviet Union in the interwar period and the concentration camps of Germany and Italy during World War II represent the most extreme use, among all European nations to date, of the deprivation of liberty as a form of punishment.

The search for a better method of punishment not only gave rise to the prison but also led to its transformation and its partial obsolescence. The search as it continues today is necessarily rooted in the national experiences of this important period in the history of the modern European prison.

THE PRISON AND LIFE WITHIN, 1865–1914

Inmates and Guards

From their origins in the early nineteenth century, prisons had been primarily intended to house populations who were poor, unskilled, unemployed, and judged to be in need of social and moral instruction and discipline. Public fears about idle young men crowding the cities in search of work fueled middle-class fears of political unrest. The idea of rehabilitation through punishment became a panacea for a variety of perceived social ills. By the middle of the nineteenth century, penitentiaries were performing their assigned task of disciplining populations of mostly young and single men, who, in age, marital status, class, and occupational experience, were remarkably similar to the rank and file of European conscript armies. The profile of French prison populations in the last quarter of the nineteenth century was typical of those of the continent as a whole: two out of every five French male prisoners were between the ages of twenty-one and thirty; men between thirty-one and forty years old constituted, on average, about 20 percent of the male prison population, with declining percentages in the older age groups.

Female prisoners, who made up 20 percent of the total prison population in the mid-nineteenth century, dropped to 12 to 13 percent by the end of the century. The women inmates, like the men, were made up of the young. Again the French experience exemplifies the trend: two out of every three women in French penitentiaries were between the ages of twenty-one and forty; and women in their twenties outnumbered women in their thirties by about three to two. Most women in prison, like the men, were single (65 percent), but most female prisoners had children, whereas two out of every three men were listed as single and without children.

After mid-nineteenth century, prison populations emerged as significantly and disproportionately urban. Repeat offenders were especially likely to come from urban areas. Prisoners possessed few or no job skills; women were consistently less skilled than men, and those who did list occupations identified themselves as seamstresses, domestics, and day laborers. In spite of considerable difficulties with the recorded occupational identifications of prisoners, we are able to observe that the percentage of vagrant and unskilled workers in the prisons declined in the second half of the nineteenth century, revealing a more occupationally—and criminally—experienced population. Most male prisoners were convicted of theft and other property crimes. Domestic theft by servants, prostitution, and vagrancy figured significantly in the female prison profile.

Guards were not very different in social origins and class from the prisoners. They too came from poor backgrounds and had little or no specialized training. Because of the deliberate recruitment policies of prison administrations, most guards came from military backgrounds. As the role of the prison guard came to be more highly valued as a moralizing force in a progressive penitentiary system, the background and training of the recruit received greater administrative scrutiny and attention. In France in 1872 a parliamentary inquest studying the failure of the prison to rehabilitate prisoners recommended "special training" for guards. And in 1879 the International Penitentiary Congress voted in favor of creating special normal schools to instruct prison guards.

This endorsement of the principle of formal education for guards was controversial in France, as elsewhere, because, critics insisted, guards were best trained as apprentices, learning their skills on the job and in the prison. This tension helps explain the failure of the movement to develop a significant training school program for guards. In France, regardless of the parliamentary inquest in 1872 and the vote by the International Penitentiary Congress in 1879, such an institution was not created until 1893 and never took firm root. It closed in 1908, reopened in 1927, was abolished in 1934, and was reestablished after World War II as part of more general prison reforms. In fact, instruction for prison personnel in programs such as these often consisted of basic courses in reading and writing, with little attention being paid either to the rehabilitation of prisoners or to their humane control.

Perhaps the single most important characteristic of prison populations after 1865 was their shrinking size after decades of growth, a reduction reflecting the development of a new array of punitive sanctions. Such a contraction was common in Western European nations, except in those countries that came late to the prison solution. Thus in these decades, Italy, Russia, and Spain experienced no such diminution in either reported crime or prison populations. But whatever rise or fall occurred within the prison population, there continued to be a heated and contentious debate about the efficacy of the prison as a mechanism of control and about what standards should characterize life inside its walls. This debate often revolved around such specific issues as the proper physical structure of the prison and the appropriateness of labor within the prison but also addressed such larger and more inchoate issues as whether the prison created a subculture of deviance.

Prison Architecture

The architecture of European prisons throughout the period drew on a small repertoire of forms that pointed to a common and international penal philosophy and on shared ideas of how to achieve goals of security, sanitary conditions, and rehabilitation. Two broad models emerged: the Pentonville radial design (wings radiating around a central rotunda), which achieved complete separation of prisoners; and the "telephone pole" model (multiple cell blocks at right angles to a long central corridor), as in the American facilities of Auburn and Sing Sing, which provided single cells for night separation and communal workrooms and refectories for the day.

The Pentonville model inflicted a harsher life on its prisoners; it was also more expensive to construct and to maintain. Nevertheless Pentonville-type, radial prisons continued to be built in Holland, Belgium, Spain, Switzerland, Scandinavia, Austria, Hungary, and Portugal in the latter half of the nineteenth century, even after the efficacy of solitary confinement had been called into question. The cruelty and harshness of total isolation of prisoners came under frequent attack as statistics revealed higher rates of death, suicide, and madness among isolated populations.

Even in countries endorsing the principle of solitary confinement, financial pressures caused prisons to be constructed with common dormitories and common workrooms, thereby reflecting a kind of institutional schizophrenia between articulated goals and economic realities. Although France, Russia, and Italy built single-cell prisons, they also tended, often out of fiscal necessity, to rely on buildings converted from other purposes, such as convents and military barracks, to fulfill the need for more prisons. In Spain, as late as 1880, old, poorly ventilated buildings were the order of the day for offenders of all types, who were mixed together in communal arrangements. Extreme overcrowding and inadequate food allotments were not uncommon.

In 1872, on the heels of the French military defeat by Prussia, the French National Assembly commissioned an inquest to examine the state of French prisons in a system where isolation, in principle, was endorsed. Two great social fears informed the deliberations: the fear of homosexual promiscuity among prison populations, and the fear of rising recidivism rates. The conclusions of that inquest reaffirmed that single cells were absolutely essential for just and rehabilitative punishment. It was hoped that as a result of separating prisoners from each other and eliminating common dormitory arrangements, the moralizing influence of isolation would reform behavior denounced as promiscuous and degenerate. Yet few prisons complied with the laws that were passed in the wake of the committee reports. By the turn of the century, and in spite of new prison construction, the number of single cells in France remained about the same as fifty years earlier: five thousand, which accommodated only half of the penitentiary inmates. Only Belgium among Western European nations claimed to have completed a standardized penitentiary regime composed of single-cell prisons, and it did so by spreading the cost of twenty million francs over forty years.

By 1900, the efficacy of confining and isolating prisoners for long periods was called into question by high and steady recidivism rates. Yet the momentum of solitary confinement in the first half of the nineteenth century was so firmly established in state institutions that new prison edifices continued to be designed according to principles once considered enlightened, even though the prisons were being built at a time when the principles of punishment themselves were judged to be bankrupt and in need of replacement.

Work in Prison

By the end of the nineteenth century, many Western European penitentiaries engaged in manufacturing. They produced for an external market or responded to the institution's own internal demand for uniforms, shoes, bedding, baskets, and the like. Some were profit-oriented in their operations and distributed nominal wages to prisoners. Others employed prisoners in the maintenance of the prison: cooking, baking, cleaning, doing laundry, working in the infirmary, shepherding, farming, gardening, landscaping, and raising animals. The Russian anarchist Peter Kropotkin captured well this aspect of prison life in his description of the French penitentiary Clairvaux: "When one approaches the immense outer wall of Clairvaux, which extends along the slopes of the hills for about the length of four kilometers, one rather believes he is looking at a little manufacturing city. Smoking factories, four large smokestacks, steam engines, one or two turbines, and the punctuated rhythm of the factories, that's what strikes one from the very first" (Pierre Kropotkine, *Les Prisons* [Paris, 1890], p. 7).

Labor was the central and organizing factor of the daily life of the nineteenth-century penitentiary. On a typical day in 1880 in a Belgian prison, inmates rose at 5 A.M. to the sound of organ music as a call to prayer; breakfast followed a half hour later, with work beginning at 6 A.M. and lasting until 5:30 P.M., punctuated by visits from prison officials, weekly lectures, lunch, and walks in the prison garden. After a half-hour dinner break, the prisoners returned to work from 6 to 8:45 P.M. and retired, after fifteen minutes of prayer and organ music, at 9 P.M. In Austrian prisons, inmates typically worked ten and one-half to eleven hours a day, following similar breaks for instruction, exercise, and meals.

Even before the creation of the penitentiary, prisoners had performed work tasks as part of their punishment. Some had served in forced labor, as galley slaves exemplified. By the same token, workhouses relied on labor as a tool of reform and improvement; in response to the rising costs of poor relief in the eighteenth century, the indigent poor were put to work in these new workhouses under the strict control of overseers and a harsh disciplinary regime. Though work in such institutions often consisted only of spinning and weaving, the idea that inmates should be occupied in productive labor spread from the workhouse to the prison.

Just as nineteenth-century politicians, theorists, and social reformers stressed the redemptive value of work in creating a disciplined work force in free society, so too did prison reformers count on the moral benefits of productive labor to transform the most hardened criminals into useful citizens. Although prisons were not simply mirror images of production in the marketplace, the prison was dynamically linked to the cultural changes of the broader society and economy. By the end of the nineteenth century, the shift from craftwork to piecework had, both in the community at large and in the prison, produced an insistence on new expectations about discipline and productivity.

Even though the rehabilitative value of prison work was recognized throughout Europe, debate continued from country to country into the twentieth century over the appropriate form of work—should it be performed in isolation or in groups, as occupation for its own sake or as productive activity determined in relation to markets? Early-nineteenth-century English experiments with implements like the treadwheel or treadmill had been aimed at keeping prisoners occupied; in certain instances, these wheels and mills could be harnessed to the tasks of raising water or grinding grain, but on the whole, they were certainly not intended for productive labor. It was not until mid-century that English penal reformers and administrators began to consider the rehabilitative values of productive labor among prison populations.

The possibilities for real profits from efficiently organized prison work systems led to a new kind of moral reasoning in the last quarter of the nineteenth century: some reformers now argued that profitable and productive prison labor was immoral because it succeeded by denying employment to unconvicted and therefore more worthy workers in free society. Beginning at mid-century in France, community worker associations periodically objected to the unfair competition presented by the vastly reduced wages of the prison work force. In periods of revolutionary activity—and notably in 1848—craftworkers demanded the cessation of prison production. In Prussia, businessmen and manufacturers—not workers—protested over low labor costs in prisons; they resented what they considered the state's unfair advantage of a captive work force whose minimal cost could undercut prices and destroy their businesses. These bourgeois preferred a prisoner on a treadmill to an inmate textile worker; critics of a work system oriented to markets argued that prisons that aimed to be self-supporting by the sweat of their inmates' brows did so to the detriment of the true penal goals of education and rehabilitation.

Nevertheless, many countries remained committed to the goal of the prison as a financially self-sustaining institution. Some did so not by competing with local businessmen for markets but by working as partners with manufacturers and producers through a labor contract system. Free employers, in other words, paid the prison administration a fee for the labor of prison inmates. Among German states, Brunswick claimed that its system of inmate labor contracted out to local businessmen nearly covered the cost of operating the prison, whereas Baden, under a work system administered by the state, was said to have supplied two-thirds of the institution costs and taught useful trades to inmates. French prison administrators sought to establish self-sustaining institutions whose operating expenses were defrayed by prison labor contracted out to community entrepreneurs. Subcontracting was also common: the principal entrepreneur could act as an agent by entering into agreements with other local producers who sought cheap, short-term, inmate workers, already under contract to him. Italian prison authorities sought, less successfully than the French, whom they emulated, to make prisons economically self-sufficient by offering specific services in the prison to local entrepreneurs or by allowing for the subcontracting of whole prison populations.

Prison work organized by entrepreneurs rather than the state responded necessarily to local factors and not to central planning; the complexion and the organization of work systems, at the very heart of the nineteenth-century penal philosophy, were, therefore, often in the hands of private individuals. In France, penitentiaries adopted one of two models that maximized work for profit: either the prison administration directly supervised production or, more commonly, the prison director contracted with a private entrepreneur who assumed the provisioning and maintenance of the prison in return for which he had total control over the organization of work. Choosing among competing bids by local businessmen, the director of a particular prison and the local prefect aimed to ensure that the prisoner was always working and that the prison was self-supporting. Neither the kind of work nor the rehabilitative and educational value of particular occupations figured heavily in the selection process. As a result, occupational practices varied widely from prison to prison. Gaillon, for example, was the only

French prison that engaged in accordion-making, and umbrellas were manufactured exclusively at Melun prison by about three dozen men.

The role of outside businessmen, trying to turn the prison into a profitable enterprise, created many tensions. There were problems for prison personnel, paid by the state but now serving the interests of entrepreneurs. And there were problems for prisoners, with some entrepreneurs economizing on overhead costs, which for the most part meant food, light, and heating for prisoners. Abuses were rife. In France, a declining standard of life in prison due to entrepreneurial neglect came to light at the end of the nineteenth century and fueled public debate and calls for reform. An additional source of profits—and abuse—was the prison store, or *cantine,* where prisoners could buy foodstuffs, beverages, soap, clothing, and stamps with the wages they earned through the prison work system. The standard fare in prison was a notoriously bland diet often consisting of bread, soup, gruel, and occasionally meat and vegetables. Although seldom starved, prisoners could escape the monotony of their diet only through purchases from what was essentially a company store. With the increased ability of the state to monitor and inspect, these arrangements came under reforming scrutiny by the end of the century.

Around the mid-nineteenth century, certain countries, including Bavaria, Italy, and Spain, initiated experiments that allowed prisoners to choose the trades in which they wished to be apprenticed. Reformers argued that by allowing choice, prison administrators would reduce recidivism rates. In spite of the best intentions to stress the utility of work in prison as preparation for return to free society, however, vocational training in marketable skills, whether by choice or by assignment, was either neglected or ineffectively implemented for adults in most European prisons. In the rhetoric surrounding new punishments that emerged in the twentieth century, penal reformers were curiously silent about the rehabilitative benefits of work in prison, a principle at the heart of the nineteenth-century program of punishment. Individualization of the punishment to fit the offender as well as the crime meant that new, noncustodial punishments took the place of organized work systems within the prison.

Prison Subcultures

Not all aspects of prison life were organized by those in charge. To an extent that varied from institution to institution, it was the prisoners who shaped the daily regime. The majority of prisoners, especially those in long-term facilities, adapted to life within the institution by forming their own informal communities, networks of power, and cultural identifications. Rather than being stripped of their personalities, prisoners seem to have adjusted their identities and experiences to the penal environment. Common features of life within prison included coded vocabularies, "argot," tattooing, and social networks based on homosexual relations. Although inmate subcultures transgressed the formal rules of prison life, they appear to have taken root to varying degrees in many European prisons.

The growing presence of recidivism in European prison populations after 1865 helps explain the continuity in content and form of inmate culture. Even in countries like France, where the most frequent offenders were isolated or sent abroad after 1885, recidivists served as the primary conduit for transmitting knowledge from one generation of inmates to another. Those men and women who returned to prison dominated the prison hierarchy because of their experience in the system.

By means of a steady process, repeat offenders were returned to prisons to serve sentences made longer and longer by records of previous convictions. By the end of the nineteenth century in France, two of every five imprisoned men and one of every four imprisoned women were repeat offenders, and they were not necessarily the most vicious or dangerous criminals. These returning inmates, who circulated from regional to central prisons, played a critical role in shaping the ongoing subculture of the institutions.

Inmate interactions and social organization in the prison were dynamically related both to the ordered world of work and discipline in the prison and to the prisoners' experiences beyond prison walls. Prison subcultures were not simply interesting anomalies that defied the best intentions of the nineteenth-century penal reformers: they were the arena in which prisoners appropriated, distorted, and recast the values of disciplinary society. As such, prisoners did as much to define the realities of imprisonment as did the rules and regulations that governed penitentiary life. In its own way, the prison subculture was as much a regulating and disciplining force in the prison as the bells that signaled the hours of rest, prayer, meals, and work.

Special language, or argot, with its own vocabulary and distinctive patterns and word placement, brought a cohesiveness into inmate life. The secrecy of communication among prisoners who shared a separate language protected prisoners' privacy, even in the presence of intense surveillance. Coded communication allowed prisoners to define their relative status and rights, just as workers who were members of corporations and guilds had their own argot used to the same ends. Through words, whose meaning was known only to the initiated few, the group reinforced its shared identity.

Inmates in long-term facilities all over Europe appeared to have invented specialized vocabularies and idioms indigenous to prison life. In the nineteenth century, prison slang differed from the street slang of criminals and from the language of the laboring poor. Although little of this shadow world has been preserved, French ethnographers and linguists worked prodigiously at the end of the nineteenth century to compile dictionaries and collections of criminal and prisoner argot. From their work, there is every indication that while the corporate argot of workers was disappearing, the argot of the criminal class and of prisoners was expanding and flourishing.

Prisoners also chose, often with considerable pain and without sufficient hygiene, either to tattoo themselves with crudely designed images or to be tattooed with more sophisticated images by tattoo artists within the prison. It seems ironic that tattooing grew in popularity in prisons just as branding, a state-imposed mark of infamy on convicts' bodies and a means of social ostracism, was being terminated throughout Europe. Writing in 1881, Alexandre Lacassagne, professor of forensic medicine at the University of Lyon, found in tattoos a means of studying the social milieu of the criminal: "From the point of view of identity, it is a veritable talking scar." Lacassagne was one of the first medical specialists to catalogue tattoos systematically among prison populations. The categories of the twenty-four hundred "talking scars" he examined included fantasy and historical images, erotic and sexual images, metaphoric symbols, military figures, inscriptions, professional or occupational symbols, and patriotic and religious emblems.

Tattooing, as much as distinctive speech patterns, helped define the prisoner's sense of identity in the institution. The marking of one's body, an immemorial phenomenon associated with primitive societies and tribal cultures, was widely practiced in modern prisons. Beginning in the late nineteenth century, continental European criminologists and criminal anthropologists compiled detailed statistical accounts of tattooing in prisons. Just as men in the army and women in the brothel were known to mark their bodies permanently as a rite of passage and as a means of self-identification with the values of the group, so too did inmates recognize tattoos as emblems of status and distinction within the institution.

A common inventory of images of power, defiance, sex, affection, and motherhood circulated in prison systems. Prisoners most commonly tattooed their arms, chests, and backs, but no area of the body was immune from the puncturing needle as hands, faces, necks, and genitals were marked with indelible symbols of love, power, and bravado. Women more rarely inscribed their bodies, but when they did, they most frequently chose maternal, religious, and romantic depictions.

Prison regimes, then as now, attempted to obliterate the individuality of inmates, relying on uniforms, codes, rules, and regulations to transform individuals into homogeneous conforming prisoners. However, through words, images, and gestures, the prisoners themselves often managed to create their own system of values and cultural identifications. The inmate's body could record the graffiti of protest and longing. Scripted tattoos like "Martyr for liberty" and "Prison is waiting for me" expressed the negative view of the victim and outcast. "Death to the bourgeoisie" indicated more than a vague sense of protest against the social order. One early-twentieth-century French inmate serving a term for theft with three previous convictions had his entire torso tattooed, explaining: "The tattoos on my body are hidden [under my shirt] and having them is a great source of pleasure to me. They are well done, there is nothing dishonest about them, and I like to show them off. My only regret is not being tattooed from top to bottom" (quoted in Charles Perrier, *Les Criminels: Etude concernant 859 condamnes* [Lyon, 1901–5]). The particular choice of this twenty-eight-year-old inmate was a potpourri of revolutionary and Napoleonic images, flowers, a serpent, a badge of honor, a bee, a bird, an assortment of portraits of women and men, the hilt of a dagger drawn as if entering his heart, and "Souvenir de la Martinique," all crowding his upper body and arms.

The use of argot and tattooing has been common among prisoners in different penal systems, whether in late-nineteenth-century Italian or French prisons or in the Soviet gulag system and the forced labor camps of the twentieth century. In the Soviet case, for example, criminals spoke their own dialect in the camps, regardless of their place of origin outside the world of incarceration. Representational and symbolic forms were used by generations of inmates to express a shared cultural identity within the context of the prison and to defy the anonymity of the faceless, homogenized, and uniformed mass that the disciplinary system of the prison strove to create.

Sexual and affective relations were another means of adapting and adjusting to the anonymity of prison life. The prison created an arena for expressions of love, jealousy, anger, and affection and for the emergence of networks of power run by prisoners within the institution. There are many indications that homosexuality was widely practiced in nineteenth-century men's prisons, even in those where isolation by night and surveillance of communal areas by day were the organizing principles of punishment. There is, however, little solid evidence on the extent of the phenomenon. Promiscuity among inmates attracted the attention of specialists, who blamed the prison for creating an environment of deviant sexuality. Reports written by doctors who worked in prisons acknowledged sexual activity among prisoners and denounced it as immoral and unnatural. Others argued, to the contrary, that the prisoners themselves were biologically doomed and that homosexuality was proof of their fundamental degeneracy and corruption. Administrators' reports, parliamentary inquests, and "scientific" studies offered conflicting opinions on the causes and cures of the problem. One French prison doctor, Charles Perrier, who worked at the prison of Nîmes in the last decade of the nineteenth century and the early years of the twentieth century, explained the particular situation of his institution in great detail by providing floor plans and descriptions of locking and opening techniques used by prisoners to defy single-cell arrangements in order to engage in homosexual liaisons. During the day, the illicit activity continued "in the workshop, in passage from one place to another, under the stairs, in the refectory (during reading periods and on days of bad weather), in the dormitory, in a word, everywhere." In Perrier's accounts of feverish activity, homosexual activity was possible because the guards were "comrades" (Perrier, *Les Criminels* 2:196).

In the records of women's prisons, there are also indications of a strong inmate culture in which affective relationships predominated. At the turn of the century several collections of letters and notes by women inmates were published in France. These writings are similar in their repetition of key themes and images surrounding husband-and-wife and mother-and-child relationships among prisoners. Inmate letters expressed affection and fidelity, anger and jealousy, and provided a commentary on survival in the prison and a critique of life in the outside world. Commentators on these collections stressed the perversity that, they felt, had to be associated with expressions of sexual love and affection between women, but they overlooked the fact that the most often repeated pleas from one prisoner to another were for simple companionship and friendship.

In the end, the evidence we have from prisoners themselves about sexual and emotional relationships in prison remains sketchy. It is likely, however, that homosexuality was not a phenomenon unique to French and American prisons in the nineteenth and twentieth centuries, systems for which documentary evidence of homosexuality exists.

MOVING PUNISHMENT INTO SOCIETY, 1880–1914

The late nineteenth century marked a profound change in the policy of punishment. Through an odd nexus of public opinion and two widely divergent theories of criminality, imprisonment gradually lost its place as the preferred penal sanction. During this period, press reports, accounts by sociologists and criminologists, and inmate journals and diaries sensationalized life behind prison walls. The public became increasingly aware of the prison's failure to rehabilitate wrongdoers and its success in fostering a culture of recidivism.

At the same time, a variety of new disciplines influenced penal development. Experts in the social sciences incorporated a complex of factors into new theories of deviance and punishment. Two distinct schools of thought emerged. The Italian School, led by the criminologist Cesare Lombroso, posited a biologically determined theory of deviance. Lombroso and his disciples argued, from observation of physical characteristics, that criminals were regressive and biologically inferior, just as, he contended, women as a sex were physiologically and intellectually inferior to men.

The opposition to Lombroso and his disciples was led by a number of criminologists, jurists, and forensic specialists throughout Europe who argued that family and social influences "created" the criminal. Supporters of this view, who included Franz von Liszt of Germany, Adolphe Prinz of Belgium, and G. W. Van Hamel of the Netherlands, joined forces in the International Union of Penal Law, founded in 1889, to voice their critique of a penal philosophy that absolved society of responsibility. They contended that society as well as the criminal had to be held accountable for an individual's deviance. Most vocal in their critique of the Italian School were French criminologists and forensic specialists led by Alexandre Lacassagne and Gabriel Tarde, who argued that crime could be reduced by improving the material environment.

In a related but distinct vein, in 1898, the French penologist Raymond Saleilles published a highly influential work, *L'Individualisation de la peine: Etude de la criminalité sociale,* which argued that criminals could exercise free will and assume moral responsibility. According to Saleilles, scientific study could help fit the punishment to the special needs of individual criminals.

The biological determinists absolved the prison of responsibility for prisoners because, as innate deviants, these criminals were incurable. The social-environmental theorists favored individualized punishments outside the homogenizing influence of the prison, along with preventive social reforms. For very different reasons, then, both schools discredited imprisonment as a method of treatment.

In this way, public and expert opinion agreed that imprisonment did not, and could not, fulfill its original ideal of treatment aimed at reintegrating the offender into the community. In accord with this devaluation of the prison as a rehabilitative site, a large number of European states created an array of new, noncustodial punishments, including parole, suspended sentence, and probation. Although imprisonment remained central in the field of punitive alternatives, it was, in those countries, no longer the punishment of first resort.

New Noncustodial Punishments

The rise of noncustodial sanctions changed the size and complexion of prison populations. Fewer first-time offenders were sentenced to prison, and the total number of prisoners shrank. Prison inmates became a more concentrated population of recidivists and serious criminals.

One of the innovations most significant in reducing the number of prisoners in Europe was the suspended sentence. Belgium led the way for other Western European countries in making this alternative part of its penal policy in 1888, followed by France in 1891. In this punishment, courts determined the length of a prison sentence and then suspended it, allowing the first-time offender to enjoy freedom as long as the conditions of the suspension were honored. In a variant of the suspended sentence, probation, the wrongdoer's sentence was not prescribed after his conviction, but he was informed that if he did not conform to the conditions of probation imposed on him—usually, displaying good behavior while free and reporting to an officer of the court—he would be brought back to the court and sentenced for his original crime, as well as for any crime involved in the break of the conditions of his probation.

In France, the penal population was reduced by half between 1887 and 1956, for the most part owing to the new punitive alternatives of suspended sentence introduced in the late nineteenth century and of probation in the twentieth century. Early-nineteenth-century reformers had believed that punishments must fit crimes and that the best way of punishing was the deprivation of liberty through the penitentiary. By accepting the suspended sentence as a legitimate punishment, traditional reformers yielded ground to the challengers who stressed the need for individualized punishments and insisted on the corrupting rather than corrective nature of the prison.

Suspended sentencing, following the Belgian and French lead, moved across Europe to Luxembourg (1892), Portugal (1893), Norway (1894), Italy (1904), Bulgaria (1904), Denmark (1905), Sweden (1906), Spain (1908), Hungary (1908), Greece (1911), the Netherlands (1915), and Finland (1918). Two German states, Saxony and Prussia, modified their penal legislation to include the suspended sentence as early as 1895. After World War I, suspended sentencing was adopted throughout Eastern Europe: the Russian Socialist Federated Republic incorporated the measure into its first criminal code in 1919, followed over the next thirteen years by Czechoslovakia, Romania, and Poland. In the course of the twentieth century, suspended sentencing also spread to Asia, Latin America, Africa, and the Middle East.

Another noncustodial punishment, supervised parole, was first used on an experimental basis with French juveniles in the 1830s. Parole involved the release of the prisoner on the grounds of good behavior before the sentence expired; the release was conditional and supervised. Parole was enacted into law for juveniles for the first time in 1850 and was extended in 1854 to political prisoners transported to penal colonies, who were allowed to work in the community under supervised conditions. Portugal was the first country to use parole, or conditional release as it was also known, with adult criminal populations, beginning in 1861, followed by Saxony in 1862 and Germany in 1871. In 1873 Denmark passed a law creating an advanced system of classification in which prisoners progressed toward conditional liberation. For the ten years preceding enactment of the law, a Danish prison had experimented with conditional release and claimed a dramatic decline in the rate of recidivism. The International Penitentiary Congress held in Stockholm in 1878 acknowledged that, as a form of punishment, conditional release was "not contrary to principles of penal law, not harming the judgment, and presenting advantages for society and for the convicted."

The parole system established in France in 1885 was based on the concept of conditional release joined to a strong private patronage network. The state made grants to private societies and private institutions for the care of prisoners released after serving half their sentences. Although only those convicted of misdemeanors were eligible for this early form of parole, about twelve thousand prisoners were released to the care of private patrons between 1886 and 1895. Parole was approved throughout Europe at the International Prison Congress of 1910.

Patronage was an essential aspect of surveillance for released prisoners in certain Western European nations. Entrusting convicts to the oversight of private individuals, patronage societies, and state-funded agencies was not a return to traditional ideas about how best to control wrongdoers; it was instead an expansion of modern penal ideas into the society at large. Noncustodial punishments indicated the state's confidence in its ability to extend discipline and control beyond the prison and into the community. In the less-developed Russian system, local communities figured heavily in meting out harsh punishment. Instead of being sent to prison, the majority of those convicted were sentenced to exile, fines, and most commonly, whipping. Russia's reliance on physical punishments based on retribution and revenge, in community settings, horrified Western European reformers. In contrast, community-based punishments in the more industrialized states of continental Europe emphasized the beneficence of local involvement, although in fact constituting a highly standardized and centralized punitive mechanism.

French Penal Colonies

At the same time that punishments were ameliorated for first-time offenders and alternatives to the prison were identified, punishments for repeat offenders and those found guilty of serious crimes became harsher in France. Deportation, for example, was the legal term reserved for the punishment of political crimes in the first half of the nineteenth century. The sentence of deportation was replaced by the legal designation of transportation to a penal colony with the reform of the French penal code in 1885. After that date, serious offenders and hardened criminals were sentenced to overseas internment in French holdings in South America and the South Pacific.

Reliance on overseas penal colonies was at odds with punishment philosophy generally, which sought the reintegration of offenders into the community rather than their total exclusion from it. However, relegation—a lifetime sentence of preventive detention in a penal colony—was reserved for hardened criminals, whom the system had given up on reforming. René Bérenger, one of France's foremost penal reformers and critics of the 1885 law, described relegation to a penal colony as "the bloodless guillotine" because of the high mortality rate associated with serving time there. The French, who decided to adopt this new form of punishment at the time when the British convict system in Australia was being dismantled, were undoubtedly influenced in their decision by the fear of hardened criminality and the creation of a criminal class of recidivists. Some observers felt that the severity of the punishment, which resulted in the deaths of thousands of men and women in the penal colonies of New Caledonia and French Guiana, was tantamount to extermination.

An international penal congress in 1880 questioned the legitimacy of the transportation of convicts as a form of punishment and singled out the French overseas experience for special comment: "What are the results? The sad legend of Guiana, from which nearly all those whom yellow fever did not kill, have escaped. . . . Perils without end, continual escapes, millions in expenditures, that is the balance sheet. . . . Transportation is not a punishment. It is only an expedient." Transportation of forced-labor convicts to New Caledonia was suspended in 1897 and was finally expunged from the books in 1938. In 1942 the relegation of multiple offenders was also abolished.

Although the benefits of colonization and economic development motivated some of the support for sending convicts to a colony, the fear of relentlessly rising recidivism rates at home figured heavily in the French legislation of the 1880s. Half of all convicted criminals were former offenders. The high number of recidivists may have been due in part, however, to the state's increased ability to detect them. Recidivism was a culturally constructed category made possible by more accurate statistical knowledge and a new technology of identification, including anthropometric procedures and fingerprinting.

Russian Penal Reforms

While Western European nations were enacting noncustodial punishments, Russia moved at a considerably slower pace in its attempts to reform its penal and judicial systems between the 1860s and the outbreak of World War I. Tsarist officials faced the unique challenge of a strongly entrenched, extralegal system of popular justice known as samosud, which was regulated by the peasant community. Of the few defendants who appeared before state courts, only a small percentage of them went to prison. The vast majority of those convicted were exiled, fined, or whipped.

With the goal of remaking Russia in Europe's image, the tsarist government abolished corporal punishment in the 1860s. Educated Russians believed that physical punishments offended personal dignity. The peasant reactions to these reforms reveal a disparity in sensibilities: many peasants apparently feared that fines and imprisonment would weigh more heavily on them than corporal punishment. In addition, because of the massive state expenditures required to isolate prisoners effectively, Russian reformers grew discouraged about how to implement imprisonment. Even those interested in reforming the prisons faced, in a country as vast and diverse as Russia, an excessively expensive and complex task, which pressed them to rely on the punitive initiative of the local community more than in other European countries.

Exile continued as a punishment in Russia throughout the nineteenth century, although reformers repeatedly sought its abolition. Deportation with hard labor remained the most severe punishment into the twentieth century when, under Joseph Stalin, it assumed the scope and severity of exceptional brutality.

Internationalization of Reform

As we have seen, many of the alternative punishments introduced throughout Europe in the second half of the nineteenth century germinated in international congresses where government representatives, reformers, and prison specialists regularly convened to discuss the prevention of crime and the reform of punishment. These meetings and the periodical literature that flourished around them were important forums for the dissemination of ideas, language, and concepts among an increasingly international penological community.

International societies dedicated to philanthropy, criminology, criminal anthropology, penal law, and policy-related issues were created specifically to study reforms of particular facets of the penal process. In exchanging information, experiences, and ideas, reformers hoped that an international community could influence progressive changes in the correctional systems of member nations. The international meetings drove changes as much as they reflected them. Italian criminal anthropologists, for example, hoped that winning general European support at an international congress held in Rome in 1885 would strengthen their influence over the new Italian penal code then in preparation. International meetings not only reviewed the state of the field but also provided a showcase for new social science approaches, particularly for criminologists, psychiatrists, and those favoring biological explanations of criminality.

The influence of international meetings is nowhere more evident than in the widespread recognition of the suspended sentence for first-time offenders as a legitimate alternative punishment at the turn of the century. In fact, virtually every major transformation in punishment was discussed in one international forum or another before country-by-country adoption. The prison work system and the training of guards by apprenticeship were also widely discussed by reformers across national frontiers. In a typical procedure for reviewing a controversial issue, the Fifth International Penitentiary Congress held in Paris in 1895 posed the question: do prisoners have the right to a salary? The assembled representatives discussed the merits of bonuses, fixed allotments, and room-and-board payments to inmates and concluded that prisoners could be rewarded for work performed but did not have any legal claim to a salary. Similarly, the International Penitentiary Congress held in Budapest in 1905 discussed the issue of prisoners' accident insurance, which was defended on the grounds that prisoners were sentenced to a loss of liberty, not a loss of health. The content of the debate and the solutions endorsed differed from country to country, but these international forums defined the terms of the debate and helped to forge a new consciousness and new sensibilities about punishment.

Twentieth-Century Trends in Punishment, 1914–1945

The period between 1914 and 1945 was a liminal epoch in the history of modern punishment, poised as it was between nineteenth-century practices of incarceration and twentieth-century experiments in noncustodial punishment. Most penal innovations introduced before World War I were maintained and extended after 1918 from Western Europe to Russia, where reforms had been introduced late and inconclusively. Across Europe, a number of changes occurred, expanding the range of penal options. On one end of the spectrum were experiments like the Swedish furlough program and a heavier reliance on fines in place of incarceration. On the other end of the spectrum was the increased use of prisons and camps, which now housed newly defined deviant populations, sometimes in the same countries that were also testing alternatives to incarceration.

In the Soviet Union, commitment to penal reform was part of the postrevolutionary agenda of the Bolsheviks, who, in 1918, abolished courts and prisons for children and raised the age for criminal liability from ten years to seventeen. Commissions studying juvenile crime recommended that the child not only be punished but also be educated and protected, although little coordination in child care and rehabilitation actually took place because of competing jurisdictions and agencies.

In the 1920s, the Soviet Union experimented with penal forms, as well as with other institutional and cultural structures. A Ukrainian teacher, Anton S. Makarenko, established a commune for young offenders convicted for crimes of violence. Makarenko's aim was to use the pressure of the peer group as a means of moral rehabilitation through education and vocational training. Along with the emphasis on education, which re-sembled certain Western European experiments in the nineteenth century, there was also a moral concern with productive Soviet citizenship. In spite of the best intentions of reformers, however, little changed in penal practice.

Like Russia, other European countries attempted to reform their penal systems by relying on prewar advances in penology, criminology, and related disciplines. Western Europeans differed, however, in the degree to which psychoanalysis influenced the individual treatment model. The psychoanalytic case history approach also threw into relief the corrective treatment of children. Out of its concern with "international child welfare," the newly formed League of Nations created a committee whose concerns ranged beyond juvenile delinquency to include health, political, and moral issues af-fecting adult populations as well as children. The League hoped to serve as "a world documentation center" to encourage governments and private bodies to exchange in-formation and to coordinate welfare issues related to punishment.

Other countries expanded their implementation of noncustodial punishments. In the 1930s Sweden introduced the furlough system as a key component of institutional care. On a regular basis, prisoners, selected according to type of crime and length of punishment, were allowed periods of freedom following periods of imprisonment. Furloughs, normally forty-eight hours in duration, were established to maintain the prisoner's ties with the outside world and with family members and thereby, it was hoped, to facilitate the prisoner's return to free society. On the whole, Swedish penal reformers deemed the program a success.

In the 1930s there was a growing use of fines throughout Europe. Fines were a significant deviation from earlier punitive models, in which deprivation of liberty was the sine qua non of effective punishment. Fines were sometimes criticized, however, as commercializing the justice systems of the countries that used them. In countries with large numbers of impoverished citizens, including Poland, Italy, and Bulgaria, fines were less likely to be used to penalize the most common offenses.

By contrast, Germany and Italy dramatically enlarged their prison systems in the interwar years. In Germany, criminal law served as an important tool for the National Socialist state to rid itself of its enemies. Crime rates skyrocketed as a consequence of the creation of new categories of criminal behavior covering everything from sexual practices to political dissent. The higher crime rate was used in turn as a justification for enlarging the police force and giving it more authority.

In their classic study *Punishment and Social Structure,* Georg Rusche and Otto Kirchheimer acknowledged that the accession to power of Adolf Hitler advanced, rather than itself initiated, the increasing severity of punishment, whose origins are more ac-curately identified in the Weimar period. Concerned with justifying its own constitu-tional legitimacy and facing the severe economic challenges of hyperinflation and reparations payments, the Weimar Republic relied on greater use of the death penalty, penal servitude, and long-term imprisonment. These rigid penal practices had their origins in the imperial period. Yet National Socialist penal policies took severe punishments to new extremes, singled out those deemed socially unacceptable for special severity, and enlarged the number of political offenses. Imprisonment, originally intended as a more humane and rehabilitative punishment than physical torture and disfiguring punishments, was perverted into a tool of systematic repression and extermination. The achievements of nineteenth- and twentieth-century industry and technology were perverted to what one German official called "murder by assembly line."

The concentration camps of twentieth-century Germany and the work camps of the Soviet Union also facilitated the ruthless exploitation of convict labor. Ironically, the systems of forced labor under which millions suffered and died were masked by a slogan that could have been devised by a nineteenth-century penal reformer explaining the liberating value of labor: "Arbeit Macht Frei" (Work Makes You Free).

The creation of Soviet corrective labor camps, a vast network of penal institutions in Siberia and Soviet Asia begun in the 1930s, coincided with the planned growth of the Soviet economy and the purges that accompanied it. Horrifying accounts of life in forced labor camps leave no doubt that principles of rehabilitation and the creation of a productive citizenry were incompatible with Stalinist penal policies. The gold mines of the eastern Soviet Union, for example, were death camps characterized by a total disregard for the value of human life. In the Arctic camps of Kolyma, where millions are said to have died, prisoners were expected to mine even in winter.

After Stalin's death, several important changes in punishment took place. The number of forced labor camps was apparently reduced. In limited cases, authorities began to rely on social collectives for supervision of released offenders returned to the community. Within prison, work teams, quotas, and group responsibility in the prison workplace corresponded to the behavior and values of the broader society. An observer in 1965 commented on the effectiveness of the Soviet work system in measuring up to standards of outside production.

Thus, the development of European penal systems took two widely divergent paths in the first half of the twentieth century. The desire to rehabilitate and reintegrate prisoners led some countries to rely less on imprisonment and more on noncustodial punishments. Other countries saw in imprisonment an opportunity for unprecedented abuse and exploitation.

Post–World War II Penal Reforms, 1945–1965

The horrors of World War II, the imprisonment and extermination of millions in concentration camps, and the displacement and expulsion of millions more after the war provided the world with a picture of collective punishment that was brutal, unjust, and inhumane. In reaction to the events of 1940–45, postwar penal reformers devoted unprecedented attention to the legal rights of prisoners. Those who took up the cause in 1945 had two significant lessons from the war fresh in their minds: the world had just witnessed the worst perversion of punishment run amok, as eyewitness accounts and photographs chronicled the horrifying genocide of concentration camps; and an extranational juridical body at Nuremberg had recognized the existence of evil and the need to punish it. Whereas the latter affirmed the legitimacy and morality of the right to punish, the former demanded reevaluation of the whole array of penal sanctions. With a new fervor and commitment, Europeans took up the challenge of fair and humane punishment and the need to reform the institutions that enforced it.

France was among the first to change its national penal system. In May 1945, the Commission for the Reform of French Penitentiaries explicitly endorsed the humane treatment and betterment of prisoners through general and professional instruction. Medical, psychological, and social services were available in every penitentiary, and prison personnel were required to receive specialized, technical training.

In the international arena, the United Nations (UN) was in the vanguard of attempts at enlightened reform of criminal justice systems throughout the world. Just as the League of Nations had done in the interwar years, the UN worked to establish international standards for fair and humane treatment of prisoners, to undertake research of penal issues, and to compile accurate statistical information at the international level. In 1948 the UN created a section dedicated to the prevention of crime and the treatment of offenders. The Geneva Congress of the United Nations, held in 1955, passed "Minimum Rules for the Treatment of Prisoners," which observers believed opened a new era in penal corrections: the "Rules" set the standards for fair and just treatment and made recommendations for training personnel and for creating more "open" penal and correctional institutions. In addition, the European Convention on the Protection of Human Rights and Basic Freedoms, endorsed in Rome on November 4, 1950, was influential throughout Europe in its attempt to guarantee basic rights to everyone, including prisoners. Prisoners' rights were also defined by the Council of Europe, which established the European Committee on Crime Problems in 1957.

The Social Defense Movement

The treatment concept, a familiar idea in new garb, dominated international discussions in the 1950s and 1960s. One of its manifestations, the Social Defense movement, spearheaded in the postwar years by the eminent French jurist Marc Ancel, had its roots in the late-nineteenth-century reform movements, which had taken their inspiration from discoveries in biology, medicine, and the social sciences. Postwar Social Defense reformers emphasized that society would be protected best through the treatment of the offender, not through the insistence on his or her moral responsibility under the law. Much of the movement's fervor came from the prewar penal reforms of the 1930s throughout Europe and from the renewed postwar commitment to decency and humanity in punishment.

Although the Social Defense movement is difficult to define because of its doctrinal diversity and its various splinter groups and factions, in general terms it advocated treatment of the individual offender as the best way of protecting society. Treatment drew on the array of social services in the postwar welfare system, from psychiatric counseling to job training to assistance by social workers. Social Defense had a truly international dimension with its own group founded under Ancel's direction in 1947. The International Society of Social Defense hoped that through social and economic change and the application of scientific treatment measures to the criminal, the role of the prison would be greatly reduced. In spite of attempts to internationalize solutions, however, particular national concerns and cultural assumptions predominated in the process of reforming correctional systems. The indeterminate sentence, an open-ended sentencing practice intended to calibrate the length of sentence to the prisoner's performance in the institution and his or her fitness for release, is a good example of lack of agreement in international reform circles about the value of particular punishments for Social Defense. For some followers, the indeterminate sentence practiced in the United States since 1900 was viewed as enhancing rehabilitative possibilities, whereas European countries such as France saw indeterminacy as a cruel and unusual punishment.

Many critics warned that the Social Defense approach to deviance would result in both an attenuation of the authority of the courts and an emptying out of prisons because it would break the link between crime and imprisonment and displace fixed penalties. Opponents of the movement feared that sociologists, criminologists, and psychiatrists would usurp the role of judges and place their sciences over the rule of law. Yet in spite of often bitter disagreements among both followers and detractors of the movement, Social Defense stood as a marker of the general postwar emphasis on individual treatment and social protection.

The Open Prison and Autonomy within the Walls

Centralized administrative structures continued to be responsible for much of the correctional work conducted throughout Europe after World War II and continued to impose rigid, routinized regimes in all prisons. The French Fourth Republic, for example, renewed its endorsement of the deprivation of liberty as a principal form of punishment for the purposes of reforming convicted criminals and returning them to free society, even as critics of the prison system agitated for more individualized treatment.

But now, in addition to the traditional, closed prisons, which continued to operate after 1945, a new breed of penal institutions took their place in the range of punishments. Communal-based sentencing, that is, punishment taken out into the community and beyond prison walls, was the logical extension of a treatment-based model of punishment. Several European countries developed "prisons without walls": farms and open, unfenced institutions for those offenders who could be trusted not to escape and who presented no serious threat if they did. Simultaneously, there was a movement toward establishing looser regimes behind the walls of closed, secure institutions, in which the prisoner would be allowed a larger measure of autonomy than in the traditional prison.

Most European nations recognized that allowing prisoners a certain degree of freedom of movement and decision within the institution and allowing more frequent interaction with the outside world constituted the best means of returning offenders to their families and communities as productive citizens. These prisons relied on behavioral and therapeutic models of correctional treatment. The "treatment ideology" superseded the security, prevention, and deterrence rhetoric of punishment, although implementation varied widely from country to country. These developments dovetailed with a recognition in the 1960s that the idea of confinement was itself deviant, a perception confirmed by the normalization theories of radical sociology.

Leaves, vacations, and the general relaxation of punishment in Denmark and Sweden resulted in Europe's most lenient prisons. Scandinavia and the Netherlands offered extensive support to the imprisoned and the recently released by implementing a whole array of day and weekend leaves, work release programs, home furloughs, and job-hunting furloughs. The Netherlands was in the vanguard of treatment- and community-based punishments. There, the Prison Act, passed in 1953, decreed two important organizing principles for postwar Dutch prisons: first, that prisoners be involved in group interactions; and second, that a greater emphasis be placed on the prisoner's preparation for the return to free society. Sweden too endorsed the move beyond prison walls. The official Swedish policy was that prisons should be as little used and as painless as possible. Sweden was especially committed to penal policy-making by the lay public and to community-based facilities. The small size and homogeneity of the Swedish national community, reformers acknowledged, made such a system viable. On the whole, then, those countries that experimented with open prisons and more autonomous prison populations had made a firm commitment by the early 1960s to a road that led away from traditional forms of incarceration and toward the decline of the prison.

Treatment as Punishment: The Decline of the Prison

Postwar reforms stressed the need for the state to tailor punishment to the individual convicted criminal, to his or her personality, attitude, and willingness to change. Custodial sanctions and deprivation of liberty declined dramatically as punishments of first resort, and parole, probation, suspended sentence, and fines became more common sentences for first-time offenders. Above all, state agencies, social workers, and private patronage systems sought individual treatment solutions rather than relying on incarceration to transform prisoners into a uniformed and faceless population.

In 1965, Sweden enacted a new criminal code emphasizing noninstitutional alternatives to punishment. The code endorsed the goal of prevention and eliminated prevailing ideas of retribution. Conditional sentences and probation became routine for first-time offenders. Fines were the most common punishment for over three hundred prohibitions and were imposed on 95 percent of offenders. Sweden was more advanced in its rejection of custodial sanctions but was nevertheless typical of many continental European nations in the twenty years following World War II.

The popularity of probation grew dramatically in Scandinavia, the Netherlands, France, and Italy. In 1965, only Spain, Portugal, and Eastern Europe resisted the two dominant Western European models of probation: active, intense surveillance, and the more lenient monitoring. Active treatment aimed at reintegration into the community or stressed intervention and coercion over the offender's behavior by using probation as an alternative to custody. Probation caused the dramatic decline in the already small numbers of women in prison. The number of women serving long-term sentences in France, for example, was 5,231 on January 1, 1946; by January 1, 1980, the number, after a steady decline, stood at 1,121.

The Netherlands offers the most striking example of the decline in the size of sentenced populations in the two decades following World War II. The number sentenced to prison per 100,000 of the population fell from 66 in 1950 to 25 in 1965 and continued to decline to the lowest rate in Europe. The Dutch state invested heavily in the correctional system in terms of personnel, institutional construction, and intensity of treatment efforts. The shrinking prison population reflected shorter prison sentences, with an average prison term of one and one-half months.

By the same token, Sweden's use of short sentences also explains the contraction in its prison populations in the two postwar decades. By 1970 only one-tenth of all prisoners received sentences of one year or longer. Over two-thirds received sentences of less than four months. Prisons were modified and diversified, so that open prisons held one-third of all prisoners. The emphasis on treatment as punishment was linked to the open prison policy as part of the same progressive reform movement. In the 1970s, prisoners' exposure to limited periods of freedom was extended to summer vacations with members of their immediate families in specially surveilled vacation dwellings. The possibility of actually living with their families became available to those prisoners serving long sentences. Visitor hotels near certain designated prisons permitted conjugal and family visits on weekends.

In the Netherlands, religious and philanthropic groups continued to be responsible for probationary care and helped to make it common to judicial procedures. Private, communal involvement in corrections existed as well in Norway and Finland, where the governments subsidized private societies for probationary activities, and in Sweden, where probation was conducted by supervised volunteers. Social workers in the Netherlands and Sweden assumed growing responsibility for professional probationary activities; both countries relied on a combined program of volunteer aides and trained social workers. The participation of these private groups in the shift to communally based corrections should not be underestimated: reminiscent of the involvement of bourgeois philanthropists a century earlier, modern volunteers embraced the idea of a citizenry involved in the punishment and correction of criminals in a world where prisons no longer worked. By contrast, West Germany built its new correctional system by relying on professionally trained probation officers to supervise almost half of all convicts who would otherwise serve sentences of nine months or less, thus also achieving a low rate of incarceration.

Prisons and Society

In spite of common trends, one must in the end remark on the diversity that characterized European penal systems in the last quarter of the twentieth century. Among the many ways to measure the effectiveness of punishment is to calculate the care and attention that prisoners receive from their keepers. Here there appeared to be no common pattern. The ratio of prison personnel to inmates varied widely throughout Europe in the two decades following World War II. The Netherlands, heavily committed to a treatment model, had the lowest ratio, with 3,100 correctional personnel responsible for 4,500 prisoners in 1959. Sweden, with the same prison population, had half as many prison employees to supervise and treat prisoners. West Germany lagged considerably behind with 3,300 prison personnel responsible for 19,000 prisoners. However, West Germany built its new corrections system by relying on professionally trained probation officers to supervise almost half of all convicts serving sentences of nine months or less.

Regardless of how effectiveness is measured and regardless of the number of prisoners and guards in a given institution, the rhetoric that surrounded penal reform stressed less punishment rather than more. Scandinavian countries in the postwar period went so far as to call for the total abolition of the prison. These countries experienced a decline in prison populations over the long term. As a consequence of the Northern Punishment Criminal Act of 1963, Denmark, Finland, Iceland, Norway, and Sweden agreed to open up their correctional system, which had already been considerably reduced in size. The new relaxation of the exigencies of confinement included measures such as weekend and vacation passes and increased availability of leaves for prisoners.

Socialist countries, in contrast to the rest of Europe, maintained the prison sentence as the single most important sanction in the correctional repertoire. Prisons in socialist countries continued to be oriented toward "resocialization" of the offender through longer sentences, job training, education, and disciplinary techniques. Hungary was closest to the Western European model and was the exception among Eastern bloc nations because of its willingness to use conditional release as a means of facilitating the prisoner's social reentry into free society.

Dramatically different from the prison trends of most of continental Europe and much closer to the American experience was the steady growth of the prison systems in England. The number of prisoners in Britain doubled between 1950 and 1980 while the number declined rapidly in the open prison countries of the Netherlands and Scandinavia.

The diversity in state prison systems in the end reflected the political systems of the different states and, as the reformer Léon Faucher said over a century earlier, "the social state" of citizens. A common commitment to reform prevailed. By 1965 the concern for prisoners' rights inspired by the legacy of World War II had produced penal innovations that took hold in much of Western Europe. In Denmark and Sweden, prisoners were granted extensive new freedoms to maintain ties with families and communities, for the purpose of easing the eventual release from prison. Even those countries that continued to endorse traditional imprisonment also relied more and more on community-based intermediate punishments such as suspended sentence, parole, and probation. The shared values and moral consensus that emerged after the war allowed the punishment process to move into the society at large. Monitoring and surveillance, which formerly required prison walls, could be achieved in free society on a scale never before possible.

In general, however, despite reforms of the penal codes of Western European nations through the introduction of short sentences or noncustodial sentences aimed at keeping people out of prison, penal populations in Western Europe, viewed over the long term, began to expand again after 1955. Penal specialists viewed the increase in life sentences and sentences longer than five years as troubling and not easily explained. Although noncustodial punishments became increasingly prevalent throughout Europe after 1950, prison populations continued to grow even in countries, like France, committed to noncustodial arrangements. Punishment has always been expensive. Penal practices, like collective pardons due to overcrowding or the policy of wait-listing those sentenced to prison until space becomes available, required public toleration if not approval, neither of which was easily achieved in some parts of Europe. Critics also questioned how progressive noncustodial sentencing really was as community corrections and nonsegregative techniques made state control more pervasive.

Rehabilitation and control have been the twin concerns of the modern penal system from its beginnings. In the twentieth century, emphasis on treatment complemented but did not vanquish the earlier reformers' preoccupation with discipline and control. Yet the ideal prison so ardently sought by reformers in the early nineteenth century, the prison in which prisoners were made into better citizens, seemed as far from reality in 1965 as it had in 1865.

Bibliographic Note

Since the 1960s the social science literature on continental European prisons has expanded dramatically, with an emphasis on sociology, criminology, and penology. The appearance of Michel Foucault's *Discipline and Punish: The Birth of the Prison,* trans. Alan Sheridan (New York: Pantheon Books, 1977), marked a sea change in the historical literature. The impact of Foucault's work on the history of the prison was evident in the 1980s in studies of the social and cultural history of punishment. These studies include my own book, *The Promise of Punishment: Prisons in Nineteenth-Century France* (Princeton: Princeton University Press, 1982), as well as the following: Michelle Perrot, ed., *L'Impossible prison: Recherches sur le systeme penitentiaire au 19e seicle* (Paris: Seuil, 1980); Jacques Guy Petit, *La Prison, le bagne et l'histoire* (Geneva: Librairie des Meridiens, 1984) and *Ces Peines obscures* (Paris: Fayard, 1990); and Robert Roth, *Pratiques penitentiaires et theorie sociale; l'Exemple de la prison de Geneve, 1825–1862* (Geneva: Droz, 1981).

The classic Marxist study by Georg Rusche and Otto Kirchheimer, *Punishment and Social Structure* (New York: Russell and Russell, 1939), looks at the prison in relation to commercial capitalism across Europe, including Italy, Poland, Belgium, Sweden, and Germany. Dario Melossi and Massimo Pavarini, *The Prison and the Factory: Origins of the Penitentiary System*, trans. Glynis Cousin (Totowa, N.J.: Barnes and Noble Books, 1981), follows Rusche and Kirchheimer in their strict Marxist analysis by applying it to the Italian experience. Michael Ignatieff, "State, Civil Society, and Total Institutions: A Critique of Recent Social Histories of Punishment," *Crime and Justice: An Annual Review of Research* 3 (1981): 153–92, provocatively critiques the new historiography of the modern prison including his own work, *A Just Measure of Pain: The Penitentiary in the Industrial Revolution, 1750–1850* (New York: Pantheon Books, 1978), that of David Rothman on the history of the American prison, and the work of Michel Foucault.

Gordon Wright, *Between the Guillotine and Liberty: Two Centuries of the Crime Problem in France* (New York: Oxford University Press, 1983), Robert Badinter, *La Prison republicaine* (Paris: Fayard 1992), and John A. Davis, *Conflict and Control: Law and Order in Nineteenth-Century Italy* (Basingstoke, England: Macmillan Education, 1988), root the prison very much in the specific political realities of national communities. Although some recent works, including Foucault's, have implications for a comparative analysis of the prison across national borders, virtually no historical studies have undertaken this task. Penal reformers, however, constituted and continue to constitute an international professional community that generates comparative data: national commissions, conventions, international congresses, reports by the League of Nations, the United Nations, and the European Community are important sources for information on continental European prisons in the nineteenth and twentieth centuries.

Studies by Norman Johnson on prison architecture, by Harold K. Becker and Einar O. Hjellemo on the Netherlands, by Robert Gellately on Germany, by Ulla Bondeson on Sweden, and the late-nineteenth-century classic by Raymond Saleilles on individualization of punishment—*L'Individualisation de la peine: Etude de la criminalite sociale*, published in English as *The Individualization of Punishment*, trans. Rachel Szold Jastrow (Montclair, N.J.: Patterson Smith, 1968)—are among the works that have been useful in developing this chapter. Marc Ancel's many books on the Social Defense movement he founded, on suspended sentencing, and on European penal legal systems provide an important perspective on post–World War II conditions. Two studies by David Garland—*Punishment and Welfare: A History of Penal Strategies* (Aldershot, England: Gower, 1985) and *Punishment and Modern Society: A Study in Social Theory* (Chicago: University of Chicago Press, 1990)—examine the relationship between culture, especially that of the modern welfare state, and penal practices.

CHAPTER EIGHT

THE CONTEMPORARY PRISON
1965–Present

Norval Morris

By the mid-1990s, one and three-quarter million persons were held in prison or jail in the United States; more than one million, one hundred thousand were in prison. But there is an astonishing diversity to the institutions in which they are held. Prisons range in security from double-barred steel cages within high-walled, electronically monitored perimeters to rooms in unlocked buildings in unfenced fields. They range in pain from windowless rooms of close-confined, sensory-deprived isolation to work camps of no physical adversity whatsoever. There are "open prisons" indistinguishable from farms and "prisoners" who spend their days working unescorted and unsupervised in the community; there are "weekend prisons" and "day prisons"; there are "coeducational prisons"; and there are prisons of grindingly dull routine interrupted by occasional flashes of violence and brutality. There are prisons with tennis courts and prisons where the only out-of-cell exercise is an hour of pacing an outdoor cage three times a week; there are prisons of excessively crowded congregation and prisons of utter isolation. There are community-based prerelease centers, called "prisons," indistinguishable from workers' hostels; and there are "prisoners" doing time in their own homes, which for this purpose are legally classified as prisons.

It would be an error to assume that most of these late-twentieth-century mutations of the prison tend toward leniency and comfort. The most common prisons are the overcrowded prisons proximate to the big cities of America; they have become places of deadening routine punctuated by bursts of fear and violence. Nor is there a clear trend in either direction: traditional, massive prisons and modern, smaller prisons both proliferate.

Yet within this diversity, the typical prison in the United States has a distinguishable pattern of daily life. For the great bulk of prisoners, this consists of a relentlessly unchanging, grimly gray routine—always the same, never a change unless for the worse. Day in, day out, life is the same, unless there is a "lockdown." And during a lockdown it is even more of the same: twenty-four hours per day in the cell, broken only by a once-weekly shower. Otherwise there is the same routine, the same grinding repetition.

Always the same, always the same—but then, unless you have been a prisoner, you don't know that deadening sameness. It is not easy to portray life in prison; bland description would miss the inner reality. So I have used the literary device of a diary of one day and one night in the life of a typical prisoner in a typical prison adjacent to a typical industrial city. This "diary of prisoner #12345" was constructed as follows. At my request, two prisoners kept a detailed diary for one day. I chose the one prepared by Simon "Sam" Gutierrez, of F House, Cell 304, Stateville Prison, Illinois, and, with his permission, rewrote it from what I knew from observing prison life. I then shared the result with Sam Gutierrez and with the warden of Stateville and several senior correctional officials in Illinois and elsewhere. I adopted most of their suggestions for revision. The responsibility for all errors remains mine; but the pattern and, I believe, the truth are Sam's. Sam wrote a commentary around his diary, and I have retained this structure in my composite diary.

Stateville Prison, where Sam is held, is the maximum-security prison in effect serving Chicago, though prisoners come there from all over Illinois. It is a paradigm maximum-security prison; at the time the "diary" was written it housed some twenty-one hundred prisoners in a complex of buildings covering sixty-four acres, surrounded by a high and gun-manned wall.

Given the substantial differences in types of imprisonment in different countries of the contemporary Western world, this chapter will concentrate on imprisonment in the United States. And since jails, prisons for women, and institutions for juvenile offenders are dealt with elsewhere in this book, they are excluded here. Hence the typical prisoner is an adult male, and the pronouns *him* and *he* are used throughout.

ONE DAY IN THE LIFE OF #12345

You asked me to keep a diary for one day. You told me I was not to tell you that things were good or bad—just to tell you exactly what I did and what happened to me through one day. I have never done anything like this before. It is not easy to describe a day of monotony and boredom other than as monotonous and boring.

Before I start on the diary, let me say this: if you expect the usual prison tale of constant violence, brutal guards, gang rapes, daily escape efforts, turmoil, and fearsome adventures, you will be deeply disappointed. Prison life is really nothing like what the press, television, and movies suggest. It is not a daily round of threats, fights, plots, and "shanks" (prison-made knives)—though you have to be constantly careful to avoid situations or behavior that might lead to violence. A sense of impending danger is always with you; you must be careful to move around people rather than against or through them, but with care and reasonable sense you can move safely enough. For me, and many like me in prison, violence is not the major problem; the major problem is monotony. It is the dull sameness of prison life, its idleness and boredom, that grinds me down. Nothing matters; everything is inconsequential other than when you will be free and how to make time pass until then. But boredom, time-slowing boredom, interrupted by occasional bursts of fear and anger, is the governing reality of life in prison.

So, here is my diary for yesterday:

5:30 A.M.:

I was awakened by the wake-up call for the kitchen detail. I am not on that detail, but the banging on the bars of the cell near me, to awaken a prisoner who is on the kitchen detail, wakes me every morning. I knew I could doze for the next half hour, half awake but careful not to think about where I was. I heard Tyrone stirring in the bunk beneath mine, but today he did not, as he often does, celebrate the new day with a loud and odorous fart.

6:00 A.M.:

The keys were rattled across the bars of our cells, and F House came to life. F House is the roundhouse (the cell house, you told me, is a panopticon, designed by Jeremy Bentham). It has four tiers of cells around its perimeter, each tier having sixty-two cells. The cells are all the same; most of them are single cells, but recently there has been some double celling.

As F House came to life, the noise began—radios, TVs, shouting from cell to cell—and so it would go on till night, with an occasional scream of rage or fear through the night.

Tyrone and I did our best to keep out of each other's way in the space of nine feet by six in our cell while we used our toilet and washed and dressed and pulled up the blankets on our steel bunks. We change our outer clothes sometimes twice a week, sometimes once a week, and our socks and underwear every other day. If you have money, or influence, or a friend in the laundry, you can do better than this. Our dress in summer is blue jeans and a blue shirt or a white T-shirt; in winter we wear blue jeans, a blue shirt, and one of those heavy, lined, blue jackets. Our sartorial flourish is our sneakers, with Nike outranking Reebok and so on down the line; they cost a lot, but in this place they are worth it.

As we washed and dressed, we listened to my radio, which is tied to the steel support of my bunk. Tyrone and I agree about what we like to listen to in the mornings—talk shows, real people talking about real issues. My mind dives into whatever issues are discussed, pro and con; I form opinions; it represents sanity for me. It helps to give me the sense that we are still part of the world. It is often hard to hear, such is the noise from competing radios and TVs in neighboring cells, particularly the rock and country music stations turned on full blast. And there are the shouts from cell to cell and to the tower guards from prisoners trying to get their cell doors opened—the noise never ceases. Others tell me that they get used to it; Tyrone doesn't seem to mind; I must be getting old.

6:30 A.M.:

F House began to be unlocked, with the loudspeaker from the tower guards bellowing, "Three and four galleries: in the tunnel for chow." I turned off the radio and flipped the light switch at the back of the cell, on and off, on and off, the flickering light being my request to the tower guard to open the door to this cell, which he does from the controls in the central tower. Most cells in F House remain locked at this time; usually not many guys get up for breakfast except on "Donut and Sweet Rolls" days, when most everybody remembers to come for breakfast.

We lined up in rough lines, to walk through the tunnel to the mess hall. There was pushing at the front; the fat ones always seem to be there. It was semi-dark in the tunnel, and there were no lights. I was glad I had put on my jacket; it was cold in the tunnel.

The door to the section of the mess hall that our galleries use was opened. Our section is a segment, pie-shaped, of the huge round mess hall—the dangerous days of one single mess hall, holding all prisoners, are gone forever. Food is served cafeteria-style. We pick up our trays and wait in line. The food is either waiting in bowls for us to pick up, as we file by, or is served onto our plates by the kitchen detail. Knives and forks and spoons are of plastic, not particularly useful for making weapons, though they are sometimes smuggled back to the cells and narrowed and sharpened for this purpose.

We are often kept waiting, sometimes for twenty or thirty minutes, before the food service line opens, not that this matters much, but it is aggravating. They serve meals here, three times a day, to over two thousand prisoners each meal, 365 times a year, on a twelve-day repeating menu. I calculate that this comes to more than two million meals a year. I suppose I should expect it to be dull and lifeless food—and it is. But guys mostly tend to put on weight in prison; I know I do. The meals are not light on carbohydrates. The cartons of milk cannot be spoiled by our prisoner cooks, and I usually manage to collect two of them with whatever else is handed to me. I did this today.

After you get your food you walk back to the seating area, metal tables with six metal seats fixed to them. You have to be careful where you sit; there are "regulars" who sit together and expect this to be known. And, of course, the blacks and Hispanics don't welcome a white guy joining their tables. The prison is more than 90 percent black and Hispanic, but this causes no great problem—the whites tend to congregate with one another in the mess hall and in the yard. I may be a bit of an exception here; Tyrone is black, but he is also older and more sensible, and neither of us belongs to a gang. We occasionally sit at the same table, but mostly not.

Breakfast and all other meals take about fifteen minutes to eat, but often we are held in the mess hall for about forty-five minutes after our arrival. Today I walked back through the tunnel and up the three flights of stairs to my cell, carrying a carton of milk and a box of cereal for snacking. The cell house was still not fully awake; the noise level was not too bad.

7:30 A.M.:

I stood in front of my cell door. Tyrone was sitting on the toilet seat, which we have covered with a shaped piece of three-ply and a cloth. He was reading a magazine and smoking. The cell smelled of us and of cigarette smoke. The tower guard saw me and unlocked my cell door; I didn't have to pound on the bars to attract his attention. I put the carton of milk in a hammock-like contraption we have fashioned from a small towel, tied to the cell bars, to hold some of our things. They are in danger of theft by anyone passing by the cell, and this happens, but not often enough to worry about, and I never put anything there I am not willing to lose. Of course, if I know who took something, particularly if others know that I know, I have to do something about it, and the ensuing fight may well put either or both of us in the hole; but I am known to be a determined person, and my things are rarely interfered with.

8:05 A.M.:

All the cells throughout the prison, ours included, were locked for "Morning Count." I laid down on my bunk and turned the radio on. Our cell is #304. The guard came by and looked into our cell, making a mark on a pad he was carrying, and walked on. You could hear him shout in front of each cell, "302, 303, . . . 305," telling those inside to look up and be recognized as alive and not dummies. He didn't call out in front of our cell; he saw and knew us; he didn't have to speak to us, and we didn't have to reply. Our cell is different from some of the others in that we have not put up a "curtain"—some material across the bars—to achieve some privacy. We prefer to leave the cell open; it's too much trouble putting the curtain up and taking it down. These curtains are not allowed, but they are tolerated—there is much like this in Stateville. Disciplinary "tickets" are occasionally written but not routinely.

The count, usually four times a day but sometimes more, is a slow process. The early morning count and the last count around 11:30 P.M. do not interfere with the routine of the prison, since all prisoners are then locked in their cells and the count is easier to take. The other counts present more difficulty. Nothing goes on in the prison until the count is reported from every cell house and from everywhere that prisoners are supposed to be, nothing until the numbers reported reconcile exactly with the numbers that are supposed to be there. It can go on for a long time. It is the central ritual of prison life.

8:30 A.M.:

There was the sound of a factory whistle, which meant, "The count has checked." A bell rang loudly in F House, followed by the loudspeaker blaring, "School, barbershop, library . . . get ready for work." The cell-opening and door-banging began in earnest, and prisoners poured out of their cells, some joining the school or work details, others going to the showers—it was the usual rush to "nowhere."

Tyrone flipped the light switch until our cell door was opened; he knows I dislike the banging on the bars. The day officially began. I joined the crowd pouring from the cells. It is another ritual, a ritual of chaos. The work details were rounded up like straying cattle; each prisoner always has something to do, some message urgently to deliver, something to collect or to hand over, before he can leave for his work assignment.

"Yard, yard, get ready for F House yard . . . yard in the tunnel, yard." Tyrone left for the tailor shop, where he tells me he has found a peaceful job. He left with the "Industry" detail. I decided to go to the yard, since it was a fine, cool fall day, and get a workout, bench-pressing some weights. I was glad to see that only twenty or so prisoners joined the yard detail, and probably a few of those were not interested in exercise but rather in the telephones, which are often more available in the yard than in F House.

The yard is of playing-field size and of rounded, triangular shape, with a rough baseball diamond, with other areas of grass and of packed earth, surrounded by a running track and a fence. Some sparse outdoor gym equipment is in one corner. There are two telephones, protected a little from the weather by steel surrounds; a small line formed. Guys ran around the track or walked around in twos or small groups. Five or six of us worked out on the equipment.

The telephones here and in F House are monitored, and every few minutes a voice interrupts telling you and whomever you are speaking to that this is a call from a "state correctional facility." And the time you are allowed for any one call is limited, depending on whatever the prison authorities have arranged with the telephone company. Of course, only collect calls can be made, so that no one outside has to talk to a prisoner on the telephone, and this makes the telephone expensive for the person you are calling, particularly long-distance calls.

10:30 A.M.:

A new guard, a woman I had not seen before, came to unlock the chain-link fence, and the yard detail headed back to F House.

I returned to my cell, feeling better for the workout. I gave my cell a quick inventory; anything can happen while a cell is empty. TV, radio, calculator, typewriter, fan . . . I hadn't had any larcenous visitors while I was gone. There hadn't been a shakedown, everything was in place, the carton of milk was still in the "hammock." The milk was warmish by now, but I reached through the bars for the milk and drank it.

I raised my hand as if to indicate that I was going to pound on the bars to get the guard's attention. He saw me and opened the cell door. I hung up my jacket on a screw in the wall, washed my hands in the small steel basin behind and above the toilet seat, put a sheet of paper in the typewriter, and wondered to whom I should write.

I decided instead to have a shower; I felt hot and smelly from my workout. I took off my shoes and socks, rolled up my pants legs, slipped into my shower sandals, and grabbed my washcloth and towel and a green bar of state-issue soap. Many prisoners buy "commissary soap," some TV-advertised soap, on their weekly visit to the commissary; but I'm going nowhere special for some time, and state soap will do fine until I'm free. At this time all the cells were open in F House, so without having to signal the guard I walked down the three flights of stairs and along the paint-peeled ramp to the showers. Most prisoners shower "with security," that is, when there are guards about to watch the shower room. I prefer to shower "without security." The showers are dangerous places; gangs tend to shower together as a protective measure; only a very few prisoners shower alone and without security, as I do. I am known as a loner and dangerous to cross and tend therefore to be left alone. The shower room seems designed for crazies. There are these buttons you push, and then the water comes out for a couple of minutes, then it stops, and you push again. This is supposed to be for "water conservation," but of course everyone pushes all the buttons all the time so that the water is hotter and continuous. So much for saving water.

When you come to prison it is wise to leave all shyness behind. But I am not anxious for myself in the showers. Here in Stateville there aren't gang rapes or even rapes that I hear about, though they are reputed to take place occasionally, and they are certainly more frequent in the jails. Here, the gay community is largely left alone by both prisoners and guards, though there is a good deal of vulgarity directed their way. The old thing about "dropping the soap in the shower" is ancient history. Girlie magazines and a tacit acceptance of masturbation, including mutual masturbation, as well as of other relatively consensual homosexual relationships, minimize sex-related violence. And the fact that there are quite a few women guards at Stateville seems to help. Prisoners taking showers need security from gang attacks, not from sexual attacks. Still, I suppose I am always a little anxious in the showers; I avoid being alone in the showers with any one or more who might have some particular reason to dislike me. Even if violence is not all that common, still there is often tension and anxiety and, I suppose, fear.

11:30 A.M.:

I looked for some semi-clean socks, got dressed, and started typing a letter. I was waiting for the call to lunch, though I hate the mess hall at lunchtime. It is chaos at lunch; the prisoners refuse to act "orderly," and the guards do not take the trouble to enforce order. The gang element is definitely in control. Nevertheless, to the sound of "Chow going out the door," I joined the mass of prisoners heading for the tunnel. We were kept waiting outside the mess hall. The noise built up. The guy in front of me yelled at one of his buddies, who stepped up and joined him in front of me. I made no complaint; it wasn't worth it, and in the confusion nobody took any notice of such matters.

Nobody learns from the mistakes of yesterday. The door to our segment of the dining room was finally opened, the guards stepped back, and everyone tried at once to squeeze through the twenty-inch opening, rushing for the soggy vegetables and limp pasta that awaited them. Once I got my food, after ten or fifteen minutes in the surging line, with the food servers shouting at one another, spraying the food, I sat down at a table and joined my regular lunchtime group, with conversation devoted to complaints about the food and discussions of TV programs. I found myself unusually dejected, waiting for the doors to be unlocked so that I could get back to the relative peace of my cell.

1:00 P.M.:

I joined the "school" detail and with six others from F House went off to a course on computers run in the school area. Unlike all but a few prisoners in Stateville, I am a genuine high school graduate. There are a few more who claim to be such, but the truth is that a majority of my fellow prisoners in Stateville are functionally illiterate, and only a handful have any sort of a record of high school academic achievement. In earlier years in Stateville I worked in the furniture factory and in the tailor shop, earning more than I can earn at school; but the computer course interested me, and I applied for it and got it. I have now been in it for three months and am beginning to be able to write programs. The course is taught by an Indian who speaks strangely but knows what he is doing. It fills my afternoons, three days a week, two hours each day.

The better-educated have the pick of the jobs in Stateville. Though it is poorly paid, the library, particularly the law library, is probably the best job, passing prison time more swiftly than other prison jobs, having influence in the prison, and being left alone by the guards; but the computer class seems to me in some ways even better. In the distant years when I am free I may be able to use what I am learning about computer programming, but I doubt it; the point is that it helps to keep me alive here.

You may be interested in the pay scale in this prison: the low rate for all jobs, industry and maintenance, from the useful to the make-work, is $.95 per day. The top pay is $2.15 per day. These rates are based on the prisoner's working twenty-one work days per month. However one's money arrives, either from prison pay or approved payment from outside, currency is contraband, and commissary credit is all one can have without risking disciplinary punishment, including loss of "good time." There is no limit to what a prisoner (other than a prisoner under prison disciplinary sanction) may spend at the commissary, provided his account is in credit.

3:30 P.M.:

Two guards escorted the school detail back to F House. I went back to my cell. Tyrone was showering, his work in the tailor shop finished. While he was away I turned on the TV. It is my set, but I cannot control what we watch, since his friends outside could afford to give him a set if he wanted it. So, if we are to share this cell, we have to strike some bargain about what we watch. I am fortunate; he mostly falls in with my preferences, and when he doesn't, I yield.

I've never watched so much TV as I do here. My set is a thirteen-inch RCA color TV. I turned on Channel 11/WTTW Chicago, "Your Window to the World," for me an ideal program. It's just what I want, a public television news commentary program; I wish I had money to give them a contribution—they ask for it frequently. The TV is on a little table we have rigged up beside the toilet; it is best watched by lying on one's bunk. Tyrone came in and lay down on his bunk without speaking. It's the best way; avoid useless chatter.

I got sleepy and dozed.

I was awakened by the mailman rapping on the bars of our cell and giving a small package of mail to Tyrone. Nothing for me; after a year or two in prison, incoming mail dries up to a trickle, even if you write regularly.

5:00 P.M.:

I watched the local news. It was depressing, much of it about the activities of people who are on their way here. I lay on my bunk, half listening to the news, half daydreaming of freedom. Like most other prisoners, I devote much of my waking thought, and all my dream time, to being out of prison.

5:25 P.M.:

The loudspeaker blared again, "Three and four galleries, get ready for chow." The food is often worse in the evening than at lunch, but it is better to go than to stay in what is by now the thundering noise of F House, with TVs and radios blaring and, it seems to me, every prisoner shouting to another prisoner and nobody listening.

The evening meal was a less-adequate replica of lunch, with more bread and less pasta; but the pushing and shoving was also less, and the gangs were less active.

7:00 P.M.:

The evening count—it also went smoothly. Most everyone was by now back in the cell houses, and there were fewer places—schoolroom, gym, yard, industry, barbershop, kitchen, and so on—to be counted.

It was F House's turn for evening gym. Many, including Tyrone, went to throw basketballs around. I stayed in the cell and followed a batch of my favorite TV programs—they passed the time well for me, and I had had my exercise for that day.

And so the evening went: TV, reading a little in my computer training manual, TV again, and by nine o'clock Tyrone was back in the cell, and I got out of my clothes, except my undershorts, and got into my bunk. The central lights in F House stay on through the night. I wondered if perhaps we should put up some sort of curtains, and with that thought the day ended for me.

Well, that was my diary for yesterday. Let me comment a bit on it.

Yesterday was unusually uneventful. Often in prison something happens to disturb the dull flow of the day. For example, sometimes when I am wakened in the morning Tyrone is to be heard pulling himself off, and my bunk shakes slightly. I don't mind this; it is better than the homosexual habits that some others, who are not homosexual outside, fall into when they are here, but it disturbs me. Of course, I do the same sometimes, mostly at night. And Tyrone shits so noisily and with such a stench—I think there is something wrong with his digestion; after all, we eat the same food. Tyrone and I take care neither by what we say nor in any other way to let the other know about these and other ways in which, living so close to one another as we do, we annoy one another. It is better that way. We have not yet had an argument that leads to a fight, even a shouting match, but we live so close that someday that will happen, and we will both probably end up in the hole, hating one another. Cell places are supposed to be controlled by security, but the gangs manage to keep their members together in neighboring cells, which makes for peace. Unless you are very strong or influential, or for one or another reason it has been decided to leave you alone, you have to belong to a gang or be under their protection.

There are, of course, the regular variations in our days. Regularly we go to the barbershop, where our apprentice-barber fellow prisoners practice their skills on us. There is the weekly visit to the commissary. There are Sundays, with their more relaxed regimen, more open yard and gym time, more sitting or walking about in groups talking. There are times to go to the library and to the law library for those of us still appealing our convictions or pursuing prisoners' rights litigation, which they tell me is a good way to "do time" but rarely produces any success in the courts. And then there are the hard-to-avoid confrontations with some of the guards—leading to tickets and segregation and loss of "good time." Even worse are the collective punishments of the "lockdown," when cells are locked for all twenty-four hours, sometimes for months, with only one shower a week out of the cell; time moves even slower then.

Neither Tyrone nor I use prison hooch or drugs to get through the days and nights, but many prisoners do, and the disorder of prison, the frequency of punishments and of lockdowns, is increased because of it. Drugs, all drugs, are readily available at about twice their street price, payable inside or outside the prison. Some drugs come over the wall; some are brought in by guards; some make their way in with visitors, despite the administration's efforts; small quantities are hidden under the stamps or built into pockets in envelopes; one way or another, I am told, drugs are available in every large prison and jail, and they certainly are available here if you can pay for them.

Gang activity is another addiction of our prison. Gang membership is known to the prison authorities, but there is not much they can do about it. They try to move gang

Above Various forms of medieval physical punishment are illustrated in this German woodcut from 1509. In the absence of the prison, all of the punishment involved a direct assault on the body. *FotoMarburg/Art Resource, NY.*

Below In late-eighteenth-century London, the spectacle of the scaffold essentially had turned into a popular festival. Engraving after a painting from William Hogarth's *The Idle Prentice,* of a procession to the gallows at Tyburn. *The Bettman Archive.*

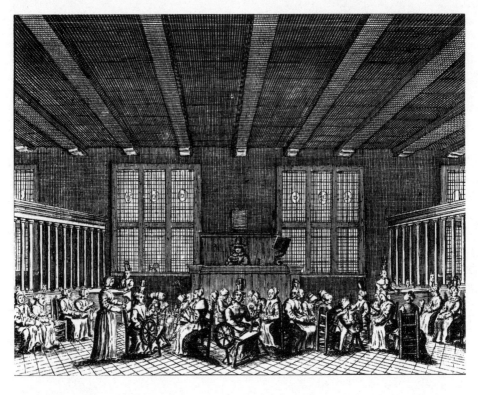

Above Among the earliest forms of confinement were the workhouses organized in seventeenth-century Amsterdam. The expectation was that through work in the spinhouse, the female prisoners would acquire steady habits. *University Library, Amsterdam.* **Below** A 1795 engraving of the Gloucester County Gaol, which was designed by architect William Blackburn. Blackburn believed that highly ordered architecture could foster self-control and rational behavior. *Gloucester Collection, Gloucestershire City Council.*

Above The exercise yard at Pentonville Prison, an institution that was inspired by the writings of Jeremy Bentham. To ensure prisoners' total isolation, inmates at Pentonville were forced to wear hoods whenever they emerged from their cells. From *The Criminal Prisons of London and Scenes of Prison Life (1862)* by Henry Mayhew and John Binny. *New York Public Library, General Research Division, Astor, Lenox, and Tilden Foundations.*

Right A view of the interior of the Surrey House of Correction. After dinner, hooded prisoners returned to their cells in single file, under close surveillance. From *The Criminal Prisons of London and Scenes of Prison Life (1862)* by Henry Mayhew and John Binny. *New York Public Library, General Research Division, Astor, Lenox, and Tilden Foundations.*

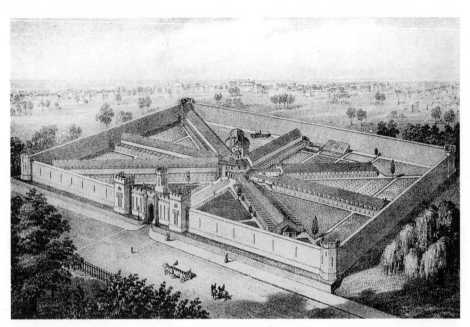

Above An aerial view of Eastern State Penitentiary in Philadelphia in 1856. The institution was the model prison of the "Pennsylvania plan," also known as the "separate system." Under this plan, prisoners served their sentences confined to individual cells, where they ate, worked, and slept in isolation. *The Library Company of Philadelphia.* **Below** Stateville's F House, the last circular cellblock in the United States. The design of this contemporary prison demonstrates the powerful influence of the past on current thinking about prison organization and purpose. *Photograph by Lloyd DeGrane.*

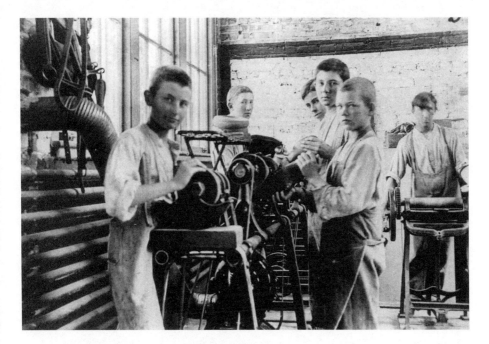

Above The favorite method for promoting inmate responsibility in England and in the United States, both for adults and for juveniles, continued to be work regimens. This vocational training class took place in an Indiana juvenile reformatory, circa 1910. *Courtesy of the American Correctional Association.*

Below The workroom of the Lancaster Industrial School for Girls, circa 1926. The girls' daily regime focused on preparing them for indenture as house servants after their release. *Courtesy of the American Correctional Association.*

Above The Fresno County jail in 1938. Even more than the state prisons, they illustrate the shortfall between rhetoric of reform and reality of conditions. *Courtesy of the American Correctional Association.* **Below** Another indication of the custodial character of the contemporary prison is the frequent reliance on "lockdowns," during which inmates are confined to their cells for weeks. Angry prisoners at Stateville litter the floor outside their cells in a futile protest effort. *Photograph by Lloyd DeGrane.*

Right A young inmate in his cell at Gardner House, a juvenile detention center in Austin, Texas, in 1972. The mood captured in the photograph conveys what it means to do "dead time." *Stock, Boston, © Bob Daemmrich.*

Below Police survey the wreckage following a 1952 riot at the State Prison of Southern Michigan at Jackson. The complaints of the Jackson rioters—such as over-crowding, inadequate medical care and food, and guard brutality—mirrored those of the many other inmates who partici-pated in a rash of prison riots in the early 1950s. *Courtesy of the State Archives of Michigan.*

Above Handcuffed and in chains, newly arrived prisoners await processing to Stateville. *Photograph by Lloyd DeGrane.*   **Below** This seventy-three-year-old inmate is Stateville's oldest prisoner. With the number of elderly prisoners growing, prisons now face the challenge of providing adequate care for the aged and infirm. *Photograph by Lloyd DeGrane.*

leaders about, from one prison to another, but this only briefly interrupts gang activity— new leaders promptly emerge. The gangs influence who moves safely in the prison and who gets into trouble with the prison authorities; they influence a great deal of life in prison. The influence of gangs in Stateville is much the same as it is on the streets, though mercifully they are not equipped with guns here, only with shanks.

I am not sure whether the average prisoner is safer physically in prison than on the streets, where most of us come from. In Stateville, we are less likely to be shot and killed but possibly slightly more likely to be knifed or injured seriously in a fight. Fights are not uncommon but they are always followed up by the prison authorities, and an effort is made to punish those responsible. There are regular and intermittent shakedowns of all the cells and other areas for shanks and other contraband. It is a violent place, but most prisoners do their time without being victimized physically unless they are looking to prove something to themselves or unless they get into trouble with betting, or hooch, or drugs, or with the gangs. Those who adhere to the main tenets of the prison culture— never "rat" on another prisoner, always keep your distance from staff, "do your own time"—have the best chance of avoiding violence.

I hope this diary is of use to you; it fails to capture the constant unhappiness of prison life and the constant sense of danger—you are never for a moment happy, except sometimes briefly on visitors days, and that is a bitter happiness. The letter misses the relentless, slow-moving routine, the dull repetitiveness, the tension mixed with occasional flashes of fear and rage; it misses the consuming stupidity of living this way. I am sorry; it is not easy. Probably prison was easier to describe many years ago when prison guards saw themselves as punishers, inflicting pain on prisoners, and prisoners joined together to resist them. Now, in prisons like Stateville, purposes are unclear, education is largely a token, idleness takes the place of work and industry, and keeping peace and safety between prisoner and prisoner is the prevailing aim. Anyhow, that is how it appears to this prisoner.

Let me know when you will next visit me; I hope soon.

Sincerely,
Prisoner #12345

THE STATE OF THE PRISONS

From 1970 to 1980 the population of the prisons of the United States doubled; from 1981 to 1995 it more than doubled again, so that a crisis of crowding overwhelmed the prison systems, both federal and state. Though there had been substantial increases in crime rates during the first of those decades, the second decade, from the early 1980s to the early 1990s, was marked overall by no increase in the rates of crimes reported and recorded in the FBI's *Uniform Crime Statistics* or by any increase in imprisonable crime as measured by the victim surveys of the National Crime Survey. By all our measures, for the period 1980 to 1985, serious crime steadily declined and then, from 1985 to 1990, steadily increased, though never reaching its earlier high rates. Thereafter, through 1996, it remained either stable or slightly declining. Nevertheless, political attitudes and sentencing policies toughened; police, prosecution, and judicial resources were supplemented; and in the result a flood of prisoners was produced.

There were similar increases for a time in the prisons of England and Wales, but nothing like the deluge in the United States. A comparison of the imprisonment rates in several countries at the beginning of 1992 gives a compelling view of this inundation. The following are incarceration rates per 100,000 of population, adding prison and jail together as is necessary for international comparisons:

Holland	36
Sweden	61
England and Wales	98
Canada	109
South Africa	332
U.S.A.	455

Because an insufficient number of new prisons was built to house this flood of inmates, by 1994 cells built for one held two and sometimes three prisoners. All the resources of the prisons were similarly stretched—health services, recreational services, classification of prisoners into manageable and trainable groups, vocational and educational services—and most important, discipline became much more difficult to impose, with the result that gangs began to flourish as never before, drugs to be more available, and brutality between prisoners to be an increasing threat.

The extent of imprisonment varies widely among the different regions of the United States. The South has the highest rate of imprisonment, incarcerating more people per capita than any other area; then, in declining rates, follow the West, the North Central, and the Northeast. And, as we saw for national crime rates, these regional differences in rates of incarceration do not mirror differences in rates of serious crime.

The Federal and State Prison Systems

There were no federal prisons, as such, until 1890. Of course, there were colonial prisons and jails, there were military prisons, and there was even a District of Columbia prison run by the Department of the Interior. But, though there were criminal offenses against congressional statutes from the first days of the Union, there were no federal prisons until the Three Prisons Act of 1890, which authorized the building of federal prisons at Leavenworth, Kansas; Atlanta, Georgia; and McNeil Island, Washington. Until 1890, those convicted of federal offenses were farmed out by contract to state institutions.

In the years between 1890 and 1930, the number of federal prisoners greatly increased, and under separate congressional authorization, the number of federal prisons grew to seven, each operated under policies and procedures established locally by each warden. In 1930 the Bureau of Prisons Act brought these scattered institutions under the control of a single bureaucracy, the Federal Bureau of Prisons. The bureau has now grown into a nationwide system of prisons, jails, and community correctional centers that will likely house more than 100,000 offenders by the mid-1990s.

The distinction between federal offenses and state offenses has never been clear, other than the obvious and formal point that the former reflect a breach of federal law, the latter of state law. Generally speaking, federal statutes aim to deal with crimes that stretch beyond the borders of a single state or that involve large-scale conspiracies, which are difficult for states to investigate and bring to justice. But, over the years, the ambit of federal law has grown and shrunk, moved largely by political fashion and changing popular concerns. Thus for many years, under the Mann Act, federal criminal law was deeply concerned with the transportation of women for immoral purposes, but there is no one now in federal prison for pimping. For many years too, the illegal distillation and distribution of alcohol was a major concern, but moonshiners no longer fill federal prisons. Then the prosecution of interstate transportation of stolen motor vehicles had its turn, but this is not a concern now. Today drug offenses are the largest single source of federal prisoners, so that currently over 60 percent stand convicted of drug offenses, and over one-fourth of all federal prisoners are not citizens of this country (they are drug carriers from south of the U.S.-Mexico border); and this figure does not include those held for breach of immigration or nationalization laws.

The range of federal offenses grows, and the number of federal prisoners burgeons. Federal prisons hold more "white-collar" criminals than state institutions, but they also hold their share of violent robbers and murderers. Federal prisons range in security from open camps to the most secure and rigidly controlled prison in the United States— the federal prison at Marion, in southern Illinois.

It is sometimes facetiously said that federal prisons attract a better class of inmates than state prisons and that they are therefore easier to control. There is some truth in this, but the high esteem in which the Bureau of Prisons is held among those informed on correctional matters is founded less on the kind of inmates than on the quality of the staff that has over the years been recruited, the staff training programs that have been developed, and the continuity of leadership that has been maintained at the bureau.

The history of state prisons has followed a very different path, as described in chapters four and six of this book. In the pattern that finally emerged, every state runs its own prison system, whereas local communities, counties, and cities run the jails. By and large, convicted felons go to prison, and convicted misdemeanants and those awaiting trial go to jail.

There are interesting financial consequences of this division of responsibility. To a degree, the sentencing judge controls who pays for punishment: if the convicted offender is sentenced as a felon to prison, the state pays; if he is sentenced as a misdemeanant to jail, or if a felon or misdemeanant is placed on a community-based sentence such as probation, the local community will pay. Such consequences sometimes cloud punishment policy.

To complete the outline of this administrative patchwork, there are a few interstate compacts by which states combine to administer institutions for particular categories of prisoners—for example, women prisoners and mentally ill prisoners. Finally, there are contractual arrangements between the states and the federal Bureau of Prisons by which individual state prisoners are held in federal institutions and vice versa. For example, the federal prison at Marion, Illinois, holds a few state prisoners who are too unremittingly aggressive and violent to be held in state institutions. Likewise, it is not unusual for a state prisoner who would be particularly vulnerable in a state institution—a convicted policeman, for example—to be held in the federal system.

Classification of Prisons and Prisoners

Every state and the federal system provide for the classification of prisoners at admission to prison and for their allocation to institutions and within institutions according to that classification. All states have prisons for those who are not escape risks and who can be held with less likelihood of violence in open and less-supervised conditions. For the other end of the prison-behavior spectrum, all prison systems run maximum-security facilities with close and constant supervision. In between there is usually a range of medium-security prisons, such as prisons for younger offenders and prisons with particular emphasis on vocational or educational training or on industrial activities.

The architecture of these diverse institutions varies greatly, from traditional concrete and brick behemoths, filled with tiers and ranks of steel-barred cages with vast congregate dining halls, to campus-like facilities with scattered houses, each holding thirty or forty inmates in home-like conditions. Architecture tends to dominate much of the texture of life in prison.

Prisoner #12345's life, hour by hour, would be different indeed were he moved to an open or even a medium-security prison. All would be different, from the noisy awakening to the separate life he created for himself in his cell in Stateville: he would spend much more of his time out of his cell; useful work would more likely be available; congregate and safer associations with other prisoners would prevail; and the guards would be less anxious and therefore less demanding. In all, he would have a greater sense of personal worth. There would be the same recognition of separateness from the world, but the daily round, the details of life, would be much less oppressive. A man of ordinary life experience, who had never before seen the inside of a jail or prison, would find no physical pain in living in many of the open and medium-security prisons, state and federal—other than the pain resulting from the sense of banishment from life. Indeed, this type of prison life is not unlike that on a rigidly disciplined military base. But the overcrowded, maximum-security prisons are quite another matter.

White-collar criminals are disproportionately to be found in open facilities, whereas those from the inner cities, those with histories of "street crime," fill the maximum-security prisons. White-collar prisoners generally are neither escape risks nor violent and dangerous; since assessment for these risks is the basis for classification of prisoners, white-collar criminals are generally found in minimum-security institutions, which, being less staff-intensive and not requiring massive walls and steel cages, are also much cheaper both to build and to run. These "open prisons" provide much "easier time" than the maximum-security institutions. There is an unevenness in suffering in such a classificatory system, but it is not an inequity that the prison authorities can or should avoid. There is no point in wasting funds and personnel resources to make conditions worse for white-collar criminals. The essential pain of imprisonment lies in the prisoner's banishment from society and his loss of autonomy; it would serve no social purpose to increase suffering for criminals in open institutions.

Minority Prisoners

In the United States as a whole, the differential rate of imprisonment of African-Americans to Caucasians, proportional to population, is in excess of 7.5 to 1. The differential rate of imprisonment of those with Hispanic surnames in proportion to Caucasians is about 5 to 1. Efforts to account for these gross differences raise important and disturbing issues. (In the cause of brevity, if not precision, the terms white, black, and Hispanic will be used, without hint of pejorative intent.)

To illuminate this problem, consider a few statistics of the racial impact of the criminal justice system in the nation's capital city, Washington, D.C. On a typical day in 1991, of all black males between the ages of eighteen and thirty-five living in Washington, 42 percent were within the control of the criminal justice system. To be more precise, 15 percent were in prison, 21 percent were on probation or parole, and 6 percent were either awaiting trial or being sought for trial.

These are deeply disturbing figures, but they appear to be exceeded in one other city and could be approximated in many others. To what extent they account for the extraordinary difference between incarceration rates in the United States and other Western countries is uncertain. By way of contrast, black males in the United States are incarcerated at a rate four times that of black males in South Africa.

Let us consider some possible explanations for this gross racial skewing. It may reflect racial prejudice on the part of the police, the prosecutors, the judges, and juries, so that, crime for crime, black and Hispanic offenders are more likely to be arrested by the police and are more likely to be dealt with severely by the courts.

Support for that view is found in the data on arrests for drug offenses. From 1970 onward, the arrest rate of whites for drug offenses has held relatively steady at about 300 per 100,000; by contrast, the arrest rate of blacks, which was also at 300 in 1968–69, shot up with the "war on drugs" to just below 1,500 per 100,000 in 1990, declining to about 1,050 in 1992. No one informed on drug usage would suggest that this huge differential reflects differential usage—it is surely the product of intense targeting, by police and prosecutors, of drug use in certain areas and not in others.

The overall reality of racial skewing in punishment practice may suggest that the officials of the criminal justice system, at every level, deal more harshly with blacks and Hispanics, so that clemency is disproportionately extended to whites and denied to blacks and Hispanics. This possibility is suggested by the fact that in 1990, even though less than 30 percent of those arrested were black, blacks accounted for 47 percent of those imprisoned, and that although whites were nearly 70 percent of those arrested, only 48 percent of prisoners were white.

The racial imbalance in the prison population may be explained in part by the fact that blacks who commit crimes against white victims, particularly serious crimes, are punished more severely than blacks whose victims are black and more severely than whites, regardless of the color of their victims. It is likely that some of the minority prison population is made up of prisoners who would not have been sent to prison, or who would have received shorter sentences, had their victims been of some other race.

Another possible cause of this racial skewing is that whereas blacks and Hispanics disproportionately commit what might be called "imprisonable crimes," white offenders express their criminality, disproportionately higher than do blacks and Hispanics, in frauds, embezzlements, and white-collar offenses, which do not so inflame public opinion and do not so readily attract imprisonment as a punishment.

Genetic factors are sometimes suggested as causally related to these differences in involvement in imprisonable crime; but this position is extremely difficult to maintain in the light of what is known about evolution and the noninheritance of acquired characteristics and for the more immediate reason that as blacks and Hispanics steadily move into the middle class, their crime rates and the delinquency rates of their children are indistinguishable from those of their white neighbors.

There is this qualification, of course: if blacks and, to a lesser extent, Hispanics have been subjected to adverse social conditions stretching over generations—if opportunities for a contributing and rewarding life have been denied them by the lack of adequate health care and the lack of reasonable educational and employment opportunities, if their children and youths over generations have been subjected to the culture of the inner-city streets, and if socially acceptable role models are denied them—then criminality becomes a much more normal and accepted social adaptation, passed on from generation to generation.

As is true of any observation about human behavior, single-factor explanations are here superficial in the extreme; all of the above suggestions, apart from the genetic, may have validity, varying from case to case, but they are extraordinarily difficult to quantify in the mass. Nevertheless, an effort toward that end was made in some research done for a panel of the National Academy of Sciences. The results suggested that about 80 percent of the black-to-white disproportion in rates of imprisonment could be explained by blacks' disproportionate involvement in serious crime and that 20 percent remained unaccounted for and may well be attributable to racial prejudice on the part of those initiating and administering the criminal justice process. This does not, of course, dispose of the allegation that, regarding their crime rates, blacks are the captives of racial prejudice; it merely shifts the focus to 20 percent attributable to racial prejudice within the criminal justice system and 80 percent attributable to what racial prejudice and imposed social adversities have contributed to society at large.

Whatever the causes, many of the prisons and jails of the United States, particularly the larger, maximum-security institutions, appear to be institutions designed to segregate from society a young black and Hispanic male underclass.

Sentencing and Release Procedures

A substantial reason for the doubling and redoubling of incarceration rates in the United States in the period from 1970 to 1994 was a profound change in sentencing practices, federal and state. Sentencing practices have two impacts on prison populations. First, they determine who out of the mass of convicted offenders will be sentenced to prison; that is, they determine who goes to prison. And second, they determine for how long criminals will stay in prison. Over the period we are considering, more convicted offenders were selected for prison, and they were sentenced to longer terms of imprisonment.

Regarding the second effect of sentencing decisions, the duration of imprisonment, there have been great changes: in the 1960s, legislatures set the maximum prison term for a particular offense and, very rarely, also set the minimum. Within that range legislatively set, the sentencing judge would order an indeterminate sentence of imprisonment, being the maximum number of years that the prisoner could be imprisoned. Then, the actual term that the prisoner would serve would later be determined by a parole board, the parole board's decision being based on the gravity of the crime, the prisoner's behavior in prison, and the parole board's prediction of his likely success during the parole release term. The parole release term, the period of conditional release under supervision, would normally be the unserved period of imprisonment, the difference between the time he actually spent in prison and the maximum that the judge had ordered. During that period the ex-prisoner could be returned to prison for breach of a condition of his parole or, of course, for commission of a crime. As a rough estimate, prisoners generally served something between one-third and two-thirds of the sentence the judge had imposed.

This type of indeterminate sentencing had as its main justification a belief in the rehabilitative purpose of imprisonment; the period of incarceration would be used to train the prisoner for a life free of crime, with educative and vocational training and psychological techniques being directed to this end. During the late 1960s and early 1970s a full-scale attack was made on this "rehabilitative ideal," led by a series of technical articles maintaining that "nothing works," that rehabilitative purposes may be fine in principle but that they failed in practice. This depressing view was exaggerated and reflected the genuine difficulties of running methodologically sound studies to test the later conduct of discharged offenders in relation to their prison experience, but it had considerable popular appeal.

During the early 1970s, crime rates increased, along with disenchantment with efforts that had been made—pursuant to the 1967 report of the President's Crime Commission—to bring principle and efficiency to the criminal justice system. Sentencing reform became a focus of political and academic interest, each tending in the same direction, though for profoundly different reasons.

The political pressure for sentencing reform was a reaction to increased and increasing serious-crime rates in the 1960s and 1970s and stemmed from the belief that crime could be inhibited by greater severity of punishment. The popular press depicted judges and parole boards as sentimentally lenient, the evidence being a parade of imprecisely described, exceptional cases. The remedies recommended were legislatively fixed and mandatory minimum sentences and an abandonment of parole release.

The academic pressure for sentencing reform had a quite different provenance. It flowed first from an appreciation of the extent of unjustified disparity in sentencing, by which like offenses by like offenders in the same jurisdiction received profoundly different sentences, and second from an understanding that to support parole release discretion on the basis of the parole board's presumed ability to predict behavior in the community from observing the offender's behavior in prison was an exercise in self-deception, since prison behavior is known to be a very poor predictor of behavior in the community.

Denunciation of the assumed leniency in sentencing moved the legislatures and influenced the judges; a quest for fairness and predictability in sentencing moved the academic reformers. Both agreed on "truth in sentencing," by which the sentence the judge proclaimed would be the sentence served, less some time off for "good behavior" in prison, but there was little else in common in their purposes. Nevertheless, this unlikely alliance between those favoring more condign punishment and those favoring fairer and more predictable sentencing practices had a great effect on increasing the severity of sentences, federal and state, throughout the United States. As a result, the extent of imprisonment for crime and of time served for each type of crime substantially increased.

Legislatures, federal and state, moved to mandatory sentences for whatever "crime of the month" for which they thought the judges had been too lenient in sentencing. These mandatory minimum sentences obliterated judicial discretion (transferring it, in effect, to the prosecutors who determine what offense the criminal is to be charged with) and achieved substantial increases both in the numbers sent to prison and in the duration of their confinement.

There were also various experiments in guiding judicial sentencing discretion to achieve rough equality in sentencing, the best known being the establishment of sentencing commissions in the federal system and in Minnesota, to draft complex sets of sentencing guidelines to channel the judges' sentencing discretion. The strong tendency of the federal system of sentencing guidelines has been toward greatly increased severity of sentencing; in the states that have followed this path of sentencing reform, particularly Minnesota and Washington, that result is less clear. In those two states, the prison population increase was held below that in comparable jurisdictions lacking such guidelines.

Fundamental changes in sentencing policies have been widespread, and though crime rates in the early 1990s were broadly the same as they were, or were slightly lower than they were, at the beginning of the 1980s, the great increase in rates of incarceration continued, in substantial part because of those sentencing "reforms."

Unhappily, these changes in sentencing practice, which have tended to eliminate or reduce the discretion of the parole releasing authorities, have also reduced parole supervision of discharged prisoners. Ideally, all prisoners, certainly all who have served long terms, should be released gradually into the community; they should be supervised and, where appropriate, assisted during the difficult period of readaptation to freedom. Some prison systems do this. For example, the Federal Bureau of Prisons has entered into contractual arrangements with 260 Community Corrections Centers, where many longer-term federal prisoners are held for the last two or three months of their period of imprisonment; these are community-based facilities from which prisoners go out each day to work or to try to find work. The bureau administers this system by contractual and supervised arrangements with nonprofit, for-profit, and public agencies.

But the bureau's release program is, regrettably, not the norm. In many state prison systems, the prisoner is set free at the prison gate in clothes ill-suited to the likely pattern of his life and with funds insufficient to support himself during the difficult period of readaptation but sufficient to buy a handgun. A few private organizations, such as the SAFER Foundation in Chicago, sometimes financially assisted by federal and state funds, do provide some training and assistance to ex-prisoners in finding employment, but the resources are swamped by the need.

The Impact of Accreditation and the Courts

The American Correctional Association (ACA) is a voluntary organization of those working in correctional programs, adult and juvenile, institutional and community-based. With over twenty-four thousand members in 1992, it has considerable influence on correctional legislation and practice. Following the example of hospital accreditation programs, in 1974 the ACA established a correctional institution accreditation program, which has defined acceptable standards for prison conditions and programs and has assisted correctional administrators in meeting them. Accreditation has assisted prison administrators in attracting funds to improve prison conditions; but a larger, similar effect has been achieved by the courts, mostly the federal district courts.

Until the early 1970s, federal and state courts adopted a "hands off" policy toward prison conditions, deferring to the assumed expertise of the prison administrators and being prepared to intervene in only the most egregious circumstances; in effect, the constitutions, federal and state, did not protect the prisoner. But since that time there has been a spate of judicial activity relating to prison conditions, with the federal district courts and, to a lesser extent, the state courts and federal appellate courts being actively involved. Class-action suits by prisoners have led the courts to the definition and enforcement of minimum standards of health care, to the establishment of minimum procedural due-process requirements for the imposition of disciplinary punishments, to the equal protection of the laws for different categories of inmates, and to the upholding of the Eighth Amendment guarantee against cruel and unusual punishments.

Overcrowding in several prisons and jails has led the courts to impose a "ceiling" on populations, which has compelled the release of some prisoners before the expiration of their sentences. Inevitably, some of those so released commit new crimes and bring vigorous press and public criticism on the correctional authorities and on the courts.

In two decades of such judicial activism, all but a few states have had a major prison or jail running under court control, and eight states at one time or another had their entire correctional system, either adult or juvenile, under court order. The most common mechanism by which the courts exercise control over the correctional institution is by the appointment of a Special Master, responsible to the court, who acts as the authorized agent of the court in ensuring that its order concerning prison or jail conditions, or the maximum number of offenders to be held in an institution at any one time, is obeyed.

Court intervention is a matter of considerable contention, with some arguing that the courts have neither the knowledge nor the ability to control prison conditions. The alternative view is that this type of litigation helps, rather than hinders, correctional administrators. Prison administrators control neither prison populations nor prison purse strings. They have no means to build new cells or hire additional staff to accommodate the constant, growing stream of prisoners or to control the resultant overcrowding; they have no way to keep new inmates out or to allow nonthreatening inmates to leave. Federal court orders mandating the reduction of prison populations or the improvement of conditions enable administrators to make their institutions safer and fairer places for both prisoners and staff.

Vocational, Educational, and Other Prison Programs

As we have seen in other chapters of this book, prisoners were traditionally sentenced to "hard labor," which was often very hard and useless labor indeed. The modern problem is quite different: to find sufficient work to keep the prisoner occupied. Opposition by both employer and labor interests has gravely impeded the availability of productive employment in prisons and jails. This is one issue on which the correctional administrator and the prisoner are in complete accord; they both desire useful, productive employment for the prisoner, preferably work of a type that would pay a small stipend for the prisoner to help his family, if he has one, and to cushion the early days of his release.

Opposition from manufacturers' associations and organized labor has stifled the growth of prison industries, which, it is argued, constitute unfair competition to labor and management. As a result, prison industries have been confined largely to a "state use" system by which prisons can produce goods and services only for governmental consumption. Restrictions of this nature have also hindered the development of vocational training programs, which work best when they can be linked to productive employment.

Nevertheless, several prison systems, notably those of the Federal Bureau of Prisons with its quasi-independent UNICOR (Federal Prison Industries) program and the Florida PRIDE (Prison Rehabilitative Industries and Diversified Enterprises) program, do give a minority of prisoners the experience of productive employment, pay them modestly for the work, and train them well for such work on release.

There has been some experimentation in Europe with the "full wages" prison, and this idea has been discussed in the United States. In such a prison, the prisoner would be employed and paid at the same scale as he would were he gainfully employed at large; he would then pay the prison for his board and keep, the remaining funds being used to compensate those he has injured, to assist in the maintenance of his family— who would likely otherwise be supported by the taxpayer on some type of social welfare—and to be saved against his release. This idea reads better in theory than it works in practice. Since the cost of maintaining a prisoner in 1993 hovered around twenty thousand dollars per year, and since no prisoner in a "full wages" prison could be expected to earn that amount, a highly artificial deduction, much less than that, would have to be assessed. The plan becomes an exercise in bookkeeping rather than economic reality.

From the perspective of the prison administrator, an ample program of prison industries is a management tool of central importance, making for a peaceful and orderly prison. If it can also help to train the prisoner for freedom and provide him with some funds to tide him over the early days of his release, so much the better; but the resistance to such programs by outside interests remains a serious impediment to their development.

Basic education programs, on the other hand, are to be found in a large number of prisons, since a substantial number of prisoners are undereducated, with many being illiterate. Likewise, there is usually an opportunity for most prisoners to pursue correspondence courses. Such self-developmental opportunities, educational and vocational, are widely available but generally lightly patronized in the larger, maximum-security prisons; the culture of those institutions does not favor them. They are more apt to flourish in the smaller, medium-security and open prisons. The same is true of psychological and counseling programs, which are to be found in rudimentary or reasonably developed form in many prisons.

Alcohol and drugs figure prominently in the etiology of imprisonable crime; more than half of all prisoners were under the influence of drugs, alcohol, or both at the time of their arrest. Because of this, efforts at alcohol and drug treatment programs in prison are widespread. Alcoholics Anonymous has had considerable success in federal and state prisons; by contrast, drug treatment programs seem more effective when they are community-based, compulsorily treating those sentenced to intermediate punishments or those released from prison on condition of involvement in such programs.

One philosophical aspect of these programs merits mention. In 1965 a major purpose of the prison was thought to be the rehabilitation of the prisoner. By a variety of reeducative programs, the prison was to turn the malefactor into a conforming and productive member of society. In the ensuing decades, these high aspirations have been rejected in public commentary, and it has become fashionable to say that "nothing works" in prison to reform criminals. The fact of the matter is that it is extremely difficult to measure the reformative effects of prison programs; clearly some prisoners are assisted to a conforming life, but equally clearly others are, by the total prison experience, confirmed in their criminality. As a result, the general posture of even the more enlightened prison administrators is to do their best to provide self-developmental opportunities and programs for those prisoners who want to pursue them.

Discipline and Punishment

It is not always appreciated by the general public that immediate power within the prison belongs to the prisoners. Ultimate power, of course, lies with the prison authorities, but guns and weapons cannot be taken into the security areas of a prison where prisoners move—unless one is running a concentration camp—since the prisoners always greatly outnumber the staff.

The reality is, of course, that most prisons are characterized by a high degree of order most of the time, since most prisoners want order and safety and thus accept its maintenance. Nevertheless, whatever the prisoners' feelings on the matter, firm and enforceable disciplinary processes are essential to effective prison governance.

Hence, prisons have their prisons, their "holes," their punishment cells. They also have a further armamentarium of disciplinary punishments, ranging from the withdrawal of privileges to the prolongation of the term to be served, as well as transfer to a higher-security, more rigidly controlled institution—or to a lower-security, more relaxed institution as a reward for conformity.

Three contemporary problems of discipline and punishment merit mention: prison gangs, protective custody, and riots. Starting in the 1960s, prison gangs began to cause acute problems of discipline and safety in several jurisdictions, particularly in California, Illinois, and Arizona. Linked to street gangs, welded to loyalties by religious or racial sentiments, they seriously challenged the preservation of order and discipline within the larger, increasingly overcrowded and understaffed big-city prisons. They remain a potent force, linked to disturbances and riots.

Partly as a product of the growing influence of prison gangs and partly as a result of overcrowding, it has become more difficult to protect the weak prisoner from the strong, the isolate from the gang, the minority prisoner from the majority (whatever their ethnicity). As a result, an increasing number of prisoners in the last two decades have had to be held, at their own request and agreed to by the prison authorities, in "protective custody"—segregated for their own safety from the general population of the prison.

It is not uncommon to find 10 percent of the population of a large prison in protective custody. This puts further pressure on the prison administrator. Unless puni-tive, near-solitary confinement is imposed on the protective custody inmate (which too often happens), there must be two distinct prison programs within the prison, one for those in the general population and one for those in protective custody: two different programs for food service, employment, visits, work, recreation, library, and religious observations, in short, for everything that is required of a prison. The task of preserving order and discipline is thus further complicated.

Sometimes discipline and order break down completely. Over the period from 1971 to 1992 there have been at least fourteen major prison riots in the United States, the two worst being at Attica, a New York State facility, in 1971 and at New Mexico State Penitentiary in 1980. In the Attica uprising, eleven prison employees and thirty-two unarmed prisoners were killed—all the prisoners and four of the prison employees being killed by the gunfire with which the authorities reclaimed the prison. The thirty-three prisoners killed in the riot in the New Mexico penitentiary were killed by other inmates in a scene of unbridled brutality. Many of those murdered were prisoners who were being held in protective custody and who, rightly or wrongly, were seen by other prisoners as informers.

The other major state prison riots during those decades resulted in more deaths: Oklahoma State Penitentiary in McAlester in 1973, three prisoners killed; Soledad in California in 1979, two inmates killed and seventeen injured in what amounted to a race riot; three riots in Michigan prisons in 1981, injuring 130 prisoners and guards and causing nine million dollars in property damage; in 1983, a riot in Conner Cor-rectional Center in Hominy, Oklahoma, in which one inmate was killed and twenty-three prisoners and guards were injured; in 1985, rioting at four Tennessee prisons; in 1985, an eighteen-hour uprising at Oklahoma State Penitentiary, in which hostages were taken and three guards stabbed; and in 1986, three inmates killed in a two-day takeover of West Virginia State Penitentiary in Moundsville.

The federal prison system has also experienced riots, but their origin is different from that of the riots in state prisons. In 1980, President Jimmy Carter decided to allow 125,000 Cuban refugees to come to this country in a boat-lift from the Cuban port of Mariel, a decision that General Fidel Castro used as an opportunity to empty Cuban long-term prisons and the back wards of Cuban mental hospitals. Many of these refu-gees eventually filled the federal correctional institutions at Atlanta, Georgia, and Talladega, Alabama, after having been convicted of crimes in the United States. The riot at Talladega, in August 1991, occurred when it became known that, pursuant to the 1984 agreement between the United States and the Castro government, a group of such detainees was soon to be forcibly repatriated.

There has been much speculation on, but no satisfactory analysis of, the causes of prison riots, other than the riots of the Marielitos. When riots start and communication is achieved between the rioters and the prison authorities, the list of complaints by the prisoners follows a common pattern—bad food, inadequate medical care, the lack of rehabilitative programs, unfair punishments—but even all these complaints taken to-gether do not seem a sufficient explanation. It is worthy of note, however, that riots seem to be confined to the larger, overcrowded prisons characterized by idleness and racial tensions.

Health Care in Prison: Physical

The accreditation movement and the involvement of federal courts from the 1970s onward in requiring minimum constitutional conditions of custody had a widespread impact on health care in prisons. Typically, the prison hospital is one of the first sites shown to a visitor to a prison. And, as we have seen in other chapters of this book, the presence of professional medical personnel in prisons has had an ameliorating effect on prison conditions generally. Nevertheless, it is often difficult to attract competent medical staff to work in prisons; salaries tend to be lower, and inmates tend to be difficult and litigious patients. Three prison medical problems of serious concern have recently emerged: HIV positivity and AIDS; a strain of treatment-resistant tuberculosis; and an increase in the number of geriatric and terminally ill patients.

In the early days of recognition of the threat of AIDS, prisons and jails were seen as likely to be fertile fields for expediting the spread of this plague—and so it has proved. After all, both institutions contain a substantial number of active homosexuals less likely than others to be protective of their own physical safety and that of their sexual partners. And of course, isolating young men from women increases the incidence of homosexual behavior. Further, although it is now less frequent, the threat of homosexual rape by an HIV-positive inmate is appalling to contemplate. Add to this the realities of a large number of drug users in prison and of the availability of drugs in most prisons and jails, and these breeding grounds for AIDS are further fertilized. Prison staffs became greatly alarmed; the spittle or bite of an HIV-positive prisoner was, without secure medical foundation, seen as a lethal threat.

There was much discussion about whether there should be compulsory regular HIV testing in prisons, and this is now generally in place. There was also discussion about whether those prisoners who had tested positive should be separated from other prisoners to impede the spread of AIDS and whether condoms should be available to the prison population. In a very few prisons, condoms were made available, but this remains a rare practice. It is also the consensus that it is unwise to try to segregate HIV-positive prisoners (though this is done in some prisons and jails), for two reasons. First, there is the problem of the window of delay, often six months, required for the HIV test accurately to establish the presence of that condition; and second, experience has shown that the spread of HIV positivity in the prison is less extensive when there is an appreciation of the risk than when the majority of prisoners have a false sense of safety, which is all that segregation would achieve.

In July 1992, the three most centrally concerned national medical associations—the American College of Physicians, the National Commission on Correctional Health Care, and the American Correctional Health Care Association—officially reported their collective view of the gravity of the problem that AIDS presented to health care in prisons and jails and to the community at large. They reported that the incidence of AIDS was fourteen times higher in state and federal correctional systems (202 cases per 100,000) than in the population at large (14.65 cases per 100,000), with 6,985 confirmed AIDS cases in prisons at the end of 1990. They estimated that many more inmates than these numbers reflect were seropositive, that is, were carrying the HIV virus. In states conducting blind epidemiological studies, rates of HIV seropositivity ranged from as low as 0.6 percent (Oregon and Wisconsin) to as high as 17 percent (New York, with 18.8 percent of women prisoners in New York being seropositive). They calculated the lifetime cost of caring for a single person with AIDS to be eighty-five thousand dollars (thirty-two thousand dollars annually) and the yearly cost of caring for an asymptomatic HIV-infected person to be over five thousand dollars.

If the patient were not in prison, he or his family would have to meet that cost; few prisoners have incomes sufficient to do so. Although the cost to prisons of providing treatment is generally less than the cost of private health care, the expense is still great. Should such a cost fall on the prison budget? Federally, and in most states, the answer has been yes, adding up to a very considerable burden on the budget. It is paradoxical that, in the absence of a national health insurance program, the punishment for crime becomes a prolongation of life.

Tuberculosis is also presenting a new and difficult problem, particularly in the light of its link with AIDS. The incidence of tuberculosis in people with AIDS is nearly five hundred times that in the general population. Given the extent of AIDS in prisons and jails, the Centers for Disease Control of the Department of Health estimated that the incidence of tuberculosis among incarcerated people in 1985 was more than three times the rate in the general population, and with the burgeoning of AIDS in prisons and jails since then, that rate is now much higher.

A few studies have attempted to calculate the frequency of tuberculosis among the incarcerated in particular states: in 1987 in New Jersey it was eleven times higher than in the general population; in the same year in California it was six times higher. In New York prisons, cases of tuberculosis increased from 15.4 to 105.5 per 100,000 in the period from 1976 to 1986, with 56 percent of cases occurring in HIV-positive inmates. These are straws in the wind of an impending and grave plague.

In the early 1990s, a virulent and difficult-to-treat strain of tuberculosis began to spread with extraordinary speed through the inmate populations of the New York jails and prisons and less swiftly in other crowded big-city institutions. With tuberculosis, unlike with AIDS, the risk to the institutional staff is both real and appreciated. In November 1991, the New York prison system reported that this treatment-resistant condition had in eleven months caused the deaths of thirteen prisoners and one guard.

As we have seen in earlier chapters, prisons and jails have a long history of being breeding grounds for infection. The problem seems to be recurring with renewed intensity, spurred by AIDS and tuberculosis, a new "gaol fever," as we approach the end of the twentieth century.

In addition, an entirely novel problem now confronts prison administrators and prison physicians—the problem of aged and infirm prisoners. Prisons have always held a disproportionate number of young male offenders, and they still do; but with the increasing numbers of people now being sent to prison and with the duration of sentences lengthening greatly, several federal and state prison systems are facing the difficult problem of incarcerating, in reasonably decent conditions, a substantial number of aged and terminally ill prisoners. AIDS and Alzheimer patients are but the most visible and challenging groups that prisons must accommodate in running a geriatric prison-hospital. Geriatric care raises the same moral paradox for the prison administrator as does AIDS patient care: if the patient-prisoner continues to be punished by imprisonment for his crime, his life will be prolonged and his medical treatment will be far better than if the punishment is remitted and he is discharged. Money and morality point, as they sometimes do, in opposite directions.

Health Care in Prison: Psychological

In the world of colonial America, the mentally ill who lacked financial or familial support were treated in the same way as the poor and the homeless, finding their way to jails, workhouses, hovels, and the streets—a condition in which too many of them are still to be found today. It was not until the first half of the nineteenth century that asylums for the mentally ill spread throughout the United States to house and treat those who could not live safely in the community.

With the spread of the asylum, it came to be recognized that certain classes of the mentally ill presented distinct problems—those who, as well as being mentally ill, were physically dangerous or were thought to be physically dangerous and those who, as well as being criminal and held as prisoners for their crimes, were also mentally ill. Hence hybrid institutions, within the mental health and correctional systems of the state, were established to house and treat these two categories of the mentally ill. Of these two hybrids, the institution closer to our present concern is the psychiatric prison.

Psychosis is more common among prisoners than in the community at large. Likewise, criminal records are more common among those in mental hospitals than in the community at large. But when both subgroups are compared with control groups of the same sex, age, and socioeconomic circumstances, those disparities largely, though not completely, disappear. It is therefore an unsafe conclusion that prisoners are disproportionately mentally ill, but it is an entirely safe conclusion that among prisoners there will be found many who are mentally ill and many who are retarded. Hence, every prison system, federal and state, has to make some provision for a substantial number of such prisoners. And since the movement to deinstitutionalize psychiatric hospitals in the 1970s, the pressure on the prisons and jails for mentally ill inmates has greatly increased; with the lack of community-based treatment facilities to help those removed from the psychiatric hospitals, many such unfortunates have found their way to prisons and jails.

Typically, in each state and in the federal system, there is a section of a prison, or a separate prison or prisons, set aside for psychiatric and severely retarded prisoners. Here they serve their prison sentences and are released at the end of their prison term. If still mentally ill and dangerous, they may, when their prison terms are served, be admitted as compulsory or voluntary patients to a state mental hospital, the tests of their commitment to such institutions being the same as for the unconvicted.

These hybrid institutions, the prison mental hospitals, vary greatly in the quality of care they provide. Some are excellent; for example, the psychiatric care available at the federal prisons at Butner and Rochester is of the highest quality. Others provide little more than secure custody and drug therapy. The reputations and careers of ambitious psychiatrists are not advanced in such institutions, and few are to be found at work in the prison mental hospitals.

State mental health systems also have to provide for some violent patients who present, or who are thought to present, a particular danger both to those in the institution and to others if the patients are at large; hence high-security mental hospitals, or sections of mental hospitals, are to be found in every state. These facilities also generally serve the criminal justice systems of each state by holding people who have been charged with crimes and found unfit to stand trial or who have been found not guilty by reason of insanity. Like the psychiatric-prison hybrid, the mental hospital–security institution hybrid also tends to provide a less-curative environment than do other state mental hospitals.

It is not surprising that prisoners who are mentally ill, and mentally ill citizens who are seen as dangerous or criminal, should receive less-adequate care than do less-stigmatized citizens; but it is a regrettable fact that, by and large, these hybrid institutions provide deeper circles of suffering and less-solicitous care than either the typical mental hospital or the typical prison.

The Other Prisoners

The "other prisoners" are, of course, the prison staff. During their working shifts, day and night, they too are within the security perimeter of the prison, subjected to a routine reflecting that of the prisoners. Over the quarter century since the report of the President's Crime Commission in 1967, there have been substantial changes in the composition of the prison guard force as well as in their working conditions and vocational roles.

At the top of the hierarchy of prison administration is the director or superintendent of prisons or the commissioner of corrections. In most states this functionary is appointed by the governor. These senior administrators of prison systems demonstrate widely differing styles of prison management: some are closely involved with their staff and inmates, adopting a hands-on approach; others spend the majority of their time outside the prison, relating to the legislature and public-interest groups.

At the next level are the wardens, responsible for the supervision of their particular institutions. They supervise the custodial and administrative staffs and the staff more concerned with what is known as "program"— education, industries, the hospital, counseling, recreation, and similar personal development programs.

The majority of the prison staff work as security officers. Individual states have different requirements, but correctional officers must usually be over eighteen or twenty-one years of age and have a high school diploma or the equivalent, although a growing number also have some college education. Applicants with a history of criminal convictions are automatically ineligible in most states, a policy that has met with criticism. The employment of ex-offenders can encourage prison inmates by demonstrating that there are career opportunities available to them after their release and that recidivism is not inevitable. It has been argued too that the corrections system should set an example for other public and private employers by hiring ex-offenders who meet the necessary requirements and who have diverted their lives from criminal activity. It is also possible that such officers would be better equipped to deal with prison inmates, by virtue of having once been in the same position.

The number of corrections officers who leave their jobs each year differs from state to state; some states have an annual turnover rate of 5 percent, whereas others lose nearly a third of their officers each year. The average career of a corrections officer lasts about ten years.

The division between those responsible for security and those responsible for "program" remains in place; but there is a larger sense of social purpose, of belonging to a profession providing a useful social service, than previously obtained. Unionization has played a role in this, with the guard force developing a voice in the governance of the prison independent of management. But a more substantial reason has been the funds and energies, federal and state, that have been devoted to staff training at every level. The National Institute of Justice and the National Institute of Corrections have provided federal funds to the states and other governmental units for staff training, and the American Correctional Association has also played an important part in giving prison staffs a sense of belonging to a vocation with standards and values worthy of respect.

Women now serve as frontline guards in most prisons. Fears that they would be less able than men to control the prisoners, that they would be subjected to rape, and that they would disproportionately be the objects of violence have all proved to be false. The number of women prison guards has steadily increased, to the benefit of safety and order in the prisons.

Likewise, because it has come to be understood, for reasons of efficiency buttressed by affirmative-action employment pressures, that the guard force should include African-American and Hispanic minorities, what used to be a predominantly Caucasian male guard force has changed its composition. (As an example, the guard force of 866 at Stateville in the year that Prisoner #12345 wrote was made up as follows: men, 663; women, 203; whites, 448; blacks, 371; Hispanic, 30; American Indian, 3; others, 14.)

A major problem in the prison staffing systems of the states is the lack of continuity in leadership at the commissioner or director level, a problem that stems from too much political interference in the governance of the prisons. Each newly appointed governor selects a new commissioner or director of corrections; when things go wrong—or are thought by the public to have gone wrong—in the administration of the prison system, the commissioner or director, at fault or not, is usually sacrificed to the political winds.

THREE EMERGING ISSUES

Private Prisons

In both the state and the federal systems, a new category of prisons is emerging: private prisons built and sometimes operated by private corporations. There are several variations among private prisons. Some are simply built by private companies and leased to the government, to be run by the same departments of corrections that currently run publicly owned prisons. Others are built and run by corporations quick to see an opportunity to establish themselves in what is, for the most part, a new field of enterprise. Still other prisons are built and owned by governments who employ private companies to operate them.

Certain limited types of privatization within the prison system are not new; for some time prison systems have contracted out for specific services such as medical care, counseling, and education. Privatization of whole facilities, however, is new to the modern prison and has raised alarm among groups as diverse as municipal employee unions and civil rights organizations. The delegation by government, to private business, of the power to imprison and, necessarily, the power to use force to maintain order, prevent escape, and the like raises troublesome legal and ethical questions. Worrisome too is the creation of an entire industry with a pecuniary interest in maintaining, or even increasing, the number of people incarcerated. Given the current influence of special interests over government decisions, the possibility that a private prison industry lobby could affect important decisions, such as whether to develop alternatives to imprisonment, seems credible.

It is unclear whether private prisons are the wave of the future of corrections. In addition to the above concerns, there is mixed evidence as to whether they are fulfilling their initial promise of less-expensive, more efficient service.

Intermediate Punishments

The problems created by the overcrowding of the prisons in the 1980s and 1990s, and the sheer expense of supporting so many prisoners, generated political pressure to substantially increase the imposition of "intermediate punishments." To confine punishments to imprisonment and probation, which broadly describes current practice, is like prescribing either surgery or an aspirin for every body pain.

The commonsense case for the expansion of intermediate punishments is as follows: there are many in prison who could safely be punished by community-based intermediate punishments; also, there are many on probation who require closer supervision than ordinary probation provides. The near vacuum between prison and probation should be filled with a range of intermediate punishments.

What, then, are these intermediate punishments, and what are the claims made for them? Intermediate punishments are house arrest, conditions of residence, periodic imprisonment, residential and nonresidential treatment programs for drugs and alcohol, the use of electronic controls on movement so that comprehensive supervision can be achieved, community service, fines and restitution, boot camp, and a wide variety of arrangements for intensive probation supervision. Throughout the United States, and more extensively in Europe, there has been extensive experimentation with all of these intermediate punishments—but nowhere in the United States have they been institutionalized into a comprehensive and graduated system of punishments.

Three claims are made for intermediate punishments: they will reduce prison crowding; they will save money; and they will reduce recidivism, thus better protecting the community. Are these claims valid? In the short run intermediate punishments will not much reduce crowding, first because of their tendency to draw more clients from those on ordinary probation than from those in prison or those who are prison-bound, and second because many criminals sentenced to intermediate punishments will fail to observe the conditions of their sentences, so that their sentences will be revoked and they will be sent to prison.

Will these punishments save money? Prison is very expensive; all intermediate punishments are much less expensive. Hence, it is argued, they will save public money. In the longer run this is probably true, but in the period of their introduction they will increase correctional costs, since new resources have to be provided if intermediate punishments are to be rigorously enforced, as they must be if they are to be effective.

It remains uncertain whether intermediate punishments will reduce recidivism and better protect the community. So far, there are very few methodologically satisfactory studies of the later conduct of criminals sentenced to intermediate punishments. All that can responsibly be claimed at present is that intermediate punishments do not appear to lead to an *increase* in recidivism rates.

That intermediate punishments have not been shown to be reductive of crime should come as no surprise—neither has any other punishment. Neither the lash nor the executioner, neither the psychiatrist nor the psychologist—and certainly not the prison—has been shown to provide measurable increments of crime control. Despite the long history of punishment, scholarship has so far failed to establish a link between punishment and crime control, other than in the individual case.

Prison as a punishment for crime differs from community-based punishments in this respect: if an increasing rate of imprisonment fails to deter criminality, fails to reduce crime rates, that very failure will contribute to a public demand, swiftly echoed by politicians, for still more imprisonment and even less use of community-based punishments. The irony is that the less effective the prisons are in reducing crime, the higher the demand for still more imprisonment. It is the "Humpty Dumpty" principle: if all the king's horses and all the king's men couldn't put Humpty together again, then, by heavens, we need more horses and more men. Generations of research have failed to disturb the commonsensical but false view that increased severity of punishment will produce less crime, that increased reliance on imprisonment is to be preferred to other nonincarcerative punishments.

Much the same analysis applies to treatment programs as part of the sentencing structure, though the Humpty Dumpty principle does not apply. Treatment programs for adult offenders, like punishment programs, seem to have only marginal effects, if any, on gross crime rates. Measurable systemwide effects have never been shown, either for increased severity as a deterrent or for increased treatment as an inoculum.

This does not mean, of course, that the criminal justice system itself does not serve to hold down crime rates. What it means is that although system effects are substantial, fine-tuning that system by using reforms toward severity or leniency has not been shown to have measurable effects. So, the case for intermediate punishments as a means of more effective crime control is a matter of belief or speculation, not knowledge.

In the United States, the criminal justice systems, federal and state, are overwhelmed, swamped beyond bailout, by the criminogenic consequences of an entrenched culture of violence and, perhaps more significant, by the existence of a locked-in underclass, denied the minimum conditions necessary for a productive and peaceful life, with race, ethnicity, and class interlocking in a unique way. Booming crime rates are one important cost of the creation and continued toleration of these evil conditions.

Ultimately, the case for intermediate punishments rests not on utilitarian crime-prevention and cost-saving grounds, though both are relevant. It rests on principles of justice. Justice, not crime control, is the major purpose of sentencing, of distributing punishments. Crime control justifies the system; principles of justice should control the imposition of sentences on convicted criminals.

Justice requires the creation of a graduated, comprehensive system of criminal punishments incorporating intermediate punishments, with much less reliance on imprisonment as the punishment of choice. Values of proportionality in punishment, limited by concepts of desert, require a range of punishments between incarceration and probation. Lacking that middle range—lacking a set of comprehensive, graduated punishments—a criminal justice system will inevitably impose many sentences that are either too severe or too lenient, too socially protective or too socially lax.

The Politics of Imprisonment

A major impediment to reducing the use of imprisonment in the United States, and to bringing its imposition into accord with that of other developed countries, lies in its having become, over the past two decades, the plaything of politics. Being "tough on crime" has become a necessary precondition of election to political office and of the retention of incumbency.

Efforts at social reform in the early 1960s have been unjustly maligned, and the public has been misled by a series of political platforms that make unreal promises of effective crime reduction by means of increased severity of punishment, by capital punishment, by the lengthening of prison terms, and by false assurances that condign incarcerative punishment will be imposed on all criminals.

Wars on crime and wars on drugs are regularly declared in powerful rhetoric promising the enemy's surrender. But success never attends these efforts; there is no victory and no armistice. Instead, a new war is declared, as if the previous war had never taken place—and not even the rhetoric changes.

I am far more skilled at retrospection than prediction; lacking a safety net, I shall not hazard a guess as to when our political masters will acknowledge that vote gathering by these mendacious means is a sin against the future. But it is entirely proper to conclude this overview of U.S. prisons of the past quarter century by stressing that it is political irresponsibility that has generated the cancerous growth of imprisonment.

The one potential break in this depressing pattern is at the state level, where an increasing number of governors and legislatures face daunting financial dilemmas. Prisons are built but cannot be opened for lack of funds to run them. Educational budgets are cut to find dollars for prisons. Perhaps the choice between schools and prisons will force a break in the political rhetoric favoring incarceration.

Bibliographic Note

For the numerical data on prisons, jails, and prisoners, see the *Sourcebook of Criminal Justice Statistics*, published annually by the Bureau of Justice Statistics of the U.S. Department of Justice. The 1993 *Sourcebook* is a nearly 800-page compendium of basic statistics on crime and criminal punishments, courts, and criminals and of federal and state criminal justice systems.

I know of no adequate current description of the "American prison," and such is the diversity of organization and practice in the prisons of the United States that I doubt that one could be written. Hence this essay relies generally on three decades of my own involvement, to a greater or less degree, in prison policy decisions in England, Australia, Scandinavia, Japan, and the United States. In recent years my focus has been on the prisons of the U.S. Bureau of Prisons and on the prisons of the state of Illinois. I also rely somewhat plagiaristically on some of my own earlier writings, in particular *The Habitual Criminal* (London: Longmans, Green, 1951) and *The Future of Imprisonment* (Chicago: University of Chicago Press, 1974).

I chose Stateville in Illinois as my paradigm prison for this essay for two reasons: first, because I have been in touch with its administration for over two decades and, for three years, served as a special master for a federal district court in a case involving living conditions in that prison; and second, because of James B. Jacobs's superb study, *Stateville: The Penitentiary in Mass Society* (Chicago: University of Chicago Press, 1977), dealing with life in that prison. The same author's *New Perspectives on Prisons and Imprisonment* (Ithaca: Cornell University Press, 1983) further analyzes aspects of the prison culture. An earlier influential effort to describe that culture is Gresham Sykes's *The Society of Captives: A Study of a Minimum Security Prison* (Princeton: Princeton University Press, 1958).

Books that provide departure points for consideration of the modern American prison are Blake McKelvey, *American Prisons: A History of Good Intentions* (Montclair, N.J.: Patterson-Smith, 1977), Donald Clemmer, *The Prison Community* (New York: Rinehart, 1958), Daniel Glaser, *The Effectiveness of a Prison and Parole System* (Indianapolis: Bobbs-Merrill, 1964), and Gordon Hawkins, *The Prison* (Chicago: University of Chicago Press, 1976).

For a history of the federal Bureau of Prisons, see Paul Keve, *Prisons and the American Conscience: A History of U.S. Federal Corrections* (Carbondale: Southern Illinois University Press, 1991).

There is a long history of articles and books on prison reform, including authors such as Jeremy Bentham, John Stuart Mill, Sir James Fitzjames Stephen, John Howard, and Montesquieu— and the flow continues. Of recent interest are William Nagel, *The New Red Barn: A Critical Look at the Modern American Prison* (New York: Walker, 1973), John Irwin, *Prisons in Turmoil* (Boston: Little, Brown, 1980), and Michael Sherman and Gordon Hawkins, *Imprisonment in America: Choosing the Future* (Chicago: University of Chicago Press, 1981).

On styles of governance of prisons, see John DiIulio, *Governing Prisons: A Comparative Study of Correctional Management* (New York: Free Press, 1987). On the impact of imprisonment on crime rates, see Franklin Zimring and Gordon Hawkins, *Incapacitation: Penal Confinement and the Restraint of Crime* (New York: Oxford University Press, 1995). On race and imprisonment, and the effect of racially disproportionate imprisonment on community groups, see Michael Tonry, *Malign Neglect: Race, Crime, and Punishment in America* (New York: Oxford University Press, 1995).

I have omitted from this bibliographic note many important studies of the history of imprisonment in the United States because they are dealt with elsewhere in this volume.

PART II

THEMES AND VARIATIONS

CHAPTER NINE

THE AUSTRALIAN EXPERIENCE

The Convict Colony

John Hirst

Throughout history convicts have been removed from the society in which they have offended. Sometimes they have been sent into exile, the policy Britain followed in sending convicts to the American colonies. Sometimes they have been sent to special penal settlements, like those the French ran in their colonies of Guiana and New Caledonia. Only once have convicts been sent to found the society in which they were to endure their punishment. This was the strange beginning of European settlement in Australia.

A REPUBLIC OF CONVICTS

In the late eighteenth century, Great Britain had to find a way to deal with growing numbers of convicted criminals. After its North American colonies won their independence, it could no longer send convicts across the Atlantic, so the British government began to search for another overseas possession where it could found a convict colony. In 1786 the cabinet decided on Botany Bay, a harbor discovered and named by English Captain James Cook on his voyage along the eastern coast of Australia in 1770. Why the British decided to colonize Botany Bay with convicts is a matter of dispute. Some experts argue that it was simply a way of ridding the kingdom of convicts. Others assert that in addition Britain hoped to use the colony to supply its navy and merchant vessels and to advance a grand strategy for dominance in the area. It is clear that Prime Minister William Pitt was himself closely involved in the deliberations over the convict colony at Botany Bay and that at this time he was preoccupied with plans to check or outmatch the other European powers in the Indian and Pacific Oceans. Since policymakers had long used convicts to advance trade and settlement within the empire, Pitt and his colleagues likely had some such thoughts in mind when they decided to dispatch convicts to Australia. That speck of new European settlement was certainly made the occasion for a large territorial claim: the eastern third of the continent, known as New South

Wales, and the adjacent islands of the Pacific Ocean.

Britain adopted the plan of sending convicts to Australia after examining and re-jecting a number of alternatives. One of these was the penitentiary, first outlined in modern form by English penal reformer John Howard in his 1777 treatise, *State of the Prisons*. Howard proposed a new kind of prison, in which convicts would receive pun-ishment according to the seriousness of their crimes. In his plan, prisoners were to be classified by their crimes, kept in cells, and put to work under strict discipline. Parlia-ment accepted the penitentiary idea in principle, passing the Penitentiary Act in 1779. But because of the huge initial expenditure required, the penitentiaries were not built. Transportation was a far more appealing alternative—it not only was cheap but also promised to reduce crime by the simple expedient of removing criminals. The govern-ment began to look for a new location to which convicts might be sent.

One option that advanced far enough to receive cabinet approval was to send con-victs to an island in the Gambia River in West Africa, where they would be left to their own devices to form, as it were, a convict republic. Convicts would be encouraged to elect a chief, who would appoint subordinate officers and maintain law and order. They were to survive by cultivating the land, a pursuit in which a few would undoubtedly do better than the rest. Those who acquired large estates would become the employers of convicts who arrived later. The British government would have no involvement with the operation of the colony, other than supplying it with the resources it needed to get started and posting a ship at the mouth of the river to prevent escape.

This scheme, abandoned after a House of Commons committee reported that the climate was too unhealthy, shows how transportation was conceived as a punishment. Clearly, the authorities had no interest in assigning convicts to different positions in this new society according to the nature of their offenses. In the free-for-all, the convicts who ended up with power over the rest would undoubtedly be not the timid first of-fenders but those hardened in crime. The British ministers believed the scheme would punish sufficiently by exiling criminals and exposing them to the uncertainties and dangers of the wilderness. Their attitude drove Jeremy Bentham, the leading English penal reformer of the time, to despair. He could not understand how ministers who had shown some interest in penitentiaries, which could offer certainty and gradation in punishment, could turn to a plan in which uncertainty and lack of discrimination were essential features. When the government finally settled on Botany Bay, he immediately began to collect information to damn the project.

The government did not leave the convicts to their own devices in Australia. A governor, a few officers of civil administration, and a detachment of marines would oversee convict life. But as it turned out, these minimal government structures did not prevent the development of something like a republic of convicts. In the Gambian case the British government was not itself to be involved in this anomalous society; in New South Wales the government became fully complicit in the moral topsy-turvydom that it entailed.

Australians commonly envision the early British outpost in Australia as a prison or penal settlement that gradually developed into a more ordinary colony. The reverse is closer to the truth. New South Wales started as a colony peopled by convicts and ex-convicts whose governors were preoccupied with ensuring the survival of the colony and enhancing its growth. Then the British government belatedly attempted to transform the colony into a conventional penal settlement, where penal principles determined convicts' fates.

Peopling the Colony

Opinion on Australia's founding population, the convicts, has changed over the course of time. After the British government abandoned transportation to New South Wales in 1840, Australians themselves came to share the world's view of the practice as shameful. This outlook caused many to lump the convicts into a single category, assuming the worst of them and preferring not to speak of them. In the early twentieth century, however, a nationalist reaction against this self-abasement caused Australians to depict the convicts as innocent victims of an unjust, hierarchical British society and a draconian law. This remains the popular view, but since the 1950s comprehensive studies of the records have shown that most convicts were ordinary criminals and ne'er-do-wells. Recently there has been an academic reaction to this view. The authors of *Convict Workers* have argued that the convicts were not a separate group but were ordinary working-class men and women who brought a great range of skills to the colony. They cite in support of this view recent British research that highlights the petty and casual nature of most crime, though the British work gives no warrant for the claim in *Convict Workers* that there were no regular criminals or a criminal underworld. Finally, variety must be accepted: among the convicts were professional London thieves, ne'er-do-wells in and out of work, skilled workers regularly employed in their trade, and country laborers who were close to being innocent victims. Statistical analysis of the convict records establishes that convicts were generally young and convicted of offenses against property; that they came disproportionately from the towns and cities; that over half had been convicted of a previous offense; and that nearly all came from the lower classes, with only a sprinkling of educated and professional people. The nonconvict marines and civilians who oversaw the convicts became well aware of the variations and knew that an individual convict's usefulness and tractability were not closely related to the nature and frequency of his crimes.

In 1787 the first fleet of eleven British ships, carrying 750 convicts and 250 marines, set sail for Botany Bay under the command of Navy Captain Arthur Phillip. The voyage was remarkably healthy, due chiefly to the care taken by Phillip. Before he sailed he insisted that the ships be brought to first-class condition and amply supplied with food and medicine. During the voyage he allowed convicts to exercise on deck and provided them with fresh food at every port of call. There were only 32 deaths before the fleet reached its destination on January 26, 1788.

By contrast, the voyage of the second fleet in 1790 was horrendous: there were 267 deaths, a rate of 25 percent. The disaster prompted official efforts to improve conditions aboard the convict ships. This was achieved not through legislation but through a number of administrative devices adopted during the next thirty years. The devices used were of the sort recommended by Jeremy Bentham in his other role, as administrative reformer. Thus indirectly Bentham did have an influence on the administration of transportation even while his strictures against it as a system of punishment were being ignored.

Britain started paying its shipping contractors according to the number of convicts who reached the colony alive, giving gratuities to captains who ran healthy ships. Naval surgeons were appointed to each ship, and captains were made subject to them in matters of the convicts' health. Captains were forbidden to engage in private trade or to carry cargo. With these measures, the convict ships were rendered remarkably safe and healthy; it was less dangerous to travel to Australia as a convict than to sail to the United States as a migrant. After 1815 the death rate was less than 1 percent, compared with an average rate of 10 percent on the eighteenth-century convict voyages to the American colonies. Not one of the voyages to Australia was as bad as the worst to America, when nearly half died. Thus one of Bentham's objections to transportation—the supposed dangers and uncertainty of convict voyages—rang hollow in light of the government's success.

Overall, 187,000 convicts were sent to Australia, nearly all of them after 1815. Between 1788 and 1815, long wars with France forced Britain to sharply curtail its transportation of convicts. Instead, convicts were more often pressed into service in the armed forces or into work on the docks. During the wars only a few hundred convicts were sent to New South Wales each year. The peace in 1815 boosted that number to 2,000–3,000 annually; in the 1830s, when transportation peaked, an average of 5,000 convicts arrived in the colony each year. Nevertheless, the British program did not produce a society in which convicts were the majority of the population. Their children were free, and from 1831 the government sponsored a large-scale migration of free working people to Australia. When transportation to New South Wales ceased in 1840, convicts and ex-convicts composed one-third of the population.

Founding the Colony

Soon after he reached Botany Bay in 1788, Phillip discovered Sydney Harbor a few miles to the north. He fixed the site of the new settlement there, on the spot where downtown Sydney now stands. The marines immediately made clear that they were nonpersons in the internal government of the new settlement. They would repel invasion and put down rebellion, but they would not supervise the work of the convicts. Even when the ground was being cleared for their own encampment, the marines would not involve themselves in the operation. Governor Phillip accordingly had to find all his overseers from among the ranks of the convicts. The supervisors' reward at first was freedom from toil. Later they were paid by being allotted one or two convicts for their own use. Some employed these convicts in businesses they ran; others allowed the convicts to work on their own account and took a portion of their earnings. Since it was difficult and expensive to attract nonconvict professional people to the settlement, the colony's government also drew on skilled convicts for services in medicine, law, architecture, and surveying. Overseers, superintendents, and professional people were further encouraged to good service by the granting or promise of pardons.

Since the marines took no interest in the maintenance of law and order, Governor Phillip also recruited convicts for the colony's first police force. When the convict police came to exercise civil authority not only over their fellows but over the marines as well, the commanding officer of the marines protested strongly. By all normal standards he was in the right: the marines were already subject to a discipline that derived from a much higher authority than that of the governor's police. Nevertheless Phillip, forced to follow the logic of a convict republic, backed his police and sent the marines' commander to the remote outpost of Norfolk Island, fifteen hundred miles away. Convicts and ex-convicts thus remained the mainstay of the colony's police force for the whole period of transportation.

Since convicts composed three-quarters of the original population of New South Wales, they were given legal rights denied to convicts in Britain. They could give evidence in court, for without it most proceedings and transactions in the colony could not have been officially known. This right was important to the convicts' own welfare, because it allowed them to give evidence in court against their overseers and masters. Convicts could also own property and sue to protect these possessions, the chief threat to which came from other convicts. The first case in the civil court of New South Wales was brought against the master of a transport ship by two convicts whose luggage was lost on the way to the colony. In Britain, convicts could not sue, but they could be sued; their status as convicts could not be allowed to shield them from the law. The governors of the new colony sought to abridge the right to sue convicts, since a convict sent to jail (for the nonpayment of a debt, for example) was not available to work. As a result, it was a penalty that convicts might seek. Shopkeepers who supplied the convicts, of course, wanted to retain the right to sue them, and it took time before the court jettisoned their interests to accommodate those of the governors.

None of these convict rights would have been necessary had the colony been run, as was initially intended, as a military government. A much more summary form of justice would then have prevailed, and any concessions made to convicts would not have borne the full implication of rights under English law. Instead, in the later stages of planning for the colony, the British government had provided for a civilian court, albeit in a military form. This court was to be presided over by a judge-advocate, who was a military officer, and its jury was to consist of six military or naval officers, who, with the judge, determined verdicts by a majority vote. However, in actuality the civilian court of the colony strictly followed English legal practice. Convicts charged with serious crimes appeared before it, and even more securely before the courts established later, as innocents whose guilt had to be proved. The standard of proof was high, and acquittals were common. (For minor crimes and offenses against the labor code, convicts appeared before a court of petty sessions; as in England, this court was composed of unpaid magistrates.)

The provision of a civilian court was likely the work of the British Home Secretary Lord Sydney, who otherwise did not play a prominent part in planning the settlement that came to bear his name. In refusing to subject convicts to some unusual and arbitrary authority, Sydney expressed a common British misgiving. Ministers who contemplated putting excess convicts to work on the roads of the kingdom always had to acknowledge that British public opinion would be outraged by such a scheme. A free-born Englishman might be hanged and flogged, but he could not be worked in chains by some tyrannical overseer. The application of the normal processes of English law to convicts in New South Wales shows how far from general acceptance was the delegated, institutional authority envisioned for the penitentiary by Bentham and other reformers.

Building the Colony's Economy

The original plan for feeding the convicts was deceptively simple: convicts would grow their own food on public farms, and ex-convicts would be given small land grants so that they could become a self-sufficient peasantry. In practice, Governor Phillip had great trouble making his public farms productive. Not only did he operate in an alien climate, but he also had to contend with reluctant laborers and overseers with no experience or interest in the work. Even the threat of famine could not motivate the convict workers, and starvation was averted only by the arrival of new shipments of food from England and deliveries arranged by Phillip from Cape Colony (South Africa) and Batavia (Djakarta, Indonesia).

When Phillip left New South Wales in 1792, the government of the colony fell, for over two years, into the hands of the military officers of the New South Wales Corps, which replaced the marines early that year. The officers abandoned public farming and redirected the convicts to private farms that the Crown had granted to the members of the corps just before Phillip's departure. In private hands and with interested supervision, Australian agriculture prospered; for the first time, the colony approached self-sufficiency in grain production. But the government still used the official store to feed the convicts who worked for the officers. The store in turn purchased its supply of grain from the officer-farmers with bills issued on the treasury in London. Thus, as originally planned, the convicts ate food they had grown themselves, but in the process military officers milked huge profits from the British taxpayer. The British government did not allow such a raid on the public funds to continue, but the two-year interregnum of the New South Wales Corps set the colony on a social and economic course that was never reversed.

The first result of the corps' profiteering was that the treasury bills gave the officers the wherewithal to begin overseas trade. Producing no product for export and only just able to feed itself, the colony now had funds in sterling courtesy of the British taxpayer. With these the officers imported tea, sugar, tobacco, and most notably rum. The rum became for a time a sort of internal currency, for it was the best inducement to get labor out of convicts. From these beginnings the officer-merchants diversified, securing their economic position by developing products for export: sealskins, sandalwood, whale oil, and from the 1830s on, wool.

The second result of the corps' interregnum was that officers started using convicts as assistants in their trading enterprises. Convicts ran the officers' shops so that the gentlemen would not sacrifice their dignity by engaging in business. On gaining freedom, some of these convicts used their newly minted skills to set up businesses themselves; some even eclipsed their patrons. Within twenty years, the richest people in the colony were ex-convict merchants and bankers. Beneath them in the colony's economy was a wide array of ex-convict shopkeepers, publicans, and tradesmen. The economic resource officially provided for ex-convicts—a thirty-acre farm—provided a precarious living for a minority.

Former officers and gentlemen migrants held large landed estates, but their wealth was more than matched by that of the ex-convict merchants and tradesmen, a few of whom bought into land. The success of all ex-convict businessmen rested on their unquestioned right to convict labor on the same terms given to those who came to the colony free. Approximately half the convicts in New South Wales had ex-convict masters a quarter-century after the founding of the colony. Thus, the British government's original scheme for the Gambia River settlement—that old convicts would employ new arrivals—was realized in Australia.

After the officers' interregnum, which ended in 1794, New South Wales returned to government by a series of civilian governors. From then on, a majority of the convicts worked for private employers. The ploy of feeding the convicts from the government store was halted after a struggle, and all employers became responsible for feeding and clothing their convicts. By the time of Governor Lachlan Macquarie (1810–22), convicts in private service were also paid a wage by their employers. This wage originated in a right claimed by convicts in the first days at Sydney. Convict overseers, ignoring the official requirement that convicts work from sunrise to sunset, assigned their charges taskwork of such a fixed nature that the convicts could finish the work by early afternoon. The convicts came to expect afternoon free time—"their own time," as they put it—and the government was finally obliged to accept this system, though it did manage to shift knock-off time to 3 P.M. In the afternoons the convicts took on extra work, for which they were paid.

This arrangement continued after most of the convicts moved into private service. The understanding was that if they worked for their master after 3 P.M., they had to be paid. If the convict's master did not have any extra work, the convict could go elsewhere in the afternoon to find it. Eventually Governor Macquarie ruled, as part of his policy to establish better order and decency, that in private service, the division of the day (which was becoming increasingly notional as more convicts worked for their own master in the afternoon) should cease. Convicts were to serve one master full time, and in return for rights foregone they were to receive an annual wage. Private masters were also required to supply their servants with the same rations as were issued to convicts in government service. From their wages, convicts could buy luxury items such as tea and sugar, which were not part of the standard flour-and-meat ration. Formerly these luxuries had been purchased out of their extra earnings.

Regulating the Colony's Citizens

Even though most convicts worked for private masters, they remained the responsibility of the government. In America, the government had taken no interest in the convicts at all: the merchants who had shipped them across the Atlantic had simply sold them to private masters for the term of their sentence. The fate of convicts in the American colonies had depended on the whim of masters and on the weak protection of the local courts. But in New South Wales, the government at a minimum had to know where the convicts were and whether they were alive or dead. On all matters concerning their detention and release the convicts had the right to petition the governor. During their confinement extra punishment could be inflicted on convicts only by order of the court; masters were prohibited from inflicting corporal punishment themselves. A master who had a complaint against a convict laborer had to take him to the same court that heard the complaints of convicts against masters.

The Australian prohibition on private punishment of convicts is surprising. In America masters had beaten convicts, and in Britain corporal punishment was still a central part of household discipline. But in Australia at first all convicts were in the hands of the government, and the government could control its subjects only through the courts. As convicts passed into private hands, the government did not relinquish its control. The reason for this becomes clear in an incident from the tenure of Governor Philip King (1800–1806). Despite the stricture, a certain military officer regularly and unashamedly beat his convict servants. Governor King pursued the officer through the military and civil courts, and the prohibition held. At the same time King, like the other early governors, was arguing with the military officers over their trading activities, which doused the colony in rum. The case of the beaten servants was clearly part of a larger trial of strength. Lowly convicts, it turns out, were protected by the Crown in order to clip the wings of overweening subjects.

The Crown also reserved the right to take convicts away from masters, the ultimate sanction against ill treatment. In the 1820s the New South Wales Supreme Court overturned this practice on the grounds that it threatened the right to private property, since if convicts were removed, land would be worthless. But both the British Parliament and British law officers overruled the colonial court, concluding that the necessity of public responsibility for convicts outweighed private interests. The colonial government's ultimate dominion over convicts would eventually allow it to establish closer control of them in the second phase of the colony's history.

Besides overseeing the use of convicts by private employers, the government of New South Wales always kept some convicts in its own hands. A number of these were employed in government administration and on public works; others were under punishment at outlying penal settlements for crimes committed in the colony. Since all these convicts had to be fed, the government store remained in business, serving as an important market for goods produced by both free and ex-convict settlers. Those who did business with the government store thus enjoyed a subsidy from the British treasury.

The most pressing requirement placed on the local government by Britain was economy in public expenditure. For governors after Phillip, this meant minimizing the number of convicts in government hands and maximizing the number in private service. But when the flow of new convicts to the colony exceeded what the private economy could absorb, the government was obliged to take direct responsibility for the excess. To ease government expenditure, Governor King introduced a device that was to have a long history in penal practice: the ticket-of-leave. Under this dispensation, convicts were allowed to make their own living while remaining convicts, but they were liable to be recalled to bond labor if they offended again. So effective was this threat that ticket-of-leave convicts became renowned for their steadiness. In its early days, the ticket was given not on the basis of good behavior or time already served but according to the convict's chance of supporting himself by wages, business, or landholding. It was, in short, a reward for enterprise and skill. Tickets were also given to gentlemen convicts who arrived with money or letters of recommendation from home.

In 1812 the British government first expressed misgivings about the readiness with which convicts were set free in New South Wales. A select committee of the House of Commons, charged with examining the transportation system, expressed surprise at the number of pardons granted, especially to convicts who received them on arrival in Australia. The secretary of state for colonies accepted the committee's recommendation that the final say on pardons should rest in London. Both the committee and the minister thought pardons were debased unless distributed carefully, to those who had shown clear signs of reformation.

Governor Macquarie was very disturbed at the prospect of being reduced to recommending pardons instead of granting them. He pleaded to keep his power, promising in return to abide by new regulations that set minimum periods of eligibility for pardons and tickets-of-leave. Macquarie himself drew up these regulations to impress the secretary of state, and the minister accepted this proposal. In practice, however, Macquarie frequently broke his own regulations. He still felt obliged to give pardons and tickets-of-leave to those who performed special duties or who brought offenders to justice, no matter how little time they had served. And of course, the claims of gentlemen could not be overlooked. For their part, the convicts put their own interpretation on the new regulations: they assumed they had a right to receive a ticket-of-leave as soon as they had served their minimum term.

In his pragmatic approach to pardons and tickets-of-leave, Macquarie embraced the logic of a republic of convicts. He saw the colony's prosperity as due overwhelmingly to the efforts of convicts and ex-convicts, and he considered that the colony belonged to them. Although he wanted a well-ordered society, he did not want that order to deny any position to an ex-convict. Free migrants who did not like this, he believed, should not come to New South Wales. In pursuit of these views, he appointed three ex-convicts as magistrates, invited them to his table at Government House, and expected the free gentlemen to treat them as equals. The ascent of ex-convicts to the seat of justice represented the full realization of the moral absurdity forecast by London wits when Britain first founded its colony of thieves: "There vice is virtue, virtue vice, / And all that's vile is voted nice."

Free gentlemen in New South Wales bitterly resented the forced social contact with ex-convicts, though in business they associated with them quite willingly. Historians usually take the part of the ex-convicts in this regard, deploring the exclusiveness and, as they see it, the hypocrisy of the free gentlemen. What the historians overlook is that no strictures had been placed on ex-convict enterprise, because free gentlemen had been confident, until Macquarie's move, that an untainted reputation before the law would ensure their superiority over any ex-convict, no matter how wealthy. The British Colonial Office was dismayed at Macquarie's policy; in fact, his action was one of several considerations that soon forced Britain to take stock of the social oddity it had created.

Male Freedom and Female Confinement

For the colony's first thirty years of existence no convict was subject to anything approaching an institutional regime of confinement or punishment. Those who lived in small establishments owned chiefly by ex-convicts worked, ate, and drank with their masters. On larger properties there was an orderly routine and a stricter work discipline, but after working hours convicts lived away from their masters in rough huts, where they cooked their own food. In the wool industry, which became the colony's prime means of support, convict shepherds and stockmen were scattered throughout the country, living and working away from their masters and subject to only intermittent surveillance.

Similarly, convicts employed as domestic servants in Sydney and the other towns usually slept outside their master's house in a detached kitchen. Although servants in London slept inside their master's house to provide added security against robbers, in New South Wales the servants were often convicted robbers, so security lay in keeping them outside. Convicts who worked for the government in the towns were not provided with housing. In their free time after 3 P.M., they earned enough to pay for rooms in private houses. The absence of strict supervision gave the convicts ample opportunity to mix with each other and to visit pubs and illicit grogshops. Approximately a quarter of the court-imposed floggings they received were for drunkenness and absenteeism.

The convicts with the most freedom and the most opportunity to abuse it were those working for the government in Sydney. To prevent them from roving freely after 3 P.M., Governor Macquarie had his convict architect construct a large barracks to house them. It opened in May 1819 and still stands, one of the glories of Georgian Sydney. Macquarie's use of the term "barracks" is significant: though it was a residence for prisoners, it did not have any of the features of the penitentiary. Its large, open sleeping rooms paid no attention to convict classification, and there were no separate cells. The standard punishment was a flogging in the barracks yard. Convicts left the barracks each day to work around town, returning at night. On Saturday and Sunday, however, they were free to roam the town for the purposes of work or play.

It was female convicts who were the first to be closely confined. Women had been sent to New South Wales from the beginning, in a ratio of about one female to every six males. From the standpoint of the British government, women convicts' chief purpose was to serve as sexual partners for the men. In the absence of an institutional regime there was no bar to sexual intercourse in the colony. The only intervention of government in this matter was to encourage marriage, since governors much preferred to free a woman convict into the control of a husband than to remain responsible for her. Married or single, the women presented a special difficulty to the governors: there was little demand for them as workers.

Domestic service was almost the sole occupation open to female convicts, and in this they so seldom gave satisfaction that numerous women were left in the government's hands. Employers, who found that female convicts disrupted their households, declared women convicts more depraved than the men. Apparently, masters failed to see that in expecting prompt and cheerful service from a female maid or cook, they asked more than they did of most men, who worked out of doors and away from the master's eye. Female convicts in private employment could not sleep and eat under their own roof or wander after hours and take extra work. Domestic service was thus a form of prison.

Since the women were unwilling to undertake such confining work, in 1804 Governor King established a cloth factory for them in a room above the jail at Parramatta, the colony's second town at the head of Sydney Harbor. There was insufficient room for all the inmates to sleep on the premises, so some women lodged outside. Most cohabited with men or raised funds to pay rent through prostitution. These solutions to the housing problem were equally immoral in the eyes of Parramatta's evangelical parson, the Reverend Samuel Marsden. Largely because of his lobbying among his English patrons the colony's government was pressured to prevent immorality. Its solution was to confine the women even more strictly.

The isolation of the women was not achieved until 1821, when Governor Macquarie built a new factory that would sometimes be called the Female Penitentiary. Women who committed offenses were sent here, as were those without a steady work assignment. In the factory, convict classification appeared for the first time on Australian soil. Women were separated into three classes, distinguished from each other by differences in diet, dress, and indulgences awarded. In the third, or penal, class were women newly sent there by sentence of the local courts. If they behaved, they then progressed through the second class to the first, from which they were eligible for assignment to outside work. Also in the first class were women convicts newly transported to New South Wales who were awaiting their first assignment, women between assignments, and women who had become pregnant. Inside the walled institution, the inmates were cut off from outside society except that members of the first class could go out to church and receive visitors.

Six cells were provided for punishment within the factory in hopes that isolation from their fellows would be a satisfactory punishment for incorrigible women. Simple confinement to the factory did not appear to have the desired effect, for many seemed to court return to its walls when on assignment outside. Women had seldom been flogged in the colony, and the prohibition of the practice in Britain in 1817 operated in the colony. In the factory, the women convicts of New South Wales were the first to experience the punishment of cellular isolation, in which British prison reformers had such faith.

The Critique of Transportation

From its beginnings, the British practice of convict transportation had its critics. Jeremy Bentham was the most persistent, and he established the arguments that the penal reformers used against the system until it was abandoned. Just as the plan to send convicts to New South Wales was being adopted, he developed his version of the penitentiary. Bentham called it the panopticon because the cells were to radiate around a central point from which an "all-seeing" supervisor would monitor them. Even while plans for transportation went forward, he offered to run such an institution for the government, since he was sure he could make a profit from the prisoners' labor. To keep attention focused on his scheme, Bentham became a fierce critic of the convict colony.

At first, the founding of New South Wales did not appear to threaten the future of Bentham's panopticon. William Pitt, the prime minister, inspected a model of the panopticon at Bentham's house and authorized him to proceed with construction, with the understanding that Bentham would run the institution. But the project met opposition from landholders on all the sites Bentham proposed, so the government dragged its feet. To Bentham's infinite frustration the scheme, shuffled between departments, was delayed and thwarted. The panopticon plan was finally discarded in 1820, after a long quarrel over the compensation that Bentham was to receive in return for the money he had spent.

At one stage in these tortuous negotiations, Bentham was told that Britain had less need for the panopticon because of improvements in New South Wales. This news prompted him to write a pamphlet, "Panopticon versus New South Wales," in 1802. The pamphlet outlined Bentham's arguments against transportation: it was costly, uncertain in the punishment it inflicted, unlikely to reform because those employing convicts were interested solely in profit, and unable to deter because punishment took place at a distance. In New South Wales, Bentham claimed, transportation had reached unprecedented lows, for convicts sent there did not enter established, moral communities as they had when transported to the American colonies. In New South Wales, convicts were under the charge of people no better than themselves, and they set the tone of the whole society. It was in fact a society of thieves committed to thieving and dissipation. The colony was awash with rum, and the calendar of new crimes was appalling. Even the worst jails, even the hulks, could claim at least to prevent their inmates from committing further major crime. On the test of the incapacitation of the criminal under sentence, the colony failed completely: "I question whether the world ever saw anything under the name of punishment bearing the least resemblance to it."

Bentham was a close student of the colony, so he did have evidence for the particular outrages and crimes he reported. What he missed was the movement of ex-convicts into business and property holding, which made them as firm supporters of law and work discipline as those who had come to the colony freely. This transformation explains why disorder never crippled the convict colony and why the prevailing tone was not that of a thieves' kitchen. Bentham was certain that transportation to the American colonies had clearly been superior to transportation to New South Wales. However, ongoing governmental supervision of the New South Wales scheme made it potentially more amenable to control and refinement. In fact, the whole enterprise of founding a convict colony signaled the growth in government capacity and reach, of which Bentham was a prophet and instructor.

Even as Bentham recorded his complaints, the colony was well launched toward economic success. Soon, however, others noticed the prosperity of ex-convicts, supplying further ammunition to critics who asked how transportation could be a deterrent when ex-convicts accumulated fortunes.

During the Napoleonic Wars few convicts were sent to New South Wales, and the government had little trouble in staving off criticisms of its convict colony. With the end of the wars in 1815 and the onset of economic depression, crime in Britain increased, and the number of transported convicts rose rapidly. The increasing numbers now sent to the colony could not all be employed privately, so government expenditure on convict maintenance rose, to the alarm of the treasury. The Home Office, worried about the English crime wave, badgered the Colonial Office to make the convicts' lot more painful. An assortment of Whigs, Radicals, and law reformers belabored the government over its convict colony and its apparent failure to deter crime in Britain.

To set all this criticism to rest, in 1818 the British government appointed John Thomas Bigge as a commissioner of inquiry into its convict colony. The government was now prepared to consider that the colony was not an appropriate place for the punishment of convicts. Bigge was charged by the colonial secretary to inquire whether a system of "general discipline, constant work and vigilant superintendence" could be created in the colony. This represented a distinct advance for the new penology—the government was now using the language of its critics to describe a proper punishment.

Transportation had been an effective punishment at first, asserted the British colonial secretary, because New South Wales had been distant, foreign, and unfathomable; now transportation had lost its terrors because the early reports of hunger and wretchedness had given way to tales of general prosperity and outstanding individual success. Some convicts were now asking to be sent to New South Wales. But the minister deluded himself when he claimed there had been a time when New South Wales was actually administered with the aim of punishing convicts and deterring potential criminals. He believed strict regulations had been uniformly enforced and "hard labour, moderate food and constant superintendence" had been the norm in the early days, when in fact convicts had been plied with rum and official tasks had been completed by midday. There had, of course, been much hard labor performed in the colony, but it had been done by those who did not have the status, skills, or influence to avoid it.

After eighteen months of inspection and inquiry in the colony, Bigge decided that New South Wales could indeed be made a fit place for punishment. Convicts, Bigge concluded, should be kept out of the towns and assigned as far as possible to the more prosperous settlers who had come as free people and who would take more care over the convicts' discipline and reformation. Nor should convicts receive wages or expect to receive tickets-of-leave or pardons as a matter of right. Further, Bigge recommended, accurate central records should be kept of all offenses committed by the convicts in the colony. Any property the convicts brought with them should be confiscated and held until the owners demonstrated they were reformed. Ex-convicts should no longer be given land or convict assistance once they became free. Bigge's plan was to reshape the society of New South Wales so that the economic distinctions between owners and workers would more closely match their distinctions in legal status. Under his system free emigrants would be employers while convicts and ex-convicts would perform hard labor for them. In these ways, Bigge believed, transportation would become a fate to dread, and fewer stories of ex-convicts accumulating wealth would circulate.

FROM COLONY TO PRISON

The British government accepted Bigge's recommendations, which formed the basis of convict colony policy for the two decades before transportation to mainland Australia was halted in 1840.

A steady stream of convicts arrived, but demand for workers for the expanding economy soon outstripped supply. When Bigge toured the colony, most settlement was still confined to the narrow plain between mountain and sea, within a radius of 50 miles from Sydney. In the twenty-two years before transportation ended, settlement would spread 500 miles north and south of Sydney, and all the good land across the mountains would be occupied. During this era wool became the staple of the colony, and criminals from British towns found themselves in isolated shepherd huts in the far interior of Australia.

The expansion of settlement was so rapid that it overtook the isolated places chosen for penal settlements to punish crime committed in the colony. First among these was the penal colony at Newcastle, located on the coast 100 miles north of Sydney, which closed in 1823. It was succeeded by Port Macquarie, 250 miles north of Sydney, and then by Moreton Bay, 500 miles to the north. Moreton Bay operated until 1839, when it became the free city of Brisbane, the capital of the future colony of Queensland. The penal settlement whose isolation was never disturbed was Norfolk Island, a tiny volcanic speck far out in the Pacific Ocean northeast of Sydney.

The first governor to assume office after the acceptance of Bigge's report was Thomas Brisbane. He complied with the instructions of the Colonial Office and made a number of important changes, but he did not respond wholeheartedly to Bigge's vision.

Brisbane repealed Macquarie's convict wage order. In doing so, he also freed masters from the obligation to supply the standard ration. Nonetheless, most masters continued to issue the same ration of meat and a more generous ration of flour. Tea, sugar, and tobacco were now supplied as indulgences that could be revoked for misbehavior. Previously, convicts could have these whenever they wanted, since these luxuries could be purchased out of their guaranteed wage. The loss of the wage was thus a clear decline in convict status, but not all convicts were reduced to the same level. Convicts in skilled and responsible jobs were still given extra rewards and indulgences, which might include money payments.

Brisbane was much stricter than Macquarie had been in ensuring that tickets-of-leave went only to those who had served the minimum time set down in the regulations. For convicts transported for seven years, Brisbane set the minimum at four years (one year more than under Macquarie); fourteen-year convicts had to serve at least six years before they were eligible and the lifers eight years. These minimums would remain the same until the end of transportation. But Brisbane still saw the need for exceptions, for instance in rewarding those who caught bushrangers (renegades who lived in the bush and survived by robbery) or those who provided information to the police.

Large-scale efforts at reforming the convict colony did not start until Brisbane's successor, Governor Ralph Darling (1826–31), took office. Darling was a military man, but his métier was administration. He set about restructuring the various government departments of New South Wales and introduced boards and committees to inquire into, report on, and process the official business of the colony. Dealing with this bureaucratic government required the colonists to become more and more adept at filling out forms. Darling's bureaucratic style showed up in the administration of convict affairs: starting on January 1, 1827, each newly arriving convict was given an identification number. If the colony could be made a satisfactory place for punishment, it now had a governor ready for the task.

On his arrival Darling was surprised to find that nearly all the clerks in the government offices were convicts. They worked in the most sensitive areas. Some handled convict indents, the lists sent from Britain detailing the dates of conviction and the sentence length for each convict. Others worked in the offices of the attorney general and the solicitor general, where charges in criminal cases were drawn up.

The convict clerks were thus well placed to collect bribes. Critics alleged that convict clerks set standard fees for altering the lengths of sentences listed in the indent: so much for a reduction from fourteen years to seven, something more if the original sentence had been for life. Darling wanted to replace all the convict clerks, but he found he could not offer enough pay to tempt educated young migrants into the service. If free migrants had any wit, they preferred to seek their fortune in livestock and land. Still, Darling was generally successful in replacing convicts in the most sensitive areas, but the cost of employing free people fostered the temptation to revert to convicts. To have created a government service staffed only with nonconvicts would have been a crippling expense.

Elsewhere, Darling succeeded in tightening government control of convicts by systematizing ticket-of-leave practices. He allowed convicts six months off their minimum term for every bushranger or two runaways they caught and twelve months for giving information on receivers of stolen property. Despite his mission to strengthen discipline, though, Darling continued to award tickets to those who undertook particularly worthy or dangerous work, such as accompanying an exploratory expedition. And for all its new concern for better order in New South Wales, the British government still wanted occasional exceptions made. In Britain, people of standing and influence could mention to the secretary of state the names of convicts in whom they were interested, and he would pass the word to the colonial governor to do whatever was possible for them.

The colonial government found it relatively easy to ensure that tickets-of-leave were given only after convicts had served a minimum time. First of all it possessed, in the form of the indents, clear records of each convict's date of conviction and period of sentence. Second, it accepted Commissioner Bigge's recommendation that the colonial government collect records from all its district courts on offenses committed by and punishments awarded to convicts. This data collection proved essential to governors interested in bringing greater discipline to the process. It allowed them to counter the self-interest of masters and the leniency of magistrates, who liberally recommended tickets-of-leave. Before records were centralized, even conscientious masters and magistrates who recommended only the well-behaved and not the merely useful could not be aware of how convicts had behaved in other districts, unless they took the trouble of asking the magistrates there. Now the governor could guarantee that only deserving convicts who had served their minimum term would receive tickets-of-leave.

Setting up the central records of punishment took some time. Under Brisbane, the collection and recording of information had proceeded sloppily. When Darling arrived, his officials started requiring magistrates who sent or sought information on convicts to give the names and numbers of the ships on which the convicts arrived, in addition to the individuals' names. Without that extra information, separating all the John Smiths from each other was impossible. Darling's assignment of a number to each convict was the best solution to the problem, but the numbers never came into general use outside government circles. For the rest of the period of transportation, the name of a convict's ship and the number of its voyage became part of the convict's identity tag.

Darling set up the Office of the Principal Superintendent of Convicts to keep convict records and transact all convict matters. There, a relatively complete and reliable record system was eventually established. By the 1830s the superintendent of convicts could report on the behavior of most convicts whose cases were referred to him. It became standard practice to inquire of the superintendent whenever any indulgences, not merely tickets-of-leave, were requested. The efficiency of this office shows up in its pattern of response to recommendations from the Goulburn magistrates for tickets-of-leave between 1838 and 1840. In this period the office approved 135 tickets but refused 78. Though recommended by the local bench, the refused convicts had central records that told against them. Darling's bureaucratic reforms brought some order to a formerly random process.

The Problem of Assignment

Darling set up a board to process applications for the assignment of all convicts. He instructed the board to grant convicts to good masters who oversaw the conduct of their servants and to refuse convicts to abusive or lax masters. From then on, the government would more regularly withdraw convicts from offending masters. Previously, the threat to withdraw servants had been largely empty, but since the demand for servants now exceeded the supply, this measure no longer burdened the government with the maintenance of extra convicts. Convicts could easily be reassigned elsewhere, and in fact Darling instituted a regular administrative process to carry out this operation.

His successor, Governor Richard Bourke (1831–37), tightened the regulations for screening potential masters and overseeing the use of servants. Bourke insisted that if a master lent a servant to someone else—a very common practice—the master had to inform Sydney and seek approval from the magistrates. As competition for servants became keener, more complex procedures were adopted for allotting servants. All told, Governor Bourke's regulations on convict assignment occupied eight tightly packed pages in the *Government Gazette,* followed by examples of Forms A through F, which were required at various stages in the assignment process. This was a far cry from the old days, when servants were obtained by a word to the governor in the street or a quick note to his office.

The thorough bureaucratic oversight of assignment attempted by Darling and Bourke depended at crucial stages on local magistrates, who might be lazy or, being masters themselves, not interested in enforcing all of Sydney's rules. As a result, cases of extreme laxity in transferring servants or permitting them too much freedom still turned up. In applying for convicts, employers learned how to find loopholes in regulations designed to ensure an equitable distribution. Darling's regulations were subverted by people applying for more convicts than they really needed; Bourke's attempt to apportion convicts according to the amount of land held was upset by masters who took out leases on uncleared land solely for this purpose. Some gave fictitious leases to their children and servants, who would then become eligible to receive convicts.

Despite efforts at reform, private assignment remained the gravest affront to penal principles. Private masters would always consider their own profit and convenience before punishment and reformation of their convict servants. Further, the diversity of tasks in private employment produced inequalities in work requirements and treatment of convicts. Commissioner Bigge would have been happy if all the convicts could have been kept out of Sydney and the other towns and set to rural labor. But the British government's attempt to follow this recommendation, which impinged directly on the operation of the colonial economy, was a signal failure.

In 1826, the British secretary of state informed Governor Darling that transportation was still not dreaded sufficiently in Britain. He then instructed Darling to remove all the skilled convicts from the towns and assign the able-bodied ones to field labor rather than shepherding. The comparatively easy task of herding sheep had replaced field labor as the rural occupation of most convicts, making transportation a less dreadful punishment. The minister pointed out that as long as skilled convicts were allowed to work at their trades, transportation would remain a light punishment; if they were kept in the towns, they would have greater opportunity to pursue the dissipation for which they were notorious. Only hard work in the country, the minister believed, would punish and reform them.

Darling refused to implement the instruction. He reported that he would attempt to assign most convicts to new settlers in the countryside but that ending assignment in Sydney would be "injurious in the highest degree." Unskilled convicts continued to be assigned for domestic service in Sydney until almost the end of transportation. Depriving Sydney of its skilled convict workers was almost unthinkable because they were the tailors, shoemakers, and other tradespeople. Further, convicts serving as building-tradesmen were employed in the government's public works and labored for private builders on the weekends: "Thus has the Town of Sydney been built." Economics was a very stubborn fact to put against the needs of punishment and reformation. So long as the British government wanted New South Wales to prosper and grow wool using convict labor, these were unanswerable arguments, and the minister did not pursue the matter further.

Among Commissioner Bigge's recommendations was one that convicts be assigned to free emigrants, whom he regarded as more suitable masters than ex-convicts. The governors could not ban employment by ex-convicts altogether, because these masters supplied jobs to so many convicts in the private sector. Britain responded to Bigge's recommendation by encouraging the immigration of free settlers with capital. Simultaneously, the growth of the sheep industry in the 1820s and 1830s made the colony more attractive to them. In parts of New South Wales, something like a plantation society developed: large estates in the hands of gentlemen employed great numbers of convict laborers. But the insatiable demand for more pastureland forced the flocks beyond the official limits of settlement. This far afield, land was held at first without any permission and then only by annual license. With the proprietors of these squatting runs frequently absent, convicts working there were actually controlled by ex-convict, ticket-of-leave, or even convict overseers. Control of any sort had to be lax when workers mounted on horseback were scattered over such a large area. This was not the disciplinary regime Bigge had envisaged.

With the growth of free migrant enterprise and the boom in the economy, the governors could have denied convict workers to ex-convicts without creating any surplus. However, such a blanket exclusion was never contemplated. The most attempted by the colonial government (in 1835) was to link an employer's entitlement to convict labor to the possession of a minimum area of land. The requirement was first set at forty acres, effectively excluding many ex-convict settlers with grants of thirty acres. Later, the requirement fell to twenty acres, which excluded almost no one. The regulation was changed because the economic interests of ex-convict and free settlers were so inextricably linked that it would have been difficult to damage the one without hurting the other. The fact that this half-hearted attempt to exclude lowly ex-convicts from access to the convict work force had to proceed by reference to size of land rather than legal status shows how firmly the colonists held to the view that legal status should not affect economic opportunity. By this time, an ex-convict party formed in the 1830s was urging self-government and full political rights for ex-convicts. It would have fiercely resisted any general exclusion of ex-convicts from the benefits of convict labor.

Reform in Van Diemen's Land

Van Diemen's Land, now known as Tasmania, was first settled as part of New South Wales in 1803. The island off the southeastern coast of Australia became a separate colony in 1825. There, the employment of convict labor by private masters was controlled for the higher purposes of punishment and reformation in a way never achieved in the parent colony. This was the work of Governor George Arthur (1824–36), a meticulous, indefatigable administrator who mastered the assignment system by taking direct charge of it himself for a year. Arthur distributed convicts according to his assessment of the order and discipline maintained in the private establishments applying for them. Certain people could be forbidden to receive convicts—innkeepers, those without free overseers, and ex-convicts. This last group could be more readily denied on the island because they did not have the wealth or prominence of their New South Wales counterparts.

To monitor the worthiness of convict masters, Arthur maintained what his opponents called a "spy" system. He placed stipendiary magistrates in each district to serve as his eyes and ears, to play the part of major generals to his Cromwell. Governors used some stipendiaries in New South Wales, but in the parent colony there was no parallel to Arthur's concerted attack on the customary right of landowners to be ruled by unpaid magistrates drawn from their own ranks. Such officials could be relied on to give a local gloss to central directives.

The convict records set up by Arthur were also more complete and comprehensive than had ever existed in New South Wales. There, a number of registers had to be consulted to establish what crimes and labor offenses a convict had committed. In Van Diemen's Land, all this information appeared in one place, the so-called Black Books (which, unlike the New South Wales records, have survived). This resource allowed Arthur to closely match punishment and indulgence to convict behavior. The control Arthur exercised over both masters and convicts was easier to achieve here than in New South Wales because settlement in Van Diemen's Land was closely confined. He would not have done so well in New South Wales, where society not only was spread over a wider area but also was older and more complex—though none of this would have daunted him. When his term was up, Arthur went home execrated by the colonists, a distinction that he took as a sign of his success.

Governor Arthur gave his name to Port Arthur, the penal settlement he designed as a place of additional punishment. Located on the rugged Tasman Peninsula, it had only a very narrow connection to the mainland and was guarded by a chain of dogs who barred escape. The ruins of this settlement are the largest physical remains of the convict era in Australia, a fact that explains why Port Arthur has come to symbolize the convict system as a whole. Port Arthur is in fact quite unrepresentative of convict life and not simply because most convicts worked out their time in civil society and not in penal settlements. It is also an atypical institution because, built first under Arthur and extended later, its buildings were designed to impose classification and solitary confinement on the inmates. This system came late to the convict colonies of Australia, where little notice had been taken of convicts' original crimes and most further offenses were punished with the lash. The ruins of Port Arthur are monuments to the attempt to modernize the system of transportation and make it conform to the principles of its critics, the proponents of the penitentiary.

Places of Dread in New South Wales

New South Wales had its own penal settlements, at Port Macquarie, Moreton Bay, and Norfolk Island. In addition to reforming policy toward the general convict population, Governor Darling made a concerted attempt to impose regular and uniform discipline at these establishments. Harsh labor and severe punishments were common in the settlements before Darling, but they were not consistently applied to everyone. Although populated by transported convicts who had been convicted of additional offenses in the colony, the penal settlements tended toward the laxity and inequity that characterized early New South Wales as a whole, for similar reasons. These were small settlements in the charge of military detachments that had no interest in penal discipline and fervently wished themselves elsewhere.

At Port Macquarie in the 1820s, the officers, like their counterparts in the first New South Wales settlements of the 1790s, employed convicts on their own farms and gardens and provided generous indulgences and taskwork. Convicts alone filled the minor administrative offices and performed the light work at the penal settlements. From the ranks of these twice-convicted prisoners, their keepers had to find overseers and constables. Skilled workers were much in demand, so they easily avoided heavy labor. Friends outside the penal settlements could send the inmates food, clothing, and other goods, carried from Sydney in government vessels free of charge. Some convicts were thus able to engage in the business of retail trading. Both men and women convicts were sent to these settlements, and wives and children were allowed to join husbands and fathers serving time there. Married men were given time to work on their own account to support their families. In forming its first penal settlements, New South Wales was clearly governed by the same beliefs that had led to its own establishment as a place of exile rather than of systematic punishment.

Governor Darling wanted to make these places more prison-like: they were to become places of dread capable of deterring the convicts from further crime, just as the British government wanted New South Wales to be a fearful place that would help keep its own population in order. Darling issued new regulations to prevent officers and convicts at the penal settlements from farming or trading on their own account. He hoped to stamp out private enterprise—which sustained irregularities and disrupted discipline—and to reduce the settlement to a prison farm. To make agricultural labor more strenuous, he forbade the use of draft beasts and the plow. But regulations could go only so far while the personnel of the penal settlements remained the same.

Wish as he might, Darling could not avoid using convicts as overseers, constables, and servants to officers. He did, however, regularize the practice by creating two classes of convicts at the penal settlements and restricting the more desirable jobs to members of the first class. Convicts gained entry to this class based on time served and good behavior. All mechanics, meanwhile, were to work in the field unless their skills were urgently required elsewhere, and then only as a temporary measure. So here, as in Sydney, it was impossible to ignore skill and to put all men to a uniform, hard labor. Even Darling was not prepared to ban families altogether from the settlements, so the wives and children of first-class inmates were still allowed to join their menfolk at Port Macquarie and Moreton Bay.

For Norfolk Island, however, Darling planned something different. One of his first acts was to order that the women there—the wives of soldiers and convicts—be removed and that no women be allowed there in the future. Darling wanted a sentence to Norfolk Island to represent the most extreme form of punishment in New South Wales short of death. Although Darling stated that the absence of women would lead to an increase in homosexuality on the island, he thought the presence of a few women would not make much difference. In any case, deterrence was the primary aim. Whether he was right about homosexuality or not, Darling correctly gauged the significance of barring women. He did not want the discipline of the prison disturbed by the comforting regularities of family life or the irregularities of casual congress between men and women, interaction that had been part of life in every other settlement in New South Wales. Norfolk Island became the closest thing New South Wales had to a prison and would in fact have been one if the convicts themselves had not been the wardens.

Hated by the other inmates as traitors and fearing always for the security of their jobs, the Norfolk Island wardens were tyrannical and cruel. There was little restraint on their power, so the convicts, isolated and degraded, were driven to desperate measures. Three times—in 1826, 1834, and 1842—the inmates attempted to seize the island. Short of mutiny, another way to throw off the yoke of a Norfolk Island sentence was to kill a fellow convict. The murderer then enjoyed the respite of a trip to Sydney for his trial, which gave him the chance of escape or, failing that, the certainty of a death sentence.

To stop this abuse, the Supreme Court instituted hearings and executions on the island. The leaders of the 1834 revolt were thus tried at the scene of the crime. One of them told the court, "Let a man's heart be what it will when he comes here, his Man's heart is taken from him and he is given the heart of a Beast." Thirty of the rebels were condemned to death, but sixteen had their sentences commuted to life imprisonment on the island. When the chaplain took this news to the condemned men, those who were to hang rejoiced at their deliverance, and those who had been reprieved were desolate.

Maintaining the penal settlements, whether at Norfolk Island, Port Macquarie, or Moreton Bay, was an expensive business. Darling, like all governors, was supposed to spend as little as possible on them. At the same time, the private economy of New South Wales had grown large enough and was expanding so rapidly that it absorbed all the convicts sent from England. The settlers clamored for more laborers. Darling decided he could reduce costs at the penal settlements and increase the labor supply in the colony if he put some of the hardened offenders to work, in irons, on mainland roads. This would free the existing road workers, ordinary convicts, for assignment to the settlers.

Work on the roads was hard, and as in all government work, the supervision was poor. Unrestrained by the interests and concerns of private masters, the overseers were either extremely harsh or far too lax with their charges. Convicts thus had plenty of incentive and opportunity to run away. Overseers sometimes arranged temporary or permanent convict absences for a price or in return for the absentee's rations. Private masters in the neighborhood of road gangs were not beyond seducing road workers into their service.

The new penal road gangs were kept in irons with their legs chained together; although this restricted motion, it did not prevent escape. As a result of Darling's policy, runaways were now seasoned offenders and more desperate to remain free. Thus, though bringing order and rule to bear in many places, in this matter the governor fostered disorder on a large scale. Hardened convicts who escaped from road gangs represented a large proportion of the bushrangers who proliferated during Darling's tenure. This was the price the colony paid for keeping some of the worst convicts inside its borders instead of sending them to penal settlements.

In the early 1830s, Governor Bourke overcame the disadvantages of Darling's policy by keeping the iron gangs locked up in crude caravans at night and by arranging for a small military detachment to guard them day and night. This last measure was a real coup. Though soldiers still did not directly supervise convict work, for the first time they served as the force that kept convicts at work. Under Bourke's system, the runaway rate dropped dramatically. But this too had its cost. Maintaining the military was expensive; in 1834 Bourke reported that he could not work any more convicts in irons unless he had more money to finance a larger garrison.

The closer supervision of convict assignment, the establishment of central records, the granting of indulgences only for good behavior, and the stiffening of punishment at the penal settlements were the changes introduced following Bigge's report to make New South Wales a credible penal colony. By the end of Bourke's tenure as governor, the most glaring anomalies of the old order had been contained if not abolished, but reform was stopped short of its goals. The pressure to contain costs constantly overwhelmed other considerations in administering the convict colony.

Just as cost-cutting led to disorder, so the need to impose order breached another penal principle. To encourage the capture of bushrangers, tickets-of-leave were granted as rewards. This violated the policy of granting indulgences only to the well-behaved, for those who caught bushrangers were more like their captives than the sober, industrious, and honest servants envisaged in the ticket-of-leave rules. Darling had issued many regulations in the cause of good order and discipline, but he sometimes regularized the indefensible, such as when he set the conditions for the employment of convicts as overseers (a practice that remained common in the colony and universal in the penal settlements). At many points the system depended on private masters and unpaid magistrates, who were keen enough about getting convicts to work but not about supporting the Sydney bureaucracy in its attempt to monitor and control convict punishment. Making communities into prisons is no easy thing.

The Convict Colony as Slave Society

The reforms made after Commissioner Bigge's evaluation did little to satisfy the critics. The zealots of the new penology, who promoted the penitentiary, would not revise their views on transportation no matter what changes were made in the colonies. If all their other arguments failed, they, like Bentham, argued that punishment at a distance was a poor deterrent.

In the 1830s, when the prospects for social reform of all sorts seemed so bright, the case against transportation was made with new vigor. The opponents of the convict colony developed a new and damning argument against it, asserting that the assignment of convicts to private masters constituted slavery. Convicts, of course, should be made to work, but private masters who controlled and profited from bond labor were likely to succumb to all the vices of slave owners. Previously, critics had claimed that transportation created an immoral society because convicts reduced their neighbors to their own level. Now the corruption of convict society was depicted as more entrenched: it arose out of the immoral relationship between masters and convict servants, and no individual, however virtuous, was immune from it. Britain had abolished slavery, and now it would have to abolish transportation.

However, the antitransportation cause by no means attracted the degree of support enjoyed by the antislavery movement. There was still plenty of support for transportation in the reformed House of Commons, on the time-honored grounds that transportation was cheap and got rid of unsavory characters. Edward George Stanley, the Whig colonial secretary in charge of the bill to abolish slavery, made a last-ditch attempt in 1833 to save transportation by making it a punishment worse than death itself. This was to be achieved by having all new convicts work on the roads in chains, a scheme that had to be abandoned when law officers declared it illegal. Two years later the Whig government, which took office in 1835 after the brief Tory interlude, made the first decisive moves against transportation. The two ministers who shaped government policy on the issue were Lord John Russell, who as home secretary initiated the first major reform of the criminal law, and Henry George Grey, Viscount Howick, who had acted as under secretary for colonies in the first Whig administration and was now secretary of state for war.

Deeply involved in the campaign to rid Africa of slavery, both men thought of New South Wales as a slave society. They were strongly influenced by *Thoughts on Secondary Punishments*, an attack on transportation written by Archbishop Richard Whately in 1832. Whately, a philosopher and an economist as well as a churchman, became the most eminent pamphleteer against New South Wales since Bentham. His work contained little detailed information on New South Wales, and much of that was wrong. Its strength lay rather in the spirited demonstration from first principles that transportation was an ineffective punishment and totally incompatible with colonization. No convict, he said, was as wicked as the person who devised the plan of transportation to New South Wales.

Arguments of this sort impressed Russell and Howick, who were determined to do what was right, not what was simply convenient. They had a high sense of their responsibility and were appalled at the state of society in New South Wales, which Whately called a "monstrous excrescence." Russell and Howick knew that if they did not act, the barbarity could well continue for some time, since transportation was a convenience both to Britain and to the colonists. Though the two ministers accepted the case against the current system of transportation, they did not want to abandon transportation completely. The two were put off by the cost of alternatives and even more by the realization that convicts, staying in Britain, would find it very hard to get work after serving their term. But one thing was clear to Russell and Howick: the assignment of convicts to private masters would have to cease. If convicts were employed on public works in the colony or confined in colonial penitentiaries, transportation would be more acceptable.

The difficulty perceived by Russell and Howick was that only a limited number of convicts could be transported because, on becoming free, they would flood into a society already overwhelmed by viciousness. Therefore, alternatives to transportation to Australia would have to be provided. Russell and Howick planned for penitentiaries at home and for more convicts to be sent to Bermuda. Finally, Russell decided to abandon transportation to New South Wales and to continue it on a reduced scale to Van Diemen's Land and Norfolk Island. From now on, convicts would of course remain in the government's hands so that punishment and reformation could be properly controlled and "slavery" avoided. Like most reformers, Russell had a touching faith in the ability of wardens and superintendents to abstain from the capriciousness and tyranny to which private masters were thought to be particularly prone.

Radical Impatience

In the House of Commons, one man steadfastly opposed transportation in any form: William Molesworth, an ambitious young Radical. The Radicals had grown increasingly impatient at the pace and scope of reform under Whig governments, to whom they had given their support. Molesworth was among those who planned either to radicalize the Whigs or to unseat them. In domestic matters, the Radicals had little hope of influencing the government, since the Tories would support the Whigs against moves for radical reform. But in colonial matters it was possible that Tories and Radicals might find a common ground against the Whigs. With this in mind, Molesworth became a keen student of colonial affairs.

Molesworth came to support Edward Gibbon Wakefield's systematic colonization plans, which were receiving their first trial in the new colony of South Australia. Wakefield's regime involved the orderly sale and settlement of land and the use of the proceeds to pay for the passage of free workers so that convicts would not have to be used. Wakefield's system convinced Molesworth that transportation to the Australian colonies should be abandoned completely, because sufficient funds could be raised to pay for the migration of a free labor force if land was sold at a higher price.

In April 1837, Molesworth successfully moved in the House of Commons to establish a select committee on transportation. Lord Russell, who had already decided that assignment must be abandoned, cooperated with him. As the instigator of the committee, Molesworth in accordance with usual practice became its chairman. Russell and Howick were among those appointed to the committee, and when it drafted its report they used their influence to prevent Molesworth from recommending the total abolition of transportation. They were satisfied to condemn the present system and to use the evidence of the committee to support the changes they had decided on.

As chairman of the committee, Molesworth was in charge of collecting evidence and cross-examining witnesses. He very easily showed that the assignment of convicts to private masters produced unequal treatment and that this inequity had nothing to do with the nature of offenders' crimes. Molesworth devoted himself to collecting evidence that would demonstrate the moral corruption of the convict colonies. He was himself a notorious libertine, but for his inquisitorial role he adopted puritanical standards and reaped a rich harvest of crime and depravity in Australia. Even so, like Bentham before him, he had to distort his evidence to support his central claim that convicts dragged the whole community down to their level. The evidence actually showed that the first generation of native-born Australians was remarkably honest. Molesworth also referred speciously to "slaves" and "slavery" to bolster his argument: one mention of these and colonial society was left without a shred of decency. Single-minded in his mission, he brushed aside any attempt to consider how the convict might differ from the slave.

Transportation Defended

Though the colonists wanted transportation to continue, they were not greatly surprised that the British government now planned to modify or abandon it. This eventuality had seemed certain enough over the years. What enraged the colonists was the wholesale denunciation of colonial society, a criticism that Molesworth enshrined in the report presented by his House of Commons select committee. The reputation of free colonists in a convict colony had always been dubious; now Molesworth had given an official endorsement to all the jokes and scorn directed at those who sought their fortunes in New South Wales or Van Diemen's Land. Even though they had little expectation of changing British government policy, the colonists were driven to defend their reputation and the system of transportation as a whole. In answer to Archbishop Whately, Governor Arthur of Van Diemen's Land, the convict colony's high priest, defended transportation in two pamphlets. These defenses are of particular interest in the history of the prison because, in explaining the advantages of transportation, they developed a scathing critique of the principles and practice of the new, penitentiary-oriented penology. Arthur's defenses contained the following chief points:

- A prisoner who is isolated in a cell with Bible and crank handle is much less likely to reform than if he is kept in civil society under the control of private masters. Convicts learn a job that they can follow later; they mix with people other than convicts while under punishment; they become accustomed to the habits of social life and so are more ready for the transition to freedom.

- When transportation is condemned for failing to deter, masters are depicted as indulgent; when condemned for failing to reform, masters are depicted as tyrants. If masters followed either of these courses, they would get very little work out of convicts. Most masters adopt the middle course of firm yet fair discipline. Private masters of decent character with an interest in the convicts' work are infinitely superior as a controlling body to the type of men who can be recruited as wardens and overseers.

- Assignment in private service admittedly cannot be finely adjusted to make punishment fit the crime, but is not this a will-o'-the-wisp? Men differ in their physical and mental characteristics, so that the same measure of pain will be felt differently by each. And if pain can be finely adjusted in a penitentiary, who is to do the adjusting? The adjusters will be wardens and guards, against whose arbitrariness and tyranny there will be little check.

- Failure to deter is allegedly the great weakness of transportation. Certainly convicts are well fed in the colonies, but given the appalling deprivation that so many of the British poor have to endure, the harshest prison regime will be superior to their lot. Since prisoners have to be fed, better to do so at a distance than at home. In any case, deterrence is not the most important requirement for the reduction of crime. The roots of crime are poverty, wretchedness, unemployment, and lack of education. By removing these, governments would do more to reduce crime than by creating severer punishment.

The most incisive of the defenders of transportation, Dr. William Bland, was himself an ex-convict who had been transported for killing his opponent in a duel. His views were contained in *Letters to Charles Buller Esq. M.P.* Dr. Bland penetrated further into the underlying assumptions of the new penology, exposing them with a wonderful clarity. He attributed the support for the new penology to "hypothetical prejudices as to vice and virtue, representing these qualities as two distinct essences; and on the moral, physical and general nature of man, through which the human being is contemplated as a mere chemical or mechanical element, requiring nothing more than a clever state chemist, or state mechanist, to be dealt with accordingly."

On the likely effects of the penitentiary regime, he wrote:

> The exclusion of Convicts from all society but their own and of their keepers, . . . divests them of all virtuous habits and sympathies and renders them, year by year, less fitted for returning to that community from which they have been entirely estranged. For, let it be remembered that the human mind cannot be divested of its store of images, but by the substitution of other images; or if the case be otherwise, that it must be left a mere blank, subject to all those morbid changes which the faculties of man, whether mental or bodily, are observed to undergo when not sustained by appropriate exercise. In such a state, far worse than that of any other species of utter seclusion, it is ill-fitted to receive or comprehend, either moral or religious truths, which can alone be advantageously introduced through the medium of the gentler feelings and sentiments.

In contrast to the individualistic orientation of the penal reformers and penitentiary backers, all of the defenders of transportation had a sense of people as social beings. This sense informed their analyses of why people became criminals and of the circumstances in which criminals were most likely to reform. Even such a stern figure as Governor Arthur reported that large numbers of transported convicts were not perversely wicked. Like everyone else, Arthur had seen people who were criminals in one social setting become good subjects in another—and not by the reformatory methods of the new penology.

An Experiment at Norfolk Island

Needless to say, none of the defenses of transportation made any impact on the British government. Lawmakers took the colonists' defense of such a corrupting institution as further evidence of its undesirable nature. Only one document from the colonies was heeded in London. This was a report on transportation from Captain Alexander Maconochie, who had gone to Van Diemen's Land as private secretary to the governor who succeeded Arthur, Sir John Franklin (1837–43). After a few months in the colony, Maconochie pronounced decisively against assignment as a punishment and denounced the character of the master class. He found the colonists harsh and overbearing in their relations to each other and to the government. Following the standard critique of the evils of slave society, Maconochie interpreted this rudeness as a carryover of habits gained in the control of convicts. That the colonists were as Maconochie described them cannot be doubted, for settlers tended toward roughness in every new colony where numbers were small, fortunes were still to be made, and the social hierarchy was uncertain.

A condemnation of colonial society was just what the critics of transportation in London wanted to hear. Their receptiveness predisposed them to consider the novel part of Maconochie's paper—his scheme for the punishment and reformation of convicts. Maconochie proposed that convicts should be sentenced not to a period of time in the colony but to a certain amount of labor, measured by a system of marks. Under this system, convicts would earn marks for work and good conduct and lose them for bad behavior. Food and clothing would be obtained only by the expenditure of marks, so the less convicts indulged themselves, the sooner they would have sufficient marks to gain freedom. Prisoners would associate and work with companions of their own choosing, and all would lose marks if one offended.

Maconochie believed his system would make corporal punishment and physical coercion unnecessary. The system would encourage a sense of individual responsibility and mutual trust, which would in turn ensure the prisoner's successful reintegration into society. In Maconochie's view, prisons should in fact be mini-societies that remained in close contact with the larger society outside. He allowed that there should be a short period of punishment at the beginning of the sentence but argued that the prime purpose of detention was reform.

Others had proposed particular points of Maconochie's scheme, but the scheme as a whole was his own. Though he was a critic of transportation as it was currently practiced, his preoccupation with the social education and reintegration of prisoners no doubt arose from his experience in Australia. What he learned by witnessing punishment in progress in the midst of civil society turned his mind away from the penal reformers' obsession with the physical structure of the prison. Maconochie's scheme, as fully elaborated later, was for the conduct of prisons, but he drew it up at first as an alternative method of conducting transportation. The first, brief punishment stage would take place in isolated spots in the colony; in the reformatory stage convicts would work on the roads and other public works. From there, they would proceed to private employment under a ticket-of-leave, the one part of the existing system that Maconochie retained.

Lord Russell invited Maconochie to institute his scheme as an experiment on Norfolk Island, not with the hardened offenders already there but with convicts sent directly from Britain, since New South Wales could no longer receive them. Maconochie argued that Norfolk Island was not an appropriate place because it was cut off from society and because two different penal systems could not operate so close to each other. But the offer applied only to Norfolk Island—perhaps precisely because it was isolated—so Maconochie accepted it. When he arrived there, he solved one of the problems he had foreseen by ignoring the instruction that his system was not to apply to the old hands. Old and new convicts alike were governed by the marks system in a modified form, made necessary because sentences and eligibility for ticket-of-leave were still officially defined by periods of time.

Maconochie took down the gibbet, threw open locked doors, removed the bars from the windows of his house, and acted as if he were in charge of a civilized community. He brought with him books and musical instruments for the prisoners' use, he encouraged the cultivation of garden plots, and he erected Protestant and Catholic chapels. With members of his family, Maconochie walked unescorted around the island and chatted with the prisoners, who were no longer expected to cringe in the presence of a government official. The lack of barriers on the island demonstrated an important part of Maconochie's system of reform: the exercise of moral power over prisoners by the person in charge. It made him an advocate of small jails and of large personal discretion for their keepers, a position that later proved his undoing.

Although circumstances on Norfolk Island were less than ideal, Maconochie rated his experiment a success. The prisoners, especially the old hands, responded well to the abolition of harsh punishments and to the freedoms they were trusted not to abuse. The dynamic of the marks did work. But in the colonists' eyes the old hands were on Norfolk Island not to be reformed but to suffer so that the rest of the convicts would be deterred from crime and keep to their work. Conflict between Maconochie and the colonists flared soon after he arrived on the island, when he gave the convicts a holiday to celebrate the queen's birthday. On that day the inmates were free to roam over the island and swim in the surf. They enjoyed a dinner with rum and lemon for every man, a play performed by convicts in the afternoon, and fireworks in the evening. When news of this event reached the mainland, the colonists were incensed. The episode convinced them that Maconochie was unhinged and that his experiment would ruin them. Lord Russell took the same view and gave the governor of New South Wales, George Gipps (1838–46), the power to dismiss Maconochie at any time. Gipps protected Maconochie for some years; when he eventually visited the island unannounced he was agreeably surprised. But his favorable report to London came too late: the Colonial Office had already decided to dismiss Maconochie. After a four-year interlude, Norfolk Island reverted to a place of terror.

Maconochie returned to Britain and in 1849 was given the chance to try his system in the new Birmingham Prison. Undermined by his deputy and by visiting justices, he was dismissed after two years. A subsequent inquiry revealed that during his tenure at Birmingham, Maconochie had used unauthorized punishments. As part of his policy that bringing a prisoner to submission was the initial stage of reform, he had inflicted whippings on one convict in daily installments. Because he had to prove his system within an inimical legal and administrative structure, Maconochie was predisposed to ignore the rules. Undaunted by criticism, Maconochie produced a stream of pamphlets in support of his system. He had no impact on the penal regime in England, but Walter Crofton, who was in charge of Irish prisons, accepted Maconochie's scheme except for the assumption of mutual responsibility among groups of prisoners. Maconochie also had an effect across the Atlantic: the 1870 "Declaration of Principles" of the American Prison Association reflected his emphasis on reformation and his understanding of the means to achieve it, even taking some language from his pamphlets. The indeterminate sentence (that is, a sentence not defined by a period of time) owes most to his advocacy.

THE FINAL DAYS

In the 1840s, with the abolition of transportation to New South Wales, all transported convicts went to Van Diemen's Land. Since private assignment was now taboo, they were kept by the government and worked in gangs. Gangs of convicts under convict overseers were notorious in Australia for inefficiency, corruption, and tyranny. The Molesworth committee had condemned them even more roundly than the system of assignment. The British government had originally planned to appoint free superintendents and overseers, but since these were difficult to obtain and expensive to pay, convicts were used instead.

More convicts were sent to Van Diemen's Land than had been expected, so the size of the gangs had to be increased. When the local economy went into recession, convicts reaching the end of their period in the gangs could not find work. Disaster loomed. The governor, Sir John Eardley-Wilmot (1843–46), continued to report positively on the gang system to the officials who had initiated it, but adverse reports reached the Colonial Office by other channels. The most disturbing news was that homosexuality was rife among the convicts. When this came to the attention of William E. Gladstone, who served briefly as secretary of state for colonies in 1846, he dismissed Governor Eardley-Wilmot. Officials in London now regretted having abandoned assignment so hastily.

Gladstone was succeeded by the third earl Grey, formerly Viscount Howick. Grey suspended transportation to Van Diemen's Land for two years and began to hunt for other places in the British Empire that could take convicts and relieve the intolerable pressure on Australia. He hoped to transport convicts who had served some part of their sentence in a penitentiary and were hence considered reformed. Referred to as "exiles" rather than convicts, they would receive tickets-of-leave once transported. Earl Grey did not think of these people as convicts, but colonies in every quarter of the globe refused to accept them. A boatload sent to South Africa aroused such opposition that the boat had to sail on to Australia.

Surviving without transportation for a decade, New South Wales refused to resume its role as a convict dumping ground. Free working people who had come to the colony on assisted passages in the 1830s and 1840s backed a massive antitransportation movement. Only the squatters in the interior, who always had difficulty obtaining labor, supported the importation of exiles. A few boatloads landed in New South Wales, but in the face of concerted opposition Earl Grey desisted. In Van Diemen's Land, to which transportation resumed in 1848, opinion was evenly divided. Giving up convicts, some argued, would imperil the colony's prosperity because it had trouble attracting free labor. Even a few leading lights of the island's antitransportation movement still hired convicts.

The issue was decided by the discovery of gold in New South Wales and Victoria in 1851, which made punishment by exile to Van Diemen's Land (separated from the goldfields by only a narrow stretch of water) an absurdity. Meanwhile, the rapid rise in prices during the gold rush made the whole exile operation much more expensive for the British government. When the defeat of the Whig government in February 1852 carried Earl Grey from office, transportation to Van Diemen's Land was abandoned. Britain did, however, continue to send convicts to Australia, for the colony of Western Australia had responded favorably to Grey's blandishments. Founded by free settlers in 1829, Western Australia had languished economically; it now sought salvation in cheap labor and the British treasury. Transportation began on a small scale in 1850 and continued until 1867. Nevertheless, Western Australia made little difference to the penal regime of Great Britain. From the early 1850s, the great majority of British convicts served out their time within their homeland's borders.

The policies adopted for Britain's post-transportation penal regime owed something to the experience of the Australian convict colonies. When a bill promulgating other punishments in lieu of transportation passed through the House of Lords in 1853, Earl Grey suggested that the Australian ticket-of-leave system be adopted in Britain. The government accepted the proposal, giving that old device for saving money a new lease of life. From the ticket-of-leave system, the practice of parole and parole supervision eventually developed.

Just when the British abandoned transportation, the French took it up, sending convicts to Guiana from 1852 and to New Caledonia from 1865. French debate over whether transportation was an appropriate punishment had gone on for decades, with both sides pointing to the British experience in Australia. One outcome of British transportation stood out very clearly: whatever its effectiveness as a punishment, it had produced prosperous colonies. This decided the matter in the mind of Emperor Louis-Napoléon. Though colonization was a strong motive, French penal settlements remained distinct institutions in the two colonies, both of which had been established by free migrants. Most of the convicts worked under government supervision, with a portion available for private employment at a fee. Further, ex-convicts were obliged to remain in the colony for a period equal to that of their sentence. Neither French colony prospered as New South Wales had, with the result that the ex-convicts had few opportunities. In Guiana, they faced a pitiful plight far worse than their original sentence. Thus, the French failed to duplicate the British experience.

Indeed, no one could have duplicated the British experience of transportation to New South Wales. There, the colony was a social oddity created by the absence of free wardens, the pressures of pioneering an alien land, and the hijacking of convicts and government stores by military officers for private gain. Early in its history the boundary between penal settlement and colony disappeared; the second had subsumed the first. Penal reformers discovered how difficult it was to reorient the colony for penal purposes. The governors of Van Diemen's Land had more success at building a penal regime, in part because they did not face the particular disadvantages present in New

South Wales. In that larger, less-contained colony, ex-convicts were an influential party in public affairs. Until the end of transportation, the logic of the republic of convicts was still working itself out in New South Wales.

The standards by which Australians judge the convict colony are usually those of civil society. Forced labor under threat of the lash appears as an oppression, and Australia's convict past is as roundly condemned as American slavery. But if the convict colony is considered as a place for the punishment of crime, then our judgment will be less confident. The principles of punishment by which transportation was condemned led to a penal regime in which we now have little confidence. The prison, still its central institution, is not a scientific instrument for the reformation of criminals but a form of barbarism. In *The Fatal Shore* (1987), the most compelling book written on the convict system, Robert Hughes spent hundreds of pages highlighting its tyranny and cruelty. He then concluded that the assignment of convicts to private masters was "by far the most successful form of penal rehabilitation that had ever been tried in English, American or European history" (p. 586).

The convict colony invites judgment by the standards of a civil society because that is how it presents itself. This is its most surprising characteristic—that a society peopled so largely by convicts nevertheless maintained the rule of law for all, imposed no disability on ex-convicts, and gave them the opportunity for economic success through employment of convict labor. It is a society without parallel, a strange, late flowering of the ancien régime in crime and punishment.

Bibliographic Note

The argument over the reasons for the British government's decision to settle Australia with convicts can be followed in Ged Martin, ed., *The Founding of Australia: The Argument about Australia's Origins* (Sydney: Hale and Iremonger, 1978), Ged Martin, "The Founding of New South Wales," in *The Origins of Australia's Capital Cities,* ed. P. Statham (Cambridge: Cambridge University Press, 1989), and Alan Frost, *Convicts and Empire: A Naval Question, 1776–1811* (Melbourne: Oxford University Press, 1980).

For the plans of the Gambia settlement and their modification for New South Wales, see Alan Atkinson, "The First Plans for Governing New South Wales, 1786–87," *Australian Historical Studies* 24 (1990): 22–40.

On Bentham's rival plan for a panopticon and his criticism of New South Wales, see J. Bentham, *The Works of Jeremy Bentham,* ed. J. Bowring, 11 vols. (Edinburgh: William Tart, 1843), and L. J. Hume, "Bentham's Panopticon: An Administrative History," *Historical Studies* 15 (1973): 703–21, 16 (1974): 36–54.

The social characteristics of the convicts are dealt with in L. L. Robson, *The Convict Settlers of Australia* (Melbourne: Melbourne University Press, 1965), and Stephen Nicholas, ed., *Convict Workers: Reinterpreting Australia's Past* (Cambridge: Cambridge University Press, 1988); the operation of the convict system in A. G. L. Shaw, *Convicts and the Colonies: A Study of Penal Transportation from Great Britain and Ireland to Australia and Other Parts of the British Empire* (London: Faber and Faber, 1966), J. B. Hirst, *Convict Society and Its Enemies: A History of Early New South Wales* (Sydney: G. Allen and Unwin, 1983), and Robert Hughes, *The Fatal Shore: A History of the Transportation of Convicts to Australia, 1787–1868* (London: Collins Harvill, 1987). The most fully worked local defense of the convict system is found in W. Bland, *Letters to Charles Buller Esq. M.P. from the Australian Patriotic Association* (Sydney, 1849).

John Ritchie, *Punishment and Profit: The Reports of Commissioner John Bigge on the Colonies of New South Wales and Van Diemen's Land, 1822–1823* (Melbourne: Heinemann, 1970), assesses the

British government's major rethink on the colony. The new departure on Norfolk Island is studied by J. V. Barry, *Alexander Maconochie of Norfolk Island: A Study of a Pioneer in Penal Reform* (Melbourne: Oxford University Press, 1958).

The following have been drawn on for the treatment of transported convicts in other locations: M. Bourdet-Pléville, *Justice in Chains: From the Galleys to Devil's Island,* trans. Anthony Rippon (London: Robert Hale, 1960); A. Roger Ekirch, *Bound for America: The Transportation of British Convicts to the Colonies, 1718–1775* (Oxford: Clarendon Press, 1987); Colin Forster, "French Penal Policy and the Origins of the French Presence in New Caledonia" (unpublished paper, Department of Economic History, Australian National University); Martyn Lyons, *The Totem and the Tricolour: A Short History of New Caledonia since 1774* (Sydney: New South Wales University Press, 1986); Charles Péan, *Conquest of Devil's Island* (London: Max Parrish, 1953).

CHAPTER TEN

LOCAL JUSTICE

The Jail

Seán McConville

That jailes should be, there is law, sense and reason,
To punish bawdry, cheating, theft and treason,
Though some against them have invective bin,
And call'd a Jaile a magazin of sin,
An Universitie of villany,
An Academy of foule blasphemy,
A sinke of drunkenesse, a den to Thieves,
A treasury for Sergeants and for Shrieves,
A mint for Baylifes, Marshals men and Jailers,
Who live by losses of captiv'd bewailers:
A nurse of Roguery, and an earthly hell,
Where Dev'ls or Jaylers in mens shapes doe dwell.

— John Taylor, "The Praise and Vertue
   of a Jayle and Jaylers," 1630

No other public institution so well embodies the contradictions among which we live. Certainly symbols and instruments of order and law to hold a prisoner implies deliberation and process rather than summary disposal—jails have equally been identified with grand and petty tyranny, sadism, corruption, extortion, debauchery, contamination, ruin, and despair. Refuges of last resort, the door from which the mad, sick, destitute, and unwanted could not be turned away, jails have also been, and are, places of terror, degradation, and suffering. They take away liberty, yet to some they impart a sense of freedom and security. Jails have always attracted philanthropic and political criticism, yet as prosperity and security advances, in some Western societies the jail does not fade away but rather grows and becomes an even more common experience.

Its paradoxical nature and functions are well reflected in the heterogeneity of its critics and supporters. Across the political spectrum, some have found the jail an indispensable instrument for maintaining Arcadia or moving toward Utopia—a platform for noblesse oblige or a university for rebellion. To some, the jail is a conduit transmitting social policy to the lower depths; to others, more romantic, jails are a price of individual liberty, since their walls hold back not only the criminal but also the coercive powers of the state: better to be captive within walls than a member of a captive community. On the eve of a new century and millennium, it remains certain that jails are with us and speak for us and shall continue to thrive on their age-old contradictory functions.

PRISONS, JAILS, AND GAOLS

Some terminological points must be made. The word *prison* is essentially generic, encompassing a range of detention institutions and devices. These include the jail and places of temporary detention such as the lockup, pound, or crib. The latter were formerly found in the smallest of towns for the overnight detention of drunks, prostitutes, and other minor offenders. The bridewell is another type of prison. This was inaugurated by the City of London in the sixteenth century in a hand-me-down royal palace converted into a reformatory for misdemeanants, nuisances, and orphans. The county institutions modeled on it were called houses of correction. These names are still used, with police stations and lockups in some jurisdictions being known as bridewells and jails being called houses of correction. Cages and stocks should also, in my view, be treated as a subspecies of prison.

Modern practice complicates this historical use of terms. In the United States it is usual to designate state prisons, whatever their names—penitentiary, reformatory for men or women, or the pallid and dishonest "correctional facility"—as prisons. Prisons run by the county or municipality are called jails. In England, no such distinction is now made. Jails were amalgamated with houses of correction in 1865 (the distinction between the two is discussed below) and called local prisons. Long-term prisons (the equivalent of the state prison in the United States) and local prisons were eventually brought together under central government administration, with all being known as prisons and with consignment thereto known as imprisonment.

In England and the rest of the United Kingdom, there are therefore no longer places called jails, although there are prisons and sections of prisons that function as jails—detaining pretrial prisoners and people serving short sentences. To confuse it all, newspaper copy editors prefer the four-letter *jail,* as verb and noun, to the six-letter *prison* and to the even more space-consuming *imprisonment,* which they usually mean. Americans are further baffled by the now preferred British spelling of jail—*gaol.* The pronunciations are exactly the same, and both forms have long been in use. Perhaps, in the *gaol* form, there is an unconscious desire to gentrify a very disreputable organization, since the tabloid newspapers are much more prone to *jail* than to *gaol,* and the quality press prefers the opposite. For clarity, I shall stick to the American spelling and practice.

A jail is a county or municipal prison, in the United States. Where I deal with the jail function in recent English imprisonment, I shall be explicit. It is difficult to find a substitute for *prisoner. Captive* is clearly not right. I see nothing illogical in describing someone as a prisoner in a jail and so shall use that term as well as the sanitizing *inmate.*

And if terminology is an irritating start to what the reader expects to be a simple story, I must warn of complications to follow. There are not many public institutions that have been around as long as the jail. In England its provenance extends through the recorded history of the country; and in the United States it existed from early colonial times. The jail's place in public administration and the life of the community has inevitably changed over the centuries, as have some of its functions and relations with derivative and substitute institutions. These developments must be mentioned. Administration, staffing, and financing inevitably affected what happened to prisoners and so will also be considered. More recently the extension of central control over jails is a significant development, whether it be through a direct administrative takeover by national government, as in England, or through regulation, legislation, and court intervention, as in the United States. These will be some of our signposts and milestones as we take a brief excursion into the dense and surprising undergrowth that is jail history.

This essay will slip to and fro across the Atlantic fairly easily, but there should be no alarm and hopefully no confusion. The shared history of the United States and Great Britain is nowhere more apparent than in the legal heritage of the two countries. Inevitably, there have been divergences, where local needs, sentiments, and inventiveness have prompted changes in policy and institutions. The story is complicated but not all that difficult to follow. As in certain other matters (speech patterns and certain usages, for example), the former colony has remained truer to the common heritage than the parent. The jail flour-ishes openly in the United States, but in England it is kept in what is felt to be the decent seclusion of a terminological and bureaucratic shrubbery. But, as we shall see, a jail by any other name . . .

Early English Jails

The Normans of the Conquest found numerous and well-established jails, which clearly were important components of English criminal justice. Seeking, a century later, to suppress the anarchy that had occurred during the reign of his predecessor, Henry II introduced criminal justice procedures and institutions that have endured the tests of more than eight centuries. Many jails belonged to local magnates, church and secular, but at the 1166 Assize of Clarendon, Henry took care that in each county there should be at least one jail, under the charge of his sheriff. The sheriff was, of course, a royal appointment, a functionary who upheld his master's interests against local powers. Five hundred years later, as strong central government faltered, all but the tiniest vestiges of the sheriff's jail powers were stripped away and, during the long period of Whig supremacy, were ceded to a magistracy that had become the voice, apparatus, and substance of local government.

Although Henry II decreed one of his jails for each county, he dared not extinguish all others. By the early thirteenth century there were only five counties that did not have sheriffs' jails. Alongside these, however, operated a swarm of municipal jails and lock-ups, as well as various franchise jails. Some of these municipal ventures were established under charters—political deals between ambitious burgesses and an avaricious Crown. The franchise jails arose from the customary rights adhering to administrative entities such as manors, divisions of counties, and liberties within towns. Belonging to ecclesiastical and secular lords, they passed through a variety of owners, gradually dwindling in number as they were squeezed by the Crown and restricted by Parliament. As profit-making debtors' jails, a few managed to survive until the latter half of the nineteenth century, when strict legislation and inspection finished them off.

All jails were theoretically the Crown's, periodically to be delivered (i.e., emptied for trial) by the king's justices. A few were even more directly connected to central government than this useful administrative fiction suggested. From the beginning, the Tower of London served as a jail for state offenders. A number of other London jails also operated ad hoc on behalf of central government. Newgate belonged to the City of London but held prisoners from all over the country on the directions of the Crown, privy council, or superior courts. Prisoners included people in trouble for reasons of state and religion, together with notorious criminals and even debtors. Other London jails acquired various specialized functions, besides their conventional local uses. The Fleet, probably England's oldest purpose-built jail, came to serve the courts of common pleas, chancery, and star chamber, whereas the Clink, originally the bishop of Winchester's jail for petty offenders, whores, and their associates, was used in Elizabeth's reign to hold recusants and added yet another term to the glossary of punishment.

Other jails were maintained in places that had special rights secured by charters, such as forests and tin-mining areas (stannaries). These institutions were needed because the activities and way of life of these localities did not fit with the conventional machinery of justice. The church, which in its secular right as a landowner maintained jails for the laity, also had detention and reformatory prisons to serve its parallel system of clerical justice. These were located in part of a church-owned lay prison, or on ecclesiastical premises, and continued in use for religious offenders until the Reformation.

Finance and Corruption

The notion of public money is of relatively recent origin, and jails were among many institutions that were financed by user fees. Just as sheriffs, tax collectors, customs and excise officers, coroners, and judges and justices, together with their subordinates and servants, were expected to obtain their income from fees, so were the jailers, turnkeys, and other minor jail functionaries. The prospect of extracting fees from prisoners may at first seem futile, since these people were drawn chiefly from the poor and powerless classes. Yet, until the beginning of the nineteenth century, English jailers and their subordinates were paid in this way. In the words of an eighteenth-century reformer, they "wrung their emolument from misery." Control over the prisoners' bodies was an effective means of securing credit, since all accounts had to be settled before the guest could depart.

In the large town jails, livelihoods were so handsome that jailerships were traded as major investments. In 1716, in the aftermath of their failed rebellion, Jacobites incarcerated in London yielded profits of three to four thousand pounds to William Pitt, Newgate's keeper. Criminal celebrities such as Jack Sheppard and Jonathan Wild were also profit-makers, since the citizenry was delighted to pay to gawk at and talk to them as they awaited trial and execution. Yet these were mere windfalls. Bread-and-butter profits came from the daily life of the prison. There were admittance and discharge fees, fees for ironing and de-ironing, fees for food, water, and lodgings. The last could range from a vermin-infested cellar to a room in the keeper's own house, depending, of course, on one's ability to pay. More money was to be made from the tap—an alehouse for prisoners and visitors. In some jails, entertainments such as skittles and the services of prostitutes were available to all with funds. It was no wonder that some jailerships had a large price tag. Turnkeys, porters, and clerks also bought and sold their positions, which yielded a modest but not miserly income and a retirement nest egg when the office was sold. Sometimes these positions were bought and sublet, with profits being shared between the owner and the worker.

The line between fee-taking and extortion is easily crossed, as is that between legitimate and illegitimate service. Eighteenth-century thieftakers, such as Jonathan Wild, had complicated but lucrative relationships with crime and criminals. Notionally they acted as a private police, rewarded by victims and protective associations to recover property and apprehend criminals. They were accepted as a type of fee-supported detective force. In the pursuit of profit, a number of corrupt relationships and tricks were developed. Thieftakers split fees with thieves for the return of property, fenced property on which deals could not be made, spotted likely targets and commissioned thefts, and from time to time turned rebellious associates over to the law and the gallows, *pour encourager les autres.*

London jailers, and probably those of other big towns, were similarly embedded in the economy of crime. Their jails were brothels, taps, criminal clubs, and asylums for thieves, robbers, and fraudsmen, and when their raw material—prisoners—threatened to run out, minions would bring false charges to replenish the supply. Whereas the petty criminal or debtor would be ground up in the jail's maw, the professional thief or pretend bankrupt could use the jail as a sanctuary, leaving and returning at will. Prison walls were as useful to exclude pursuers as they were to keep wrongdoers in custody. And if this sounds im-probable, it should be remembered that there were no professional police forces at the time; obtaining admission to a jail against the wishes of the jailer would have been extremely difficult.

How did those prisoners exist who had neither friends nor family to support them, no corrupt relationship with the jailer, no creditor on a string? Many starved to death or died from disease. For centuries, epidemics were a second form of jail delivery. The jails made no pretense at reform, did not claim to do anything other than detain, and provided almost nothing in the way of sustenance; thus prisoners were relatively free within the walls. Some—probably a minority—supported themselves in the portable trades—cobblers, tailors, and saddlemakers. Others performed services for prisoners who had funds. Young women sold their bodies. Prisoners also imposed collective levies under the name of garnish or chummage: newcomers had to pay up or strip off their clothes, which could be sold.

There was some outside support. Jails might, for example, have gratings on their street side, from which prisoners could beg from passersby; others designated official beggars, who would solicit alms while chained in the street. The pious left bequests for prisoners' relief (a form of charity that lasted in England until the late nineteenth century, when it was zealously extinguished by disapproving bureaucrats). Municipalities occasionally stirred themselves. Foodstuffs confiscated for violations of trade regulations would sometimes be sent to the prisons. In 1572, the wide-ranging Poor Law of Elizabeth I at last stipulated that the counties could use public funds to provide for poor prisoners, although this provision was very unevenly carried into effect. And on all these donations and doles, the jailer and his underlings could be expected to levy their tolls.

Functions and Conditions

Until relatively recent times the notion of using a jail to reform the offender was unknown and indeed would have seemed bizarre. People were held to await their trial and to await the execution of sentence, whether that be flogging, death, or banishment. A minority were jailed as retribution—for violating municipal trade laws, for petty criminal offenses, and for reasons of state. The jail's great inconvenience and financial demands made this a severe punishment in itself, even for the wealthy, quite apart from the perils to health. Two other groups made up the jail population—those in civil contempt (usually debt), and an unfortunate group of witnesses held to ensure their appearance.

The jail's danger, inconvenience, and generally coercive properties made it the ideal instrument to wring money due to the Crown from careless tax collectors and reluctant subjects. Edward III's Debtors' Act in 1350 extended to private creditors this most useful method of squeezing, thus inaugurating centuries of incarceration for debt. On first consideration, it probably seems counterproductive to jail a debtor, since one thereby cuts off the means of earning money and settling obligations. But the intention was to coerce, and the belief was that the debtor's property would be realized or friends and family induced to pay. This doubtless happened in many instances, but in the course of time it became obvious that people were being jailed and held, sometimes for many years, to enforce payment of trifling sums; creditors' malice and ire pulled the levers of state power, and the satisfaction sought sometimes went far beyond the purely financial. In England and the American colonies by the eighteenth century various societies settled the trifling debts of the poor and gave them freedom. Benjamin Franklin (author, after all, of the aphorism "Remember, that time is money") was one of many prominent figures on both sides of the Atlantic who had an interest in such philanthropic societies. The relief of poor debtors was also a common object of charitable bequests.

A singular weakness in procedure was fully exploited by the dishonest debtor, even while the truly destitute remained firmly within the toils of the law. Once a debtor had been incarcerated, no further action could be taken by his creditor to recover money: the creditor could not, for example, seize the debtor's chattels. This anomaly led to the emergence of a class of fraudsman well known in Shakespeare's time and probably before—the "politic debtor." Deliberately running up debt, these tricksters sat in jail, enjoying their creditor's substance, with which they would buy comfortable lodgings, good food, and servants. This would continue until the creditor agreed to settle for a percentage of the amount that had been tricked from him and that he could see was daily diminishing. The agreement released the cheat to continue his profitable game with another gull. For such tricksters, life at the Fleet could be made even easier by paying the jailer to allow them to "go abroad," that is, to move around and conduct business within a certain part of the city, escorted by a bailiff. So attractive was this privilege that some prisoners had themselves transferred to the Fleet by pretending to be Crown debtors. A more pitiful class of debtor who opted to remain in jail consisted of those who, in the knowledge that debts were canceled by death, chose lifelong captivity as a means of preserving their remains of property and possessions for family and heirs.

The hopeless plight of some debtors and the criminal pillagings of others were well-known, as John Taylor's verse shows:

> So Rorers, Rascals, Banquerouts politicke,
> With money, or with friends will find a tricke,
> Their Jaylor to corrupt, and at their will
> They walke abroad, and take their pleasure still:
> Whilst naked vertue, beggerly, despis'd,
> Beleaguered round, with miseries surpris'd,
> Of hope of any liberty defeated,
> For passing of his word is merely cheated:
> And dungeond up, may tell the wals his mones,
> And make relation to the senseless stones,
> Where sighs and grones, and tears may be his feast,
> Whilst man to man is worse than beast to beast.
> Till death he there must take his sad abode,
> Whilst craft and coozenage walke at will abroad.
>
> ("The Praise and Vertue of a Jayle and Jaylers")

Until the nineteenth century, jail life could be made comfortable for those who had funds, and it was certainly not the restricted prisoner's life of shame, discipline, and submission with which we have become familiar. There was no uniform, nor were the days shaped by a penal routine; only a minority of prisoners were locked in separate cells. Penal labor was not imposed, and there was no special diet. To the extent that the rapacity of the keeper and his acolytes, and one's fellows, could be accommodated, life could approximate that pursued outside, with the exception that one could not leave. Family and servants (if there were any) could move in and out relatively freely, as could tradesmen, friends, and gawkers. Children could be born in jail and, with their debtor parent, live out much of their life there (Dickens's *Little Dorrit* is based on such a theme). Games and recreations were unhindered by any consideration except custody. Squash rackets is thought to have originated in the Fleet; it was certainly played there.

It is tempting to describe the laissez-faire state of the jails, a state that persisted until the nineteenth century (and beyond), as benign neglect. But malign neglect is more accurate. The haphazard miseries of jails were blended into a convenient and persuasive teleological doctrine: *squalor carceris*. Danger and ruinous expense combined with appalling living conditions and loss of freedom to produce the sanction that punished the wrongdoer and coerced the debtor and contumacious. That the taxpayer was thereby justified in his unwillingness to pay to improve such conditions was a happy and convenient circumstance: parsimony and virtue united. If the jailed felon was still alive, it was by grace and favor; the misdemeanant equally deserved his punishment. James Neild, disciple of the noble penal reformer John Howard, in the early years of the nineteenth century encountered in his work of jail reform and philanthropy a common view of the misery of the prisoner. This emphasized that jails were provided for the wrongdoer "who, having opposed the *ordinances,* has abandoned *the protection of the laws.* Leave him to his doom of misery: Let him rot in the vapours of a dungeon; and drag his unwieldy chain, at the mercy of his keeper." Howard himself, when he appealed to the gentry of his county to pay jail fees out of taxes and to improve conditions (which resulted, inter alia, in people who had been found not guilty by the courts being returned to jail until they had paid their keeper) was told "'*Let them take care to keep out,*' prefaced perhaps with an angry prayer."

This fine old sentiment lives on and has been successfully transplanted to the New World. A prominent judge in Prince George's County, Maryland, was in 1982 questioned by a *Washington Post* reporter about forced acts of sodomy in the county jail. There were as many as twelve such assaults a week, in a jail of 450 prisoners, 70 percent of whom were pretrial detainees. The judge's response was blunt: "One of the reasons you shouldn't break the law is that you get raped in that jail." Another judge had a weaker stomach: "This is the kind of thing that's so bad you shut your mind to it. It's easier to blot it out than to come to grips with the fact it's happening in our society." *Squalor carceris* lives—a rationalization for neglect, administrative lawlessness, and a pandering to popular vindictiveness. Frustration with crime, class and race prejudice, and a lack of moral and political leadership ensure its longevity and vigor.

JAIL REFORM

A number of developments in the late eighteenth century began the process of bringing a new kind of order to the jails. The evangelical revival inside and outside the Church of England directed spiritual energy and practical attention to sources of misery and vice, of which jails were clearly one. Various philanthropists, including the Wesley brothers, undertook the dangerous work of ministering in the jails and cataloging their deficiencies. In the United States, republican idealism and energy provided another impetus to reform. Correspondence crossed the Atlantic as experiments in penal reform were tried and evaluated; over several generations there was to be considerable cross-fertilization. Any review of this period of penal history must acknowledge the common legal and institutional heritage of the two countries. Experiments by English county magistrates easily commended themselves to political leaders in Philadelphia and elsewhere. A generation later the spark passed in the opposite direction, with Britain and France sending emissaries to study Pennsylvania's strict system of penal discipline, which was based on separate confinement. That kindly man (and jailbird's son) Charles Dickens came and looked at the Eastern State Penitentiary. He returned horror-struck to England to wage a campaign against the rationalistic cruelties of the separate system, which was being promoted afresh in England, as a national model. Jails had begotten penitentiaries.

Before this extravagant experiment got under way there were more modest attempts to curb the lawlessness of jails. In reform-minded jurisdictions men were separated from women, children from adults, felons from misdemeanants, remands (pretrials) from the convicted, and debtors and other civil prisoners from the criminal. Jail fees were prohibited in England in 1815. This obliged counties and municipalities to pay realistic salaries, and with public money came accountability of a kind—closer county supervision and greater expectations for order and discipline. Jailers could no longer claim to "own" their positions, nor could they justify trading with prisoners. The United States, with its small-farmer ideology and residual hostility toward government and taxes, was slower to move to publicly financed jails. The leasing of prisoner labor, a form of self-financing, did not, for example, stop in Florida until 1917 and in Alabama until 1928. Vestiges of the fee system remained, and in some places as late as the 1940s jailers continued to be paid fees instead of salaries by their counties.

At different paces, maybe, both American and British politicians and administrators sought to curb jail excesses and to find new forms of punishment. Felons (with some few exceptions) had in England always been the responsibility of the Crown, which either executed them or, from the early eighteenth century onward, transported them overseas, to America and then to the conveniently discovered Australia. The twelve-year hiatus between the outbreak of the American War of Independence and the landing of felons at Botany Bay compelled the "temporary expedient" of keeping in floating prisons the felons who otherwise would have been transported. The vessels were old warships (called hulks) moored on the Thames and in Portsmouth harbor. What had been thought to be no more than a temporary local upset turned into a new nation, and American doors closed forever against British convicts. There was muddle, make-do, and scandal for a while in British convict administration, but eventually the hulks spawned land-based prisons for convicts (i.e., convicted felons), quite separate from the jails. These new prisons were administered directly by central government. In America, at about the same time, states went into the construction of penitentiaries, and a similar dual system of incarceration was established: county- and municipality-run jails for remands, misdemeanants, and debtors; state penitentiaries for felons.

At the opposite end of the continuum of culpability, reformers argued with increasing success that jailing and imprisonment were ruinous for children. Since jails corrupted, contaminated, and blasted young lives, it was argued, alternatives had to be found. Separate children's prisons, based on the theory that older criminals were the principal source of corruption (a silly notion, given what we now know of the chemistry of the peer group), increasingly took children out of the jails, where they had usually served short sentences of a few days or weeks, and put them instead into reformatories, where, in pressure-cooker conditions, they spent years and compassed ruination probably far more thoroughly than in the jails. Closer to our own times, the expense and folly of this expedient became inescapably obvious, and attempts were made to keep youthful offenders out of custody in all but the most extreme cases.

Misery, Reform, and More Misery

The philosopher and critic C. S. Lewis observed in a famous essay on punishment that it might be better to live under robber barons than under omnipotent moral busybodies. His reasoning was that the robber baron might sometimes relent, because he either slept or was satiated. On the other hand, Lewis argued, "Those who torment us for our own good will torment us without end for they do so with the approval of their own conscience." It is tempting and not a little plausible to apply this perspective to life in jail—and a comparison of reformed and unreformed jails may tilt us toward the robber baron.

The jailer and his minions were undoubtedly cast in the robber baron mold. Over every newcomer a very cold eye was cast, and the senses with which every pawnbroker and moneylender must be endowed if they are to survive gave an instant financial reading. If the prisoner was a person of substance, he might expect a greeting not too dissimilar, in all the circumstances, from that which a world-worn hotelier might extend. But if the prisoner was poor, the greeting and his prospects would be very different.

The difference can be seen in contemporary reports. John Paston, an English landowner who found his way into the Fleet (one of London's jails) in 1472, wrote to his wife in terms that tell us a lot about the jail experience of the well-to-do. "The Flet is a fayir preson, but ye had but smale lyberte therein, for ye must nedys aper when ye war callyd." Thomas Dekker, a writer of Shakespeare's time, was apt to be histrionic, but his lament for the poor prisoner smacks of authenticity (and that probably from firsthand experience): "Art thou poor and in prison? Then thou buried before thou art dead. Thou carriest thy winding-sheet on thy back. . . . Thou liest upon thy bier and treadest upon thy grave at every step. If there be any hell on earth, here thou especially shalt be sure to find it: If there be degrees of torments in hell, here thou shalt taste them."

Until the nineteenth century few observers would have found anything particularly worrying in the very different lives of the poor and the well-off in jail. Why, they would wonder, should a person who was poor, miserable, and in danger of starvation when free have his lot in any way improved when in jail? And why should a person not use his wealth to maintain himself in jail, as close as possible to the way he would if free? That was their version of equity, and it would have seemed absurd and possibly wicked to them to suggest that there should be equality in the misery of the jail.

The lives of the poor and the rich were, therefore, very different in jail, although in the past, as now, only a very select company of the rich were jailed. The only condition that both shared was that they were captives. This meant that you could not leave and, as Paston complained, had to appear when called. Both rich and poor might be chained, although since one of the jailer's devices for raising funds was to charge his prisoners for *not* wearing chains, the chances are that the prisoner with funds was free of encumbrances. But the days of the two were very different. Food and lodging in the jailer's apartments, or in a special part of the jail, were as different as they could be from necessities in the common ward. Starvation, intimidation, disease, and desperation were the lot of the poor prisoner certainly until the late eighteenth century. William Smith, a doctor who visited the London jails in the mid-1770s, described the prisoners as "vagrants and disorderly women of the very lowest and most wretched class of human beings, almost naked, with only a few filthy rags almost alive and in motion with vermin, their bodies rotting with the bad distemper, and covered in itch, scorbutic and venereal ulcers."

The incarcerated merchant or landowner, tucking into lamb chops at the jailer's table, probably had little idea of the misery that dwelt within a few score feet. Periodically, however, the common ward visited the loftier parts of the jail, and even went beyond the walls, in the form of deadly jail fever. No respecter of social position or of hefty fee-payers, these periodic epidemics swept away the jurymen, lawyers, judges, and magistrates before whom the prisoners were produced. (The stench of the prisoners, and a belief in the miasmatic transmission of disease, are the origin of the posy that senior judges still carry on the opening of new court terms in England.) Released prisoners carried the disease to their home communities. Where altruistic argument failed, the threat of plague prevailed, and some of the earliest jail reforms were preventive health measures.

A number of factors came together in the nineteenth century to make the jails egalitarian in their infliction of suffering. Although the regulation of jails (the separation of men from women, young from old, criminal from civil, felon from misdemeanant, convicted from untried) probably did not make too many inroads into the differential treatment of rich and poor, it began to establish order in the place of locked-up anarchy. The next stage in the reform process, however, was inimical to a diversity of jail lifestyles. Step one had been to stop jails from killing people through disease or from making prisoners more hardened offenders; step two was to imagine that jails could be used to make criminals better. Prisoners were to become better by being subject to controls on every aspect of daily life: sleeping, eating, working, associating with others, reading—and in religion, dress, and exercise. Through the deterrence of carefully calculated discomfort or pain, or by coerced habits of regularity, or through educationally and religiously structured reform, or by combinations of these, offenders could be changed into law-abiding citizens—so ran the theory. Such a determina-tion to control all aspects of the environment was clearly going to make the jail experience highly uniform. There would be no place for the carousing and unregulated misery of earlier centuries.

It would be foolish for the sake of argument to claim that these changes left the poor prisoner worse off than before. The moral busybodies at least ensured minimum food, hygiene, and medical treatment. But the price of these improvements was a different kind of misery. To prevent mutual contamination, solitude was imposed on the prisoners. It is hard for a free person to imagine the impact of prolonged separate confinement on the human mind; and even though most of those in jails served only days or weeks, this was a very heavy punishment. Forms of labor were devised that could be minutely measured and that machines made inescapable. Much thought went into food that would keep body and soul together but would do no more. Sleep was seen as an indulgence and was regulated accordingly.

In truth, the misery of the robber baron and the reformers is hard to measure. Certainly any exercise of imagination would prevent one from joining in what until recent times was a paean of unquestioned praise for the work of the early (and later) prison reformers. The squalor, danger, and barbarism of the premodern jail evoke our pity and wonder at the cheapness of human life. But how are we to react to those who designed, implemented, and constantly refined a system of hygienic suffering? Surely one must recoil from what was either an abundance of imagination or none at all. Samuel Coleridge's derisive indignation was not excessive when he wrote of Cold Bath Fields, one of London's pioneering reformed jails:

As he went through Cold-Bath Fields he saw
   A solitary cell;
And the Devil was pleased, for it gave him a hint
   For improving his prisons in Hell.

Uniformity of punishment might be defended as another aspect of equality before the law: riches should not shield one from just punishment, nor poverty expose one to an excess of it. But what about those who are sent to jail not for punishment but simply to ensure their court appearance? The nineteenth- and early-twentieth-century reformers stressed that all—including pretrial detainees—should be treated in the same way. But why should an unconvicted person be obliged to forgo the comfort and privileges of his means simply because he is in detention? There must, of course, be such restrictions as are necessary to provide secure and safe custody, but other than these, what right—moral or political—can there be to impose deprivations on the unconvicted? For this injustice we must also blame those prison reformers who looked far more to administrative convenience than to right and who in their hearts probably believed that it all mattered little, since to be accused and detained was to be guilty. About half the average daily population of the jails today consists of pretrial prisoners. Here clearly is another reform to make the devil grin.

Moving Debtors out of Jail

Debtors were gradually cleared out of the jails, although the fiction that one was being jailed for contempt of court, and not for debt, allowed people to be imprisoned in England for private debts until the 1960s and for public debt, such as local taxes, even now. In America, coercive imprisonment for private debt ceased in most jurisdictions in the nineteenth century, although other forms of debtor imprisonment, often masked by a contempt of court or criminal citation, have continued into modern times. Certainly the English found the issue perplexing. One school of thought was apt to think of all debtors as criminals, since by recklessness or dishonesty they had caused a loss to their creditors, which was viewed much as if they had stolen. This view was vigorously espoused, for example, by members of the supposedly liberal Gladstone Committee on prisons as late as 1895. To others, the pettiness of the sums involved, debtors' and defaulters' miserable lives, and the misfortune, rather than malice, that marked the progress of most debtors into custody spurred campaigns for changes in the law.

Debt raised certain difficult issues in political and legal thought. Was government entitled to intervene in what was essentially a matter of private contract and property? What damage might such intervention inadvertently do to commerce? Conversely, when the jail was being used to enforce a contract, was there not, ipso facto, a public interest? In the later eighteenth century there was no clear answer to these questions. Piecemeal solutions were found in periodic Insolvent Debtors Acts, which released debtors from the English jails, eased overcrowding, and salved the public conscience. In 1813 Parliament set up a court to deal with insolvent debtors, thus obviating the need for regular legislative action. But new ways of handling the problems were not easily adopted, and in the succeeding thirty years there were more than forty such acts.

An increase in wealth and the ease of credit led to laws that, in the latter part of the nineteenth century, began again to increase the number of jailed debtors. Door-to-door salesmen, known as tallymen, brought household goods on credit to the working classes, and inevitably a crop of defaulters was produced for the jails. Husbands were liable for their wives' debts at this time, and there was much public criticism of the resultant family disasters. Public and commercial opinion was confused and divided, but the frequent tinkering with the law eventually had an effect. In 1776 John Howard had found that debtors constituted some 60 percent of jail inmates. By 1877 debtors accounted for only 3 percent of English jail committals. The last jail in England exclusively for debtors—the Queen's Prison—closed in 1862 and was demolished in 1868. The privately committed debtor became a dwindling element in the population and life of the jails. Today, in most common-law jurisdictions, he has all but vanished.

One American colony (Georgia) was founded with the intention that it should be a haven for poor debtors, and there was a sense that the New World should mean a fresh start. This history, and a republican distaste for coercive incarceration, made Americans uneasy with the jailing of debtors. Some states prohibited the practice in their constitutions, but others continued in the English tradition. Pennsylvania, for example, both as colony and as state, showed its concern with the evils of jailing for debt by successive steps of amelioration but did not actually forbid the practice until 1842. Indeed, as recently as 1969 Maine debtors were jailed for failing to obey the repayment instructions of court-appointed officials. This type of prisoner—a person who was in contempt of court because he failed to follow schedules concerning debt—continues to be found in the American jails in small numbers. The civil nature of the offenses is concealed, since in most jurisdictions they have been subjected to the criminal code.

There are more of those who are incarcerated because of their failure to obey laws or court orders to pay family support. Some of these men plead inability but go to jail if they fail to convince the court. This path to custody may follow either a civil or a criminal process, and the objective of punishment continues to be intermingled with that of coercion. The numbers are not great, but neither do they seem to be totally negligible. Unfortunately, our knowledge of the national statistics is far from complete. In 1968–69 almost 7 percent of those committed to jails in Nebraska had been found guilty of failing to support their families; at the Milwaukee, Wisconsin, county jail in 1966 just under 4 percent of prisoners were there for the same reason. Some of these men are obdurate and angry and will not pay; others are feckless and could pay were they to put their lives in order; and probably a small number do not pay because they cannot. Under budgetary, social, and political pressures a number of states have recently begun more aggressively to seek and prosecute family-support defaulters. If these efforts result in an increased number of cases coming before the courts, we may again see a significant debtor population. Whether such jailings are cost-effective is questionable. Payment coerced through incarceration can hope to work in only a general and long-term way and will always be thwarted by a federal system of administration and diverse jurisdictions.

Incarceration for an offense of dishonesty or dishonor has always carried a stigma in respectable circles, but when jailing for debt was fairly widespread the experience was treated more lightly and did not permanently damage reputations. To have been an imprisoned debtor sometimes provoked sympathy for one's misfortune or, in the case of otherwise respectable young men, was seen as no more than the sowing of wild oats—adding the spice of youthful recklessness to the staidness of middle-age. Montagu Williams, a distinguished Queen's Counsel, wrote his widely read memoirs, *Leaves of a Life,* in the 1890s. He recalled his own youthful escapades with debt, spunging houses (a type of profit-making halfway house for debtors), moneylenders, and bailiffs, as well as the experiences of family friends. One of the latter was a nobleman who, because of his debts, was obliged to lodge with Williams's family to escape arrest. The immunity arose from the fact that the family lived in The Cloisters at Windsor, and debtors could not be arrested within the precincts of a royal palace. To make his semicaptive life tolerable, the Williams's guest took advantage of another indulgence of the law, and each Sunday he would go to London, safe in the knowledge that all arrests for debt were stayed on that day. He eventually fell into the bailiffs' hands when a clock was set back, and he tarried in London past the midnight hour and into the first minutes of an arrestable Monday. These and other adventures Williams relates with aplomb, though had he, in bourgeois middle age returned to the ways of the feckless nobility and his youth, he would quickly have forfeited both social position and legal practice.

Changes in Jail Procedure and Function

Bail

As has been seen, from the earliest times one of the main functions of the jail has been to hold accused people pending their trial. From equally early times there was an alternative means of ensuring appearance at trial—to provide securities in the community. Indeed the roots of peacekeeping in the English-speaking nations go back to the mutual surveillance and collective responsibilities of Anglo-Saxon England. Groups of ten families were responsible, under a tithingman, for ensuring obedience to the law in their area. Part of this obligation included the duty to produce a wrongdoer. Failure to locate or give up an offender meant the imposition of a collective fine, called a "grithbryce" or "fightwitt." The knowledge that all could suffer through the misdeeds of one was a powerful and simple means of enforcing the law. It also accorded with one of the inclinations of the Anglo-Saxon tradition—a weak state and decentralization of power.

The enforcement of collective responsibility is, of course, entirely practical when people live a settled agrarian life. Not only does everyone know everyone else in such communities, but there is nowhere for a fugitive to go, since all other communities would look with suspicion and hostility on a stranger unable to account for himself. Collective responsibility may not be practical in modern urbanized conditions, which are marked by mobility, anonymity, and a lack of ties between people. But the notion of giving security to ensure appearance remains. Bail has come to mean monetary or other property being pledged to guarantee appearance—the pledge being either the accused's or that of a relative, friend, or supporter.

In modern times, a major drawback in the notion of accepting a pledge of security to appear has been that many accused people are from the poorest sections of society, and neither they nor their families and friends have property to pledge. The solution is, of course, to jail such people. But the problem with this is that the jails are overcrowded in many jurisdictions. It is, moreover, expensive to hold a person in jail, and it undoubtedly hampers one's ability to prepare a defense. Under the pressure of numbers, expense, and concerns about equity, schemes have been developed that involve a personal assessment of the accused and of the chances of his honoring a promise to appear if allowed to be at large pending trial.

There are bound to be failures with such schemes, but for the most part they work well enough. We may not live in the glass bowl of Anglo-Saxon England, but modern bureaucracy and technology make it difficult to live the life of a fugitive, and most people realize that running is not a solution to their problems and will simply make things worse. To some extent, therefore, the jail has spilled out into society, but without major ill effects. Considerations of cost and fairness now make bail schemes essential to the administration of justice, and the problem for those who have the responsibility of risk assessment is to refine their procedures (including statistically based risk-assessment tables) to give the accused as much latitude as is compatible with the protection of society.

Apart from release on a promise to appear (which is called release on own recognizance), there are various forms of hybrid custody, involving some release and some confinement. An accused person who does not have a home or settled accommodation, for example, might be granted bail on condition that he reside in a hostel—in the United States usually called a halfway house or (for those hopelessly addicted to euphemisms) a community correctional facility. In the last decade the jail has become electronic, with the development and use of devices that oblige the wearer to remain at home. Certain liberal and libertarian critics have issued dire warnings about these devices, variously called "tags" or "electronic handcuffs." The worry is that an authoritarian government might abuse them. The use or not of devices is, of course, no defense against authoritarian government, and perhaps some comfort will be taken from the absence so far of reports of dissident professors being electronically handcuffed to their homes. Far from being a sinister development, these devices, though not without problems, have saved both expense and hardship in the case of the limited group of offenders on whom they can be used (people with a minimum level of maturity, telephones, and homes).

In the United States, but not in England, a commercial bail-bonding industry developed. This is also based on risk assessment, but by a profit-making concern rather than a probation officer or other official. Once bail is set, a person unable to deposit the whole amount with the court can apply to a bail-bonding agency, which, for a fee of 10 percent of the total bail, will pledge the full sum required by the court. Should the client abscond, the bonder forfeits bail, and the 10 percent fee is payment for assuming that risk. The courts are happy to accept such guarantees, which allow people to be at large who otherwise would have to be in custody, and the bonder has a considerable inducement realistically to assess risk and to pursue and return to the court any bonded fugitives.

It is difficult to account for the nondevelopment of the bail-bonding industry in England. In at least one English jail, until the nineteenth century, it was possible for a debtor to pay the jailer for the privilege of being at large within a certain area adjacent to the jail. The fee was justified on the basis that a bailiff had to accompany the debtor outside the jail. Even more to the point, common law provided that the jailer was liable for the debts of an escaped debtor, and so it was argued that the jailer who charged a debtor to go outside the jail was charging for the extra risk he assumed.

But despite this precedent for payment to assume risk, commercial bail bonding failed to develop in England. A number of differences in the administration of the two countries are suggestive but not conclusive explanations. The multiple jurisdictions of the United States and the consequent problems of retrieving a fugitive may constitute one reason American law-enforcement agencies prefer to permit a commercial concern to assume that risk and inconvenience, and clearly there is a strong demand for the service from accused and indicted people. The rise of strong central government in Britain during the nineteenth century, and the concomitant extinction of most user fees as a method of financing public services, may be another consideration. In this, as in several other matters, the United States long remained more faithful to the common-law tradition than its administrative parent. Over the last twenty years or so the bail bondsman has, however, lost much of his trade because of court-administered bail-bonding schemes, which are thought to be fairer and less scandal-prone.

The Jail, the Workhouse, and the House of Correction

For some centuries the jail competed with other institutions for the pauper. English laws against able-bodied beggars go back at least as far as the Ordinance of Labourers of 1349, which sought to counter some of the economic devastation and social upheaval that followed the Black Death. The vagabond was for many reasons deemed to be a particularly dangerous threat to social harmony and stability. He could but would not work. When he wandered the country alone he was a seductive example to those bent to the discipline of labor; traveling with companions, he threatened the peace. Whipping, branding, mutilation, and even hanging were used to suppress the menace, but all in fits and starts. The dissolution of the monasteries and the sixteenth-century wave of agricultural enclosures swept a great number of people from the land and a way of life and added to fears that a tide of vagabonds was lapping at the piles of society. Henry VIII and his successors—notably Elizabeth I—brought in various remedial and conservative laws. In essence these provided upkeep for the deserving poor, work for those who were unemployed, and punishment for those who could but would not work. The house of correction and the poorhouse thus rapidly became rivals of the jail.

The common view of the unworthy poor and the petty criminal may best be seen in the catalog of such types in Elizabeth's first Poor Law of 1572. All were defined as "vagabonds." They included proctors and procurators and people who conducted "Subtyll craftye unlawful Games," those pretending to have knowledge of "Phisnmye, Palmestrye, and other abused Scyences," landless and masterless people who could not account for the means by which they earned their livelihood, entertainers such as "fencers, Bearwardes; Common Players in Enterludes and minstrels" who were not attached to a nobleman, wanderers without a magistrate's license, "Juglars, Pedlars, Tynkers and Petye Chapmen" as well as shipmen and liberated prisoners. Laborers who refused to work for customary wages were included in this roster of petty criminality, as were the manufacturers of counterfeit passes, which were necessary for the poor to move around the country. Finally, there were those scholars of Oxford and Cambridge who did not possess a license from their chancellor or vice-chancellor. A great ragbag of the suspicious, disreputable, and idle.

Work was prescribed for all these drones. Used as deterrents to continued idleness were various corporal punishments: whipping and ear-boring for a first offense; involuntary service for the second; and hanging for a third. For those who were not vagabonds but who were without work, Elizabeth's act of 1575 provided that work should be provided and that every county was to establish a house of correction for those who refused to do this work. These houses of correction were modeled after London's Bridewell, which, as has been mentioned, was a type of reformatory prison for vagabonds, petty offenders, and orphans. Penal labor, trade-training, and a generous recourse to the whip were the principal elements in the regime. These measures were consolidated and extended by acts in 1597. Thereafter the relief of the poor and the policing of the petty criminal remained closely associated tasks of the magistracy and a triumvirate of institutions—jail, workhouse, and house of correction.

An overlapping clientele did not mean that assignment to one of the three was completely random, but there was a degree of chance. How did one decide that someone was willfully idle as distinct from unfortunate, inept at an assigned workhouse task, or unwilling to work? The overlap and a reluctance of the counties to provide proper funding resulted in the gradual assimilation of the house of correction into the jail. There was an attempted revival at the end of the eighteenth century, but by then most houses of correction were simply wings of the jail, used for the punishment of misdemeanants and usually sharing the same keeper. Some legal distinctions remained, the most important being that the house of correction could not be used for the confinement of debtors or condemned felons. But the distinctions were maintained by doors and a few feet of corridor rather than separate institutions, philosophies, and administrations. In contemporary documents one occasionally finds references to the "sheriff's side" (the jail part of the hybrid) or the "magistrates' side" (the house of correction portion). In 1865, legislation amalgamated the houses of correction and jails in England. Strictly speaking, after that date England no longer had jails but only the assimilated jail and house of correction, which ought more properly to be known by the generic "prison."

There was a late challenge from the jail's other rival, the workhouse. The Elizabethan Poor Law had been intended to give stability to an unsettled agrarian society. By the nineteenth century the doles and subsidies of the old Poor Law were seen as impediments to that freedom of movement of labor—or, as some would see it, the subjugation of labor to market forces that was deemed essential for the prosperity of a country ever more entranced by the enormous possibilities of the first industrial revolution. Political economists such as Jeremy Bentham and his disciple Edwin Chadwick argued for a much more stringent administration of poor relief. This would have the effect, they contended, of forcing labor onto the market at its true and unsubsidized price. In the long term, the country would benefit from increased productivity; in the short term, the laboring classes would live a life of declining hardship rather than dole-supported underemployment and indolence. By the Poor Law Amendment Act of 1834, workhouses were set up throughout the country, financed by a local poor-rate. The workhouses served groups or unions of parishes, about six hundred in all. (The terms *workhouse* and *union* thereafter cast a shadow over English working-class life, a shadow that has only now faded from memory.)

The problem with the deterrent workhouse—and they were self-consciously, relentlessly, and minutely deterrent—was that jails had to be even more deterrent. If workhouse food was reduced to minimum levels and deliberately made unpalatable, if a shameful pauper's uniform was provided and hard penal labor enforced, if "casuals" (the itinerant poor) were obliged to sleep on boards—how much more severe would it be necessary to make the discipline of the jail? And unless the jail was more deterrent, the vagabond might decide to take his lodgings there, instead of the workhouse, by the simple expedient of committing some audacious petty offense (the jail being the one public institution that cannot keep out someone who is determined to enter). There also had to be somewhere to send those who misbehaved in the workhouse, and unless jail conditions were more severe, what threat could be held over the rebellious pauper? Yet if science and official determination had reduced the workhouse diet to the minimum that would support life, how could the jails go further? And since the shame of being a workhouse inmate was so great, what margin of shame was left for the jailbird?

This conundrum, which arose entirely from the simplistic psychology of the utilitarians, principally Bentham and Chadwick, was never resolved. Into the twentieth century, governors of English local prisons (that is, prisons that by then were performing jail functions) and keepers of workhouses sniped at each other over matters of diet and discipline. If workhouse conditions were less stringent, argued the governors, there would be fewer instances of paupers breaking equipment or destroying their clothes (two favorite offenses) in order to be removed to jail. But if incarceration really punished, countered poor law administrators, and governors ceased fattening up criminals, then the paupers' calculations would be different, and they would submit to the discipline of the workhouse and the labor market.

More generous social policy, which began just before World War I, and new ideas about the social dimensions of citizenship, together with higher standards of living among the poor, combined to make these debates moot. State-provided old-age pensions did much to eliminate one large group of the poor. There was an increasing recognition of the effects of the trade cycle, and classic political economy (on which the workhouse had been based) had to acknowledge that unemployment was frequently not a matter of character and choice. Surveys showed that dire poverty could be experienced even by those in full-time employment. The workhouse became an asylum for the elderly and sick and lost much of its deterrent function. Workhouse infirmaries treated the paupers as patients rather than social criminals. Social policy again allowed for "outdoor relief" (doles and allowances, as distinct from institutionalization), which the political economists of early capitalism had pronounced anathema.

Yet, for all its unpleasant deterrence and moral tyrannizing, institutionalization had provided control, support, and asylum for the lower strata of society—those who teetered among unemployability, homelessness, acute material deprivation, personal inadequacies and hardships, sickness, insanity, and petty wrongdoing. Most, but not all, of this pitiful residue was swept up by the welfare provisions of the post-1945 period in Britain and by developments that had similar effects in the United States. Yet political, economic, and administrative changes, as well as developments in psychiatry, have again raised a tide of vagabonds and swept them into the indispensable jail. Asylums are no longer available for the mildly mentally ill or social inadequates. A belief that welfare support is a path to integration for the marginal has been replaced by a concern that state support all too frequently is a cause of indolence and dependence. Albeit in modern terminology, antiwelfare arguments uncannily echo the sentiments of Bentham and his nineteenth-century followers, contending that human action can be understood merely as pleasure-seeking and pain-avoidance and that the task of public administration is to compute the optimum application of both. Coercion, condemnation, and control of the pauper (the poor who seek public support) are again fashionable. The answers to complicated economic and social problems are sought in simple formulas. The terms *pauper* and *vagabond* have been abandoned, replaced by *welfare dependant* and *petty persistent offender*, as social and penal policymakers, administrators, and philanthropists try to deal with this group.

But whatever it is called, this body of the homeless and unconnected will be difficult to handle. It has nothing to lose and nowhere to go; it has nothing and wants nothing and is therefore immune from penal threat; it lives only in the present and is largely indifferent to any but immediate inducement. Although on any given day these modern vagabonds compose only a small percentage of the total population of the jails, their frequent recommittal makes them a significant drain and a major management problem. Workless, homeless, and hopeless, addicted to alcohol and drugs, prey to various mental and physical ills—here again is a group of nuisances that, in the last decades of the twentieth century, some politicians and administrators have concluded may be ethically and economically dealt with by means of criminal rather than social policy.

The Mentally Ill

The trend toward using the jail as a substitute mental hospital has been reinforced by changes in mental health policy. The marked decline since the 1960s in the use of mental hospitals as asylums and the greater reliance on medication to treat the mentally ill doubtless have arguments in their favor. Too many lives were unnecessarily lived out in the shade of the asylum. But one consequence of this development has been to feed the mentally ill into the jails.

They have always gone there, of course. Two acts of Parliament in 1845 ensured that by the 1850s all English counties had lunatic asylums, locally financed and managed, overseen and inspected by central government's Lunacy Commission. It would be foolish to take at face value statistics that showed an apparent subsequent decline in jail committals of lunatics or imbeciles. Prison medical services, obsessed with malingering, have always been more at ease in dealing with bodily rather than mental illness. Even today such are the uncertainties of diagnosis that few reliable estimates can be obtained for the proportion of the mentally ill among prisoners, but the numbers are probably substantial. (A 1991 English study concluded that 37 percent of males and 56 percent of females serving sentences of more than six months were suffering from a medically identifiable mental disorder.)

In the nineteenth century, statistics were further distorted because one authority was financially responsible for the care of the mentally ill and another for criminals. For example, when local authorities had to support the institutionalized insane in England in the 1890s, magistrates, acting in what they saw as the local interest, seem frequently to have committed to the jails (by then controlled by central government) people whom they thought might be mentally ill. Central government met the costs of diagnosis and, if insanity was confirmed, committed the patient to the county asylum at central government expense. If insanity was not confirmed, well and good. From the local authority's perspective the problem was satisfactorily solved either way. This shell game continues in some jurisdictions today.

JAILS AS CINDERELLA INSTITUTIONS

In England

English municipalities and counties had been jail-holders for more than seven hundred years when, in 1876, it was decided to bring them under central government administration. This step was decided almost entirely for party political reasons. A great reduction in taxes was promised by Tory leader Benjamin Disraeli in what was to be his last election campaign. To those who argued that shifting jail costs from local to national taxpayers was an illusionary savings, the response was that a unitary administration would be able to close the smaller jails, combine their populations, and thereby cut overhead costs and generally rationalize the system. These calculations were based on erroneous, misleading, and superficial assumptions, and the savings never materialized. The jails, however, fell under the control of central government, whose administrator, Sir Edmund Du Cane, determined to make them uniformly deterrent. That story is told elsewhere in this book, but it needs to be noted here that from this time England, unlike the United States, no longer had locally operated jails. It was not that jails ceased to exist but simply that their form of administration had been changed. Within a generation, one central government department was running the jails (known as remand prisons or local prisons) and another the convict prisons (for long-term prisoners). Although unitary and central control meant that standards could more easily be brought to a certain level, it did not mean that this level was a particularly desirable one.

A major consequence of nationalization (as central government's takeover came to be called) was that uniformity in punishment—which had been put forward as an additional reason for the takeover—became an administrative fetish. It also meant that the jails were totally cut off from the magistracy, which had been their principal source of experiment and innovation. Jails could no longer be adapted to the requirements and resources of a community but instead were managed in accordance with the views of a very small group of senior government officers. Inertia fell like a curtain. And since central government's reputation was invested in the new administration, the jails became obsessively secret as civil servants sought to guard against political embarrassment. The protective curtain was penetrated by an occasional journalistic exposé, coroner's inquiry, or book of memoirs, but these merely heightened official defensiveness.

It has not been until very recent years that the near paranoia of British officialdom has been replaced by a qualified willingness to allow academics, journalists, and television cameras behind the walls. Political directives have gone so far as to arrange open days, during which events are staged and the public is admitted. The spectacle of relatively free public access—albeit annual and necessarily carefully regulated—has a certain historical resonance, recalling Charles Dickens's Marshalsea and the customs and practices of previous centuries. It is certainly to be welcomed in the interests of public education and official accountability.

As noted, the term *jail* has continued to be applied colloquially to the centralized system of local prisons that operated in England after 1877, even though government preferred the term *local prison*. At the time central government took control of the jails, it was operating its own system of convict prisons. The longest, and rarely imposed, jail (local prison) sentence was two years, whereas the minimum convict sentence was three years. (In the United States the jail cutoff point is usually one year: any longer sentence will send the offender to state prison.) Sir Edmund Du Cane, appointed to run the newly acquired local prisons for central government, had come into prison work as a soldier seconded to manage the convict system. Administering convict and local prisons in tandem, he naturally stuck to his own tested ways of doing things and gave preference to trusted convict prison staff, whom he appoin- ted to senior positions in the local prisons. Blatantly, but largely unchallenged, convict prisons were accorded more standing, and their staff continued to be paid more and to enjoy better working conditions, even though both types of prison were under the same central control.

Although an integrated system of prison staffing and management eventually emerged, it occurred after Sir Edmund Du Cane's departure from the scene. Even then various distinctions, necessary and unnecessary, were drawn between convict prisons (which, in a trope characteristic of modern officialdom, came to be called training prisons) and local prisons. Local prisons have remained the poor relatives, with inferior conditions and premises. This is a very curious inversion of what equity and common sense might indicate, since a substantial portion of their inmates are pretrial detainees, who are legally innocent yet who are obliged to endure premises that are vastly inferior to those provided for convicted criminals and conditions of confinement that are all too frequently uncivilized.

Equally curious is the continued political and official toleration of these disparities, for which it is hard to find any functional basis. In Sir Edmund Du Cane's day, convict prisons undoubtedly had custody of some wicked and dangerous criminals, but local prisons handled the bulk of the country's prison business. In 1877, when there were just over 20,000 persons in English local prisons, convict prisons held half that number. But that gives only part of the picture. There were more than 187,000 committals to local prisons in that year, whereas the equivalent figure for the convict prisons was only 1 percent of that, or some 1,900 committals (including license revocations).

And although security was undoubtedly a central task in convict prisons, probably only a minority of convicts were grave risks. Convict prisons took prisoners already sorted and classified, medically examined, deloused, and reasonably decent and clean. Over the years that they were held, the risks posed by individual prisoners could be assessed. Jails, on the other hand, received people directly from the streets or the police lockup, in a great variety of conditions—emotional, mental, physical, and hygienic—of all ages and degrees of criminal experience, having committed or at least having been accused of committing every kind of crime, from petty theft to murder. Because of the stressful conditions under which they were received, and since so many of them were unknown qualities, these seemingly minor offenders all had to receive maximum-security treatment. In the big cities this was compounded by an enormous daily turnover, since in the late nineteenth century the average stay per committal was only about ten days. Control of this daunting stage army was undoubtedly more demanding than management of the supposedly more hardened inmates of the convict prison. Yet the latter continued, on some topsy-turvy scale, to be more prestigious. One can understand this in criminals' inverted rankings. But the reasoning of the official who saw himself as achieving the success of his career when he was promoted into a convict prison is more difficult to follow, until one recognizes that the supposed wickedness of his captives is the measure of a prison manager's status, rather than the difficulty of his task. Official status rankings thus mimic those of the underworld. Propinquity results in some odd transferences.

Transference cannot (or so one hopes) be offered as an explanation of scholarly indifference toward the jail. Of several academic studies in penal history, only one or two have dealt with jails, and by far the most acclaimed have in recent times concentrated on convict policy in England and state imprisonment in the United States. Yet in terms of the amount of punishment doled out by the state, convict prisons and their American equivalents were relatively insignificant. It has been the jails, not the convict prisons, that have most touched the lives of the rough and poor. Could it be that, like the officials, politicians, and reformers they study, most scholars attach a higher significance to the experiences of a minority of "serious" prisoners than to the conditions and consequences of a system of mass punishment?

In the United States

Ignorance of or indifference toward the jail is as evident in the United States as in England. The structure of public administration in the United States, especially the jealous preservation of local powers, expresses basic antigovernment concerns of eighteenth-century Whig thought, which was the principal source of the country's constitutional arrangements. The pattern of penal administration inherited from colonial government, and developed within a federal structure of power, led to an enormous proliferation of local authorities and therefore of jails. As in England, they were municipality- and county-based and were well established long before the states dipped their toes in the water of penal administration.

At the national level this administrative caution was even more pronounced. The federal government at first contracted with states and counties to lodge the limited number of prisoners produced by federal courts. This population increased, rising in 1895 to some twenty-five hundred federal prisoners in state prisons and fifteen thousand in local jails. States became less inclined to act as underpaid hosts, and in 1895 the first federal prison for civilians opened at Fort Leavenworth. Thenceforward there were to be three levels of penal administration in the United States—local, state, and federal. Although there was reasonably good information about the last two, little systematic information was collected about the jails. The total jail population, annual committals, and even the number of jails in the country were unknown until well into the twentieth century. Elementary judicial, social, and demographic information has only recently become available, although there remain many gaps in our knowledge of the national jail picture. In part, this has reflected the restricted role and truncated apparatus of the federal government, which generally impedes the collection of national information about local administration and often gives it a low priority; and in part this lack of knowledge results from the extraordinary and expanding dimensions of local government. The first national survey of American jails was not published until 1931, and the survey method is used even today. Periodic jail censuses started only in 1978 and are now conducted every five years.

Although there were American penal reformers who claimed to follow the example of John Howard, none were prepared or able to cover the United States in the way that Howard surveyed the jails, houses of correction, and prisons of the United Kingdom and parts of continental Europe. A vast and continually expanding territory and the difficulties and dangers of frontier life probably made such an enterprise impossible. Historical uncertainty about the basic statistics is therefore compounded by our ignorance about jail conditions. That there were some appalling jails is clear, but we would be on very uncertain ground if we asserted that all were in a similar state. In the early days of the new nation there were jails that the historian John McMaster, looking back a century from the 1880s, claimed "would now be thought unfit places of habitation for the vilest and most loathsome of beasts." He mentioned two Massachusetts jails. In the jail at Northampton, cells barely four feet high were filled with gases from the sewers that were supposed to ventilate them. Worcester's jail had cells of a similar height—and without window, chimney, or even a hole in the wall for light. And such institutions survived into the next generation. The District of Columbia jail in the 1820s, described as "the foulest prison in the United States," consisted of sixteen cells built over a sewer; convicted, unconvicted, and even witnesses, up to eighty in number, were confined in the cells.

McMaster was writing for a generation that took pride in its investments in a vast range of penitentiaries, reformatories, asylums, and houses of correction and of refuge and that, in most states, had installed in these places emblems and instruments of progress and humanity such as infirmaries, workshops, and libraries. It was understandable that, with evidence of material progress all around him, he should regard the conditions of the young republic as having vanished completely. He certainly did not have information to persuade him otherwise. But around the time of McMaster's self-satisfied retrospective, Eugene Debs, the socialist and labor organizer, experienced his first incarceration, in Cook County Jail. There he found cells so infested with insects that the prisoners were bloody from scratching. It was impossible, indeed, to find a place on the floor that was not covered with vermin. The jail was also home to large and vicious rats, of such a size that a guard's fox terrier beat a retreat when confronted by them. Debs may have been given to the agitator's exaggeration, but his reliability is enhanced by the fact that when he later served time at other jails and prisons, he did not hesitate to commend humane conditions, treatment, and staff.

In truth, there has never been a "golden age" in America's prisons and jails. As befits a young and idealistic nation there have been some notable and well-scripted experiments and even some successes in promoting humane and nonharmful conditions of confinement. But for one generation after another, the overcrowding, underfunding, and brutality of the jails have been an inescapable part of the American experience. It is a telling comment on official and scholarly priorities that a major responsibility of public administration and of national life should have received such disproportionately small attention.

The forces of state legislation and inspection and, since the 1970s, a willingness of the federal courts to involve themselves in prison and jail matters have undoubtedly brought about improvements in organization and conditions. As late as 1931, for example, Hastings Hart's jail survey showed that in small rural jails there was little provision for the separation of men from women, juveniles from adults, or the convicted from those awaiting trial. These conditions have largely been corrected, although the continuing success of numerous suits alleging violation of federal law regarding overcrowding, treatment, security, physical conditions, and essential services shows substantial continuing problems. In 1988 one-eighth of American jails were under court order to limit their populations or to improve conditions.

Another consequence of greater federal and state intervention in jail administration has been a continuing trend in jail closures. This has also been encouraged by the movement of population out of many rural counties and small towns as the U.S. economic and social structures change. In a move reminiscent of England in the nineteenth century, many localities have met their jail responsibilities by contracting with a neighboring authority rather than maintaining their own operations. In 1970 there were 4,037 jails in the United States. Numbers fell to 3,316 in 1988 and to 3,304 in 1993. Small jails were particularly prone to closure. The rated capacity (i.e., the officially determined population limits) of jails holding fewer than fifty prisoners fell by 28 percent between 1978 and 1988 and by 45 percent between 1988 and 1993. Problems remain with these small institutions, particularly questions about their economic viability. Yet they continue to be the predominant type of institution. Almost 70 percent of American jails in 1988 had average daily populations of less than fifty; by 1993 this was true of only 57 percent.

JAILS AND THE COURTS

Both Britain and the United States have experienced a considerable growth in prison and jail populations from the mid-1970s to the mid-1990s. Insufficient investment has meant overcrowding and a deterioration of conditions and basic services. In Britain, the principal response to these problems has been administrative. Lobbyists, politicians, and the mass media have exerted pressures, and government has responded to the extent it thinks fit. In the absence of a written constitution, the courts play a very limited role in overseeing the actions of British government. But since the United Kingdom gave its citizens the right of individual petition to the European Court at Strasbourg, under the European Convention on Human Rights, several cases on prison conditions have been heard, decisions critical of the British government have been handed down, and changes in various aspects of administration have been made. The European Court's overall impact on imprisonment (including jailing) has not, however, been great.

In the United States, the developments have been very different. With a written constitution and relatively straightforward means for evoking its protection, thousands of suits have successfully been brought to oblige federal, state, and local authorities to comply with their constitutional obligations. Mirroring the curiously low institutional status of jails, it has been prisons rather than jails that have attracted most of this legal and philanthropic attention. The most experienced and successful prison litigation group in the United States is the American Civil Liberties Union Prison Project. This was established in 1972, but it was not until 1983 that its Jail Project was set up. It would perhaps be futile to argue that the needs of either the prisons or the jails should have precedence, but the sheer volume of business conducted by the jails and the truly appalling conditions in some of them make their cause as pressing as that of the prisons.

Perhaps an element in the judgment of the litigators who must allocate finite resources is that individuals spend much less time in jails than in prisons and that therefore the damage of unconstitutional conditions is less. This is a questionable conclusion. The number of committals to jails (10 million in 1990, as compared with about 320,000 committals to prison) makes jail conditions a prime issue. But there are other considerations. A person attacked in jail, or so disoriented through disorderly and unsafe conditions that he cannot prepare an adequate defense, suffers lifelong consequences as surely as if he had spent several years in prison.

Remedies possibly granted by the court that finds a violation of constitutional rights range from directions to correct a specific condition to a complete takeover of the jail or even of an entire jail system. Orders commonly touch on crowding, food, clothing, medical care, security, and the physical state of the jail. When multiple unconstitutional conditions have been found, and the court is convinced that administrators cannot or will not remedy them, a takeover may be ordered. This is always intended to be a temporary solution (although such direct control may last for several months or even years), and when constitutional conditions have been established the court bows out. Court-appointed experts administer the jail during the period of the takeover and may subsequently monitor for the court conditions and for compliance with directions.

Sometimes jail administrators have been tacit supporters of court intervention, since the jail problems have resulted from political neglect or miscalculation and the courts are seen as the only means of providing funds for what is an electorally unpopular cause. At other times administrators—perhaps acting on political instructions, overt or by nod and wink—may obstruct or seek to evade court orders. At one large city jail, a population limitation cap was imposed by the court, which subsequently discovered that "surplus" inmates were being kept in school buses outside the jail until the evening count was completed. The results of this childish but effective ruse were that the authorities were able surreptitiously to breach the court order—but only for a time.

The courts cannot be a substitute for responsible executive government. They are not equipped for administration. Legal action takes time, problems are often urgent, circumstances may change rapidly, and the costs of litigation and of the appointment of experts are always high. And sometimes, of course, the court will come to an ill-advised decision. It can safely be said, nevertheless, that in decades during which the number of arrests, political and popular despair about crime, and fiscal retrenchment have increased, only the courts could defend minimal jail standards in many jurisdictions. There are neither votes nor party preference in providing decent conditions for prisoners or even in promising to meet the obligations imposed by the U.S. Constitution (though apparently much political advantage lies in vows to increase the incarceration rate), and so the judiciary has had to be the civilized conscience of the nation.

Of the 683 largest jail jurisdictions in the United States (those with an average daily population of more than one hundred) in 1993, 135 were under court order to limit crowding. In the early 1990s Cook County Jail, the world's largest single-site jail, was chronically overcrowded and under federal court order, as were many other large jails. Considering that many of the smaller jurisdictions escape legal action because litigators prefer to direct their efforts to places where a large number of people are confined, or because rural remoteness protects the smaller jails, it can be seen that a large and important number of U.S. jails have been found to be in violation of the constitution, or are in violation and have not yet become the subject of litigation.

THE OBTRUSIVE AND INDESTRUCTIBLE JAIL

Who goes to jail also remains a worrisome issue. In 1946 it was found that there were some 40,000 children in America's jails. Federal legislation in 1974 required most juveniles to be completely separated from adults (the exception being those who were to be tried as adults), and a 1980 amendment required the removal from jails of all juveniles who were not there to be tried as adults. Children remain in jails, therefore, and in significant numbers. The average daily population of juveniles in American jails for the year ending in June 1990 was more than 2,000.

The jail experience in the United States is much more widespread than in Britain and appears to be growing. The average daily population of the American jails in 1978 was just under 158,000. By 1990 it was estimated to be more than 405,000. Given the rate of turnover in the jails, however, it can be seen that jails touch the lives of a very large number of Americans. In 1989–90 there were approximately *10 million* receptions into American jails. And although there is a stage army that winds its way through the jail year after year, there are many who go only once or twice to jail. Even allowing for a proportion of readmissions, this is a vast number. Add family members, whose lives are touched by the jailing of a relative or partner, and one realizes that the jail intrudes significantly into national life. A rough estimation suggests that over a ten-year period perhaps one-fifth of the U.S. population directly experiences jail, with a much larger segment indirectly involved through the jailing of a friend or family member. Indeed, with these figures, in some communities it is unusual for someone *not* to have been in jail.

Jailing and imprisonment on such a large scale must necessarily affect national attitudes. Generally speaking, Americans seem much more prepared than Europeans to forgive a jailing. Perhaps because there is a tendency to regard all politicians as rascals, a jailing does not break political careers, as it almost universally would in Europe. This is possibly a consequence of the more fluid American social structure, but it surely also has to do with the prevalence of imprisonment and jailing. The 1993 U.S. jailing rate was 188 per 100,000, and the imprisonment rate was 351 per 100,000, giving a combined incarceration rate of 539 per 100,000. (The jailing rate is lower because, despite the high jail committal rate, time spent in jail is only a fraction of that spent in prison; in consequence, on any given day, the prison population is about twice that of the jails.) By contrast, England and Wales (which probably have the highest incarceration rate in Europe), in the latest figures available, show a combined incarceration rate of 97 per

100,000. Another consideration in the United States is possibly that the institutional distinction between the jail and the prison has been much more rigidly maintained than in Britain. Time in jail may more easily be seen as indicating less culpability than a spell of imprisonment. Because jails and prisons have been amalgamated in England, such a judgment would not be possible there.

Possibly as a result of this obtrusiveness, determined opponents of the jail have made many nobly motivated attempts to dispense with or greatly restrict its services. Jails have had offspring, supposedly more humane and scientific and intended to replace the anachronistic and atavistic parent. Alternatives have proliferated, from reformatories to probation to the electronic handcuff and house arrest. Some of these ventures have been failures, producing more tyranny and suffering than the jails they were intended to replace. Others have been reasonably successful, assisting both in rehabilitation and in keeping offenders out of custody. There have been valid criticisms that these alternatives often dealt with those who would not in any case have been jailed. Yet without such innovations, historically high jail populations would probably be greater still.

And in all of this the paradox remains. More than in ancient Greece or Rome or China, more than in Tzarist Russia or Anglo-Saxon England or medieval England, the jail flourishes in the United States and Great Britain today. As our economies produce abundance, wealth, power, and convenience, the jail endures. As our culture refines and exalts sensibilities, as we seek enlightenment as nations and individuals, rituals and relationships that were thought by our ancestors to be passing barbarism continue in our midst. More than ever, the jail is indispensable to the way we live. An institutional talisman, it forever reminds us of our imperfections, our unmalleability and unfitness for this, and perhaps any other, brave new world. We fear it, and it shames us, but may we not also draw a curious encouragement from its persistence?

Bibliographic Note

There are numerous histories of imprisonment, but not many deal exclusively with the jail. An exception, and an essential starting point for a study of the Anglo-American jail, is Ralph Pugh's *Imprisonment in Medieval England* (London: Cambridge University Press, 1968). Sidney Webb and Beatrice Webb's *English Prisons under Local Government* (London: Longmans, Green, 1922; reprint, London: Cass, 1963) deals mainly with the late eighteenth and the nineteenth centuries. My own *History of English Prison Administration* (London: Routledge and Kegan Paul, 1981) spans the two periods; the second volume, *English Local Prisons 1860–1900: Next Only to Death* (London and New York, Routledge, 1994), deals exclusively with jails. There is still no satisfactory detailed history of jails in the early modern period. Two accounts of the Elizabethan demimonde fill some of the gaps: Gamini Salgado's *The Elizabethan Underworld* (London: J. M. Dent, 1977) and A. V. Judge's *The Elizabethan Underworld* (New York: E.P. Dutton, 1930; reprint, London: Routledge and Kegan Paul, 1965).

Some eighteenth- and early-nineteenth-century jail surveys are available as reprints or through libraries. Preeminent among them is John Howard's *The State of the Prisons in England and Wales*, 3d ed. (Warrington: Privately published, 1784); I prefer this edition or the fourth edition, published in 1792. James Neild followed Howard's example a generation later, and in 1812 he produced *The State of the Prisons in England, Scotland, and Wales* (London: Privately published, 1812). Much less famous than either of these is the work of Dr. William Smith, who published *State of the Gaols in London, Westminister, and Borough of Southwark* (London: Privately published, 1776).

It is more difficult to get an overview of the history of the jail in America because of the proliferation of local authorities and the sheer size of such a project. David Rothman's much acclaimed books *The Discovery of the Asylum: Social Order and Disorder in the New Republic* (Boston: Little, Brown, 1971) and *Conscience and Convenience: The Asylum and Its Alternatives in Progressive America* (Boston: Little, Brown, 1980) analyze American penal and social policy from colonial to comparatively recent times. The focus is beyond the jail, however, concentrating on reformatory institutions and measures. Two nineteenth-century studies that are still reasonably accessible through libraries should provide useful starting points for more specialized reading. The descriptions of jails and punishment in John Bach McMaster's *History of the People of the United States*, 8 vols. (New York: D. Appleton and Co., 1885–1937) have the advantage of having been collected from a great variety of sources and the drawback of being largely unrelated to broader developments in jurisprudence and public administration. Condensed versions of this monumental work are currently available. The survey conducted by Enoch C. Wines and Theodore W. Dwight, *Report on the Prisons and Reformatories of the United States and Canada* (Albany: Van Benthuysen, 1867), gives an excellent sense of the hopes and illusions of the times, although the authors, like Rothman, look over the shoulder of the jail to its reformatory offspring.

There is a paucity of recent work. Ronald Goldfarb's account of modern jails, *Jails: The Ultimate Ghetto* (Garden City, N.Y.: Anchor Press, 1975), is written with passion and to high standards. The first two chapters bring together much material of historical interest. Goldfarb's critique of the American bail system is provocatively entitled *Ransom* (New York: Harper and Row, 1965) and is also stimulating reading. John Irwin's *The Jail: Managing the Underclass in American Society* (Berkeley: University of California Press, 1985) is also a provocative read, for those who seek an introduction to the contemporary American jail. Hans W. Mattick was another member of the small band of scholars with an interest in the jail. He wrote mainly about Illinois jails but drew broader conclusions. His *Selected Bibliography on the American Jail* (Chicago: University of Chicago, Center for Studies in Criminal Justice, 1972) is of course dated but remains an excellent starting point for further studies. Peter J. Coleman's *Debtors and Creditors in America: Insolvency, Imprisonment for Debt, and Bankruptcy, 1607–1900* (Madison: State Historical Society of Wisconsin, 1974) is a very helpful introduction to the use of the jail for civil prisoners in America. Such limited jail statistics as are available at the national level are collected and published by the U.S. government's Bureau of Justice Statistics, in Washington, D.C.

When one turns from general surveys and accounts to the histories of particular jails and prisons, titles become more prolific, and local history journals and societies will nearly always produce something of interest. There have been too many such histories of English jails to list here. Fifty years ago, Margery Bassett published two excellent pioneering articles: "Newgate Prison in the Middle Ages," *Speculum* 18 (1943), and "The Fleet Prison in the Middle Ages," *University of Toronto Law Journal* 5, no. 2 (1944). Henry Mayhew and John Binny compiled (but never completed) a large and very well-illustrated account of the jails of 1850s London: *The Criminal Prisons of London and Scenes of London Life* (1862; reprint, London: Frank Cass, 1968). "The Clink" gave its name as slang for jails in general, and its history is given in E. J. Burford's *In the Clink* (London: New English Library, 1977). The jail immortalized by Oscar Wilde is given a history in Peter Southerton's *The Story of a Prison* (Reading: Osprey, 1975), and the jail associated with another literary figure (John Bunyan) is the subject of Eric Stockdale's *A Study of Bedford Prison, 1660–1877* (London: Phillimore, 1977). Those who would like to pursue Dickens's connection with jails must start with Philip Collins's *Dickens and Crime* (London: Macmillan, 1962).

Given the dearth of nationally published material, the most likely sources on individual American jails are probably state, regional, and local history journals and societies. Socialist organizer and labor agitator Eugene Debs recollects jail and prison experiences over a turbulent thirty-year period in his 1927 *Walls and Bars* (reprint, Chicago: Charles H. Kerr and Co., 1973). (For the sake of brevity and convenience, I have listed English jail and convict memoirs at the end of chapter 5.) Philadelphia, because of its place in the history of the American penitentiary, has received much attention. Negley K. Teeters's *The Cradle of the Penitentiary: The Walnut Street Jail at Philadelphia, 1773–1835* (Philadelphia: Philadelphia Prison Society, 1955) contains much that is interesting about the jail, as well as about the penitentiary it spawned. In the same manner, jail and penitentiary are dealt with in W. David Lewis's *From Newgate to Dannemora: The Rise of the Penitentiary in New York, 1796–1848* (Ithaca: Cornell University Press, 1965).

CHAPTER ELEVEN

Wayward Sisters

The Prison for Women

Lucia Zedner

Fear not! I do not exact vengeance for evil, but compel you to be good. My hand is stern, but my heart is kind.

Thus read the motto over the entrance to the first prison built for women: the Spinhuis, opened in 1645 in Amsterdam, Holland. The Spinhuis (so called because inmates were employed mainly in spinning for the Dutch textile industry) was a model institution admired far and wide. People traveled to Amsterdam specifically to visit this, "the biggest sight of the city." At first it held only poor, "disrespectful" women and girls, but within a few years it had established cells for women who could not "be kept to their duties by parents or husbands" and separate dormitories for prisoners, drunks, prostitutes, and "for those whipped in public."

Across Europe, houses of correction were set up on the Dutch model of incessant labor intended both to punish and to instill habits of discipline. Women prisoners were to be employed not only in supplying productive labor—as spinners, weavers, and sewers—but also in providing services to the prison community—as cooks, cleaners, and laundresses. Unhappily, in England, at least, the Protestant ethic of reformative, penal labor degenerated over the course of the following centuries. The governors of the London Bridewell, for example, ran their prison as a highly profitable brothel by persuading women inmates to provide sexual services. Those who would not prostitute themselves "voluntarily" were coerced by threats and beatings to join in this unorthodox form of prison employment.

The order, the systematic labor, and the segregation of the Dutch Spinhuis shone out against the dank, filthy disarray and corruption that overtook most early houses of correction. And as a separate prison for women, it remained virtually unique. Throughout Europe, women were generally housed within male prisons and often herded alongside men with little concern for the likely results. They were poorly supervised by day and often left completely to their own devices at night. Similarly, in prerevolutionary

America, city jails held "in one common herd . . ., by day and night, prisoners of all ages, colours, and sexes!"

The mass of petty offenders were held in local prisons. More serious offenders faced physical punishment or death. From the mid-seventeenth century until well into the nineteenth century, many were transported to the colonies on "convict ships." Although conditions on board these ships were appalling for both sexes, women particularly suffered because they were commonly assumed to be prostitutes. As such, they were considered fair game for the sexual attentions of sailors and fellow convicts alike. The plight of women on convict ships remained little changed until the 1820s, when the reformer Elizabeth Fry instituted a major campaign to improve conditions on board. Important changes included outlawing the use of leg irons on women, allowing children under seven to accompany their mothers, and not transporting nursing mothers until their babies were weaned.

Many women simply did not survive the journey; for those who did, conditions in the colonies were hard. For example, women arriving in New South Wales were sent to live and work in a "factory" set up at Parramatta in 1821. But Parramatta quickly came to be used as a sort of brothel and marriage mart by male convicts and settlers. Men came to the factory and made their choice, often after no more than a brief conversation. If selected, the woman had no option but to accept her "assignment" and move in with her new master. Even those fortunate enough to be assigned proper positions in domestic service fared badly. Often isolated, they had little protection from the male members of the household. Pregnancy meant immediate expulsion and a disgraced return to the factory.

Given the availability of women on such terms, there was little incentive for male settlers to marry them. The hope that women sent to the colonies would act as a moralizing influence over the rough masculine society of settlers and ex-convicts was quickly dispelled. As one disillusioned colonial official admitted, "The influence of female convicts is wholly valueless upon male convicts; women of depraved character do them no good whatsoever." Officials failed to recognize that the very nature of life within the colonies, and the huge imbalance of the sexes, made it all but impossible for even well-intentioned women to retain their "character."

For as long as women were banished to the harsh life of the colonies or dumped alongside men in local jails and houses of correction, there was little hope for reform. Only with the advent of separate prisons for women, opened across Europe and the United States in the first half of the nineteenth century, was there any prospect of protecting female offenders from further corruption and of instituting distinctive treatment that might actually lead to their reform. What prompted the establishment of these first prisons for women? Who decided what form they should take? And how far did they fulfill their supposed aims? An important theme must be how prisons for women compared with those for men. In what ways was the regime of the female prison distinctive? And in what ways did the character of the women, both warders and inmates, bring different qualities to life inside? This chapter will trace developments in prisons for women through the emergence of specialist institutions for women toward the end of the nineteenth century and into the twentieth. And it will conclude by observing the continuing impact of this historical legacy on prisons for women today.

DEVELOPMENTS LEADING TO THE SEPARATE WOMEN'S PRISONS

Women in Local Prisons

By the nineteenth century, the vast majority of women who committed petty offenses were sentenced to local prisons, mostly for only a few days, weeks, or months. Conditions inside varied enormously. Since these were run and financed at the local level, much depended on the generosity of local administrators and the honesty of individual jailers. Women formed only a small minority of the prison population. In the first half of the nineteenth century, in Britain about 20 percent, in France 14–20 percent, and in the United States as little as 4–19 percent of prisoners were women. They found themselves greatly outnumbered by male prisoners and often completely alone among the men. Even in the best-run jails, providing accommodation for women continued to be an afterthought, to be achieved with the least effort and expense.

Lack of concern, or worse, systematic exploitation meant that women often endured much poorer conditions than men convicted of similar offenses. In the United States men were provided with individual cells at a far earlier date than women. Across the East and the Midwest, accommodating women in prisons, whose architects had not foreseen their presence, often made for miserable conditions. At Albany Jail in New York, "Fifteen females were in one room with beds, so far as they had beds, on the floor." Even where women were provided with segregated accommodation within the male prison, they were often locked up with supposedly vulnerable male prisoners, such as lunatics or men who had given evidence against friends. In any case, wherever women were housed within the male prison, it was all but impossible to prevent communication. A governor of one English jail admitted, "I frequently detect communication going on by notes and otherwise, between the male and female prisoners, and often hear obscene conversation between them." If supervision was lax, prisoners were quick to exploit any possibility for getting together. The chaplain of Preston Jail, England, revealed: "I have known even females to climb over the chevaux-de-frise [a fence], which I should have thought utterly impossible, in order to get into the ward of the other sex." Prostitutes could continue to ply their busy trade inside the prison, but many girls and younger women faced appalling sexual exploitation by turnkeys and fellow prisoners alike. Prison pregnancies were a recurrent scandal.

The impetus behind setting up prisons for women in the early nineteenth century was, therefore, in large part disciplinary. The opening of a detached building for women at Wakefield Prison in England was hailed as a great success in this respect. "Women are found a great deal easier to manage when removed to a distance from the men. The spirit of reckless stubbornness and bravado dies within them when they know that they are out of sight, hearing, and notice of their fellows of the other sex." Apart from keeping order within the prison, segregation of the sexes also prevented the embarrassment of prison pregnancies, and it minimized corruption. Who was corrupting whom was a moot point, for it was not at all clear that women were necessarily always the victims of this association. The view that "female[s] are, as a class, even more morally degraded than men" meant that protecting men from the corrupting influences of female prisoners was considered as important as saving women from sexual assault.

Descriptions of criminal women by Victorian commentators are highly revealing of the moral context in which women's prisons were set up and their form and purpose established. The well-known English journalist and social investigator Henry Mayhew summed up a common view of criminal women when he declared: "In them one sees the most hideous picture of all human weakness and depravity—a picture the more striking because exhibiting the coarsest and rudest moral features in connection with a being whom we are apt to regard as the most graceful and gentle form of humanity."

This dualistic view of women had its roots in Christian imagery of the female as madonna and whore. The good woman was a moral exemplar, but the bad woman was even more depraved than any criminal man. As the directors of one London prison saw it, "The gentler sex, as a whole, are superior in virtue to the sterner sex; but when woman falls, she seems to possess a capacity almost beyond man, for running into all that is evil." All agreed that separating the sexes was the only possible way of creating an environment conducive to reform.

By the 1820s almost all French jails provided segregated daytime and nighttime accommodation for men and women. A law passed in 1828 in the United States required that all county prisons segregate male and female prisoners. In Britain, Sir Robert Peel's Gaol Act of 1823 required that women be held separately from men, that they be supervised only by women, and that no man be allowed to visit the female part of the prison unless accompanied by a female officer. Implementation of this legislation was somewhat haphazard. A few local prisons were set up specifically for women in England: at Wyndmondham in Cambridge and at Borough Comptor and Tothill Fields, both in London. But, for the most part, segregation meant little more than finding rooms or wards within the male prison to which women could be assigned.

The segregation of prisoners by sex was one of the major achievements of nineteenth-century penal reform. More than any other single aspect of reform, it rescued women from the degradation and exploitation of eighteenth-century prison life.

Elizabeth Fry and Prison Reform

Segregation was largely the result of energetic campaigning by a new breed of middle-class women who, in the early years of the nineteenth century, came to take an intense interest in the welfare of female prisoners. One of the earliest and most influential figures in shaping prison life for women on both sides of the Atlantic was Elizabeth Fry. A strict Quaker committed to religious and philanthropic work, she tirelessly campaigned to expose the plight of women in prison and to promote better conditions for them. Whereas prison reformers following the ideas of Jeremy Bentham stressed impersonal, disciplinary techniques of reform, Quakers such as Fry laid their trust in personal influence and the power of religion. Her interest was first aroused by the visit of a group of American Quakers to London in 1813. Entering the notorious London jail at Newgate, they were horrified to find "blaspheming, fighting, dram-drinking, half-naked women." Their report of this encounter prompted Elizabeth Fry to visit Newgate for herself some months later. Like her American precursors, she was shocked by the conditions of "riot, licentiousness, and filth" in which women prisoners were held. Gathering around her a number of other Quaker women, she began to campaign for the reform of both prison conditions and women prisoners themselves.

Combining missionary visits with energetic publicity, Fry quickly gained a high profile for her work. Her pioneering Ladies Association for the Reformation of Female Prisoners in Newgate was soon followed by the wider reaching British Ladies Society for the Reformation of Female Prisoners. Promotional travels throughout the British Isles during the 1820s and 1830s by Fry and her followers led to the formation of numerous ladies prison associations. Together these organizations put considerable energy into improving standards of accommodation, establishing special regimes for women, and promoting programs of moral treatment.

Fry's work for the reform of women's prisons became internationally renowned. In 1837 and 1838 she toured French prisons and was shocked by the exploitation of female inmates by male guards. The number of women who became pregnant while in prison indicated the frequency with which women, willingly or not, submitted to the sexual attentions of their captors. For example, at the central prison at Montpelier in 1829, several women had become pregnant after a year or more of captivity. Writing several years later, Fry deplored the continuing presence of men in French female prisons: "The Guards! This is the plague of prisons where women are kept."

Even as Fry's interest in prisons had been prompted by that of American Quakers, news of her own work spread quickly back across the Atlantic. The first to take up Fry's call was a group of Quaker women in Philadelphia who began in 1823 to make regular visits to women in Arch Street Prison. According to Dorothea Dix, "Every Monday afternoon throughout the year . . . you may see them there seriously and perseveringly engaged in their merciful vocation." They read from the Scriptures, provided basic educational instruction, and sought to extend their moral influence over individual inmates. American women were shocked by the prison conditions they discovered. Almost everywhere they found women at best ignored, at worst abused. In the Indiana state prison, for example, women prisoners were systematically exploited by corrupt officials who forced them into prostitution to provide sexual services for male guards. Like their British counterparts, middle-class American women sought to draw public attention to the plight of female prisoners and to campaign for better conditions. One particularly influential group of women reformers established the Female Department of the Prison Association of New York in a bid to draw attention to the plight of women in the city jails.

Their work gave rise to a strong tradition of prison reform by middle-class women in the United States. Many were members of liberal sects, mainly Quakers or Unitarians. And many were deeply involved in a variety of other social campaigns, for example, temperance, social purity, pacifism, and antislavery. Their class, education, campaigning skills, and determination to draw attention to the welfare of women prisoners ensured that the state of the female prison became a subject for public concern and debate.

Unlike hard-pressed prison staff, these upper-middle-class women had the leisure to develop close, lasting relationships with individual inmates, relationships intended to sustain the prisoners throughout their sentences. The women reformers used this as a diplomatic excuse for intruding on the role of the prison warders. "Official staff may do their duty and achieve much, but it is not possible for them to give the individual sympathy and patient attention to every member of a community . . . needed to win the confidence of persons made suspicious and distrustful by years of guilt, and many of ill-usage too." Their very name, "Lady Visitors," set them apart from the formal prison hierarchy. This was vital if they were to succeed in their mission of raising women out of the spiritual mire of imprisonment. They worked on a one-to-one basis in the belief, as expressed by one Lady Visitor, that "confidence can only be won through the medium of the sympathy of woman with woman." Ideally, the bonds they developed would continue even after release, allowing the ex-prisoner to fall back on the advice and patronage of the Lady Visitor in times of need.

The fact that the Lady Visitors concentrated their efforts on women is hardly surprising. Upper-class ladies could scarcely have been expected to entertain the risks necessarily involved in carrying out similar work with men. Also, their relationships with women inmates were modeled, to a large extent, on the pastoral concern that the mistresses of larger households were supposed to foster for the moral welfare of their female servants. The receptivity of prisoners to their efforts was predicated on the assumption that women were more impressionable than men. Women, it was believed, could be won over by a personal appeal to the heart in a way that men could not.

In the longer term, women were thought more likely to develop an abiding trust in their benefactors and give enduring loyalty to the higher ideal of femininity exemplified by the Lady Visitor. This ideal set high moral standards, of which innocence, purity, modesty, passivity, and altruism were just a few of the essential traits. The fact that criminal women were seen to fall far from this ideal set a hard task for those seeking to reform them. Lady Visitors sought to establish a regime that might successfully overcome "the seemingly indomitable obstinacy and perversity of the female character, when all the barriers are down and only vileness and depravity remains." Such attitudes toward criminal women raised serious doubts over the role of the prison for its female inmates, and some suggested that "they were beyond the reach of reformation." Yet such was the high optimism surrounding the prison in the first half of the nineteenth century that the challenge posed by women only redoubled the determination of reformers and Lady Visitors to instill those attributes thought essential to the female character. Quietly confident that they, as upper- and middle-class women, could wield a powerful influence over members of their own sex, the Lady Visitors held themselves up as models of piety and respectability to which women prisoners might aspire.

At first their work attracted considerable publicity, but sustaining commitment to their program of prison visiting proved far harder. The early enthusiasm that had prompted the proliferation of Lady Visitors all too often proved insufficient to sustain the difficult and often thankless task of prison visiting. Many prisoners, far from falling at their feet in penitent gratitude, as the Lady Visitors expected, simply derided their efforts. Often their visits were greatly resented by prison officials, who saw their work as no more than amateurish meddling. At worst, among more devious inmates, they could prove a temptation to lip service and hypocrisy, which did not fool more worldly-wise prison warders. Indeed, those working full time in prisons considered women prisoners to be particularly adept at simulating penitence in order to attract praise or other rewards. The time, interest, and attention of outside visitors had a strong attraction, not least because it broke the monotony of daily life. Unsurprisingly, then, in some prisons, the Lady Visitors came to be seen as a hindrance to good order—disrupting the routine, unwittingly encouraging dishonesty, and provoking jealousies among inmates. Unpaid and apparently unwanted, many Lady Visitors simply gave up.

Despite the mixed record of Elizabeth Fry's prison visiting campaign, it is for this that she is best remembered today. Arguably, her wide-ranging ideas for penal reform had a more profound and lasting impact. Perhaps the most important exposition of her ideas was *Observations on the Siting, Superintendence, and Government of Female Prisoners* (1825). Whereas many writings on penal reform of this period were full of grand theories but little practical advice, Fry gave detailed, concrete proposals for how prisons should be run. In line with prevailing penal thought, Fry argued for continuous surveillance and an unremitting regime of labor, education, and daily religious observance. Especially important for women, she argued, were cleanliness, plain decent clothing, and warm, orderly surroundings. As a matter of first principle she insisted, "It is absolutely essential to the proper order and regulation of every prison, that the female prisoners should be placed under the superintendence of officers of their own sex." Fry had secured this provision in Britain under Peel's Gaol Act of 1823, but it remained common for women to be guarded by men in many continental prisons. Quite apart from saving women from the exploitation that inevitably resulted if they were left under male guards, Fry argued that "respectable" female warders might play a positive role as a "consistent example of propriety and virtue."

Fry's vision of the prison for women was clearly very different from that of the prisons being set up for men. Whereas proposals for male prison reform emphasized uniform treatment, formal direction, and rigid adherence to rules, Fry advocated that women be "tenderly treated" with gentleness and sympathy so that they would submit cheerfully to the rules and cooperate willingly in their own reform.

The End of Transportation and the Establishment of Convict Prisons

While local jails continued to cater to the mass of offenders throughout the nineteenth century, the problem of how to deal with more serious offenders prompted one of the most important developments in Victorian penology—the growth of state or central government prisons. Historically, serious offenders had faced hanging or transportation. In the first half of the nineteenth century, however, growing discontent with capital punishment and the increasing reluctance of the colonies to admit convicts, particularly women, prompted the building of the first national penitentiaries. These central, state, or convict prisons, holding serious offenders sentenced to longer terms, formed the second tier of imprisonment.

In Britain, the ending of transportation provided the impetus for more rapid development of convict prisons for women. The colonies had always been resistant to accepting women convicts. Western Australia refused to take them from the start, and when New South Wales closed down as a penal colony in 1840, Van Diemen's Land was persuaded to accept women only after vehement opposition. In 1852 it too refused to admit any more female convicts, thus bringing an abrupt halt to the transportation of women. Joshua Jebb, who was then chairman of the Directors of Convict Prisons, calculated that one thousand prison places, in addition to those already at Millbank Prison in London, would be needed to house women who would previously have been shipped abroad. In 1852 the government bought the house of correction at Brixton from the county of Surrey for thirteen thousand pounds to provide an extra seven hundred to eight hundred places. Under immense pressure to take the growing body of women who could no longer be sent abroad, the government converted the house of correction and had it open and ready for use in less than a year.

Under the Penal Servitude Act (1853) the new female convict prisons at Millbank, Brixton, and Fulham, also in London, were to be governed by all the rules and regulations that already applied in male convict prisons. But prison administrators were far from convinced that the male model could simply be lifted wholesale and applied to women. Their worries were only amplified when both prison staff and outside lobbyists insisted that women required differentiated treatment appropriate to their sex. How convict prisons for women were to be organized was far from clear. One bewildered medical officer at Brixton admitted in 1856, "The present mode of treating female convicts, and the collecting of so large a number of female prisoners in a prison expressly prepared for women, are circumstances altogether new in this country." To provide a punishment that seemed in some sense equivalent to transportation, the government set sentences of penal servitude at a minimum of five years. The implications of holding prisoners for such long periods raised a series of problems not previously confronted by the prison system.

The first separate state prison for women in the United States was set up in 1835, when New York opened Mount Pleasant Female Prison. Established largely in response to overcrowding in existing New York prisons, it remained the only such prison for women in the country until the 1870s. Although the management of Mount Pleasant was officially the responsibility of inspectors at nearby Sing Sing, in practice, day-to-day management was left to the prison's matrons. Prisoners labored under a monotonous regime of sewing, button-making, and hat-trimming, apart from a brief period, from 1844 to 1847, when, under matron Eliza Farnham, a period of radical experimentation was instituted.

Under Farnham's leadership the prisoners enjoyed better conditions than those found at the male prison at Sing Sing. She instituted personal tuition, exhorted staff not to rely on punishment, and abolished the rule of silence. Such reforms provoked angry opposition from critics who argued that this milder regime for women sowed discontent among male prisoners in neighboring Sing Sing. Farnham was obliged to resign, and this brief period of innovation gave way to a longer decline characterized by increasing overcrowding. In 1865 the population at Mount Pleasant reached nearly twice its capacity. The state refused to finance further expansion and instead closed the prison, dispersing inmates to local prisons. Mount Pleasant was in many ways an institution ahead of its time. It sat alone as the first and only state prison for women, suggesting a model for women's imprisonment that found favor only with the development of the women's reformatory movement in the last quarter of the century.

A major schism developed over two rival models on which prison regimes might be organized: the "silent system" (in which prisoners were not allowed to talk to one another) and the "separate system" (in which prisoners were isolated in individual cells so as to keep contact between them to a minimum). These two systems originated in experiments in two English local prisons at Gloucester and Southwell. But the major controversy over their rival merits centered around the silent regime developed at Au-

burn Penitentiary, New York, and the separate system imposed at the Western Penitentiary, Philadelphia.

Many of the criticisms that were made of the silent system in relation to men were
also applied to women: that it would be virtually impossible to enforce and that it would
send punishment rates soaring as prison guards tried to quash every infraction. In addition, imposing the silent system on women was seen to involve special problems.
Since women were thought to be naturally more sociable and more excitable than men,
silence might be more damaging to their nervous system. Women, it was said, lacked
self-control, so enforcing silence among them would require even more careful supervision than among men. Inevitably inmates would find ways around the silent regime,
and here, again, worries were voiced about the supposed impressionability of women.
Lurid pictures were painted of innocent first-time offenders becoming prey to the whis-
pered exploits of hardened "thieves, brothel-servants, [and] prostitutes." If silence was
to be effective at all, every infringement had to be noted and punished. Yet continual
reprimands would do little to foster good relations between staff and inmates, as the
matron of one English prison that tried to enforce the silent system soon discovered.
"Older criminals . . . upon being reported for breaches of silence . . . almost invariably
pour forth upon the Officers a torrent of obscene and blasphemous abuse." Even at
Auburn Prison in New York, the supposed model of the silent system, women were
crammed into a cramped and fetid attic room above the kitchen while men were locked
in separate cells at night. Officially supervised by the head of the kitchen, the women
were left largely to their own devices, with little to do. Their plight was summed up by
Auburn's chaplain, who wrote in 1833, "To be a male convict in this prison would be
quite tolerable; but to be a *female* convict, for any protracted period, would be worse
than death."

Due to all these drawbacks of the silent system, in England a modified version of
the separate system (in which prisoners were isolated in single cells where they worked,
ate, and slept alone) was widely advocated. Penal reformers thought that separation
was particularly suitable for women. In one prison where separation was introduced,
the chaplain claimed that women who, "under the old system, must have gone out
corrupted and ruined by the association with the most depraved and basest of their sex"
were now, under the new system, "discharged from prison impressed with better principles, and possessed of a real desire to retrieve their characters and to become useful
members of society." Prison reformers had worried whether men would be able to tolerate the inactivity and lack of exercise that being confined to their cells entailed. But
few of these concerns seemed to apply to women, who were said to be passive, even
"naturally sedentary." Accordingly, staying in their cells all day would not be the hardship for women that it was for men. That this view was widely held is clear from the
contributions made at international penological conferences. At the Congress of
Stockholm, one delegate argued, "The woman is more docile, more resigned, she has
more sedentary habits and as a consequence will reconcile herself, if not better than, at
least as well as a man to solitary confinement."

Curiously this sanguine approach to subjecting women to solitary confinement
was not shared in France. Here, in contrast, it was feared that women would not be able
to stand up to the demoralizing effects of isolation. Women were said to be naturally

sociable creatures who would not have the inner resources to survive alone. And yet, despite these worries, in France as in Britain, the benefits of separation for women were reluctantly accepted on the grounds that "women contaminate each other even more than men do." Since women were thought to be more impressionable, they needed even greater protection from bad influences than did men. Total separation was a radical, but effective, means of removing the younger, more innocent women from all possible sources of corruption. In much of Europe, separation became the dominant characteristic of long-term imprisonment.

Life inside Nineteenth-Century Women's Prisons

By the mid-nineteenth century, the prison system for both men and women was generally organized on two distinct tiers: the local prisons or jails, and the convict or state penitentiaries. The basic components of prisons at both levels looked roughly alike. Both had cells, workrooms, chapel, school, and nursery. But in many other respects they differed markedly. Clearly, holding a prisoner for several years made demands on the system quite unlike those imposed by the continual flux of prisoners held perhaps for only a few weeks or even days. In what follows we shall attempt to draw out these differences, to give some flavor of what it was like to be a woman in a local or a convict prison.

Prison Structure

To a great extent, for both men and women, the nature of life in prison was determined by the constraints of the buildings. Unsurprisingly, many local authorities were unable or unwilling to meet the costs of constructing the individual cells necessary to run prisons on the separate system. Where cells were built, their walls were often too thin to prevent communication. Poor design and inadequate funding meant that, in many local prisons, cells were small, dark, cold, and damp. Physical conditions in convict prisons tended to be better, but other problems arose from the fact that female convicts were mostly housed in buildings built for men and only later adapted for women. Women convicts inherited prisons built with individual cells for each inmate at a time when growing evidence of the psychological burden of separation was raising doubts about its desirability. Worried about the contaminating effects of allowing women to associate, yet equally concerned that total separation would prove too much for the "weaker sex" to bear, prison administrators allowed women to spend time together during the day. However, prison officials were heavily constrained by the existing architecture: one mid-century engraving (see p. 328) shows the women at Brixton Prison working silently and in evident discomfort on the narrow landings outside their cells.

Quite apart from their architectural constraints, prisons built for men tended to be dour, formal places that did not fit well with the aim of encouraging women to develop feelings of femininity and a sense of domestic pride. In 1844 Eliza Farnham, on taking charge of Mount Pleasant prison for women in New York, introduced flowers and music in an attempt to mitigate the grim character of the place. In London, when Brixton Prison was reopened for women, they were "allowed" to whitewash the interior of the prison and encouraged to cultivate small plots of flowers and plants that were dotted around the exercise yards. One mid-century visitor, the social investigator and journalist Henry Mayhew, proclaimed such efforts a success, declaring that the prison had "nothing of the ordinary prison character or gloomy look." Contemporary sketches and engravings, however, even in Mayhew's own massive compendium *The Criminal Prisons of London and Scenes of Prison Life* (1862), do little to support such an optimistic impression. Prisons for women in France tended to be less formidable places, not least because many of them were established by religious orders in former convents. The St. Lazare House of Correction for Women in Paris, for example, was originally a convent, which, even when converted for prison use, retained much of its former character. Given the emphasis on the individual redemption and moral reform of female prisoners, convents such as these provided a far more conducive atmosphere than did the austere setting of many former male prisons.

Purposes of the Regime

We have seen how Victorians' perceptions of criminal women differed markedly from their views of criminal men. These differences were clearly reflected in the regimes set up for women in prison. Since, by committing crime, women were seen to have fallen from the ideal of femininity to which all women were supposed to aspire, the main aim was to provide inmates with the opportunity and means to reform. Although the ideal of the "lady," by definition, presumed a social class most criminal women could never hope to attain and set standards remote from the realities of the life they faced outside, this fact did not deter reformers from holding the ideal up as the ultimate goal.

Short sentences in local prisons allowed little scope to achieve any lasting change in the inmates. Over the course of the nineteenth century the proportion of very short sentences increased as more women came before the courts for the most trivial offenses of drunkenness, disorderly conduct, prostitution, and petty theft. For example, by the time local prisons were nationalized in Britain in 1877, of the women entering Tothill Fields House of Correction in London, over half were sentenced to terms of less than fourteen days, three-quarters to less than one month, and well below one-tenth to more than six months. Such short terms led to attitudes very different from those prevalent in convict prisons. Whereas convicts were likely to be demoralized by the prospect of years in prison and feel isolated from the outside world, a woman held for only a few days was unlikely to be very amenable to whatever influences the prison brought to bear. She was probably still in contact with her family and friends outside and knew that she could soon escape the pains of punishment and return to her former life. All these factors gave women in local prisons little reason to cooperate with the prison authorities. Quite apart from the prisoners' attitudes, the huge turnover of inmates in local prisons created an administrative burden that threatened to take up the energies of the staff entirely. "The prison-vans bring them, fifty or sixty a day, from all the police-courts of the metropolis, as well as from the criminal courts and sessions. So many came in every day: so many discharged, mostly to come again. What a work for the chaplains! What a work for the reformers!" In practice, of course, reform was a hopeless task when time was so short and resources were so heavily diverted by the burdens of administering the continual flood of admissions.

Longer terms in state or convict prisons allowed greater scope for implementing a reform program intended to bring about lasting change in inmates. Male convict prisons were characterized by a militaristic discipline, in which inmates remained anonymous, known only by their number. Relations with staff were terse and formal. In women's custodial institutions in the United States, routines and punishments were very similar to those of the male prisons with which they were associated. But in England, although regulations governing male prisoners were extended to cover female convict prisons, the emphasis here was on moral treatment intended to restore criminal women to respectability and "womanliness." One anonymous writer summed up the purpose of the regime as follows, "A woman on entering a convict prison should feel that however vicious her past life has been, she is come to a place where she has a character to regain and support."

The female convict system mimicked the "progressive stage system" set up for men in that a series of classes was established, through which convicts moved during the period of their sentence depending on their behavior. For men, the central feature of this system was the "public works" stage, in which they were employed in hard-labor quarrying, stone-breaking, and building. There was no comparable work available or, at any rate, deemed suitable for women. As Joshua Jebb only too clearly recognized, "Females must of necessity be employed chiefly indoors, and will have neither the varied work, nor the complete change afforded to Male Convicts, by removal to the public works." Whereas chain gangs of men could leave the prison each day, women faced a monotonous daily round of highly contrived and often petty employment within the prison walls.

Jebb worried at length about confining women long term, particularly because he believed that they did "not have the same physical and mental powers which enable them to bear up against the depressing influence of imprisonment." French penologists were similarly alarmed by the signs of nervous decline and even madness manifest in women prisoners. Their inability to adapt to institutional life was put down to their "defective" nature. Records of mental disorders and nervous illness among women prisoners were anxiously scrutinized by mid-nineteenth-century psychiatrists for signs of impending breakdown. In fact, however, in national prisons in both Britain and France, women had lower records of attempted and successful suicide than men.

Obviously the men's daily escape from the confines of the prison should not be glamorized. They were obliged to do backbreaking work in all weather, often at the cost of their health or at the risk of serious injury. Nonetheless, it did provide for a change of scene, vigorous physical exercise, and possibly some relief from the routine of life inside. Although being spared the harshness of the male prison regime, women were, in many respects, subject to a regime of greater tedium and more intrusive surveillance. They not only had to obey the formal prison rules and regulations but also had to live up to notions of appropriate feminine behavior in every aspect of their carriage, conduct, and conversation. Under the "mark system," set up to encourage good behavior, men were rewarded for diligence and productivity, but significantly, women earned their marks for good conduct, honesty, propriety, and "moral improvement."

In Britain, female convicts were received at Millbank and then moved through two "stages" or classes to Brixton. If they were well behaved, they progressed through two further stages to Fulham. Brixton offered a series of small improvements and privileges that appear petty but no doubt took on great importance against the background of prison routine—for example, women were allowed tea three evenings a week instead of gruel, and they could wear a different dress denoting their new status. For the very best behaved women who reached Fulham, life took a markedly different turn. Significantly, at least initially, Fulham was not called a prison but a "refuge," bringing to mind those charitable institutions set up by philanthropic Victorian ladies for impoverished gentle-women. The thinking behind this maneuver was highly pragmatic. Whereas men could generally find rough work whatever their background, women were likely to be look-ing for domestic service where a good "character" or reference was vital for gaining a position. Employers reluctant to take servants from a prison might, it was hoped, be persuaded to take them from a refuge. Prison officials were well aware that a double standard operated for female convicts, with the result that they were judged more harshly than their male counterparts. "The difficulties in the way of a woman of the character of the majority of these prisoners returning to respectability are too notorious to require description. They beset her in every direction the moment she is discharged."

Fulham was, then, the most distinctively feminine of the early convict prisons. Practically, it sought to provide its inmates with the sorts of skills that women might actually need on release, such as household cleaning, cooking, and laundering. Disci-pline was "relaxed as far as possible," and the women were allowed to talk together on suitable subjects with the aim of encouraging responsibility and restoring self-respect. Great emphasis was placed on "softening and civilising" and on inculcating the women with higher social aspirations. In part it was simply a public relations exercise, to con-vince potential employers that they could safely take such women into their homes as servants. And in part it was, in a sense, a luxury, an experiment that could be tried only because the numbers of women were relatively small. Such an institution would simply not have been possible within the massive machinery of the male convict system.

The Prison Nursery

Undoubtedly the most distinct aspect of the female prison was the nursery, de-scribed by one observer as "the most touching part of the female . . . prison, and what distinguishe[d] it essentially from all the penal institutions appropriated to male prisoners." Women could take their babies and infants into both local and, in the early years, convict prisons. Babies born to pregnant inmates were also al-lowed to remain, often to the end of their mothers' sentences. Yet prison condi-tions were hardly suitable for children. For example, before the opening of the first state prison nursery at Mount Pleasant Female Prison in the United States, every baby born at nearby Sing Sing had died.

Inevitably the prison nursery set the disciplinary regime at odds. Rules and regula-tions had to be waived in the interests of the children. But the authorities were reluctant to allow mothers a privileged existence that might be the envy of other inmates. Result-ing compromises often bordered on the ridiculous. At one local prison, mothers in the nursery were allowed to talk to their babies but not to one another. It takes little imagi-nation to see how easily such a rule would be subverted. Where labor requirements were waived, prison mothers often found themselves in a far easier position than women outside prison who were struggling to earn enough to support their offspring. In convict or state prisons there was the more serious problem of whether children could be incarcerated alongside their mothers for long periods without serious harm to their development. Inmates' children showed utter terror on meeting rare male visitors to the prison, and they lacked stimulus and experience of the world. The journalist Henry Mayhew found "one little thing had been kept so long incarcerated, that on going out of the prison it called a horse a cat." Officials worried also that children raised in the dismal surroundings of the prison and under the influence of their criminal mothers were inevitably doomed to a life of crime themselves.

Unsurprisingly, there were continual demands to remove children from both local and state prisons. Efforts were made to persuade a woman's parish or community to take responsibility for her children. Partial success in this campaign was achieved in Britain under the 1866 Industrial Schools Act, which provided for the children of women who had been twice previously convicted to be removed to industrial schools. In 1871, the Prevention of Crimes Act extended the 1866 act to cover women with only a single previous conviction. Thereafter, children under fourteen with no other means of subsistence or proper guardianship became liable to be sent to an industrial school. The feelings of mothers obliged to surrender their children seem to have attracted little discussion, and opposition to this concerted deprivation of women's rights of custody over their own children was soon overcome.

Female Prison Staff

With the notable exception of the chaplain, prisons for women were staffed almost entirely by women. In Britain, after the passing of Peel's Gaol Act in 1823, men had been barred from any access to female prisoners. Even the chaplain had to be accompanied on his pastoral visits around the prison, though whether this was to protect inmates or to save him from embarrassing accusations is unclear. In the United States, it was argued: "A matron [is] necessary for the special superintendence of the female prisoners, she is quite indispensable if the Auburn system is applied to women as well as men; she alone can enforce the order of this system, while it is nearly impossible for male keepers."

The responsibilities placed on the female staff were almost unparalleled at a time when men ran most institutions of comparable size. And they were increased by the fact that the demands made of staff in female prisons were very different from those made of staff in prisons for men. Since male prisons tended to operate on quasi-militaristic lines, officers there were required to enforce the massive body of rules strictly and uniformly. In women's prisons, discipline tended to be relaxed, and in its place warders were expected to maintain order by setting a personal example, gaining the trust of the prisoners, and instilling a sense of loyalty. They were expected to set themselves up as models of feminine decorum, good temper, and compassion, traits that inmates might then seek to emulate. The directors of the Millbank convict prison, for example, insisted that staff should show "patience, a disposition to discover, and give credit for, the least evidence of improvement, and a sympathy which can understand and feel for the trials and difficulties even of the outcast." Arguably, such a requirement imposed greater burdens on female staff, who were, therefore, required to keep a close watch on their demeanor whenever in contact with prisoners. In stark contrast to the practice at men's prisons, warders at female prisons were encouraged to get to know the women personally and to develop close relationships with them. Rules were bent or even ignored to allow discipline to be adapted to individual temperaments. In theory, at least, every effort was to be made to encourage moral reform by a process that combined an uneasy mix of coercion, encouragement, and manipulation.

In practice, long hours (female warders worked a twelve- or even fifteen-hour day) and poor staff-inmate ratios meant that the ideal of zealous women patiently encouraging the penitent to reform was rarely achieved. "Towards the close of the day . . . some of the officers get irritable and extremely cross with the prisoners, and . . . other officers get so tired out, they really do not much care whether the prisoners about them conduct themselves well or ill." The caliber of women recruited to the prison service was a further hindrance. Most were from a social background scarcely distinct from that of the prisoners themselves, and many lacked the education, intelligence, or ability to meet the demands made of them. In the United States, the matrons were often older women, and many were widows obliged to take up prison posts out of force of circumstances. Elizabeth Fry deplored the "very poor Sort of Matrons" employed on both sides of the Atlantic and even claimed, "Some of the Women [prisoners] are superior to themselves in point of Power and Talent, so that they have scarcely any Influence over them."

French prisons also experienced major difficulties in recruiting suitable women staff. Yet here the large population of Catholic nuns provided a readily available recruiting ground for women whose morals, religious faith, and commitment were unimpeachable. Entire religious orders, like the sisters of Marie-Joseph, dedicated themselves to staffing women's prisons. They acted as models of femininity and piety that British prison administrators could only envy. Not everyone in France was quite so uncritical of the work of these religious orders, however. Anticlerical republicans objected to the employment of nuns by state-run institutions. Others objected to their activities on more pragmatic grounds. For example, the *maisons de refuges* set up and run by the sisters of Marie-Joseph for women finishing their prison sentences were criticized: "The sisters think of the interests of their religious community above all else; they choose the best subjects from the central prisons, those who are capable of easily earning a living." Selectively, the nuns thus equipped themselves with groups of hard-working, manageable women, leaving the rest of those discharged from the central prisons to face the outside world without help or shelter.

Formally, warders exercised control over inmates by applying a series of rules and regulations and consistently sanctioning any infringement, however minor. We know relatively little of the internal life of the male prison in the nineteenth century, of whether or not male prisons were in fact run along these lines. In female prisons, however, order was not maintained by discipline alone but by a complex set of relationships between warders and inmates. Officially, the rulebook forbade undue familiarity with inmates. In practice, the common assumption that women were more susceptible to personal influence than men justified a greater level of intimacy than was ever countenanced in male prisons. It was generally accepted that the female warder could exert good moral influence by showing a personal interest in and giving advice to individual women.

The dividing line between legitimate interest and undue intimacy was not always easy to establish. "Tampering" was the coy and conveniently euphemistic term used to describe cases of lesbianism by female staff. Cases of tampering with prisoners are recorded with surprising frequency in the discipline books of female prisons. In male prisons, homosexuality was abhorred and heavily punished. In female prisons, the reaction of the prison authorities was much less predictable and, surprisingly, often resulted in no more than a simple reprimand to the warder concerned. Part of the problem was that the common use of sentimental terms by Victorian women to one another blurred the distinction between emotional relations and those of sexual intimacy. What should one make of the effusive letters sent by one subwarder to a former female prisoner, Susan W. Fletcher? One letter began: "MY DEAR DARLING BABY—if I may still call you so,—and I think you will let me, for indeed you are very dear to me,—you don't know how miserable and unhappy I feel, now you are gone. It is not like the same place. It was very bad, but now it is much worse. As I am passing that old cell, I look in. It is empty—no one there. Then I don't know what to do with myself. Oh, *do* forgive me! I ought not to remind you of this dreadful place, but I do miss you so much!" The warder who wrote this letter was found out and was, in fact, dismissed. Her letter reveals much of the miserable life of the female prison warder. Because women were obliged to resign when they married, those who remained tended to be even more cut off from the outside world than their male counterparts and all the more dependent on the life of the prison for emotional sustenance.

Other relationships were rather more straightforwardly subversive. The records of one London prison, Tothill Fields, reveal a variety of illegal arrangements between warders and prisoners. These ranged from the simple bartering of services by inmates in return for petty privileges to sophisticated systems for trafficking goods into the prison. In September 1860, four female prisoners at Tothill Fields "confessed they had done both plain and embroidery work for these Officers in return for which they received bread, butter, cheese, tea, fruit, and cake." Given the meager and monotonous rations of the prison diet, these must have seemed luxuries indeed. Access to a warder who was prepared to bring in food and drink on a regular basis must have done much to mitigate the rigors of prison life. Organized trafficking—where a prisoner's friends outside the prison paid a warder to take in highly illicit goods such as meat or even alcohol—formed the basis of an illegal economy within the prison. In prison records, reports of trafficking are so frequent, and the penalties imposed so minor, that one can only assume that such illegalities were very common. At Tothill Fields Prison one warder, Charlotte Howe, posed as a potential trafficker and was offered ten shillings and a gold watch by one woman to take in "some Grub, Meat, and a little Wine" to a relative inside. At the same prison, an inmate, Emma Steiner, told the authorities that warder Ann Bailey was trafficking goods to a number of her peers, though, significantly, not to Steiner herself. She said, "The prisoners say subwarder Bailey receives so much a week to bring parcels into them: it is talked about outside, and when a prisoner gets her sentence they say never mind she has a good screw inside."

Obviously it was largely up to prison warders to develop covert, illegal relationships of any sort with the inmates. But to choose to do so tipped the balance of power between them. Any relationship that strayed beyond that strictly allowed immediately involved a series of illegalities. The warder then placed herself at the mercy of the prisoners, for she risked being reported by them. Prisoners stored up contraventions of the rules and regulations by warders as ammunition when threatened with punishment themselves.

Reading between the lines of prison daybooks and punishment records suggests that order inside the female prison was precariously maintained by a web of favors, illicit agreements, and even blackmail. Although female prison staff were encouraged to build up relationships with prisoners in the hope of exercising personal influence over them, the result was that staff and inmates were pushed together into a relationship of mutual dependency. Inevitably this was closer, more claustrophobic, and possibly more open to abuse than that which operated in the more regimented, strictly hierarchical world of the male prison.

Inmates

The lives of female prisoners and their relationships with one another in nineteenth-century prisons are all but hidden from us today. For the most part their experiences remained unrecorded. Building up any picture of what their lives were like relies on those occasions when their misbehavior was so blatant as to attract the attention of the prison authorities. Inmates' own accounts are so rare that we can only question how typical they were. One of the few memoirs by a female inmate of a local prison in Britain was Susan Willis Fletcher's *Twelve Months in an English Prison* (1884). Fletcher's story is eloquently written and informative. But Fletcher was an upper-class American who operated as a spiritualist and was convicted of obtaining jewels and clothing "of great value" by false pretenses—hardly a typical inmate of a local prison.

In France there is a far richer source in the form of "biftons," or notes and letters, sent between women inmates, seized by the authorities, and published by prison commentators to expose the underlife of women's prisons. These letters provide an important counter to the views of those in authority. Yet they too are a somewhat suspect source. Questions about their authenticity, their typicality, and the very purposes for which they were published all raise doubts about their validity. The largest published collection of these letters, *Les Enracinees,* was edited by Arnauld Galopin; according to a recent study, these letters were published largely for "their prurient appeal." As such, even they constitute a questionable basis for discovering what life was really like in women's prisons.

Official records and writings give some glimpses into the lives of female prisoners. But they are heavily colored by the writers' personal beliefs about criminal women. Contemporary commentaries often dwell on the plight of relatively innocent women imprisoned for petty offenses only to find themselves subjected to "the foul language of the stews, the unchecked blasphemy and ribaldry of the lowest prostitutes, and the outpourings of thieves." Criminal women were also thought to be more difficult, as Reverend Walter Clay, a well-known prison chaplain, declared: "It is well known that women are far worse to manage, and resist what is for their good far more vehemently than men." Such statements probably tell us more about contemporary attitudes than about what actually went on within women's prisons. Although chaplains and prison administrators alike insisted that women caused them far more disciplinary problems, actual punishment records suggest that women were neither much worse nor much better behaved than men.

To assuage the loneliness of prison life, many women developed highly charged relationships with one another. Prison authorities were deeply worried by the prevalence of "unnatural practices" in male prisons and stamped them out by severely punishing those involved. Perhaps through lack of imagination, many British officials insisted that female relationships were strictly affectionate and refused to accept that they had any sexual content. As a result, women prisoners were much freer to develop intense though often short-lived relationships, known in the prison argot as "palling-in." Rows between lovers were common, and the swapping of allegiances often sparked off tempestuous jealousies upsetting to the order of the prison. In convict prisons, where women were cut off from their families for many years, such attachments tended to be longer-lasting. Based on affection and fidelity, they were an important source of friendship.

Homosexuality among women prisoners was more openly recognized by French prison officials. The concierge at one Parisian prison for prostitutes, the Petite Force, insisted that nearly all the inmates there practiced "commerce contre nature." And the overcrowded, crumbling dormitories and shared cells at St. Lazare prison for women in Paris were condemned for encouraging blatant promiscuity. Generally French penal reformers claimed that women's prisons, quite as much as men's, were "schools for vice."

Just how far women's relationships formed the basis of counterculture within the prison remains unclear. Certainly prison officials in Britain believed that a secret "sisterhood" existed among the women and was used to pass information about such practices as prostitution, abortion, and even infanticide. The snatches of conversation on which these beliefs were based give only the barest indication of the "subculture" of the women's prison and of the degree to which it operated to undermine official ideology.

A core of women persistently refused to comply with the demands made of them. Labeled "incorrigible" by desperate prison authorities, they flouted the prison rules and created disturbances at every opportunity. In the British convict system these women were confined in the "penal class" at Millbank and later at Parkhurst. The journalist Henry Mayhew described them as "the very worst women in existence." He added, "I don't fancy their equal could be found anywhere." Their behavior prompted one prison director to declare: "The language of the penal class women is fouler than anyone who had not heard it could possibly imagine. Nothing but the gag can restrain the abominations they utter." Similarly, in America a report on the Ohio penitentiary in the 1840s claimed that its nine female inmates were more troublesome than the prison's five hundred men: "The women fight, scratch, pull hair, curse, swear and yell, and to bring them to order a keeper has frequently to go among them with a horsewhip." Whether these women really were so bad, or whether prevailing ideas about how women ought to behave created false expectations that could only be rudely shattered, is unclear. Certainly the description of one woman convict as showing a "deadness to all feminine decency" would seem to suggest the latter explanation.

There was, however, a phenomenon that was peculiar to the female convict prison and that was unparalleled in male prisons. "Breaking-out" was a form of riotous behavior by women "amounting almost to a frenzy, smashing their windows, tearing up their clothes, destroying every useful article within their reach, generally yelling, shouting or singing as if they were maniacs." For example, when overcrowding reached a peak at

Mount Pleasant Female Prison in New York in 1843, the women responded by almost continuous riot. The prison report for that year recorded, "Violent battles are frequent and knives have been known to be drawn among them." Overcrowding continued, and the management problems it provoked proved so insuperable that eventually Mount Pleasant was shut down in 1865.

Similarly, after the ending of transportation in England, the first women convicts were devastated to find themselves facing years in prison instead of a "new life" in the colonies. Uncertain about their ultimate fate, they "broke-out" with terrifying frequency. Overcrowding in Millbank Prison created a catalyst by which the violence of one woman sparked similar frenzy in many others. Throughout the 1850s and 1860s, women's extreme frustration with the monotonous prison regime continued to lead to dramatic outbursts of anger and destruction. Generally these outbursts were of such violence and intensity that they came at once to the attention of prison authorities—in a single year 154 such cases were recorded in Millbank alone. Evidence from France is more sketchy, but there are recorded instances of women prisoners rioting in protest against harsh regimes. Their protests seem to have taken a very similar form to those in Britain. For example, at Bon-Pasteur Prison in Limoges, women recently transferred from Paris reportedly went on a rampage, breaking furniture and attacking the Catholic nuns who guarded them.

In this particularly intense form, such outbreaks seem to have been confined to women's prisons and were always considered to be a peculiarly female response to long-term incarceration. Explanations of "breaking-out" rested on the belief that women were incapable of controlling their more violent passions and so, under the intense pressure of imprisonment, gave way to hysteria. Dismissively labeled as irrational, such outbreaks were, nonetheless, a terrifying spectacle as windows and furniture were smashed and clothing was torn to shreds.

Punishing such behavior was problematic, not least because many of the sanctions imposed on men simply could not be applied to women. Notions of women, even criminal women, as the "weaker sex" meant that corporal punishments, such as whipping, were ruled out. In the United States, Mount Pleasant Female Prison resorted to straitjackets, the gag, and even the "shower bath" in an attempt to subdue the more recalcitrant inmates. But in Britain the use of physical restraints was thought inappropriate, and they were rarely applied. That such sanctions were not available for women was clearly regretted by some prison warders. As one prison governor, G. L. Chesterton, noted in *Revelations of Prison Life* (1856), "The female attendants, in the extremity of their disgust and horror, used to exclaim `what a blessing it would be, if we could employ some stout-armed woman to give them the rod!'" Instead, warders had to rely on a range of lesser sanctions, all of which seemed unequal to the task. The most common form of punishment—short-term confinement in a solitary cell known as "the dark"—was simply derided by women who, knowing there was little prospect of further punishment, took the opportunity to behave even more badly. As Dr. Guy of Millbank Prison observed: "If they are put into a dark cell, they shout and sing and make merry. They know that there are prisoners not very far off them who can hear their noise, and they like to go on in that strange way."

Curiously then, women seem to have been a greater disciplinary problem than men. High expectations of how women should behave, plainly riotous behavior by some, and the limited sanctions available all combined to create the impression that women were worse behaved. The deputy-governor of Millbank, Arthur Griffiths, asserted that it was "a well-established fact in prison logistics" that the women were far worse than the men. He noted, "When given to misconduct they are far more persistent in their evil ways, more outrageously violent, less amenable to reason or reproof." Little thought was given to why women were so fiercely resistant to the imposed regime. Instead female convict prisons were subject to a continuing round of reorganization, which had little administrative justification but rather reflected a profound sense of dissatisfaction with attempts to subject women to long-term imprisonment.

One final aspect of the ways in which women subverted the purpose of nineteenth-century imprisonment is especially curious. Women in desperate straits of destitution or sickness saw the local prison as a place of asylum. Brought up to consider themselves naturally dependent, women looked to the prison as a somewhat unlikely benefactor in times of need. Sick women, and especially diseased prostitutes, looked on the prison as a sort of hospital where they could expect a reasonable standard of free medical care. Similarly, pregnant women saw it "as a comfortable asylum or lying-in hospital," where they were "properly cared for during their confinement, or while nursing their little ones." A window pane deliberately smashed was enough to secure admission so that they would be housed, fed, and looked after through pregnancy and childbirth. No doubt destitute men would also resort to such stratagems during periods of illness or harsh weather. But among women this phenomenon seems to have been remarkably common. Indeed, the governors of the Tothill Fields prison for women in London were horrified to discover that their prison enjoyed "an undesirable popularity amongst Prisoners generally."

Release from Prison

Quite apart from the many limitations on the ability of the prison to reform, attitudes toward criminal women were a major stumbling block for women prisoners seeking to start life anew. In America, the leader of the Female Department of the Prison Association of New York, Abby Hopper Gibbons, recognized that the powerful stigma attached to women when convicted meant that women also faced greater difficulties when released. In 1845, after conducting a public campaign for funds, she opened the Isaac Hopper Home (named after her father) as a refuge for women ex-prisoners who would promise to forsake smoking, drinking, and cursing in favor of domestic labor and religious study. From 1845 to 1864, the home provided shelter for 2,961 women, found posts for 1,083 of them, and condemned only 480 as "unworthy or without hope of being reclaimed."

In Britain, innumerable voluntary bodies set up similar refuges and shelters, catering almost exclusively to women, under the umbrella organization of the Discharged Prisoners' Aid Societies. The government too set up three state refuges: the Carlisle Memorial Refuge for Protestant women, the Winchester Memorial Refuge, and the Eagle House Refuge for Catholic women. The proliferation of refuges during the 1860s and 1870s led to a state-run scheme whereby women "whose conduct and character" justified "the hope of complete amendment" were released on license nine months before the end of their sentence into the care of either a voluntary or a state refuge. If by persistent misbehavior or trying to escape a woman forfeited her license, she was immediately returned to prison, where she would remain until the end of her term.

In France too, Catholic sisters who interested themselves in the plight of women prisoners recognized similar problems facing women discharged into society without friends to help them. The sisters of Marie-Joseph, for example, established *maisons de refuge,* to which women with no families of their own might turn for help when released. Finding respectable employment was all but impossible for women who bore the label of convict. From a "refuge," it was hoped, they had some chance of making a fresh start.

INNOVATION AND DEVELOPMENTS INTO THE TWENTIETH CENTURY

The last quarter of the nineteenth century was a period of considerable innovation for women's prisons on both sides of the Atlantic. Developments in Britain and the United States were very different in their origin, perspective, and purpose. In America, the impetus to reform came mainly from a powerful body of women who, much influenced by reformatories already established for juvenile delinquents, campaigned to set up similar institutions for adult women. Many of these reformers had been active in "child saving," and others had gained experience in a range of social, educational, and welfare reform movements. A central tenet of their philosophy was that women required separate treatment appropriate to their sex.

Women's involvement in prison reform had begun with voluntary prison visiting—an activity that had always been regarded by prison authorities as marginal, at best. In the latter years of the nineteenth century and into the twentieth, women occupied a much more central role. They were, for example, influential in founding the American Prison Association in 1870, a body dedicated to reviving debate about penal methods and promoting penal reform. In this and other similar organizations, women philanthropists developed new ideas about the government and, indeed, the purpose of female prisons. Many espoused a new creed of "social feminism," arguing that they, as women, had unique feminine virtues that could be fruitfully applied in developing institutions better able to respond to the special needs of their sex. The new female reformatories were a direct outcome of their endeavors.

On the other side of the Atlantic in Europe, the development of medical science, particularly psychiatry, was the primary force in penal reform. This "medicalization" of deviance promoted a new way of thinking. As one French doctor, Dr. Eugene Dally, explained, "One must treat criminals as sick, having with regard to neither hate nor anger nor the spirit of vengeance and limit oneself to preserving society from the dangers their presence brings." According to this view, punishment of those who were inadequate or sick was scarcely justifiable. Instead, containment in benign conditions was acceptable only in proportion to the danger an individual posed to society. At the same time, the growing influence of Social Darwinism focused attention on the potential of criminal women to produce future generations of "neurotic, vicious children." As one Scottish physician, Dr. Clouston, dramatically warned, "When illegitimate children are born by such young women, the chances are enormously in favour of their turning out to be either imbeciles, degenerates, or criminals." Incapacitation took priority over punishment as the primary purpose of female custody.

Despite these very different sources of penal thinking in Europe and America, a number of similarities suggest themselves. Significantly, on both sides of the Atlantic, it was penal policy for women that attracted the most innovation in this period. Whether this was because the smaller scale of female imprisonment allowed flexibility for experimentation in a way that men's prisons did not, or whether it reflected a deeper unease about the appropriate treatment of women, remains unclear, however. As we shall see, the emergent view in America of female offenders as "wayward" or errant and the growing recognition in Europe of medical reasons for offending by women both, in their different ways, tended to raise questions about the utility of punishing those who could not be held fully responsible for their crimes. It led to the removal of many women from custodial prisons on the grounds that conventional punishment was inappropriate. They were sentenced instead to new reformatories whose ostensible purpose was not to punish but to cure or redeem. And yet the effect of this tacit decriminalization of women was in fact to extend control over women by replacing short sentences for petty offenses in local prisons with indeterminate terms in these new specialist institutions. Women were liable to be held until they were considered to be reformed or cured. Those who proved recalcitrant or incurable, as in the case of mentally deficient women, were liable to be confined indefinitely. If the mainstream prison population decreased, therefore, it was more than replaced by the growth in numbers of those held long term in specialist institutions and reformatories.

The American Reformatory Movement

Whereas France had established prisons specifically for women as early as the 1820s and Britain by the 1850s, in America demands that prisons for women be set up completely independently of those for men and be run solely by women did not bear significant fruit until 1870. In that year, the state of Michigan opened a "house of shelter" for women, in which inmates were to "receive intellectual, moral, domestic, and industrial training." Just a few years later, in 1874, Indiana opened the Indiana Reformatory Institution, the first completely independent and physically separate prison for women in America. Massachusetts Reformatory Prison for Women opened only three years later in 1877, New York House of Refuge for Women in 1887, Western House of Refuge at Albion in 1893, and Bedford Hills Reformatory, New York, in 1907. Together these institutions pioneered structures and techniques that were to become central to the reformatory movement.

Highly instrumental in achieving the establishment of these first reformatories were social feminists who campaigned for institutions oriented toward the special characteristics and needs of female prisoners. That the institutions set up took the form of reformatories rather than straightforward prisons was largely due to changing conceptions of the female offender in late-nineteenth-century America. Whereas women had previously been thought more depraved and more thoroughly corrupt than men, increasingly they were seen as "wayward girls" who had been led astray and who could, therefore, be led back to the paths of "proper" behavior: "childlike, domestic, and asexual." This view was greatly encouraged by the fact that many reformatories refused to take experienced, hardened offenders, preferring those who had only "recently begun lives of crime" over those who had "spent years in prisons and almshouses" and had "lost ambition for better lives."

In some respects the twenty reformatories set up for women in the period from 1870 to 1935 echoed the ethos and organization of the first prisons for women established in Britain around the middle of the century. Significantly, many influential American reformers had visited Mount Joy Female Convict Prison in Dublin and were impressed by the advantages of a separate institution governed and run entirely by women. In many respects, however, the new American reformatories differed markedly. Whereas prisons for women in Britain were heavily constrained by their architectural setting, American reformatories started afresh in buildings that mirrored the ideals they sought to inculcate in their inmates. Most were set in rural areas, often on vast plots. The Massachusetts Reformatory Prison for Women occupied thirty acres, the House of Refuge at Hudson, New York, was set on forty acres, and the Western House of Refuge opened on a one-hundred-acre campus. Ellen Cheny Johnson encapsulated the supposed value of this rural location: "To rouse an interest in country life and pursuits is likely to make the woman more contented when she is placed in a quiet home away from the city."

Following the model established by the House of Refuge at Hudson, the reformatories were generally built as a series of cottages, each housing "families" of twenty or more inmates, grouped around a central administrative building. The philosophy behind this organization was clear: "Each cottage should be a real home, with an intelligent, sympathetic woman at the head to act as mother." At Indiana Reformatory, for example, in an attempt to create a truly domestic atmosphere, the women dressed in gingham frocks and ate at tables set with tablecloths and decorated with flowers. This domestic setting allowed ample opportunity to train inmates in the housewifely skills of cooking, cleaning, and serving. Many of the women were subsequently paroled to positions as domestic servants, but if they did not perform satis-factorily, parole was revoked and they were returned to the reformatory to complete their sentence.

Unlike ordinary custodial prisons, reformatories also provided extensive educational facilities. Many of the early reformatories were well equipped with workshops, classrooms, and gymnasiums. Women spent several hours a day in class learning the basic skills of reading, writing, and health care. Remunerative skills were also considered an essential part of the reformatory program. At Indiana, the industrial laundry employed about half the prisoners, and experts were brought in to teach the women the secrets of starching, ironing, and other similar skills. Outside of classes and domestic duties, women were kept busy with an array of recreational pursuits including outdoor sports, singing, picnics, and nature walks.

Central to the development of these reformatories was the aim that women should direct and staff them. At first, men retained top positions as prison managers and doctors. However, women struggled to realize their thesis that female prisoners were best managed and treated by other women. In 1877, for example, Indiana Reformatory threw out its male board of managers. And throughout the 1880s and 1890s female doctors were appointed at Indiana and New York reformatories. By the turn of the century, women had largely gained control over the administration of reformatories. At Massachusetts it was proudly noted, "Every officer, from the head to the lowest matron, is a female, and no man goes into the institution for any official business whatever." Many of those now in charge were women with strong personalities and pronounced views on the management of female prisoners. Women like Eliza Mosher at Framington Reformatory and Sarah Smith at Indiana Reformatory had a marked impact on the character and life of the institutions they governed. But even for these most determined women, finding competent female staff willing to undertake the poorly paid and burdensome work of the prison matron proved an almost insuperable barrier. As a result, they were all too often forced to revert to traditional methods of managing their prisons.

In many ways, life in these reformatories was far less severe than in male prisons at that time, and yet in important respects the reformatory represented a greater infringement on women's freedom. Although sentencing practices varied from state to state, the norm was an indeterminate three-year sentence. This meant that women could be held for up to this maximum if they failed to show signs of reform. Moreover, they could be committed to reformatories for misdemeanors or even lesser offenses, whereas men could be sentenced for such long terms only if they had committed felonies. Judicial authority for differential sentencing was provided by the 1919 Kansas decision *State v. Heitman,* which allowed women to be given maximum indeterminate sentences in reformatories while men served shorter terms in local jails. This differential was justified on the basis that women were sent to reformatories not to be punished in proportion to the seriousness of their offense but to be reformed and retrained, a process that, it was argued, required time. Increasingly, the pressure to hold women for such long periods came not only from would-be reformers but also from the growing Eugenics Movement, which sought to have "genetically inferior" women removed from social circulation for as many of their childbearing years as possible.

Innovations in Britain

If reformatories in the United States were used as a covert means of incapacitating women in order to prevent them from reproducing, in Britain these eugenic purposes were far more overt. Special institutions were developed specifically to incarcerate those women who seemed to present a risk to the future health of the race. Many of these women were "habitual offenders," who defied all reformatory efforts and returned to the prison time and again. They presented a major problem for penal discipline, raising serious doubts about the feasibility of the moral reform program that had once been seen as the main purpose of the female prison. The atmosphere of moral regeneration and religious awakening that had prevailed under the directorship of Sir Joshua Jebb now disappeared under the regime of Sir Edmund Du Cane (director of prisons from 1865 to 1898), a strict disciplinarian who favored, instead, a highly militaristic order. The nationalization of local prisons in 1877 sounded a further death knell to innovation and individual treatment. Earlier efforts to respond to women on a personal basis were subsumed by the obsessive concern for uniformity that had long characterized male prisons.

With their reformatory purpose largely abandoned, prisons were increasingly seen as dumping grounds for the socially inadequate. Prison officials were disturbed to find that there was a sizable core of criminal women who seemed to be almost immune to the pains of imprisonment. Although women formed less than one-fifth of all prisoners in Britain, they actually outnumbered men in the class of those who had ten or more previous convictions—the "hardened habituals." For much of the second half of the nineteenth century, women made up well over two-thirds of those who had been imprisoned more than ten times. Du Cane argued that the repeated appearance of the same core of offenders actually signified a measure of success in that it indicated that "new recruits" were being deterred from entering the prison system. Certainly, the number of women committed to penal servitude in Britain declined steadily from an annual high of 1,050 in 1860 to a mere 95 in 1890. Similarly, in France the number of women committed to central prisons was halved in the final quarter of the century, with the result that seven of the country's eleven central prisons were closed by 1885. Whether this decline represented, as Du Cane maintained, the success of the prison as an agent of deterrence or whether it merely signified growing disillusionment with the prison and a consequent reluctance to impose long custodial sentences remains unclear.

Those who remained in the central prisons represented the most hardened offenders, apparently impervious to moral reform. In its annual report for 1880 a leading penal reform agency, the Howard Association, declared, "It is well known that the least hopeful subjects of moral influence are habitual criminals, and most of all, criminal and debased women." Yet many of the worst female recidivists were not dangerous criminals so much as petty offenders, social inadequates, and outcasts incapable of surviving in outside society. Repeatedly sentenced to short terms of a few days or so for petty theft and public-order offenses, drunken and mentally deficient women were a serious source of disruption to the prison regime. To commit them to prison time and again was clearly both inappropriate and unproductive. As the chaplain of Brixton Prison pointed out, "It does seem important that women of this class should be treated in a special manner and in a *special place,* and that they should be placed under medical treatment, as their presence among other prisoners operates most injuriously upon those around them, and constitutes one of the chief difficulties in carrying out the discipline of this prison."

The case for removing such women from prisons became overwhelming. After much public pressure and parliamentary debate, the Inebriates Act passed in 1898 removed alcoholics from the prison system by setting up a two-tier system of local "certified" and state reformatories. These were to hold two main groups—habitual drunkards and those who had committed serious crimes while drunk—for up to three years. Although there was nothing in the legislation to indicate that the act was directed primarily at women, in practice the common view that female alcoholism was the greater social problem ensured that women filled the places. By 1904, women made up 91 percent of admissions to the local reformatories; even in the state-run institutions they outnumbered men by two to one.

Inebriate reformatories were run much on the model of reformatories established for women in America. For the most part they were set up in remote, often idyllic, rural locations. Modeled on the cottage system, they formed their inmates into "families" who spent much of their days pursuing a traditional vision of the rural life that was fast disappearing. Turning their backs on the filth and demoralization of the growing urban slums to which most of the women would one day return, the reformatories attempted to re-create a rural way of life apparently free from the temptations of alcoholism and crime.

Another group to attract the attention of turn-of-the-century reformers consisted of those prison habitues whose offenses seemed to owe more to mental inadequacy than malice. Penal administrators had always maintained that women prisoners, as a class, were of weaker intellect and were less able to control their emotions than men. Consequently, women were seen not only as less reformable but also as less able to comply with the strictures of the penal regime. "They are a source of great trouble to those who have to deal with them, as they are not amenable to ordinary prison discipline and need to be treated differently from other prisoners." Such assumptions about women's weaker mental health both necessitated and justified the development of more flexible regimes in women's prisons. Even then a minority of women were so mentally inadequate that they were incapable of complying with prison rules. As such, they posed problems of management out of all proportion to their numbers.

The attempt to classify and to separate those deemed "feeble-minded," and to develop appropriate institutions for them, was one of the main areas of innovation in penal policy for women in the early twentieth century. The aim was to create easier conditions for these women but also to allow a tougher regime to be imposed on the remaining inmates. Segregation within the prison was only a partial solution. There was growing pressure for feeble-minded women to be removed completely from the rigors of the penal regime. In 1907, Aylesbury Convict Prison for Women became the first prison in Britain to segregate its feeble-minded in an entirely separate wing ("D" Hall), where they were supervised by specially selected officers and "treated in all respects with exceptional leniency." By contrast the continuing lack of specialist provision for the feeble-minded in local prisons was found increasingly intolerable. The prison commissioners, in their report for 1909, declared that such prisoners, "especially in the case of women," constituted "one of the saddest and most unprofitable features of prison administration."

The Demise of the Reformatory Movement

The early twentieth century was a period of disillusionment with late-nineteenth-century innovations on both sides of the Atlantic. Faith in a cure for chronic alcoholism in Britain and early optimism about the potential for reforming women in America both declined. In part this was due to changes in the female prison population. Programs to control the growth of prostitution during World War I sent thousands of women to prison in both Britain and America. Little attempt was made to reform these "fallen women"; rather, their sentences served simply as a way of protecting servicemen from the spread of venereal disease.

In America the imprisonment of prostitutes during the war and of increasing numbers of alcoholics and drug addicts in the following decade continued to transform the reformatory population. Sympathy for the vulnerable, young women who had populated the early reformatories was less forthcoming for their "hardened" successors. Similarly, the growing numbers of black female prisoners attracted less compassion and understanding than their predominantly white precursors. These trends were exacerbated by funding cutbacks, which prevented the expansion of buildings to house the growing number of women sent to reformatories. For example, serious overcrowding at Bedford Hills New York Reformatory for Women forced inmates to share rooms and even sleep in corridors. Classification of inmates broke down while tensions rose and were exacerbated by the discovery that many inmates were forming homosexual relations. The discovery that "most undesirable sex relations" had grown out of this "mingling of the two races" led to a series of urgent investigations into discipline within Bedford Hills. Despite attempts to classify and separate inmates, growing overcrowding was such that, by the 1920s, the institution was forced to recognize that it was no longer in any real sense serving its original reformatory purpose.

By the mid-1930s the reformatory movement had fallen into general decline. Re- ·formatories had proved highly expensive to maintain alongside regular custodial prisons for women. By the onset of the Great Depression, most states had stopped building on the reformatory model, and many were even driven to shutting down existing custodial prisons. As a result, those reformatories already built were obliged to take increasing numbers of more serious offenders, to relinquish many of their distinctive features and, indeed, their idealistic reformatory aims, and to provide more secure, more strictly punitive accommodation. As the historian Nicole Hahn Rafter has gracefully commented: "Gone were the days of nature hikes over the reformatories' rolling hills. Women now had less freedom within the institution, and security measures were intensified. Whatever benefits had accrued to inmates from the reformatory movement dwindled and disappeared." The impetus that had fired the reformatory movement appeared to have died. Former reformatories became conventional custodial institutions, and across many of the southern and western states women continued to be held in accommodations adjoining male penitentiaries. The failure of the reformatory experiment left policymakers seemingly bereft of new ideas about how to deal with women prisoners.

In Britain a similar pattern of disillusionment and decline can be seen. By the 1920s, all the reformatories opened for female alcoholics only fifteen or twenty years before had been closed down. The vast numbers of women convicted of drunk and disorderly behavior were again sent to prison, so that by 1926 the governor of Holloway Prison for women was once more arguing, "If some proper method were devised for dealing with this unfortunate class the greater part of this prison could be closed." The report of the Committee on Persistent Offenders in 1932 recorded that drunkenness accounted for just short of half the women sent to prison. Most female drunks were sentenced for only a few weeks to local prisons. Often highly disruptive, they could not be fitted into any program of training or reform. For weary prison officials, simply keeping order took precedence over any other higher aim. The demise of reformatory movements on both sides of the Atlantic left little energy or enthusiasm for innovation in women's prisons.

Undoubtedly the most important change in women's prisons in the first half of the twentieth century was the staggering decline in their populations. In Britain, for example, more than 33,000 convicted women had been imprisoned in 1913; by 1921, this number had fallen to 11,000, and by the 1960s, to less than 2,000. In part this may have been attributable, as contemporaries maintained, to "the improvement in social conditions and social behaviour." But it was also triggered by declining faith in the value of imprisonment and by concurrent pressures to move women into other, more suitable institutions. Across Britain, as a matter of policy, the wards and wings of many local prisons were closed down. For example, in 1921 women prisoners were removed from Ipswich, Oxford, Plymouth, Shrewsbury, Swansea, and Carlisle; the following year the women's wing at Bristol closed, and by the end of 1925, the women's wings at Newcastle, Leeds, Maidstone, and Norwich had all been shut down. Their inmates were sent instead to a few chosen institutions, like Holloway Prison in London, which soon became the largest and most important prison for women in England and Wales. Yet even here, innovations in the interwar period were few and unexciting. Such changes as there were related mainly to improvements in physical conditions and in the classification of women as a means of better segregating young from old and recalcitrant from reformable. Impetus in penal reform in this period was located firmly outside the prison, in the development of alternatives to custody. Discharges, suspended sentences, fines, compensation, and most innovative of all, the introduction of probation orders in large measure replaced the futile round of short sentences for both women and men.

The United States did not witness closure of women's prisons on the same scale as did Britain in the interwar years. Nonetheless, virtually no new institutions opened in the northeastern or north central states, and no more than a handful opened in the South. Even these were opened not as a result of reforming zeal but as a simple matter of expediency when women's units attached to male penitentiaries became intolerably overcrowded. For example, women were held next to the male prison at Raleigh in North Carolina until 1933, when lack of space obliged the authorities to move them to old prison buildings on the outskirts of the town. In some southern states, prisons for women came into existence more or less by chance: female offenders employed on farms and plantations were housed in separate camps that eventually became prisons for women in their own right. The development of prisons for women by either route was, then, largely pragmatic. It bore little resemblance to the vision and drive that had inspired earlier developments.

Only in the 1960s did interest in women's prisons become once more a topic of research and innovation. The conjunction of a number of factors explains this renewed interest. First, the rise of modern feminism encouraged a reappraisal of women's role in society in general and, as a result, a growing body of empirical research on women as offenders and sociological studies of their life in prison. Second, crime rates among women began to rise, apparently at a faster rate than for men, prompting a veritable "moral panic" about the "new female criminal." Unsurprisingly, women's prisons attracted new attention as a means of combating this unwelcome trend. Finally, the view that female offenders require differentiated treatment appropriate to the perceived attributes of their sex led, at last, to changes in mainstream prisons for women. The most important prison for women in Britain—Holloway—was redesigned in the late 1960s on the assumption that "most women and girls in custody require some form of medical, psychiatric or remedial treatment." Holloway was rebuilt on the basis that it would operate as "basically a secure hospital to act as the hub of the female prison system." According to the plan, its medical and psychiatric facilities would be "its central feature," and normal custodial facilities would form "a relatively small part of the establishment." In fact, Holloway has developed much more like a "conventional" prison than its originators intended. Yet its special facilities for mentally disturbed prisoners are testament to the continuing view of criminal women as mentally ill or inadequate.

The view that a proportion of the female prison population was mentally inadequate now seems to have spread to envelop the female prison population as a whole. Today psychotropic drugs are dispensed in far larger quantities in prisons for women than in those for men, ostensibly in response to women prisoners' greater mental problems. The tendency to self-mutilate has at times become almost endemic in female prisons, but there seems to be no self-destructive equivalent among male prisoners. The fact that women in prison are punished for infringements of prison discipline nearly twice as often as men is also cited as evidence of women's greater psychiatric disturbance. As a result of all these factors, the expectation that women in prison are likely to be in some way mentally inadequate or ill is now common among penal policymakers.

Though the demands of differential treatment for criminal women have historically tended to mitigate the harshness and uniformity of the regime in female prisons, it would be dangerous to assume that women were, therefore, treated more leniently. The pressure to protect these more "vulnerable" prisoners from corruption and to restore them to prevailing ideals of femininity tended to create regimes that were in many senses more claustrophobic and more oppressive than those found in male prisons. Moreover, in a bid to maintain ideal standards of feminine conduct, demeanor, and conversation, women were more closely surveilled than their male counterparts. Above all, diagnoses of women prisoners as errant, sick, or mentally deficient have justified indeterminate sentencing and even permanent incarceration, in contrast to the more strictly proportional sentences imposed on men. Whether women prisoners are, in fact, more prone to mental illness or inadequacy remains unresolved. Yet the historical legacy of poorer prison conditions, the greater stigma applied to women who offend, and the amalgamation of female prisons, which has caused many women to be held far from home, may together go some way to explaining why women appear to have a harder time than men in coming to terms with imprisonment.

Bibliographic Note

This chapter draws on my own work on the history of women's prisons: *Women, Crime, and Custody in Victorian England* (1991; reprint, Oxford: Clarendon Press, 1994) and "Women, Crime and Penal Responses: A Historical Account" in *Crime and Justice: A Review of Research,* vol. 14, ed. Michael Tonry (Chicago: University of Chicago Press, 1991). Important accounts of the prison for women in Britain are Russell P. Dobash, R. Emerson Dobash, and Sue Gutteridge, *The Imprisonment of Women* (Oxford: B. Blackwell, 1986), and Ann Smith, *Women in Prison* (London: Stevens, 1962), and in the United States, Estelle B. Freedman, *Their Sisters' Keepers: Women's Prison Reform in America, 1830–1930* (Ann Arbor: University of Michigan Press, 1981), and Nicole Hahn Rafter, *Partial Justice: Women, Prisons, and Social Control,* 2d ed. (New Brunswick, N.J.: Transaction Publishers, 1990). For France, Patricia O'Brien, *The Promise of Punishment: Prisons in Nineteenth-Century France* (Princeton: Princeton University Press, 1982), contains good material on women's prisons.

On the history of women's transportation to the colonies, see Robert Hughes, *The Fatal Shore: A History of the Transportation of Convicts to Australia, 1787–1868* (London: Collins Harvill, 1987), and Anne Summers, *Damned Whores and God's Police: The Colonization of Women in Australia* (Victoria: Penguin Books, 1975). On responses to women prostitutes in the nineteenth century, see Frances Finnegan, *Poverty and Prostitution: A Study of Victorian Prostitutes in York* (Cambridge:

Cambridge University Press, 1979), Judith Walkowitz, *Prostitution and Victorian Society: Women, Class, and the State* (Cambridge: Cambridge University Press, 1980), and Linda Mahood, *The Magdalenes: Prostitution in the Nineteenth Century* (London: Routledge, 1990). On women murderesses and their punishments, see Peter C. Hoffer and N.E.H. Hull, *Murdering Mothers: Infanticide in England and New England, 1558–1803* (New York: New York University Press, 1981), Mary S. Hartman, *Victorian Murderesses: A True History of Thirteen Respectable French and English Women Accused of Unspeakable Crimes,* 2d ed. (London: Robson Books, 1985), and Ruth Harris, *Murders and Madness: Medicine, Law, and Society in the Fin de Siecle* (Oxford: Clarendon Press, 1989).

Important nineteenth-century books on the imprisonment of women quoted in the text include the following: Elizabeth Fry, *Observations on Visiting, Superintending, and Government of Female Prisons* (London: John and Arthur Arch, 1827); George Laval Chesterton, *Revelations of Prison Life,* 2d ed. (London: Hurst and Blackett, 1856); Henry Mayhew and John Binny, *The Criminal Prisons of London and Scenes of Prison Life* (London: Griffin, 1862); Mary Carpenter, *Our Convicts* (London: Longman, 1864); Susan Willis Fletcher, *Twelve Months in an English Prison* (London: Lee and Shepard, 1884); and Mary Gordon, *Penal Discipline* (London: Routledge, 1922).

To situate the prison for women within the wider history of the prison, see the following: Michel Foucault, *Discipline and Punish: The Birth of the Prison,* trans. Alan Sheridan (Harmondsworth, England: Peregrine, 1975); Michael Ignatieff, *A Just Measure of Pain: The Penitentiary in the Industrial Revolution, 1750–1850* (London: Macmillan, 1978); Christopher Harding, Bill Hines, Richard Ireland, and Philip Rawlings, *Imprisonment in England and Wales: A Concise History* (London: Croom Helm, 1985); William James Forsythe, *The Reform of Prisoners, 1830–1900* (London: Croom Helm, 1987); and Leon Radzinowicz and Roger Hood, *The Emergence of Penal Policy in Victorian and Edwardian England* (Oxford: Clarendon Press, 1990).

CHAPTER TWELVE

DELINQUENT CHILDREN
The Juvenile Reform School

Steven Schlossman

Of the many and valuable institutions sustained in whole, or in part, from the public treasury, we may safely say, that none is of more importance, or holds a more intimate connection with the future prosperity and moral integrity of the community, than one which promises to take neglected, wayward, wandering, idle and vicious boys, with perverse minds and corrupted hearts, and cleanse and purify and reform them, and thus send them forth in the erectness of manhood and in the beauty of virtue, educated and prepared to be industrious, useful and virtuous citizens.

> —Massachusetts Governor George Briggs, address at opening of the Lyman Industrial School for Boys, Massachusetts, 1848

The child must be placed where he will gradually be restored to the true position of childhood . . . he must in short be placed in a *family*. Love must lead the way; faith and obedience will follow. . . . This is the fundamental principle of all true reformatory action with the young.

> —English child advocate Mary Carpenter, *Athenaeum*, March 19, 1853

What is a "reform school"? What is a "juvenile delinquent"? What is "rehabilitation"? These terms, familiar though they may be, occasion as much puzzlement as any in the lexicon of criminal justice. Definitions have changed since the early 1800s, when the reform school was first envisioned as a field of dreams on which to plan grand schemes for salvaging errant youth. Today, with the brutality rather than the innocence of youth trumpeted in the media and the rehabilitative ideal all but abandoned as a goal of corrections policy, the very notion of a juvenile reform school seems like an oxymoron. Few other criminal justice legacies of the nineteenth century—not even the prison—have so thoroughly lost their credibility as an instrument of sound public policy.

The path by which the reform school evolved from a popular child-saving venture in the early nineteenth century to an unwanted orphan of the corrections and educational systems in the late twentieth century has never been fully explored. The classic texts in criminology deal with the reform school in passing, if at all. Perhaps this is because its history has been rather quiet: no Panopticon, no Auburn, no Elmira, no Attica to inspire high hopes or dread doubts. The reform school produced few highlights of the kind likely to secure its place in correctional lore.

Yet the reform school was a full-fledged partner in the burst of institution building that saw the invention of such new approaches to transforming human behavior as prisons, mental hospitals, and public schools in the nineteenth-century Western world. Like these other institutions, the reform schools of the United States attracted many famous foreign visitors (such as Charles Dickens, Alexis de Tocqueville, and Gustave de Beaumont), who portrayed them as models for worldwide emulation. This chapter will pay particular attention to the American experience in tracing the history of the reform school. At the same time, it will situate the reform school in a context of international experimentation that marked it as an invention shared by the Western world rather than one of American origin alone.

JUVENILE DELINQUENCY AND THE INVENTION OF REFORM SCHOOLS IN THE NINETEENTH CENTURY

Although it is possible to identify a few institutional precedents to the reform school in sixteenth-, seventeenth-, and eighteenth-century Europe, it is clear that until the early 1800s, families, not institutions, were the principal instrument through which communities disciplined children. The laws regulating children's behavior and upholding parental prerogatives were quite rigid and comprehensive, and the penalties that were authorized as appropriate for juvenile offenders were often severe (most notably, the Massachusetts law of 1646, which specified the death penalty for children over age sixteen who cursed or refused to obey their parents). Yet, in reality, the more stringent laws were rarely enforced. Magistrates were more likely to order parents and guardians to administer punishment within the household to incorrigible and law-breaking children than to confine the children in adult penal institutions or to have them publicly subjected to the corporal punishments (especially whipping) that would be commonly dispensed to adult offenders.

At the same time, judges and juries retained considerable discretion in enforcing the statutes that authorized harsh punishments for juvenile offenders. In the eighteenth century, it was relatively common for magistrates to sentence preteen as well as teenage children to local and state jails and prisons for relatively minor offenses. This practice continued and may well have expanded in the early nineteenth century. Yet it is also clear that judges and juries often determined that neither the interests of justice nor a child's well-being would be served by committing him or her to an adult penal facility and that it would be better to exonerate and release than to incarcerate the child. This practice of absolving children from punishment, however clear-cut their crime and criminal intent, stimulated grave social concern and fed the early-nineteenth-century interest in establishing separate penal facilities for juveniles.

The term "juvenile delinquency" underwent an important transformation in the early nineteenth century. Vague public concern about tendencies toward misbehavior among the young in general (such as being disorderly in church or attaching lit candles to paper kites) gave way to a newly heightened and focused concern about misbehavior among urban lower-class children. "Juvenile delinquency" was increasingly used to single out the suspicious activities of groups of lower-class (often immigrant) children who occupied a netherworld in the bowels of the nation's growing cities and who were perceived to be either living entirely free of adult supervision or serving as pawns of depraved parents. Well before Dickens set the archetype to fiction, dire portraits of youthful urban predators were quite common among social commentators who popularized the new image of dangerous street urchins and campaigned for special institutions to house and rehabilitate them.

Houses of Refuge

Although the New York House of Refuge (which opened on January 1, 1825) is generally acknowledged to be the first of the early reform schools, several institutions of somewhat similar character already existed in England and Europe. Indeed, these predecessors significantly shaped the ideas of the founders of the New York facility. The Quaker teacher and philanthropist John Griscom, a longtime member of the New York Society for the Prevention of Pauperism, brought their experience to the attention of American reformers. Griscom was especially influenced by the work of the London Philanthropic Society, which had been founded in 1788 "for the Prevention of Crimes, and for a Reform Among the Poor; by training up to Virtue and Industry the Children of Vagrants and Criminals, and such who are in the Paths of Vice and Infamy." By the time Griscom visited the society in 1818, its institution had begun to accept juvenile offenders as well as impoverished and abandoned children, ignoring the distinction between vagrants and criminals. Particularly impressed by the society's educational and industrial program, he concluded: "It was cheering to find that so many wretched children were `snatched as fire brands' from criminality and ruin, and restored to the prospects of respectable and honourable life." The reform school was thus not exclusively an American invention. Rather, it represented a transatlantic cross-fertilization of philanthropic ideas and designs, especially among Quakers.

The founders of reform schools assumed that their clientele would not be exclusively serious offenders but a motley group of lower-class children—some who had already been convicted of criminal acts, others whose incorrigible behavior predicted future confrontations with the law, and still others whose life chances were so circumscribed by poverty and bad example that it would be an act of charity (in the founders' view) to incarcerate them and prevent a lifetime of poverty and crime. The term "delinquency" was used rather elastically to legitimate the incarceration of any youngster who, in the judgment of a court or of a reform school's managing directors, might benefit from a highly structured regime of discipline and instruction. True, formal legislation enabling a reform school to house criminal with noncriminal children was sometimes politically controversial and often did not appear until the institution was already long in operation. Moreover, outside of the United States, particularly in England, diligent efforts were made to distinguish institutions for young criminals from those housing merely incorrigible or neglected children. Nonetheless, most early reform schools brought all these groups together. The founders emphasized the commonalities rather than the differences among them.

Legal Foundations of the Reform School

The principal legal justification for reform schools in the United States in the 1820s (as for juvenile courts three-quarters of a century later) was the doctrine of *parens patriae*. A medieval English doctrine of nebulous origin and meaning, *parens patriae* originally sanctioned the right of the Crown to intervene in natural family relations whenever a child's welfare was threatened. As part of its legal inheritance from England, every American state in the nineteenth century affirmed its right to stand as guardian, or superparent, of all minors.

The seminal legal decision incorporating *parens patriae* into American juvenile law was *Ex parte Crouse*, delivered by the Pennsylvania Supreme Court in 1838. The case involved a young girl who, on the complaint of her mother, had been committed to the Philadelphia House of Refuge. Under an expansive commitment law, the Pennsylvania juvenile institution was permitted to do officially what it had always been doing in practice, namely, incarcerating incorrigible as well as criminal children, sometimes on complaints from parents and with little concern for formal criminal procedure. Mr. Crouse did not approve of his wife's actions and filed a *habeas corpus* petition to obtain his daughter's release. When his petition was denied, he hired a lawyer to press suit on Sixth Amendment grounds, charging that his daughter's incarceration without a jury trial was unconstitutional. The Supreme Court denied Mr. Crouse's allegations and in so doing established the reform school's practice on a solid legal foundation.

The court's argument was in two parts. First, it affirmed the binding nature of the English common law tradition in general and of the *parens patriae* doctrine in particular. Asserting the government's power to incarcerate noncriminal as well as criminal children on the grounds that their families were incapable of raising them properly, the court asked rhetorically:

> May not the natural parents, when unequal to the task of education, or unworthy of it, be superseded by the *parens patriae,* or common guardian of the community? It is to be remembered that the public has a paramount interest in the virtue and knowledge of its members, and that, of strict right, the business of education belongs to it. That parents are ordinarily entrusted with it, is because it can seldom be put into better hands; but where they are incompetent and corrupt, what is there to prevent the public from withdrawing their faculties, held as they obviously are, at its sufferance?

Mr. Crouse's daughter, the court concluded, "had been snatched from a course which must have ended in confirmed depravity: and not only is the restraint of her person lawful, but it would have been an act of extreme cruelty to release her from it." Thus, the court clearly established the legal right of a reform school to try to reform an inmate, whether or not the child had officially been convicted (or accused, for that matter) of a crime.

In its second argument, the court was equally vigorous in affirming that a reform school was indeed a school; the Philadelphia House of Refuge, for legal purposes, was best understood as an expansion of the city's fledgling system of public schools, not of its prisons. "As to the abridgement of indefeasible rights by confinement of the person," the court insisted, "it is no more than what is borne, to a greater or less extent, in every school; and we know of no natural right to exemption from restraints which conduce to an infant's welfare." In sum, a reform school was a residential public school for confirmed and incipient delinquents. The government had every right, if not a moral duty, to create reform schools without serious concern for whether children *qua* children held indefeasible rights other than to be brought up properly. Except for one maverick appellate court decision in Illinois in 1870 (People v. Turner), the legal standing of reform schools underwent no significant challenge for many years. (Turner itself was overruled several years later.) Not until the U.S. Supreme Court issued its famous In re Gault decision in 1967 would the logic of the Ex parte Crouse decision be seriously challenged.

Reform Schools Triumphant

It is all too easy to view the spread of reform schools in the nineteenth century as inevitable, as conforming to a self-evident growth pattern whereby the example set by the pioneer urban institutions in the 1820s stimulated a flurry of imitative activity throughout the United States and the Western world. Yet the urgency of establishing reform schools was not generally evident until mid-century. Outside of a few major industrial cities, such as Boston, Philadelphia, Bristol, Hamburg, and Paris, the reform school did not initially carry wide appeal in the United States or in Europe (where the sponsorship of reform schools was overwhelmingly private rather than public). Additionally, in the United States the issue of reform schools lacked the degree of consensus that had helped build widespread support for prisons, mental asylums, and public schools in the 1830s and 1840s. From the start, the reform schools were rent by internal discord over proper architectural design, disciplinary methods, and religious and educational strategies for rehabilitating juvenile delinquents.

A true reform school movement did emerge, however, after mid-century in both the United States and Western Europe. In Europe, reform schools generally emerged under private auspices and private management but often with more or less public funding. The pioneer efforts of Johann Wichern and the Rauhe Haus in Germany in the 1830s and of Frédéric Demetz and the Colonie Agricole in France in the 1840s, both of whom looked to normal schools to produce trained cadres of reform school personnel, spawned dozens of imitators in their respective countries as well as in Switzerland, Belgium, Holland, and Denmark. Mary Carpenter's renowned work with delinquents at the Kingswood and Red Lodge reform schools in the 1850s not only helped popularize the Wichern and Demetz models in England but also facilitated the passage of England's first comprehensive juvenile justice legislation, the Youthful Offenders Act of 1854, and the Industrial Schools Act of 1866.

Reform schools were also popular after mid-century in the United States, where they were generally created under public rather than private authority. However, joint public and private financing was not uncommon, and the schools' internal affairs were often supervised by local private boards. The number of reform schools in America grew from only three in the mid-1840s to twenty in 1860, ten of them sponsored by states (the first was at Westborough in Massachusetts in 1847), seven by municipalities, and three by private sponsors but with substantial public funding. The number of reform schools grew to over fifty in the mid-1870s. By the end of the nineteenth century, reform schools were ubiquitous in every region except the South, which generally lagged behind the other regions in all phases of institutional development.

The most provocative interpretation of reform schools in the United States is by David Rothman, who contends in *The Discovery of the Asylum* (1971) that the reform schools, like the prisons, mental hospitals, poorhouses, and orphan asylums founded around the same time, served important symbolic as well as functional purposes for nineteenth-century American society. This entire class of custodial institutions, he argues, was invented in response to widespread fears—real and imagined—of social and family disintegration. The new institutions would isolate "deviant" from law-abiding citizens to prevent "contamination," teach inmates the necessity of highly disciplined behavior in a rapidly evolving social order, and—Rothman's most far-reaching hypothesis—create exemplars of order for the citizenry at large. For parents, the well-ordered reform school would model the virtues of demanding unquestioned obedience from children in order to prepare them to cope with the uncertainties fostered by accelerated and unregulated social change.

Deference to authority was the organizing principle of most reform schools. Adherence to elaborate prescribed rules of conduct was both an end in itself and the means by which inmates and their keepers would learn to live harmoniously. Absolute obedience was demanded, and officials were quite ready to quell insubordination with physical thrashings. Corporal punishment was the norm; inmates were whipped or placed in solitary confinement for failing to conform to the daily regimen.

There were many ways of instilling deference and self-discipline, but the one prized most highly by reform school officials was the imposition of elaborate fixed routines. By scheduling every minute of every inmate's day, the officials hoped not only to maintain order and keep children from mischief but also to imbue them with the ethic of orderly and purposeful living. The degree of regimentation was startling. Consider the following typical day reported by the New York House of Refuge in 1835:

> At sunrise, the children are warned, by the ringing of a bell, to rise from their beds. Each child makes his own bed, and steps forth, on a signal, into the Hall. They then proceed, in perfect order, to the Wash Room. Thence they are marched to parade in the yard, and undergo an examination as to their dress and cleanliness; after which, they attend morning prayer. The morning school then commences, where they are occupied in summer, until 7 o'clock. A short intermission is allowed, when the bell rings for breakfast; after which, they proceed to their respective workshops, where they labor until 12 o'clock, when they are called from work, and one hour allowed them for washing and eating their dinner. At one, they again commence work, and continue at it until five in the afternoon, when the labor of the day terminates. Half an hour is allowed for washing and eating their supper, and at half-past five, they are conducted to the school room where they continue their studies until 8 o'clock. Evening Prayer is performed by the Superintendent; after which, the children are

conducted to their dormitories, which they enter, and are locked up for the night, when perfect silence reigns throughout the establishment. The foregoing is the history of a single day, and will answer for every day in the year, except Sundays, with slight variation during stormy weather, and the short days in winter.

Although the work and school routines of reform schools varied somewhat, the basic patterns were everywhere evident. Schooling received more attention than in adult prisons, but it was subordinated to work. Even when inmates received several hours of instruction, it was scheduled so as not to conflict with work schedules. As the century progressed, formal schooling was accorded more time, sometimes up to half a day. The instruction, however, rarely went beyond the elementary level, and the teachers usually lacked qualifications for the task.

The work required of reform school inmates was generally less demanding than that prescribed for adult prisoners; similarly, there was somewhat less pressure on reform schools than on prisons to defray costs by selling the products of inmates' labor. At institutions with farms, many inmates spent the summer months tending crops, usually for internal consumption but sometimes to meet the needs of other philanthropic institutions and occasionally for sale. Even the few institutions with thriving farms had to employ the inmates in other pursuits during the nonsummer months, however, so that farming never became as central to the routine as many reform school officials would have preferred.

The employments for delinquents were chosen as much for alleged character-building quality as for potential market value or any productive skills that inmates might learn. The stated goal was not to prepare inmates for particular employment but to instill industrial habits that would prepare them to become apprentices—not, ideally, in their old city haunts but in farm families. By the latter part of the century, the ability of reform schools to secure apprenticeships for their inmates declined precipitously, and delinquent children were simply released outright to shift for themselves and live where they might (usually their original residences). Although the practice of unsupervised release was certainly of concern, it was in fact not inconsistent with the policy orientation of reform schools. Institution officials rarely investigated the homes to which they apprenticed inmates, nor did they pay much attention to the difficulties delinquents faced in readjusting to conventional society.

Making nails and cheap shoes and caning wicker chairs were probably the most common employments at reform schools. As in adult prisons, contract labor was sometimes relied on to provide machines and materials, but the financial incentives for contractors to employ children were understandably less than for adults, as was the degree to which the contractors might exploit inmates or punish those who did not meet production quotas. Contract labor in reform schools did become more exploitative in the post–Civil War decades. The reform schools had greater budgetary needs because inflation and competition with newer types of charitable institutions reduced their public subsidies. To run the institutions with less money, superintendents were ready to delegate more authority to contractors in order to attract better contracts, increase inmate production, and thereby meet operating costs.

One of the more heated debates in juvenile corrections during the second half of the nineteenth century occurred between the advocates of the "congregate" and "cottage" systems. The congregate system used large, heterogeneous group living and work arrangements, whereas the cottages gathered (ideally) one to three dozen inmates to live and work in small "homes" under the supervision of full-time surrogate parents. At issue were not only broad questions of penal philosophy and design but also the appropriation, by both sides in the debate, of the same domestic language to describe their goals and practices: "family," "home," "love," "nurture." Could any institution that incarcerated young children against their will for several years' duration—whether it be the New York House of Refuge or Mary Carpenter's Kingswood in Bristol—truly be considered a substitute family or home?

The most curious aspect of the debate was that neither side was willing to concede the inherent limitations of custodial facilities to serve as family surrogates. Advocates of the cottage system confidently claimed that reform schools based on congregate organization could never aspire to be more than junior prisons but that cottage reform schools could rehabilitate their charges provided the surrogate parents were chosen with great care. The defenders of congregate institutions rejected this contention. As insistently as the advocates of the cottage system, they invoked family metaphors to describe their intent and their actual programs. An affectional mode of discipline was possible regardless of whether inmates slept and worked in cottages of thirty or in dormitories and workplaces of several hundred. Sentiment, not architectural design, held the key.

That neither cottage nor congregate reform schools provided substitute "homes" is readily demonstrable and not surprising. Domestic metaphors provided both Europeans and Americans with a new rhetoric for describing reform schools in terms consonant with the sentimental patterns of social thought common in the Victorian era, but the metaphors obscured the harsh realities of daily regimens and the impossibility of bending children's wills entirely to the wishes of their keepers, however benign.

Female Delinquency and Gender-Segregated Reform Schools

The first group of delinquent children delivered in 1825 to the New York House of Refuge consisted of six girls and three boys. Although girls thereafter never formed more than a small fraction of the refuge's inmates, the founders always intended to include girls, albeit in entirely separate residential quarters and under the supervision of a matron. Because of their isolation, the girls could not participate in most of the activities planned for boys, but they were still expected to contribute, through their cooking, sewing, and washing, to the institution's domestic maintenance. As with boys, the hope was that the industrial habits acquired in the institution, quite as much as any particular skills learned, would enable the girls to acquire apprentice positions as domestic servants in rural families far removed from their original, corrupting homes and communities.

From the first, the difficulties of keeping boy and girl delinquents entirely separated were recognized, occasionally through the embarrassing discovery that a girl had become pregnant while incarcerated. With little more to occupy their time than endless housekeeping and Bible chats, the female inmates often became obstreperous and offended Victorian sensibilities to a degree that their overseers could not tolerate. Although several American reform schools founded after mid-century excluded girls, the common practice was to house each sex in separate departments (if possible, in separate buildings) at the same institution. By 1880 there were only eleven separate girls' reform schools in the United States. Not until after the turn of the century did a true reform school movement for girls emerge.

Of the two female reform schools to achieve international reputations in the nineteenth century—Mary Carpenter's Red Lodge in England and the Lancaster Industrial School for Girls in Massachusetts—the Lancaster facility is of more abiding historical interest because of its innovations in cottage design. The founders would have preferred family-like cottages for ten or fewer girls rather than the residences that were actually built, boarding-school type homes with space for thirty or forty, but the difference did not dull their enthusiasm for being the first to embark on a new reform school tradition in America. "It is to be a *home*. Each house is to be a *family*, under the sole direction and control of the matron, who is to be the *mother* of the family. The government and discipline are strictly parental. . . . It is to educate, to teach them, industry, self-reliance, morality and religion, and prepare them to go forth qualified to become useful and respectable members of society. All this is to be done, without stone walls, bars or bolts, but by the more sure and effective restraining power—*the cords of love*." The nineteenth-century reform schools for girls had their own regimen, which was not as relentlessly grinding, production-oriented, or harsh as in male reform schools. Formal schooling and religious observances were more central to the routines of the girls' schools as well. Housekeeping, though, was the principal means of filling the girls' time and preparing them for indenture after release.

The rather idyllic early years of the cottage reform school for girls in Lancaster were not long sustained. Reflecting broader shifts in Massachusetts child welfare policy, younger girls were gradually eliminated from the institution and placed directly in farm families; they were replaced by girls with more confirmed patterns of sexual misconduct (including prostitution) and petty criminal behavior. Furthermore, the growing appeal in the late nineteenth century of hereditarian explanations of female delinquency (which culminated in the belief that sexual experimentation by girls indicated "feeble-mindedness") helped to undermine faith that "the cords of love" could rehabilitate female delinquents.

This experience was not, of course, unique to the girls' institutions. It occurred also in the cottage reform schools for boys in such states as Ohio and Wisconsin. The reputed ability to classify inmates according to different degrees of "badness" became the principal advantage that the new cottage design gave to superintendents. Rather than a means toward intense, affection-driven personal interaction between staff and inmates, the cottage system became mainly a tool by which management isolated younger delinquents from older, smaller ones from larger, and malcontents from everyone else.

Assessing the Nineteenth-Century Heritage

By the end of the nineteenth century, in both Europe and the United States, the reform school could count on only a handful of strong proponents, in penological or educational circles, to articulate its ideals for salvaging errant youth. One such proponent was the Columbia University educationist David Snedden, who believed that reform schools were pedagogical pioneers in developing new methods to educate lower-class youth, especially in vocational training. Equally positive assessments of steady progress and of better times ahead came from corrections professionals, particularly after the establishment of a new interest group in the United States, the National Conference on the Education of Truant, Backward, Dependent, and Delinquent Children.

A much more negative judgment was rendered by Homer Folks, a well-known social worker and secretary of the Children's Aid Society of Pennsylvania. His review of the history of reform schools led him to discount both their claims of success and their future utility. These institutions, he argued, offered temptations to parents to shirk their child-rearing responsibilities, subjected younger, relatively innocent inmates to the educational influences and sexual advances of older, more confirmed delinquents, imparted an ineradicable stigma that hampered inmates' postrelease adjustment, treated individuals en masse rather than individually, and by their very nature, were incapable of preparing children for life outside an institution. By the 1880s similar criticisms began to be heard in Europe, even with reference to such one-time institutional exemplars as the Colonie Agricole. Folks's viewpoint was becoming the prevailing wisdom of child welfare reformers throughout the Western world.

In retrospect, the nineteenth-century reform school was an altogether unadventurous institution. Having separated juvenile from adult offenders and thereby sparing the former (or so it was claimed) from the dangers of sexual exploitation and education in crime, the overwhelming majority of reform school administrators were unable to turn the institution into something more than a mini-prison for children—despite the fact that liberal commitment laws sent a relatively young and criminally inexperienced cohort to the schools. To the extent that doubts about design and purpose emerged, they centered more on form than substance, particularly on the alleged benefits of a cottage plan that encouraged a rhetoric of domesticity that bordered on the silly. The cottage ideal became a substitute for, rather than a spur to, original thinking about rehabilitating juvenile delinquents.

REFORM SCHOOLS IN THE FIRST HALF OF THE TWENTIETH CENTURY

At the turn of the twentieth century, the number of reform schools in the United States was still less than one hundred. They were located mainly in the North Atlantic and North Central states. Although boys' institutions were generally much larger than girls', they varied greatly in size, with some housing as many as one thousand delinquents. The American reform schools tended to be substantially larger than their European counterparts, in part because the American institutions were built anew whereas the European reform schools were often located in preexisting buildings.

Boys composed around 80 percent of the American reform school population. At commitment they were on average fourteen years old, the girls were somewhat older, and some institutions accepted children as young as age ten. The average length of stay was a little under two years. Most inmates had immigrant parents (in some states the overwhelming majority did). African-American youth composed around 15 percent of the inmates.

Generally speaking, girls were less likely to be charged with a specific criminal offense than boys. However, few boys in reform schools were serious criminals either.

The majority belonged "to the wayward, incorrigible, or vagrant class, and the special offence alleged in commitment" was usually "but an incident in a more or less extended career of anti-social activity." Whereas the girls' offenses were mainly linked to early sexual exploration or to victimization (the distinction between the two was not often observed—vice was vice), the boys' offenses, if they involved a property crime at all, were limited to petty larceny and only rarely involved a personal injury offense.

The number of American reform schools grew slowly but steadily in the first half of the twentieth century; the bulk of the increase came in the South and in the creation of separate facilities for girls. Although the great majority of inmates were white, progressively fewer among them had immigrant parents (a product of the reduced immigration from Europe), and progressively more were African-American (following the large-scale migration of southern blacks to northern cities). By the 1930s, nearly 25 percent of reform school inmates were African-American.

At the same time, the average length of stay declined nearly in half—from almost two years to one—and the median age at commitment increased from fourteen to sixteen. The former trend probably reflected an unstated policy of paroling inmates early to compensate for the failure of states to build reform schools at a pace commensurate with population growth. The latter trend probably reflected the impact of juvenile court-sponsored probation in siphoning off status offenders and minor property offenders from reform schools.

Variations on a Nineteenth-Century Theme

The story of the twentieth-century reform school is largely the perpetuation of scaled-down prisons for juveniles. Innovations were modest in design and even more modest in implementation, no more than a variation on adult prison routines. Several features, however, distinguished twentieth-century reform schools from their antecedents: they were much less prone to epidemic illness; they relied somewhat less on severe corporal punishments; they placed greater emphasis on academic education; they used rudimentary behavioral science methods to diagnose and classify inmates; and—to a limited degree—they paid more attention to monitoring the postrelease experiences of inmates. These changes notwithstanding, to enter most reform schools in America and Europe in the mid-twentieth century was to return to a remnant of the Dickensian era.

Most reform schools were virtually impervious to change. Even when serious efforts to transform correctional philosophy, design, and practice were contemplated and planned, the implementation was usually so faulty as to abort the experiment. These failures were generally as evident in the cottage as in the congregate institutions.

Consider, for example, the typically disappointing experience of the Ohio Boys' Industrial School (BIS)—originally known as the Ohio Farm School—which in the late nineteenth century was the best-known American imitator (for males) of the Colonie Agricole. According to its founders, the Ohio Farm School had two main advantages over its "house of refuge" predecessors. First, it relied mainly on agricultural labor to teach inmates self-reliance and usable vocational skills. Second, its cottage design facilitated close personal contact and communication between the staff and inmates.

The fame of the Ohio Farm School spread in the post–Civil War era, but the institution soon experienced difficulties in maintaining its agricultural work. Periodic crop failures and other mishaps undermined the institution's boast of maintaining self-sufficiency. Superintendent George Howe began to introduce various industries to service the institution and defray costs. As government expenses to maintain the institution mounted, much of its early legislative support eroded. Howe was fired, and he was replaced by a superintendent who was far less committed to the school's original philosophy. Then, in 1884, the name of the institution was changed to the Ohio Boys' Industrial School to incorporate a growing orientation to factory-like work. Apart from its rural location, the BIS was becoming increasingly indistinguishable from such traditional reform schools as the New York House of Refuge.

During the last decades of the century, administrative turmoil and harsh discipline characterized the institution. Even its cottage design was no longer a distinguishing feature as the inmate population soared to over eight hundred without a commensurate expansion in residences. As it became clear that the legislature would turn a deaf ear toward complaints about overcrowding, the superintendents resorted to early release (parole) to regulate population size.

In the early 1900s, the BIS introduced three major innovations to try to bring its program in line with the "individual treatment" methods that were becoming popular among penologists and educators. Influenced by such authors as William Healy, Edward Thorndike, and Lewis Terman, this orientation emphasized inmate classification, vocational education, and upgraded academic instruction. Potential benefits from a more sophisticated classification of inmates received the greatest attention, especially after the Ohio Bureau of Juvenile Research, founded in 1913, began to screen inmates with psychological and psychiatric tests. Yet aside from administering a battery of examinations to identify "feebleminded" boys for exclusion, the superintendents did not have much use for the psychological information. The available educational and vocational programs were simply not advanced or diverse enough to allow much refinement in selection procedures. In practice, the assignment of boys to institutional programs or living quarters proceeded according to traditional criteria such as age, race, religion, and offense.

As with classification, the introduction of new forms of vocational training changed work routines very little. The state legislature's professed enthusiasm for vocational programs was mainly rhetorical; the limited funding available usually purchased equipment that was obsolete from the start and prone to regular breakdown. Other problems emerged in the poor match between required work skills and inmate abilities. The typing instructor, for example, was perfectly satisfied with her equipment but soon found that few inmates possessed the level of reading skill necessary to train them for possible future employment as "type-writers."

These difficulties in implementing vocational programs paled before two more basic realities. First was the limited number of vocational offerings available to the huge inmate population. The vast majority of inmates did not have access to even a modicum of vocational training. For African-American inmates the prospects of gaining entry into a vocational program were even poorer, since they were shunted into specific service jobs, such as tending the kitchen and dining facilities, where their postrelease job prospects were alleged to be brighter. Second was the undeniable need, in light of inadequate legislative appropriations, to use the great bulk of inmate labor to maintain the institution. Maintenance needs at an institution as large as the BIS were literally endless. So-called force work, such as tending the garden, mending and sewing, and painting walls, occupied most inmates during the bulk of their stay at the BIS. This was especially the case if the boys were older or lacked skills developed in prior employments.

On the surface, more impressive changes occurred in academic programs than in either vocational training or inmate classification. Schooling occupied an increasing segment—often half—of most inmates' days. Serious efforts were made to upgrade the level and variety of instruction available to inmates and to improve the teaching staff. Though innovation was clearly attempted, the BIS educators tended to exaggerate their achievements. Such a basic reform as grading, for example, was often undermined by the inmates' major reading deficiencies. Moreover, reforms could rarely be sustained. Attracting or holding onto good teachers was a never-ending problem, for obvious reasons. In reality, pedagogical flexibility never displaced the highly didactic instructional style that was common in the nineteenth-century houses of refuge. Furthermore, despite the strong rhetorical emphasis placed on formal schooling, there was never a doubt that institutional work requirements took precedence. Hence, it remained common for inmates to be removed from school for several weeks at a time to harvest crops or to be removed from day classes entirely if they were needed to meet production quotas and attend to pressing maintenance needs.

Far more easily integrated into institutional routines than "individual treatment" was the military regimen—in fact, military routines were already common in many nineteenth-century European institutions. Like most reform schools, the BIS had relied primarily on one or another version of a merit-demerit system and its attendant series of punishments—loss of privileges, assignment to the "correctional cottage" for corporal punishment, and solitary confinement—to regulate inmate behavior and schedule release times. Although the superintendents were forever engaged in refining the merit system, the principal addition to the institution's disciplinary apparatus after 1900—coinciding with the declining legitimacy of corporal punishments—was a heavy reliance on military drill. This was supplemented by extensive use of inmate monitors (not unlike prison trustees) to provide surveillance and to secure obedience.

Under this routine, inmates were placed in regiments and divided into ranks ranging from officers to cadets; inspections were held every Sunday, followed by a dress parade. The inmates drilled for forty-five minutes daily and were even taken away from work assignments to drill more. Superintendents at the BIS believed that military training offered multiple physical and disciplinary benefits to the inmates of a reform school. The military program also served an important public relations function. Through weekly parades, annual field days, and occasional excursions off the grounds, the inmates demonstrated to the public at large the institution's capacity to mold delinquents' behavior.

By the 1930s, the highly structured and formalized relationships characteristic of a military outpost had penetrated every aspect of staff-inmate relations. The boys marched to and from every activity in total silence. "The general impression . . . was that the whole spirit at this school was rather that of an old-fashioned institution running on institutional precedents established during the long years of existence, with only such staff teamwork as comes from a somewhat militaristic organization."

Central to the military organization was the monitor system, which promoted some boys to supervisory positions over their fellow inmates. In the shops, fields, and cottages, the monitors kept inmates under constant surveillance. They could pull inmates out of line and inform staff of any misbehavior; when staff were absent for any reason, the monitors were left in charge. The BIS administrators were aware that this system tended to undermine their ability to build trust among the boys. Nonetheless, they argued that, given the facility's financial constraints and its perpetual overcrowding, they had no other option to maintain order. "We've got to handle them on a mass basis," acknowledged one superintendent in the 1940s. The monitor system was, of course, subject to serious abuse. "Manned by the toughest bullies in the school," some monitors were "authorized to beat up or otherwise discipline their fellow inmates—to make flunkies of the weaker boys, to extort bribes, to inflict sadistic punishments, and even force homosexual relationships."

Between the 1920s and the 1940s, the BIS administrators still boasted of the institution's cottage organization. However, severe overcrowding "precluded the possibility of any real family atmosphere." One superintendent unhesitatingly admitted, "The school is operated along semi-military lines." Consistent with this view was another superintendent's description of the inmates' living arrangements: "We have nine drill families. The family company is made up of forty boys." The superintendent's mixed metaphors nicely synthesized both the institution's origins as a cottage reform school and its transformation into a military outpost.

Experimental Reform Schools: The George Junior Republic and the Whittier State Reform School

The evolutionary path traced by the BIS reflected broader patterns of reform school development in the first half of the twentieth century in both Europe and America. In the early 1900s, however, a number of fascinating experiments in juvenile corrections were launched in the United States and soon acquired an international reputation. These experiments, under both public and private auspices, were few in number and without extensive influence. Nonetheless, they helped sustain the quasi-utopian tradition that such institutions as the Rauhe Haus and the Colonie Agricole had brought to juvenile corrections in the nineteenth century. Two examples were the George Junior Republic and the Whittier State Reform School.

Probably the best-known innovator in juvenile corrections in the early twentieth century was William "Daddy" George. George's unique blend of modern educational ideas and conservative economic principles in his Junior Republic in Freeville, New York, won him a large following among child welfare workers in the United States and, eventually, throughout the Western world. The organizational centerpiece of the Junior Republic was inmate self-government. The inmates' day-to-day life was regulated mainly by their peers, who were elected to the institution's offices of president, senator, representative, and so forth. In addition to re-creating the basic political structure of the United States, the Junior Republic established such community institutions as banks, stores, police, and a judiciary to resolve conflicts, all of which were run by the inmates. In addition, the Junior Republic issued its own money and expected every inmate to earn his keep, including the costs of food and lodging. Though George established the ground rules and occasionally intervened in the process, the inmates of the Junior Republic controlled their fate to a remarkable degree.

George was clearly trying to re-create in a reform school the aura of a normal embryonic community (including girls as well as boys) of the kind envisioned by the most famous progressive educator, John Dewey. This functioning community, George believed, prepared inmates for effective citizenship far better than the pious lectures and ineffective civics lessons that were standard in most reform schools (or American public schools, for that matter). Undergirding the legal framework of the Junior Republic was the moral principle of "nothing without labor." George had fewer qualms than many child welfare workers about the virtues of laissez-faire capitalism. He offered inmates regular opportunities to earn a sufficient income not only to pay for basic food and lodging but to accumulate savings and even to live in a degree of luxury (at the "Hotel Waldorf" rather than at the "Beanery"). As long as social distinctions arose from effort and achievement, George had no desire to enforce the same life-style on inmates simply because they all resided at the same institution.

Just as George offered material incentives for extraordinary effort and achievement, he did not hesitate to punish sloth and improvidence. The "nothing without labor" principle did not lead to starvation or exposure for uncooperative, lazy, or economically imprudent inmates. It did mean, however, that they would be sentenced to the Junior Republic's jail, followed by a symbolic "repayment" for upkeep by being forced to crush stones.

Although the Junior Republic was known mainly for its reliance on inmate self-government and the "nothing without labor" principle, the rhythm of daily life centered on diverse vocational and academic tasks, just as at many less innovative reform schools. The differences were mainly two: first, George implemented the vocational programs more comprehensively and the academic programs more creatively than did directors of other correctional institutions; and second, George embedded his instructional programs within a much broader rehabilitative credo.

Most children at the Junior Republic divided their days equally between vocational and academic pursuits. The institution early gained a reputation as a model vocational school. The "nothing without labor" principle was not expended on the kinds of make-work or institutional maintenance chores that occupied inmates at most reform schools but rather on well-conceived projects that combined theory and practice. Moreover— in a radical departure from other reform schools' policies—George kept in close contact with local businessmen and thereby facilitated the employment of nearly all of his charges after their release. (At least this was true of the boys; it is less certain what became of the girls after release.)

At the beginning, George was skeptical that academic instruction had a place in his work-centered, earn-your-own-way institution. But he soon devised a means to integrate academics into the Junior Republic so that it was congruent with and reinforced his correctional philosophy. Rather than offer conventional instruction to children who, in the main, had failed at prior schooling, George opened instead a "Publishing House." Like their work assignments, the inmates' academic assignments were completed through a contract with the foremen-teachers who ran the "Publishing House"; inmates were remunerated for their academic efforts at a rate comparable to that paid for other tasks at the institution.

Bits and pieces of William George's correctional ideas penetrated into many public and private reform schools in the United States and Europe in the first half of the twentieth century, especially the self-government scheme. Nonetheless, the penetration was almost always superficial, isolated not only from George's comprehensive educational philosophy but also, inevitably, from the unique context in which the institution had evolved in upstate New York.

The second example of a unique experiment in juvenile reform was the Whittier State Reform School. As noted earlier, most twentieth-century reform schools in the United States did little more to integrate individual treatment into their operations than subject their inmates to a battery of mental tests. Those reform schools that did attempt to make use of their diagnoses found it difficult to translate new knowledge into new modes of treatment, either because their grounding in psychology was superficial or because the urgency of maintaining secure custody overrode individual treatment considerations. But a few correctional institutions did try more diligently and comprehensively than others to implement the individual treatment ideal, probably none more so than Whittier, California's principal public correctional institution for delinquent boys.

In 1912, the reform-minded governor of California, Hiram Johnson, appointed a Los Angeles businessman, Fred Nelles, as superintendent at Whittier. Built earlier on the congregate design, Whittier was reputed to be nothing more than a scaled-down prison for juveniles. Determined to push California to the vanguard of correctional practice, Nelles cultivated substantial personal support from legislators during the next fifteen years and fundamentally overhauled the structure and operations of the institution. The extent of his efforts demonstrated what it took to make individual treatment more than empty rhetoric.

To realize his goals, Nelles felt that it was essential to control his immediate environment. This meant, first, restructuring the facility according to the cottage rather than the congregate design. It took over ten years for Nelles to rebuild the institution so that the great majority of inmates lived in cottages, but when the process was complete he had no doubt of the superiority of this approach. Nelles's plan of individual treatment also presumed, as at private reform schools in both the United States and Europe, considerable control over admissions and a select, fairly young population on whom to translate theory into practice. He quickly gained the authority to exclude boys over the age of sixteen and to transfer refractory inmates, and by the early 1920s, he was able to rid the institution of inmates who scored exceptionally low on intelligence tests.

Unlike William George, Nelles made clinical diagnosis of inmates' behavior problems a centerpiece of his treatment plans. With the active participation of the psychology departments at UCLA and Stanford University, Nelles developed his own research department (later called the California Bureau of Juvenile Research) to provide extensive psychological testing and, to a lesser extent, psychiatric counseling of inmates. The bureau's prime objects were to formulate individual treatment plans that took into account inmates' special needs and to pursue scientific research into the causes and cures for delinquency. The bureau also recommended specific placements in cottage, school, work assignment, and recreation. The behavioral sciences, in Nelles's view, held the key to individualizing treatment.

Although the cottage system, a selective admissions process, and clinical evaluation and assignment provided a framework for innovation, Nelles still had to specify rehabilitative goals and establish specific programs to fulfill them. It was more in the execution than in the articulation of goals or programs that Whittier differed from most public reform schools.

Though he often spoke the language of the behavioral sciences, Nelles was quite traditional in portraying character development as the primary goal of a reform school. Accordingly, there were minimal restraints on inmates' movements within the institution. They rarely marched in formation, and there were no fences or guards to prevent escapes. Whittier did not insist on uniforms, so the boys wore their own clothing. They even had individual lockers for personal possessions. Corporal punishment was prohibited. The most severe punishment—and one rarely used—was assignment to one of four quarantine rooms in the lost-privilege cottage. However, even when isolated, inmates received normal food provisions and were regularly interviewed to determine whether they were ready to resume regular activities. Nelles's scheme of punishment was less harsh than the one in place at the George Junior Republic.

Academic schooling, vocational training, and experience in teamwork via athletic and other recreational activities were the main vehicles through which Nelles sought to transform inmates' character. During the early part of his administration, Nelles gave primary attention to building up formal vocational training at Whittier. By the 1920s, though not denigrating vocational preparation, he placed increasing emphasis on academics, particularly now that the "feebleminded" boys and those over the age of sixteen had been reduced. All boys under fourteen, and those over fourteen who had not completed fourth grade, attended academic school for approximately five and one-half hours every day. Nelles, like George, introduced an individualized contract-learning plan to structure academic instruction above the sixth grade level. The flexibility of this plan was particularly well suited to a reform school, Nelles believed, because the arrival and departure of inmates throughout the year was irregular and because the contracts of boys who were failing could be altered without embarrassing them (as was often the case in public schools).

Whereas Nelles's pedagogical innovations were most apparent in the academic arena, he placed great faith in his elaborate vocational training programs. He claimed that many former inmates continued working on the outside at the same occupations for which Whittier had trained them. Though Whittier taught (with fairly up-to-date equipment) some dozen trades, the line separating training from institutional maintenance was hard to draw. This was not a major concern to Nelles, who saw vocational training principally as a form of character development and a spur to emotional maturation.

No less vital to Nelles's correctional program were the formally organized athletic and recreational activities. In addition to daily gym class for everyone, the sports program emphasized cottage-based, competitive intramural contests. Participation was carefully limited to boys who were performing well in school and who exhibited acceptable behavior. The prime aim of the program was not victory but, as in vocational training, character development.

Recreation was not considered as therapeutic as athletics, but it was no less organized and central to Nelles's plans. Responding to the widely shared view that children were generally delinquent during their leisure hours, Nelles considered it essential to teach boys the wholesome use of free time. For example, he equipped each cottage with a loudspeaker on which he played radio programs designed to improve inmates' musical tastes and on which he often read stories and books aloud at night. In addition— and very important to Nelles because it substituted for the military trappings that marked most European and many American institutions in the 1920s—the Whittier State Reform School sponsored a thriving Boy Scouts program. Scout executives in the city of Whittier were heavily involved in the program's administration, and when inmates were paroled, special efforts were made to enroll them in a local Scout unit.

In sum, the Whittier State Reform School embodied several features that differentiated it in both design and implementation from most public reform schools: small cottages staffed by surrogate parents; no walls; selective admissions; no corporal punishment and a mild disciplinary apparatus; clinical diagnosis as a routine service; on-site experimentation and evaluation monitored by a research unit with strong academic links; a balance between academic and vocational instruction, with strong programs in both; highly developed athletic and recreational programs; regular exposure of inmates to outsiders through athletics and recreational events; and private-sector subsidy of institutional activities. All these elements placed Whittier in the vanguard of juvenile corrections in the first half of the twentieth century.

Girls' Reform Schools: Domesticating Sexual Misconduct

In the decades preceding and following World War I, female delinquency began attracting increasing attention as a separate and pressing social problem in the United States. Whereas between 1850 and 1920 an average of fewer than five new reform schools for females were opened per decade, twenty-three such facilities began operation between 1910 and 1920. Equally important, a number of states took over girls' reform schools that had been founded under private auspices.

Many American reform schools for girls resembled traditional prisons and regularly employed flogging, solitary confinement, cold-water baths, nausea-inducing drugs, severely restricted diets, and head-shaving as disciplinary measures. But a number of institutions—such as Sleighton Farms in Pennsylvania, El Retiro in Los Angeles, Sauk Center in Minnesota, the State School for Girls in Connecticut, and Clinton Farms in New Jersey—earned reputations for educational innovation that equaled or surpassed those attained by the Junior Republic and the Whittier State Reform School. The best-known publicists for new approaches to female juvenile corrections were Martha Falconer, the superintendent of Sleighton Farms, and Miriam Van Waters, the superintendent of El Retiro. As described by them, the modern reform school for girls shared the characteristics of a psychological clinic, a sanatorium, a summer camp, a country day school, a working farm, a home economics department, a pastoral college campus, and a George Junior Republic.

Unfortunately, empirical investigation of twentieth-century American reform schools for girls lags behind even that of reform schools for boys (the scholarship on European institutions is more meager still). It is not yet possible to describe their characteristics in detail or to be certain whether new ideas were fully translated into daily programs. Nonetheless, one characteristic of the experimental girls' institutions is clear: like their nineteenth-century predecessors, they defined female delinquency in gender-specific terms. This attitude was no less characteristic of El Retiro and Sleighton Farms than of dozens of other institutions that functioned solely as holding tanks until the girls reached their eighteenth birthdays.

Unlike boys, girls continued to be branded delinquent and incarcerated primarily for out-of-wedlock sexual activity. Illicit sex by female youth was presented as both a medical and a biological threat to society. On the one hand, the "sex delinquent" was alleged to be a key carrier of venereal disease. On the other, the "sex delinquent," by giving birth to children alleged to be mentally or biologically inferior, was identified as a major threat to the genetic purity of the population. Indeed, female "sex delinquents" were a prime object of the eugenicists' most prominent policy instrument, sterilization. Girls' reform schools played a key role in identifying inmates for the sexual surgery, usually by discharging them from the reform school and having them placed at special state hospitals for "feebleminded" and/or recalcitrant "sex delinquents."

Conclusion

For all the enthusiasm that innovative programs created, neither in the United States nor in Europe did the models provided by the George Junior Republic, the Whittier State Reform School, El Retiro, and Sleighton Farms transform the institutional treatment of juvenile delinquents. The quiet deterioration of the nineteenth-century status quo, rather than new departures, characterized the history of reform schools during the first half of the twentieth century. Indeed, the most notable change during this period may have been the decline of and, finally, the abolition of the Colonie Agricole in 1937. With its demise, there was no international model to serve as a counterforce to the predominant view of the reform school as a mini-prison for children.

Some child welfare reformers on both sides of the Atlantic did achieve a modicum of success in challenging prevailing opinion and practice. In England, for example, the passage of the Children's and Young Person's Act of 1933 created a new generation of "approved schools" for juvenile delinquents and stirred more serious discussion about reform schools than at any other time since Mary Carpenter's campaigns in the 1850s and 1860s. Yet the "approved schools" constituted only a modest alteration of the status quo. In collapsing the nineteenth-century industrial school and reformatory to form a single new type of "approved school," England mainly followed the well-established American example in consolidating institutions whose clientele had never been clearly differentiated in the first place. (It should be noted that Britain's most famous contribution to penology in the first half of the twentieth century, the Borstal, was aimed at young men between the ages of sixteen and twenty-one rather than the customary reform school cohort of fifteen and under.)

In some ways, the publicity received by the quasi-utopian American reform schools may have created or perpetuated an illusion of more genuine interest in change than actually existed among corrections practitioners or the larger public. Nonetheless, the experimental American reform schools introduced a breath of fresh air into an institution that for nearly three-quarters of a century had undergone only cosmetic change. One need not claim strong external influence for these experiments to acknowledge how inventive they were and to wonder how other delinquent youth might have fared if these examples had been more widely imitated.

THE LAST HURRAH AND BEYOND:
THE REFORM SCHOOL AND DEINSTITUTIONALIZATION

Several major changes in the characteristics of American reform schools and their inmates emerged after World War II. First, the total number of juveniles in reform schools
increased substantially. Between 1950 and 1970, the population under confinement
jumped by over 75 percent, from 35,000 to 62,000 inmates. The rate of juvenile incarceration increased as well, from 127 to 156 per 100,000 juveniles. Second, the number
of publicly operated reform schools grew to nearly two hundred—and this figure excluded several hundred more camps, group homes, and private institutions that might
fairly be regarded as mini-reform schools. Third, the share of reform school inmates
who were female declined from its mid-century high of approximately 33 percent to
approximately 20 percent (the same as in the late nineteenth century). Fourth, while
the share of immigrant youth in reform schools declined dramatically, the share of
African-American youth grew rapidly, reaching 40 percent by 1970. Finally, although
the average age at commitment remained steady at sixteen, the average length of stay
continued its century-long decline, so that by 1970 it was under one year.

The early 1970s were an especially discordant period in the history of American
juvenile corrections. As a result, two of the trends just outlined were reversed: both the
number of youth incarcerated and the rate of juvenile incarceration declined during
this decade. However, there is good reason for skepticism about the real import of this
change. It may be that many juveniles who once would have been incarcerated in reform schools were sent to smaller group homes and private custodial institutions. In
any event, the rate of juvenile incarceration was soon on the rise again and by the mid-
1980s reached an all-time high of over 200 per 100,000 juveniles. By the early 1980s,
the total reform school population was also expanding, fueled by the growing share of
African-American youth, who now composed more than 50 percent of the inmates.

The early-twentieth-century search for new strategies in juvenile corrections came
to a resounding end in the third quarter of the twentieth century. Most professionals in
child welfare and law enforcement had already lost faith in the reform school as a desirable placement for delinquent youth. But the new commitment to the
deinstitutionalization and community treatment movements of the 1960s and 1970s
was built on different presumptions. These movements represented, first, a transformation of earlier discouragement and skepticism into total despair and, second, an utter
denial of the traditional claims that—even on a theoretical level—reform schools could
function more like schools than prisons. The rehabilitative ideal was virtually denied,
for children as well as adults, as a legitimate or feasible purpose of corrections.

The Last Hurrah: The Youth Correction Authority

Curiously, the deinstitutionalization and community treatment movements emerged in
the aftermath of one final attempt, in the 1940s and 1950s, to revive confidence in
reform schools as potentially effective environments in which to deliver individual treatment to delinquent youth. This renewed confidence centered as much on new ideas
about the administration of reform schools as on any original therapeutic approaches to
correcting delinquent behavior.

Starting in the 1930s, several prominent American advocates in the fields of corrections and law advanced the view that the next great step forward in the treatment of delinquent youth would be for each state to create a "Youth Authority" or "Youth Correction Authority." These new agencies, it was believed, would remove the commitment decision from a scattered, unregulated judiciary and centralize it in a single body whose placement decisions would derive impartially, indeed scientifically, from elaborate psychiatric, psychological, medical, and social casework assessments conducted by experts. By centralizing control over placement and assigning behavioral evaluations to experts, each state would maximize its chances of rehabilitating delinquent youth and would provide an effective match between individual need and rehabilitative program.

Of course, like many institutional classification schemes that had been proposed over the years, the Youth Correction Authority idea assumed the existence of both a scientific ability to diagnose problem behaviors in youth *and* the ready availability of specialized programs to offer treatment. The tendency among advocates was to assume that prior difficulties in rehabilitating delinquent youth would virtually disappear once placements were rationalized under expert control. Characteristic were the comments of the well-known penologists Harry Elmer Barnes and Negley Teeters: "There is little doubt that this Youth Authority innovation is the most important advance in correctional thought since the 1870's."

This emerging concept took concrete form in a model "Youth Correction Authority Act" formulated in 1940. Five states (California, Minnesota, Wisconsin, Massachusetts, and Texas) created one or another version of a Youth Correction Authority during the next decade. The California Youth Authority (CYA) was created in 1941 and was given administrative responsibility for the state's reform schools in 1942. Essentially updating and expanding the 1920s individual treatment philosophy of the Whittier State Reform School, the CYA particularly emphasized the role to be played by "diagnostic centers," to which all delinquent youth would be sent before placement in a particular institution. The diagnostic center would identify the distinctive problems and needs of each youth with the expectation that an appropriate treatment already existed or could be devised to solve his or her individual problems.

Throughout the 1950s, the CYA used its considerable political clout to gain legislative support for a monumental building program to expand and diversify the state's reform schools. The confidence of many corrections leaders in the state grew as increasingly sophisticated diagnostic technologies were developed under CYA auspices. These culminated in the invention of the "Interpersonal Maturity Level," or "I-Level," screening device to define inmate personality types for purposes of classification and assignment to specific treatment programs.

In addition to building several large reform schools, often organized internally by cottages, the CYA popularized a new model of what might be termed a mini-reform school, in the form of correctional "camps." Originated in the 1930s by the juvenile probation staff in Los Angeles County, the camps were initially created to serve as vehicles for providing depression-era transient youth with a means of earning train fare to return home. As sponsored by the CYA, the camps usually housed between fifty and seventy boys who had been carefully screened for admission. They usually kept the boys incarcerated for not more than six months, after which (as in the state's other reform schools) the boys were returned to the community on parole. In addition to intensive individual counseling, other programs centered on park development, road construction, conservation, and farming. The California model of a mini-reform school became fairly popular in the 1950s in such states as Michigan, Wisconsin, Ohio, Minnesota, Illinois, and Washington.

The renewed confidence in reform schools as potential diagnostic and treatment centers in mid-century America exerted considerable influence in several European juvenile correctional systems. The publications of the CYA, as Gordon Hawkins and Franklin Zimring have observed, were widely read in Europe, and American theories provided a conceptual basis for a new approach to corrections.

The Reform School Scorned: Deinstitutionalization and Community Treatment

Although it orchestrated a boom in reform-school building, the CYA intended from the start to explore new community-based approaches to delinquency prevention and treatment. The idea that delinquents would be best served by noninstitutional treatment had its origins in the mid-nineteenth century; in the 1950s, the more immediate stimulus for the growing interest in community-based programs was a number of well-known social experiments, notably the Chicago Area Project, the Cambridge-Somerville project, and the Highfields project. In 1961 the CYA—building upon these models as well as upon its own creative work in assisting delinquents in their neighborhoods—launched the Community Treatment Project (CTP) in several sections of Sacramento and Stockton. As much as any single event, the creation of the CTP inaugurated the commitment to deinstitutionalization and to community treatment movements in American juvenile corrections.

The CTP was a carefully planned social experiment that, at least in its ideal form, grouped delinquents scientifically by I-Level, assigned them randomly to reform schools or community treatment (oftentimes to their own homes), and compared the effectiveness of institutional versus community programs. A select group of CYA parole agents was trained in I-Level diagnosis and treatment strategies to provide intensive supervision and counseling to youth in the experimental group. Caseloads were unusually small, around eight youth per agent, and additional resources (such as money to purchase foster care, tutors, expert consultants, and transportation) were provided to enlarge the agents' range of community-based treatment options.

The preliminary results from the CTP were very positive and received wide publicity. They were alleged to demonstrate clearly the superiority of community-based treatment over reform school placement as a means of treating juvenile delinquents, superiority not just in rehabilitative effectiveness but in financial savings as well. Evidence from the CTP was widely used to challenge the jurisdiction of reform schools over all but the most hardened juvenile offenders. The initial findings from the CTP were rapidly integrated into the deliberations of two national policy-making bodies in the United States, the President's Commission on Law Enforcement and the Administration of Justice (1967) and the National Commission on the Causes and Prevention of Violence (1969). Both reports concluded that incarceration had failed either to deter crime or to cure criminals.

Despite evidence suggesting that the social scientific foundations for the initial glowing evaluations of the CTP were shallow and misleading (as presented in Paul Lerman's devastating 1975 critique of the CTP, *Community Treatment and Social Control*), momentum in favor of community-based treatment grew dramatically in the late 1960s and early 1970s. Reflecting in various ways the impact of the children's rights movement, the civil rights movement, and the growing distrust of law enforcement as an agent of coercive paternalism, the credibility of all components of the juvenile justice system—but especially of reform schools—came under withering review by the courts, legislatures, and a growing army of academicians. Within a remarkably short period of time, new policies were inaugurated in most states to protect juveniles from placement in reform schools unless they had committed persistently serious criminal offenses and to house less serious offenders in small community-based facilities, if not to divert them altogether from formal contact with any part of the juvenile justice system.

The CTP, in short, heralded an anti-institutional shift in American juvenile correctional philosophy as radical as that which had led to the initial creation of reform schools in the early nineteenth century. For many vocal critics in the 1970s, the state had a moral obligation not to subject the innocence of youth to the cruelty of the reform school. No doubt the most dramatic exemplification of this viewpoint was the 1972 decision by Jerome Miller, the commissioner of the Massachusetts Department of Youth Services, to close its several reform schools and to substitute a network of small, generally nonsecure group homes. Though Miller was generally viewed as unique for his political daring and skill, his closing of traditional custodial institutions for juveniles reflected the consensus, emerging during the 1970s and early 1980s, that the reform school could not redeem errant youth—a consensus reflected in the rapid expansion of a dizzying array of government-subsidized, privately sponsored, community-based treatment alternatives.

In both rhetoric and law, Miller's sentiments came to a rather remarkable culmination in 1974 with the passage of the Juvenile Justice and Delinquency Prevention Act, which gave the imprimatur of Congress to deinstitutionalization as a correctional ideal. After 1974, it was unlikely that the American reform school would ever again be portrayed as a field of dreams on which to plan grand schemes for rehabilitating juvenile delinquents. That the reform school would continue to exist, most corrections leaders on both sides of the Atlantic grudgingly accepted. But no longer would there be even a pretense that it had a heroic child-saving mission to fulfill.

Bibliographic Note

This chapter draws in part on my own work, especially the following: *Love and the American Delinquent: The Theory and Practice of "Progressive" Juvenile Justice, 1825–1920* (Chicago: University of Chicago Press, 1977); "The Crime of Precocious Sexuality: Female Juvenile Delinquency in the Progressive Era," *Harvard Educational Review* 48 (February 1978) [with Stephanie Wallach]; "Identifying and Treating Serious Juvenile Offenders: The View from California and New York in the 1920s," in *Intervention Strategies for Chronic Juvenile Offenders: Some New Perspectives*, ed. Peter Greenwood (Westport, Conn.: Greenwood Press, 1986) [with Alexander Pisciotta]; and *The California Experience in American Juvenile Justice: Some Historical Perspectives* (Sacramento: Bureau of Criminal Statistics, California State Department of Justice, 1989).

Several overviews and critical interpretations of the juvenile justice system provide considerable insight on the development of reform schools. Recent works dealing with the United States include the following: Mary Odem, *Delinquent Daughters: Protecting and Policing Adolescent Female Sexuality in the United States, 1885–1920* (Chapel Hill: University of North Carolina Press, 1996). Eric Schneider, *In the Web of Class: Delinquents and Reformers in Boston, 1810s–1930s* (New York: New York University Press, 1992); Peter Halloran, *Boston's Wayward Children: Social Services for Homeless Children, 1830–1930* (Rutherford, N.J.: Fairleigh Dickinson University Press, 1989); John Sutton, *Stubborn Children: Controlling Delinquency in the United States, 1640–1981* (Berkeley: University of California Press, 1988); LeRoy Ashby, *Saving the Waifs: Reformers and Dependent Children, 1890–1917* (Philadelphia: Temple University Press, 1984); Barbara Brenzel, *Daughters of the State: A Social Portrait of the First Reform School for Girls in North America, 1856–1905* (Cambridge: MIT Press, 1983); and David J. Rothman, *Conscience and Convenience: The Asylum and Its Alternatives in Progressive America* (Boston: Little, Brown and Co., 1980).

Earlier, very useful monographic and synthetic studies dealing primarily with the United States include the following: Joseph Hawes, *Children in Urban Society: Juvenile Delinquency in Nineteenth-Century America* (New York: Oxford University Press, 1971); Robert Mennel, *Thorns and Thistles: Juvenile Delinquents in the United States, 1825–1940* (Hanover, N.H.: University Press of New England, 1973); Robert Pickett, *House of Refuge: Origins of Juvenile Reform in New York State, 1815–1857* (Syracuse, N.Y.: Syracuse University Press, 1969); Jack Holl, *Juvenile Reform in the Progressive Era: William R. George and the Junior Republic Movement* (Ithaca: Cornell University Press, 1971); David J. Rothman, *The Discovery of the Asylum: Social Order and Disorder in the New Republic* (Boston; Little, Brown and Co., 1971); Anthony Platt, *The Child Savers: The Invention of Delinquency* (Chicago: University of Chicago Press, 1969); and Michael Katz, *The Irony of Early School Reform: Educational Innovation in Mid-Nineteenth Century Massachusetts* (Cambridge: Harvard University Press, 1968). Also invaluable are Wiley Sanders, ed., *Juvenile Offenders for a Thousand Years: Selected Readings from Anglo-Saxon Times to 1900* (Chapel Hill: University of North Carolina Press, 1970), and Robert Bremner et al., eds., *Children and Youth in America*, 3 vols. (Cambridge: Harvard University Press, 1970–1974).

On the Ohio Boys' Industrial School, see the following: Robert Mennel, "The Family System of Common Farmers: The Origins of Ohio's Reform Farm, 1840–1858," *Ohio History* (Spring 1980), and "The Family System of Common Farmers: The Early Years of Ohio's Reform Farm, 1858–1884," *Ohio History* (Summer 1980); Joseph Stewart, "A Comparative History of Juvenile Correctional Institutions in Ohio" (Ph.D. diss., Ohio State University, 1980); and Jared Day, "From Family Cottage to Military Drill: A Study of Changing Policies and Programs at the Ohio Boys' Industrial School, 1858–1940" (Internship Paper, Department of History, Carnegie Mellon University, December 1990). For additional information on the New York House of Refuge and nineteenth-century reform schools, see Alexander Pisciotta, "Race, Sex, and Rehabilitation: A Study of Differential Treatment in the Juvenile Reformatory, 1825–1900," *Crime and Delinquency* (April 1983), and "Saving the Children: The Promise and Practice of *Parens Patriae*, 1838–1898," *Crime and Delinquency* (July 1982). On Massachusetts, see John Wirkkala, "Juvenile Delinquency and Reform in Nineteenth-Century Massachusetts: The Formative Years in State Care, 1846–1879" (Ph.D. diss., Clark University, 1973).

On the Youth Authority concept, particularly in California, see Edwin Lemert, *Social Action and Legal Change* (Chicago: Aldine Publishing Co., 1970), Paul Lerman, *Community Treatment and Social Control: A Critical Analysis of Juvenile Correctional Policy* (Chicago: University of Chicago Press, 1975), and Jane Bolen, "The California Youth Authority, 1941–1971: Structure, Policies, and Practices" (Ph.D. diss., School of Social Work, University of Southern California, 1972). The new cynicism regarding institutional treatment in the 1970s was captured best by Robert Martinson, "What Works? Questions and Answers about Prison Reform," *Public Interest* (Spring 1974). On the origins and results of the deinstitutionalization movement in juvenile corrections, especially in Massachusetts, see Jerome Miller, *Over the Wall: The Massachusetts Experiment in Closing Reform Schools* (Columbus: Ohio State University Press, 1991), and Robert Coates, Alden Miller, and Lloyd Ohlin, *Diversity in a Youth Correctional System: Handling Delinquents in Massachu-*

setts (Cambridge, Mass.: Ballinger Publishing Co., 1978). On recent developments in juvenile justice in New York State, see Edmund McGarrell, *Juvenile Correctional Reform: Two Decades of Policy and Procedural Change* (Albany: State University of New York Press, 1988).

The most comprehensive recent history examining twentieth-century juvenile justice policies outside of the United States is Victor Bailey, *Delinquency and Citizenship: Reclaiming the Young Offender, 1914–1948* (New York: Oxford University Press, 1987), which deals with England. A biographical study by Jo Manton, *Mary Carpenter and the Children of the Streets* (London: Heinemann Educational Books, 1976), contains much important information on English reform schools in the nineteenth century. Still useful on England is David Owen, *English Philanthropy, 1660–1960* (Cambridge: Harvard University Press, 1966). On the Borstal system and its broader influence from the 1920s to the 1950s, see Roger Hood, *Borstal Reassessed* (London: Heinemann Educational Books, 1965), and Gordon Hawkins and Franklin Zimring, "Cycles of Reform in Youth Corrections: The Story of Borstal," in Greenwood, *Intervention Strategies*. On nineteenth-century French reform schools, see John Ramsland, "The Agricultural Colony at Mettray: A Nineteenth Century Approach to the Institutionalization of Delinquent Boys," in *Melbourne Studies in Education, 1987–1988*, ed. D. Stockley (Bundoora, Victoria: La Trobe University Press, 1989). On Australian child welfare in the nineteenth century, see John Ramsland, *Children of the Back Lanes: Destitute and Neglected Children in Colonial New South Wales* (Kensington: New South Wales University Press, 1986). On recent European approaches to juvenile justice policy, see Gordon Hawkins and Franklin Zimring, "Western European Perspectives on the Treatment of Young Offenders," in Greenwood, *Intervention Strategies*.

CHAPTER THIRTEEN

CONFINING DISSENT

The Political Prison

Aryeh Neier

In January 1638, English dissenter and leader of the "Levelers" John Lilburne was arraigned in the Star Chamber before the archbishop of Canterbury and other judges and charged with distributing "factious and scandalous" books promoting Puritan ideas. It was said he had violated the licensing system that had been decreed by the Star Chamber more than a half century earlier, on June 23, 1585. Under this system, books could not be published or distributed in England unless they had first been cleared by, among others, the bishop of the appropriate diocese, so as to make certain that they did not contain anything that might impugn either the monarch or the state. Lilburne was convicted and sentenced to pay a fine and to be whipped, pilloried, and imprisoned. Even as he was being punished, however, Lilburne continued to speak out, using the pillory as a platform until Archbishop William Laud had him gagged.

Public outrage over the punishment meted out against Lilburne helped to bring about the abolition of the Star Chamber a few years later, and he was freed from prison at the initiative of Protector Oliver Cromwell. Lilburne's ordeal apparently had not suppressed his insistence on challenging authority, and he was soon in difficulty again for, among other things, being the first to call publicly for a written constitution that would be binding on those who promulgated the laws. He was imprisoned three more times for his peaceful expression of dissenting views. On one occasion, it was Oliver Cromwell's government that sent him to the Tower of London; though Cromwell had secured Lilburne's release from his first imprisonment, "freedom John"—as he became known—had gone on to call for his erstwhile benefactor's impeachment for treason.

Over the years many political prisoners have been imprisoned not only for the peaceful expression of their views but for the expression of those views in order to champion individual rights. In that respect, as in many others, including his stubborn refusal to bend under pressure, the seventeenth-century English dissenter John Lilburne may be regarded as the prototype of the political prisoner.

Though Lilburne was treated harshly for standing up for his beliefs, the fact that his punishment was not even more severe than imprisonment represented an advance.

A century before Lilburne's case, Sir Thomas More, chancellor of England, had been imprisoned in the Tower of London for refusing to recognize not only Anne Boleyn's marriage to King Henry the Eighth after Henry's divorce from his first queen, Catherine of Aragon, but also Henry's supremacy over the Church of England. After fifteen months in the Tower (where the rigors of confinement were eased by his servant, who was confined with him), More was brought to trial but maintained his loyalty to the authority of the pope, and on July 7, 1535, he was executed. Before the seventeenth century, this was the likely fate of anyone who challenged the monarch. By comparison, Lilburne's treatment was not so harsh, since it spared his life.

The Tower of London had been used to incarcerate important political figures long before King Henry the Eighth, two of whose queens were executed there. The main part of the building had been constructed in the eleventh century, shortly after the Norman conquest, and from the start it was used as a prison for those who mattered. (Lowlier prisoners, from the fourteenth century on, were confined at the Marshalsea, a prison that also remained in use for several hundred years and eventually became the setting for Charles Dickens's great novel *Little Dorritt*.) Unlike Lilburne or More, most of those who were confined in the Tower were imprisoned not merely because they expressed views that challenged the policies of the monarch; rather, they were rivals for power, even claimants to the throne, or they were suspects in palace intrigues. The British religious and political dissenters of the sixteenth and seventeenth centuries, on the other hand, were not themselves aspirants for the office and perquisites of the monarch, nor were they courtiers out of favor. In common with many millions worldwide who would become political prisoners in more recent times, it was their opinions, their beliefs, their manner of expression or worship, or their associations that led to their incarceration.

Implicit in the designation of such nonviolent dissenters as forerunners of contemporary political prisoners is a definition of the term. It is not a definition that is universally recognized, however. In much of the world, the term "political prisoner" is applied to anyone confined for a politically motivated offense, violent or nonviolent. In Latin America, for example, the term *preso politico* has been widely applied to imprisoned guerrilla combatants or even to political assassins, as well as to those confined for expressing their views peacefully. In the United States and Britain, on the other hand, the term has generally been used more restrictively. We do not regard Sirhan Sirhan, Robert F. Kennedy's killer, or James Earl Ray, the murderer of the Reverend Martin Luther King, Jr., as political prisoners.

The confusion over definitions is one reason that a prominent organization, Amnesty International, has employed another term: "prisoner of conscience," someone imprisoned for his or her views or associations and who has neither used nor advocated violence. The organization limits its efforts to secure releases to those it considers to be prisoners of conscience. Amnesty also works on behalf of political prisoners—defining the term more broadly to include those who used or advocated violence—to see that they obtain fair trials and to protect them against torture.

To civil libertarians imbued with the thinking reflected in U.S. constitutional jurisprudence, this approach may appear too restrictive. American civil liberties proponents have been concerned for several decades to see that the law distinguishes between those who actually use or incite violence and those who advocate violence. For example, in opposing the Smith Act—the 1940 law that made it a crime to *advocate* the forcible overthrow of the United States—American civil libertarians objected to the punishment of "mere advocacy." Eventually, in cases decided in the late 1950s and in the 1960s, they persuaded the U.S. Supreme Court to accept this view, effectively making the Smith Act a nullity.

The definition of a political prisoner used here is that which would be used by civil libertarians in the United States: someone who is incarcerated for his or her beliefs or for peaceful expression or association. This definition is broader than that used by Amnesty International for a prisoner of conscience in that those who have merely advocated violence are included; it is narrower than the definition of political prisoners in much of the world in that those who have employed violence, or imminently incited violence, are excluded.

THE SEVENTEENTH AND EIGHTEENTH CENTURIES

Some cases of political imprisonment in the seventeenth and eighteenth centuries, like the case of Lilburne, are considered landmarks in the history of civil liberty. These include the imprisonment of the future founder of Pennsylvania, William Penn, in England in 1670 on charges of unlawful assembly for preaching a sermon to a group of Quakers; of newspaper editor John Peter Zenger in New York in 1735 for publishing "seditious libel" in his newspaper; and of John Wilkes on more than one occasion in the 1760s for his satirical and virulent denunciation of King George III. Wilkes survived imprisonment and by 1774 had become lord mayor of London and, during the American Revolutionary War, was an outspoken defender of the cause of the colonists in the House of Commons. Penn and Zenger were acquitted at trial, but Penn was not immediately released; he was sent back to jail for contempt of court, and the twelve jurors who acquitted him were themselves jailed briefly for disobeying the court instructions to convict him. Penn was imprisoned for another six months the following year for another unauthorized sermon.

In France, the Bastille in Paris became a symbol of political imprisonment during the eighteenth century because it had been used to confine a number of well-known dissenters. The building was almost as old as the Tower of London and had also been used as a prison from the start; legend has it that its architect became its first inmate. Among those confined there whom we might call political prisoners was Voltaire, who was incarcerated in the Bastille for several months in 1717–18 for libeling the regent of Orléans; Voltaire again spent a brief period in the Bastille in 1725. Yet even in the eighteenth century, not all the inmates of the Bastille were imprisoned there for political dissent; a larger number were charged with common crimes. Indeed when the Bastille was stormed in 1789, and thereby earned its special place in history, none of the seven inmates who were freed by the crowd were political prisoners. That did not prevent the fall of that institution from coming to symbolize the triumph of liberty over tyranny.

Though "liberty," "fraternity," and "equality" were the expressed goals, the Revolution itself produced a far larger number of political prisoners than were ever confined in the Bastille or anywhere else in prerevolutionary France. Generally, however, their imprisonment did not endure long: they were either killed or freed.

On the evening of August 29, 1792, at the instigation of Jacobins such as Jean-Paul Marat and Georges-Jacques Danton, a series of arrests began of priests, nobles, and many ordinary people who were considered suspect by the Paris Commune and its Committee of Surveillance. In all, it is estimated that some four thousand persons were rounded up and arrested.

At about this time a band of toughs, including many known criminals, had arrived in Paris, recruited from Marseilles by the Girondins, the opponents of the Jacobins in the Assembly, to help shore up their own strength. When the toughs arrived, however, they made an agreement with Marat and, a few days after the arrests of the priests and the others began, were set loose in the prisons and began killing the prisoners. Some of those who had been imprisoned had already been released and escaped death; others, such as Abbé Roch-Ambroise Sicard, the renowned teacher of the deaf who had been swept up because he was a priest, were spared because soldiers intervened in their behalf at the last moment. But at least fourteen hundred persons were murdered in the prisons in what became known as the "September massacres." The journey of these cutthroats from Marseille to Paris became associated with a song written by Claude-Joseph Rouget de Lisle several months earlier, apparently because they sang it along the route. This association helped to convey the impression that they were a group of freedom-loving volunteers defending liberty. Though Rouget's song was originally entitled "Chant de guerre pour l'armee du Rhin" for the patriotic struggle against the Germans that inspired its composition, it soon became known as "La Marseillaise."

The following year, on June 2, 1793, the period known as the "Reign of Terror" began when a mob incited by Marat entered the Tuileries and seized twenty-two elected representatives to the Assembly from the Girondins Party. They were imprisoned and, several months later, were executed. For the next year, Girondins were hunted down, imprisoned, and in many cases, guillotined. Marat did not live to see the completion of his triumph over the Girondins however. On July 13, 1793, as he sat in the bath in which he spent nearly all his time, trying to relieve the pain caused by a skin disease, he was stabbed to death by Charlotte de Corday, a young admirer of the Girondins. The Reign of Terror continued for another year, however, until others of its architects, such as Louis Saint-Just and Maximilien Robespierre themselves, fell victim and were guillotined without trial on July 28, 1794. Considerable killing continued even thereafter in several provincial areas of France during the period known as the "Counter-Terror."

There is no known precedent in the seventeenth and eighteenth centuries for the phenomenon of extended mass political imprisonment that has become familiar to subsequent generations. Somewhat larger numbers of peaceful political dissenters were incarcerated in the nineteenth century, though it is difficult to determine the numbers because systematic efforts to compile information on such matters are a more recent phenomenon. Much of the information that is available on nineteenth-century practices is to be found in the writings of political dissenters who themselves experienced imprisonment for expressing their views.

THE NINETEENTH AND TWENTIETH CENTURIES

Russia in the Nineteenth Century

Perhaps the largest number of political prisoners in any country in the nineteenth century was in Russia. An important account of political imprisonment under the tsar was
provided by the great Russian memoirist Alexander Herzen. A scion of one of the most
aristocratic families of Russia, Herzen was arrested in 1834 when he was twenty-two
years old. Herzen's arrest was apparently due to his participation in a circle in which the
utopian ideas of the Fourierists and the Saint-Simonists in France were discussed en-
thusiastically and which sympathized with the Poles, whose insurrection against Russian rule had recently been suppressed.

Herzen's memoir, *My Past and Thoughts,* also recounts the arrest of several of his
fellow young aristocrats who were active in discussing such matters. In custody, they
were treated badly, but their social status apparently provided some protection. Herzen
wrote: "To know what the Russian prisons, the Russian lawcourts and the Russian
police are like, one must be a peasant, a house-serf, an artisan or a town workman.
Political prisoners, who for the most part belong to the upper class, are kept in close
custody and punished savagely, but their fate bears no comparison with the fate of the
poor. With them the police do not stand on ceremony. To whom can the workman go
afterwards to complain? Where can he find justice?"

Herzen tells us that those who were taken into custody were commonly abused in
detention. As in more recent times, the most dangerous period was before trial, when
the prisoner was in the hands of the police. The prisoner, he wrote, "looks forward with
impatience to the time he will be sent to Siberia; his martyrdom ends with the beginning of this punishment."

Martyrdom at the hands of the police, according to Herzen, included torture. As in
other times and places, ostensibly such practices were not officially sanctioned. He wrote:

Peter III abolished torture and the Secret Chamber.
Catherine II abolished torture.
Alexander I abolished it *again.*
Answers given "under intimidation" are not recognized by law. The official who
    tortures an accused man renders himself liable to trial and severe punishment.
And yet all over Russia, from the Bering Straits to Taurogen, men are tortured.

Herzen was sent to a prison at Perm, a town near the Urals that remained a favorite spot
for the confinement of political prisoners for the next century and a half until most—if
not all—were freed by Mikhail Gorbachev. From Perm, like political prisoners in subsequent generations, Herzen was sent into internal exile in Siberia, not to return to
Moscow until six years after his arrest.

Another Russian writer who spent several years as a political prisoner was Fyodor
Dostoyevsky. He was arrested in 1849 for his participation in a group known as "the
Petrashevsky circle," a group of young men who—like those with whom Herzen had
been associated a decade and a half earlier—met to study the works of the French
socialists and the possible application of their ideas in Russia. Dostoyevsky's treatment
included a purported death sentence followed by a mock execution, which he thought

was real until the moment that the shots from the firing squad failed to materialize. With ten-pound fetters around his ankles, he was sent on a two-thousand-mile sled ride to the prison at Omsk in western Siberia, where he was incarcerated. Dostoyevsky's novel Memoirs From the House of the Dead—of which Leo Tolstoy said, "I know no better book in all modern literature"—is an only slightly fictionalized account of his four years at Omsk, where most of his fellow prisoners were serving sentences for common crimes.

Though Anton Chekhov was not a political activist like some of his predecessors among Russia's great writers, and accordingly never got to see a prison as an inmate, he did spend three months in the enormous penal colony on the island of Sakhalin in 1890 as a doctor undertaking a medical survey of the prisoners. Chekhov had sought permission to interview the convicts and obtained it readily, but his permit prohibited him from talking to the relatively small number of political prisoners among them, an indication of official sensitivities.

Though the number of political prisoners remained small by the standards of our own century, the growing use of imprisonment to punish peaceful expression and association during the nineteenth century reflected the emergence and spread of ideologies such as socialism, syndicalism, communism, and anarchism, which threatened the monarchies of Europe. In addition, those European powers that were completing the colonization of most of Africa, Asia, and the Middle East feared native insurrections against their rule and, when they did not resort to more draconian forms of punishment, imprisoned those who they thought were stirring up trouble.

Political Prisoners in the United States and Great Britain

In the United States, activists in a number of causes were imprisoned during the nineteenth century for peaceful expression or association. Among them were abolitionists in the years before the Civil War (for example, the crusading newspaper editor William Lloyd Garrison was committed to jail after he declined to pay a fine for libeling the owner of a slave ship), opponents of the draft during the Civil War, women's suffragists and labor organizers during the second half of the century, objectors to Jim Crow legislation in the southern states in the 1880s and 1890s, and also during those decades, participants in the various radical movements of the times.

One of the most hotly disputed cases of the latter part of the nineteenth century, and for long thereafter, was the imprisonment of eight men for the Haymarket Square bombing in Chicago on May 4, 1886. As police arrived in the square to disperse a crowd that had gathered to protest an earlier episode in which police had beaten striking employees of the McCormick Harvester Company, a bomb exploded. Several of the police were killed, and many more were wounded. Those arrested were the speakers at the rally, which the police were in the process of dispersing. Their sympathizers contended that the men were imprisoned for the expression of their views and that those arrested had nothing to do with the bombing. Nevertheless, four of the defendants were hung, one committed suicide, and three of the men were sentenced to long prison terms. Those convicted for the Haymarket bombing were widely regarded as "martyrs"; protest demonstrations against their conviction, and on the anniversaries of the hangings, became occasions on which many activists in the labor and radical movements of the times were imprisoned for the peaceful expression of their political views.

One of those who was especially stirred by the fate of the Haymarket convicts was Emma Goldman, a young Russian immigrant. Already an adherent of radical causes, she became a fervent anarchist and was soon arrested and tried on charges of "inciting to riot" for a speech she made in New York. Goldman, like many who have been arrested for their political views over the years, saw her arrest as an opportunity: "I had suddenly become an important personage, though I could not understand why, since I had done or said nothing that merited distinction. But I was glad to see so much interest in my ideas. . . . My trial would give me a wonderful chance for propaganda. I must prepare for it. My defence in open court should carry the message of anarchism to the whole country."

A quarter of a century later, in 1917, after repeated arrests and sojourns in jails for expressing her anarchist views, Goldman was one of those imprisoned for opposing conscription during World War I. With the exception of the Japanese-Americans interned during World War II—who represent a somewhat distinct category—the opponents of the draft arrested at that time, and those arrested in the two years following the war on charges relating to the "red scare" that swept the country, constituted by far the largest number of political prisoners in American history. Goldman, along with several hundred other immigrants among the accused radicals, was deported from the United States in December 1919, three months after her release from prison.

The foremost historian of freedom of speech in the United States in the first half of the twentieth century, Harvard Professor Zechariah Chafee, Jr., wrote, "Over nineteen hundred prosecutions and other judicial proceedings during the war, involv[ed] speeches, newspaper articles, pamphlets and, books." In Minnesota, a man named Freerks was convicted under the state Espionage Act and sent to prison for discouraging women from knitting for the troops when he remarked, "No soldier ever sees these socks." A prominent opponent of the war, Rose Pastor Stokes, was convicted in a federal court and sentenced to ten years in prison for writing in a letter, "I am for the people and the government is for the profiteers." Judge Van Valkenburgh, who presided at her trial, stated in his charge to the jury, "Our armies in the field and our navies upon the seas can operate and succeed only so far as they are supported and maintained by the folks at home." (A year and a half after the war ended, Stokes's conviction was set aside by a U.S. Court of Appeals.)

Perhaps the best known of the wartime prosecutions was the case of Eugene Victor Debs, leader and presidential candidate of the Socialist Party. In Debs's most extreme statement in the antiwar speech for which he was prosecuted, he noted, "You need to know that you are fit for something better than slavery and cannon fodder." On the basis of such pronouncements, Debs was sentenced at trial to ten years in prison, and astonishing as it seems in retrospect, his conviction was upheld unanimously by the U.S. Supreme Court. The Court's decision in *Debs* was written by no less than Justice Oliver Wendell Holmes, Jr., also the author of the landmark opinion for a unanimous Supreme Court earlier in the year in the case upholding the conviction of Charles Schenck.

Schenck, general secretary of the Socialist Party in Philadelphia, had been convicted under the Espionage Act of 1917 for circulating a leaflet describing the draft as unconstitutional and saying, "A conscript is little better than a convict . . . ASSERT YOUR RIGHTS." In upholding his six-month prison sentence, Holmes wrote for the Court, in words that have been quoted and misquoted countless times all over the world in justifying political imprisonment:

> We admit that in many places and in ordinary times the defendants in saying all that was said in the circular would have been within their constitutional rights. But the character of every act depends on the circumstances in which it is done. . . . The most stringent protection of free speech would not protect a man in falsely shouting fire in a crowded theater and causing a panic. . . . The question in every case is whether the words are used in such circumstances and are of such a nature as to create a clear and present danger that they will bring about the substantive evils that Congress had a right to prevent. It is a question of proximity and degree. When a nation is at war, many things that might be said in time of peace are such a hindrance to its efforts that they will not be endured so long as men fight and that no court could regard them as protected by any Constitutional right.

Given his own opinion for the Court in *Schenck*, Holmes apparently considered that he had no choice but also to uphold the savage sentence imposed on Debs. Accordingly, Debs, at the age of sixty-three, began his prison sentence on April 13, 1919. The following year, he was nominated for the fifth time as the Socialist Party's presidential candidate and, though he remained in prison, received 919,799 votes. Debs was released from prison on Christmas Day 1921 at the direction of President Warren G. Harding.

In Britain, also, opponents of the war were imprisoned. Among them was the philosopher Bertrand Russell, who wrote in his autobiography about interceding with his friend Prime Minister Herbert Asquith to help secure commutation of the sentences of thirty-seven conscientious objectors who had been condemned to death. Subsequently Russell became acting chairman of the No Conscription Fellowship—"after all the original committee had gone to prison"—and was sentenced to six months in prison himself in 1918 for writing an article for the fellowship's newsweekly, in which he said: "The American garrison which will by that time be occupying England and France, whether or not they will prove efficient against the Germans, will no doubt be capable of intimidating strikers, an occupation to which the American Army is accustomed when at home." This statement was apparently the cause for Russell's imprisonment. His class connections, however, ensured that Russell—like some of the Russian aristocrats in the previous century—obtained better treatment than most prisoners. In his autobiography he recalled:

> By the intervention of Arthur Balfour [then foreign secretary], I was placed in the first division, so that while in prison I was able to read and write as much as I liked, provided I did no pacifist propaganda. I found prison in many ways quite agreeable. I had no engagements, no difficult decisions to make, no fear of callers, no interruptions to my work. I read enormously; I wrote a book, *Introduction to Mathematical Philosophy*, a semi-popular version of *The Principles*

of Mathematics, and began the work for *Analysis of Mind.* I was rather interested in my fellow-prisoners, who seemed to me in no way morally inferior to the rest of the population, though they were on the whole slightly below the usual level of intelligence, as was shown by their having been caught. For anybody not in the first division, especially for a person accustomed to reading and writing, prison is a severe and terrible punishment; but for me thanks to Arthur Balfour, this was not so.

In the United States, the end of the war produced no slackening in the imprisonment of peaceful political dissenters. In 1919, with the Bolsheviks in power in Russia, communism making great gains in several European countries, and an unprecedented wave of labor strikes in the United States reflecting resentments that had been kept in check during the war years when work stoppages might have seemed disloyal, a worldwide Communist revolution seemed to many to be a realistic possibility. Tensions were heightened considerably when letter bombs were sent to the homes of several prominent public figures over the course of a few weeks from April to June of 1919. Among the recipients of the letter bombs was U.S. Senator Thomas Hardwick of Georgia; the bomb tore off the hand of his maid, who opened the letter. Targets of other bombings were U.S. Senator Lee Overman; Justice Holmes; Judge Kenesaw Mountain Landis, subsequently commissioner of baseball and, at the time, famous or infamous for presiding over the political trials in which labor leader Big Bill Haywood and socialist Victor Berger, a former member of Congress, had been sentenced to prison terms; John D. Rockefeller; J. P. Morgan; Postmaster General Albert Burleson; Secretary of Labor William Wilson; and Attorney General A. Mitchell Palmer.

Just who sent the bombs was never established. Most of the bombs did little harm. The one that had the greatest effect was the bomb thrown into the home of Attorney General Palmer on the night of June 2, 1919; it injured no one but wrecked his house. Though there was no evidence as to who had thrown the bomb, the New York Times immediately asserted, "The crimes are plainly of Bolshevik or IWW origin." The bombing of his home spurred Palmer to launch raids on radicals, raids with which his name became associated.

The first of the raids took place on November 7, 1919, the second anniversary of the Russian Revolution, and involved coordinated roundups of suspected radicals in twelve cities. Some of those who were rounded up were among the 249 persons deported to Russia the following month on a ship, the Buford. This was also the sailing on which Emma Goldman was deported. In preparation for subsequent raids, more than 3,000 federal arrest warrants were prepared, and the number actually taken into custody was larger still. The Palmer raids were stopped by a lawsuit brought in federal court in June 1920 by the newly established American Civil Liberties Union. The suit had been filed in Massachusetts with the help of such prominent lawyers as Harvard Professors Zechariah Chafee, Jr., and Felix Frankfurter, and its immediate legal effect was to free eighteen persons who had been seized in Boston. The testimony elicited during the proceedings by Federal Judge George W. Anderson about the casual methods of identifying targets for the raids so embarrassed the Justice Department and its Bureau of Investigation that the case also turned the tide nationally. From then on, the red scare was on the wane. That did not mean that all radicals were freed immediately; some of those imprisoned during the war for speaking against the draft remained in prison for years and were not released until after President Calvin Coolidge took office in 1923. Moreover, many radicals continued to be arrested throughout the 1920s and 1930s for violating such laws as those, passed by virtually all the states, requiring the display of an American flag. (The Massachusetts law prohibiting a red or a black flag had to be repealed because it made the Harvard crimson illegal.) Others were imprisoned for unlawful assembly for their efforts to organize labor unions or for their public speeches in support of various radical causes.

The Japanese-Americans who were interned during World War II do not precisely fit the definition of political prisoners used here. Even so, they must be mentioned. Some 120,000 were forcibly evacuated from the West Coast and interned in concentration camps from early 1942 to January 1945. They were deprived of liberty not for expression or association but solely on the ground of their ethnic identity. Aliens, naturalized citizens, and citizens by birth were all assumed to be ready to assist the Japanese enemy, who had launched a surprise attack on Pearl Harbor on December 7, 1941.

Among the most vigorous proponents of the exclusion of the Japanese-Americans from the West Coast was Earl Warren, then attorney general of California. He argued, "Every alien Japanese should be considered in the light of a potential fifth columnist." According to Warren, the absence of any sabotage attributable to the Japanese-Americans in the early weeks of the war only proved that they were biding their time to engage in sabotage later on. (According to Jack Harrison Pollack, a biographer of Warren, in later years, "There was nothing that Chief Justice Warren regretted more poignantly than his vehement—even rabid support . . . [for] the forced resettlement of Japanese-Americans into West Coast concentration camps." Immediately after the war, Warren became a champion of their right to return to their homes and communities.) The actual exclusion took place under an order signed on February 19, 1942, by President Franklin D. Roosevelt, and internment followed when the governors of the states in which relocation centers had been constructed refused to allow the resettlement of the Japanese-Americans. At that point, the relocation centers were transformed into detention facilities, and the War Relocation Authority set criminal penalties for those leaving the camps without permission. The American Civil Liberties Union brought a series of court cases challenging the restrictions on the Japanese-Americans, but these did not succeed. Several Supreme Court justices who were noted at other times for their defense of individual rights—including Harlan Fiske Stone, Hugo Black, and William O. Douglas—were among those who upheld the restrictions on the Japanese-Americans entirely on the basis of ancestry or racial identity.

After World War II, the United States did not again experience mass political imprisonments for extended periods. Certain controversies—the post–World War II red scare, the civil rights movement of the late 1950s and the 1960s, and the protests against the Vietnam War of the late 1960s and the early 1970s—produced political prisoners. On some occasions, such as civil rights demonstrations in the South or antiwar gatherings in Washington, D.C., thousands of peaceful protesters were arrested at one time. In May 1971, for example, the Washington, D.C., police herded more than twelve thousand persons whom they had arrested in antiwar demonstrations into the Robert F.

Kennedy Memorial Stadium because it was the only place large enough to hold them while they were processed for arraignment in court on such charges as disorderly conduct. Their incarceration was brief, however, and the number imprisoned for extended periods for peaceful protest in the United States at any time after the 1920s was relatively small. Perhaps the greatest number in the latter category consisted of those imprisoned during the Vietnam War era either because the courts had rejected their claims to be classified as conscientious objectors, among them those who sought exemption from military service on grounds of conscientious scruples against service in a particular war rather than such opposition to all wars, or because the courts were unwilling to apply freedom of speech protections to such symbolic protest as the burning of draft cards. At its highest point, the number of those serving prison sentences at one time in such cases was in the low hundreds; in contrast, during World War I and in the red scare following the war, the United States confined thousands of political prisoners for the peaceful expression of their views.

Russia in the Twentieth Century

The deportation of Emma Goldman to Russia produced a consequence that was probably not anticipated by those who put her aboard the *Buford*: she became one of the first outspoken critics of political imprisonment in the Soviet state.

Goldman arrived in Russia in January 1920 full of hope. In her autobiography she described her first reactions: "Soviet Russia! Sacred Ground, Magic People! You have come to symbolize humanity's hope, you alone are destined to redeem mankind. I have come to serve you, beloved *matushka*. Take me to your bosom, let me pour myself into you, mingle my blood with yours, find my place in your heroic struggle, and give to the uttermost to your needs!" Soon, however, her disillusionment began. She wrote:

> I had been asked to attend a conference of anarchists in Petrograd, and I was amazed to find that my comrades were compelled to gather in secret in an obscure hiding-place. . . . Presently came the answer—from workers in the Putilov Ironworks, from factories and mills, from the Kronstadt sailors, from Red Army men, and from an old comrade who had escaped while under sentence of death. . . . They spoke of the Bolshevik betrayal of the Revolution, of the slavery forced upon the toilers, the emasculation of the soviets, the suppression of speech and thought, the filling of prisons with recalcitrant peasants, workers, soldiers, sailors, and rebels of every kind. They told of the raid with machine-guns upon the Moscow headquarters of the anarchists by the order of Trotsky; of the Cheka and wholesale executions without hearing or trial. These charges and denunciations beat upon me like hammers and left me stunned.

At first, Goldman was unable to accept what she heard, but as she encountered efforts by some of her fellow American radicals to justify what was happening, Goldman's determination to face the truth increased. One of her arguments was with John Reed, a friend from her years in the United States and the author of a dramatic account of the Russian Revolution. He told her that counterrevolutionaries should be dealt with harshly. "To the wall with them I say," she recalls him as saying. "I learned one mighty expressive Russian word, 'razstrellyat'! (execute by shooting)." Goldman recalled: "'Stop, Jack! Stop!' I cried; 'this word is terrible enough in the mouth of a Russian. In your hard American accent it freezes my blood. Since when do revolutionists see in wholesale execution the only solution of their difficulties?'" The autobiography goes on to describe an argument in which Reed acknowledged to Goldman that five hundred prisoners had been executed as counterrevolutionaries; Goldman denounced this as "a dastardly crime, the worst counter-revolutionary outrage committed in the name of the Revolution."

After many arguments with others, including Maxim Gorky, along similar lines, Goldman and her longtime companion and erstwhile lover, Alexander (Sasha) Berkman, arranged to see Lenin to take their complaints to him. Why were anarchists in Soviet prisons, Berkman asked. Goldman recalled:

> "Anarchists?" Ilich interrupted; "nonsense! Who told you such yarns, and how could you believe them? We do have bandits in prison, and Makhnovtsky [followers of Makhno, a counterrevolutionary military leader] but no *udeiny* anarchists."
>
> "Imagine," I broke in, "capitalist America also divides the anarchists into two categories, philosophic and criminal. The first are accepted in the highest circles: one of them is even high in the councils of the Wilson Administration. The second category, to which we have the honour of belonging, is persecuted and often imprisoned. Yours also seems to be a distinction without a difference. Don't you think so?" Bad reasoning on my part, Lenin replied, sheer muddleheadedness to draw similar conclusions from different premises. Free speech is a *bourgeois* prejudice. . . . The proletarian dictatorship was engaged in a life-and-death struggle, and small considerations could not be permitted to weigh in the scale.

The political situation in the new Soviet state deteriorated thereafter; repression grew worse, and less than two years after her arrival full of hope and enthusiasm, Goldman felt fortunate to be able to escape Soviet Russia. Out of the country, she tried to publish her findings in a liberal publication in the United States, but her articles were rejected, and after first turning down an offer from the *New York World*, she eventually agreed to publish a series of seven articles in that "capitalist" publication.

Though Emma Goldman was clear-eyed about Soviet Russia and its successor, the Soviet Union, most other liberals and leftists from the West who traveled there from the 1920s through the 1950s—Theodore Dreiser, George Bernard Shaw, Jean-Paul Sartre, and many more—refused to see what was going on, even when the number of political prisoners under Joseph Stalin soared to levels that would have seemed inconceivable in the period when Goldman was arguing with Lenin. Despite all the revelations during Mikhail Gorbachev's tenure as head of state in the late 1980s and subsequent to his fall, it is not yet possible at this writing to establish with certainty even an approximate figure for the number of those who were imprisoned under Stalin for expressing their views or for associating with others peacefully. That it was in the millions has been known for a long time, but not how many millions.

Robert Conquest, a historian who has attempted for decades to document the extent of repression under Stalin, published a "reassessment" in 1990 drawing on *glasnost*-era revelations to supplement his previous research. Conquest wrote that at the point when Stalin's terror was at its peak—that is, the end of 1938, following the Moscow purge trials—the number of political prisoners in the Soviet Union was seven million or a little less, a figure that was somewhat lower than the eight million he had previously estimated but one that remains so enormous that it is virtually incomprehensible.

The calculations cited by Conquest in support of his figures are not wholly persuasive. That is not to say that his figure is wrong or too high; it could be right, and it could even be too low. But trying to determine numbers of prisoners a half century later in a vast country with a totalitarian system that practiced political imprisonment on an enormous scale and that sought to conceal such information is very difficult. Few records containing actual names, dates, and numbers have yet come to light. Inevitably, under these circumstances, it is necessary for those intent on establishing figures to extrapolate from sources such as the testimony of survivors. At best, it may be possible to determine a range from such limited data, but even suggesting an approximate number of political prisoners involves considerable guesswork.

If one assumes that Conquest is right in calculating that the number of political prisoners at the end of 1938 in the Soviet Union was close to seven million, that figure represents about one person in every thirty in the country, or one in every fifteen or sixteen adults. Taken another way, the figure means that one in every six or seven families of four or five persons throughout the entire Soviet Union had a member who was imprisoned for political reasons at that moment. Moreover, when one considers that Stalin ruled the Soviet Union for nearly three decades and that the number of those imprisoned for political reasons was always high throughout—particularly from the mid-1930s until his death in 1953—the total was far larger than the number imprisoned at any particular moment. (Conquest suggests that, by 1952, the year before Stalin's death, the prison camp population had swelled to twelve million. No basis for this figure is provided, and it is difficult to know what to make of it. Nevertheless, the general point that the number remained enormous seems well-founded.) It appears that hardly any individual or family was not directly and immediately affected by political imprisonment. The testimonies we have from survivors establish that conditions were extremely harsh, that large numbers of prisoners were executed, and that many more died from the combined effects of hunger, cold, disease, and ill-treatment in the prison camps. Except for what took place in the same era in Nazi-occupied Europe and in Japanese-occupied China, this was repression on a scale perhaps never previously known in human history. Conquest, Alexander Solzhenitsyn, and others who have written about political imprisonment under Stalin have rendered a great service in conveying the enormity of the crimes committed against the inmates of the Gulag Archipelago. Revelations yet to come in the post-Communist era may permit future historians to document Stalin's repression more fully and to provide numbers that may not be different but that may be better supported.

The Nazis

Large-scale political imprisonment by the Nazis began less than a month after Adolf Hitler was appointed chancellor of Germany on January 30, 1933. The pretext was the

Reichstag fire.

On February 24, Hermann Göring's police conducted a search of Karl Liebknecht House, formerly the headquarters of the Communist Party, and claimed to have discovered, in a basement, documents showing that the Communists planned to launch a revolution by setting fire to vital government buildings. On February 27, the Reichstag caught fire. Harry Kessler, an aristocrat and a patron of the arts whose diary is one of the most vivid accounts of the Weimar years and of the advent of the Nazi regime, provided this entry on February 28, 1933:

> Marinas van der Lubbe, a poor wretch of an alleged Dutch Communist has been arrested as the incendiary responsible for the Reichstag fire. He promptly confessed that he was suborned by Communist deputies to perform the deed and that he was also in touch with the SPD [Social Democratic Party]. This twenty-year-old youth is supposed to have stored inflammable material at thirty different spots in the Reichstag and to have kindled it without either his presence, his activity, or his bestowal of this enormous quantity of material being observed by anyone. And finally he ran straight into the arms of the police, having carefully taken off all his clothes except for his trousers and depositing them in the Reichstag so as to ensure that no sort of mistake could fail to result in his identification. He is even supposed to have waved with a torch from a window.
>
> Göring had immediately declared the entire Communist Party guilty of the crime and the SPD as being at least suspect. He has seized this heaven-sent, uniquely favorable opportunity to have the whole Communist Reichstag party membership as well as hundreds or even thousands of Communists all over Germany arrested. . . .
>
> There appear to be no limits set to the continuation of arrests, prohibitions, house searches, and closure of Party offices. The operation proceeds to the tune of blood-thirsty speeches by Göring.

Ernst Torgler, the leader of the Communists in the Reichstag, and Georgi Dimitrov, a Bulgarian who was a leader of the Communist International, were among those arrested and were tried with van der Lubbe on charges of setting the fire. The young, mentally unbalanced Dutchman was convicted, but Torgler and Dimitrov were acquitted.

Konrad Heiden, who was later a biographer of Hitler and who was still in Germany at the time, described the manner in which the arrests of the Communists and SPD members took place: "By truck loads the storm troopers thundered through cities and villages, broke into houses, arrested their enemies at dawn; dragged them out of bed into S.A. barracks where hideous scenes were enacted in the ensuing weeks and months. . . . At first one was lucky to be arrested on the strength of Göring's big blacklist. These men were sent to ordinary police prisons and as a rule were not beaten. But terrible was the fate of those which the S.A. arrested for their own `pleasure.'"

At this juncture, for the most part, Jews were not arrested for being Jews; Jews who happened to be Communists or Social Democrats were arrested for their political affiliations, though they were treated especially brutally in detention because they were

Jews. As Heiden wrote, "In the National Socialist formulation [in early 1933], the political weapon of Jewry must be broken, not yet Jewry itself."

The first time significant numbers of Jews were arrested for being Jews was for violating Nazi racist laws that prohibited marriages or extramarital relationships between Jews and Aryans. Under the Law for the Protection of German Blood and Honor, of September 15, 1935, both men and women could be punished for mixed marriages, but only the man could be imprisoned for extramarital intercourse. Reinhard Heydrich, the security police chief whose name is indelibly associated with the "final solution," effectively overrode this exception, however, by issuing orders to send Jewish women to concentration camps if their German partners were jailed.

The Nazis had started to develop the concentration camp system in 1933. Initially, these were camps in Germany, as at Dachau near Munich, used to confine all sorts of people whom the Nazis considered their enemies, including members of rival Nazi factions. In the years before the outbreak of the war, according to Raul Hilberg, the leading historian of the Holocaust, the Nazis confined the following groups:

1. Political prisoners:
    a. Communists (systematic round-up)
    b. Active Social Democrats
    c. Jehovah's Witnesses
    d. Clergymen who made undesirable speeches or otherwise manifested opposition
    e. People who made remarks against the regime and were sent to camps as an example to others
    f. Purged Nazis, especially S.A. men
2. So-called asocials, consisting primarily of habitual criminals and sex offenders
3. Jews sent to camps in *Einzelaktionen* [individual encounters]

After the war broke out, concentration camps were also established in Nazi-occupied Poland. These became the killing centers to which millions of Jews, hundreds of thousands of Gypsies, and large numbers of "asocials" and political enemies of the Nazis were deported and at which they were exterminated, particularly during the last three years of the war.

Gandhi

During World War I, the British colonial authorities in India convened secret tribunals that sentenced thousands of nationalists to prison terms for such offenses as sedition. The prisoners included Bal Gangadhar Tilak, the foremost nationalist leader of the time, and Annie Besant, a British-born theosophist and renowned orator of Irish descent who established the Indian Home Rule League and became its president in 1916 and who served as president of the Indian National Congress in 1917. It had been widely expected that the British would restore civil liberties in India after the war, but this did not happen, and in the years following the war, the number of nationalists imprisoned for political offenses rose even higher. By the beginning of 1922, the prisoners included virtually all the leaders of the Indian National Congress (forerunner of the Congress Party) including Motilal Nehru. The next three generations of Nehru's family would each provide India with a prime minister: Jawaharlal Nehru, Indira Gandhi, and Rajiv Gandhi. On March 10, 1922, the man who came to symbolize the worldwide decolonization movement, Mohandas K. Gandhi, was arrested for the first time in India; he had been arrested previously during one of his sojourns in South Africa in connection with a strike by indentured Indian workers.

Gandhi was charged with sedition on the basis of three articles that he had written. In the first, published on September 19, 1921, he had written, "I have no hesitation in saying that it is sinful for anyone, either soldier or civilian, to serve this government . . . sedition had become the creed of Congress." In the second, published on December 21, 1921, he wrote: "Lord Reading [the viceroy] must understand that Nonco-operators are at war with the government. They have declared rebellion against it." In the third, published on February 23, 1922, he wrote: "How can there be any compromise whilst the British lion continues to shake his gory claws in our face? . . . The rice-eating, puny millions of India seem to have resolved upon achieving their own destiny without further tutelage and without arms."

In court, Gandhi offered no defense against the indictment. He told the judge, "I am here . . . to invite and cheerfully submit to the highest penalty that can be inflicted upon me for what in law is a deliberate crime and what appears to me to be the highest duty of a citizen." He invited the court to impose on him "the severest penalty provided by law."

According to Gandhi biographer Louis Fischer, Justice Broomfield, who presided at the trial, responded to this statement by bowing to Gandhi and pronouncing his sentence: "The law is no respecter of persons. Nevertheless, it will be impossible to ignore the fact that you are in a different category from any person I have ever tried or am likely to have to try. It would be impossible to ignore the fact that, in the eyes of millions of your countrymen, you are a great patriot and a great leader. Even those who differ from you in politics look upon you as a man of high ideals and of noble and even saintly life." With this, Justice Broomfield sentenced Gandhi to six years in prison.

Gandhi served less than two years of his sentence. In prison, he suffered an attack of acute appendicitis, and when the operation he underwent resulted in complications, the government considered it expedient to release him. Thereafter, he was arrested repeatedly, and though he was imprisoned a number of times, he was never again given the opportunity to speak in court by being brought to trial.

Many of Gandhi's colleagues in the struggle in India were also imprisoned for taking part in peaceful protest, as were their counterparts in a great many countries. (Indeed, in India and almost everywhere else, political prominence in the postcolonial period was hardly possible without a record of imprisonment during the struggle for independence.) Nonviolent protests such as those in which Gandhi engaged were by no means the rule in anticolonial struggles, however. Nor were Gandhi's refusal to contest his punishment and his request for the maximum punishment generally emulated. Yet some participants in the anticolonial struggle and in some subsequent protest movements—including the civil rights struggle and the anti–Vietnam War protests in the United States—did try to follow Gandhi's lead. Just as Emma Goldman had regarded her trial as an opportunity for propaganda, Gandhi and those who tried to model their behavior on his grasped that they could employ their own willingness to accept punishment as a means to advance their causes.

THE HUMAN RIGHTS ERA

The experience of World War II caused a dramatic shift in attitudes toward human rights generally of governments and citizens worldwide. Previously, the way a government treated its own citizens was considered to be primarily and almost exclusively a matter for concern within that country and was not an appropriate basis for action by other governments or by the international community generally. There were exceptions. In 1876, to cite a notable example, Turkish atrocities against the Bulgarians—at a time when Bulgaria was still part of the Ottoman Empire—and the failure of the government of Queen Victoria's prime minister, Benjamin Disraeli, to respond appropriately became a major political issue in Britain. One reason for British outrage was that it was a case of Muslims abusing Christians. Disraeli's rival, William Gladstone, his predecessor and successor as prime minister, wrote a pamphlet entitled *The Bulgarian Horrors and the Question of Evil*, which sold two hundred thousand copies within a month and may be regarded as a precursor to the international human rights reports that started to become familiar a century later. Other atrocities that stirred a measure of international protest before the outbreak of World War II in Europe were Italy's use of mustard gas against the Emperor Haile Selassie's forces in Ethiopia in 1935 and 1936 and the "rape of Nanking" by Japanese troops in 1937. Yet both of these were abuses committed against another country by invading armies; they did not involve a government's mistreatment of its own citizens. The imprisonment of millions in the 1930s in Stalin's Soviet Union and the deaths of large numbers because of the conditions of incarceration aroused little or no protest from other governments and only a few isolated denunciations from citizens' groups aroused by such critics as Emma Goldman. This was not only a consequence of the willful blindness of many visitors to the Soviet Union; it also reflected the prevailing worldwide consensus that such matters were not an international concern. When political leaders in the West spoke of their differences with the Soviet Union in the 1930s, it was mainly to espouse the superiority of capitalism over communism, not to uphold civil liberty against totalitarianism.

The revelations at the end of World War II about what happened in the Nazi concentration camps were the principal cause of the shift in thinking worldwide. One factor in this shift was that it was evident that the cruelties practiced by the Nazis against Jews and other inhabitants of Germany could not be separated from their role as an international aggressor. The tribunal at Nuremberg considered three kinds of crimes committed by the Nazis: crimes of aggressive war, which involved the Nazi invasions; war crimes, which included their treatment of foreign combatants such as the wounded and prisoners of war; and crimes against humanity, such as their extermination of Jews and others in Germany and in Nazi-occupied Europe. The links between these crimes were apparent. Accordingly, in language whose revolutionary significance was not fully grasped at the time, the United Nations Charter, adopted in 1945, committed the institution to promote "universal respect for, and observance of, human rights" and committed the member states "to take joint and separate action in cooperation with the Organization" to promote human rights. By joining the United Nations, the governments of the world acknowledged that the manner in which they dealt with the human rights of their own citizens was not solely an internal affair; henceforth, it would be a legitimate concern of the United Nations and of all the member states.

In 1948, the United Nations adopted the Universal Declaration of Human Rights with no negative votes but with abstentions by the Soviet bloc, South Africa, and Saudi Arabia. The declaration spelled out the meaning of the "human rights" referred to in the charter. The provisions of the declaration made political imprisonment a violation of the commitment made by governments when they ratified the United Nations Charter and became members of the international body. The declaration explicitly guaranteed such rights as "freedom of thought, conscience and religion," "freedom of opinion and expression," and "freedom of peaceful assembly and association." In subsequent years, several additional international agreements were adopted incorporating these provisions. Among them were the International Covenant of Civil and Political Rights (1966), the European Convention on Human Rights (1950), the American Convention on Human Rights (1969), the Helsinki Accords (1975), and the African Charter on Human and Peoples' Rights (1981).

Such declarations and treaties did not instantly ensure, of course, that all governments that were parties to them would acknowledge that domestic practices regarding political imprisonment were appropriate matters for international concern. Though the Soviet Union ratified the International Covenant of Civil and Political Rights and signed the Helsinki Accords in the 1970s, in the years before the Communist system began to collapse in the late 1980s it regularly insisted that political imprisonment was an internal affair. In the 1990s, the People's Republic of China and India remained among the major nations that continued, at least intermittently, to insist that international concern with their domestic practices on human rights was illegitimate.

Despite the failure of the provisions of the United Nations Charter to gain universal acceptance in the half a century during which the nations of the world formally subscribed to them, it may be said that today they are widely accepted, at least in principle. Moreover, with each passing year, fewer and fewer governments have resorted to the claim that international concern with their human rights practices is improper. For the most part, governments that are criticized on such grounds as political imprisonment now dispute their critics on the facts. They claim that those people they have imprisoned were not merely engaged in peaceful expression or association but were, in fact, engaged in violence or conspiracies to commit violence. Accordingly, over time, the international effort to free political prisoners has increasingly required proponents of human rights to enter into disputes with governments over the facts. Intergovernmental groups, foreign governments, and nongovernmental groups—especially the latter—seeking freedom for political prisoners increasingly rely on reporting by groups such as Human Rights Watch and Amnesty International in opposing imprisonment for peaceful expression and association. The modus operandi of these organizations has become investigative. They go far beyond mere assertions that prisoners are confined for political reasons or are mistreated in custody; instead their reports are filled with detailed discussions of the evidentiary basis for such allegations because, for the most part, the predictable response from governments will not be to try to justify practices but to deny that prisoners are being held for peaceful expression or association and to insist that prisoners have been treated well. The aim of organizations promoting human rights is to prevail in these debates about the facts by persuasively documenting their allegations.

Political Imprisonment in the Human Rights Era

In the period following the adoption of international agreements to respect human rights, many countries in all parts of the world have practiced mass political imprisonment. A far-from-complete list would include Ethiopia, Sudan, Uganda, Guinea, Zaire, and South Africa in Africa; China, Indonesia, India, Afghanistan, Burma, Cambodia, and Vietnam in Asia; Iraq, Syria, Iran, Israel, Egypt, and Morocco in the Middle East; Argentina, Chile, Uruguay, Brazil, Haiti, and Cuba in Latin America; the Soviet Union, Poland, Turkey, Greece, and Yugoslavia in Europe.

In some cases, the number of such prisoners has been known and not subject to significant dispute. An example is Uruguay, a tiny country of three million persons where, for a decade following a 1973 military coup, the number of political prisoners at any given moment was about six thousand; elsewhere, as in Iran, whether under the shah or under the Islamic Republic, it has been difficult to gather the information that would permit a confident estimate. What is plain is that political imprisonment was practiced extensively by many governments aligned with either side in the four decades of the cold war struggle: by democracies such as India and Israel as well as by dictatorships of the Right and the Left; by countries with long democratic traditions, such as Chile and Uruguay, before they succumbed to dictatorship; and by both sides in such regional disputes as those between Iraq and Iran, or Greece and Turkey. Though a Communist country, the People's Republic of China undoubtedly ranks first by a large margin in the total number of political prisoners that it confined during this era; a fiercely anti-Communist country, Indonesia, ranks second. Indeed, with more than one million political prisoners at a time confined during the latter part of the 1960s and hundreds of thousands of them detained until the late 1970s, the ratio of political prisoners to population in Indonesia was probably comparable to that in China during those years. Since the decade beginning in 1966 was also the period of the Cultural Revolution in China, these two Asian countries with violently antagonistic political systems experienced the most intense political repression at the same time.

China and Indonesia

The term "political imprisonment" is somewhat imprecise in the Chinese context because the great majority of the victims of repression were sent to the countryside rather than placed behind walls or fences. In many respects, however, their treatment was similar to that of prisoners: they were taken from their homes; separated from their families; required to live at a particular place; not permitted to leave that place; and required to work at particular tasks. Many endured great hardships. Members of the intelligentsia, who were taken from their urban environments and sent to remote parts of the country for periods of six, eight, or ten years, were punished in this manner solely on the basis of their class background.

Liu Binyan, China's most renowned journalist, has described his experience during the Cultural Revolution in his memoirs, *A Higher Kind of Loyalty*. At the outset, in

1966, the offices of his newspaper were invaded from time to time by groups of Red Guards who "would drop into the courtyard of [his] offices and `struggle' against the capitalist roaders." Liu and his colleagues would be insulted and humiliated in these sessions. Worse was to come. In June 1968, he was detained in a cowshed along with some of his professional colleagues. "They were ordered to stand together in front of Mao's image every morning and every night to show contrition for their sins, and to recite Mao's quotations; they were punished if they made a mistake." That lasted a year. Then he was sent to Henan Province, five hundred miles from Beijing, to spend eight years planting rice, making adobe bricks, and raising pigs. Throughout this period, he was cut off from books and forced to participate in sessions in which he found he was "a handy tool" for those trying "to prove their revolutionary zeal, to outdo their opponents in political mudslinging." He noted, "Shouts, insults, banging on tables, and stamping of feet became part of the burden I had to bear; this became the means by which Party members demonstrated their class and Party loyalty, non-Party members demonstrated their solidarity with the Party as a steppingstone to membership, and those from bad social backgrounds demonstrated their change of class allegiance."

Though the treatment of members of the intelligentsia sent to the countryside was harsh, the class enemies who were actually sent to prison during the Cultural Revolution generally suffered even more. One of the outstanding memoirs from this period— a classic of prison literature, worthy of comparison to such works as Dostoyevsky's *Memoirs from the House of the Dead*—is Nien Cheng's *Life and Death in Shanghai*.

Nien, a well-to-do woman who had been educated abroad, and her husband had chosen to remain in China after the Communist triumph in 1949 because they sympathized with the revolution. When the Cultural Revolution began in 1966, she was working for the Shell Oil Company in Shanghai, where her husband had been general manager before his death some years earlier. In 1966, she was fifty-one and lived with her daughter, a twenty-four-year-old film actress.

Her ordeal began when Red Guards invaded her home and initially held her there under house arrest. After a few weeks, she was taken to prison in Shanghai, amid demands that she "confess." Initially, it was not clear what she was supposed to confess; over time, however, as she underwent interrogations in prison, it appeared that she was supposed to admit to passing information to "British agents"—that is, colleagues with whom she had worked at Shell. Nien Cheng was a stubborn woman who apparently took a certain amount of pleasure from her frequent verbal battles with her interrogators. Inevitably, however, her captors became increasingly annoyed with her intransigence, leading to the following episode that occurred in January 1971, more than four years after the start of her imprisonment and the beginning of the demands for her confession:

> At the door of the interrogation room, the guard suddenly gave . . . a hard shove, so that I staggered into the room rather unceremoniously. I found five guards in the room. As soon as I entered, they crowded around me, shouting abuse at me.
>
> "You are a running dog of the imperialists," said one. "You are a dirty exploiter of workers and peasants," shouted another. "You are a counterrevolutionary," yelled a third.

Their voices mingled and their faces became masks of hatred as they joined in the litany of abuse with which I had become so familiar during the Cultural Revolution. While they were shouting, they pushed me to show their impatience. I was passed around from one guard to another like a ball in a game.

Nien Cheng was bounced against the wall, slapped several times on the cheek, and pulled by the hair. She vomited, and nearly passed out, but did not confess. She was then handcuffed behind her back and told the handcuffs would remain on until she confessed. Though they were kept on for many days—making it extremely difficult and painful for her to relieve herself, sleep, or eat—and though her hands and feet swelled enormously, she still refused to confess. Eventually Nien Cheng was released in 1973 after six and a half years in prison—without ever confessing. When she emerged from prison, she discovered that her daughter had died as a consequence of persecution. Several years later, Nien was permitted to emigrate to the United States, where she wrote her prison memoirs.

The demand for confessions has been a characteristic of political repression in many countries but perhaps never to the extent that it has figured in the Communist period in China, particularly during the Cultural Revolution. A government document from the period asserted: "Disclosure is better than no disclosure; early disclosure is better than late disclosure; thorough disclosure is better than reserved disclosure. If one sincerely discloses his whole criminal story and admits his crimes to the people humbly, he will be treated leniently and given a way for safe conduct, and his case will not affect his family."

Confessions may also reflect the need of political oppressors for confirmation, from the mouths of their victims, of the justice of their actions. This is probably one of the factors that has made torture so frequently a concomitant of political imprisonment; by inflicting pain on detainees, the captors obtain the confessions that they seek. In addition, of course, torture is a means for extracting from detainees the names of other participants in suspected conspiracies, and it may be used simply as a punitive measure. No doubt, there is sometimes also a sadistic element.

The Cultural Revolution accounted for the highest level of political imprisonment in China, but it was by no means the only period since the Communist triumph when great numbers were incarcerated because they participated in peaceful expression or association or simply because they were considered to be class enemies. In the antirightist campaign of 1957, the period at the end of the 1970s and in the early 1980s when the Democracy Wall movement was crushed, and the crackdown following the Tiananmen Square protest of 1989 and into the 1990s, many political prisoners were confined. In addition, when challenges to central authority have emerged in regions such as Tibet and Inner Mongolia, the confinement of great numbers of political prisoners has been the inevitable consequence. As to how many, estimates vary greatly, and reliable figures are not available.

In Indonesia, the era of mass political imprisonment began with a purported coup attempt on October 1, 1965, attributed by the Indonesian armed forces to the PKI, the Communist Party of Indonesia. This was followed by a bloodbath in which large numbers of suspected PKI members were massacred; the usual estimate is that half a million people were killed over the course of the six months following the coup. Previously, the Indonesian Communist Party had been the third largest in the world—after the Soviet Union and China—and the survivors of the massacres were imprisoned, most without charge or trial. Many remained in prison for more than a decade. In 1985, an Indonesian military official gave the number who had been imprisoned as 1,459,107. At other times different figures have been used. In the late 1980s, some of those imprisoned since 1966 were executed for their part in the events of 1965. By then, the majority were men in their sixties. Those who were released from prison continued to suffer prohibitions on various forms of employment, and the Indonesian government also imposed such restrictions on their children. A small number of those imprisoned in connection with the alleged coup attempt—whether there was an actual attempt to overthrow the government has always been disputed—remained in prison in the mid-1990s.

By and large, neither China nor Indonesia figured significantly in international denunciations for abuses of human rights during most of the period in which they practiced mass political imprisonment. For a variety of reasons, international attention focused far more on other regions: the Soviet Union and its Communist allies in Eastern Europe; the right-wing military dictatorships of Central and South America; South Africa; and Israel. Several factors combined to produce the relative neglect of the two countries that practiced political imprisonment on the most massive scale.

Though the Universal Declaration of Human Rights was adopted by the United Nations in 1948 and Amnesty International was founded in 1961, the human rights cause did not become a focus for major public attention until the latter half of the 1970s. By then, the Cultural Revolution in China and the mass imprisonment of PKI members in Indonesia were drawing to a close.

In addition, during the cold war era, the human rights cause was often exploited by partisans of the two superpowers to denounce the practices of their antagonists. That is, proponents of the Western cause denounced the human rights abuses of the Soviet Union and its clients from Vietnam to Poland to Cuba. Critics of the United States, on the other hand, focused many of their denunciations on Latin American military regimes that depended heavily on support from Washington. China occupied a peculiar slot in the cold war: it was a Communist state that was more or less aligned with the United States against the Soviet Union. Neither side in the cold war debate was particularly eager to try to discredit China by denouncing its abuses of human rights.

Another factor was that most international human rights campaigns originated in and derived the largest part of their support from the public in the United States and Western Europe. Indonesia was remote, its language was unfamiliar, and there were not many Indonesian exiles in the West to arouse interest in their country. (There is a significant international human rights movement in Australia, and its greater proximity has stimulated more concern there than elsewhere with Indonesia.) As for China, it too was far away, the language was also difficult for Westerners, and Chinese names tended to sound alike. In addition, after China was "opened" in the 1970s, the West experienced a collective romantic infatuation with all things Chinese; the country was epitomized by Ping-Pong, panda bears, and its seemingly benign leader, Deng Xiaoping.

Indonesia's invasion of East Timor in 1975 and subsequent abuses there aroused some human rights denunciations in the West; and the democracy demonstrations and massacre in Beijing in 1989 ended China's capacity to evade international campaigns for human rights. Yet both countries had failed to attract international attention to their abuses of human rights on a scale commensurate with their extreme practice of political imprisonment and other forms of repression. That had become less true in the case of China by the 1990s, but Indonesia continued to be largely neglected.

Latin America

From the 1960s to the 1980s, political imprisonment was practiced in a large number of Latin American countries. During this period, however, the authors of political repression in many of these countries began to adjust their methods to the emergence of organized international human rights campaigns that could mobilize effectively around cases of political prisoners. A case involving a political prisoner was proving the ideal focus for such a campaign: such a case involved an identifiable individual; the government that incarcerated the person generally could not evade its responsibility for the prisoner's incarceration; and political imprisonment, by its nature, endured for a long period, giving human rights groups outside the country time to organize a campaign and making it possible to sustain the campaign for months or years. Frequently a family member, friend, lawyer, or other advocate for the prisoner was out of the country, or in some cases could travel from the country, making it possible to convene meetings at which that person would speak about the prisoner and allowing testimony before legislative bodies or interviews with the press. When freed—often in response to an international campaign—the former prisoner could contribute to international denunciations by giving press interviews or writing a memoir. This happened, for example, in the case of the Argentine editor and publisher Jacobo Timerman. He had been imprisoned in April 1977 and was tortured, but as a consequence of an international campaign that was mobilized speedily, and unlike many less-prominent journalists, he was not murdered in detention. In September 1977, a military tribunal released him from prison, but he was placed under a bizarre form of house arrest in which his military watchers moved into his Buenos Aires apartment with him. The campaign for Timerman continued during this period, and two years later he was expelled from the country. In exile, Timerman helped to bring down the Argentine military dictatorship by publishing his account of his ordeal, *Prisoner without a Name, Cell without a Number*. The book attracted enormous attention just at the moment that the newly installed administration of President Ronald Reagan in the United States had assumed office and was proposing to end the existing prohibition on economic and military aid to the Argentine military government, a prohibition imposed by the predecessor administration of President Jimmy Carter because of Argentine human rights abuses. Timerman and his book figured crucially in the U.S. political debates that made it impossible for the Reagan administration to implement that plan, which might well have prevented the military regime in Argentina from collapsing in 1983.

The Decline of Political Imprisonment
and the Rise of Alternative Modes of Repression

The cases of political prisoners were made to order for the emerging international human rights movement, which launched campaigns to free the prisoners, and conversely, were extremely damaging to the governments that confined such prisoners. As a consequence, by the end of the 1980s, the only Latin American country that continued to confine political prisoners for extended periods was Cuba, and even in that country, the number had declined to the low hundreds from a high of fifteen thousand to twenty thousand at a time in the 1960s. Yet the elimination of political imprisonment in the rest of Latin America did not signify an end to political repression—far from it. In some countries, more sinister means were devised, which had the advantage, from the standpoint of the governments practicing these measures, of enabling them to deny responsibility.

The forms of political repression that became the hallmarks of certain Latin American countries in the last quarter of a century were death squad killings and "disappearances." Typically, a death squad is a group of heavily armed men in civilian clothes who apprehend an individual at his or her home, or place of work or some other place that the person frequents, and either kill the person on the spot or kill him or her at some place nearby and dump the body at a spot where the sight of it is likely to spread terror. The number of killers in a death squad is usually determined by the size of the vehicle in which they travel: as many as eight or ten when it is a van; four or five when it is an ordinary car.

The Latin American country in which such death squad killings were most prevalent was El Salvador. Of the fifty thousand or so civilian noncombatants killed during the 1980s while a war was under way between left-wing guerrillas and government troops, about one-third were murdered by death squads; most of the rest died in indiscriminate attacks by Salvadoran armed forces. It was the death squad killings that inspired the greatest fear, helping to cause the flight from the country of more than one million people, about 20 percent of the population. When these killings were denounced, the Salvadoran government disclaimed responsibility. During much of the 1980s, the administration of President Ronald Reagan in the United States, which financed and armed the Salvadoran armed forces, echoed these denials, blaming the killings on "extremists of the right and the left." On the other hand, human rights groups such as Americas Watch attributed the killings to the Salvadoran security forces, noting varied circumstantial evidence: the death squads were never apprehended by the police; sometimes the police blocked traffic in a neighborhood to allow the death squads to operate uninterruptedly; the death squads passed through military checkpoints without difficulty; during the early 1980s, when a curfew was in effect and anyone on the street at night would be shot on sight, the death squads operated safely during curfew hours; random stops and searches of vehicles, which were common during many of the war years, never turned up the weapons carried by the death squads; and so on. (In Argentina in the late 1970s there had been another refinement: shortly before several heavily armed men broke into their victim's home, the electricity in the area had been turned off.)

During the 1980s, the Salvadoran government often imprisoned several hundred persons at a time for politically motivated offenses. The number would fluctuate because periodic amnesties would be declared, followed by new rounds of arrests, which would quickly restore the prison population. Some of these prisoners warranted designation as political prisoners; others may well have been involved in violence. It was difficult to determine in which category they belonged because almost none were ever brought to trial.

In neighboring Guatemala, the phenomenon of political imprisonment has been virtually unknown. Since "disappearances" were invented in that country in 1966, that mode of repression has been the principal means employed against dissenters. (In the early 1980s, the Guatemalan army conducted a counterinsurgency campaign in which tens of thousands were killed in massacres that wiped out a large number of villages in the western highlands. The victims were the predominantly Indian residents, who may or may not have been dissenters.) According to the definition of human rights organizations, individuals have "disappeared" when they are known to have been taken into custody and subsequently their whereabouts cannot be determined. In fact, such persons are almost invariably killed by those who take them into custody, but—since no body is located—their families cling to the hope that their fathers, husbands, and sons are actually alive. Where disappearances have been practiced, it is common to hear accounts of secret detention centers in which the disappeared have been kept alive, but these accounts usually turn out to represent wishful thinking. When government officials are questioned about the disappeared, they claim to know nothing and, from time to time, assert that such individuals have left the country or joined a guerrilla group. (Indeed, when partisans of the disappeared are careless and include on their lists someone who is missing but not actually known to have been taken into custody, it may turn out that the person is alive and did leave the country or join the guerrillas. Any case in which that can be demonstrated will be seized on by those denying governmental responsibility as a way to discredit reports of disappearances.)

There is no reliable count of the number of disappearances in Guatemala in the past quarter of a century, but the most commonly repeated estimate is more than forty thousand. This could be too high or too low; what is certain is that the number is in the tens of thousands, but the scarcity of effective domestic human rights monitoring due to the great danger of such efforts during most of that period makes a more reliable figure unavailable.

The other Latin American country in which the greatest number of disappearances took place was Argentina in the period in which the military ruled that country, from March 1976 to December 1983. In the Argentine case, detailed information on disappearances was compiled by human rights organizations throughout the period of military repression. A government commission that investigated the disappearances following the transition to democratic government was able to draw on this information and confirmed 8,960 disappearances by the armed forces during their seven and a half years in power. (The commission described this count as "not exhaustive.") The Argentine military also practiced political imprisonment and held about 8,000 persons without trial or charge during most of the period from 1976 to 1983. Though many of these people were tortured or otherwise abused in detention, they were considered the fortunate ones because they survived.

Brazil, Chile, Nicaragua, and Uruguay were among the Latin American countries that confined substantial numbers of political prisoners in the 1970s. Some disappearances also took place in all these countries, particularly in Chile in the five years following General Augusto Pinochet's accession to power by means of a military coup in September 1973. But by the mid-1980s, political imprisonment had come to an end in all these countries except Nicaragua, where the Sandinistas confined thousands of former members of the National Guard, captured when the Sandinistas overthrew the regime of Anastasio Somoza in July 1979, as well as numerous "contra" combatants, captured during the war that began about two and a half years later, along with political opponents imprisoned for peaceful expression or association. The last group varied in number from a handful to several hundred at different periods of Sandinista rule. Many critics of the Sandinistas within the country and internationally regularly counted the guardsmen and the contras in denouncing the Sandinistas for holding great numbers of political prisoners. Indeed, the U.S. State Department and other critics published claims that the Sandinistas held ten thousand or more political prisoners at a time, more than doubling the actual number even if the guardsmen and contras were included and multiplying twentyfold the largest number of peaceful dissenters held at any moment of Sandinista rule. Such denunciations reflected the significance that political imprisonment had acquired as a factor in international relations by the mid-1980s. Its importance helps to explain why this practice fell into disuse in parts of the world, such as Latin America, that were the focus of international human rights attention.

In the 1990s, the human rights situation in Latin America remained particularly dire in such countries as Brazil, Colombia, Guatemala, Haiti, and Peru. Death squad killings, assassinations, disappearances, and torture are the means of repression practiced in these countries, but none of them confine prisoners for extended periods for peaceful expression or association. Cuba alone in the Western Hemisphere continues to practice what, at least in its part of the world, is an outdated means of repression.

In the post-Stalin era, the Soviet Union and its client states in Eastern and Central Europe continued to practice political imprisonment, though the numbers were greatly reduced. Relatively large numbers were imprisoned in Poland and East Germany after the anti-Soviet protests in 1956, in Hungary following the crushing of the revolution in 1956, in Czechoslovakia after Soviet tanks rolled in to end the "Prague Spring" of 1968, and in Poland after the declaration of martial law in an effort to suppress Solidarity in December 1981.

By the time thousands of Solidarity activists were rounded up and imprisoned in the hours and days following the imposition of martial law, the human rights issue had achieved a firm place on the agenda of relations among nations. The United States and Western Europe immediately imposed economic sanctions on Poland, and at least in the case of the United States, most of these measures remained in place until all the political prisoners were freed several years later.

While they were held in prison, the Solidarity prisoners caused the Polish government no end of discomfort, leading the minister of internal affairs, General Czeslaw Kiszcak, to propose to one of the best known, historian and political essayist Adam Michnik, that he could spare himself a trial at which he would be convicted and given a long sentence if he would leave the country. Michnik, General Kiszcak suggested, had only to agree to this proposition and he could spend Christmas on the Côte d'Azur instead of in the Rakowiecka Street prison. Michnik responded in a letter dated December 10, 1983. Smuggled out of prison and circulated widely throughout the Solidarity underground that flourished in Poland after the organization was declared illegal and that also became well known in the West, the letter read:

I have reached the conclusion that your proposal to me means that:

1. You admit that I have done nothing that would entitle a law-abiding prosecutor's office to accuse me of "preparing to overthrow the government by force" or "weakening the defensive capacity of the state" or that would entitle a law-abiding court to declare me guilty.
    I agree with this.
2. You admit that my sentence has been decided long before the opening of my trial.
    I agree with this.
3. You admit that the indictment written by a compliant prosecutor and the sentence pronounced by a compliant jury will be so nonsensical that no one will be fooled and that they will only bring honor to the convicted and shame to the convictors.
    I agree with this.
4. You admit that the purpose of the legal proceeding is not to implement justice but to rid the authorities of embarrassing political adversaries.
    I agree with this.

From here on, however, we begin to differ. For I believe that:

1. To admit one's disregard for the law so openly, one would have to be a fool.
2. To offer a man, who has been held in prison for two years, the Côte d'Azur in exchange for his moral suicide, one would have to be a swine.
3. To believe that I could accept such a proposal is to imagine that everyone is a police collaborator.

Just as the imprisonment of Jacobo Timerman helped to bring down the Argentine military regime, the imprisonment of Adam Michnik in the age of international human rights hastened the end of the Communist government in Poland. At least in the case of countries on which organized efforts to promote human rights have focused during the past decade and a half, the pens of such political prisoners have proven mightier than the swords of their captors.

The failure of political imprisonment to achieve its purposes in Poland allowed that country to lead the way in bringing about the revolutions that swept the rest of Eastern Europe in 1989 and brought about the disintegration of the Soviet Union in 1991. Before those momentous events, the Soviet Union had released the majority of its political prisoners in 1987 and 1988; earlier in the decade, about a thousand at a time had been confined in prisons and labor camps. Many of their names—physicists Yuri Orlov and Anatoly Shcharansky, psychiatrist Anatoly Koryagin and poet Irina Ratushinskaya—had become familiar in the rest of the world. When Mikhail Gorbachev came to power in the Soviet Union in the mid-1980s, freeing them proved an essential means of demonstrating to the rest of the world that he represented something new and different. Indeed, if there was a single event in which Gorbachev demonstrated his bona fides internationally, it was on December 16, 1986, when he telephoned Andrei Sakharov in Gorky (the phone had been installed in the apartment the previous evening), where Sakharov had been exiled seven years earlier, to inform Sakharov that he could return to Moscow.

Almost immediately after Gorbachev was ousted five years later and the Soviet Union dissolved, the president of one of the newly independent republics that formerly constituted the Soviet Union, Zviad Gamsakhurdia of Georgia, was himself overthrown in an armed uprising. The foremost complaint of Gamsakhurdia's opponents was that he was holding political prisoners. Though Gamsakhurdia had won 87 percent of the vote in an election less than a year earlier, he was driven out of office in January 1992 in large part because the means of political repression in which he was engaged were those that were particularly associated with the discredited Communist regimes of the past; indeed Gamsakhurdia himself had been a political prisoner of the Soviet Union in previous years. Though the ethnic tensions and economic difficulties of the former Soviet Union have led to repression—as in the massive bombardment of Chechnya starting at the end of 1994 to crush that republic's separatist movement—its forms differ from that which particularly characterized the era that began with Lenin and ended with Gorbachev. As in Latin America, political imprisonment is out of date in the former Soviet Union and the former Soviet bloc in Eastern Europe.

Political Imprisonment in the 1990s

Certain countries in Africa, Asia, and the Middle East continued to practice political imprisonment extensively into the 1990s. In South Africa the political prisoners confined at various times following the advent of the apartheid regime in the late 1960s numbered many thousands and, for those jailed for violating the pass laws (restricting the movements of blacks), in the tens of thousands at a time. That country largely ended political imprisonment in 1991 through negotiations with former long-term prisoner Nelson Mandela and through an effort to meet the conditions for ending international sanctions. Political developments in several other sub-Saharan African countries, among them Angola, Benin, Ethiopia, Kenya, and Malawi, sharply reduced the number of political prisoners elsewhere on the continent. Releases in those countries were partially offset, however, by a dramatic increase in political imprisonment in Sudan following a June 30, 1989, coup that brought to power the Islamic fundamentalist military government of General Omar el Bashir.

By the early 1990s, the Middle East had not been greatly affected by the decline in political imprisonment under way elsewhere. For the most part, the countries of the region had not been a focus of international human rights pressure to anything like the degree experienced in the previous decade and a half to free political prisoners in the Soviet bloc countries or in Latin America. That began to change in the 1990s, but such countries as Iraq, Iran, Syria, Israel, Egypt, and Turkey continued to confine many political prisoners. Of these countries, Turkey was the target of the most sustained pressure, including from the Council of Europe, which demanded an improvement of human rights practices. This led to a sharp decline in political imprisonment in Turkey over the course of the 1980s, but not an end to the practice. On the other hand, political imprisonment by Israel of Palestinians from the Occupied Territories reached a high point at the beginning of the 1990s, reflecting the government's response to the intifada, which began in December 1987. With the advent of Palestinian autonomy in Gaza in 1994, a new phenomenon emerged: Palestinians held as political prisoners by their fellow Palestinians.

In Asia, large numbers of political prisoners were confined in the 1970s and for much of the 1980s by the Soviet-backed governments in Afghanistan and Vietnam. In the latter country, these included many thousands of people who had been associated with the government of South Vietnam and who were confined for "reeducation" after that government fell. India imprisoned several thousand political opponents of the government during the "emergency" declared by Prime Minister Indira Gandhi from 1975 to 1977 but subsequently did not hold large numbers of such prisoners. It has never been possible to gather much information about political imprisonment in North Korea, though it is widely believed that the number incarcerated for peaceful expression or association is high. South Korea still confined several hundred political prisoners at the beginning of the 1990s, including some elderly men accused of supporting the North Korean side in the war at the beginning of the 1950s. By then, they were the longest-term political prisoners anywhere in the world. Burma (now Myanmar), which largely cut itself off from the rest of the world after General Ne Win seized power in 1962, maintained the extensive use of political imprisonment from then until the 1990s. It remains to be seen whether an international human rights focus on the country in the wake of the award of the Nobel Peace Prize in 1991 to the country's best-known dissenter, Aung San Suu Kyi, will reduce political imprisonment. In 1995, she continued to be held under house arrest, and the country's military rulers seemed intent on maintaining the suppression of all opposition.

The foremost symbols of political imprisonment worldwide in the 1990s were the democracy activists in China imprisoned after the Tiananmen Square demonstrations. In the immediate aftermath of the massacre in Beijing on June 4, 1989, many thousands were imprisoned. A large number of them were released in the subsequent months without being brought to trial. Six years later, in 1995, Human Rights Watch had detailed information on more than five hundred who were still imprisoned. Given the difficulty of gathering information on such cases in China, it is impossible to say how large a proportion this was of the actual number of such prisoners. Those who were considered the ringleaders—or "black hands," as the Chinese authorities refer to them—had been sentenced to long prison terms. For example, Wang Juntao and Chen Ziming, two young intellectual leaders who had previously been associated with *Beijing Spring,* an influential unofficial journal of the earlier, Democracy Wall period, were each sentenced to thirteen years in prison, though they were released in 1994, ostensibly for medical reasons but actually to ensure that U.S. President Bill Clinton would renew most-favored-nation (MFN) trading status. Previously it had been the practice of the Chinese authorities to require prisoners to serve their sentences to the last day; but Wei Jingsheng, the best-known prisoner from the Democracy Wall period, who had been sentenced to fifteen years in prison in 1979, was released six months early, in October 1993, also because of the impending MFN decision. However, he was rearrested after China won renewal of MFN, as were other prominent dissenters. Accordingly, barring a dramatic turn of events in China, or a great increase in the effectiveness of human rights campaigns focusing on that country, China can be expected to be a leader in political imprisonment for many years to come.

THE FUTURE OF POLITICAL IMPRISONMENT

Though it is too soon to predict the end of political imprisonment, the increased use in many countries of alternative modes of repression suggests that we will not again see anything resembling what occurred during the middle decades of the twentieth century. In some instances, as in Latin American countries such as Colombia, Guatemala, or Peru, or in Asian countries such as India and Sri Lanka, more violent abuses may be practiced, both because they are less susceptible to human rights campaigns and because they inspire more terror. Elsewhere, in countries with as widely varying political systems as Vietnam, Saudi Arabia, and Kenya, governments may suppress dissent by controlling employment, education, travel, and other aspects of daily life. Actions such as denial of a job, or of a child's right to attend college, or of a passport, lend themselves far less readily to international campaigns for human rights than political imprisonment. Even so, they may be effective in suppressing dissent.

Political imprisonment flourished during an era in which the weapon that governments feared most was the printing press. Imprisonment was used to try to suppress the spread of information and ideas, from the books distributed by John Lilburne to the leaflets handed out in Tiananmen Square by the Chinese dissidents. The practice of political imprisonment reached its apogee in the twentieth century, when some governments believed that by imprisoning millions of their citizens, they could hold back ideas that had infected entire populations. This proved to be effective so long as the rest of the world went along with the tradition that what any state does within its own borders is not the proper concern of governments and citizens elsewhere.

The decline of political imprisonment in the past decade, and the prospect that it will decline further, reflect the inability of governments to silence their external critics by the same means that they had been using to deal with domestic dissenters. Indeed, repressive states have become aware that political imprisonment, as the perfect symbol of their repression, makes them relatively easy targets for those outside the country denouncing them for their abuses of human rights. Though they may try to shrug off such criticism for a time, few governments find that it is comfortable to be identified over the long term as pariah states because of their human rights abuses. Unfortunately for the cause of human rights, it is more common for repressive regimes to seek alternate means of repression, ones that are less susceptible to international denunciations, than to end their efforts to suppress dissent.

For those who continue to suffer imprisonment for peaceful expression or association, of course, there is little comfort to be derived from the knowledge that they may be victims of an anachronistic mode of repression. Yet there may be some solace in their awareness that they are in distinguished company. The dissenters who were imprisoned for their views and associations during the past three centuries or so include a disproportionate number of the outstanding thinkers and writers of our era.

Bibliographic Note

The memoirs of former political prisoners are a distinctive and rich literary genre. Among those that I particularly benefited from in writing about the history of political imprisonment are Alexander Herzen's *My Past and Thoughts*, trans. Constance Garnett (New York: Vintage Books, 1974) and Fyodor Dostoyevsky's lightly fictionalized *Memoirs from the House of the Dead*, trans. Jessie Coulson, ed. Ronald Hingley, World's Classics (Oxford: Oxford University Press, 1990). Among more recent Russian authors, I relied on Andrei Sakharov's *Memoirs*, trans. Richard Lourie (New York: Alfred A. Knopf, 1990). Among non-Russians writing about Russia, I cited Robert Conquest's *The Great Terror: A Reassessment* (New York: Oxford University Press, 1990) in discussing political imprisonment under Stalin.

Another country that must figure significantly in any discussion of political imprisonment is China. Among recent memoirs, two notable works are Liu Binyan's *A Higher Kind of Loyalty*, trans. Zhu Hong (New York: Pantheon Books, 1990) and Nien Cheng's *Life and Death in Shanghai* (New York: Grove Press, 1986). Jonathan Spence's *The Search for Modern China* (New York: Norton, 1990) is an excellent general history. In discussing other Communist countries, one may choose from a plethora of important memoirs by dissenters who were imprisoned; if a single book had to be chosen to represent this extensive literature, Adam Michnik's *Letters from Prison and Other Essays*, trans. Maya Latynski (Berkeley: University of California Press, 1985), seems to me outstanding for its political insights and its eloquence.

To illustrate political imprisonment in the United States, I cite the memoirs of two of the leading radicals of the early decades of the twentieth century: Emma Goldman's *Living My Life*, 2 vols. (1931; reprint, New York: Dover Publications, 1970), and Big Bill Haywood's *Autobiography* (New York: International Publishers, 1929; reprint, Westport, Conn.: Greenwood Press, 1983). An essential overview of that era is Zechariah Chafee's *Free Speech in the United States*, new ed. (New York: Atheneum, 1964). A different kind of political imprisonment in the United States, the incarceration of the Japanese-Americans during World War II, is discussed in Peter Irons's *Justice at War* (New York: Oxford University Press, 1983) and also in biographies of leading participants in that shameful episode, such as Jack Harrison Pollack's *Earl Warren: The Judge Who Changed America* (Englewood Cliffs, N.J.: Prentice Hall, 1979). A biography that tells a lot about the role of the Federal Bureau of Investigation in the imprisonment of dissenters is Curt Gentry's *J. Edgar Hoover: The Man and the Secrets* (New York: Norton, 1991).

The only Latin American memoir that I cite is Jacobo Timerman's account of his imprisonment under the military dictatorship in Argentina: *Prisoner without a Name, Cell without a Number*, trans. Toby Talbot (New York: Knopf, 1981). Two other important works on repression in the region are *Nunca Mas: The Report of the Argentine National Commission on the Disappeared* (New York: Farrar, Straus, Giroux, 1986) and Michael McClintock's *The American Connection*, 2 vols. (London: Zed Books, 1985).

Important sources on political imprisonment in Nazi Germany and Nazi-occupied Europe include two classic works: Konrad Heiden, *Der Fuehrer: Hitler's Rise to Power*, trans. Ralph Manheim (Boston: Houghton-Mifflin, 1944), and Raul Hilberg, *The Destruction of the European Jews* (New York: Quadrangle, 1961; reprint, New York: Harper Colophon, 1979). For the period in which the Nazis were rising to power, perhaps the outstanding memoir is Harry Kessler, *In the Twenties*, trans. Charles Kessler (New York: Holt, Rinehart and Winston, 1971).

Finally, I relied on Bertrand Russell's *Autobiography*, 3 vols. (Boston: Atlantic/Little, Brown, 1967–69) and Louis Fischer's biography *Gandhi: His Life and Message for the World* (New York: New American Library, Signet Key Book, 1954) in discussing the experiences of two of the most famous political prisoners of the twentieth century.

CHAPTER FOURTEEN

THE LITERATURE OF CONFINEMENT

W. B. Carnochan

There is no material content, no formal category of an artistic creation, however mysteriously changed and unknown to itself, which did not originate in the empirical reality from which it breaks free.

—Theodor Adorno, "Commitment"

In "Commitment" (1962), Theodor Adorno argued, on the one hand, against explicitly political art and denied, on the other, claims that the art of the avant-garde, represented by writers like Franz Kafka and Samuel Beckett, could be thought of as autonomous: the iconoclasm of the avant-garde originates in empirical reality, nor could it be otherwise. Adorno's figure of speech—art "breaks free" from empirical reality—evokes the prison theme that, broadly defined, has played a large part in a culture that understands artistic creation as an act, forever being repeated, of release from constraints.

Whether fictional or autobiographical, the literature of the prison concerns the interplay of constraint and freedom and therefore, analogously, also concerns its own creation. Prison fictions are often told in the first person, and even when they are not, they imply the question, how does mind break free? Following Adorno, we could say that in a secular context freedom is always and only the figure; prison, the essential ground. A text that gives expression to this paradoxical relationship is the Marquis de Condorcet's *Sketch for a Historical Picture of the Progress of the Human Mind* (1795): it was composed while Condorcet was under friendly house arrest to escape prosecution during the French Revolution's "Reign of Terror."

The prison theme is not encompassed by dungeons, debtors' prisons, penal colonies, internment camps, jails, or penitentiaries alone; such a list, though something of a practical necessity, overlooks the larger, metaphorical pattern that includes all manner of restraint on human action. The overarching category is confinement; its subcategories are captivity of any sort and the particular experience of imprisonment. Confinement restricts the free movement of body or mind.

Originary fictions of confinement in the Western tradition, quite different in surface meanings yet linked by a common thread of feeling, include the story of Zeus's antagonist, the rebel Prometheus, whose punishment is to be chained to a rock in the Caucasus; Plato's image of the soul locked helplessly within the body; and Adam and Eve, whose expulsion from the walled garden can be seen, on one interpretation, as merely the beginning of their woe but, on another, as a release, a fortunate fall into the world of the human. If Western experience is conceived as having originated in a sense of confinement, the theme of imprisonment may then be thought of as one metaphorical convenience among others for rendering that original feeling. Confinement comes in many forms—on islands, in madhouses, in abbeys and convents, in domestic households, in underground apartments in Harlem, where we last see the protagonist of Ralph Ellison's *Invisible Man* (1952), in claustral settings like those in which Kafka or Beckett immure their characters, as well as in jails, penitentiaries, and prisoner-of-war camps; in the human imagination, prison is where one finds it. Not only are there countless texts—poems, dramas, opera, fictions, and works by those who write of their own prison experience—but if every artistic expression exemplifies a breaking free from empirical reality, the subject also has no natural limit.

Prisons of the self and mind may be called imaginary in that imagination forms them. Others are as realistic as fiction, or the descriptive powers of the prisoner, can make them. If the mythical prison comes in as many guises as mind can conceive, representations of what may be simply called the real or actual prison rely on the accumulation of grim detail—the physical surroundings, the behavior of guards or wardens, and in modern instances, the physical brutality and erotic violence of prison life. In the one case, all is mind; in the other, all is body. Yet these paradigms in practice flow into each other and merge in unpredictable combinations. In the first case, the subject is the self; in the other, society. In either case, imprisonment means being imprisoned by someone or by some force, whether external or internal; hence prison literature concerns the workings of power and resistance to power, whether represented by Zeus, by the state, or by compulsions and needs within.

Ideas of struggle underlie the plot of prison literature, although the very absence of struggle, the radical acceptance of confinement—the desire not to escape or even the love of being imprisoned—is sometimes the real story. Lord Byron's "The Prisoner of Chillon" (1816) ends on such a note:

> My very chains and I grew friends,
> So much a long communion tends
> To make us what we are:—even I
> Regain'd my freedom with a sigh. (IV.16)

Yet the desire not to be free, which may be read allegorically either as submission or existential indifference, may itself be a version, if not quite the usual one, of transcendence; prison stories commonly share a hope of transcendence, as represented by the overcoming of limitation or of degradation, whether by the exercise of mind or by interventions of providence. The protagonist of John Cheever's *Falconer* (1977), named Farragut, is one of Cheever's suburban characters but with a difference: a drug addict who has murdered his brother, he is sent to Falconer Prison, where he becomes prisoner #734-508-32. On the book jacket the publishers described the tale: "This is the story of what happens to Farragut—how he moves toward the essence of his ardor for life and beauty, how he falls in love unexpectedly and profoundly; how he experiences those hours of imprisonment that open the way to his astonishing salvation." Though imperfectly true of the tale Cheever actually tells, the rhetoric and its religious overtones, the litany of "essence," of "love," of "salvation," mark the prison theme. Prison is hell; getting out of it, or overcoming degradation, a pathway to heaven. Alternatively, prison may itself be a type of paradise. One of Jean Genet's fictions of the prison, told as autobiography, is *The Miracle of the Rose* (1946).

THE CLAIMS OF ORDER AND FREEDOM

Yet transcendence is uncertain. Interpreting prison fictions requires a judgment on the character whose story is told; in the process, opposing claims of order and freedom, of authority and the individual, must be weighed. That the prison became common fictional currency in the eighteenth and nineteenth centuries reflects the historical moment when individualism became the dominant ideology of the West. But the theme of individualism was hardly new, and the figure of Prometheus, capable of inspiring quite different feelings among different onlookers, remains at the ambiguous center of Western consciousness.

To be sure, the Prometheus figure lodged in the Western mind since Percy Shelley enshrined him among Romantic heroes in *Prometheus Unbound* (1820) represents martyred virtue; he stands for compassion and humanity in the face of the gods' tyrannical unreason. That is his role also in Aeschylus's *Prometheus Bound* (460–450 B.C.) but not his only one; more subtle than Shelley's, the Prometheus of Aeschylus is suspiciously given to rant and rapture. The curious figure of Ocean who enters, ridiculously, riding a four-footed bird and then offers counsels of prudence—"Keep quiet, don't run off at the mouth" and "calm down"—deflates the Promethean rhetoric. For a moment, the hero seems a silly blowhard full of noise and fustian. "What I wish to give you (smart as you are)," says Ocean, "is the best advice of all: *know thyself*." (45, 44) That is even more provocative, less comic: all that sound and fury, does it signify some absence in the Promethean self? Why all this posturing? Is it truly such a splendid thing to have stolen Zeus's fire?

Elsewhere in the play the chorus utters words that one may write off as merely pious—"Can the plans of things that live and die ever overstep the orchestrated universe of Zeus?" (55)—but the rendering of power as celestial harmony compels a second thought; and when Zeus's messenger Hermes comes on stage, he gives as good as he gets, providing another view of the Promethean character. "You there!" says Hermes, "Yes, you . . . are, I presume, the bitter . . . intellectual who committed crimes against the Gods" (76). Prometheus stole Zeus's fire by cunning, not by heroic action, and Hermes challenges the Promethean image: in Hermes's eyes, Prometheus is not the heroic rebel but the agile intellectual and sharp-tongued satirist who has himself been tricked in turn by the superior power and wit of Zeus. It is a part that fictional prisoner-heroes often play. The antagonist of authority opposes his own strength, often wittily and satirically, against the superior weaponry of society or the gods. Another hero of the Romantics, John Milton's Satan in *Paradise Lost* (1667), fits the profile too: the guise of the venomous serpent in whose form he tempts and seduces Eve conceals the trickster and is the emblem of his sinister yet faintly comic masking. The prisoner-hero, like the satirist whose verbal or artistic antagonisms the prisoner acts out, evokes double feelings. Is the chance of transcendence, intimated by the atmospheric horrors of the prison, really a mirage? The words of Ocean, "*know thyself,*" and of Hermes warn against taking too much for granted. Only after Shelley and other of the Romantics could Prometheus or Satan have seemed a complete hero.

The ambiguity of the captive hero, ambiguous by virtue of being captive (if nothing more), rubs off on other fictional characters whom one would not otherwise place in the company of Prometheus or Satan. Few figures in English fiction are more familiar than the heroes of Daniel Defoe's *Robinson Crusoe* (1719) or Jonathan Swift's *Gulliver's Travels* (1726), and they have much in common (including a role unanticipated by their creators in the growth of a literature for children). Both fictions depict captivities, and every reader remembers Crusoe on his island, umbrella raised, utterly alone yet lording it over his nonexistent kingdom, or the prostrate Gulliver awakening in the land of tiny Lilliputians, bound by thousands of exquisitely thin ties, blinded by the sun, pricked by volleys of tiny arrows, unable to move. But even though Crusoe and Gulliver, who undergoes one strange captivity after another in the four voyages that make up his *Travels*, are etched on Western memory, neither is a simple case.

On one view, Gulliver's ultimate, violent misanthropy, which makes him incapable even of sitting at the table with his own family, is grounded on a true estimate of human wickedness; on another, it marks his blindness to human decency. And Crusoe exemplifies either (as Jean-Jacques Rousseau believed) the natural self-reliance of mankind or (as readers are more likely to believe now) the colonizing mentality at work, an economic man in his island kingdom, waiting to people it with subjects as compliant as the man he will call Friday. Conflicting interpretations of literary texts are nothing new, but these divergences are sharp and partly depend on the natural psychology of response to the prisoner theme. In the eyes of some higher power—the Christian God, for example, who punishes Crusoe for his wandering ways by confining and testing him in solitary—the captive has earned captivity. Though often calling up deep human sympathies, the case of the prisoner cannot be abstracted from considerations of lawfulness, hence with claims of order as well.

Nor, it should here be added, can the literature of the prison be abstracted from considerations of gender, associated as they are with those of the social order. Though not exclusively male, the literature of the prison is largely so. Any survey that focused on women and prison literature would yield a different account of how claims of order compete with those of freedom.

Poetry; Drama; Opera and the French Revolution

Literature of the prison includes, on the one hand, fictions written about prison experience and, on the other, writings of every sort by inmates. Yet the categorical division is not watertight and overlaps other distinctions of period and genre. Prisoners write fictions, not always about prison experience: Thomas Malory is thought to have written *Le Morte Darthur* (1485) in prison, and Cervantes, who spent time both as a captive and as a prisoner, describes *Don Quixote* (1605) in the prologue as the sort of thing that might be conceived in a jail. Because these texts are not directly concerned with the experience of confinement, they are not considered here. This account begins with poetry, early modern drama, and—with an eye to the mythography of the French Revolution—operas and some postrevolutionary texts; then the historically more recent genre of prose fiction, including, when it comes to the twentieth century, a side glance at dramas by Jean-Paul Sartre and Beckett; then autobiographical and other writings by prisoners; and finally texts in which boundaries between the kinds of prison literature are put in question.

Poetry

Prison experience has not produced much poetry in English that has entered the canon, though the concentrated power of a collection like *The Light from Another Country: Poetry from American Prisons* (1984) suggests that the canon could be amended in this area, as it has been in others. In the seventeenth century Richard Lovelace addressed verses "To Althea, from Prison" (1642), but they have more to do with the imprisonment of love, a medieval metaphor here made literal, than with Lovelace's imprisonment for his political activities. Byron somewhat improbably turned the story of François Bonivard, the prisoner of Chillon's castle, into poetry. Oscar Wilde's last work, the hugely popular *Ballad of Reading Gaol* (1898), memorialized a trooper of the Royal Horse Guards, hanged for the murder of his wife while Wilde was confined in Reading Prison on conviction of sodomy. And Robert Lowell, who served five months in federal prison in 1943–44 on charges of draft evasion, wrote about the experience in "In the Cage" (1946) and again in "Memories of West Street and Lepke" (1959). Short and powerful, "In the Cage" is a flashing surrealistic glimpse into the prisoner's mind. It ends: "Fear, / The yellow chirper, beaks its cage" (23).

From the royal hostage Charles d'Orléans (1394–1465) to Genet, who produced a small body of verse, the prison has been a more fertile source of poetry in France than in England and America. Other French poets of the prison experience are the picaresque troubadour François Villon; the revolutionary André Chénier, imprisoned and executed during the Terror; and Paul Verlaine, who shot and wounded his fellow poet Arthur Rimbaud in a crime of passion. During his two years in prison Verlaine composed a lyric, "Le ciel est, par-dessus le toit" (1875), that beautifully expresses the sensory and psychological deprivation of one separated from, yet acutely conscious of, life beyond prison walls. Even in translation, the lyric retains its fragile beauty:

> The sky, above the roof,
>   Is so blue, so calm!
> A tree, above the roof,
>   Sways its crown.
>
> The bell, in the sky one sees,
>   Softly rings.
> A bird on the tree one sees
>   Sings its lament.
>
> My God, my God, life is there,
>   Simple and quiet.
> This peaceful music there
>   Comes from the town.

And as the outside world fades from view, the poet's gaze turns inward:

> What have you done, o you there
> Who weep so endlessly,
> Say, what have you done, o you there,
> With your youth?

In its crystalline lucidity, Verlaine's lyric captures and purifies an experience resistant to the usual impulses of lyricism.

Early Modern Drama: Shakespeare and Gay

More common in plays than in poetry, prisons are scattered through the drama of early modern Europe. Yet in these settings they are usually incidental, not thematically central. When the king is imprisoned in William Shakespeare's *Richard II* (1595), his being captive matters less than the larger turnings of the wheel of fortune, whose revolutions bring princes down. In a famous soliloquy Richard reflects on his fate: "let us sit upon the ground / And tell sad stories of the death of kings" (III.ii.155–56), thus anticipating his own end. Being in prison counts less than having been dethroned.

Nor are prisons usually at the heart of either comedy or tragedy in their purer forms. The wall that separates Pyramus and Thisbe in the play-within-a-play of Shakespeare's *Midsummer Night's Dream* (1595–96)—perhaps the purest of comedies— is palpably unreal; comedy, though often relying on metaphorical confinement and release, seldom relies on the prison image to effect its meanings. Prisons are too real for comedy and, Prometheus notwithstanding, too confining for conventional tragedy. Unlike other classical tragedies, *Prometheus Bound* lacked all of the action that Aristotle thought essential. Tragedy thrives on the drama of all-or-nothing; its destination is death. King Lear, in Shakespeare's play (1605), having recovered the shreds of his reason after the storm on the heath and having been taken captive, imagines passing his remaining days with his daughter Cordelia in the quiet shelter of prison. "Come, let's away to prison; / We two alone will sing like birds i' th' cage," there to outlast "packs and sects of great ones / That ebb and flow by th' moon" (V.iii.8–9, 18–19). But the logic of the tragedy defeats any resolution in which prison might offer sanctuary: only death can measure up to all that Lear has undergone.

The prison theme better suits tragicomedy, or "dark" comedy, the mixed and difficult-to-classify form that has become, not just in drama, a dominant strain in modern literature. Of all Shakespeare's plays, the dark comedy *Measure for Measure* (1604), a meditation on the uncertainties of justice, depends most on the prison as a vehicle of its meanings, and its most memorable dialogue occurs in prison. Disguised as a friar, Vincentio, the Duke of Vienna, addresses Claudio, under sentence of death for violating a long unenforced law against fornication: "Thou hast nor youth, nor age, / But as it were an after-dinner's sleep / Dreaming on both" (III.i.32–34). This underscores the duke-friar's admonition to come to terms with death, "Be absolute for death: either death or life / Shall thereby be the sweeter" (III.i.5–6), but the dreamlike sense of stasis fits the speaker's homiletic moral to the hearer's situation: prison represents a halfway house between the random mobility of life and the calm enclosure of the grave. In prison, time stops. Yet because *Measure for Measure* is a type of comedy, Vincentio also implies to Claudio the consolation that he may, at least this once, awaken from the after-dinner dream of prison and escape his sentence. This is how it turns out. But for every reader or spectator who recalls the play's resolution, more will remember the duke's words, speaking as he does to the condition of life and calling up the image of body and flesh as a bondage from which time at last brings release. The combined roles of Vincentio—duke and friar alike, the double image of civil authority and of religious consolation—mirror those of prison as the real place where authority, sometimes unjustly, consigns us and as the metaphorical condition of earthly life. In either case, the only good advice in the long run is the same: "Be absolute for death."

If *Measure for Measure*, as a so-called dark comedy, is hard to situate within Shakespeare's canon, John Gay's musical drama *The Beggar's Opera* (1728) not only is the work on which its author's reputation mainly depends, holding the stage to the present both in its own right and as the source for Bertolt Brecht's *The Threepenny Opera* (1928), but also so wittily reflected the social and political environment as to make it, along with *Gulliver's Travels* and *Robinson Crusoe*, a central text of its time. Using popular tunes and based on the life of the notorious outlaw Jonathan Wild, *The Beggar's Opera* satirizes the conventions of Italian opera and, at the same time, the corruptions of Robert Walpole's government. The play is said to have originated in Jonathan Swift's suggestion to his friend Gay that he write a "New-gate pastoral." Rich in irony, the notion of a Newgate pastoral, like Vincentio's double role, captures the contrasting values of prison as a place both of confinement and of sanctuary. Gay also sports with the irony of death as the last sanctuary. At the end, the im-prisoned highwayman Macheath (Brecht's model for Mac the Knife in *The Threepenny Opera*) longs for the gallows to release him from the importunities of his numerous wives; because prisons before the rise of the penitentiary were places of public coming and going, the profligate Macheath, though in Newgate, cannot escape his past. But the hero is rescued by a totally implausible reprieve—"an Opera must end happily"—and returned to his wives "in Triumph" (64). Whether the triumph belongs to Macheath, to his wives, or to the one wife, Polly Peachum, who has the best claim on him, is the final uncertainty in Gay's acidic mix of musical parody and political caricature. Like other successes of its kind, *The Beggar's Opera* spawned many imitations; it can be called the first musical comedy. Yet with its Newgate setting it is a comedy—or a farce—as dark in some ways as *Measure for Measure*.

Opera and the French Revolution

If musical comedy begins in Newgate, the nineteenth-century tradition of grand opera also begins in a prison setting. Just as the French Revolution and the fall of the Bastille came to symbolize the meanings of modern history, the prison came to serve as the principal image of political oppression. Beethoven's *Fidelio*, first performed in 1805 and later revised, sets to music the psychic drama of the Revolution as release. Based on Jean-Nicolas Bouilly's *Léonore, or Conjugal Love* (1799), a drama said to have been based on an actual incident of the Revolution, *Fidelio* dramatizes the power of love and fidelity with no inflections of doubt. The political prisoner Florestan lies in prison, condemned to die. His wife, Léonore, disguised as the young man Fidelio and serving as assistant to the chief jailer, ultimately saves Florestan with some last-minute help from the king's minister, friendly to Florestan, who arrives to the sound of trumpets and in the usual nick of time. The first act closes with a chorus of prisoners, briefly released into the courtyard of the prison; the next act opens with Florestan, chained in his dungeon, lamenting his lost freedom. "In des Lebens Frühlingstagen," he sings, "in the springtime of life." Literature of the prison often relies on fragments of memory or imperfect glimpses, caught through windows and bars, of the world out there, and memory may re-form itself as vision; now Florestan cries out to a vision of Léonore, and she appears, though unrecognizable to Florestan in her disguise. In prison, as in ordinary life, mind may seem to make the reality it seeks. When Florestan is freed and reunited with Léonore, he sings of "unutterable" joy: "O namenlose Freude"—a redemption that in other settings might be in doubt.

The operatic tradition that begins in Florestan's dungeon might be said to end in the prison of St. Lazare, where André Chénier awaits execution, in Umberto Giordano's *Andrea Chénier* (1896), or in the Italian prison of Giacomo Puccini's *Tosca* (1900), set in the Rome of 1800 after the Napoleonic coup of 1799, where Tosca's lover, Cavaradossi, awaits the same fate. Condemned during the Terror, Giordano's Chénier writes his last poem at night in his cell. Like Florestan's "In des Lebens Frühlingstagen," the poem is redolent of spring: in Chénier's original of 1794 (which was not, historical legend notwithstanding, written immediately before his execution), "Comme un dernier rayon, comme un dernier zéphyre" ("Like a final ray, like a final breeze"); or in the version of Giordano's librettist, "Come un bel di di Maggio" ("Like a lovely day in May"). But unlike Florestan's aria, this one foreshadows death. With his lover, Maddalena, who has bribed the jailer to substitute her name for another woman's on the list of the condemned, Chénier goes to execution. In *Tosca,* Puccini's heroine bargains with the villainous Scarpia for Cavaradossi's life, then kills Scarpia, only to see Cavaradossi executed by Scarpia's treachery before her eyes, and those of the audience. In a famous climax, Tosca hurls herself off a parapet. The revolutionary triumph of love's release into joy, celebrated by Beethoven, is now a memory.

Like prisons themselves, the Revolution—and the idea of revolution—have bewitched the Western imagination, not only in operas but also in dramas like Georg Büchner's *Danton's Death* (1835) or Peter Weiss's *The Persecution and Assassination of Jean-Paul Marat as Performed by the Inmates of the Asylum of Charenton under the Direction of the Marquis de Sade,* more commonly known as *Marat/Sade* (1964), or in fictions like Charles Dickens's *Tale of Two Cities* (1859). Since the Revolution, the prison in literature has carried meanings inseparable, psychologically and politically, from the events in France two centuries ago.

PROSE FICTION

Prose fiction first makes the prison a dominant image, and for a time perhaps *the* dominant image, in Western or at least in British literature. To pin down the reasons would require an account of "the rise of the novel," an event so deeply embedded in social and economic history that no brief account will serve. But why, in a narrower question, is the literature of the prison decisively, though far from exclusively, one of prose?

For one thing, prose has simply become more common than poetry. For another, the constraints of the ordinary—and prose is nothing if not "ordinary"—and of realistic narrative embody the confinement theme itself. For all its suppleness, the ordinariness of the language we speak can be felt as a constraint. For that reason, it may be felt as the very limitation that literary expression seeks to overcome. Yet realistic fiction has typically relied on the powers and limitations of ordinary language—its grammar, its syntax, its diction. At the heart of the realistic tradition, therefore, lies a paradox: though aiming to represent things as they really are and language as it really is, realism also participates in art's aspiration to reach beyond the quotidian. This paradox grows increasingly hard to support and in the twentieth century has generated all manner of efforts to overcome it. The modern tradition, as represented by a writer like James Joyce, often violently disrupts the terrain of ordinary language while still using, as in Joyce's *Finnegans Wake* (1939), what can only be called prose. But Joyce comes after several centuries of the realistic novel; and in the history of the realistic novel the prison is conspicuous at its start.

Lazarillo of Tormes *and the Origin of the Picaresque*

A Spanish novel of uncertain authorship, *Lazarillo of Tormes* (1553), began the mode of the picaresque novel that dominated European fiction for at least two centuries and has left a strong trace throughout the history of later fiction. *Picaro* means "rogue," and picaresque fictions tell a formulaic story: a young boy or girl, left an orphan or otherwise having to survive alone in the world, learns street wisdom through experience and hard knocks. In this milieu, jail lies around the corner of the next misadventure, and Lazarillo first learns the harshness of the world when his father is sent to jail, confesses (though the charges against him may be false), then is released to join an expedition against the Moors and is killed during the journey. Lazarillo's nonchalance in the face of this story expresses his defiance of harsh realities: "When I was eight years old, they accused my father of gutting the sacks that people were bringing to the mill. They took him to jail, and without a word of protest he went ahead and confessed everything, and he suffered persecution for righteousness' sake. But I trust God that he's in heaven because the Bible calls that kind of man blessed" (5). Colloquial piety, largely ironic, joins with uncertainty. Was his father guilty or not? The answer does not matter much. Piety is a stock response, and Lazarillo's offhandedness radiates wry awareness, as much as to say "well, that's how things are, everybody knows it, there's not much to be done about it, let's get on with it," which is also to say, let's get on with the story. This attitude dominated the early picaresque. As an ordinary feature of the picaresque landscape, the prison carried less intellectual and psychological freight than it has gathered over time.

Eighteenth-Century Fiction

In the eighteenth century the literary image of the prison veered by fits and starts from the relative straightforwardness of the picaresque toward the anxieties of the modern. This shift can best be traced in British prose fiction. Although prisons or their counterparts are present in *Manon Lescaut* (1731), the Abbé Prévost's tale of the Chevalier des Grieux's implacable passion for the courtesan Manon; in Denis Diderot's *The Nun* (1780), the story of a young woman who enters a convent and finds a prison-like world of clandestine sexual encounters; or in the tortured sexual fantasies of the Marquis de

Sade, who himself spent years in prison (and had been transferred from the Bastille to Charenton only days before the Bastille was stormed on July 14, 1789), the French tradition cannot match the sheer multitude of prisons in Defoe, Henry Fielding, and Tobias Smollett, among writers whose affiliations are with the picaresque, or the tense claustrophobia throughout the seven volumes of Samuel Richardson's *Clarissa* (1747–48), or the fascination of Gothic fiction, an English invention, with dungeons, vaults, closets, convents, monasteries, madhouses, and every variety of claustral space. A history of the prison theme in eighteenth-century Britain could come remarkably close to being an account of the literature of the age. What follows charts some points on a curve that any such history would plot in more detail.

Among those novels identified with the picaresque, Defoe's *Moll Flanders* (1722) and Fielding's *Tom Jones* (1749) reflect a shifting toward increased self-consciousness in representations of the prison. The heroine of *Moll Flanders,* as the title page relates, was born in Newgate, was twelve years a whore, twelve years a thief, and eight years a felon before at last growing rich and dying "a Penitent." Moll's roguery is even more directly the consequence of social conditions than in the early picaresque, but she does not live life unreflectively. Quite the contrary, she dwells on her sinfulness and also on the cruelty of an environment that leaves her little room but to do what she does. For someone of such self-reflectiveness, prison is a place for looking inward. In Newgate, under threat of execution, Moll claims to undergo a "sincere repentance" (288) and, when she obtains a reprieve, thinks it a rebirth. Yet important though the prison may be in her self-reflective mood, it also remains a natural episode in the life of a picaresque heroine. Though a symptom of injustice, even an image of hell, the prison represents a stage of Moll's life, leading not to the gallows but, when she is reprieved and her sentence changed from execution to transportation, to the new world. In Defoe's novel the prison is not quite yet at the vital heart of the fiction.

In Fielding's *Tom Jones,* the prison comes closer to a spiritual center of things. Despite its roots in the picaresque, *Tom Jones* differs from its predecessors in being more tightly plotted and differs even more substantially in its hero, an impetuous but good-hearted orphan whose troubles arise from imprudence, animal spirits, and instinctive benevolence—a hero, that is, for whom prison is not a completely predictable interlude. When Tom ends up in the Gatehouse after many misadventures and picaresque wanderings across the English countryside, it is not only a crisis but also the moment before everything is finally made right. Just as all seems lost, a visitor arrives with dramatic news. Tom's true parentage is revealed, he and Sophia Western are at last united, his persecutors get what they deserve. Prison here is the darkness before the comic dawn. As such it has antecedents in drama (Fielding was a dramatist before he became a novelist), but the structural role assigned the prison in *Tom Jones* is new to the novel and announces the prison's hold on the modern literary imagination.

As the eighteenth century wore on, the prison solidified this hold, but with a gathering difference. At the same time as the reformer John Howard was investigating conditions in European prisons, novelists came more and more to portray prisoners as victims and prison itself as the site of intolerable hardship. Whether in *Clarissa,* whose heroine is trapped by the repeated stratagems of her would-be seducer; in Mary Wollstonecraft's unfinished *Maria; or, The Wrongs of Woman* (1798), whose heroine is incarcerated in a private madhouse by her husband's order; in images like the caged starling of Laurence Sterne's *A Sentimental Journey through France and Italy* (1768), who has been taught to speak but can only repeat, over and over, "I can't get out—I can't get out" (71); or in Smollett's five principal novels—*Roderick Random* (1748), *Peregrine Pickle* (1751), *Ferdinand, Count Fathom* (1753), *Sir Launcelot Greaves* (1762), and *Humphry Clinker* (1771), each of them emphasizing the ugliness of prison life—in every case the story represents social oppression or indifference, though the victims, in keeping with the custom of prison fiction, may be complicit in their own victimization. Three novels that will illustrate this new understanding of social realities are Fielding's last fiction, *Amelia* (1751), Oliver Goldsmith's *The Vicar of Wakefield* (1766), and William Godwin's *Caleb Williams* (1794).

A lawyer by training, Fielding had spent two years as a London magistrate and had grown disillusioned with the legal system when he wrote *Amelia*. Reflecting this disillusion and his never-quite-extinguished hopes of reform, *Amelia* could almost be called his last legal tract as well as his last novel, and it has a claim to be the first novel in the Anglo-American tradition of fictions with injustice as their subject and reform as their goal. Much of *Amelia* takes place inside Newgate, where we first meet both the heroine and her husband, where the secret that Amelia has been defrauded of her inheritance is at last exposed and where the villainous lawyer who aided the fraud is eventually taken to await execution. Amelia's husband, perpetually in prison for debt or one step away, is the exemplary victim of a system of corrupt laws and unjust penal practices. In default of just laws, London risks anarchy and mob rule. Indeed the London mob is always at hand, commenting like a Greek chorus and forever threatening to administer justice in its own rough terms.

The Vicar of Wakefield, Goldsmith's only novel, is less pervasively grim than *Amelia*, but Goldsmith's reforming instincts are as strong as Fielding's. The vicar and his family are committed to county jail, in wintry weather, at a moment when everything has come to the worst—which is also the moment, as in *Tom Jones*, before everything turns out for the best. The prison provides the vicar a chance to exhibit the ideal benevolence of a late-eighteenth-century hero. He conducts worship, preaches to his fellow prisoners, endures their jests, and "in less than six days some were penitent, and all attentive." He sets the prisoners to work, establishes a system of fines and rewards, and having miraculously ("in less than a fortnight") reformed them all, regards himself none too modestly "as a legislator, who had brought men from their native ferocity into friendship and obedience" (148). Seldom is the language of the social reformer transplanted so directly into a fictional setting as in the vicar's reflections on crime and its punishments:

> And it were highly to be wished, that legislative power would thus direct the law rather to reformation than severity. That it would seem convinced that the work of eradicating crimes is not by making punishments familiar, but formidable. Then instead of our present prisons, which find or make men guilty, which enclose wretches for the commission of one crime, and return them, if returned alive, fitted for the perpetration of thousands; we should see, as in other parts of Europe, places of penitence and solitude, where the accused

might be attended by such as could give them repentance if guilty, or new motives to virtue if innocent. And this, but not the increasing punishments, is the way to mend a state. (148–49)

This is the authentic voice of the hopeful reformer in an age before disillusion set in.

But for their common concern with reform, two novels less alike than *The Vicar of Wakefield* and *Caleb Williams* could hardly be imagined: the one a domestic comedy, the other a nightmare fantasy of Gothic voyeurism and social tyranny. The author of *Political Justice* (1793), William Godwin was a Utopian anarchist who sought in *Caleb Williams*, subtitled *Things as They Are*, to display political and social injustice in a system founded on the false hierarchy of class. As servant to the aristocratic Ferdinando Falkland, Caleb spies on Falkland, discovers a murder in his past, is caught spying, is relentlessly pursued across the countryside, is falsely accused of robbery, is committed to prison, and finally is brought face to face in the courtroom with his master, persecutor, and accuser. At this point in the narrative Godwin faltered, in the presence of feelings at odds with his ostensible theme. Uncertain how to close his story, he wrote two conclusions, one in which Falkland repents his persecution of Caleb and another in which he does not. The human drama of victims and oppressors runs deeper than Godwin's political theory allows for. If *The Vicar of Wakefield* unself-consciously appropriates the words and ideas of the reformers, *Caleb Williams* displays the danger of transplanting ideology into fiction, namely that the life of the fiction will undermine the ideology. In any case, it is a long way from the picaresque offhandedness of *Lazarillo* to the almost operatic fervors of *Caleb Williams*. The emotional temperature of prison fiction had gone up.

The Nineteenth Century: Stendhal and Dickens

Although the prison theme dominates fiction less completely after the eighteenth century, as the novel leaves its picaresque origins farther behind and adds to its repertory the tale of manners and the historical romance, the theme by no means fades from view, appearing as it does in some of the next century's most magisterial fictions. In Stendhal's *The Red and the Black* (1830) or *The Charterhouse of Parma* (1839), the theme coincides with a new concern for character. In *The Red and the Black* Julien Sorel is sentenced to execution for attempting to murder a former lover; in prison he learns most fully to understand himself and even to regret that its doors cannot be locked from inside. Prison is where Julien Sorel comes to know what is most important: who he is. At the close of *The Charterhouse of Parma,* set in the world of post-Napoleonic Europe with its shadowy political intrigues, the prisons of Parma are emptied, but the fortunes of its lovers, Fabrice and Clélia, have been shattered, and they are dead. For them, as for Julien Sorel, prison has taught them something of felicity: their lives come together when Fabrice, in prison, falls in love with Clélia, his jailer's daughter. And, fittingly, the emptying of the prisons closes their story. In *The Red and the Black* and *The Charterhouse of Parma,* the prison experience is indispensable yet inseparable from claims of individual character. In Stendhal, the experience of prison is a habit of mind.

In Dickens's *Little Dorrit* (1855–57), however, the prison theme is still more comprehensive, drawing the characters so much under its spell as to deprive them of (or some might say to spare them) the individuality of a Julien Sorel. For many years William Dorrit has been an imprisoned debtor in the Marshalsea prison; for many years his loving daughter, Amy, known as Little Dorrit, has cared for him. And in his working notes for the novel, Dickens seems to have realized the foundation of his story in a sudden, sharp, parenthetic insight: "(Society like the Marshalsea)" (704). The habitual metaphor of the "prison of experience" owes much to Dickens, especially to *Little Dorrit*. The representation of society or life as an imprisonment seeps into all the corners of the tale. Old Dorrit, the Father of the Marshalsea, grows proud of being the prison's senior citizen, welcomes newcomers with impeccable gentility, and when he is finally released, lapses into delusion followed by death, unable to imagine himself anywhere but in prison. If redemption exists, as Dickens wants to believe, it is in Amy's devotion to her father and to Arthur Clennam, whom she finally marries. Yet her love plays itself out against the backdrop of a world so constrained that the conclusion seems less like the joyful outcome of *Fidelio* and more like a triumph of hope over experience. A famous passage near the end strikes a dominant chord: "The last day of the appointed week touched the bars of the Marshalsea gate. Black, all night, since the gate had clashed upon Little Dorrit, its iron stripes were turned by the early-glowing sun into stripes of gold. Far aslant across the city, over its jumbled roofs, and through the open tracery of its church towers, struck the long bright rays, bars of the prison of this lower world" (636–37). As the sun casts its rays like celestial bars into the haze of Victorian London, how can love's redemption be believed in?

The prison figures in many of Dickens's novels: not only in *The Tale of Two Cities*, with its pervasive evocation of prisons and of the Revolution, but also in *The Pickwick Papers* (1836–37), whose hero allows himself to be imprisoned for debt rather than pay unjustified damages; in *Oliver Twist* (1837–39), with its vivid description of Fagin in prison the night before his hanging; and in *Barnaby Rudge* (1841), whose hero goes to Newgate for his part in the Gordon riots of 1780. In *Martin Chuzzlewit* (1843–44), one of the characters epitomizes the prison theme: "Life's a riddle: a most infernally hard riddle to guess. . . . My own opinion is, that like that celebrated conundrum, `Why's a man in jail like a man out of jail?' there's no answer to it" (48). But in *Little Dorrit*, Dickens created a prison novel unsurpassable in its panoramic intensity—if only because social panoramas in the manner of Dickens, William Thackeray, or Honoré de Balzac are no longer present in the novelist's imagination. After *Little Dorrit*, what else was to be done?

The Prison of Consciousness

The answer to the post-Dickensian dilemma lay in the tradition represented by Stendhal's Julien Sorel and traceable to Victor Hugo's *The Last Day of the Condemned Man* (1829)—the account "of a mind's self-observation as it watches itself move toward death" (Brombert, 92). Condemned for some unspecified crime, Hugo's prisoner records every nuance of feeling as he vacillates between horror and the hope of reprieve, the fiction closing with the sound of footsteps on the stairs, bringing (presumably) either pardon or a final order for execution. As panoramic vistas are replaced by narrower visions, Hugo's floridly painted existential view from within the prison becomes a model. For all its imaginative power, *Little Dorrit* embodied a contradiction. Though the prison is pervasive, the omniscient narrator escapes constraints, except the inescapable ones of language, by moving freely in and out of the Marshalsea, from England to France and back again, by going, in short, wherever he wants, thus announcing his independence of his fictional world. Recent prison fictions, like other contemporary fictions, renounce narrative omniscience and, by looking outward from the confinement of a cell, intensify the conditions of narrative self-reflexivity. Recent prison fictions enact the modern drama of consciousness and self-consciousness.

Self-consciousness may be conceived as either a captivity or a glory, a doubleness figured by the enclosed spaces of prison and its analogues. Whether in Kafka's *The Metamorphosis* (1915) or dramas like Sartre's *No Exit* (1946) or Beckett's *Waiting for Godot* (1953), all of them reflecting the bleak restraints of the modern, or whether in Albert Camus's *The Stranger* (1942), Cheever's *Falconer* (1977), or John Banville's *The Book of Evidence* (1989), all first-person narratives of a gratuitous murder committed by the narrator, in each case, the interplay of hope and resignation within the thinking, perceiving, feeling, and self-conscious self sets the psychological boundaries of the narrative. These texts will illustrate the ambiguous grandeur of confinement in some of its modern versions. In the metaphor of confinement, modernity has inherited an image to embody its sense of what Blaise Pascal, one of modernity's patron saints, was first to call the "human condition," that of being trapped in a tiny cell in some remote corner of the universe.

No writer has a stronger claim to being at the beginning of the modern than Kafka, whose novels *The Trial* (written in 1914 and posthumously published in 1925) and *The Castle* (written in 1922 and published in 1926) and whose shorter fictions like "In the Penal Colony" (1919) and "A Hunger-Artist" (1924) relentlessly portray the human condition as a suffering for unknown offenses that nonetheless inspire guilt, a trial without hope of acquittal. Of all Kafka's fictions, *The Metamorphosis* has most captured the popular imagination, so much so that it inspired a Broadway production with the dancer Mikhail Baryshnikov in the principal role. *The Metamorphosis* recounts Gregor Samsa's improbable transformation into a huge, awkward insect. Trapped inside his grotesque new body, Gregor struggles for a look at a vanishing world:

> He nerved himself to the great effort of pushing an armchair to the window, then crawled up over the window sill and, braced against the chair, leaned against the windowpanes, obviously in some recollection of the sense of freedom that looking out of a window always used to give him. . . . [T]hings that were even a little way off were growing dimmer to his sight; the hospital across the street, which he used to execrate for being all too often before his eyes, was now quite beyond his range of vision, and if he had not known that he lived in Charlotte Street, a quiet street but still a city street, he might have believed that his window gave on a desert waste where gray sky and gray land blended indistinguishably into each other. (112–13)

With modest alteration, the passage could describe the experience of any prisoner, seeking a view of the world out there. And as the representation of diminishing insight and shrinking horizons, Gregor's view of gray skies and gray land enacts the epistemology of the modern. Kafka's story has become an emblem. Why (I once heard a puzzled observer ask) would Baryshnikov want to play an insect? Leaving aside the lure of virtuosity, why would any artist not want to play a part so compelling in its emblematic power?

At the end of his story, Gregor Samsa has withered into nonbeing. At the same time, the conflict of desolation and hope, of despair and its transcendence, of constraint and love, along with the uncertain metamorphosis of old traumas into new beginnings, comes into play. Released by his death, Gregor's family finds reasons to hope. His sister has "bloomed into a pretty girl with a good figure," and her parents look forward to seeing her married. The family moves elsewhere. "And it was like a confirmation of their new dreams and excellent intentions" that when they came to the end of the journey, Gregor's sister "sprang to her feet first and stretched her young body" (139). The reader wonders how these buoyant hopes can be fulfilled.

Like *The Metamorphosis*, *No Exit* and *Waiting for Godot* also end in doubtful affirmations, a natural conclusion to these dramas of enclosure. In the drawing room that is the site of hell in Sartre's drama, three characters come to the insight that hell is "other people." "So here we are, forever," says one; another answers, "Forever. My God, how funny! Forever." They break into laughter, and as the laughter dies out, the third character says, "Well, well, let's get on with it," and the curtain falls (61). Sartre anticipates and influences *Waiting for Godot*, for each act of Beckett's fantasy on the theme of living in a world after the gods have departed also ends on a note of affirmation that is at once alluring and futile. At the end of act 1, Estragon asks Vladimir, "Well, shall we go?" and Vladimir answers, "Yes, let's go" (36). At the end of act 2, Vladimir asks Estragon, "Well? shall we go?" and it is Estragon who answers, "Yes, let's go" (61). Each time the stage direction reads: "They do not move." *The Metamorphosis*, *No Exit*, and *Waiting for Godot* all announce, however hopelessly, the paradoxical solace of hopefulness under circumstances of inescapable confinement and cosmic solitude.

In these circumstances, gratuitous violence offers a release that, combined with ambiguities of outcome, lies at the center of *The Stranger*, *Falconer*, and *The Book of Evidence*. All follow the tradition of Hugo's *The Last Day of the Condemned Man* but depend for their suspensefulness not on a possible pardon but on the larger question of what can be salvaged from the wreck of a life. In *The Stranger*, set in Algiers, the altogether ordinary protagonist Meursault, thinking an Arab has threatened him, kills him by shooting him five times. In prison, after trial and sentence to the guillotine, Meursault rages at a prison chaplain who has come to offer comfort. The outburst is a kind of baptism: "It was as if that great rush of anger had washed me clean, emptied me of hope, and, gazing up at the dark sky spangled with its signs and stars, for the first time, the first, I laid my heart open to the benign indifference of the universe. To feel it so like myself, indeed, so brotherly, made me realize that I'd been happy, and that I was happy still." But the happiness of a hero who finds brotherhood in the indifference of the universe requires his own martyrdom. Only if huge crowds greet him "with howls of execration," Meursault believes, can he escape the loneli-ness of being (154). Disdain of the world requires an answer in kind if happiness is not to be swallowed up in solitude. Tension comes not from the hope of pardon but from the chance that his execution will elicit not execration but rather some unwanted scraps of human sympathy.

Cheever's *Falconer* also ends with a vision of brotherhood, the more usual brotherhood of one human being and another. The murderer Farragut escapes in a burial sack intended for another inmate. He cuts his way out and at a bus stop meets an alcoholic stranger, just evicted from his lodgings. They board the bus, the stranger insists that Farragut take one of his coats for warmth, and Farragut gets off at the next stop. "Stepping from the bus onto the street, he saw that he had lost his fear of falling and all other fears of that nature. He held his head high, his back straight, and walked along nicely. Rejoice, he thought, rejoice" (211). Yet as in *The Metamorphosis*, hope or joy cannot be guaranteed beyond the fiction's temporal boundaries, even though fear has receded. Farragut has no place to go. His epiphany is sufficient only as a fiction, a transient illumination in the context of a future that cannot be foretold.

The conclusion of *The Book of Evidence* once again evokes yet holds up to question the possibility of human comradeship. The picaresque aristocrat Frederick Charles St. John Vanderveld Montgomery, known as Freddie, brutally kills a woman who has interfered with his theft of a painting that has long obsessed him. Awaiting trial, he decides to plead guilty to first-degree murder, a decision that releases him from pain and even allows him to hope that he is "not wholly lost." On his way to a hearing, he finds himself in a police van with an "ancient wino," who claims to have been arrested for killing a friend. He has a bloodied eye and a huge running sore on his mouth. Freddie tries to ignore him, but as they round a sharp corner, the drunk falls off his seat. "I found myself holding the old brute in my arms. The smell was appalling, of course, and the rags he wore had a slippery feel to them that made me clench my teeth, but still I held him, and would not let him fall to the floor, and I even—surely I am embroidering—I think I may even have clasped him to me for a moment, in a gesture of, I don't know, of sympathy, of comradeship, of solidarity, something like that" (217). Yet the ending puts the whole story in doubt. Perhaps Freddie has been more than "embroidering." He requests that his narrative be placed in his file "with the other, official fictions." An inspector wonders whether the narrative includes all the improbable details Freddie has given the police. He replies: "It's my story, I said, and I'm sticking to it" (220). The wordplay binds together the prisoner's story and the storyteller's story, a characteristic turn of the modern by which fiction is revealed as fictional. In this case the turn proposes the ultimate question about any prisoner's tale, whether real or fictional: why believe it when the teller of the story has little choice but to stick to it?

WRITINGS FROM PRISON

Even prison narratives canonized by history raise the question, implicit in any text but especially pointed in narratives by those whom society has judged as criminals, of whether the narrator is trustworthy and his actions are justified. On the other hand, the prisoner's situation may be felt as conferring special understanding. From suffering, we suppose, comes insight. These conflicting responses, as well as the intensity of the experience under narration, underlie the allure of these writings. And, for the prisoner, confinement constitutes an invitation to reflection.

Classics of prison writing that have entered the collective memory of the West include Boethius's *The Consolation of Philosophy* (524), John Bunyan's *Grace Abounding to the Chief of Sinners* (1666) and *The Pilgrim's Progress* (1678), Oscar Wilde's *De Profundis* (written in 1897 and posthumously published in 1905), and Antonio Gramsci's *Prison Notebooks* (written between 1929 and 1935; selections posthumously published in 1947–51). Boethius might be called the Christian stoic; Bunyan, the evangelist; Wilde, the martyr; and Gramsci, the political thinker. These categories, though far from airtight, exemplify the range of feelings that run through personal narratives composed in prison.

Boethius and Bunyan, the one a moral philosopher and the other a religious visionary, both transform prison experience into spiritual exercise and the habit of meditation. An officer of the Roman administrative system, Boethius was imprisoned in 523 on charges of political misconduct and, awaiting execution, wrote *The Consolation of Philosophy*, a dialogue between the narrator and Lady Philosophy, who appears to him in a vision. Her message is stoical: the wheel of Fortune turns, and its turnings are beyond human power. "Really," therefore, "the misfortunes which are now such a cause of grief ought to be reasons for tranquility" (22). True security of mind comes only after being forsaken by Fortune.

Where Boethius finds consolation in natural philosophy, Bunyan finds it in belief. Forbidden to preach after the Restoration of King Charles II in 1660, Bunyan spent the greater part of the years 1660–72 in Bedford Jail, where he wrote his spiritual autobiography, *Grace Abounding*. And while briefly imprisoned again in 1675, he dreamed the dream that became the foundation of *The Pilgrim's Progress*: "As I walk'd through the wilderness of this world, I lighted on a certain place, where was a Denn; And I laid me down in that place to sleep: And as I slept I dreamed a Dream" (9). From that dream of an imaginary den, his prison cell, Bunyan created an allegory of spiritual testing and salvation, one that has probably had more readers, the Bible excepted, than any other text in English.

If Boethius and Bunyan offer consolation, Wilde and Gramsci express the indignation of martyrdom and the hope of justice. Imprisoned for having been, in the words of the presiding judge, "the centre of a circle of extensive corruption of the most hideous kind among young men" (Ellmann, 477), Wilde wrote *De Profundis* in a spirit of Christ-like martyrdom: "Where there is sorrow there is holy ground" (XI, 35). On his way to prison, he is mocked by the crowd: "I stood there in the grey November rain surrounded by a jeering mob." And being in prison is to suffer: "To those who are in prison tears are a part of every day's experience" (XI, 140).

However little he resembled Wilde, the tough-minded Italian Communist Gramsci, sentenced to twenty years after a show trial in 1928, also saw himself as a sufferer, in his case one like Job: "Only the Greeks could have imagined Prometheus, but the Hebrews were more realistic, more pitiless, and their hero more true to life" (xciii). And throughout his strenuous theoretical meditations on history, society, and the state, there runs a sense of forces operating on the "masses," who give their spontaneous-seeming but in fact enforced consent to a social order determined by the dominant group. Prometheus acts and suffers consciously, knowing the reasons behind and the sources of his pain. Gramsci's masses, subject to the hegemony of the dominant group, more resemble Job, remaining loyal to a mysterious order of things that requires their consent as well as their suffering.

Boethius, then, offers counsels of wisdom and endurance; Bunyan, the comforts of grace and the heroism of salvation. Wilde offers the solace, if that be the word, of anguish; Gramsci, that of awareness and enlightened resistance. In the English-speaking world, it is Bunyan whose influence has run deepest, representing as he does the values of individual conscience against those of the state (he could at any time have set himself free by agreeing not to preach) and by the strength of his prose. But if *The Pilgrim's Progress* has had more readers, the less familiar *Grace Abounding* occupies an even more central place in the history of writings from inside the prison. Bunyan not only composed it in Bedford Jail but also included in it a "brief account" of his imprisonment, naming the scriptural texts that comforted him as he contemplated going to jail, then admitting his vulnerability to human frailty and human feeling:

> But notwithstanding these helps, I found myself a man, and compassed with infirmities; the parting with my Wife and poor Children hath oft been to me in this place as the pulling the flesh from my bones, and that not onely because I am somewhat too fond of these great mercies, but also because I should have often brought to my mind the many hardships, miseries and wants that my poor family was like to meet with, should I be taken from them, especially my poor blind Child, who lay nearer my heart than all I had besides; O the thoughts of the hardships I thought my blind one might go under, would break my heart to pieces. . . . but yet recalling my self, thought I, I must venture you all with God, though it goeth to the quick to leave you. (98)

Bunyan's plain prose makes the perfect, utterly unsentimental vehicle for his mixed narrative of comfort and suffering.

Among other published narratives—and many more narratives have undoubtedly not survived—several have made a mark on history, whereas others are known largely because scholars have gone in search of them. In the first category are Silvio Pellico's *My Prisons* (1832), a quietly pious account of the author's ten years of imprisonment by the Austrian government that ruled northern Italy, Henry David Thoreau's "Civil Disobedience" (1849), a secular protest against war and slavery, written on the occasion of Thoreau's one night of imprisonment in Concord Jail for not paying his poll tax, and Martin Luther King's "Letter from Birmingham City Jail" (1963).

In Italy Pellico's narrative "is on every curriculum" (xxiii); one of his translators calculated in the 1960s that an average of six editions had appeared in Italy each year since its first publication and that it had been translated into some dozen languages (including no less than twenty-two French translations). In the United States, "Civil Disobedience" is also—or used to be—a staple of the school curriculum as well as a founding text for movements of social protest. Thoreau combines a sense of the mock-heroic with a strenuous Yankee rhetoric that is by now deeply etched in the American grain. On the one hand, he knows that his imprisonment, which came to an end when someone else paid the poll tax for him the morning after his arrest, is more than a little comic. Having been put in jail on his way to pick up a shoe that had been mended, he proceeds, after being let out, "to finish [his] errand" and then to go picking huckleberries. This, he says, with a wry allusion to Pellico's long incarceration, "is the whole history of 'My Prisons'" (654). On the other hand, Thoreau speaks the language of authentic heroism: "Under a government which imprisons any unjustly, the true place for a just man is also a prison" (646).

In the tradition of Thoreau, and with as deep a historic resonance, is King's "Letter from Birmingham City Jail," his reply to critics within the church who urged him to take a more moderate course. Unlike "Civil Disobedience," King's "Letter" is grounded in a religious vocation: "One day the South will recognize its real heroes. . . . One day the South will know that when these disinherited children of God sat down at lunch counters they were in reality standing up for the best in the American dream" (302). Written at lightning speed on the margins of a newspaper and a few sheets of note paper, then smuggled out of jail by King's attorney, "Letter from Birmingham City Jail" was a manifesto of crucial importance to the civil rights movement of the time.

Less memorable than Pellico or Thoreau or King—because more self-consciously literary and without their concern for social justice—is *The Enormous Room* (1922), E. E. Cummings's narrative of his internment in France in 1917. Whatever its limitations, the book flowered into fame between the two world wars and was applauded as a masterpiece. Then, after World War II, it largely fell from public view. Set beside the incommensurable horrors of the later war, Cummings's internment, however harsh, seems only an inconvenience. His Bunyanesque stance—one chapter is called "A Pilgrim's Progress"—is overblown, especially if compared with the cool precision of Primo Levi's *Se Questo e un Uomo* (1947)—literally, *If This Is a Man* but translated as *Survival in Auschwitz*—or *The Drowned and the Saved* (1986). The simplicity and moral beauty of Levi's exposition express as well as can be the inexpressibility of the experience.

Of narratives that have been searched out by scholars, the anonymous *Female Convict* (1934), forgotten until it was unearthed in 1978 by H. Bruce Franklin, affords a good example. A vivid autobiographical tale ("as told to Vincent Burns"), *Female Convict* recounts the deprivations of the author's childhood and her experience in prison on conviction of writing bad checks. In it the passion of resistance combines with a sharp eye for descriptive detail; among the narrator's fellow prisoners are "Laura, the Candy Kid, seventeen year old shoplifter, prostitute and drug-addict, an inveterate thief, pretty as a picture"; "Old Lady Cuno, eighty-seven, arrested for begging, always swearing in German and smelling like a fish factory"; and "Ethel Kingsley, morose murderess" (Franklin, 171–72). This lineup, a stock property of prison writing, could stand beside its masculine counterparts in Genet; instead of Genet's baroque extravagance, it offers the rough colloquialism of genre art.

Finally, among narratives of prison experience, that of Polish Resistance leader Kazimierz Moczarski is curious in its presentation of an enforced intimacy as to deserve mention, though it falls outside the limits of this volume. In 1949, Moczarski was placed in a Warsaw jail cell with two Germans, one of whom turned out to be Jürgen Stroop, liquidator of the Warsaw ghetto. After his release, Moczarski wrote an account of the experience; published in 1977, two years after his death, the work was later translated as *Conversations with an Executioner* (1981). Despite the astonishing circumstances, his account on one occasion resembles nothing so much as a jailhouse comedy of manners. There is only one bunk in the three-man cell. Stroop has been using it; his subordinate has been sleeping on a mattress on the floor. When Moczarski is assigned to the cell, Stroop offers him the bunk because Moczarski is "a member of the victorious and ruling nation here, and therefore the *Herrenvolk*" (4–5). Moczarski declines on the grounds that in prison, all inmates are equal. Thereafter, during the more than eight months that they share the cell, all three sleep on mattresses on the floor.

Personal narrative accounts for much but not all of prisoners' writings. In addition to the occasional writer, like Malory or Verlaine, who carries on his natural vocation while imprisoned, there are also those, like Genet, who discover their powers in prison. Among these was the African-American novelist Chester Himes, who spent more than seven years in Ohio State Penitentiary on conviction of armed robbery, published his earliest stories and a novella before his release in 1936, and went on to a long career of writing. His prison novel, *Cast the First Stone* (1952), was fifteen years in finding a publisher, no doubt the result of its homoeroticism and the protagonist's final redemption in his unconsummated love for a fellow convict. Soon after publication of *Cast the First Stone*, Himes left the United States for France, where he found an audience more receptive to his work and where he lived until his death in 1984.

Nor should the extraordinary case of Robert Stroud (1890–1963), the "bird-man of Alcatraz," pass unnoticed, though his works do not fall into conventional categories of the literary. At the age of eighteen, Stroud killed a man in Alaska and, while in Leavenworth, killed a guard. Woodrow Wilson commuted his death sentence to life imprisonment. In all, Stroud spent fifty-four years in prison, the largest part of them in isolation, where he taught himself the care and breeding of small birds. In 1933 he published *Diseases of Canaries* and, in 1943, his *Digest on the Diseases of Birds*. As the subject of a film (1962), he became a folk hero. Despite Stroud's disclaimer in *Digest*, "I make no pretense of literary style" (vi), he was capable of eloquence that fairly takes the breath away, especially coming from one whose formal education ended with the third grade:

> Years of work, of study, of careful observation; the lives of literally thousands of birds, the disappointments and heartbreaks of hundreds of blasted hopes have gone into these pages; almost every line, every word, is spattered with sweat and blood. For every truth I have outlined to you, I have blundered my way through a hundred errors. I have killed birds when it was almost as hard as killing one's children. I have had birds die in my hand when their death brought me greater sadness than that I have ever felt over the passing of a member of my own species. And I have dedicated all this to the proposition that fewer birds shall suffer and die because their diseases are not understood. (312–13).

The solitary prisoner's obsession with birds both captive and free plays out his own interior drama of confinement and flight.

Prisons Without and Within: Mailer, Styron, Genet

Since literature of the prison evokes at some level of consciousness the theme of art and artistic expression as liberation, this literature sometimes, predictably, blurs the distinction between personal narratives of prisoners and authorial fictions about the experience of prison. Norman Mailer's *The Executioner's Song* (1979), William Styron's *The Confessions of Nat Turner* (1966), and the whole corpus of Genet's writing illustrate this manner of sustaining the analogy between the experience of prison and that of life.

The documentary story of the life and execution of the murderer Gary Gilmore, told "as if it were a novel" (1022), *The Executioner's Song* begins and closes with what Mailer calls an "old prison rhyme":

> Deep in my dungeon
> I welcome you here
> Deep in my dungeon
> I worship your fear
> Deep in my dungeon,
> I dwell.
> I do not know
> if I wish you well.

In the version of the rhyme at the close, a second stanza is added, identical to the first except for its final two lines: "A bloody kiss / from the wishing well" (1019). In an afterword, however, Mailer admits to his "own creations": this "is not, alas, an ancient ditty but a new one, and was written by this author ten years ago" (1021). If there is a false step in the more than one thousand pages of *The Executioner's Song*, it is Mailer's arch "alas." A signature piece, the rhyme marks the narrator's identity both as the teller of this "true life story" (1022) and as a partaker of the story told. Like the murderer, the narrator does not know at the start if he wishes "you well" but, at the end, imagines himself proffering a "bloody kiss." The writer and the killer are secret sharers, joined with their audience by a common destiny and purpose.

Mailer's Gilmore and Styron's Nat Turner offer their creators alter egos: in Mailer's case, the experience depends on recognizing sameness; in Styron's, on overcoming difference. In the summer of 1831, the slave preacher Nat Turner led a fierce but unsuccessful rebellion. He was executed, and his confessions, as recorded by an otherwise unknown lawyer, were published in November of the same year. Using the original document as a starting point, Styron re-creates Turner's private history in the first person, combining lyrical narrative with dialogue modeled on Turner's own speech and that of his contemporaries. In choosing his subject, Styron has said that he was remembering "the cosmic loneliness of Meursault" and that he saw "a spiritual connection between Meursault's frigid solitude and the plight of Nat Turner" (*Darkness Visible*, 21). But like Mailer, Styron thinks of his work as not quite classifiable, neither a novel nor not a novel, "a work that is less an 'historical novel' in conventional terms than a meditation on history" (ix). The crossing of boundaries between documentary and novel, or between a historical novel and a meditation, yields a narrative identification with a subject across the boundaries of time, or of race, or of prison walls. Prison walls and bars represent whatever separates or divides.

It is Genet, however, who most completely effaces boundary lines between the prison and the world beyond. He is the author as picaro, his life a work in the manner of the picaresque, a writer whom history may come to regard as this century's exemplary instance of literary self-fashioning. That is how Sartre saw and defined him, in *Saint Genet: Actor and Martyr* (1952), a massive celebration of the artist as criminal and outsider. Genet lives out the prison theme and in doing so may even have brought this long-lived strain in the Western literary tradition to a climax. Predictions of the end of art or the end of the novel have always been wrong, or at least premature, but it would be hard to carry the prison theme further than Genet.

Born illegitimate in Paris in 1910 and abandoned by his mother, he became a ward of the state and then the foster child of a peasant family, was sent to Mettray Reformatory at the age of fifteen, joined the army on his release in 1929, was declared a deserter in 1936, wandered across Europe begging, thieving, and selling himself as a male prostitute, was committed to Fresnes Prison when he returned to Paris, and in his early thirties, began the career as poet, novelist, and playwright that won him the attention of the French literary establishment and, in 1949, a presidential pardon. It is as if a sixteenth-century fictional picaro had found himself in the mid-twentieth century—and famous.

Before his pardon, Genet wrote *Our Lady of the Flowers* (1943), *The Miracle of the Rose* (1946), and other fictions; in 1947, *The Maids* was his first play to be performed; and in 1948 he published *The Thief's Journal*, the autobiographical meditation that Sartre in his foreword called the *Dichtung und Wahrheit* (referring to Goethe's autobiography, *Poetry and Truth*) of homosexuality and "the most beautiful" of Genet's works (8). Though he continued writing plays after his pardon—and became a political gadfly, traveling in the United States on behalf of the radical Black Panthers, supporting Palestinian liberation, and, in an essay originally called "Violence and Brutality," providing an introduction to the prison letters of the German anarchist Ulrike Meinhof and others of her group—it is by *The Thief's Journal*, his most accessibly picaresque work, that Genet is best known.

A meditation on two photographs of himself from the criminal archives, the first when he was sixteen or seventeen, the second when he was thirty, defines Genet's love affair with the prison. Going to prison the first time released him from the solitudes of his childhood: "When I was a farmhand, when I was a soldier, when I was at the orphanage, despite the friendship and, occasionally, the affection of my masters, I was alone, rigorously so. Prison offered me the first consolation, the first peace, the first friendly fellowship: I experienced them in the realm of foulness" (85). Later, prison becomes his habitual refuge: "Prison offers the same sense of security to the convict as does a royal palace to a king's guest. . . . The masonry, the materials, the proportions and the architecture are in harmony with a moral unity which makes these dwellings indestructible so long as the social form of which they are the symbol endures. The prison surrounds me with a perfect guarantee" (87). Yet the very security of the prison, in Genet's account, will be its ruin: were prisons "established on the ground and in the world with more casualness, they might perhaps hold out for a long time." But, he added: "Their gravity makes me consider them without pity. I recognize that they have their foundations within myself; they are the signs of the most violent of my extreme tendencies, and my corrosive spirit is already working at their destruction" (88).

Genet's affair of the heart with prisons mingles love and hate. The security of prisons depends both on the unity of life within their walls and on those rough constraints that keep society safe from the inmates, though seldom keeping the inmates wholly safe from one another. Genet's feelings incorporate self-love and self-hatred: the foundations of prison are within himself, the prison once more serving as a metaphorical looking-glass. On the one hand, it signifies companionship, security, even kingly grandeur;

on the other, violence, destruction, and terror. It sums up the multiplicity of human possibility and experience. In this completeness it comes closest to achieving the transcendence that is often one of its themes.

Acknowledgments

I am indebted to colleagues for reading this chapter in draft and making helpful suggestions: Hans Ulrich Gumbrecht, Elisabeth Hansot, Herbert Lindenberger, and Robert Polhemus. I am also grateful to Victor Brombert and Kenneth Fields for their advice and interest, to Robert Harrison for his fine translation of Verlaine, and to Edmund White for generously providing information about Genet's life before the publication of his biography. Toni Bowers and Jeff Erickson were diligent and thoughtful research assistants. Paul Neimann was also extremely helpful. Dr. Stancil Johnson loaned me, with the consent of its author, a manuscript composed in prison—a tangible reminder of how many prison manuscripts must be unknown to history. I am also grateful to Stefan Amsterdamski for bringing Moczarski's narrative to my attention. Prisons and literature make a subject that stirs the memory and imagination, and I am grateful, finally, to other colleagues with whom I have shared the topic. They have made many contributions, and this chapter has been a collaborative effort, with the customary but essential qualification that I alone am responsible for lapses of fact or interpretation that undoubtedly have crept in.

Works Cited

Adorno, Theodor W. "Commitment." In *The Essential Frankfurt School Reader*, ed. Andrew Arato and Eike Gebhardt. New York: Urizen Books, 1978.

Aeschylus. *Prometheus Bound*. Trans. James Scully and John Herington. New York: Oxford University Press, 1975.

Banville, John. *The Book of Evidence*. New York: Scribner's, 1989.

Beckett, Samuel. *Waiting for Godot: Tragicomedy in Two Acts*. New York: Grove Press, 1954.

Boethius. *The Consolation of Philosophy*. Trans. Richard Green. Indianapolis: Bobbs-Merrill, 1962.

Brombert, Victor. *The Romantic Prison: The French Tradition*. Princeton: Princeton University Press, 1978.

Bruchac, Joseph, ed. *The Light from Another Country: Poetry from American Prisons*. Greenfield Center, N.Y.: Greenfield Review Press, 1984.

Bunyan, John. *Grace Abounding to the Chief of Sinners*. Ed. Roger Sharrock. Oxford: Clarendon Press, 1962.

———. *The Pilgrim's Progress from This World to That Which Is to Come*. Ed. James Blanton Wharey. Oxford: Clarendon Press, 1960.

Byron, Lord. *The Complete Poetical Works*. 7 vols. Ed. Jerome J. McGann. Oxford: Clarendon Press, 1980–93.

Camus, Albert. *The Stranger*. Trans. Stuart Gilbert. New York: Knopf, 1946.

Cheever, John. *Falconer*. New York: Knopf, 1977.

Chénier, André. *Oeuvres Complètes*. Ed. Gérard Walter. Paris: Gallimard, 1958.

Defoe, Daniel. *The Fortunes and Misfortunes of the Famous Moll Flanders*. Ed. G. A. Starr. New York: Oxford University Press, 1981.

Dickens, Charles. *Little Dorrit*. Ed. Harvey Peter Sucksmith. New York: Oxford University Press, 1982.

———. *Martin Chuzzlewit*. Ed. Margaret Cardwell. Oxford: Clarendon Press, 1982.

Ellmann, Richard. *Oscar Wilde*. New York: Knopf, 1988.

Franklin, H. Bruce. *Prison Literature in America: The Victim as Criminal and Artist*. Expanded ed. New York: Oxford University Press, 1989.

Gay, John. *The Beggar's Opera. In John Gay: Dramatic Works*. 2 vols. Ed. John Fuller. Oxford: Clarendon Press, 1983.

Genet, Jean. *The Thief's Journal*. Foreword by Jean-Paul Sartre. Trans. Bernard Frechtman. New York: Grove Press, 1964.

Goldsmith, Oliver. *The Vicar of Wakefield: A Tale Supposed to Be Written by Himself*. Ed. Arthur Friedman. New York: Oxford University Press, 1974.

Gramsci, Antonio. *Selections from the Prison Notebooks*. Ed. and trans. Quintin Hoare and Geoffrey Nowell-Smith. New York: International Publishers, 1971.

Kafka, Franz. *Complete Stories*. Ed. Nahum N. Glatzer. London: Allen Lane, 1983.

King, Martin Luther, Jr. *A Testament of Hope: The Essential Writings*. Ed. James Melvin Washington. San Francisco: Harper and Row, 1986.

The Life of Lazarillo of Tormes: His Fortunes and Misfortunes as Told by Himself. Trans. Robert S. Rudder. New York: Ungar, 1973.

Lowell, Robert. *Selected Poems*. New York: Farrar, Straus and Giroux, 1976.

Mailer, Norman. *The Executioner's Song*. Boston: Little, Brown, 1979.

Moczarski, Kazimierz. *Conversations with an Executioner*. Ed. Mariana Fitzpatrick. Englewood Cliffs, N.J.: Prentice-Hall, 1981.

Pellico, Silvio. *My Prisons*. Trans. I. G. Capaldi. New York: Oxford University Press, 1963. Reprint. Westport, Conn.: Greenwood Press, 1978.

Sartre, Jean-Paul. *No Exit and The Flies*. Trans. Stuart Gilbert. New York: Knopf, 1947.

————. *Saint Genet: Actor and Martyr*. Trans. Bernard Frechtman. London: W. H. Allen, 1964.

Shakespeare, William. *King Lear*. Ed. Kenneth Muir, based on W. J. Craig. London: Methuen, 1952.

————. *King Richard II*. Ed. Peter Ure. London: Methuen, 1956.

————. *Measure for Measure*. Ed. J. W. Lever. London: Methuen, 1965.

Sterne, Laurence. *A Sentimental Journey through France and Italy, by Mr. Yorick, to Which Are Added The Journal to Eliza and A Political Romance*. Ed. Ian Jack. London: Oxford University Press, 1968.

Stroud, Robert. *Stroud's Digest on the Diseases of Birds*. St. Paul, Minn.: Webb, 1943.

Styron, William. *The Confessions of Nat Turner*. New York: Random House, 1967.

————. *Darkness Visible: A Memoir of Madness*. New York: Random House, 1990.

Thoreau, Henry David. *Walden and Other Writings*. New York: Random House, 1937.

Wilde, Oscar. *The First Collected Edition of the Works of Oscar Wilde, 1908–1922*. Ed. Robert Ross. 15 vols. London: Dawson's, 1969.

Bibliographic Note

Most texts mentioned in this chapter are the subject of commentary that at least touches on themes of confinement and the prison. Relative to the number of fictional texts that incorporate these themes, however, more general studies are rare. Nor is analysis of the writing of inmates very frequent. Commentary on fictions of the prison usually examines formal characteristics of texts more closely than the historical prison. Commentary on prisoners' writings often displays a commitment to the cause of the imprisoned. The material might be more fully served, in the first case, by greater recognition of the social conditions underlying the theme and, in the second, by closer attention to the nature and history of the type and its habitual patterns.

Like other of Michel Foucault's work, *Surveiller et Punir: Naissance de la Prison* (Paris: Gallimard, 1975) (*Discipline and Punish: The Birth of the Prison,* trans. Alan Sheridan [New York: Vintage Books, 1979]) has influenced the study of literary texts. Foucault's analysis of the social organization of modern life represents the prison as parallel to other institutions equally "complete and austere." He asks, "Is it surprising that prisons resemble factories, schools, barracks, hospitals, which all resemble prisons?" (228) Foucault offers a mode of entry, almost too convenient in its historical and ideological neatness, to any number of individual texts. For all of its imaginative power, Foucault's analysis is a selective vision. Although the penitentiary develops in the last two centuries, confinement as an imaginative category is far older. Revision of Foucault's argument might stress imaginative continuities rather than historical discontinuities.

Studies that examine aspects of literature and the prison, as represented (largely) from the outside, include the following: John Bender, *Imagining the Penitentiary: Fiction and the Architecture of Mind in Eighteenth-Century England* (Chicago: University of Chicago Press, 1987); Victor Brombert, *The Romantic Prison: The French Tradition* (Princeton: Princeton University Press, 1978), originally published as *La Prison Romantique: Essai sur L'imaginaire* (Paris: Jose Corti, 1975); W. B. Carnochan, *Confinement and Flight: An Essay on English Literature of the Eighteenth Century* (Berkeley: University of California Press, 1977); Janet Ann Juhnke, "The Prison Theme in the Eighteenth-Century Novel" (Ph.D. diss., University of Kansas, 1974); and Mary Ann Frese Witt, *Existential Prisons: Captivity in Mid-Twentieth-Century French Literature* (Durham, N.C.: Duke University Press, 1985), which includes a chapter, "From Inside," about Genet.

Studies that examine writings (largely) "from inside" include the following: Ioan Davies, *Writers in Prison* (Oxford: Basil Blackwell, 1990); Françoise d'Eaubonne, *Les Ecrivains en Cage* ([Paris]: André Balland, 1970); H. Bruce Franklin, *The Victim as Criminal and Artist: Literature from the American Prison* (New York: Oxford University Press, 1978), reprinted and expanded as *Prison Literature in America: The Victim as Criminal and Artist* (New York: Oxford University Press, 1989); Elissa D. Gelfand, *Imagination in Confinement: Women's Writings from French Prisons* (Ithaca: Cornell University Press, 1983); and Jean-Marc Varaut, *Poètes en Prison de Charles d'Orléans à Jean Genet* (Paris: Perrin, 1989). Davies, Franklin, and Gelfand include useful bibliographies. Jolene Babyak's *Bird Man: The Many Faces of Robert Stroud* (Berkeley: Ariel Vamp Press, 1994) presents Stroud not as a popular hero but as a violent sociopath.

An essay that combines discussion of the picaresque tradition and recent autobiographical narratives by Malcolm X and others is Anthony N. Zahareas, "The Historical Function of Picaresque Autobiographies: Toward a History of Social Offenders," in *Autobiography in Early Modern Spain,* ed. Nicholas Spadaccini and Jenaro Talens (Minneapolis, Minn.: Prisma Institute, 1988), 129–62.

Collections of writings by prisoners and about the prison experience include the following: Judith A. Scheffler, ed., *Wall Tappings: An Anthology of Writings by Women Prisoners* (Boston: Northeastern University Press, 1986), its earliest entry being an English Quaker's account of her imprisonment by the Inquisition at Malta in 1659; Cynthia Owen Philip, comp., *Imprisoned in America: Prison Communications 1776 to Attica* (New York: Harper and Row, 1973); Olivier Blanc, *Last Letters: Prisons and Prisoners of the French Revolution, 1793–1794,* trans. Alan Sheridan (London: Andre Deutsch, 1987); Philip Priestley, ed., *Victorian Prison Lives: English Prison Biography, 1830–1914* (London: Methuen, 1985); Philip Priestley, ed., *Jail Journeys: The English Prison Experience since 1918, Modern Prison Writings* (London: Routledge, 1989); *Who Took the Weight? Black Voices from Norfolk Prison* (Boston: Little, Brown, 1972); and Joseph Bruchac, ed., *The Light from Another Country: Poetry from American Prisons* (Greenfield Center, N.Y.: Greenfield Review Press, 1984).

Brombert's *The Romantic Prison* opens with a perception that is also a summary: "Prison haunts our civilization" (3). Jean-Paul Sartre's immense *Saint Genet: Comedien et Martyr* (Paris:

Gallimard, 1952), translated by Bernard Frechtman, *Saint Genet: Actor and Martyr* (London: W. H. Allen, 1964), marks the power of the prison over the critical as well as the artistic imagination. In canonizing the criminal-artist, Sartre sets a seal on Genet as the Prometheus of his times. Edmund White's *Genet* (New York: Knopf, 1993) is the fullest, most reliable account of Genet's life.

CONTRIBUTORS

THE EDITORS

NORVAL MORRIS is the Julius Kreeger Professor of Law and Criminology, Emeritus, at the University of Chicago. He is a Fellow of the American Academy of Arts and Sciences and serves on numerous federal and state government and scholarly councils and commissions. Before coming to Chicago, he directed a crime prevention and treatment institute for the United Nations in Japan. He has taught at the University of London, the Universities of Melbourne and Adelaide in Australia, and at Harvard, New York, and Columbia Universities as well as the University of Chicago in the United States. His last four books were *The Future of Imprisonment* (1974), *Madness and the Criminal Law* (1982), *Between Prison and Probation* (1990, with Michael Tonry), and *The Brothel Boy and Other Parables of the Law* (1992).

DAVID J. ROTHMAN is Professor of History, Bernard Schoenberg Professor of Social Medicine, and Director of the Center for the Study of Society and Medicine at the Columbia College of Physicians and Surgeons. Trained in social history at Harvard University, he is the author of *The Discovery of the Asylum* (1971), co-winner of the Albert J. Beveridge Prize. He has also published *Conscience and Convenience: The Asylum and Its Alternatives in Progressive America* (1980), *The Willowbrook Wars* (1984, with Sheila M. Rothman), and *Strangers at the Bedside: A History of How Law and Bioethics Transformed Medical Decision-Making*. In 1987, he received an honorary Doctor of Law Degree from the John Jay School of Criminal Justice. He has served as Samuel Paley Lecturer at Hebrew University, as Fulbright Lecturer in India, as Distinguished Lecturer at Kyoto, and as fellow at the Rockefeller Foundation Study Center at Bellagio.

THE AUTHORS

W. B. CARNOCHAN is Richard W. Lyman Professor of the Humanities, Emeritus, at Stanford University. From 1985 to 1991, he was director of the Stanford Humanities Center. Among his writings on eighteenth-century literature is *Confinement and Flight: An Essay on English Literature of the Eighteenth Century*. His most recent book is *The Battleground of the Curriculum: Liberal Education and the American Experience*.

JOHN HIRST is Reader in History at La Trobe University, Melbourne, Australia. He has written extensively on Australia's colonial history. His book *Convict Society and Its Enemies* was the first in the "normalizing" school, which regards New South Wales as a society with convicts rather than a convict society.

SEÁN McCONVILLE is Professorial Research Fellow and Professor of Criminal Justice in the Department of Law, Queen Mary and Westfield College, University of London.

He has taught, researched, and consulted on both sides of the Atlantic and has published widely on criminal and penal policy, both comparatively and historically. His most recent book is *English Local Prisons, 1860–1900: Next Only to Death.*

RANDALL McGOWEN is Associate Professor of History at the University of Oregon. He is the author of a number of articles on punishment and on the reform of the criminal law in England. He is currently at work on a book on the crime of forgery and the debate over the death penalty.

ARYEH NEIER is President of The Open Society Fund. Previously, he served as Executive Director of Human Rights Watch and, before that, as Executive Director of the American Civil Liberties Union. His books include *Dossier, Crime and Punishment: A Radical Solution, Defending My Enemy,* and *Only Judgment.*

PATRICIA O'BRIEN is Director of the University of California Humanities Research Institute and Professor of History at the University of California, Irvine. She has written on a range of subjects including French female criminality, urban history, and the new cultural history. She is the author of *The Promise of Punishment: Prisons in Nineteenth-Century France* and has coauthored, with Mark Kishlansky and Patrick Geary, *Civilization in the West.* She is currently working on a study of the political culture of the liberal professions in nineteenth-century Europe.

EDWARD M. PETERS is the Henry Charles Lea Professor of History at the University of Pennsylvania. He is a Fellow of the Royal Historical Society and the Medieval Academy of America and the author of *Heresy and Authority in Medieval Europe, Torture,* and *Inquisition,* as well as several dozen other books and scholarly articles. From 1970 to 1995 he was the editor of the series *The Middle Ages* at the University of Pennsylvania Press.

EDGARDO ROTMAN is the foreign and international law librarian at the University of Miami. He teaches, among other courses, one on prisoner litigation. He has written for numerous publications on prisons and prison law in the United States, Europe, and Latin America. He is the author of *Beyond Punishment: A New View on the Rehabilitation of Criminal Offenders.*

STEVEN SCHLOSSMAN is Professor of History and Head of the History Department at Carnegie Mellon University, where he teaches courses in American social history and policy history. He has written *Love and the American Delinquent: The Theory and Practice of "Progressive" Juvenile Justice* and many additional articles on the history of criminal justice. His most recent publications deal with the histories of African Americans, women, and gays in the military.

PIETER SPIERENBURG is Professor of History at Erasmus University, Rotterdam, the Netherlands. He is Secretary of the International Association for the History of Crime and Criminal Justice. He is the author of several books and many articles on European sociocultural history. Among his publications is *The Broken Spell: A Cultural and Anthropological History of Preindustrial Europe*.

LUCIA ZEDNER is Fellow and Tutor in Law at Corpus Christi College, Oxford, and an associate of the Centre for Criminological Research, University of Oxford. She is the author of *Women, Crime, and Custody in Victorian England* and has also published widely on contemporary issues in criminal justice. She is currently working, with Nicole Lacey, on a comparison of criminal justice in Britain and Germany.

INDEX